Microeconomics
BRIEF EDITION

Third Edition

Campbell R. McConnell
University of Nebraska

Sean M. Flynn
Scripps College

Stanley L. Brue
Pacific Lutheran University

With the special assistance of
Randy R. Grant
Linfield College

Mc Graw Hill Education

THE MCGRAW-HILL SERIES ECONOMICS

ESSENTIALS OF ECONOMICS

Brue, McConnell, and Flynn
Essentials of Economics
Fourth Edition

Mandel
Economics: The Basics
Second Edition

Schiller
Essentials of Economics
Eighth Edition

PRINCIPLES OF ECONOMICS

Colander
Economics, Microeconomics, and Macroeconomics
Ninth Edition

Frank and Bernanke
Principles of Economics, Principles of Microeconomics, Principles of Macroeconomics
Fifth Edition

Frank and Bernanke
Brief Editions: Principles of Economics, Principles of Microeconomics, Principles of Macroeconomics
Second Edition

McConnell, Brue, and Flynn
Economics, Microeconomics, and Macroeconomics
Twentyfirst Edition

McConnell, Brue, and Flynn
Brief Editions: Economics, Microeconomics, and Macroeconomics
Third Edition

Miller
Principles of Microeconomics
First Edition

Samuelson and Nordhaus
Economics, Microeconomics, and Macroeconomics
Nineteenth Edition

Schiller
The Economy Today, The Micro Economy Today, and The Macro Economy Today
Thirteenth Edition

Slavin
Economics, Microeconomics, and Macroeconomics
Ninth Edition

ECONOMICS OF SOCIAL ISSUES

Guell
Issues in Economics Today
Sixth Edition

Sharp, Register, and Grimes
Economics of Social Issues
Twentieth Edition

ECONOMETRICS

Gujarati and Porter
Basic Econometrics
Fifth Edition

Gujarati and Porter
Essentials of Econometrics
Fourth Edition

MANAGERIAL ECONOMICS

Baye and Prince
Managerial Economics and Business Strategy
Eighth Edition

Brickley, Smith, and Zimmerman
Managerial Economics and Organizational Architecture
Fifth Edition

Thomas and Maurice
Managerial Economics
Eleventh Edition

INTERMEDIATE ECONOMICS

Bernheim and Whinston
Microeconomics
Second Edition

Dornbusch, Fischer, and Startz
Macroeconomics
Eleventh Edition

Frank
Microeconomics and Behavior
Eighth Edition

ADVANCED ECONOMICS

Romer
Advanced Macroeconomics
Fourth Edition

MONEY AND BANKING

Cecchetti and Schoenholtz
Money, Banking, and Financial Markets
Third Edition

URBAN ECONOMICS

O'Sullivan
Urban Economics
Eighth Edition

LABOR ECONOMICS

Borjas
Labor Economics
Sixth Edition

McConnell, Brue, and Macpherson
Contemporary Labor Economics
Tenth Edition

PUBLIC FINANCE

Rosen and Gayer
Public Finance
Ninth Edition

Seidman
Public Finance
First Edition

ENVIRONMENTAL ECONOMICS

Field and Field
Environmental Economics: An Introduction
Sixth Edition

INTERNATIONAL ECONOMICS

Appleyard and Field
International Economics
Eighth Edition

King and King
International Economics, Globalization, and Policy: A Reader
Fifth Edition

Pugel
International Economics
Fifteenth Edition

THE SEVEN VERSIONS OF MCCONNELL, BRUE, FLYNN

Chapter	Economics	Economics: Brief Edition	Microeconomics	Microeconomics: Brief Edition	Macroeconomics	Macroeconomics: Brief Edition	Essentials of Economics
1. Limits, Alternatives, and Choices	x	x	x	x	x	x	x
2. The Market System and the Circular Flow	x	x	x	x	x	x	x
3. Demand, Supply, and Market Equilibrium	x	x	x	x	x	x	x
4. Market Failures: Public Goods and Externalities	x	x	x	x	x	x	x
5. Government's Role and Government Failure	x	x	x	x	x	x	x
6. Elasticity	x	x	x	x			x
7. Utility Maximization	x	x	x	x			x
8. Behavioral Economics	x	x	x	x			
9. Businesses and the Costs of Production	x	x	x	x			x
10. Pure Competition in the Short Run	x	x	x	x			x
11. Pure Competition in the Long Run	x	x	x	x			x
12. Pure Monopoly	x	x	x	x			x
13. Monopolistic Competition	x	x	x	x			x
14. Oligopoly and Strategic Behavior	x	x	x	x			x
15. Technology, R&D, and Efficiency	x		x				
16. The Demand for Resources	x		x				
17. Wage Determination	x	x	x	x			
18. Rent, Interest, and Profit	x		x				
19. Natural Resource and Energy Economics	x		x				
20. Public Finance: Expenditures and Taxes	x	x	x	x			
21. Antitrust Policy and Regulation	x		x				x
22. Agriculture: Economics and Policy	x		x				
23. Income Inequality, Poverty, and Discrimination	x	x	x	x			
24. Health Care	x				x		
25. Immigration	x				x	x	
26. An Introduction to Macroeconomics	x	x			x	x	x
27. Measuring Domestic Output and National Income	x	x			x	x	x
28. Economic Growth	x	x			x	x	x
29. Business Cycles, Unemployment, and Inflation	x	x			x	x	x
30. Basic Macroeconomic Relationships	x				x		x
31. The Aggregate Expenditures Model	x				x		
32. Aggregate Demand and Aggregate Supply	x	x			x	x	x
33. Fiscal Policy, Deficits, and Debt	x	x			x		x
34. Money, Banking, and Financial Institutions	x	x			x	x	x
35. Money Creation	x				x		
36. Interest Rates and Monetary Policy	x	x			x	x	
37. Financial Economics	x				x		
38. Extending the Analysis of Aggregate Supply	x	x	x		x	x	x
39. Current Issues in Macro Theory and Policy	x		x		x		
40. International Trade	x	x		x	x	x	x
41. The Balance of Payments, Exchange Rates, and Trade Deficits	x	x	x	x	x	x	x
42. The Economics of Developing Countries	x				x		

*Chapter numbers refer to *Economics: Principles, Problems, and Policies*.
*A Red "X" indicates chapters that combine or consolidate content from two or more *Economics* chapters.

MICROECONOMICS: BRIEF EDITION, THIRD EDITION

Published by McGraw-Hill Education, 2 Penn Plaza, New York, NY 10121. Copyright © 2019 by McGraw-Hill Education. All rights reserved. Printed in the United States of America. Previous editions © 2013 and 2010. No part of this publication may be reproduced or distributed in any form or by any means, or stored in a database or retrieval system, without the prior written consent of McGraw-Hill Education, including, but not limited to, in any network or other electronic storage or transmission, or broadcast for distance learning.

Some ancillaries, including electronic and print components, may not be available to customers outside the United States.

This book is printed on acid-free paper.

1 2 3 4 5 6 7 8 9 LWI 21 20 19 18

ISBN   978-1-260-32497-6 (bound edition)
MHID   1-260-32497-4 (bound edition)
ISBN   978-1-260-32506-5 (loose-leaf edition)
MHID   1-260-32506-7 (loose-leaf edition)

Portfolio manager: *Anke Weekes*
Associate portfolio manager: *Adam Huenecke*
Lead product developer: *Kelly Delso*
Product developer: *Kelly Pekelder*
Marketing manager: *Bobby Pearson*
Content project managers: *Harvey Yep (Core); Bruce Gin (Assessment)*
Buyer: *Laura Fuller*
Designer: *Matt Diamond*
Content licensing specialist: *Shawntel Schmitt*
Cover image: *©Kativ/Getty Images*
Compositor: *Aptara®, Inc.*

All credits appearing on page or at the end of the book are considered to be an extension of the copyright page.

Library of Congress Control Number: 2018954871

To Mem, to Terri and Craig, and to past instructors

CAMPBELL R. MCCONNELL earned his PhD from the University of Iowa after receiving degrees from Cornell College and the University of Illinois. He taught at the University of Nebraska–Lincoln from 1953 until his retirement in 1990. He is also coauthor of *Contemporary Labor Economics,* eleventh edition, and *Essentials of Economics,* third edition, and has edited readers for the principles and labor economics courses. He is a recipient of both the University of Nebraska Distinguished Teaching Award and the James A. Lake Academic Freedom Award and is past president of the Midwest Economics Association. Professor McConnell was awarded an honorary Doctor of Laws degree from Cornell College in 1973 and received its Distinguished Achievement Award in 1994. His primary areas of interest are labor economics and economic education. He has an extensive collection of jazz recordings and enjoys reading jazz history.

STANLEY L. BRUE did his undergraduate work at Augustana College (South Dakota) and received its Distinguished Achievement Award in 1991. He received his PhD from the University of Nebraska–Lincoln. He is retired from a long career at Pacific Lutheran University, where he was honored as a recipient of the Burlington Northern Faculty Achievement Award. Professor Brue has also received the national Leavey Award for excellence in economic education. He has served as national president and chair of the Board of Trustees of Omicron Delta Epsilon International Economics Honorary. He is coauthor of *Economic Scenes,* fifth edition (Prentice-Hall); *Contemporary Labor Economics,* eleventh edition; *Essentials of Economics,* third edition; and *The Evolution of Economic Thought,* eighth edition (Cengage Learning). For relaxation, he enjoys international travel, attending sporting events, and going on fishing trips.

SEAN M. FLYNN did his undergraduate work at the University of Southern California before completing his PhD at U.C. Berkeley, where he served as the Head Graduate Student Instructor for the Department of Economics after receiving the Outstanding Graduate Student Instructor Award. He teaches at Scripps College (of the Claremont Colleges) and is the author of *Economics for Dummies,* second edition (Wiley), and coauthor of *Essentials of Economics,* third edition. His research interests include finance, behavioral economics, and health economics. An accomplished martial artist, he has represented the United States in international aikido tournaments and is the author of *Understanding Shodokan Aikido* (Shodokan Press). Other hobbies include running, traveling, and enjoying ethnic food.

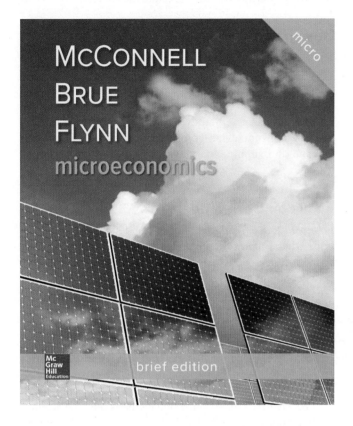

Welcome to *Economics: Brief Edition,* third edition, the trimmed and edited version of *Economics,* twenty-first edition, the nation's best-selling economics textbook.

Fundamental Objectives

We have three main goals for *Economics: Brief Edition*:

- Help the beginning student master the principles essential for understanding the economizing problem, specific economic issues, and the policy alternatives.
- Help the student understand and apply the economic perspective and reason accurately and objectively about economic matters.
- Promote a lasting student interest in economics and the economy.

Integrated, Distinct Book

Although *Economics: Brief Edition* is a spin-off of *Economics,* twenty-first edition, it is not a cut-and-paste book that simply eliminates several chapters of *Economics* and reorders and renumbers the retained content. We can prepare such books via custom publication. Instead, the *Brief Edition* is a very concise, highly integrated economics textbook that is distinct in purpose, style, and coverage from *Economics* and its Micro and Macro splits.

What's New and Improved?

One of the benefits of writing a successful text is the opportunity to revise—to delete the outdated and install the new, to rewrite misleading or ambiguous statements, to introduce more relevant illustrations, to improve the organizational structure, and to enhance the learning aids.

We trust that you will agree we have used this opportunity wisely and fully. Some of the more significant changes include the following:

New Behavioral Economics Chapter

Placed at the end of the text for those instructors who want to supplement the primary material, this chapter on behavioral economics provides insights for those students wrestling with some of the standard assumptions and conclusions of traditional economics. Topics covered include time inconsistency, myopia, decision-making heuristics, framing effects, mental accounting, loss aversion, the endowment effect, and reciprocity. The discussion is couched in terms of consumer decision making and includes numerous concrete examples to bring the material home for students.

We have also striven to make clear to students the ways in which behavioral economics builds upon and augments the insights of traditional neoclassical economics. Thus the chapter opens with a section comparing and contrasting behavioral economics and neoclassical economics so that students will be able to see how both can be used in tandem to help understand and predict human choice behavior.

Updated End-of-Chapter Questions and Problems

We have updated the end-of-chapter questions, adding new problems to reflect revised and enhanced content. The questions are analytic and often ask for free responses, whereas the problems are mainly quantitative. We have aligned the questions and problems with the learning objectives presented at the beginning of the chapters. All of the questions and problems are assignable through McGraw Hill's *Connect,* and many contain additional algorithmic variations and can be automatically graded within the system.

Chapter-by-Chapter Changes

In addition to the changes and new features listed above, chapter-specific revisions include:

Chapter 1: Limits, Alternatives, and Choices features updated examples of opportunity cost, and the **Chapter One Appendix: Graphs and Their Meaning** has been converted from Web-Only content into the main product.

Chapter 2: The Market System and the Circular Flow includes several updates, including the example of consumer sovereignty, business and household sector data in the United States, and global data.

Chapter 3: Demand, Supply, and Market Equilibrium provides a new "Applying the Analysis" piece on Uber and dynamic pricing. The **Chapter Three Appendix: Additional Examples of Supply and Demand** has been converted from Web-Only content and relocated into the main product.

Chapter 5: Market Failures: Public Goods and Externalities features updated information on the U.S. tax structure. Taxes to correct negative externalities are now referred to as "Pigovian taxes" (versus "specific taxes" in previous editions).

Chapter 8: Pure Monopoly presents a new "Applying the Analysis" on monopoly power in the Internet age, replacing the De Beers diamond monopoly example.

Chapter 9: Monopolistic Competition and Oligopoly includes a new "Applying the Analysis" piece on Internet oligopolies, replacing the example of oligopoly in the beer industry.

Chapter 10: Wage Determination features revised discussion and updated data on occupational employment trends, wage differentials, and the minimum wage.

Chapter 11: Income Inequality and Poverty contains improved discussion and significant updates to the data on the distribution of income, poverty, and income-maintenance programs.

Chapter 12: Public Finance: Expenditures and Taxes contains significant data updates, including those resulting from the "Tax Cuts and Jobs Act" that went into effect in January 2018.

Chapter 13: International Trade and Exchange Rates includes updated material on recent U.S. trade deficits and a revised discussion related to Fed policy and changes in the relative value of the U.S. dollar.

Chapter 14: Behavioral Economics is a new chapter to this edition that incorporates a scientific understanding of decision making into the study of economics.

Distinguishing Features

Economics: Brief Edition includes several features that encourage students to read and retain the content.

Design and Pedagogy

The *Brief Edition* incorporates a single-column design with a host of pedagogical aids, including chapter learning objectives, definitions in the margins, combined tables and graphs, complete chapter summaries, lists of key terms, carefully constructed study questions, connections to our website, appendixes on graphs and additional examples of demand and supply, an extensive glossary, and historical statistics.

Focus on Core Models

Economics: Brief Edition shortens and simplifies explanations where appropriate but stresses the importance of the economic perspective, including explaining and applying core economic models. Our strategy is to develop a limited set of essential models, illustrate them with analogies or anecdotes, explain them thoroughly, and apply them to real-world situations. Eliminating unnecessary graphs and elaborations makes perfect sense in the one-semester course, but cutting explanations of the truly *essential* graphs does not. In dealing with the basics, brevity at the expense of clarity is false economy.

We created a student-oriented textbook that draws on the methodological strengths of the discipline and helps students improve their analytical reasoning skills. Regardless of students' eventual occupations, they will discover that such skills are highly valuable in their workplaces.

Illustrating the Idea

Numerous analogies, examples, and anecdotes are included throughout the book to help drive home central economic ideas in a lively, colorful, and easy-to-remember way. For instance, elastic versus inelastic demand is illustrated by comparing the stretch of an Ace bandage and that of a tight rubber tie-down. A piece on Mark Zuckerberg, Taylor Swift, and Jennifer Lawrence illustrates the importance of opportunity costs in decision making. Art in the public square brings clarity to public goods and the free-rider problem. A pizza analogy walks students through the equity-efficiency trade-off, and a discussion of credit cards helps explain what money is and is not. These brief vignettes flow directly from the preceding content and segue to the content that follows, rather than being "boxed off" away from the flow and therefore easily overlooked.

Applying the Analysis

A glance though this book's pages will demonstrate that this is an application-oriented textbook. *Applying the Analysis* pieces immediately follow the development of economic analysis and are part of the flow of the chapters, rather than segregated from the main body discussion in a traditional boxed format. For example, the basics of the economic perspective are applied to why customers choose the shortest checkout lines. Differences in elasticity of supply are contrasted by the changing prices of antiques versus reproductions. The book describes the principal–agent problem via the problems of corporate accounting and financial fraud. The concept of price discrimination is illustrated by the difference in adult and child pricing for ballgame tickets compared to the pricing at the concession stands. McDonald's sandwich "McHits" and "McMisses" over the years apply the concept of consumer sovereignty. The graphics of fiscal policy are followed by a discussion of recent fiscal policy, and the Federal Reserve's role in the economy is demonstrated through an application of its responses to the mortgage debt crisis and the recession. These and many other applications clearly demonstrate the relevance and usefulness of mastering the basic economic principles and models to beginning students.

Photo Ops

Photo sets under the title *Photo Op* are included throughout the book to add visual interest, break up the density, and highlight important distinctions. Just a few of the many examples are sets of photos on traffic congestion and holiday lighting to contrast negative and positive externalities, Social Security checks and food stamps to highlight the differences between social insurance and public assistance, and photos of lumber and newly constructed homes to illustrate the difference between intermediate and final goods. Other photo sets illustrate normal versus inferior goods, complements versus substitutes in consumption, homogeneous versus differentiated products, substitute resources versus complementary resources, and more.

Global Snapshots

Global Snapshot pieces include bar charts and line graphs that compare data for a particular year or other time period among selected nations. Examples of these lists and comparisons include income per capita, the world's 10 largest corporations, the world's top brand names, the index of economic freedom, the differing economic status of North Korea and South Korea, and so forth. These *Global Snapshots* join other significant international content to help convey that the United States operates in a global economy.

Digital Solutions

Extensive Algorithmic and Graphing Assessment

Robust, auto-gradable question banks for each chapter now include even more questions that make use of the *Connect®* graphing tool. More questions featuring algorithmic variations have also been added.

Interactive Graphs

This new assignable resource within Connect® helps students see the relevance of subject matter by providing visual displays of real data for students to manipulate. All graphs are accompanied by assignable assessment questions and feedback to guide students through the experience of learning to read and interpret graphs and data.

Videos

New to this edition are videos that provide support for key economic topics. These short, engaging explanations are presented at the moment students may be struggling to help them connect the dots and grasp challenging concepts.

Math Preparedness Tutorials

Our math preparedness assignments have been reworked to help students refresh on important prerequisite topics necessary to be successful in economics.

McGraw-Hill *Connect®*

McGraw-Hill's Connect® is an online assessment solution that connects students with the tools and resources they'll need to achieve success.

McGraw-Hill's Connect Features Connect offers a number of powerful tools and features to make managing assignments easier, so faculty can spend more time teaching. With *Connect*, students can engage with their coursework anytime and anywhere, making the learning process more accessible and efficient. *Connect* offers the features as described here.

Simple Assignment Management With *Connect*, creating assignments is easier than ever, so you can spend more time teaching and less time managing. The assignment management function enables you to

- Create and deliver assignments easily with selectable end-of-chapter questions and test bank items.
- Streamline lesson planning, student progress reporting, and assignment grading to make classroom management more efficient than ever.
- Go paperless with the eBook and online submission and grading of student assignments.

Smart Grading *Connect* helps students learn more efficiently by providing feedback and practice material when they need it, where they need it. The grading function enables you to

- Score assignments automatically, giving students immediate feedback on their work and side-by-side comparisons with correct answers.
- Access and review each response; manually change grades or leave comments for students to review.
- Reinforce classroom concepts with practice tests and instant quizzes.

Instructor Library The *Connect* Instructor Library is your repository for additional resources to improve student engagement in and out of class. You can select and use any asset that enhances your lecture. The *Connect* Instructor Library includes all of the instructor supplements for this text.

Student Resources

Any supplemental resources that align with the text for student use will be available through Connect.

Student Progress Tracking *Connect* keeps instructors informed about how each student, section, and class is performing, allowing for more productive use of lecture and office hours. The progress-tracking function enables you to

- View scored work immediately and track individual or group performance with assignment and grade reports.
- Access an instant view of student or class performance relative to learning objectives.
- Collect data and generate reports required by many accreditation organizations, such as AACSB and AICPA.

Connect Insight The first and only analytics tool of its kind, Connect Insight™ is a series of visual data displays that are each framed by an intuitive question and provide at-a-glance information that allows instructors to leverage aggregated information about their courses and students to provide a more personalized teaching and learning experience.

Lecture Capture Increase the attention paid to lecture discussion by decreasing the attention paid to note taking. Lecture Capture offers new ways for students to focus on the in-class discussion, knowing they can revisit important topics later. Lecture Capture enables you to

- Record and distribute your lecture with a click of a button.
- Record and index PowerPoint presentations and anything shown on your computer so they are easily searchable, frame by frame.

- Offer access to lectures anytime and anywhere by computer, iPod, or mobile device.
- Increase intent listening and class participation by easing students' concerns about note taking. Lecture Capture will make it more likely you will see students' faces, not the tops of their heads.

Test Bank The Test Bank has been rigorously revised for this third edition of *Economics: Brief* by Randy Grant. All questions are coded according to chapter learning objectives, AACSB Assurance of Learning, and Bloom's Taxonomy guidelines. The computerized Test Bank is available in EZ Test, a flexible and easy-to-use electronic testing program that accommodates a wide range of question types, including user-created questions. You can access the test bank through McGraw-Hill *Connect*.

Computerized Test Bank Online TestGen is a complete, state-of-the-art test generator and editing application software that allows instructors to quickly and easily select test items from McGraw Hill's test bank content. The instructors can then organize, edit, and customize questions and answers to rapidly generate tests for paper or online administration. Questions can include stylized text, symbols, graphics, and equations that are inserted directly into questions using built-in mathematical templates. TestGen's random generator provides the option to display different text or calculated number values each time questions are used. With both quick-and-simple test creation and flexible and robust editing tools, TestGen is a complete test generator system for today's educators.

You can use our test bank software, TestGen, or *Connect* to easily query for learning outcomes and objectives that directly relate to the learning objectives for your course. You can then use the reporting features to aggregate student results in a similar fashion, making the collection and presentation of assurance-of-learning data simple and easy.

Diagnostic and Adaptive Learning of Concepts: LearnSmart

Adaptive Reading Experience SmartBook contains the same content as the print book, but actively tailors that content to the needs of the individual through adaptive probing. Instructors can assign SmartBook reading assignments for points to create incentives for students to come to class prepared.

▉LEARNSMART® Students want to make the best use of their study time. The LearnSmart adaptive self-study technology within *Connect* provides students with a seamless combination of practice, assessment, and remediation for every concept in the textbook. LearnSmart's intelligent software adapts to every student response and automatically delivers concepts that advance students' understanding while reducing time devoted to the concepts already mastered. The result for every student is the fastest path to mastery of the chapter concepts. LearnSmart

- Applies an intelligent concept engine to identify the relationships between concepts and to serve new concepts to each student only when he or she is ready.
- Adapts automatically to each student, so students spend less time on the topics they understand and practice more those they have yet to master.
- Provides continual reinforcement and remediation, but gives only as much guidance as students need.
- Integrates diagnostics as part of the learning experience.
- Enables you to assess which concepts students have efficiently learned on their own, thus freeing class time for more applications and discussion.

SMARTBOOK Smartbook is an extension of LearnSmart—an adaptive eBook that helps students focus their study time more effectively. As students read, Smartbook assesses comprehension and dynamically highlights where they need to study more.

Digital Image Library Every graph and table in the text is available in the Instructor's Resource section in Connect.

McGraw-Hill's Customer Experience Group We understand that getting the most from your new technology can be challenging. That's why our services don't stop after you purchase our products. You can e-mail our Product Specialists 24 hours a day to get product-training online. Or you can search our knowledge bank of Frequently Asked Questions on our support website. For Customer Support, call **800-331-5094,** or visit **www.mhhe.com/support.**

Tegrity *Tegrity Campus: Lectures 24/7* Tegrity Campus is a fully automated lecture capture solution used in traditional, hybrid, "flipped classes," and online courses to record lessons, lectures, and skills. Its personalized learning features make study time incredibly efficient and its ability to affordably scale brings this benefit to every student on campus. Patented search technology and real-time LMS integrations make Tegrity the market-leading solution and service.

create™ McGraw-Hill Create™ is a self-service website that allows you to create customized course materials using McGraw-Hill's comprehensive, cross-disciplinary content and digital products. You can even access third-party content such as readings, articles, cases, videos, and more. Arrange the content you've selected to match the scope and sequence of your course. Personalize your book with a cover design and choose the best format for your students—eBook, color print, or black-and-white print. And, when you are done, you'll receive a PDF review copy in just minutes!

Assurance-of-Learning Ready

Many educational institutions today are focused on the notion of *assurance of learning,* an important element of some accreditation standards. *Economics: Brief* is designed specifically to support your assurance-of-learning initiatives with a simple yet powerful solution.

Each test bank question for *Economics: Brief* maps to a specific chapter learning outcome/objective listed in the text. You can use our test bank software, EZ Test and EZ Test Online, or *Connect® Economics* to easily query for learning outcomes/objectives that directly relate to the learning objectives for your course. You can then use the reporting features of EZ Test to aggregate student results in similar fashion, making the collection and presentation of assurance-of-learning data simple and easy.

AACSB Statement

McGraw-Hill Education is a proud corporate member of AACSB International. Understanding the importance and value of AACSB accreditation, *Economics: Brief,* 3th edition, recognizes the curricula guidelines detailed in the AACSB standards for business accreditation by connecting selected questions in the text and the test bank to the six general knowledge and skill guidelines in the AACSB standards.

The statements contained in *Economics: Brief,* 3rd edition, are provided only as a guide for the users of this textbook. The AACSB leaves content coverage and assessment within the purview of individual schools, the mission of the school, and the faculty. While *Economics: Brief,* 3rd edition, and the teaching package make no claim of any specific AACSB qualification or evaluation, we have labeled within *Economics: Brief,* 3rd edition, selected questions according to the eight general knowledge and skills areas emphasized by AACSB.

Instructor Aids

PowerPoint Presentations Developed using Microsoft PowerPoint software, these slides are a step-by-step review of the key points in each of the book's 21 chapters. They are equally useful to the student in the classroom as lecture aids or for personal review at home or the computer lab. The slides use animation to show students how graphs build and shift.

Solutions Manual This manual provides detailed answers to the end-of-chapter questions.

Student Aids

Built-in Student Problem Set The built-in student problem set is found at the end of every chapter of *Economics: Brief*. Each chapter has 8 to 10 numerical and graphing problems tied to the content of the text.

Acknowledgments

We give special thanks to Randy R. Grant of Linfield College, who served as the content coordinator for *Economics: Brief Edition*. Professor Grant modified and seamlessly incorporated appropriate new content and revisions that the authors made in the twenty-first edition of *Economics* into this third edition of the *Brief Edition*. He also updated the tables and other information in *Economics: Brief Edition* and made various improvements that he deemed helpful or were suggested to him by the authors, reviewers, and publisher.

Finally, we wish to acknowledge William Walstad and Tom Barbiero (the coauthors of the Canadian edition of *Economics*) for their ongoing ideas and insights.

We are greatly indebted to an all-star group of professionals at McGraw-Hill—in particular Mark Christianson, Harvey Yep, Bruce Gin, Doug Ruby, Adam Huenecke, Anke Weekes, and Bobby Pearson for their publishing and marketing expertise. Matt Diamond provided the vibrant interior design and cover.

The third edition has benefited from a number of perceptive formal reviews. The reviewers, listed at the end of the preface, were a rich source of suggestions for this revision. To each of you, and others we may have inadvertently overlooked, thank you for your considerable help in improving *Economics: Brief Edition*.

Stanley L. Brue
Sean M. Flynn
Campbell R. McConnell

REVIEWERS

Mark Abajian, *San Diego City College*

Rebecca Arnold, *San Diego Mesa College*

Benjamin Artz, *University of Wisconsin, Milwaukee*

Clare Battista, *California Polytechnic State University*

Derek Berry, *Calhoun Community College*

Laura Jean Bhadra, *Northern Virginia Community College, Manassas*

Philip Bohan, *Ventura College*

Kalyan Chakraborty, *Emporia State University*

Jan Christopher, *Delaware State University*

Donald Coffin, *Indiana University Northwest*

Diana Denison, *Red Rocks Community College*

John Allen Deskins, *Creighton University, Omaha*

Caf Dowlah, *Queensborough Community College*

Mariano Escobedo, *Columbus State Community College*

Charles Fairchild, *Northern Virginia Community College, Manassas*

Charles Fraley, *Cincinnati State Tech and Community College*

Amy Gibson, *Christopher Newport University*

John Gibson, *Indiana University Northwest*

Robert Harris, *IUPUI, Indianapolis*

Mark Healy, *William Rainey Harper College*

Melinda Hickman, *Doane College*

Glenn Hsu, *Kishwaukee College*

Scott Hunt, *Columbus State Community College*

John Ifcher, *Santa Clara University*

Vani Kotcherlakota, *University of Nebraska, Kearney*

Marie Kratochvil, *Nassau Community College*

Teresa Laughlin, *Palomar College*

Melissa Lind, *University of Texas, Arlington*

Keith Malone, *University of North Alabama*

Khalid Mehtabdin, *College of Saint Rose*

Jennifer Kelleher Michaels, *Emmanuel College*

Babu Nahata, *University of Louisville*

Jim Payne, *Calhoun Community College*

Michael Petrowsky, *Glendale Community College*

Mitchell Redlo, *Monroe Community College*

Belinda Roman, *Palo Alto College*

Dave St. Clair, *California State University, East Bay*

Courtenay Stone, *Ball State University*

Gary Stone, *Winthrop University*

Anh Le Tran, *Lasell College*

Miao Wang, *Marquette University*

Timothy Wunder, *University of Texas, Arlington*

BRIEF CONTENTS

CONTENTS

Microeconomics
BRIEF EDITION

Third Edition

Introduction

1

©Tatiana Belova/Shutterstock

1 Chapter

Limits, Alternatives, and Choices

Learning Objectives

LO1.1 Define economics and the features of the economic perspective.

LO1.2 Describe the role of economic theory in economics.

LO1.3 Distinguish microeconomics from macroeconomics.

LO1.4 List the categories of scarce resources and delineate the nature of the economizing problem.

LO1.5 Apply production possibilities analysis, increasing opportunity costs, and economic growth.

LO1.6 (Chapter appendix) Understand graphs, curves, and slopes as they relate to economics.

(An appendix on understanding graphs follows this chapter. If you need a quick review of this mathematical tool, you might benefit by reading the appendix first.)

Economics is about wants and means. Biologically, people need only air, water, food, clothing, and shelter. But in modern society people also desire goods and services that provide a more comfortable or affluent standard of living. We want bottled water, soft drinks, and fruit juices, not just water from the creek. We want salads, burgers, and pizzas, not just berries and nuts. We want jeans, suits, and coats, not just woven reeds. We want apartments, condominiums, or houses, not just mud huts. And, as the saying goes, "That's not the half of it." We also want flat-panel TVs, Internet service, education, homeland security, cell phones, and much more.

Fortunately, society possesses productive resources such as labor and managerial talent, tools and machinery, and land and mineral deposits. These resources, employed in the economic system (or simply the economy), help us produce goods and services that satisfy many of our economic wants. But the blunt reality is that our economic wants far exceed the productive capacity of our scarce (limited) resources. We are forced to make choices. This unyielding truth underlies the definition of **economics,** which is the social science concerned with how individuals, institutions, and society make choices under conditions of scarcity.

The Economic Perspective

Economists view things through a particular perspective. This **economic perspective,** or economic way of thinking, has several critical and closely interrelated features.

Scarcity and Choice

From our definition of economics, it is easy to see why economists view the world through the lens of scarcity. Scarce economic resources mean limited goods and services. Scarcity restricts options and demands choices. Because we "can't have it all," we must decide what we will have and what we must forgo.

At the core of economics is the idea that "there is no free lunch." You may be treated to lunch, making it "free" to you, but someone bears a cost. Because all resources are either privately or collectively owned by members of society, ultimately, scarce inputs of land, equipment, farm labor, the labor of cooks and waiters, and managerial talent are required. Because these resources could have been used to produce something else, society sacrifices those other goods and services in making the lunch available. Economists call such

economics The study of how people, institutions, and society make economic choices under conditions of scarcity.

economic perspective A viewpoint that envisions individuals and institutions making rational decisions by comparing the marginal benefits and marginal costs associated with their actions.

ILLUSTRATING THE IDEA

Did Zuckerberg, Swift, and Lawrence Make Bad Choices?

The importance of opportunity costs in decision making is illustrated by different choices people make with respect to college. Average salaries of college graduates are nearly twice as high as those earned by persons with just high school diplomas. For most capable students, "Go to college, stay in college, and earn a degree" is very sound advice.

Yet Facebook founder Mark Zuckerberg dropped out of college, pop singer Taylor Swift never started classes, and Jennifer Lawrence dropped out of high school. What were they thinking? Unlike most students, Zuckerberg faced enormous opportunity costs for staying in college. He had a vision for his company, and dropping out helped to ensure Facebook's success. Swift knew that staying on top in the world of pop takes unceasing work. So after her first album became a massive hit for her at the age of 16, it made sense for her to skip college in order to relentlessly pursue continuing success. And Lawrence was discovered by a talent scout at the age of 14, quit high school, and has become one of America's highest paid film stars. Finishing high school might have interrupted the string of successes that made her career possible.

So Zuckerberg, Swift, and Lawrence understood opportunity costs and made their choices accordingly. The size of opportunity costs matters greatly in making individual decisions.

QUESTION: Professional athletes sometimes return to college after they retire from professional sports. How does that college decision relate to opportunity costs?

opportunity cost The value of the good, service, or time forgone to obtain something else.

sacrifices **opportunity costs:** To obtain more of one thing, society forgoes the opportunity of getting the next best thing. That sacrifice is the opportunity cost of the choice.

Purposeful Behavior

Economics assumes that human behavior reflects "rational self-interest." Individuals look for and pursue opportunities to increase their **utility:** pleasure, happiness, or satisfaction. They allocate their time, energy, and money to maximize their satisfaction. Because they weigh costs and benefits, their decisions are "purposeful" or "rational," not "random" or "chaotic."

utility The want-satisfying power of a good or service; the satisfaction or pleasure a consumer obtains from the consumption of a good or service (or from the consumption of a collection of goods and services).

Consumers are purposeful in deciding what goods and services to buy. Business firms are purposeful in deciding what products to produce and how to produce them. Government entities are purposeful in deciding what public services to provide and how to finance them.

"Purposeful behavior" does not assume that people and institutions are immune from faulty logic and therefore are perfect decision makers. They sometimes make mistakes. Nor does it mean that people's decisions are unaffected by emotion or the decisions of those around them. People sometimes are impulsive or emulative. "Purposeful behavior" simply means that people make decisions with some desired outcome in mind. (In Chapter 21 on behavioral economics, we examine the sources and impacts of certain systematic errors in economic decision making that people regularly commit.)

Nor is rational self-interest the same as selfishness. We will find that increasing one's own wage, rent, interest, or profit normally requires identifying and satisfying somebody else's want. Also, many people make personal sacrifices to others without expecting any monetary reward. They contribute time and money to charities because they derive pleasure from doing so. Parents help pay for their children's education for the same reason. These self-interested, but unselfish, acts help maximize the givers' satisfaction as much as any personal purchase of goods or services. Self-interested behavior is simply behavior designed to increase personal satisfaction, however it may be derived.

Marginalism: Comparing Benefits and Costs

marginal analysis The comparison of marginal ("extra" or "additional") benefits and marginal costs, usually for decision making.

The economic perspective focuses largely on **marginal analysis**—comparisons of marginal benefits and marginal costs. To economists, "marginal" means "extra," "additional," or "a change in." Most choices or decisions involve changes in the status quo, meaning the existing state of affairs.

Should you attend school for another year? Should you study an extra hour for an exam? Should you supersize your fries? Similarly, should a business expand or reduce its output? Should government increase or decrease its funding for a missile defense system?

Each option involves marginal benefits and, because of scarce resources, marginal costs. In making choices rationally, the decision maker must compare those two amounts. Example: You and your fiancée are shopping for an engagement ring. Should you buy a $\frac{1}{2}$-carat diamond, a $\frac{5}{8}$-carat diamond, a $\frac{3}{4}$-carat diamond, a 1-carat diamond, or something even larger? The marginal cost of a larger-size diamond is the added expense beyond the cost of the smaller-size diamond. The marginal benefit is the perceived greater lifetime pleasure (utility) from the larger-size stone. If the marginal benefit of the larger diamond exceeds its marginal cost (and you can afford it), buy the larger stone. But if the marginal cost is more than the marginal benefit, you should buy the smaller diamond instead—even if you can afford the larger stone!

In a world of scarcity, the decision to obtain the marginal benefit associated with some specific option always includes the marginal cost of forgoing something else. The money spent on the larger-size diamond means forgoing some other product. An opportunity cost, the value of the next best thing forgone, is always present whenever a choice is made.

APPLYING THE ANALYSIS

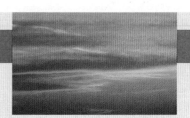

Fast-Food Lines

The economic perspective is useful in analyzing all sorts of behaviors. Consider an everyday example: the behavior of fast-food customers. When customers enter the restaurant, they go to the shortest line, believing that line will minimize their time cost of obtaining food. They are acting purposefully; time is limited, and people prefer using it in some way other than standing in a long line.

If one fast-food line is temporarily shorter than other lines, some people will move to that line. These movers apparently view the time saving from the shorter line (marginal benefit) as exceeding the cost of moving from their present line (marginal cost). The line switching tends to equalize line lengths. No further movement of customers between lines occurs once all lines are about equal.

Fast-food customers face another cost-benefit decision when a clerk opens a new station at the counter. Should they move to the new station or stay put? Those who shift to the new line decide that the time saving from the move exceeds the extra cost of physically moving. In so deciding, customers must also consider just how quickly they can get to the new station compared with others who may be contemplating the same move. (Those who hesitate in this situation are lost!)

Customers at the fast-food establishment do not have perfect information when they select lines. Thus, not all decisions turn out as expected. For example, you might enter a short line and find someone in front of you is ordering hamburgers and fries for 40 people in the Greyhound bus parked out back (and the employee is a trainee)! Nevertheless, at the time you made your decision, you thought it was optimal.

Finally, customers must decide what food to order when they arrive at the counter. In making their choices, they again compare marginal costs and marginal benefits in attempting to obtain the greatest personal satisfaction for their expenditure.

Economists believe that what is true for the behavior of customers at fast-food restaurants is true for economic behavior in general. Faced with an array of choices, consumers, workers, and businesses rationally compare marginal costs and marginal benefits in making decisions.

QUESTION: Have you ever gone to a fast-food restaurant only to observe long lines and then leave? Use the economic perspective to explain your behavior.

Theories, Principles, and Models

Like the physical and life sciences, as well as other social sciences, economics relies on the **scientific method.** That procedure consists of several elements:

- Observing real-world behavior and outcomes.
- Based on those observations, formulating a possible explanation of cause and effect (hypothesis).
- Testing this explanation by comparing the outcomes of specific events to the outcome predicted by the hypothesis.
- Accepting, rejecting, or modifying the hypothesis, based on these comparisons.

scientific method The procedure for the systematic pursuit of knowledge involving the observation of facts and the formulation and testing of hypotheses to obtain theories, principles, and laws.

- Continuing to test the hypothesis against the facts. As favorable results accumulate, the hypothesis evolves into a *theory.* A very well-tested and widely accepted theory is referred to as a *law* or *principle.* Combinations of such laws or principles are incorporated into *models,* which are simplified representations of how something works, such as a market or segment of the economy.

Economists develop theories of the behavior of individuals (consumers, workers) and institutions (businesses, governments) engaged in the production, exchange, and consumption of goods and services. Economic theories and **principles** are statements about economic behavior or the economy that enable prediction of the probable effects of certain actions. They are "purposeful simplifications." The full scope of economic reality itself is too complex and bewildering to be understood as a whole. In developing theories and principles, economists remove the clutter and simplify.

Economic principles and models are highly useful in analyzing economic behavior and understanding how the economy operates. They are the tools for ascertaining cause and effect (or action and outcome) within the economic system. Good theories do a good job of explaining and predicting. They are supported by facts concerning how individuals and institutions actually behave in producing, exchanging, and consuming goods and services.

There are some other things you should know about economic principles:

- *Generalizations*   Economic principles are *generalizations* relating to economic behavior or to the economy itself. Economic principles are expressed as the tendencies of typical or average consumers, workers, or business firms. For example, economists say that consumers buy more of a particular product when its price falls. Economists recognize that some consumers may increase their purchases by a large amount, others by a small amount, and a few not at all. This "price-quantity" principle, however, holds for the typical consumer and for consumers as a group.
- *Other-things-equal assumption*   Like other scientists, economists use the *ceteris paribus* or **other-things-equal assumption** to construct their theories. They assume that all variables except those under immediate consideration are held constant for a particular analysis. For example, consider the relationship between the price of Pepsi and the amount of it purchased. It helps to assume that, of all the factors that might influence the amount of Pepsi purchased (for example, the price of Pepsi, the price of Coca-Cola, and consumer incomes and preferences), only the price of Pepsi varies. The economist can then focus on the relationship between the price of Pepsi and purchases of Pepsi in isolation without being confused by changes in other variables.
- *Graphical expression*   Many economic models are expressed graphically. Be sure to read the special appendix at the end of this chapter as a review of graphs.

Microeconomics and Macroeconomics

Economists develop economic principles and models at two levels.

Microeconomics

Microeconomics is the part of economics concerned with decision making by individual consumers, households, and business firms. At this level of analysis, we observe the details of their behavior under a figurative microscope. We measure the price of a specific product, the number of workers employed by a single firm, the revenue or income of a particular firm or household, or the expenditures of a specific firm, government entity, or family.

principles Statements about economic behavior that enable prediction of the probable effects of certain actions.

other-things-equal assumption The assumption that factors other than those being considered are held constant; *ceteris paribus* assumption.

microeconomics The part of economics concerned with such individual units as a household, a firm, or an industry and with individual markets, specific goods and services, and product and resource prices.

PHOTO OP Micro versus Macro

Figuratively, microeconomics examines the sand, rock, and shells, not the beach; in contrast, macroeconomics examines the beach, not the sand, rocks, and shells.

Source: NPS Photo

©Shutterstock/holbox

Macroeconomics

Macroeconomics examines either the economy as a whole or its basic subdivisions or aggregates, such as the government, household, and business sectors. An **aggregate** is a collection of specific economic units treated as if they were one unit. Therefore, we might lump together the millions of consumers in the U.S. economy and treat them as if they were one huge unit called "consumers."

In using aggregates, macroeconomics seeks to obtain an overview, or general outline, of the structure of the economy and the relationships of its major aggregates. Macroeconomics speaks of such economic measures as total output, total employment, total income, aggregate expenditures, and the general level of prices in analyzing various economic problems. Very little attention is given to specific units making up the various aggregates.

> **macroeconomics** The part of economics concerned with the economy as a whole; with such major aggregates as the household, business, and government sectors; and with measures of the total economy.

> **aggregate** A collection of specific economic units treated as if they were one. For example, all prices of individual goods and services are combined into a price level, or all the units of output are aggregated into gross domestic product.

Individual's Economic Problem

It is clear from our previous discussion that both individuals and society face an **economic problem:** They need to make choices because economic wants are unlimited, but the means (income, time, resources) for satisfying those wants are limited. Let's first look at the economic problem faced by individuals. To explain the idea, we will construct a very simple microeconomic model.

> **economic problem** The choices necessitated because society's economic wants for goods and services are unlimited but the resources available to satisfy these wants are limited (scarce).

Limited Income

We all have a finite amount of income, even the wealthiest among us. Sure Bill Gates earns a bit more than the rest of us, but he still has to decide how to spend his money! And the majority of us have much more limited means. Our income comes to us in the form of wages, interest, rent, and profit, although we may also receive money from government programs or family members. As Global Snapshot 1.1 shows, the average income of Americans in 2016 was $56,810. In the poorest nations, it was less than $500.

Average Income, Selected Nations

Average income (total income/population) and therefore typical budget constraints vary greatly among nations.

Country	Per Capita Income, 2016*
Norway	$82,240
United States	56,810
Sweden	54,590
Singapore	51,880
France	38,720
South Korea	27,600
Mexico	9,040
China	8,250
Iraq	5,420
India	1,670
Madagascar	400
Malawi	320

*U.S. dollars, based on exchange rates.
Source: World Bank, **www.worldbank.org.**

Unlimited Wants

For better or worse, most people have virtually unlimited wants. We desire various goods and services that provide utility. Our wants extend over a wide range of products, from *necessities* (food, shelter, clothing) to *luxuries* (perfumes, yachts, sports cars). Some wants such as basic food, clothing, and shelter have biological roots. Other wants, for example, specific kinds of food, clothing, and shelter, arise from the conventions and customs of society.

Over time, economic wants tend to change and multiply, fueled by new and improved products. Only recently have people wanted iPods, Internet service, digital cameras, or camera phones because those products did not exist a few decades ago. Also, the satisfaction of certain wants may trigger others: The acquisition of a Ford Focus or a Honda Civic has been known to whet the appetite for a Lexus or a Mercedes.

Services, as well as goods, satisfy our wants. Car repair work, the removal of an inflamed appendix, legal and accounting advice, and haircuts all satisfy human wants. Actually, we buy many goods, such as automobiles and washing machines, for the services they render. The differences between goods and services are often smaller than they appear to be.

For most people, the desires for goods and services cannot be fully satisfied. Bill Gates may have all that he wants for himself, but his massive charitable giving suggests that he keenly wants better health care for the world's poor. Our desires for a *particular* good or

PHOTO OP Necessities versus Luxuries

Economic wants include both necessities and luxuries. Each type of item provides utility to the buyer.

©David Sachs/Getty Images   ©Ingram Publishing

service can be satisfied; over a short period of time we can surely obtain enough toothpaste or pasta. And one appendectomy is plenty. But our broader desire for more goods and services and higher-quality goods and services seems to be another story.

Because we have only limited income but seemingly insatiable wants, it is in our self-interest to economize: to pick and choose goods and services that maximize our satisfaction, given the limitations we face.

A Budget Line

The economic problem facing individuals can be depicted as a **budget line** (or, more technically, *budget constraint*). It is a schedule or curve that shows various combinations of two products a consumer can purchase with a specific money income.

To understand this idea, suppose that you received a Barnes & Noble gift card as a birthday present. The $120 card is soon to expire. You take the card to the store and confine your purchase decisions to two alternatives: DVDs and paperback books. DVDs are $20 each, and paperback books are $10 each. Your purchase options are shown in the table in Figure 1.1.

At one extreme, you might spend all of your $120 "income" on 6 DVDs at $20 each and have nothing left to spend on books. Or, by giving up 2 DVDs and thereby gaining $40, you can have 4 DVDs at $20 each and 4 books at $10 each. And so on to the other extreme, at which you could buy 12 books at $10 each, spending your entire gift card on books with nothing left to spend on DVDs.

The graph in Figure 1.1 shows the budget line. As elsewhere in this book, we represent discrete (separate element) numbers in tables as points on continuous-data smooth curves. Therefore, note that the line (curve) in the graph is not restricted to whole units of DVDs and books as is the table. Every point on the line represents a possible combination of DVDs and books, including fractional quantities. The slope of the graphed budget line measures the ratio of the price of books (P_b) to the price of DVDs (P_{dvd}); more precisely, the slope is $P_b/P_{dvd} = \${-10}/\$+20 = -\frac{1}{2}$ or $-.5$. So you must forgo 1 DVD (measured on the vertical axis) to buy 2 books (measured on the horizontal axis). This yields a slope of $-\frac{1}{2}$ or $-.5$.

The budget line illustrates several ideas.

budget line A line that shows the different combinations of two products a consumer can purchase with a specific money income, given the products' prices.

FIGURE 1.1 A consumer's budget line. The budget line (or budget constraint) shows all the combinations of any two products that can be purchased, given the prices of the products and the consumer's money income.

The Budget Line: Whole-Unit Combinations of DVDs and Paperback Books Attainable with an Income of $120		
Units of DVDs (Price = $20)	Units of Books (Price = $10)	Total Expenditure
6	0	$120 = ($120 + $0)
5	2	$120 = ($100 + $20)
4	4	$120 = ($80 + $40)
3	6	$120 = ($60 + $60)
2	8	$120 = ($40 + $80)
1	10	$120 = ($20 + $100)
0	12	$120 = ($0 + $120)

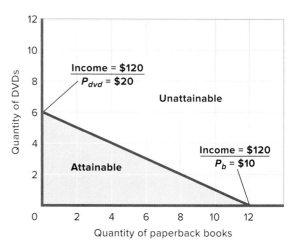

Attainable and Unattainable Combinations All the combinations of DVDs and books on or inside the budget line are *attainable* from the $120 of money income. You can afford to buy, for example, 3 DVDs at $20 each and 6 books at $10 each. You also can obviously afford to buy 2 DVDs and 5 books, thereby using up only $90 of the $120 available on your gift card. But to achieve maximum utility, you will want to spend the full $120. The budget line shows all combinations that cost exactly the full $120.

In contrast, all combinations beyond the budget line are *unattainable*. The $120 limit simply does not allow you to purchase, for example, 5 DVDs at $20 each and 5 books at $10 each. That $150 expenditure would clearly exceed the $120 limit. In Figure 1.1, the attainable combinations are on and within the budget line; the unattainable combinations are beyond the budget line.

Trade-offs and Opportunity Costs The budget line in Figure 1.1 illustrates the idea of trade-offs arising from limited income. To obtain more DVDs, you have to give up some books. For example, to acquire the first DVD, you trade off 2 books. So the opportunity cost of the first DVD is 2 books. To obtain the second DVD, the opportunity cost is also 2 books. The straight-line budget constraint, with its constant slope, indicates **constant opportunity cost.** That is, the opportunity cost of 1 extra DVD remains the same (= 2 books) as more DVDs are purchased. And, in reverse, the opportunity cost of 1 extra book does not change (= $\frac{1}{2}$ DVD) as more books are bought.

constant opportunity cost An opportunity cost that remains the same for each additional unit as a consumer (or society) shifts purchases (production) from one product to another along a straight-line budget line (production possibilities curve).

Choice Limited income forces people to choose what to buy and what to forgo to fulfill wants. You will select the combination of DVDs and paperback books that you think is "best." That is, you will evaluate your marginal benefits and your marginal costs (here, product price) to make choices that maximize your satisfaction. Other people, with the same $120 gift card, would undoubtedly make different choices.

Income Changes The location of the budget line varies with money income. An increase in money income shifts the budget line to the right; a decrease in money income shifts it to the left. To verify this, recalculate the table in Figure 1.1, assuming the card value (income) is (a) $240 and (b) $60, and plot the new budget lines in the graph. No wonder people like to have more income: That shifts their budget lines outward and enables them to buy more goods and services. But even with more income, people will still face spending trade-offs, choices, and opportunity costs.

Society's Economic Problem

Society must also make choices under conditions of scarcity. It, too, faces an economic problem. Should it devote more of its limited resources to the criminal justice system (police, courts, and prisons) or to education (teachers, books, and schools)? If it decides to devote more resources to both, what other goods and services does it forgo? Health care? Homeland security? Energy development?

Scarce Resources

Society's economic resources are limited or scarce. By **economic resources** we mean all natural, human, and manufactured resources that go into the production of goods and services. That includes the entire set of factory and farm buildings and all the equipment, tools, and machinery used to produce manufactured goods and agricultural products; all transportation and communication facilities; all types of labor; and land and mineral resources.

economic resources The land, labor, capital, and entrepreneurial ability that are used in the production of goods and services; productive agents; factors of production.

Resource Categories

Economists classify economic resources into four general categories.

Land Land means much more to the economist than it does to most people. To the economist **land** includes all natural resources ("gifts of nature") used in the production process. These include mineral and oil deposits, arable land, forests, and water resources.

land Natural resources ("free gifts of nature") used to produce goods and services.

Labor The resource **labor** consists of the physical actions and mental activities that people contribute to the production of goods and services. The work-related activities of a logger, retail clerk, machinist, teacher, professional football player, and nuclear physicist all fall under the general heading "labor."

labor People's physical and mental talents and efforts that are used to help produce goods and services.

Capital For economists, **capital** (or *capital goods*) includes all manufactured aids used in producing consumer goods and services. Included are all factory, storage, transportation, and distribution facilities, as well as all tools and machinery. Economists use the term **investment** to describe spending that pays for the production and accumulation of capital goods.

Capital goods differ from consumer goods because consumer goods satisfy wants directly, while capital goods do so indirectly by aiding the production of consumer goods. For example, large commercial baking ovens (capital goods) help make loaves of bread (consumer goods). Note that the term "capital" as used by economists refers not to money but to tools, machinery, and other productive equipment. Because money produces nothing, economists do not include it as an economic resource. Money (or money capital or financial capital) is simply a means for purchasing goods and services, including capital goods.

capital Human-made resources (buildings, machinery, and equipment) used to produce goods and services; goods that do not directly satisfy human wants; also called *capital goods* and *investment goods*.

investment Spending for the production and accumulation of capital and additions to inventories.

Entrepreneurial Ability Finally, there is the special human resource, distinct from labor, called **entrepreneurial ability.** The entrepreneur performs several socially useful functions:

- The entrepreneur takes the initiative in combining the resources of land, labor, and capital to produce a good or a service. Both a spark plug and a catalyst, the entrepreneur is the driving force behind production and the agent who combines the other resources in what is hoped will be a successful business venture.

entrepreneurial ability The human resource that combines the other resources to produce a product, makes nonroutine decisions, innovates, and bears risks.

- The entrepreneur makes the strategic business decisions that set the course of an enterprise.
- The entrepreneur innovates. He or she commercializes new products, new production techniques, or even new forms of business organization.
- The entrepreneur bears risk. Innovation is risky, as nearly all new products and ideas are subject to the possibility of failure as well as success. Progress would cease without entrepreneurs who are willing to take on risk by devoting their time, effort, and ability—as well as their own money and the money of others—to commercializing new products and ideas that may enhance society's standard of living.

Because land, labor, capital, and entrepreneurial ability are combined to produce goods and services, they are called the **factors of production** or simply inputs.

factors of production Economic resources: land, capital, labor, and entrepreneurial ability.

Production Possibilities Model

Society uses its scarce resources to produce goods and services. The alternatives and choices it faces can best be understood through a macroeconomic model of production possibilities. To keep things simple, we assume

- *Full employment* The economy is employing all of its available resources.
- *Fixed resources* The quantity and quality of the factors of production are fixed.
- *Fixed technology* The state of technology (the methods used to produce output) is constant.
- *Two goods* The economy is producing only two goods: food products and manufacturing equipment. Food products symbolize **consumer goods,** products that satisfy our wants directly; manufacturing equipment symbolizes **capital goods,** products that satisfy our wants indirectly by making possible more efficient production of consumer goods.

consumer goods Products and services that satisfy human wants directly.

capital goods Items that are used to produce other goods and therefore do not directly satisfy consumer wants.

Production Possibilities Table

A production possibilities table lists the different combinations of two products that can be produced with a specific set of resources, assuming full employment. Figure 1.2 contains such a table for a simple economy that is producing pizza and industrial robots; the data

FIGURE 1.2 The production possibilities curve. Each point on the production possibilities curve represents some maximum combination of two products that can be produced if resources are fully and efficiently employed. When an economy is operating on the curve, more industrial robots means fewer pizzas, and vice versa. Limited resources and a fixed technology make any combination of industrial robots and pizza lying outside the curve (such as at *W*) unattainable. Points inside the curve are attainable, but they indicate that full employment is not being realized.

Type of Product	Production Alternatives				
	A	**B**	**C**	**D**	**E**
Pizzas (in hundred thousands)	0	1	2	3	4
Industrial robots (in thousands)	10	9	7	4	0

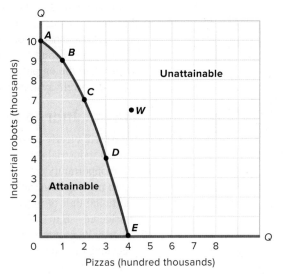

are, of course, hypothetical. At alternative A, this economy would be devoting all its available resources to the production of industrial robots (capital goods); at alternative E, all resources would go to pizza production (consumer goods). Those alternatives are unrealistic extremes; an economy typically produces both capital goods and consumer goods, as in B, C, and D. As we move from alternative A to E, we increase the production of pizza at the expense of the production of industrial robots.

Because consumer goods satisfy our wants directly, any movement toward E looks tempting. In producing more pizza, society increases the satisfaction of its current wants. But there is a cost: More pizzas mean fewer industrial robots. This shift of resources to consumer goods catches up with society over time because the stock of capital goods expands more slowly, thereby reducing potential future production. By moving toward alternative E, society chooses "more now" at the expense of "much more later."

By moving toward A, society chooses to forgo current consumption, thereby freeing up resources that can be used to increase the production of capital goods. By building up its stock of capital this way, society will have greater future production and, therefore, greater future consumption. By moving toward A, society is choosing "more later" at the cost of "less now."

Generalization: At any point in time, a fully employed economy must sacrifice some of one good to obtain more of another good. Scarce resources prohibit such an economy from having more of both goods. Society must choose among alternatives. There is no such thing as a free pizza or a free industrial robot. Having more of one thing means having less of something else.

Production Possibilities Curve

The data presented in a production possibilities table can also be shown graphically. We arbitrarily represent the economy's output of capital goods (here, industrial robots) on the vertical axis and the output of consumer goods (here, pizza) on the horizontal axis, as shown in Figure 1.2.

production possibilities curve
A curve showing the different combinations of two goods or services that can be produced in a full-employment, full-production economy where the available supplies of resources and technology are fixed.

Each point on the **production possibilities curve** represents some maximum output of the two products. The curve is a "constraint" because it shows the limit of attainable outputs. Points on the curve are attainable as long as the economy uses all its available resources. Points lying inside the curve are also attainable, but they reflect less total output and therefore are not as desirable as points on the curve. Points inside the curve imply that the economy could have more of both industrial robots and pizzas if it achieved full employment. Points lying beyond the production possibilities curve, like *W*, would represent a greater output than the output at any point on the curve. Such points, however, are unattainable with the current availability of resources and technology.

Law of Increasing Opportunity Costs

Figure 1.2 clearly shows that more pizzas mean fewer industrial robots. The number of units of industrial robots that must be given up to obtain another unit of pizzas, of course, is the opportunity cost of that unit of pizzas.

In moving from alternative A to alternative B in the table in Figure 1.2, the cost of 1 additional unit of pizza is 1 less unit of industrial robots. But when additional units are considered—B to C, C to D, and D to E—an important economic principle is revealed: The opportunity cost of each additional unit of pizzas is greater than the opportunity cost of the preceding one. When we move from A to B, just 1 unit of industrial robots is sacrificed for 1 more unit of pizzas; but in going from B to C, we sacrifice 2 additional units of industrial robots for 1 more unit of pizzas; then 3 more of industrial robots for 1 more of pizzas; and finally 4 for 1. Conversely, confirm that as we move from E to A, the cost of an additional unit of industrial robots (on average) is $\frac{1}{4}$, $\frac{1}{3}$, $\frac{1}{2}$, and 1 unit of pizzas, respectively, for the four successive moves.

law of increasing opportunity costs The principle that as the production of a good increases, the opportunity cost of producing an additional unit rises.

Our example illustrates the **law of increasing opportunity costs:** The more of a product that society produces, the greater is the opportunity cost of obtaining an extra unit.

Shape of the Curve   The law of increasing opportunity costs is reflected in the shape of the production possibilities curve: The curve is bowed out from the origin of the graph. Figure 1.2 shows that when the economy moves from *A* to *E*, it must give up successively larger amounts of industrial robots (1, 2, 3, and 4) to acquire equal increments of pizzas (1, 1, 1, and 1). This is shown in the slope of the production possibilities curve, which becomes steeper as we move from *A* to *E*.

Economic Rationale   The law of increasing opportunity costs is driven by the fact that economic resources are not completely adaptable to alternative uses. Many resources are better at producing one type of good than at producing others. Consider land. Some land is highly suited to growing the ingredients necessary for pizza production. But as pizza production expands, society has to start using land that is less bountiful for farming. Other land is rich in mineral deposits and therefore well-suited to producing the materials needed to make industrial robots. That land will be the first land devoted to the production of industrial robots. But as society steps up the production of industrial robots, it must use resources that are less and less suited to making their components.

If we start at *A* and move to *B* in Figure 1.2, we can shift resources whose productivity is relatively high in pizza production and low in industrial robots. But as we move from *B* to *C*, *C* to *D*, and so on, resources highly productive of pizzas become increasingly scarce. To get more pizzas, resources whose productivity in industrial robots is relatively great will be needed. It will take increasingly more of such resources, and hence greater sacrifices of industrial robots, to achieve each 1-unit increase in pizzas. This lack of perfect flexibility, or interchangeability, on the part of resources is the cause of increasing opportunity costs for society.

Optimal Allocation

Of all the attainable combinations of pizzas and industrial robots on the curve in Figure 1.2, which is optimal (best)? That is, what specific quantities of resources should be allocated to pizzas and what specific quantities to industrial robots in order to maximize satisfaction?

Recall that economic decisions center on comparisons of marginal benefits (MB) and marginal costs (MC). Any economic activity should be expanded as long as marginal benefit exceeds marginal cost and should be reduced if marginal cost exceeds marginal benefit. The optimal amount of the activity occurs where MB = MC. Society needs to make a similar assessment about its production decision.

Consider pizzas. We already know from the law of increasing opportunity costs that the marginal cost of additional units of pizzas will rise as more units are produced. At the same time, we need to recognize that the extra or marginal benefits that come from producing and consuming pizzas decline with each successive unit of pizzas. Consequently, each successive unit of pizzas brings with it both increasing marginal costs and decreasing marginal benefits.

The optimal quantity of pizzas is indicated by the intersection of the MB and MC curves: 200,000 units in Figure 1.3. Why is this amount the optimal quantity? If only 100,000 units of pizzas were produced, the marginal benefit of an extra unit of them would exceed its marginal cost. In money terms, MB is $15, while MC is only $5. When society gains something worth $15 at a marginal cost of only $5, it is better off. In Figure 1.3, net gains of decreasing amounts can be realized until pizza production has been increased to 200,000.

In contrast, the production of 300,000 units of pizzas is excessive. There the MC of an added unit is $15 and its MB is only $5. This means that 1 unit of pizzas is worth only $5 to society but costs it $15 to obtain. This is a losing proposition for society!

So resources are being efficiently allocated to any product when the marginal benefit and marginal cost of its output are equal (MB = MC). Suppose that by applying the above analysis to industrial robots, we find its optimal (MB = MC) quantity is 7,000. This would mean that alternative *C* (200,000 units of pizzas and 7,000 units of industrial robots) on the production possibilities curve in Figure 1.2 would be optimal for this economy.

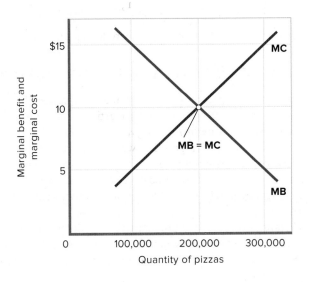

FIGURE 1.3 **Optimal output: MB = MC.** Achieving the optimal output requires the expansion of a good's output until its marginal benefit (MB) and marginal cost (MC) are equal. No resources beyond that point should be allocated to the product. Here, optimal output occurs when 200,000 units of pizzas are produced.

The Economics of War

Production possibilities analysis is helpful in assessing the costs and benefits of waging the war on terrorism, including the wars in Afghanistan and Iraq. At the end of 2015, the estimated cost of these efforts exceeded $1.7 trillion, with some projecting the total cost to reach $6 trillion, including interest costs, over the next 40 years.

If we categorize all of U.S. production as either "defense goods" or "civilian goods," we can measure them on the axes of a production possibilities diagram such as that shown in Figure 1.2. The opportunity cost of using more resources for defense goods is the civilian goods sacrificed. In a fully employed economy, more defense goods are achieved at the opportunity cost of fewer civilian goods—health care, education, pollution control, personal computers, houses, and so on. The cost of waging war is the other goods forgone. The benefits of these activities are numerous and diverse but clearly include the gains from protecting against future loss of American lives, assets, income, and well-being.

Society must assess the marginal benefit (MB) and marginal cost (MC) of additional defense goods to determine their optimal amounts—where to locate on the defense goods–civilian goods production possibilities curve. Although estimating marginal benefits and marginal costs is an imprecise art, the MB-MC framework is a useful way of approaching choices. Efficient allocation requires that society expand production of defense goods until MB = MC.

The events of September 11, 2001, and the future threats they posed increased the perceived marginal benefits of defense goods. If we label the horizontal axis in Figure 1.3 "defense goods," and draw in a rightward shift of the MB curve, you will see that the optimal quantity of defense goods rises. In view of the concerns relating to September 11, the United States allocated more of its resources to defense. But the MB-MC analysis also reminds us we can spend too much on defense, as well as too little. The United States should not expand defense goods beyond the point where MB = MC. If it does, it will be sacrificing civilian goods of greater value than the defense goods obtained.

QUESTION: Would society's costs of war be lower if it drafted soldiers at low pay rather than attracted them voluntarily to the military through market pay?

Unemployment, Growth, and the Future

In the depths of the Great Depression of the 1930s, one-quarter of U.S. workers were unemployed and one-third of U.S. production capacity was idle. Subsequent downturns have been much less severe. During the deep 2007–2009 recession, for instance, production fell by a comparably smaller 5.1 percent, and 1 in 10 workers was without a job.

Almost all nations have experienced widespread unemployment and unused production capacity from business downturns at one time or another. Since 2000, for example, several nations—including Argentina, Italy, Russia, Japan, and France—have had economic downturns and unemployment.

How do these realities relate to the production possibilities model? Our analysis and conclusions change if we relax the assumption that all available resources are fully employed. The five alternatives in the table of Figure 1.2 represent maximum outputs;

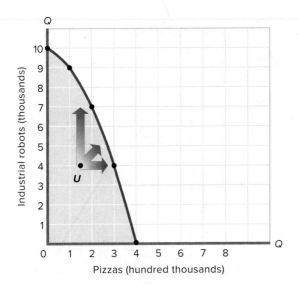

FIGURE 1.4 Unemployment and the production possibilities curve. Any point inside the production possibilities curve, such as *U*, represents unemployment or a failure to achieve full employment. The arrows indicate that, by realizing full employment, the economy could operate on the curve. This means it could produce more of one or both products than it is producing at point *U*.

they illustrate the combinations of pizzas and industrial robots that can be produced when the economy is operating at full employment. With unemployment, this economy would produce less than each alternative shown in the table.

Graphically, we represent situations of unemployment by points inside the original production possibilities curve (reproduced in Figure 1.4). Point *U* is one such point. Here the economy is falling short of the various maximum combinations of pizzas and industrial robots represented by the points on the production possibilities curve. The arrows in Figure 1.4 indicate three possible paths back to full employment. A move toward full employment would yield a greater output of one or both products.

A Growing Economy

When we drop the assumptions that the quantity and quality of resources and technology are fixed, the production possibilities curve shifts positions, and the potential maximum output of the economy changes.

Increases in Resource Supplies Although resource supplies are fixed at any specific moment, they change over time. For example, a nation's growing population brings about increases in the supplies of labor and entrepreneurial ability. Also, labor quality usually improves over time. Historically, the economy's stock of capital has increased at a significant, though unsteady, rate. And although some of our energy and mineral resources are being depleted, new sources are also being discovered. The development of irrigation systems, for example, adds to the supply of arable land.

The net result of these increased supplies of the factors of production is the ability to produce more of both consumer goods and capital goods. Thus, 20 years from now, the production possibilities in Figure 1.5 may supersede those shown in Figure 1.2. The greater abundance of resources will result in a greater potential output of one or both products at each alternative. The economy will have achieved economic growth in the form of expanded potential output. Thus, when an increase in the quantity or quality of resources occurs, the production possibilities curve shifts outward and to the right, as illustrated by the move from the inner curve to curve *A′ B′ C′ D′ E′* in Figure 1.5. This sort of shift represents growth of economic capacity, which, when used, means **economic growth:** a larger total output.

economic growth (1) An outward shift in the production possibilities curve that results from an increase in resource supplies or quality or an improvement in technology; (2) an increase of real output (gross domestic product) or real output per capita.

FIGURE 1.5 **Economic growth and the production possibilities curve.** The increase in supplies of resources, the improvements in resource quality, and the technological advances that occur in a dynamic economy move the production possibilities curve outward and to the right, allowing the economy to have larger quantities of both types of goods.

Type of Product	Production Alternatives				
	A′	**B′**	**C′**	**D′**	**E′**
Pizzas (in hundred thousands)	0	2	4	6	8
Industrial robots (in thousands)	14	12	9	5	0

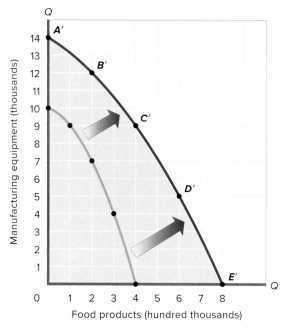

Advances in Technology

An advancing technology brings both new and better goods and improved ways of producing them. For now, let's think of technological advance as being only improvements in the methods of production, for example, the introduction of computerized systems to manage inventories and schedule production. These advances alter our previous discussion of the economic problem by allowing society to produce more goods with available resources. As with increases in resource supplies, technological advances make possible the production of more manufacturing equipment *and* more food products.

Conclusion: Economic growth is the result of (1) increases in supplies of resources, (2) improvements in resource quality, and (3) technological advances. The consequence of growth is that a full-employment economy can enjoy a greater output of both consumption goods and capital goods. While static, no-growth economies must sacrifice some of one good to obtain more of another, dynamic, growing economies can have larger quantities of both goods.

Present Choices and Future Possibilities

An economy's current choice of positions on its production possibilities curve helps determine the future location of that curve. Let's designate the two axes of the production possibilities curve as "goods for the future" and "goods for the present," as in Figure 1.6. Goods for the future are such things as capital goods, research and education, and preventive medicine. They increase the quantity and quality of property resources, enlarge the stock of technological information, and improve the quality of human resources. As we have already seen, goods for the future, such as capital goods, are the ingredients of economic growth. Goods for the present are consumer goods such as food, clothing, and entertainment.

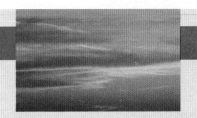

APPLYING THE ANALYSIS

Information Technology and Biotechnology

A real-world example of improved technology is the recent surge of new technologies relating to computers, communications, and biotechnology. Technological advances have dropped the prices of computers and greatly increased their speed. Improved software has greatly increased the everyday usefulness of computers. Cellular phones and the Internet have increased communications capacity, enhancing production and improving the efficiency of markets. Advances in biotechnology have resulted in important agricultural and medical discoveries. These and other new and improved technologies have contributed to U.S. economic growth (outward shifts of the nation's production possibilities curve).

QUESTION: How have technological advances in medicine helped expand production possibilities in the United States?

Now suppose there are two hypothetical economies, Presentville and Futureville, which are initially identical in every respect except one: Presentville's current choice of positions on its production possibilities curve strongly favors present goods over future goods. Point *P* in Figure 1.6a indicates that choice. It is located quite far down the curve to the right, indicating a high priority for goods for the present, at the expense of less goods for the future. Futureville, in contrast, makes a current choice that stresses larger amounts of future goods and smaller amounts of present goods, as shown by point *F* in Figure 1.6b.

FIGURE 1.6 Present choices and future locations of production possibilities curves. A nation's current choice favoring "present goods," as made by Presentville in (a), will cause a modest outward shift of the production possibilities curve in the future. A nation's current choice favoring "future goods," as made by Futureville in (b), will result in a greater outward shift of the curve in the future.

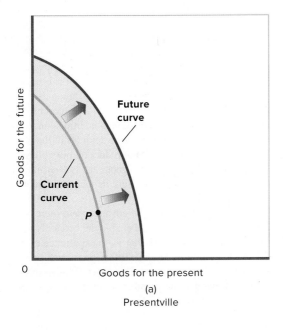

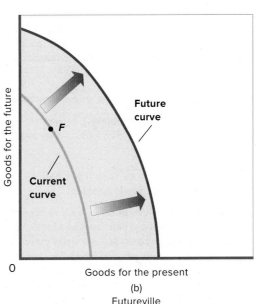

Now, other things equal, we can expect Futureville's future production possibilities curve to be farther to the right than Presentville's future production possibilities curve. By currently choosing an output more favorable to technological advances and to increases in the quantity and quality of resources, Futureville will achieve greater economic growth than Presentville. In terms of capital goods, Futureville is choosing to make larger current additions to its "national factory" by devoting more of its current output to capital than Presentville. The payoff from this choice for Futureville is greater future production capacity and economic growth. The opportunity cost is fewer consumer goods in the present for Futureville to enjoy.

Is Futureville's choice thus necessarily "better" than Presentville's? That, we cannot say. The different outcomes simply reflect different preferences and priorities in the two countries. But each country will have to live with the consequences of its choice.

SUMMARY

LO1.1 Define economics and the features of the economic perspective.

Economics is the social science that studies how people, institutions, and society make choices under conditions of scarcity. Central to economics is the idea of opportunity cost: the value of the good, service, or time forgone to obtain something else.

The economic perspective includes three elements: scarcity and choice, purposeful behavior, and marginalism. It sees individuals and institutions making rational decisions based on comparisons of marginal costs and marginal benefits.

LO1.2 Describe the role of economic theory in economics.

Economists employ the scientific method, in which they form and test hypotheses of cause-and-effect relationships to generate theories, laws, and principles. Economists often combine theories into representations called models.

LO1.3 Distinguish microeconomics from macroeconomics.

Microeconomics examines the decision making of specific economic units or institutions. Macroeconomics looks at the economy as a whole or its major aggregates.

LO1.4 List the categories of scarce resources and delineate the nature of the economic problem.

Individuals face an economic problem. Because their wants exceed their incomes, they must decide what to purchase and what to forgo. Society also faces an economic problem. Societal wants exceed the available resources necessary to fulfill them. Society therefore must decide what to produce and what to forgo.

Graphically, a budget line (or budget constraint) illustrates the economic problem for individuals. The line shows the various combinations of two products that a consumer can purchase with a specific money income, given the prices of the two products.

Economic resources are inputs into the production process and can be classified as land, labor, capital, and entrepreneurial ability. Economic resources are also known as factors of production or inputs.

Society's economic problem can be illustrated through production possibilities analysis. Production possibilities tables and curves show the different combinations of goods and services that can be produced in a fully employed economy, assuming that resource quantity, resource quality, and technology are fixed.

LO1.5 Apply production possibilities analysis, increasing opportunity costs, and economic growth.

An economy that is fully employed and thus operating on its production possibilities curve must sacrifice the output of some types of goods and services to increase the production of others. The gain of one type of good or service is always accompanied by an opportunity cost in the form of the loss of some of the other type.

Because resources are not equally productive in all possible uses, shifting resources from one use to another results in increasing opportunity costs. The production of additional units of one product requires the sacrifice of increasing amounts of the other product.

The optimal point on the production possibilities curve represents the most desirable mix of goods and is determined by expanding the production of each good until its marginal benefit (MB) equals its marginal cost (MC).

Over time, technological advances and increases in the quantity and quality of resources enable the economy to produce more of all goods and services, that is, to experience economic growth. Society's choice as to the mix of consumer goods and capital goods in current output is a major determinant of the future location of the production possibilities curve and thus of the extent of economic growth.

TERMS AND CONCEPTS

economics	macroeconomics	investment
economic perspective	aggregate	entrepreneurial ability
opportunity cost	economic problem	factors of production
utility	budget line	consumer goods
marginal analysis	constant opportunity cost	capital goods
scientific method	economic resources	production possibilities curve
principles	land	law of increasing opportunity costs
other-things-equal assumption	labor	economic growth
microeconomics	capital	

QUESTIONS

The following and additional problems can be found in ▓ connect

1. Ralph Waldo Emerson once wrote: "Want is a growing giant whom the coat of have was never large enough to cover." How does this statement relate to the definition of economics? **LO1.1**

2. "Buy 2, get 1 free." Explain why the "1 free" is free to the buyer but not to society. **LO1.1**

3. Which of the following decisions would entail the greater opportunity cost: allocating a square block in the heart of New York City for a surface parking lot or allocating a square block at the edge of a typical suburb for such a lot? Explain. **LO1.1**

4. What is meant by the term "utility," and how does it relate to purposeful behavior? **LO1.1**

5. Cite three examples of recent decisions that you made in which you, at least implicitly, weighed marginal cost and marginal benefit. **LO1.1**

6. What are the key elements of the scientific method, and how does this method relate to economic principles and laws? **LO1.2**

7. Indicate whether each of the following statements applies to microeconomics or macroeconomics: **LO1.3**
   a. The unemployment rate in the United States was 5.1% in September 2015.
   b. A U.S. software firm discharged 15 workers last month and transferred the work to India.
   c. An unexpected freeze in central Florida reduced the citrus crop and caused the price of oranges to rise.
   d. U.S. output, adjusted for inflation, increased by 2.4% in 2014.
   e. Last week Wells Fargo Bank lowered its interest rate on business loans by one-half of 1 percentage point.
   f. The consumer price index rose by 0.2% from August 2014 to August 2015.

8. What are economic resources? What categories do economists use to classify them? Why are resources also called factors of production? Why are they called inputs? **LO1.4**

9. Why isn't money considered a capital resource in economics? Why is entrepreneurial ability considered a category of economic resource, distinct from labor? What are the major functions of the entrepreneur? **LO1.4**

10. Specify and explain the typical shapes of marginal-benefit and marginal-cost curves. How are these curves used to determine the optimal allocation of resources to a particular product? If current output is such that marginal cost exceeds marginal benefit, should more or fewer resources be allocated to this product? Explain. **LO1.5**

11. Explain how (if at all) each of the following events affects the location of a country's production possibilities curve: **LO1.5**
   a. The quality of education increases.
   b. The number of unemployed workers increases.
   c. A new technique improves the efficiency of extracting copper from ore.
   d. A devastating earthquake destroys numerous production facilities.

12. Suppose that, on the basis of a nation's production possibilities curve, an economy must sacrifice 10,000 pizzas domestically to get the 1 additional industrial robot it desires but that it can get the robot from another country in exchange for 9,000 pizzas. Relate this information to the following statement: "Through international specialization and trade, a nation can reduce its opportunity cost of obtaining goods and thus 'move outside its production possibilities curve.'" **LO1.5**

PROBLEMS

1. Potatoes cost Janice $1 per pound, and she has $5.00 that she could possibly spend on potatoes or other items. If she feels that the first pound of potatoes is worth $1.50, the second pound is worth $1.14, the third pound is worth $1.05, and all subsequent pounds are worth $0.30, how many pounds of potatoes will she purchase? What if she only had $2 to spend? LO1.1

2. Pham can work as many or as few hours as she wants at the college bookstore for $9 per hour. But due to her hectic schedule, she has just 15 hours per week that she can spend working at either the bookstore or at other potential jobs. One potential job, at a café, will pay her $12 per hour for up to 6 hours per week. She has another job offer at a garage that will pay her $10 an hour for up to 5 hours per week. And she has a potential job at a day care center that will pay her $8.50 per hour for as many hours as she can work. If her goal is to maximize the amount of money she can make each week, how many hours will she work at the bookstore? LO1.1

3. Suppose you won $15 on a lotto ticket at the local 7-Eleven and decided to spend all the winnings on candy bars and bags of peanuts. The price of candy bars is $.75 and the price of peanuts is $1.50. LO1.4
   a. Construct a table showing the alternative combinations of the two products that are available.
   b. Plot the data in your table as a budget line in a graph. What is the slope of the budget line? What is the opportunity cost of one more candy bar? Of one more bag of peanuts? Do these opportunity costs rise, fall, or remain constant as each additional unit of the product is purchased?
   c. How, in general, would you decide which of the available combinations of candy bars and bags of peanuts to buy?
   d. Suppose you had won $30 on your ticket, not $15. Show the $30 budget line in your diagram. Why would this budget line be preferable to the old one?

4. Suppose that you are on a desert island and possess exactly 20 coconuts. Your neighbor, Friday, is a fisherman, and he is willing to trade 2 fish for every 1 coconut that you are willing to give him. Another neighbor, Kwame, is also a fisherman, and he is willing to trade 3 fish for every 1 coconut. LO1.4
   a. On a single figure, draw budget lines for trading with Friday and for trading with Kwame. (Put coconuts on the vertical axis.)
   b. What is the slope of the budget line from trading with Friday?

c. What is the slope of the budget line from trading with Kwame?
d. Which budget line features a larger set of attainable combinations of coconuts and fish?
e. If you are going to trade coconuts for fish, would you rather trade with Friday or Kwame?

5. Below is a production possibilities table for consumer goods (automobiles) and capital goods (forklifts): LO1.5

| | Production Alternatives | | | | |
Type of Production	A	B	C	D	E
Automobiles	0	2	4	6	8
Forklifts	30	27	21	12	0

   a. Show these data graphically. Upon what specific assumptions is this production possibilities curve based?
   b. If the economy is at point C, what is the cost of two more automobiles? Of six more forklifts? Explain how the production possibilities curve reflects the law of increasing opportunity costs.
   c. If the economy characterized by this production possibilities table and curve were producing 3 automobiles and 20 forklifts, what could you conclude about its use of its available resources?
   d. What would production at a point outside the production possibilities curve indicate? What must occur before the economy can attain such a level of production?

6. Referring to the table in problem 5, suppose improvement occurs in the technology of producing forklifts but not in the technology of producing automobiles. Draw the new production possibilities curve. Now assume that a technological advance occurs in producing automobiles but not in producing forklifts. Draw the new production possibilities curve. Now draw a production possibilities curve that reflects technological improvement in the production of both goods. LO1.5

7. On average, households in China save 40 percent of their annual income each year, whereas households in the United States save less than 5 percent. Production possibilities are growing at roughly 9 percent annually in China and 3.5 percent in the United States. Use graphical analysis of "present goods" versus "future goods" to explain the differences in growth rates. LO1.5

Chapter One Appendix

Graphs and Their Meaning

If you glance quickly through this text, you will find many graphs. These graphs are included to help you visualize and understand economic relationships. Most of our principles or models explain relationships between just two sets of economic data, which can be conveniently represented with two-dimensional graphs.

Construction of a Graph

A graph is a visual representation of the relationship between two variables. The table in Figure 1A.1 is a hypothetical illustration showing the relationship between income and consumption for the economy as a whole. Because people tend to buy more goods and services when their incomes go up, it is not surprising to find in the table that total consumption in the economy increases as total income increases.

The information in the table is also expressed graphically in Figure 1A.1. Here is how it is done: We want to show visually or graphically how consumption changes as income changes. Since income is the determining factor, we follow mathematical custom and represent it on the horizontal axis of the graph. And because consumption depends on income, it is represented on the vertical axis of the graph.

The vertical and horizontal scales of the graph reflect the ranges of values of consumption and income, marked in convenient increments. As you can see, the values on the scales cover all the values in the table.

Because the graph has two dimensions, each point within it represents an income value and its associated consumption value. To find a point that represents one of the five income-consumption combinations in the table, we draw lines from the appropriate values on the vertical and horizontal axes. For example, to plot point *c* (the $200 income–$150 consumption point), lines are drawn up from the horizontal (income) axis at $200 and across from the vertical (consumption) axis at $150. These lines intersect at point *c*, which represents this particular income–consumption combination. You should verify that the other income–consumption combinations shown in the table in Figure 1A.1 are properly located in the graph that is there.

Finally, by assuming that the same general relationship between income and consumption prevails for all other incomes, we draw a line or smooth curve to connect these points. That line or curve represents the income–consumption relationship.

If the graph is a straight line, as in Figure 1A.1, the relationship is said to be *linear*.

Direct and Inverse Relationships

The line in Figure 1A.1 slopes upward to the right, so it depicts a **direct relationship** between income and consumption. A direct relationship, or positive relationship, means that two variables (here, consumption and income) change in the same direction. An increase in consumption is associated with an increase in income; a decrease in consumption accompanies a decrease in income. When two sets

> **direct relationship** The relationship between two variables that change in the same direction, for example, product price and quantity supplied.

FIGURE 1A.1 Graphing the direct relationship between consumption and income. Two sets of data that are positively or directly related, such as consumption and income, graph as an upsloping line.

Income per Week	Consumption per Week	Point
$ 0	$ 50	a
100	100	b
200	150	c
300	200	d
400	250	e

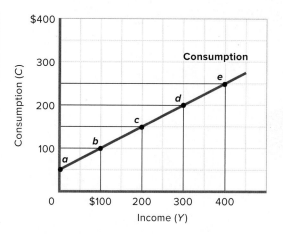

of data are positively or directly related, they always graph as an upsloping line, as in Figure 1A.1.

In contrast, two sets of data may be inversely related. Consider the table in Figure 1A.2, which shows the relationship between the price of basketball tickets and game attendance for Big Time University (BTU). Here there is an **inverse relationship,** or negative relationship, because the two variables change in opposite directions. When ticket prices for the games decrease, attendance increases. When ticket prices increase, attendance decreases. The six data points in the table are plotted in the graph in Figure 1A.2. This inverse relationship graphs as a downsloping line.

> **inverse relationship**
> The relationship between two variables that change in opposite directions, for example, product price and quantity demanded.

Dependent and Independent Variables

Economists seek to determine which variable is the "cause" and which the "effect." Or, more formally, they seek the independent variable and the dependent variable. The **independent variable** is the cause or source; it is the variable that changes first. The **dependent variable** is the effect or outcome; it is the variable that changes because of the change in the independent variable. As in our income–consumption example, income generally is the independent variable and consumption the dependent variable. Income causes consumption

> **independent variable** The variable causing a change in some other (dependent) variable.
>
> **dependent variable**
> A variable that changes as a consequence of a change in some other (independent) variable; the "effect" or outcome.

to be what it is rather than the other way around. Similarly, ticket prices (set in advance of the season and printed on the ticket) determine attendance at BTU basketball games; attendance at games does not determine the printed ticket prices for those games. Ticket price is the independent variable, and the quantity of tickets purchased is the dependent variable.

Mathematicians always put the independent variable (cause) on the horizontal axis and the dependent variable (effect) on the vertical axis. Economists are less tidy; their graphing of independent and dependent variables is more arbitrary. Their conventional graphing of the income-consumption relationship is consistent with mathematical convention, but economists historically put price and cost data on the vertical axis of their graphs. Contemporary economists have followed the tradition. So economists' graphing of BTU's ticket price–attendance data differs from normal mathematical procedure. This does not present a problem, but we want you to be aware of this fact to avoid any possible confusion.

Other Things Equal

Our simple two-variable graphs purposely ignore many other factors that might affect the amount of consumption occurring at each income level or the number of people who attend BTU basketball games at each possible ticket price. When economists plot the relationship between any two variables, they employ the *ceteris paribus* (other-things-equal) assumption. Thus, in Figure 1A.1 all factors other than income that might affect the amount of consumption are presumed to be

---

FIGURE 1A.2 Graphing the inverse relationship between ticket prices and game attendance. Two sets of data that are negatively or inversely related, such as ticket price and the attendance at basketball games, graph as a downsloping line.

Ticket Price	Attendance, Thousands	Point
$50	0	a
40	4	b
30	8	c
20	12	d
10	16	e
0	20	f

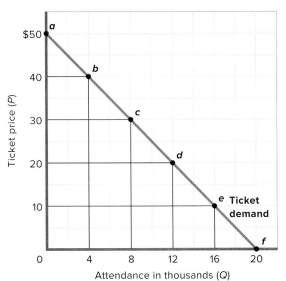

constant or unchanged. Similarly, in Figure 1A.2 all factors other than ticket price that might influence attendance at BTU basketball games are assumed constant. In reality, "other things" are not equal; they often change, and when they do, the relationship represented in our two tables and graphs will change. Specifically, the lines we have plotted would *shift* to new locations.

Consider a stock market "crash." The dramatic drop in the value of stocks might cause people to feel less wealthy and therefore less willing to consume at each level of income. The result might be a downward shift of the consumption line. To see this, you should plot a new consumption line in Figure 1A.1, assuming that consumption is, say, $20 less at each income level. Note that the relationship remains direct; the line merely shifts downward to reflect less consumption spending at each income level.

Similarly, factors other than ticket prices might affect BTU game attendance. If BTU loses most of its games, attendance at BTU games might be less at each ticket price. To see this, redraw Figure 1A.2, assuming that 2,000 fewer fans attend BTU games at each ticket price.

Slope of a Line

Lines can be described in terms of their slopes. The **slope of a straight line** is the ratio of the vertical change (the rise or drop) to the horizontal change (the run) between any two points of the line.

> **slope of a straight line** The ratio of the vertical change (the rise or fall) to the horizontal change (the run) between any two points on a line. The slope of an upward-sloping line is positive, reflecting a direct relationship between two variables; the slope of a downward-sloping line is negative, reflecting an inverse relationship between two variables.

Positive Slope Between point b and point c in the graph in Figure 1A.1, the rise or vertical change (the change in consumption) is +$50 and the run or horizontal change (the change in income) is +$100. Therefore:

$$\text{Slope} = \frac{\text{vertical change}}{\text{horizontal change}} = \frac{+50}{+100} = \frac{1}{2} = .5$$

Note that our slope of $\frac{1}{2}$ or .5 is positive because consumption and income change in the same direction; that is, consumption and income are directly or positively related.

Negative Slope Between any two of the identified points in the graph of Figure 1A.2, say, point c and point d, the vertical change is −10 (the drop) and the horizontal change is +4 (the run). Therefore

$$\text{Slope} = \frac{\text{vertical change}}{\text{horizontal change}} = \frac{-10}{+4} = -2\frac{1}{2} = -2.5$$

This slope is negative because ticket price and attendance have an inverse relationship.

Slopes and Marginal Analysis Economists are largely concerned with changes in values. The concept of slope is important in economics because it reflects marginal changes—those involving 1 more (or 1 fewer) unit. For example, in Figure 1A.1 the .5 slope shows that $.50 of extra or marginal consumption is associated with each $1 change in income. In this example, people collectively will consume $.50 of any $1 increase in their incomes and reduce their consumption by $.50 for each $1 decline in income. Careful inspection of Figure 1A.2 reveals that every $1 increase in ticket price for BTU games will decrease game attendance by 400 people and every $1 decrease in ticket price will increase game attendance by 400 people.

Infinite and Zero Slopes Many variables are unrelated or independent of one another. For example, the quantity of wristwatches purchased is not related to the price of bananas. In Figure 1A.3a the price of bananas is measured on the vertical axis and the quantity of watches demanded on the horizontal axis. The graph of their relationship is the line parallel to the vertical axis, indicating that the same quantity of watches is purchased no matter what the price of bananas. The slope of such a line is infinite.

Similarly, aggregate consumption is completely unrelated to the nation's divorce rate. In Figure 1A.3b we put

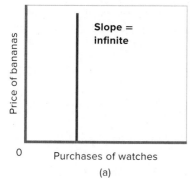
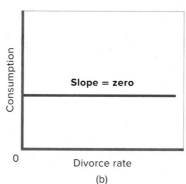

FIGURE 1A.3 Infinite and zero slopes. (a) A line parallel to the vertical axis has an infinite slope. Here, purchases of watches remain the same no matter what happens to the price of bananas. (b) A line parallel to the horizontal axis has a slope of zero. In this case, total consumption remains the same no matter what happens to the divorce rate. In both (a) and (b), the two variables are totally unrelated to one another.

consumption on the vertical axis and the divorce rate on the horizontal axis. The line parallel to the horizontal axis represents this lack of relatedness. This line has a slope of zero.

Slope of a Nonlinear Curve We now move from the simple world of linear relationships (straight lines) to the somewhat more complex world of nonlinear relationships. The slope of a straight line is the same at all its points. The slope of a line representing a nonlinear relationship changes from one point to another. Such lines are always referred to as *curves*.

Consider the downsloping curve in Figure 1A.4. Its slope is negative throughout, but the curve flattens as we move down along it. Thus, its slope constantly changes; the curve has a different slope at each point.

To measure the slope at a specific point, we draw a straight line tangent to the curve at that point. A line is tangent at a point if it touches, but does not intersect, the curve at that point. So line *aa* is tangent to the curve in Figure 1A.4 at point *A*. The slope of the curve at that point is equal to the slope of the tangent line. Specifically, the total vertical change (drop) in the tangent line *aa* is −20 and the total horizontal change (run) is +5. Because the slope of the tangent line *aa* is −20/+5, or −4, the slope of the curve at point *A* is also −4.

FIGURE 1A.4 Determining the slopes of curves. The slope of a nonlinear curve changes from point to point on the curve. The slope at any point (say, B) can be determined by drawing a straight line that is tangent to that point (line bb) and calculating the slope of that line.

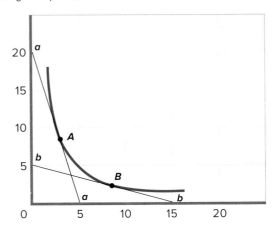

Line *bb* in Figure 1A.4 is tangent to the curve at point *B*. Using the same procedure, we find the slope at *B* to be −5/+15, or −$\frac{1}{3}$. Thus, in this flatter part of the curve, the slope is less negative.

Several of the Appendix questions are of a "workbook" variety, and we urge you to go through them carefully to check your understanding of graphs and slopes.

APPENDIX SUMMARY

LO1.6 Understand graphs, curves, and slopes as they relate to economics.

Graphs are a convenient and revealing way to represent economic relationships.

Two variables are positively or directly related when their values change in the same direction. The line (curve) representing two directly related variables slopes upward. Two variables are negatively or inversely related when their values change in opposite directions. The curve representing two inversely related variables slopes downward.

The value of the dependent variable (the "effect") is determined by the value of the independent variable (the "cause"). When the "other factors" that might affect a two-variable relationship are allowed to change, the graph of the relationship will likely shift to a new location.

The slope of a straight line is the ratio of the vertical change to the horizontal change between any two points. The slope of an upsloping line is positive; the slope of a downsloping line is negative. The slope of a line or curve is especially relevant for economics because it measures marginal changes. The slope of a horizontal line is zero; the slope of a vertical line is infinite. The slope of a curve at any point is determined by calculating the slope of a straight line tangent to the curve at that point.

APPENDIX TERMS AND CONCEPTS

direct relationship

inverse relationship

independent variable

dependent variable

slope of a straight line

APPENDIX QUESTIONS

The following and additional problems can be found in ▇connect

1. Briefly explain the use of graphs as a way to represent economic relationships. What is an inverse relationship? How does it graph? What is a direct relationship? How does it graph? **LO1.6**
2. Describe the graphical relationship between ticket prices and the number of people choosing to visit amusement parks. Is that relationship consistent with the fact that, historically, park attendance and ticket prices have both risen? Explain. **LO1.6**

3. Look back at Figure 1A.2, which shows the inverse relationship between ticket prices and game attendance at Big Time University. (a) Interpret the meaning of the slope. (b) If the slope of the line were steeper, what would that say about the amount by which ticket sales respond to increases in ticket prices? **LO1.6**

APPENDIX PROBLEMS

1. Graph and label as either direct or indirect the relationships you would expect to find between (a) the number of inches of rainfall per month and the sale of umbrellas, (b) the amount of tuition and the level of enrollment at a university, and (c) the popularity of an entertainer and the price of her concert tickets. **LO1.6**
2. Indicate how each of the following might affect the data shown in the table and graph in Figure 1A.2 of this appendix: **LO1.6**
   a. BTU's athletic director hires away the coach from a perennial champion.
   b. An NBA team locates in the city where BTU plays.
   c. BTU contracts to have all its home games televised.
3. The following table contains data on the relationship between saving and income. Rearrange these data into a meaningful order and graph them on the accompanying grid. What is the slope of the line? What would you predict saving to be at the $12,500 level of income? **LO1.6**

Income per Year	Saving per Year
$15,000	$1,000
0	−500
10,000	500
5,000	0
20,000	1,500

4. Construct a table from the data shown on the graph below. Which is the dependent variable and which the independent variable? **LO1.6**

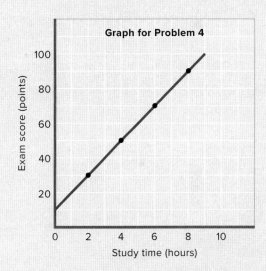

5. Suppose that when the price of gold is $100 an ounce, gold producers find it unprofitable to sell gold. However, when the price is $200 an ounce, 5,000 ounces of output (production) is profitable. At $300, a total of 10,000 ounces of output is profitable. Similarly, total production increases by 5,000 ounces for each successive $100 increase in the price of gold. Describe the relevant relationship between the price of gold and the production of gold in a table and on a graph. Put the price of gold on the vertical axis and the output of gold on the horizontal axis. **LO1.6**

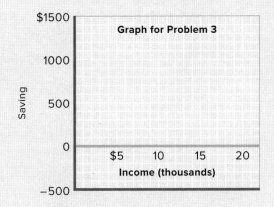

6. The accompanying graph shows curve *XX'* and tangents to the curve at points *A*, *B*, and *C*. Calculate the slope of the curve at each of these three points. LO1.6

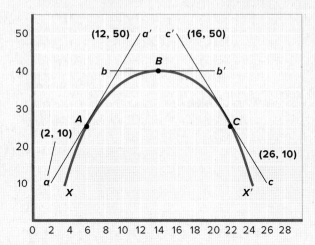

7. In the accompanying graph, is the slope of curve *AA'* positive or negative? Does the slope increase or decrease as we move along the curve from *A* to *A'*? Answer the same two questions for curve *BB'*. LO1.6

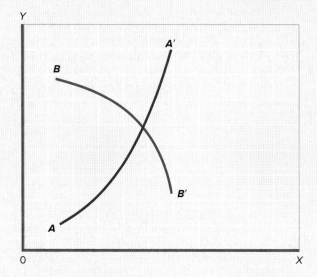

©Tatiana Belova/Shutterstock

The Market System and the Circular Flow

Learning Objectives

LO2.1 Differentiate between a command system and a market system.

LO2.2 List the main characteristics of the market system.

LO2.3 Explain how the market system answers the four fundamental questions.

LO2.4 Discuss how the market system adjusts to change and promotes progress.

LO2.5 Describe the mechanics of the circular flow model.

You are at the mall. Suppose you were assigned to compile a list of all the individual goods and services there, including the different brands and variations of each type of product. That task would be daunting and the list would be long! And even though a single shopping mall contains a remarkable quantity and variety of goods, it is only a tiny part of the national economy.

Who decided that the particular goods and services available at the mall and in the broader economy should be produced? How did the producers determine which technology and types of resources to use in producing these particular goods? Who will obtain these products? What accounts for the new and improved products among these goods? This chapter will answer these questions.

Economic Systems

Every society needs to develop an **economic system**—a particular set of institutional arrangements and a coordinating mechanism—to respond to the economic problem. The economic system has to determine what goods are produced, how they are produced, who gets them, and how to promote technological progress.

Economic systems differ as to (1) who owns the factors of production and (2) the method used to motivate, coordinate, and direct economic activity. There are two general types of economic systems: the command system and the market system.

economic system A particular set of institutional arrangements and a coordinating mechanism for solving the economizing problem; a method of organizing an economy, of which the market system and the command system are the two general types.

The Command System

The **command system** is also known as *socialism* or *communism*. In a command system, government owns most property resources and economic decision making occurs through a central economic plan. A central planning board appointed by the government makes nearly all the major decisions concerning the use of resources, the composition and distribution of output, and the organization of production. The government owns most of the business firms, which produce according to government directives. The central planning board determines production goals for each enterprise and specifies the amount of resources to be allocated to each enterprise so that it can reach its production goals. The division of output between capital and consumer goods is centrally decided, and capital goods are allocated among industries on the basis of the central planning board's long-term priorities.

A pure command economy would rely exclusively on a central plan to allocate the government-owned property resources. But, in reality, even the preeminent command economy—the Soviet Union—tolerated some private ownership and incorporated some markets before its collapse in 1992. Recent reforms in Russia and most of the eastern European nations have to one degree or another transformed their command economies to capitalistic, market-oriented systems. China's reforms have not gone as far, but they have greatly reduced the reliance on central planning. Although there is still extensive government ownership of resources and capital in China, the nation has increasingly relied on free markets to organize and coordinate its economy. North Korea and Cuba are the last remaining examples of largely centrally planned economies. Global Snapshot 2.1 reveals how North Korea's centrally planned economy compares to the market economy of its neighbor, South Korea. Later in this chapter, we will explore the main reasons for the general demise of the command systems.

command system A method of organizing an economy in which property resources are publicly owned and government uses central economic planning to direct and coordinate economic activities; command economy; communism.

The Market System

The polar alternative to the command system is the **market system,** or *capitalism*. The system is characterized by the private ownership of resources and the use of markets and prices to coordinate and direct economic activity. Participants act in their own self-interest. Individuals and businesses seek to achieve their economic goals through their own decisions regarding work, consumption, or production. The system allows for the private ownership of capital, communicates through prices, and coordinates economic activity through *markets*—places where buyers and sellers come together to buy and sell goods, services, and resources. Goods and services are produced and resources are supplied by whoever is willing and able to do so. The result is competition among independently acting buyers and sellers of each product and resource. Thus, economic decision making is widely dispersed. Also, the high potential monetary rewards create powerful incentives for existing firms to innovate and entrepreneurs to pioneer new products and processes.

In *pure* capitalism—or *laissez-faire* capitalism—government's role would be limited to protecting private property and establishing an environment appropriate to the operation of the market system. The term "laissez-faire" means "let it be," that is, keep government

market system All the product and resource markets of a market economy and the relationships among them; a method that allows the prices determined in those markets to allocate the economy's scarce resources and to communicate and coordinate the decisions made by consumers, firms, and resource suppliers.

GLOBAL SNAPSHOT 2.1

The Two Koreas

North Korea is one of the few command economies still standing. After the Second World War, Korea was divided into North Korea and South Korea. North Korea, under the influence of the Soviet Union, established a command economy that emphasized government ownership and central government planning. South Korea, protected by the United States, established a market economy based upon private ownership and the profit motive. Today, the differences in the economic outcomes of the two systems are striking:

	North Korea	South Korea
GDP	$40 billion*	$1.6 trillion*
GDP per capita	$1,800*	$35,700*
Exports	$4.4 billion	$638 billion
Imports	$5.6 billion	$524.1 billion
Agriculture as % of GDP	37 percent	2.3 percent

*Based on purchasing power equivalencies to the U.S. dollar.

Source: CIA World Fact Book, 2013–2014, **www.cia.gov.**

from interfering with the economy. The idea is that such interference will disturb the efficient working of the market system.

But in the capitalism practiced in the United States and most other countries, government plays a substantial role in the economy. It not only provides the rules for economic activity but also promotes economic stability and growth, provides certain goods and services that would otherwise be underproduced or not produced at all, and modifies the distribution of income. The government, however, is not the dominant economic force in deciding what to produce, how to produce it, and who will get it. That force is the market.

Characteristics of the Market System

It will be very instructive to examine some of the key features of the market system in more detail.

Private Property

In a market system, private individuals and firms, not the government, own most of the property resources (land and capital). It is this extensive private ownership of capital that gives capitalism its name. This right of **private property,** coupled with the freedom to negotiate binding legal contracts, enables individuals and businesses to obtain, use, and dispose of property resources as they see fit. The right of property owners to designate who will receive their property when they die sustains the institution of private property.

> **private property** The right of private persons and firms to obtain, own, control, employ, dispose of, and bequeath land, capital, and other property.

The most important consequence of property rights is that they encourage people to cooperate by helping to ensure that only *mutually agreeable* economic transactions take place. In a world without legally enforceable property rights, the strong could simply take whatever they wanted from the weak without giving them any compensation. But in a world of legally enforceable property rights, any person wanting something from you has to get you to agree to give it to them. And you can say no. The result is that if that person really wants what you have, she must offer you something that you value more highly in return. That is, she must offer you a mutually agreeable economic transaction—one that benefits you as well as her.

Property rights also encourage investment, innovation, exchange, maintenance of property, and economic growth. Why would anyone stock a store, build a factory, or clear land for farming if someone else, or the government itself, could take that property for his or her own benefit?

Property rights also extend to intellectual property through patents, copyrights, and trademarks. Such long-term protection encourages people to write books, music, and computer programs and to invent new products and production processes without fear that others will steal them and the rewards they may bring.

Moreover, property rights facilitate exchange. The title to an automobile or the deed to a cattle ranch assures the buyer that the seller is the legitimate owner. Also, property rights encourage owners to maintain or improve their property so as to preserve or increase its value. Finally, property rights enable people to use their time and resources to produce more goods and services, rather than using them to protect and retain the property they have already produced or acquired.

Freedom of Enterprise and Choice

Closely related to private ownership of property is freedom of enterprise and choice. The market system requires that various economic units make certain choices, which are expressed and implemented in the economy's markets:

- **Freedom of enterprise** ensures that entrepreneurs and private businesses are free to obtain and use economic resources to produce their choice of goods and services and to sell them in their chosen markets.
- **Freedom of choice** enables owners to employ or dispose of their property and money as they see fit. It also allows workers to enter any line of work for which they are qualified. Finally, it ensures that consumers are free to buy the goods and services that best satisfy their wants.

These choices are free only within broad legal limitations, of course. Illegal choices such as selling human organs or buying illicit drugs are punished through fines and imprisonment. (Global Snapshot 2.2 reveals that the degree of economic freedom varies greatly from nation to nation.)

Self-Interest

In the market system, **self-interest** is the motivating force of the various economic units as they express their free choices. Self-interest simply means that each economic unit tries to achieve its own particular goal, which usually requires delivering something of value to others. Entrepreneurs try to maximize profit or minimize loss. Property owners try to get the highest price for the sale or rent of their resources. Workers try to maximize their utility (satisfaction) by finding jobs that offer the best combination of wages, hours, fringe benefits, and working conditions. Consumers try to obtain the products they want at the lowest possible price and apportion their expenditures to maximize their utility. The motive of self-interest gives direction and consistency to what might otherwise be a chaotic economy.

Competition

The market system depends on **competition** among economic units. The basis of this competition is freedom of choice exercised in pursuit of a monetary return. Very broadly defined, competition requires

- Independently acting sellers and buyers operating in a particular product or resource market.
- Freedom of sellers and buyers to enter or leave markets, on the basis of their economic self-interest.

freedom of enterprise The freedom of firms to obtain economic resources, to use those resources to produce products of the firm's own choosing, and to sell their products in markets of their choice.

freedom of choice The freedom of owners of property resources to employ or dispose of them as they see fit, of workers to enter any line of work for which they are qualified, and of consumers to spend their incomes in a manner that they think is appropriate.

self-interest The most-advantageous outcome as viewed by each firm, property owner, worker, or consumer.

competition The presence in a market of independent buyers and sellers competing with one another along with the freedom of buyers and sellers to enter and leave the market.

GLOBAL SNAPSHOT 2.2

Index of Economic Freedom, Selected Economies

The Index of Economic Freedom measures economic freedom using 10 broad categories such as trade policy, property rights, and government intervention, with each category containing more than 50 specific criteria. The index then ranks 179 economies according to their degree of economic freedom. A few selected rankings for 2015 are listed below.

FREE

1 Hong Kong

3 New Zealand

5 Switzerland

MOSTLY FREE

12 United States

20 Japan

28 Colombia

MOSTLY UNFREE

117 Brazil

128 India

143 Russia

REPRESSED

169 Argentina

171 Iran

178 North Korea

Source: The Heritage Foundation, **www.heritage.org.**

Competition diffuses economic power within the businesses and households that make up the economy. When there are independently acting sellers and buyers in a market, no one buyer or seller is able to dictate the price of the product or resource because others can undercut that price.

Competition also implies that producers can enter or leave an industry; there are no insurmountable barriers to an industry's expanding or contracting. This freedom of an industry to expand or contract provides the economy with the flexibility needed to remain efficient over time. Freedom of entry and exit enables the economy to adjust to changes in consumer tastes, technology, and resource availability.

The diffusion of economic power inherent in competition limits the potential abuse of that power. A producer that charges more than the competitive market price will lose sales to other producers. An employer who pays less than the competitive market wage rate will lose workers to other employers. A firm that fails to exploit new technology will lose profits to firms that do. And a firm that produces shoddy products will be punished as customers switch to higher-quality items made by rival firms. Competition is the basic regulatory force in the market system.

Markets and Prices

Markets and prices are key components of the market system. They give the system its ability to coordinate millions of daily economic decisions. A **market** is an institution or mechanism that brings buyers (demanders) and sellers (suppliers) into contact. A market system conveys the decisions made by buyers and sellers of products and resources. The decisions made on each side of the market determine a set of product and resource prices that guide resource owners, entrepreneurs, and consumers as they make and revise their choices and pursue their self-interest.

Just as competition is the regulatory mechanism of the market system, the market system itself is the organizing mechanism. It is an elaborate communication network through which innumerable individual free choices are recorded, summarized, and balanced. Those who respond to market signals and heed market dictates are rewarded with greater profit and income; those who do not respond to those signals and choose to ignore market dictates are penalized. Through this mechanism society decides what the economy should produce, how production can be organized efficiently, and how the fruits of production are to be distributed among the various units that make up the economy.

Technology and Capital Goods

In the market system, competition, freedom of choice, self-interest, and personal reward provide the opportunity and motivation for technological advance. The monetary rewards for new products or production techniques accrue directly to the innovator. The market system therefore encourages extensive use and rapid development of complex capital goods: tools, machinery, large-scale factories, and facilities for storage, communication, transportation, and marketing.

Advanced technology and capital goods are important because the most direct methods of production are often the least efficient. The only way to avoid that inefficiency is to rely on capital goods. It would be ridiculous for a farmer to go at production with bare hands. There are huge benefits to be derived from creating and using such capital equipment as plows, tractors, storage bins, and so on. The more efficient production means much more abundant outputs.

Specialization

The extent to which market economies rely on **specialization** is extraordinary. Specialization is using the resources of an individual, region, or nation to produce one or a few goods or services rather than the entire range of goods and services. Those goods and services are then exchanged for a full range of desired products. The majority of consumers produce virtually none of the goods and services they consume, and they consume little or nothing of the items they produce. The person working nine to five installing windows in commercial aircraft may rarely fly. Many farmers sell their milk to the local dairy and then buy cheese at the local grocery store. Society learned long ago that self-sufficiency breeds inefficiency. The jack-of-all-trades may be a very colorful individual but is certainly not an efficient producer.

Division of Labor   Human specialization—called the **division of labor**—contributes to a society's output in several ways:

- *Specialization makes use of differences in ability*   Specialization enables individuals to take advantage of existing differences in their abilities and skills. If LeBron is strong, athletic, and good at shooting a basketball and Beyoncé is beautiful, agile, and

---

market Any institution or mechanism that brings together buyers (demanders) and sellers (suppliers) of a particular good or service.

specialization The use of the resources of an individual, a firm, a region, or a nation to concentrate production on one or a small number of goods and services.

division of labor The separation of the work required to produce a product into a number of different tasks that are performed by different workers; specialization of workers.

PHOTO OP LeBron James and Beyoncé Knowles

It makes economic sense for LeBron James and Beyoncé Knowles to specialize in what they do best.

©Ezra Shaw/Getty Images   ©Ethan Miller/Getty Images for ABC

can sing, their distribution of talents can be most efficiently used if LeBron plays professional basketball and Beyoncé records songs and gives concerts.

- *Specialization fosters learning by doing* Even if the abilities of two people are identical, specialization may still be advantageous. By devoting time to a single task rather than working at a number of different tasks, a person is more likely to develop the skills required and to improve techniques. You learn to be a good lawyer by studying and practicing law.
- *Specialization saves time* By devoting time to a single task, a person avoids the loss of time incurred in shifting from one job to another.

For all these reasons, specialization increases the total output society derives from limited resources.

Geographic Specialization Specialization also works on a regional and international basis. It is conceivable that oranges could be grown in Nebraska, but because of the unsuitability of the land, rainfall, and temperature, the costs would be very high. And it is conceivable that wheat could be grown in Florida, but such production would be costly for similar geographical reasons. So Nebraskans produce products—wheat in particular—for which their resources are best suited, and Floridians do the same, producing oranges and other citrus fruits. By specializing, both economies produce more than is needed locally. Then, very sensibly, Nebraskans and Floridians swap some of their surpluses—wheat for oranges, oranges for wheat.

Similarly, on an international scale, the United States specializes in producing such items as commercial aircraft and computers, which it sells abroad in exchange for digital video players from Japan, bananas from Honduras, and woven baskets from Thailand. Both human specialization and geographic specialization are needed to achieve efficiency in the use of limited resources.

Use of Money

A rather obvious characteristic of any economic system is the extensive use of money. Money performs several functions, but first and foremost it is a **medium of exchange.** It makes trade easier.

Specialization requires exchange. Exchange can, and sometimes does, occur through **barter**—swapping goods for goods, say, wheat for oranges. But barter poses serious problems because it requires a *coincidence of wants* between the buyer and the seller. In our example, we assumed that Nebraskans had excess wheat to trade and wanted oranges. And we assumed that Floridians had excess oranges to trade and wanted wheat. So an exchange occurred. But if such a coincidence of wants is missing, trade is stymied.

Suppose that Nebraska has no interest in Florida's oranges but wants potatoes from Idaho. And suppose that Idaho wants Florida's oranges but not Nebraska's wheat. And, to complicate matters, suppose that Florida wants some of Nebraska's wheat but none of Idaho's potatoes. We summarize the situation in Figure 2.1.

In none of the cases shown in the figure is there a coincidence of wants. Trade by barter clearly would be difficult. Instead, people in each state use **money,** which is simply a convenient social invention to facilitate exchanges of goods and services. Historically, people have used cattle, cigarettes, shells, stones, pieces of metal, and many other commodities, with varying degrees of success, as money. To serve as money, an item needs to pass only one test: It must be generally acceptable to sellers in exchange for their goods and services. Money is socially defined; whatever society accepts as a medium of exchange *is* money.

Today, most economies use pieces of paper as money. The use of paper dollars (currency) as a medium of exchange is what enables Nebraska, Florida, and Idaho to overcome their trade stalemate, as demonstrated in Figure 2.1.

medium of exchange Any item sellers generally accept and buyers generally use to pay for a good or service; money; a convenient means of exchanging goods and services without engaging in barter.

barter The exchange of one good or service for another good or service.

money Any item that is generally acceptable to sellers in exchange for goods and services.

FIGURE 2.1 Money facilitates trade when wants do not coincide. The use of money as a medium of exchange permits trade to be accomplished despite a noncoincidence of wants. (1) Nebraska trades the wheat that Florida wants for money from Floridians; (2) Nebraska trades the money it receives from Florida for the potatoes it wants from Idaho; (3) Idaho trades the money it receives from Nebraska for the oranges it wants from Florida.

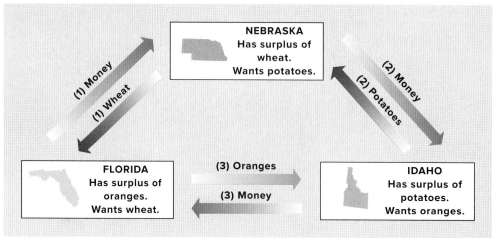

On a global basis, specialization and exchange are complicated by the fact that different nations have different currencies. But markets in which currencies are bought and sold make it possible for people living in different countries to exchange goods and services without resorting to barter.

Active, but Limited, Government

An active, but limited, government is the final characteristic of market systems in real-life advanced industrial economies. Although a market system promotes a high degree of efficiency in the use of its resources, it has certain inherent shortcomings. We will discover in Chapter 5 that government can increase the overall effectiveness of the economic system in several ways.

Four Fundamental Questions

The key features of the market system help explain how market economies respond to four fundamental questions:

- What goods and services will be produced?
- How will the goods and services be produced?
- Who will get the goods and services?
- How will the system promote progress?

These four questions highlight the economic choices underlying the production possibilities curve discussed in Chapter 1. They reflect the reality of scarce resources in a world of unlimited wants. All economies, whether market or command, must address these four questions.

What Will Be Produced?

How will a market system decide on the specific types and quantities of goods to be produced? The simple answer is this: The goods and services that can be produced at a continuing profit will be produced, while those whose production generates a continuing loss will be discontinued. Profits and losses are the difference between the total revenue (TR) a firm receives from the sale of its products and the total cost (TC) of producing those products. (For economists, total costs include not only wage and salary payments to labor, and interest and rental payments for capital and land, but also payments to the entrepreneur for organizing and combining the other resources to produce a product.)

Continuing economic profit (TR > TC) in an industry results in expanded production and the movement of resources toward that industry. The industry expands. Continuing losses (TC > TR) in an industry lead to reduced production and the exit of resources from that industry. The industry contracts.

In the market system, consumers are sovereign (in command). **Consumer sovereignty** is crucial in determining the types and quantities of goods produced. Consumers spend their income on the goods they are most willing and able to buy. Through these **"dollar votes"** they register their wants in the market. If the dollar votes for a certain product are great enough to create a profit, businesses will produce that product and offer it for sale. In contrast, if the dollar votes do not create sufficient revenues to cover costs, businesses will not produce the product. So the consumers are sovereign. They collectively direct resources to industries that are meeting consumer wants and away from industries that are not meeting consumer wants.

The dollar votes of consumers determine not only which industries will continue to exist but also which products will survive or fail. Only profitable industries, firms, and products survive.

consumer sovereignty Determination by consumers of the types and quantities of goods and services that will be produced with the scarce resources of the economy; consumers' direction of production through their dollar votes.

dollar votes The "votes" that consumers and entrepreneurs cast for the production of consumer and capital goods, respectively, when they purchase those goods in product and resource markets.

APPLYING THE ANALYSIS

McHits and McMisses

McDonald's has introduced several new menu items over the decades. Some have been profitable "hits," while others have been "misses." Ultimately, consumers decide whether a menu item is profitable and therefore whether it stays on the McDonald's menu.

- Hulaburger (1962)—McMiss
- Filet-O-Fish (1963)—McHit
- Strawberry shortcake (1966)—McMiss
- Big Mac (1968)—McHit
- Hot apple pie (1968)—McHit
- Egg McMuffin (1975)—McHit
- Drive-thru (1975)—McHit
- Chicken McNuggets (1983)—McHit
- Arch Deluxe (1996)—McMiss
- McSalad Shaker (2000)—McMiss
- McGriddle (2003)—McHit
- Snack Wrap (2006)—McHit
- Fish McBites (2013)—McMiss

QUESTION: Do you think McDonald's premium salads will be a lasting McHit, or do you think they eventually will become a McMiss?

Source: Dyan Machan, "Polishing the Golden Arches," *Forbes,* June 15, 1998, pp. 42–43, updated. Forbes Media LLC © 2011. "McDonald's Fish McBites Flounders," *Forbes,* March 12, 2013, **forbes.com.**

How Will the Goods and Services Be Produced?

What combinations of resources and technologies will be used to produce goods and services? How will the production be organized? The answer: In combinations and ways that minimize the cost per unit of output. This is true because inefficiency drives up costs and lowers profits. As a result, any firm wishing to maximize its profits will make great efforts to minimize production costs. These efforts will include using the right mix of labor and capital, given the prices and productivity of those resources. They also mean locating production facilities optimally to hold down production and transportation expenses, and finally, using the most appropriate technology in producing and distributing output.

Those efforts will be intensified if the firm faces competition, as consumers strongly prefer low prices and will shift their purchases over to the firms that can produce a quality product at the lowest possible price. Any firm foolish enough to use higher-cost production methods will go bankrupt as it is undersold by its more efficient competitors who can still make a profit when selling at a lower price. Simply stated: Competition eliminates high-cost producers.

Who Will Get the Output?

The market system enters the picture in two ways when determining the distribution of total output. Generally, any product will be distributed to consumers on the basis of their ability and willingness to pay its existing market price. If the price of some product, say, a small sailboat, is $3,000, then buyers who are willing and able to pay that price will "sail, sail away." Consumers who are unwilling or unable to pay the price will "sit on the dock of the bay."

The ability to pay the prices for sailboats and other products depends on the amount of income that consumers have, along with the prices of, and preferences for, various goods. If consumers have sufficient income and want to spend their money on a particular good, they can have it. And the amount of income they have depends on (1) the quantities of the property and human resources they supply and (2) the prices those resources command in the resource market. Resource prices (wages, interest, rent, profit) are key in determining the size of each household's income and therefore each household's ability to buy part of the economy's output.

How Will the System Promote Progress?

Society desires economic growth (greater output) and higher standards of living (greater output *per person*). How does the market system promote technological improvements and capital accumulation, both of which contribute to a higher standard of living for society?

Technological Advance

The market system provides a strong incentive for technological advance and enables better products and processes to supplant inferior ones. An entrepreneur or firm that introduces a popular new product will gain revenue and economic profit at the expense of rivals. Firms that are highly profitable one year may find they are in financial trouble just a few years later.

Technological advance also includes new and improved methods that reduce production or distribution costs. By passing part of its cost reduction on to the consumer through a lower product price, the firm can increase sales and obtain economic profit at the expense of rival firms.

Moreover, the market system promotes the *rapid spread* of technological advance throughout an industry. Rival firms must follow the lead of the most innovative firm or else suffer immediate losses and eventual failure. In some cases, the result is **creative destruction:** The creation of new products and production methods completely destroys the market positions of firms that are wedded to existing products and older ways of doing business. Example: The advent of compact discs largely demolished long-play vinyl records before MP3 players and then online streaming subsequently supplanted MP3 players.

creative destruction The hypothesis that the creation of new products and production methods simultaneously destroys the market power of existing monopolies.

Capital Accumulation

Most technological advances require additional capital goods. The market system provides the resources necessary to produce additional capital through increased dollar votes for those goods. That is, the market system acknowledges dollar voting for capital goods as well as for consumer goods.

But who counts the dollar votes for capital goods? Answer: Entrepreneurs and business owners. As receivers of profit income, they often use part of that income to purchase capital goods. Doing so yields even greater profit income in the future if the technological innovation that required the additional capital goods is successful. Also, by paying interest or selling ownership shares, the entrepreneur and firm can attract some of the income of households to cast dollar votes for the production of more capital goods.

The "Invisible Hand"

"invisible hand" The tendency of firms and resource suppliers that seek to further their own self-interests in competitive markets to also promote the interest of society.

In his 1776 book *The Wealth of Nations,* Adam Smith first noted that the operation of a market system creates a curious unity between private interests and social interests. Firms and resource suppliers, seeking to further their own self-interest and operating within the framework of a highly competitive market system, will simultaneously, as though guided by an **"invisible hand,"** promote the public or social interest. For example, we have seen that in a competitive environment, businesses seek to build new and improved products to increase profits. Those enhanced products increase society's well-being. Businesses also use the least costly combination of resources to produce a specific output because it is in their self-interest to do so. To act otherwise would be to forgo profit or even to risk business failure. But at the same time, to use scarce resources in the least costly way is clearly in the social interest as well. It "frees up" resources to produce something else that society desires.

Self-interest, awakened and guided by the competitive market system, is what induces responses appropriate to the changes in society's wants. Businesses seeking to make higher profits and to avoid losses, and resource suppliers pursuing greater monetary rewards, negotiate changes in the allocation of resources and end up with the output that society wants. Competition controls or guides self-interest such that self-interest automatically and quite unintentionally furthers the best interest of society. The invisible hand ensures that when firms maximize their profits and resource suppliers maximize their incomes, these groups also help maximize society's output and income.

QUESTION: Are "doing good for others" and "doing well for oneself" conflicting ideas, according to Adam Smith?

The Demise of the Command Systems

Now that you know how the market system answers the four fundamental questions, you can easily understand why command systems of the Soviet Union, eastern Europe, and prereform China failed. Those systems encountered two insurmountable problems.

The first difficulty was the *coordination problem.* The central planners had to coordinate the millions of individual decisions by consumers, resource suppliers, and businesses. Consider the setting up of a factory to produce tractors. The central planners had to establish a realistic annual production target, for example, 1,000 tractors. They then had to make available all the necessary inputs—labor, machinery, electric power, steel, tires, glass, paint, transportation—for the production and delivery of those 1,000 tractors.

Because the outputs of many industries serve as inputs to other industries, the failure of any single industry to achieve its output target caused a chain reaction of repercussions. For example, if iron mines, for want of machinery or labor or transportation, did not supply the steel industry with the required inputs of iron ore, the steel mills were unable to fulfill the input needs of the many industries that depended on steel. Those steel-using industries (such as tractor, automobile, and transportation) were unable to fulfill their planned production goals. Eventually the chain reaction spread to all firms that used steel as an input and from there to other input buyers or final consumers.

The coordination problem became more difficult as the economies expanded. Products and production processes grew more sophisticated, and the number of industries requiring planning increased. Planning techniques that worked for the simpler economy proved highly inadequate and inefficient for the larger economy. Bottlenecks and production stoppages became the norm, not the exception.

A lack of a reliable success indicator added to the coordination problem in the Soviet Union and prereform China. We have seen that market economies rely on profit as a success indicator. Profit depends on consumer demand, production efficiency, and product quality. In contrast, the major success indicator for the command economies usually was a quantitative production target that the central planners assigned. Production costs, product quality, and product mix were secondary considerations. Managers and workers often sacrificed product quality because they were being awarded bonuses for meeting quantitative, not qualitative, targets. If meeting production goals meant sloppy assembly work, so be it.

It was difficult at best for planners to assign quantitative production targets without unintentionally producing distortions in output. If the production target for an enterprise manufacturing nails was specified in terms of *weight* (tons of nails), the producer made only large nails. But if its target was specified as a *quantity* (thousands of nails), the producer made all small nails, and lots of them!

The command economies also faced an *incentive problem*. Central planners determined the output mix. When they misjudged how many automobiles, shoes, shirts, and chickens were wanted at the government-determined prices, persistent shortages and surpluses of those products arose. But as long as the managers who oversaw the production of those goods were rewarded for meeting their assigned production goals, they had no incentive to adjust production in response to the shortages and surpluses. And there were no fluctuations in prices and profitability to signal that more or less of certain products was desired. Thus, many products were unavailable or in short supply, while other products were overproduced and sat for months or years in warehouses.

The command systems of the Soviet Union and prereform China also lacked entrepreneurship. Central planning did not trigger the profit motive, nor did it reward innovation and enterprise. The route for getting ahead was through participation in the political hierarchy of the Communist Party. Moving up the hierarchy meant better housing, better access to health care, and the right to shop in special stores. Meeting production targets and maneuvering through the minefields of party politics were measures of success in "business." But a definition of business success based solely on political savvy is not conducive to technological advance, which is often disruptive to existing products, production methods, and organizational structures.

QUESTION: In market economies, firms rarely worry about the availability of inputs to produce their products, whereas in command economies input availability was a constant concern. Why the difference?

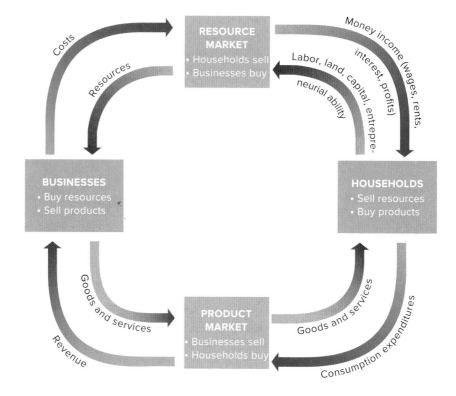

The Circular Flow Model

The dynamic market economy creates continuous, repetitive flows of goods and services, resources, and money. The **circular flow diagram,** shown in Figure 2.2, illustrates those flows for a simplified economy in which there is no government. Observe that in the diagram we group this economy's decision makers into *businesses* and *households.* Additionally, we divide this economy's markets into the *resource market* and the *product market.*

Households

circular flow diagram The flow of resources from households to firms and of products from firms to households. These flows are accompanied by reverse flows of money from firms to households and from households to firms.

The blue rectangle on the right side of the circular flow diagram in Figure 2.2 represents **households,** which are defined as one or more persons occupying a housing unit. There are currently about 125 million households in the U.S. economy. Households buy the goods and services that businesses make available in the product market. Households obtain the income needed to buy those products by selling resources in the resource market.

household An economic unit (of one or more persons) that provides the economy with resources and uses the income received to purchase goods and services that satisfy economic wants.

All the resources in our no-government economy are ultimately owned or provided by households. For instance, the members of one household or another directly provide all of the labor and entrepreneurial ability in the economy. Households also own all of the land and all of the capital in the economy either directly, as personal property, or indirectly, as a consequence of owning all of the businesses in the economy (and thereby controlling all of the land and capital owned by businesses). Thus, all of the income in the economy—all wages, rents, interest, and profits—flows to households because they provide the economy's labor, land, capital, and entrepreneurial ability.

Businesses

business A firm that purchases resources and provides goods and services to the economy.

The blue rectangle on the left side of the circular flow diagram represents **businesses,** which are commercial establishments that attempt to earn profits for their owners by offering goods and services for sale. Businesses sell goods and services in the product market in order to obtain revenue, and they incur costs in the resource markets when they purchase the labor, land, capital, and entrepreneurial ability that they need to produce their respective goods and services.

Product Market

The red rectangle at the bottom of the diagram represents the **product market,** the place where goods and services produced by businesses are bought and sold. Households use the income they receive from the sale of resources to buy goods and services. The money that consumers spend on goods and services flows to businesses as revenue. Businesses compare those revenues to their costs in determining profitability and whether or not a particular good or service should continue to be produced.

product market A market in which products are sold by firms and bought by households.

Resource Market

Finally, the red rectangle at the top of the circular flow diagram represents the **resource market** in which households sell resources to businesses. The households sell resources to generate income, and the businesses buy resources to produce goods and services. The funds that businesses pay for resources are costs to businesses but are flows of wage, rent, interest, and profit income to the household. Productive resources therefore flow from households to businesses, and money flows from businesses to households.

resource market A market in which households sell and firms buy resources or the services of resources.

The circular flow model depicts a complex, interrelated web of decision making and economic activity involving businesses and households. For the economy, it is the circle of life. Businesses and households are both buyers and sellers. Businesses buy resources and sell products. Households buy products and sell resources. As shown in Figure 2.2, there is a counterclockwise *real flow* of economic resources and finished goods and services and a clockwise *money flow* of income and consumption expenditures.

PHOTO OP   Resource Markets and Product Markets

The sale of a grove of orange trees would be a transaction in the resource market; the sale of oranges to final consumers would be a transaction in the product market.

©Zu Sanchez Photography/Getty Images

©renaschild/Getty Images

Some Facts about U.S. Businesses

Businesses constitute one part of the private sector. The business population is extremely diverse, ranging from giant corporations such as Walmart, with 2017 sales of $485 billion and 2.3 million employees, to neighborhood specialty shops with one or two employees and sales of only $200 to $300 per day. There are three major legal forms of businesses: sole proprietorships, partnerships, and corporations.

A *sole proprietorship* is a business owned and operated by one person. Usually, the proprietor (the owner) personally supervises its operation. In a *partnership,* two or more individuals (the partners) agree to own and operate a business together.

A *corporation* is a legal creation that can acquire resources, own assets, produce and sell products, incur debts, extend credit, sue and be sued, and perform the functions of any other type of enterprise. A corporation sells stocks (ownership shares) to raise funds but is legally distinct and separate from the individual stockholders. The stockholders' legal and financial liability is limited to the loss of the value of their shares. Hired executives and managers operate corporations on a day-to-day basis.

Figure 2.3a shows how the business population is distributed among the three major legal forms. About 72% of firms are sole proprietorships, whereas only 18% are corporations. But as Figure 2.3b indicates, corporations account for 82% of total sales revenue (and therefore total output) in the United States. Virtually all the nation's largest business enterprises are corporations. Global Snapshot 2.3 lists the world's largest corporations.

QUESTION: Why do you think sole proprietorships and partnerships typically incorporate (become corporations) when they experience rapid and sizable increases in their production, sales, and profits?

FIGURE 2.3 The business population and shares of total revenue. (a) Sole proprietorships dominate the business population numerically, but (b) corporations dominate total sales revenue (total output). *Source:* U.S. Census Bureau, **www.census.gov.**

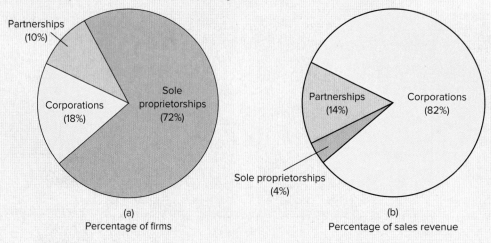

(a)
Percentage of firms

(b)
Percentage of sales revenue

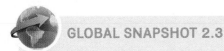

GLOBAL SNAPSHOT 2.3

The World's 10 Largest Corporations

Six of the world's ten largest corporations, based on dollar revenue in 2015, were head-quartered in the United States or China. Japan, Germany, Britain, and The Netherlands account for the rest of the top ten.

Walmart (USA) $482 billion
State Grid (China) $330 billion
China National Petroleum (China) $299 billion
Sinopec (China) $294 billion
Royal Dutch Shell (Netherlands) $272 billion
ExxonMobil (USA) $355 billion
Volkswagen (Germany) $237 billion
Toyota Motor (Japan) $237 billion
Apple (USA) $234 billion
BP (Britain) $226 billion

Source: "Global 500," *Fortune Magazine,* **www.fortune.com.** Retrieved January 10, 2017.

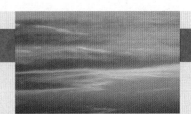

APPLYING THE ANALYSIS

Some Facts about U.S. Households

Households constitute the second part of the private sector. The U.S. economy currently has about 125 million households. These households consist of one or more persons oc-cupying a housing unit and are both the ultimate suppliers of all economic resources *and* the major spenders in the economy.

The nation's earned income is apportioned among wages, rents, interest, and profits. *Wages* are paid to labor; *rents* and *interest* are paid to owners of property resources; and *profits* are paid to the owners of corporations and unincorporated businesses.

Figure 2.4a shows the categories of U.S. income earned in 2015. The largest sources of income for households are the wages and salaries paid to workers. Notice that the bulk of total U.S. income goes to labor, not to capital. Proprietors' income—the income of doctors, lawyers, small-business owners, farmers, and owners of other unincorporated enterprises—also has a "wage" element. Some of this income is payment for one's own labor, and some of it is profit from one's own business.

The other three types of income are self-evident: Some households own corporate stock and receive dividend incomes as their share of corporate profits. Many households also own bonds and savings accounts that yield interest income. And some households receive rental income by providing buildings and natural resources (including land) to businesses and other individuals.

U.S. households use their income to buy (spend), save, and pay taxes. Figure 2.4b shows how households divide their spending among three broad categories of goods and services:

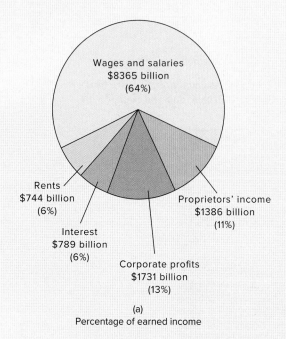

Wages and salaries
$8365 billion
(64%)

Rents
$744 billion
(6%)

Interest
$789 billion
(6%)

Corporate profits
$1731 billion
(13%)

Proprietors' income
$1386 billion
(11%)

(a)
Percentage of earned income

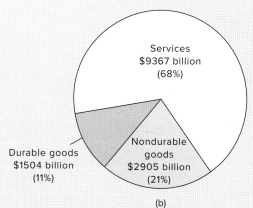

Services
$9367 billion
(68%)

Durable goods
$1504 billion
(11%)

Nondurable
goods
$2905 billion
(21%)

(b)
Percentage of consumer expenditures

FIGURE 2.4 Sources of U.S. income and the composition of spending. (a) About 64% of U.S. income is received as wages and salaries. Income to property owners—corporate profit, interest, and rents—accounts for about 25% of total income. (b) Consumers divide their spending among durable goods, nondurable goods, and services. Roughly 68% of consumer spending is for services; the rest is for goods. *Source:* Bureau of Economic Analysis, **www.bea.gov.**

consumer durables (goods such as cars, refrigerators, and personal computers that have expected lives of 3 years or longer), *nondurables* (goods such as food, clothing, and gasoline that have lives of less than 3 years), and *services* (the work done by people such as lawyers, physicians, and recreational workers). Observe that approximately 68% of consumer spending is on services. For this reason, the United States is known as a *service-oriented economy.*

QUESTION: Over the past several decades, the service share of spending in the United States has increased relative to the goods share. Why do you think that trend has occurred?

PHOTO OP Durable Goods, Nondurable Goods, and Services

Consumers collectively spend their income on durable goods (such as the washer-dryer combo), nondurable goods (such as the pizza), and services (such as hair care).

©2/Ryan McVay/Ocean/Corbis

©Maren Caruso/Getty Images

©Plush Studios/Blend Images LLC

SUMMARY

LO2.1 Differentiate between a command system and a market system.

The market system and the command system are the two broad types of economic systems used to address the economic problem. In the market system (or capitalism), private individuals own most resources, and markets coordinate most economic activity. In the command system (or socialism or communism), government owns most resources, and central planners coordinate most economic activity.

LO2.2 List the main characteristics of the market system.

The market system is characterized by the private ownership of resources, including capital, and the freedom of individuals to engage in economic activities of their choice to advance their material well-being. Self-interest is the driving force of such an economy, and competition functions as a regulatory or control mechanism.

In the market system, markets, prices, and profits organize and make effective the many millions of individual economic decisions that occur daily.

Specialization, use of advanced technology, and the extensive use of capital goods are common features of market systems. Functioning as a medium of exchange, money eliminates the problems of bartering and permits easy trade and greater specialization, both domestically and internationally.

LO2.3 Explain how the market system answers the four fundamental questions.

Every economy faces four fundamental questions: (a) What goods and services will be produced? (b) How will the goods and services be produced? (c) Who will get the goods and services? (d) How will the system promote progress?

The market system produces products whose production and sale yield total revenue sufficient to cover total cost. It does not produce products for which total revenue continuously falls short of total cost. Competition forces firms to use the lowest-cost production techniques.

Economic profit (total revenue minus total cost) indicates that an industry is prosperous and promotes its expansion. Losses signify that an industry is not prosperous and hasten its contraction.

Consumer sovereignty means that both businesses and resource suppliers are subject to the wants of consumers. Through their dollar votes, consumers decide on the composition of output.

The prices that a household receives for the resources it supplies to the economy determine that household's income. This income determines the household's claim on the economy's output. Those who have income to spend get the products produced in the market system.

LO2.4 Discuss how the market system adjusts to change and promotes progress.

The market system encourages technological advance and capital accumulation, both of which raise a nation's standard of living.

Competition, the primary mechanism of control in the market economy, promotes a unity of self-interest and social interests. As if directed by an invisible hand, competition harnesses the self-interested motives of businesses and resource suppliers to further the social interest.

LO2.5 Describe the mechanics of the circular flow model.

The circular flow model illustrates the flows of resources and products from households to businesses and from businesses to households, along with the corresponding monetary flows. Businesses are on the buying side of the resource market and the selling side of the product market. Households are on the selling side of the resource market and the buying side of the product market.

TERMS AND CONCEPTS

economic system	market	creative destruction
command system	specialization	"invisible hand"
market system	division of labor	circular flow diagram
private property	medium of exchange	households
freedom of enterprise	barter	businesses
freedom of choice	money	product market
self-interest	consumer sovereignty	resource market
competition	dollar votes	

QUESTIONS

The following and additional problems can be found in ■ connect

1. Contrast how a market system and a command economy try to cope with economic scarcity. LO2.1

2. How does self-interest help achieve society's economic goals? Why is there such a wide variety of desired goods and services in a market system? In what way are entrepreneurs and businesses at the helm of the economy but commanded by consumers? LO2.2

3. Why is private property, and the protection of property rights, so critical to the success of the market system? How do property rights encourage cooperation? LO2.2

4. What are the advantages of using capital in the production process? What is meant by the term "division of labor"? What are the advantages of specialization in the use of human and material resources? Explain why exchange is the necessary consequence of specialization. LO2.2

5. What problem does barter entail? Indicate the economic significance of money as a medium of exchange. What is meant by the statement "We want money only to part with it"? LO2.2

6. Evaluate and explain the following statements: LO2.2
   a. The market system is a profit-and-loss system.
   b. Competition is the disciplinarian of the market economy.

7. In the 1990s thousands of "dot-com" companies emerged with great fanfare to take advantage of the Internet and new information technologies. A few, like Google, eBay, and Amazon, have generally thrived and prospered, but many others struggled and eventually failed. Explain these varied outcomes in terms of how the market system answers the question "What goods and services will be produced?" LO2.3

8. Some large hardware stores such as Home Depot boast of carrying as many as 20,000 different products in each store. What motivated the producers of those individual products to make them and offer them for sale? How did the producers decide on the best combinations of resources to use? Who made those resources available, and why? Who decides whether these particular hardware products should continue to be produced and offered for sale? LO2.3

9. What is meant by the term "creative destruction"? How does the emergence of streaming music technology relate to this idea? LO2.3

10. In a sentence, describe the meaning of the phrase "invisible hand." LO2.4

11. Distinguish between the resource market and the product market in the circular flow model. In what way are businesses and households both sellers and buyers in this model? What are the flows in the circular flow model? LO2.5

12. What are the three major legal forms of business enterprises? Which form is the most prevalent in terms of number of firms? Which form is dominant in terms of total sales revenues? LO2.5

13. What are the major forms of household income? Contrast the wage and salary share to the profit share in terms of relative size. Distinguish between a durable consumer good and a nondurable consumer good. How does the combined spending on both types of consumer goods compare to the spending on services? LO2.5

PROBLEMS

1. Suppose Natasha currently makes $50,000 per year working as a manager at a cable TV company. She then develops two possible entrepreneurial business opportunities. In one, she will quit her job to start an organic soap company. In the other, she will try to develop an Internet-based competitor to the local cable company. For the soap-making opportunity, she anticipates annual revenue of $465,000 and costs for the necessary land, labor, and capital of $395,000 per year. For the Internet opportunity, she anticipates costs for land, labor, and capital of $3,250,000 per year as compared to revenues of $3,275,000 per year. (a) Should she quit her current job to become an entrepreneur? (b) If she does quit her current job, which opportunity would she pursue? LO2.3

2. With current technology, suppose a firm is producing 400 loaves of banana bread daily. Also assume that the least-cost combination of resources in producing those loaves is 5 units of labor, 7 units of land, 2 units of capital, and 1 unit of entrepreneurial ability, selling at prices of $40, $60, $60, and $20, respectively. If the firm can sell these 400 loaves at $2 per unit, what is its total revenue? Its total cost? Its profit or loss? Will it continue to produce banana bread? If this firm's situation is typical for the other makers of banana bread, will resources flow toward or away from this bakery good? LO2.3

3. Let's put dollar amounts on the flows in the circular flow diagram of Figure 2.2. LO2.5
   a. Suppose that businesses buy a total of $100 billion of the four resources (labor, land, capital, and entrepreneurial ability) from households. If households receive $60 billion in wages, $10 billion in rent, and $20 billion in interest, how much are households paid for providing entrepreneurial ability?
   b. If households spend $55 billion on goods and $45 billion on services, how much in revenues do businesses receive in the product market?

PART TWO

Price, Quantity, and Efficiency

2

©Tatiana Belova/Shutterstock

©Tatiana Belova/Shutterstock

Demand, Supply, and Market Equilibrium

Learning Objectives

LO3.1 Describe *demand* and explain how it can change.

LO3.2 Describe *supply* and explain how it can change.

LO3.3 Relate how supply and demand interact to determine market equilibrium.

LO3.4 Explain how changes in supply and demand affect equilibrium prices and quantities.

LO3.5 Identify what government-set prices are and how they can cause product surpluses and shortages.

LO3.6 (Appendix) Illustrate how supply and demand analysis can provide insights on actual economic decisions.

The model of supply and demand is the economics profession's greatest contribution to human understanding because it explains the operation of the markets on which we depend for nearly everything that we eat, drink, or consume. The model is so powerful and so widely used that to many people it *is* economics.

Markets bring together buyers ("demanders") and sellers ("suppliers") and exist in many forms. The corner gas station, an e-commerce site, the local bakery shop, a farmer's roadside stand—all are familiar markets. The New York Stock Exchange and the Chicago Board of Trade are markets where buyers and sellers of stocks and bonds and farm commodities from all over the world communicate with one another to buy and sell. Auctioneers bring together potential buyers and sellers of art, livestock, used farm equipment, and, sometimes, real estate.

Some markets are local, while others are national or international. Some are highly personal, involving face-to-face contact between demander and supplier; others are faceless, with buyer and seller never seeing or knowing each other. But all competitive markets involve demand and supply, and this chapter discusses how the model works to explain both the *quantities* that are bought and sold in markets as well as the *prices* at which they trade.

Demand

Demand is a schedule or a curve that shows the various amounts of a product that consumers will purchase at each of several possible prices during a specified period of time.[1] The table in Figure 3.1 is a hypothetical demand schedule for a *single consumer* purchasing a particular product, in this case, lattes. (For simplicity, we will categorize all espresso drinks as "lattes" and assume a highly competitive market.)

The table reveals that, if the price of lattes were $5 each, Joe Java would buy 10 lattes per month; if it were $4, he would buy 20 lattes per month; and so forth.

The table does not tell us which of the five possible prices will actually exist in the market. That depends on the interaction between demand and supply. Demand is simply a statement of a buyer's plans, or intentions, with respect to the purchase of a product.

To be meaningful, the quantities demanded at each price must relate to a specific period—a day, a week, a month. Here that period is 1 month.

demand A schedule showing the amounts of a good or service that buyers (or a buyer) wish to purchase at various prices during some time period.

Law of Demand

A fundamental characteristic of demand is this: Other things equal, as price falls, the quantity demanded rises, and as price rises, the quantity demanded falls. In short, there is an

---

[1]This definition obviously is worded to apply to product markets. To adjust it to apply to resource markets, substitute the word "resource" for "product" and the word "businesses" for "consumers."

FIGURE 3.1 Joe Java's demand for lattes. Because price and quantity demanded are inversely related, an individual's demand schedule graphs as a downsloping curve such as *D*. Other things equal, consumers will buy more of a product as its price declines and less of the product as its price rises. (Here and in later figures, *P* stands for price and *Q* stands for quantity demanded or supplied.)

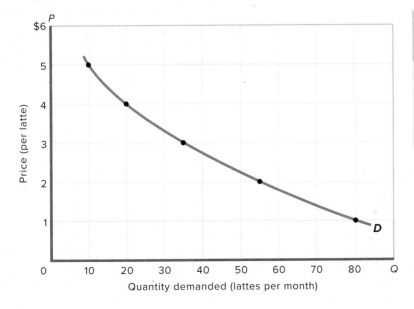

Joe Java's Demand for Lattes	
Price per Latte	Quantity Demanded per Month
$5	10
4	20
3	35
2	55
1	80

inverse relationship between price and quantity demanded. Economists call this inverse relationship the **law of demand.**

law of demand The principle that, other things equal, an increase in a product's price will reduce the quantity of it demanded, and conversely for a decrease in price.

The other-things-equal assumption is critical here. Many factors other than the price of the product being considered affect the amount purchased. The quantity of lattes purchased will depend not only on the price of lattes but also on the prices of such substitutes as tea, soda, fruit juice, and bottled water. The law of demand in this case says that fewer lattes will be purchased if the price of lattes rises while the prices of tea, soda, fruit juice, and bottled water all remain constant.

The law of demand is consistent with both common sense and observation. People ordinarily *do* buy more of a product at a low price than at a high price. Price is an obstacle that deters consumers from buying. The higher that obstacle, the less of a product they will buy; the lower the obstacle, the more they will buy. The fact that businesses reduce prices to clear out unsold goods is evidence of their belief in the law of demand.

The Demand Curve

demand curve A curve illustrating demand.

The inverse relationship between price and quantity demanded for any product can be represented on a simple graph, in which, by convention, we measure *quantity demanded* on the horizontal axis and *price* on the vertical axis. In Figure 3.1 we have plotted the five price-quantity data points listed in the table and connected the points with a smooth curve, labeled *D*. This is a **demand curve.** Its downward slope reflects the law of demand: People buy more of a product, service, or resource as its price falls. They buy less as its price rises. There is an inverse relationship between price and quantity demanded.

The table and graph in Figure 3.1 contain exactly the same data and reflect the same inverse relationship between price and quantity demanded.

Market Demand

So far, we have concentrated on just one consumer, Joe Java. But competition requires that more than one buyer be present in each market. By adding the quantities demanded by all consumers at each of the various possible prices, we can get from *individual* demand to *market* demand. If there are just three buyers in the market (Joe Java, Sarah Coffee, and Mike Cappuccino), as represented by the table and graph in Figure 3.2, it is relatively easy to determine the total quantity demanded at each price. We simply sum the individual quantities demanded to obtain the total quantity demanded at each price. The particular price and the total quantity demanded are then plotted as one point on the market demand curve in Figure 3.2.

Competition, of course, ordinarily entails many more than three buyers of a product. To avoid hundreds or thousands of additions, let's simply suppose that the table and curve D_1 in Figure 3.3 show the amounts all the buyers in this market will purchase at each of the five prices.

determinants of demand Factors other than price that determine the quantities demanded of a good or service.

In constructing a demand curve such as D_1 in Figure 3.3, economists assume that price is the most important influence on the amount of any product purchased. But economists know that other factors can and do affect purchases. These factors, called **determinants of demand,** are held constant when a demand curve like D_1 is drawn. They are the "other things equal" in the relationship between price and quantity demanded. When any of these determinants changes, the demand curve will shift to the right or left. For this reason, determinants of demand are sometimes referred to as *demand shifters.*

The basic determinants of demand are (1) consumers' tastes (preferences), (2) the number of consumers in the market, (3) consumers' incomes, (4) the prices of related goods, and (5) expected prices.

FIGURE 3.2 Market demand for lattes, three buyers. We establish the market demand curve *D* by adding horizontally the individual demand curves (D_1, D_2, and D_3) of all the consumers in the market. At the price of $3, for example, the three individual curves yield a total quantity demanded of 100 lattes.

Price per Latte	Joe Java		Sarah Coffee		Mike Cappuccino		Total Quantity Demanded per Month
		Quantity Demanded					
$5	10	+	12	+	8	=	30
4	20	+	23	+	17	=	60
3	35	+	39	+	26	=	100
2	55	+	60	+	39	=	154
1	80	+	87	+	54	=	221

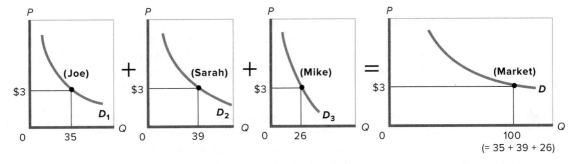

FIGURE 3.3 Changes in the demand for lattes. A change in one or more of the determinants of demand causes a change in demand. An increase in demand is shown as a shift of the demand curve to the right, as from D_1 to D_2. A decrease in demand is shown as a shift of the demand curve to the left, as from D_1 to D_3. These changes in demand are to be distinguished from a change in *quantity demanded*, which is caused by a change in the price of the product, as shown by a movement from, say, point *a* to point *b* on fixed demand curve D_1.

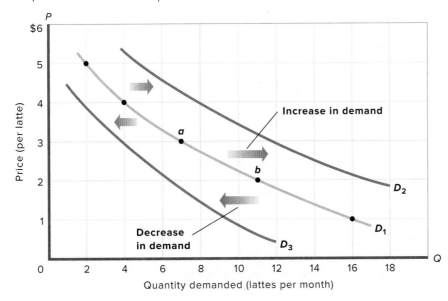

Market Demand for Lattes (*D*)	
(1) Price per Latte	(2) Total Quantity Demanded per Week
$5	2,000
4	4,000
3	7,000
2	11,000
1	16,000

Changes in Demand

A change in one or more of the determinants of demand will change the underlying demand data (the demand schedule in the table) and therefore the location of the demand curve in Figure 3.3. A change in the demand schedule or, graphically, a shift in the demand curve is called a *change in demand*.

If consumers desire to buy more lattes at each possible price, that *increase in demand* is shown as a shift of the demand curve to the right, say, from D_1 to D_2. Conversely, a *decrease in demand* occurs when consumers buy fewer lattes at each possible price. The leftward shift of the demand curve from D_1 to D_3 in Figure 3.3 shows that situation.

Now let's see how changes in each determinant affect demand.

Tastes

A favorable change in consumer tastes (preferences) for a product means more of it will be demanded at each price. Demand will increase; the demand curve will shift rightward. For example, greater concern about the environment has increased the demand for hybrid cars and other "green" technologies. An unfavorable change in consumer preferences will decrease demand, shifting the demand curve to the left. For example, the recent popularity of low-carbohydrate diets has reduced the demand for bread and pasta.

Number of Buyers

An increase in the number of buyers in a market increases product demand. For example, the rising number of older persons in the United States in recent years has increased the demand for motor homes and retirement communities. In contrast, the migration of people away from many small rural communities has reduced the demand for housing, home appliances, and auto repair in those towns.

Income

The effect of changes in income on demand is more complex. For most products, a rise in income increases demand. Consumers collectively buy more airplane tickets, projection TVs, and gas grills as their incomes rise. Products whose demand increases or decreases *directly* with changes in income are called *superior goods,* or **normal goods.**

normal good A good or service whose consumption increases when income increases and falls when income decreases, price remaining constant.

Although most products are normal goods, there are a few exceptions. As incomes increase beyond some point, the demand for used clothing, retread tires, and soy-enhanced hamburger may decline. Higher incomes enable consumers to buy new clothing, new tires, and higher-quality meats. Goods whose demand increases or decreases *inversely* with money income are called **inferior goods.** (This is an economic term; we are not making personal judgments on specific products.)

inferior good A good or service whose consumption declines as income rises, prices held constant.

Prices of Related Goods

A change in the price of a related good may either increase or decrease the demand for a product, depending on whether the related good is a substitute or a complement:

- A **substitute good** is one that can be used in place of another good.
- A **complementary good** is one that is used together with another good.

substitute goods Products or services that can be used in place of each other. When the price of one falls, the demand for the other product falls; conversely, when the price of one product rises, the demand for the other product rises.

Beef and chicken are substitute goods or, simply, *substitutes.* When two products are substitutes, an increase in the price of one will increase the demand for the other. For example, when the price of beef rises, consumers will buy less beef and increase their demand for chicken. So it is with other product pairs such as Nikes and Reeboks, Budweiser and Miller beer, or Colgate and Crest toothpaste. They are *substitutes in consumption.*

complementary goods Products and services that are used together. When the price of one falls, the demand for the other increases (and conversely).

Complementary goods (or, simply, *complements*) are products that are used together and thus are typically demanded jointly. Examples include computers and software, cell phones and cellular service, and snowboards and lift tickets. If the price of a complement (for example, lettuce) goes up, the demand for the related good (salad dressing) will decline. Conversely, if the price of a complement (for example, tuition) falls, the demand for a related good (textbooks) will increase.

The vast majority of goods that are unrelated to one another are called *independent goods.* There is virtually no demand relationship between bacon and golf balls or pickles and ice cream. A change in the price of one will have virtually no effect on the demand for the other.

PHOTO OP Normal versus Inferior Goods

New television sets are normal goods. People buy more of them as their incomes rise. Hand-pushed lawn mowers are inferior goods. As incomes rise, people purchase gas-powered mowers instead.

©Robert Daly/Caia Image/Glow Images

©Pixtal/AGE Fotostock

Expected Prices Changes in expected prices may shift demand. A newly formed expectation of a higher price in the future may cause consumers to buy now in order to "beat" the anticipated price rise, thus increasing current demand. For example, when freezing weather destroys much of Brazil's coffee crop, buyers may conclude that the price of coffee beans will rise. They may purchase large quantities now to stock up on beans. In contrast, a newly formed expectation of falling prices may decrease current demand for products.

Changes in Quantity Demanded

Be sure not to confuse a *change in demand* with a *change in quantity demanded*. A **change in demand** is a shift of the demand curve to the right (an increase in demand) or to the left (a decrease in demand). It occurs because the consumer's state of mind about purchasing the product has been altered in response to a change in one or more of the determinants of demand. Recall that "demand" is a schedule or a curve; therefore, a "change in demand" means a change in the schedule and a shift of the curve.

In contrast, a **change in quantity demanded** is a movement from one point to another point—from one price–quantity combination to another—on a fixed demand curve. The cause of such a change is an increase or decrease in the price of the product under consideration. In the table in Figure 3.3, for example, a decline in the price of lattes from $5 to $4 will increase the quantity of lattes demanded from 2,000 to 4,000.

In the graph in Figure 3.3, the shift of the demand curve D_1 to either D_2 or D_3 is a change in demand. But the movement from point a to point b on curve D_1 represents a change in quantity demanded: Demand has not changed; it is the entire curve, and it remains fixed in place.

change in demand A change in the quantity demanded of a good or service at every price; a shift of the demand curve to the left or right.

change in quantity demanded A movement from one point to another on a demand curve.

PHOTO OP Substitutes versus Complements

Different brands of soft drinks are substitute goods; goods consumed jointly such as hot dogs and mustard are complementary goods.

Supply

supply A schedule showing the amounts of a good or service that sellers (or a seller) will offer at various prices during some period.

Supply is a schedule or curve showing the amounts of a product that producers will make available for sale at each of a series of possible prices during a specific period.[2] The table in Figure 3.4 is a hypothetical supply schedule for Star Buck, a single supplier of lattes. Curve *S* incorporates the data in the table and is called a *supply curve*. The schedule and curve show the quantities of lattes that will be supplied at various prices, other things equal.

_____
[2]This definition is worded to apply to product markets. To adjust it to apply to resource markets, substitute "resource" for "product" and "owners" for "producers."

FIGURE 3.4 Star Buck's supply of lattes. Because price and quantity supplied are directly related, the supply curve for an individual producer graphs as an upsloping curve. Other things equal, producers will offer more of a product for sale as its price rises and less of the product for sale as its price falls.

Star Buck's Supply of Lattes	
Price per Latte	Quantity Supplied per Month
$5	60
4	50
3	35
2	20
1	5

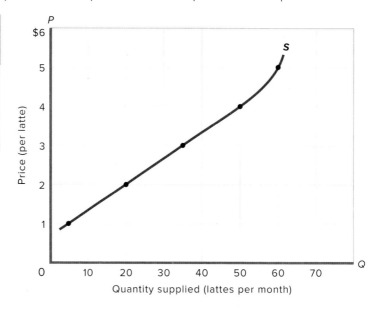

Law of Supply

Figure 3.4 shows a positive or direct relationship that prevails between price and quantity supplied. As price rises, the quantity supplied rises; as price falls, the quantity supplied falls. This relationship is called the **law of supply.** A supply schedule or curve reveals that, other things equal, firms will offer for sale more of their product at a high price than at a low price. This, again, is basically common sense.

Price is an obstacle from the standpoint of the consumer (for example, Joe Java), who is on the paying end. The higher the price, the less the consumer will buy. But the supplier (for example, Star Buck) is on the receiving end of the product's price. To a supplier, price represents *revenue,* which is needed to cover costs and earn a profit. Higher prices therefore create a profit incentive to produce and sell more of a product. The higher the price, the greater this incentive and the greater the quantity supplied.

law of supply The principle that, other things equal, an increase in the price of a product will increase the quantity of it supplied, and conversely for a price decrease.

Market Supply

Market supply is derived from individual supply in exactly the same way that market demand is derived from individual demand (Figure 3.2). We sum (not shown) the quantities supplied by each producer at each price. That is, we obtain the market **supply curve** by "horizontally adding" (also not shown) the supply curves of the individual producers. The price and quantity-supplied data in the table in Figure 3.5 are for an assumed 200 identical producers in the market, each willing to supply lattes according to the supply schedule shown in Figure 3.4. Curve S_1 is a graph of the market supply data. Note that the axes in Figure 3.5 are the same as those used in our graph of market demand (Figure 3.3). The only difference is that we change the label on the horizontal axis from "quantity demanded" to "quantity supplied."

supply curve A curve illustrating supply.

Determinants of Supply

In constructing a supply curve, we assume that price is the most significant influence on the quantity supplied of any product. But other factors (the "other things equal") can and do affect supply. The supply curve is drawn on the assumption that these other things are

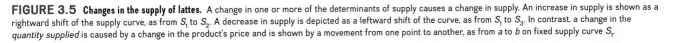

FIGURE 3.5 Changes in the supply of lattes. A change in one or more of the determinants of supply causes a change in supply. An increase in supply is shown as a rightward shift of the supply curve, as from S_1 to S_2. A decrease in supply is depicted as a leftward shift of the curve, as from S_1 to S_3. In contrast, a change in the *quantity supplied* is caused by a change in the product's price and is shown by a movement from one point to another, as from a to b on fixed supply curve S_1.

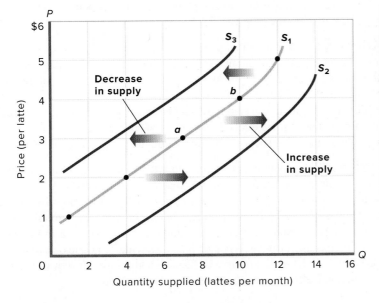

Market Supply of Lattes, (S_1)	
(1) Price per Latte	(2) Total Quantity Supplied per Month
$5	12,000
4	10,000
3	7,000
2	4,000
1	1,000

fixed and do not change. If one of them does change, a *change in supply* will occur, meaning that the entire supply curve will shift.

> **determinants of supply** Factors other than price that determine the quantities supplied of a good or service.

The basic **determinants of supply** are (1) resource prices, (2) technology, (3) taxes and subsidies, (4) prices of other goods, (5) expected price, and (6) the number of sellers in the market. A change in any one or more of these determinants of supply, or *supply shifters*, will move the supply curve for a product either right or left. A shift to the *right*, as from S_1 to S_2 in Figure 3.5, signifies an *increase* in supply: Producers supply larger quantities of the product at each possible price. A shift to the *left*, as from S_1 to S_3, indicates a *decrease* in supply: Producers offer less output at each price.

Changes in Supply

Let's consider how changes in each of the determinants affect supply. The key idea is that costs are a major factor underlying supply curves; anything that affects costs (other than changes in output itself) usually shifts the supply curve.

Resource Prices
The prices of the resources used in the production process help determine the costs of production incurred by firms. Higher *resource* prices raise production costs and, assuming a particular *product* price, squeeze profits. That reduction in profits reduces the incentive for firms to supply output at each product price. For example, an increase in the prices of coffee beans and milk will increase the cost of making lattes and therefore reduce their supply.

In contrast, lower *resource* prices reduce production costs and increase profits. So when resource prices fall, firms supply greater output at each product price. For example, a decrease in the prices of sand, gravel, and limestone will increase the supply of concrete.

Technology
Improvements in technology (techniques of production) enable firms to produce units of output with fewer resources. Because resources are costly, using fewer of them lowers production costs and increases supply. Example: Technological advances in producing flat-panel computer monitors have greatly reduced their cost. Thus, manufacturers will now offer more such monitors than previously at the various prices; the supply of flat-panel monitors has increased.

Taxes and Subsidies
Businesses treat sales and property taxes as costs. Increases in those taxes will increase production costs and reduce supply. In contrast, subsidies are "taxes in reverse." If the government subsidizes the production of a good, it in effect lowers the producers' costs and increases supply.

Prices of Other Goods
Firms that produce a particular product, say, soccer balls, can usually use their plant and equipment to produce alternative goods, say, basketballs and volleyballs. The higher prices of these "other goods" may entice soccer ball producers to switch production to those other goods in order to increase profits. This *substitution in production* results in a decline in the supply of soccer balls. Alternatively, when basketballs and volleyballs decline in price relative to the price of soccer balls, firms will produce fewer of those products and more soccer balls, increasing the supply of soccer balls.

Expected Prices
Changes in expectations about the future price of a product may affect the producer's current willingness to supply that product. It is difficult, however, to generalize about how a new expectation of higher prices affects the present supply of a product. Farmers anticipating a higher wheat price in the future might withhold some of their current wheat harvest from the market, thereby causing a decrease in the current supply of wheat. In contrast, in many types of manufacturing industries, newly formed expectations that price will increase may induce firms to add another shift of workers or to expand their production facilities, causing current supply to increase.

Number of Sellers Other things equal, the larger the number of suppliers, the greater the market supply. As more firms enter an industry, the supply curve shifts to the right. Conversely, the smaller the number of firms in the industry, the less the market supply. This means that as firms leave an industry, the supply curve shifts to the left. Example: The United States and Canada have imposed restrictions on haddock fishing to replenish dwindling stocks. As part of that policy, the federal government has bought the boats of some of the haddock fishers as a way of putting them out of business and decreasing the catch. The result has been a decline in the market supply of haddock.

Changes in Quantity Supplied

The distinction between a *change in supply* and a *change in quantity supplied* parallels the distinction between a change in demand and a change in quantity demanded. Because supply is a schedule or curve, a **change in supply** means a change in the schedule and a shift of the curve. An increase in supply shifts the curve to the right; a decrease in supply shifts it to the left. The cause of a change in supply is a change in one or more of the determinants of supply.

In contrast, a **change in quantity supplied** is a movement from one point to another on a fixed supply curve. The cause of such a movement is a change in the price of the specific product being considered. In Figure 3.5, a decline in the price of lattes from $4 to $3 decreases the quantity of lattes supplied per month from 10,000 to 7,000. This movement from point *b* to point *a* along S_1 is a change in quantity supplied, not a change in supply. Supply is the full schedule of prices and quantities shown, and this schedule does not change when the price of lattes changes.

> **change in supply** A change in the quantity supplied of a good or service at every price; a shift of the supply curve to the left or right.

> **change in quantity supplied** A movement from one point to another on a fixed supply curve.

Market Equilibrium

With our understanding of demand and supply, we can now show how the decisions of Joe Java and other buyers of lattes interact with the decisions of Star Buck and other sellers to determine the price and quantity of lattes. In the table in Figure 3.6, columns 1 and 2 repeat

FIGURE 3.6 Equilibrium price and quantity. The intersection of the downsloping demand curve *D* and the upsloping supply curve *S* indicates the equilibrium price and quantity, here $3 and 7,000 lattes. The shortages of lattes at below-equilibrium prices (for example, 7,000 at $2) drive up price. The higher prices increase the quantity supplied and reduce the quantity demanded until equilibrium is achieved. The surpluses caused by above-equilibrium prices (for example, 6,000 lattes at $4) push price down. As price drops, the quantity demanded rises and the quantity supplied falls until equilibrium is established. At the equilibrium price and quantity, there are neither shortages nor surpluses of lattes.

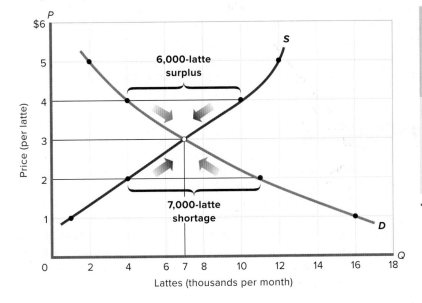

Market Supply of and Demand for Lattes			
(1) Total Quantity Supplied per Month	(2) Price per Latte	(3) Total Quantity Demanded per Month	(4) Surplus (+) or Shortage (−)*
12,000	$5	2,000	+10,000 ↓
10,000	4	4,000	6,000 ↓
7,000	3	7,000	0
4,000	2	11,000	−7,000 ↑
1,000	1	16,000	−15,000 ↑

*Arrows indicate the effect on price.

the market supply of lattes (from Figure 3.5), and columns 2 and 3 repeat the market demand for lattes (from Figure 3.3). We assume this is a competitive market, so neither buyers nor sellers can set the price.

Equilibrium Price and Quantity

equilibrium price The price in a competitive market at which the quantity demanded and the quantity supplied are equal, there is neither a shortage nor a surplus, and there is no tendency for price to rise or fall.

equilibrium quantity (1) The quantity demanded and supplied at the equilibrium price in a competitive market; (2) the profit-maximizing output of a firm.

We are looking for the equilibrium price and equilibrium quantity. The **equilibrium price** (or *market-clearing price*) is the price at which the intentions of buyers and sellers match. It is the price at which quantity demanded equals quantity supplied. The table in Figure 3.6 reveals that at $3, *and only at that price,* the number of lattes that sellers wish to sell (7,000) is identical to the number that consumers want to buy (also 7,000). At $3 and 7,000 lattes, there is neither a shortage nor a surplus of lattes. So 7,000 lattes is the **equilibrium quantity:** the quantity at which the intentions of buyers and sellers match so that the quantity demanded and the quantity supplied are equal.

Graphically, the equilibrium price is indicated by the intersection of the supply curve and the demand curve in Figure 3.6. (The horizontal axis now measures both quantity demanded and quantity supplied.) With neither a shortage nor a surplus at $3, the market is *in equilibrium*, meaning "in balance" or "at rest."

To better understand the uniqueness of the equilibrium price, let's consider other prices. At any above-equilibrium price, quantity supplied exceeds quantity demanded. For example, at the $4 price, sellers will offer 10,000 lattes, but buyers will purchase only 4,000. The $4 price encourages sellers to offer lots of lattes but discourages many consumers from buying them. The result is a **surplus** or *excess supply* of 6,000 lattes. If latte sellers made them all, they would find themselves with 6,000 unsold lattes.

surplus The amount by which the quantity supplied of a product exceeds the quantity demanded at a specific (above-equilibrium) price.

Surpluses drive prices down. Even if the $4 price existed temporarily, it could not persist. The large surplus would prompt competing sellers to lower the price to encourage buyers to step in and take the surplus off their hands. As the price fell, the incentive to produce lattes would decline and the incentive for consumers to buy lattes would increase. As shown in Figure 3.6, the market would move to its equilibrium at $3.

shortage The amount by which the quantity demanded of a product exceeds the quantity supplied at a particular (below-equilibrium) price.

Any price below the $3 equilibrium price would create a shortage; quantity demanded would exceed quantity supplied. Consider a $2 price, for example. We see in column 4 of the table in Figure 3.6 that quantity demanded exceeds quantity supplied at that price. The result is a **shortage** or *excess demand* of 7,000 lattes. The $2 price discourages sellers from devoting resources to lattes and encourages consumers to desire more lattes than are available. The $2 price cannot persist as the equilibrium price. Many consumers who want to buy lattes at this price will not obtain them. They will express a willingness to pay more than $2 to get them. Competition among these buyers will drive up the price, eventually to the $3 equilibrium level. Unless disrupted by supply or demand changes, this $3 price of lattes will continue.

Rationing Function of Prices

The ability of the competitive forces of supply and demand to establish a price at which selling and buying decisions are consistent is called the *rationing function of prices.* In our case, the equilibrium price of $3 clears the market, leaving no burdensome surplus for sellers and no inconvenient shortage for potential buyers. And it is the combination of freely made individual decisions that sets this market-clearing price. In effect, the market outcome says that all buyers who are willing and able to pay $3 for a latte will obtain one; all buyers who cannot or will not pay $3 will go without one. Similarly, all producers who are willing and able to offer a latte for sale at $3 will sell it; all producers who cannot or will not sell for $3 will not sell their product.

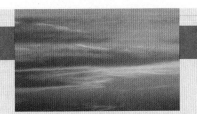

APPLYING THE ANALYSIS

Uber and Dynamic Pricing

The ride-sharing service known as Uber rose to prominence in 2013 by offering consumers an alternative to government-regulated taxi companies. Uber works via the Internet, matching people who need a ride with people willing to use their own vehicles to provide rides. Both parties can find each other easily and instantly via a mobile phone app and Uber makes its money by taking a percentage of the fare.

Uber is innovative in many ways, including empowering anybody to become a paid driver, breaking up local taxi monopolies, and making it effortless to arrange a quick pickup. But Uber's most interesting feature is dynamic pricing, under which Uber sets equilibrium prices in real time, constantly adjusting fares so as to equalize quantity demanded and quantity supplied. The result is extremely short waiting times for both riders and drivers as Uber will, for instance, set a substantially higher "surge price" in a given location if demand suddenly increases due to, say, a bunch of people leaving a concert all at once and wanting rides. The higher fare encourages more Uber drivers to converge on the area, thereby minimizing wait times for both drivers and passengers.

The short wait times created by Uber's use of dynamic pricing stand in sharp contrast to taxi fares, which are fixed by law and therefore unable to adjust to ongoing changes in supply and demand. On days when demand is low relative to supply, drivers sit idle for long stretches of time. All of that inefficiency and inconvenience is eliminated by Uber's use of market equilibrium prices to equalize the demand and supply of rides.

QUESTION: How would you expect the introduction of Uber to affect the market for traditional taxi services? Does your answer depend on whether taxi fares (prices) are fixed by law or can move based on changes in demand and supply?

Changes in Demand, Supply, and Equilibrium

We know that prices can and do change in markets. For example, demand might change because of fluctuations in consumer tastes or incomes, changes in expected price, or variations in the prices of related goods. Supply might change in response to changes in resource prices, technology, or taxes. How will such changes in demand and supply affect equilibrium price and quantity?

Changes in Demand

Suppose that the supply of some good (for example, health care) is constant and the demand for the good increases, as shown in Figure 3.7a. As a result, the new intersection of the supply and demand curves is at higher values on both the price and the quantity axes. Clearly, an increase in demand raises both equilibrium price and equilibrium quantity. Conversely, a decrease in demand, such as that shown in Figure 3.7b, reduces both equilibrium price and equilibrium quantity.

FIGURE 3.7 Changes in demand and supply and the effects on price and quantity. The increase in demand from D_1 to D_2 in (a) increases both equilibrium price and equilibrium quantity. The decrease in demand from D_3 to D_4 in (b) decreases both equilibrium price and equilibrium quantity. The increase in supply from S_1 to S_2 in (c) decreases equilibrium price and increases equilibrium quantity. The decrease in supply from S_3 to S_4 in (d) increases equilibrium price and decreases equilibrium quantity. The boxes in the top right summarize the respective changes and outcomes. The upward arrows in the boxes signify increases in equilibrium price (P) and equilibrium quantity (Q); the downward arrows signify decreases in these items.

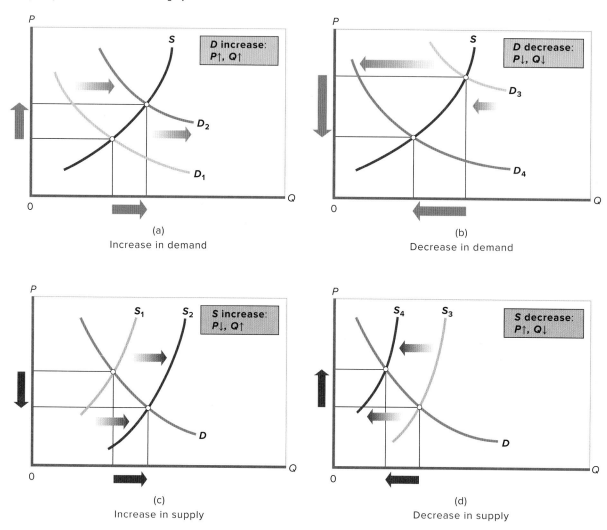

Changes in Supply

What happens if the demand for some good (for example, cell phones) is constant but the supply increases, as in Figure 3.7c? The new intersection of supply and demand is located at a lower equilibrium price but at a higher equilibrium quantity. An increase in supply reduces equilibrium price but increases equilibrium quantity. In contrast, if supply decreases, as in Figure 3.7d, equilibrium price rises while equilibrium quantity declines.

Complex Cases

When both supply and demand change, the effect is a combination of the individual effects.

Supply Increase; Demand Decrease What effect will a supply increase for some good (for example, apples) and a demand decrease have on equilibrium price? Both

changes decrease price, so the net result is a price drop greater than that resulting from either change alone.

What about equilibrium quantity? Here the effects of the changes in supply and demand are opposed: The increase in supply increases equilibrium quantity, but the decrease in demand reduces it. The direction of the change in equilibrium quantity depends on the relative sizes of the changes in supply and demand. If the increase in supply is larger than the decrease in demand, the equilibrium quantity will increase. But if the decrease in demand is greater than the increase in supply, the equilibrium quantity will decrease.

Supply Decrease; Demand Increase   A decrease in supply and an increase in demand for some good (for example, gasoline) both increase price. Their combined effect is an increase in equilibrium price greater than that caused by either change separately. But their effect on the equilibrium quantity is again indeterminate, depending on the relative sizes of the changes in supply and demand. If the decrease in supply is larger than the increase in demand, the equilibrium quantity will decrease. In contrast, if the increase in demand is greater than the decrease in supply, the equilibrium quantity will increase.

Supply Increase; Demand Increase   What if supply and demand both increase for some good (for example, sushi)? A supply increase drops equilibrium price, while a demand increase boosts it. If the increase in supply is greater than the increase in demand, the equilibrium price will fall. If the opposite holds, the equilibrium price will rise. If the two changes are equal and cancel out, price will not change.

The effect on equilibrium quantity is certain: The increases in supply and in demand both raise the equilibrium quantity. Therefore, the equilibrium quantity will increase by an amount greater than that caused by either change alone.

Supply Decrease; Demand Decrease   What about decreases in both supply and demand for some good (for example, new homes)? If the decrease in supply is greater than the decrease in demand, equilibrium price will rise. If the reverse is true, equilibrium price will fall. If the two changes are of the same size and cancel out, price will not change. Because the decreases in supply and demand both reduce equilibrium quantity, we can be sure that equilibrium quantity will fall.

Government-Set Prices

In most markets, prices are free to rise or fall with changes in supply or demand, no matter how high or low those prices might be. However, government occasionally concludes that changes in supply and demand have created prices that are unfairly high to buyers or unfairly low to sellers. Government may then place legal limits on how high or low a price or prices may go. Our previous analysis of shortages and surpluses helps us evaluate the wisdom of government-set prices.

APPLYING THE ANALYSIS

Price Ceilings on Gasoline

A **price ceiling** sets the maximum legal price a seller may charge for a product or service. A price at or below the ceiling is legal; a price above it is not. The rationale for establishing price ceilings (or ceiling prices) on specific products is that they purportedly enable consumers to obtain some "essential" good or service that they could not afford at the equilibrium price.

price ceiling A legally established maximum price for a good or service.

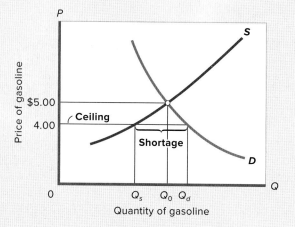

FIGURE 3.8 A price ceiling. A price ceiling is a maximum legal price, such as $4, that is below the equilibrium price. It results in a persistent product shortage, here shown by the distance between Q_d and Q_s.

Figure 3.8 shows the effects of price ceilings graphically. Let's look at a hypothetical situation. Suppose that rapidly rising world income boosts the purchase of automobiles and increases the demand for gasoline so that the equilibrium or market price reaches $5 per gallon. The rapidly rising price of gasoline greatly burdens low- and moderate-income households, which pressure government to "do something." To keep gasoline prices down, the government imposes a ceiling price of $4 per gallon. To impact the market, a price ceiling must be below the equilibrium price. A ceiling price of $6, for example, would have no effect on the price of gasoline in the current situation.

What are the effects of this $4 ceiling price? The rationing ability of the free market is rendered ineffective. Because the $4 ceiling price is below the $5 market-clearing price, there is a lasting shortage of gasoline. The quantity of gasoline demanded at $4 is Q_d, and the quantity supplied is only Q_s; a persistent excess demand or shortage of amount $Q_d - Q_s$ occurs.

The $4 price ceiling prevents the usual market adjustment in which competition among buyers bids up the price, inducing more production and rationing some buyers out of the market. That process would normally continue until the shortage disappeared at the equilibrium price and quantity, $5 and Q_0.

How will sellers apportion the available supply Q_s among buyers, who want the greater amount Q_d? Should they distribute gasoline on a first-come, first-served basis, that is, to those willing and able to get in line the soonest or stay in line the longest? Or should gas stations distribute it on the basis of favoritism? Since an unregulated shortage does not lead to an equitable distribution of gasoline, the government must establish some formal system for rationing it to consumers. One option is to issue ration coupons, which authorize bearers to purchase a fixed amount of gasoline per month. The rationing system might entail first the printing of coupons for Q_s gallons of gasoline and then the equal distribution of the coupons among consumers so that the wealthy family of four and the poor family of four both receive the same number of coupons.

But ration coupons would not prevent a second problem from arising. The demand curve in Figure 3.8 reveals that many buyers are willing to pay more than the $4 ceiling price. And, of course, it is more profitable for gasoline stations to sell at prices above the ceiling. Thus, despite a sizable enforcement bureaucracy that would have to accompany the price controls, *black markets* in which gasoline is illegally bought and sold at prices above the legal limits will flourish. Counterfeiting of ration coupons will also be a problem. And since the price of gasoline is now "set by government," there might be political pressure on government to set the price even lower.

QUESTION: Why is it typically difficult to end price ceilings once they have been in place for a long time?

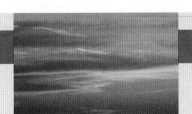

APPLYING THE ANALYSIS

Rent Controls

About 200 cities in the United States, including New York City, Boston, and San Francisco, have at one time or another enacted price ceilings in the form of rent controls—maximum rents established by law—or, more recently, have set maximum rent increases for existing tenants. Such laws are well intended. Their goals are to protect low-income families from escalating rents caused by demand increases that outstrip supply increases. Rent controls are designed to alleviate perceived housing shortages and make housing more affordable.

What have been the actual economic effects? On the demand side, the below-equilibrium rents attract a larger number of renters. Some are locals seeking to move into their own places after sharing housing with friends or family. Others are outsiders attracted into the area by the artificially lower rents. But a large problem occurs on the supply side. Price controls make it less attractive for landlords to offer housing on the rental market. In the short run, owners may sell their rental units or convert them to condominiums. In the long run, low rents make it unprofitable for owners to repair or renovate their rental units. (Rent controls are one cause of the many abandoned apartment buildings found in some larger cities.) Also, insurance companies, pension funds, and other potential new investors in housing will find it more profitable to invest in office buildings, shopping malls, or motels, where rents are not controlled.

In brief, rent controls distort market signals, and thus resources are misallocated: Too few resources are allocated to rental housing, and too many to alternative uses. Ironically, although rent controls are often legislated to lessen the effects of perceived shortages, controls in fact are a primary cause of such shortages. For that reason, most American cities either have abandoned rent controls or are gradually phasing them out.

QUESTION: Why does maintenance tend to diminish in rent-controlled apartment buildings relative to maintenance in buildings where owners can charge market-determined rents?

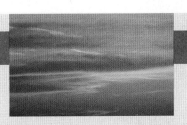

APPLYING THE ANALYSIS

Price Floors on Wheat

A **price floor** is a minimum price fixed by the government. A price at or above the price floor is legal; a price below it is not. Price floors above equilibrium prices are usually invoked when society feels that the free functioning of the market system has not provided a sufficient income for certain groups of resource suppliers or producers. Supported prices for agricultural products and current minimum wages are two examples of price (or wage) floors. Let's look at the former.

price floor A legally determined price above the equilibrium price.

FIGURE 3.9 A price floor. A price floor is a minimum legal price, such as $3, that results in a persistent product surplus, here shown by the distance between Q_s and Q_d.

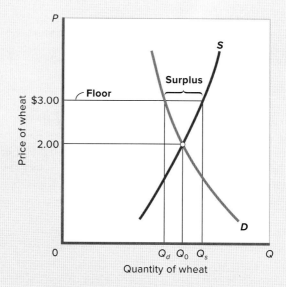

Suppose that many farmers have extremely low incomes when the price of wheat is at its equilibrium value of $2 per bushel. The government decides to help out by establishing a legal price floor (or "price support") of $3 per bushel.

What will be the effects? At any price above the equilibrium price, quantity supplied will exceed quantity demanded—that is, there will be a persistent surplus of the product. Farmers will be willing to produce and offer for sale more wheat than private buyers are willing to buy at the $3 price floor. As we saw with a price ceiling, an imposed legal price disrupts the rationing ability of the free market.

Figure 3.9 illustrates the effect of a price floor graphically. Suppose that S and D are the supply and demand curves for wheat. Equilibrium price and quantity are $2 and Q_0, respectively. If the government imposes a price floor of $3, farmers will produce Q_s but private buyers will purchase only Q_d. The surplus is the excess of Q_s over Q_d.

The government may cope with the surplus resulting from a price floor in two ways:

- It can restrict supply (for example, by instituting acreage allotments by which farmers agree to take a certain amount of land out of production) or increase demand (for example, by researching new uses for the product involved). These actions may reduce the difference between the equilibrium price and the price floor and that way reduce the size of the resulting surplus.

- If these efforts are not wholly successful, then the government must purchase the surplus output at the $3 price (thereby subsidizing farmers) and store or otherwise dispose of it.

Price floors such as $3 in Figure 3.9 not only disrupt the rationing ability of prices but also distort resource allocation. Without the price floor, the $2 equilibrium price of wheat would cause financial losses and force high-cost wheat producers to plant other crops or abandon farming altogether. But the $3 price floor allows them to continue to grow wheat and remain farmers. So society devotes too many scarce resources to wheat production and too few to producing other, more valuable, goods and services. It fails to achieve an optimal allocation of resources.

That's not all. Consumers of wheat-based products pay higher prices because of the price floor. Taxpayers pay higher taxes to finance the government's purchase of the surplus. Also, the price floor causes potential environmental damage by encouraging wheat farmers to bring hilly, erosion-prone "marginal land" into production. The higher price also prompts imports of wheat. But since such imports would increase the quantity of wheat supplied and thus undermine the price floor, the government needs to erect tariffs (taxes on imports) to keep the foreign wheat out. Such tariffs usually prompt other countries to retaliate with their own tariffs against U.S. agricultural or manufacturing exports.

QUESTION: To maintain price floors on milk, the U.S. government has at times bought out and destroyed entire dairy herds from dairy farmers. What's the economic logic of these actions?

It is easy to see why economists "sound the alarm" when politicians advocate imposing price ceilings or price floors such as price controls, rent controls, interest-rate lids, or agricultural price supports. In all these cases, good intentions lead to bad economic outcomes. Government-controlled prices lead to shortages or surpluses, distort resource allocations, and cause negative side effects.

For additional examples of demand and supply, view the appendix at the end of this chapter. There, you will find examples relating to such diverse products as lettuce, corn, salmon, gasoline, sushi, and Olympic tickets. Several of the examples depict simultaneous shifts in demand and supply curves—circumstances that often show up in exam questions!

SUMMARY

LO3.1 Describe demand and explain how it can change.

Demand is a schedule or curve representing the willingness of buyers in a specific period to purchase a particular product at each of various prices. The law of demand implies that consumers will buy more of a product at a low price than at a high price. So, other things equal, the relationship between price and quantity demanded is inverse and is graphed as a downsloping curve.

Market demand curves are found by adding horizontally the demand curves of the many individual consumers in the market.

Changes in one or more of the determinants of demand (consumer tastes, the number of buyers in the market, the money incomes of consumers, the prices of related goods, and expected prices) shift the market demand curve. A shift to the right is an increase in demand; a shift to the left is a decrease in demand. A change in demand is different from a change in the quantity demanded, the latter being a movement from one point to another point on a fixed demand curve because of a change in the product's price.

LO3.2 Describe supply and explain how it can change.

Supply is a schedule or curve showing the amounts of a product that producers are willing to offer in the market at each possible price during a specific period. The law of supply states that, other things equal, producers will offer more of a product at a high price than at a low price. Thus, the relationship between price and quantity supplied is positive or direct, and supply is graphed as an upsloping curve.

The market supply curve is the horizontal summation of the supply curves of the individual producers of the product.

Changes in one or more of the determinants of supply (resource prices, production techniques, taxes or subsidies, the prices of other goods, expected prices, or the number of suppliers in the market) shift the supply curve of a product. A shift to the right is an increase in supply; a shift to the left is a decrease in supply. In contrast, a change in the price of the product being considered causes a change in the quantity supplied, which is shown as a movement from one point to another point on a fixed supply curve.

LO3.3 Relate how supply and demand interact to determine market equilibrium.

The equilibrium price and quantity are established at the intersection of the supply and demand curves. The interaction of market demand and market supply adjusts the price to the point at which the quantities demanded and supplied are equal. This is the equilibrium price. The corresponding quantity is the equilibrium quantity.

LO3.4 Explain how changes in supply and demand affect equilibrium prices and quantities.

A change in either demand or supply changes the equilibrium price and quantity. Increases in demand raise both equilibrium price and equilibrium quantity; decreases in demand lower both equilibrium price and equilibrium quantity. Increases in supply lower equilibrium price and raise equilibrium quantity; decreases in supply raise equilibrium price and lower equilibrium quantity.

LO3.5 Identify what government-set prices are and how they can cause product surpluses and shortage.

A price ceiling is a maximum price set by government and is designed to help consumers. Effective price ceilings produce persistent product shortages, and if an equitable distribution of the product is sought, government must ration the product to consumers.

A price floor is a minimum price set by government and is designed to aid producers. Price floors lead to persistent product surpluses; the government must either purchase the product or eliminate the surplus by imposing restrictions on production or increasing private demand.

Legally fixed prices stifle the rationing function of prices and distort the allocation of resources.

TERMS AND CONCEPTS

demand	change in demand	change in quantity supplied
law of demand	change in quantity demanded	equilibrium price
demand curve	supply	equilibrium quantity
determinants of demand	law of supply	surplus
normal good	supply curve	shortage
inferior good	determinants of supply	price ceiling
substitute good	change in supply	price floor
complementary good		

QUESTIONS

The following and additional problems can be found in ▤ connect

1. Explain the law of demand. Why does a demand curve slope downward? How is a market demand curve derived from individual demand curves? **LO3.1**
2. What are the determinants of demand? What happens to the demand curve when any of these determinants change? Distinguish between a change in demand and a change in the quantity demanded, noting the cause(s) of each. **LO3.1**
3. What effect will each of the following have on the demand for small automobiles such as the Mini Cooper and Smart car? **LO3.1**
   a. Small automobiles become more fashionable.
   b. The price of large automobiles rises (with the price of small autos remaining the same).
   c. Income declines and small autos are an inferior good.
   d. Consumers anticipate that the price of small autos will greatly come down in the near future.
   e. The price of gasoline substantially drops.
4. Explain the law of supply. Why does the supply curve slope upward? How is the market supply curve derived from the supply curves of individual producers? **LO3.2**
5. What are the determinants of supply? What happens to the supply curve when any of these determinants change? Distinguish between a change in supply and a change in the quantity supplied, noting the cause(s) of each. **LO3.2**
6. What effect will each of the following have on the supply of auto tires? **LO3.2**
   a. A technological advance in the methods of producing tires.
   b. A decline in the number of firms in the tire industry.

c. An increase in the price of rubber used in the production of tires.
   d. The expectation that the equilibrium price of auto tires will be lower in the future than currently.
   e. A decline in the price of the large tires used for semitrucks and earth-hauling rigs (with no change in the price of auto tires).
   f. The levying of a per-unit tax on each auto tire sold.
   g. The granting of a 50-cent-per-unit subsidy for each auto tire produced.
7. "In the latte market, demand often exceeds supply and supply sometimes exceeds demand." "The price of a latte rises and falls in response to changes in supply and demand." In which of these two statements are the concepts of supply and demand used correctly? Explain. **LO3.4**
8. In 2001 an outbreak of hoof-and-mouth disease in Europe led to the burning of millions of cattle carcasses. What impact do you think this had on the supply of cattle hides, hide prices, the supply of leather goods, and the price of leather goods? **LO3.4**
9. Critically evaluate: "In comparing the two equilibrium positions in Figure 3.7a, I note that a larger amount is actually demanded at a higher price. This refutes the law of demand." **LO3.4**
10. For each stock in the stock market, the number of shares sold daily equals the number of shares purchased. That is, the quantity of each firm's shares demanded equals the quantity supplied. So, if this equality always occurs, why do the prices of stock shares ever change? **LO3.4**

11. Suppose the total demand for wheat and the total supply of wheat per month in the Kansas City grain market are as shown in the table below. Suppose that the government establishes a price ceiling of $3.70 for wheat. What might prompt the government to establish this price ceiling? Explain carefully the main effects. Demonstrate your answer graphically. Next, suppose that the government establishes a price floor of $4.60 for wheat. What will be the main effects of this price floor? Demonstrate your answer graphically. **LO3.5**

Thousands of Bushels Demanded	Price per Bushel	Thousands of Bushels Supplied
85	$3.40	72
80	3.70	73
75	4.00	75
70	4.30	77
65	4.60	79
60	4.90	81

12. What do economists mean when they say "price floors and ceilings stifle the rationing function of prices and distort resource allocation"? **LO3.5**

PROBLEMS

1. Suppose there are three buyers of candy in a market: Tex, Dex, and Rex. The market demand and the individual demands of Tex, Dex, and Rex are shown below. **LO3.1**
   a. Fill in the table for the missing values.
   b. Which buyer demands the least at a price of $5? The most at a price of $7?
   c. Which buyer's quantity demanded increases the most when the price is lowered from $7 to $6?
   d. Which direction would the market demand curve shift if Tex withdrew from the market? What if Dex doubled his purchases at each possible price?
   e. Suppose that at a price of $6, the total quantity demanded increases from 19 to 38. Is this a "change in the quantity demanded" or a "change in demand"?

Price per Candy	Individual Quantities Demanded			Total Quantity Demanded
	Tex	Dex	Rex	
$8	3 +	1 +	0 =	___
7	8 +	2 +	___ =	12
6	___ +	3 +	4 =	19
5	17 +	___ +	6 =	27
4	23 +	5 +	8 =	___

2. The figure below shows the supply curve for tennis balls, S_1, for Drop Volley Tennis, a producer of tennis equipment. Use the figure and the table below to give your answers to the following questions. **LO3.2**

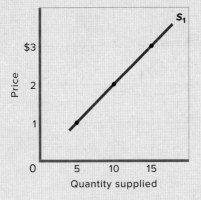

a. Use the figure to fill in the quantity supplied on supply curve S_1 for each price in the table below.

Price	S_1 Quantity Supplied	S_2 Quantity Supplied	Change in Quantity Supplied
$3	_15_	4	_-11_
2	_10_	2	_-8_
1	_5_	0	_-5_

b. If production costs were to increase, the quantities supplied at each price would be as shown by the third column of the table ("S_2 Quantity Supplied"). Use that data to draw supply curve S_2 on the same graph as supply curve S_1.
c. In the fourth column of the table, enter the amount by which the quantity supplied at each price changes due to the increase in product costs. (Use positive numbers for increases and negative numbers for decreases.)
d. Did the increase in production costs cause a "decrease in supply" or a "decrease in quantity supplied"? _curve moves_ _so actual supply_

3. Refer to the expanded table below from question 11. **LO3.3**
   a. What is the equilibrium price? At what price is there neither a shortage nor a surplus? Fill in the surplus-shortage column and use it to confirm your answers.
   b. Graph the demand for wheat and the supply of wheat. Be sure to label the axes of your graph correctly. Label equilibrium price P and equilibrium quantity Q.
   c. How big is the surplus or shortage at $3.40? At $4.90? How big a surplus or shortage results if the price is 60 cents higher than the equilibrium price? 30 cents lower than the equilibrium price?

Thousands of Bushels Demanded	Price per Bushel	Thousands of Bushels Supplied	Surplus (+) or Shortage (−)
85	$3.40	72	_____
80	3.70	73	_____
75	4.00	75	_____
70	4.30	77	_____
65	4.60	79	_____
60	4.90	81	_____

4. How will each of the following changes in demand and/or supply affect equilibrium price and equilibrium quantity in a competitive market; that is, do price and quantity rise, fall, or remain unchanged, or are the answers indeterminate because they depend on the magnitudes of the shifts? Use supply and demand graphs to verify your answers. **LO3.4**

   a. Supply decreases and demand is constant.

   b. Demand decreases and supply is constant.

   c. Supply increases and demand is constant.

   d. Demand increases and supply increases.

   e. Demand increases and supply is constant.

   f. Supply increases and demand decreases.

   g. Demand increases and supply decreases.

   h. Demand decreases and supply decreases.

5. Use two market diagrams to explain how an increase in state subsidies to public colleges might affect tuition and enrollments in both public and private colleges. **LO3.4**

6. **ADVANCED ANALYSIS** Assume that demand for a commodity is represented by the equation $P = 10 - .2Q_d$ and supply by the equation $P = 2 + .2Q_s$, where Q_d and Q_s are quantity demanded and quantity supplied, respectively, and P is price. Using the equilibrium condition $Q_s = Q_d$, solve the equations to determine equilibrium price. Now determine equilibrium quantity. **LO3.4**

7. Suppose that the demand and supply schedules for rental apartments in the city of Gotham are as given in the table below. **LO3.5**

Monthly Rent	Apartments Demanded	Apartments Supplied
$2,500	10,000	15,000
2,000	12,500	12,500
1,500	15,000	10,000
1,000	17,500	7,500
500	20,000	5,000

   a. What is the market equilibrium rental price per month and the market equilibrium number of apartments demanded and supplied?

   b. If the local government can enforce a rent-control law that sets the maximum monthly rent at $1,500, will there be a surplus or a shortage? Of how many units? And how many units will actually be rented each month?

   c. Suppose that a new government is elected that wants to keep out the poor. It declares that the minimum rent that can be charged is $2,500 per month. If the government can enforce that price floor, will there be a surplus or a shortage? Of how many units? And how many units will actually be rented each month?

   d. Suppose that the government wishes to decrease the market equilibrium monthly rent by increasing the supply of housing. Assuming that demand remains unchanged, by how many units of housing would the government have to increase the supply of housing in order to get the market equilibrium rental price to fall to $1,500 per month? To $1,000 per month? To $500 per month?

Chapter Three Appendix

Additional Examples of Supply and Demand

Our discussion has clearly demonstrated that supply and demand analysis is a powerful tool for understanding equilibrium prices and quantities. The information provided in the main body of this chapter is fully sufficient for moving forward in the book, but you may find that additional examples of supply and demand are helpful. This optional appendix provides several concrete illustrations of changes in supply and demand.

Your instructor may assign all, some, or none of this appendix, depending on time availability and personal preference.

Changes in Supply and Demand

As Figure 3.7 of this chapter demonstrates, changes in supply and demand cause changes in price, quantity, or both. The following applications illustrate this fact in several real-world markets. The simplest situations are those in which either supply changes while demand remains constant or demand changes while supply remains constant. Let's consider two such simple cases first, before looking at more complex applications.

Lettuce

Every now and then we hear on the news that extreme weather has severely reduced the size of some crop. Suppose, for example, that a severe freeze destroys a sizable portion of the lettuce crop. This unfortunate situation implies a significant decline in supply, which we represent as a leftward shift of the supply curve from S_1 to S_2 in Figure 3A.1. At each price, consumers desire as much lettuce as before, so the freeze does not affect the demand for lettuce. That is, demand curve D_1 does not shift.

What are the consequences of the reduced supply of lettuce for equilibrium price and quantity? As shown in Figure 3A.1, the leftward shift of the supply curve disrupts the previous equilibrium in the market for lettuce and drives the equilibrium price upward from P_1 to P_2. Consumers respond to that price hike by reducing the quantity of lettuce demanded from Q_1 to Q_2. Equilibrium is restored at P_2 and Q_2.

Consumers who are willing and able to pay price P_2 obtain lettuce; consumers unwilling or unable to pay that price do not. Some consumers continue to buy as much lettuce as before, even at the higher price. Others buy some lettuce but not as much as before, and still others opt out of the market completely. The latter two groups use the money they would have spent on lettuce to obtain other products, say, carrots. (Because of our other-things-equal assumption, the prices of other products have not changed.)

Exchange Rates

Exchange rates are the prices at which one currency can be traded (exchanged) for another. Exchange rates are normally determined in foreign exchange markets. One of the largest foreign exchange markets is the euro-dollar market in which the currency used in most of Europe, the *euro*, is exchanged for U.S. dollars. In the United States, this market is set up so that euros are priced in dollars—that is, the "product" being traded is euros and the "price" to buy that product is quoted in dollars. Thus, the market equilibrium price one day might be $1.25 to buy 1 euro, while on another day it might be $1.50 to buy 1 euro.

Foreign exchange markets are used by individuals and companies that need to make purchases or payments in a different currency. U.S. companies exporting goods to Germany, for instance, wish to be paid in U.S. dollars. Thus, their German customers will need to convert euros into dollars. The euros that they bring to the euro-dollar market will become part of the overall market supply of euros. Conversely, an American mutual fund may wish to purchase some French

FIGURE 3A.1 The market for lettuce. The decrease in the supply of lettuce, shown here by the shift from S_1 to S_2, increases the equilibrium price of lettuce from P_1 to P_2 and reduces the equilibrium quantity from Q_1 to Q_2.

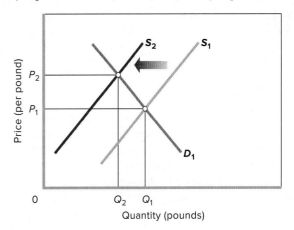

FIGURE 3A.2 **The market for euros.** The increase in the demand for euros, shown here by the shift from D_1 to D_2, increases the equilibrium price of one euro from $1.25 to $1.50 and increases the equilibrium quantity of euros that are exchanged from Q_1 to Q_2. The dollar has depreciated.

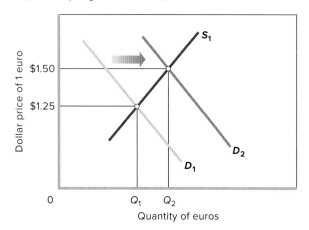

FIGURE 3A.3 **The market for pink salmon.** In the last several decades, the supply of pink salmon has increased and the demand for pink salmon has decreased. As a result, the price of pink salmon has declined, as from P_1 to P_2. Because supply has increased by more than demand has decreased, the equilibrium quantity of pink salmon has increased, as from Q_1 to Q_2.

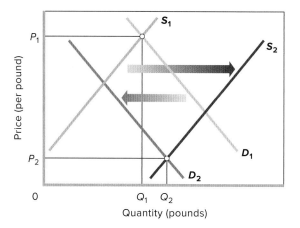

real estate outside of Paris. But to purchase that real estate, it will need to pay in euros because the current French owners will only accept payment in euros. Thus, the American mutual fund has a demand to purchase euros that will form part of the overall market demand for euros. The fund will bring dollars to the euro-dollar foreign exchange market in order to purchase the euros it desires.

Sometimes, the demand for euros increases. This might be because a European product surges in popularity in foreign countries. For example, if a new German-made automobile is a big hit in the United States, American car dealers will demand more euros with which to pay for more units of that new model. This will shift the demand curve for euros to the right, as from D_1 to D_2 in Figure 3A.2. Given the fixed euro supply curve S_1, the increase in demand raises the equilibrium exchange rate (the equilibrium number of dollars needed to purchase 1 euro) from $1.25 to $1.50. The equilibrium quantity of euros purchased increases from Q_1 to Q_2. Because a higher dollar amount is now needed to purchase one euro, economists say that the dollar has *depreciated*—gone down in value—relative to the euro. Alternatively, the euro has *appreciated*—gone up in value—relative to the dollar because one euro now buys $1.50 rather than $1.25.

Pink Salmon

Now let's see what happens when both supply and demand change at the same time. Several decades ago, people who caught salmon earned as much as $1 for each pound of pink salmon—the type of salmon most commonly used for canning. In Figure 3A.3 that price is represented as P_1, at the intersection of supply curve S_1 and demand curve D_1. The corresponding quantity of pink salmon is shown as Q_1 pounds.

As time passed, supply and demand changed in the market for pink salmon. On the supply side, improved technology in the form of larger, more efficient fishing boats greatly increased the catch and lowered the cost of obtaining it. Also, high profits at price P_1 encouraged many new fishers to enter the industry. As a result of these changes, the supply of pink salmon greatly increased and the supply curve shifted to the right, as from S_1 to S_2 in Figure 3A.3.

Over the same years, the demand for pink salmon declined, as represented by the leftward shift from D_1 to D_2 in Figure 3A.3. That decrease was caused by increases in consumer income and reductions of the price of substitute products. As buyers' incomes rose, consumers shifted demand away from canned fish and toward higher-quality fresh or frozen fish, including more-valued Atlantic, chinook, sockeye, and coho salmon. Moreover, the emergence of fish farming, in which salmon are raised in ocean net pens, lowered the prices of these substitute species. That, too, reduced the demand for pink salmon.

The altered supply and demand reduced the price of pink salmon to as low as $.10 per pound, as represented by the drop in price from P_1 to P_2 in Figure 3A.3. Both the supply increase and the demand decrease helped reduce the equilibrium price. However, in this particular case the equilibrium quantity of pink salmon increased, as represented by the move from Q_1 to Q_2. Both shifts reduced the equilibrium price, but equilibrium quantity increased because the increase in supply exceeded the decrease in demand.

Gasoline

The price of gasoline in the United States has increased rapidly several times in the past decade. For example, the average price of a gallon of gasoline rose from around $2.60 in October 2010 to about $3.90 in May 2011. What caused this 50 percent rise in the price of gasoline? How would we diagram this increase?

We begin in Figure 3A.4 with the price of a gallon of gasoline at P_1, representing the $2.60 price. Simultaneous supply and demand factors disturbed this equilibrium. Supply uncertainties relating to Middle East politics and warfare and expanded demand for oil by fast-growing countries such as China pushed up the price of a barrel of oil from $80 per barrel in October 2010 to $100 per barrel in May 2011. Oil is the main input for producing gasoline, so any sustained rise in its price boosts the per-unit cost of producing gasoline. Such cost rises decrease the supply of gasoline, as represented by the leftward shift of the supply curve from S_1 to S_2 in Figure 3A.4. At times refinery breakdowns in the United States also contributed to this reduced supply.

While the supply of gasoline declined between October 2010 and May 2011, the demand for gasoline increased, as depicted by the rightward shift of the demand curve from D_1 to D_2. Incomes in general were rising over this period because the U.S. economy was expanding after the Great Recession. Rising incomes raise demand for all normal goods, including gasoline. An increased number of low-gas-mileage SUVs and light trucks on the road also contributed to growing gas demand.

The combined decline in gasoline supply and increase in gasoline demand boosted the price of gasoline from $2.60 to $3.90, as represented by the rise from P_1 to P_2 in Figure 3A.4. Because the demand increase outweighed the supply decrease, the equilibrium quantity expanded, here from Q_1 to Q_2.

In other periods the price of gasoline has *declined* as the demand for gasoline has increased. Test your understanding of the analysis by explaining how such a price decrease could occur.

Sushi

Sushi bars are springing up like Starbucks in American cities (well, maybe not that fast!). Consumption of sushi, the raw-fish delicacy from Japan, has soared in the United States in recent years. Nevertheless, the price of sushi has remained relatively constant.

Supply and demand analysis helps explain this circumstance of increased quantity and constant price. A change in tastes has increased the U.S. demand for sushi. Many consumers of sushi find it highly tasty when they try it. And, as implied by the growing number of sushi bars in the United States, the supply of sushi has also expanded.

We represent these supply and demand changes in Figure 3A.5 as the rightward shift of the demand curve from D_1 to D_2 and the rightward shift of the supply curve from S_1 to S_2. Observe that the equilibrium quantity of sushi increases from Q_1 to Q_2 and equilibrium price remains constant at P_1. The increase in supply, which taken alone would reduce price, has perfectly offset the increase in demand, which taken alone would raise price. The price of sushi does not change, but the equilibrium quantity greatly increases because both the increase in demand and the increase in supply expand purchases and sales.

Simultaneous increases in demand and supply can cause price to either rise, fall, or remain constant, depending on the relative magnitudes of the supply and demand increases. In this case, price remained constant.

FIGURE 3A.4 The market for gasoline. An increase in the demand for gasoline, as shown by the shift from D_1 to D_2, coupled with a decrease in supply, as shown by the shift from S_1 to S_2, boosts equilibrium price (here from P_1 to P_2). In this case, equilibrium quantity increases from Q_1 to Q_2 because the increase in demand outweighs the decrease in supply.

FIGURE 3A.5 The market for sushi. Equal increases in the demand for sushi, as from D_1 to D_2, and in the supply of sushi, as from S_1 to S_2, expand the equilibrium quantity of sushi (here from Q_1 to Q_2) while leaving the price of sushi unchanged at P_1.

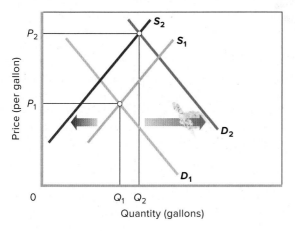

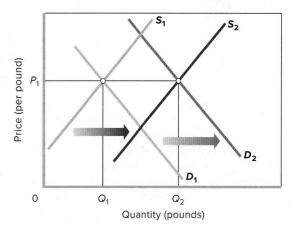

Preset Prices

In the body of this chapter, we saw that an effective government-imposed price ceiling (legal maximum price) causes quantity demanded to exceed quantity supplied—a shortage. An effective government-imposed price floor (legal minimum price) causes quantity supplied to exceed quantity demanded—a surplus. Put simply: Shortages result when prices are set below, and surpluses result when prices are set above, equilibrium prices.

We now want to establish that shortages and surpluses can occur in markets other than those in which government imposes price floors and ceilings. Such market imbalances happen when the seller or sellers set prices in advance of sales and the prices selected turn out to be below or above equilibrium prices. Consider the following two examples.

Olympic Figure Skating Finals

Tickets for the women's figure skating championship at the Olympics are among the world's "hottest tickets." The popularity of this event and the high incomes of buyers translate into tremendous ticket demand. The Olympic officials set the price for the tickets in advance. Invariably, the price, although high, is considerably below the equilibrium price that would equate quantity demanded and quantity supplied. A severe shortage of tickets therefore occurs in this *primary market*—the market involving the official ticket office.

The shortage, in turn, creates a *secondary market* in which buyers bid for tickets held by initial purchasers rather than the original seller. Scalping tickets—selling them above the original ticket price—may be legal or illegal, depending on local laws.

Figure 3A.6 shows how the shortage in the primary ticket market looks in terms of supply and demand analysis. Demand curve D represents the strong demand for tickets and supply curve S represents the supply of tickets. The supply curve is vertical because a fixed number of tickets are printed to match the capacity of the arena. At the printed ticket price of P_1, the quantity of tickets demanded, Q_2, exceeds the quantity supplied, Q_1. The result is a shortage of ab—the horizontal distance between Q_2 and Q_1 in the primary market.

If the printed ticket price had been the higher equilibrium price P_2, no shortage of tickets would have occurred. But at the lower price P_1, a shortage and secondary ticket market will emerge among those buyers willing to pay more than the printed ticket price and those sellers willing to sell their purchased tickets for more than the original price. Wherever there are shortages and secondary markets, it is safe to assume the original price was set below the equilibrium price.

FIGURE 3A.6 The market for tickets to the Olympic women's figure skating finals. The demand curve D and supply curve S for the Olympic women's figure skating finals produce an equilibrium price that is above the P_1 price printed on the ticket. At price P_1 the quantity of tickets demanded, Q_2, greatly exceeds the quantity of tickets available (Q_1). The resulting shortage of ab ($= Q_1 - Q_2$) gives rise to a legal or illegal secondary market.

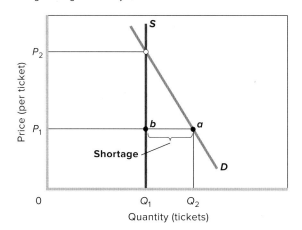

Olympic Curling Preliminaries

Contrast the shortage of tickets for the women's figure skating finals at the Olympics to the surplus of tickets for one of the preliminary curling matches. For the uninitiated, curling is a sport in which participants slide a heavy round object called a "stone" down the ice toward a target while teammates called "sweepers" use brooms to alter the course of the stone when desired.

Curling is a popular spectator sport in a few nations such as Canada, but it does not draw many fans in most countries. So the demand for tickets to most of the preliminary curling

FIGURE 3A.7 The market for tickets to the Olympic curling preliminaries. The demand curve D and supply curve S for the Olympic curling preliminaries produce an equilibrium price below the P_1 price printed on the ticket. At price P_1 the quantity of tickets demanded is less than the quantity of tickets available. The resulting surplus of ba ($= Q_1 - Q_2$) means the event is not sold out.

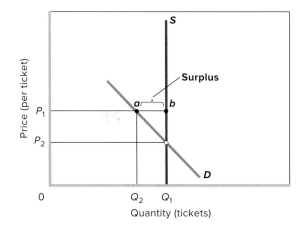

events is not very strong. We demonstrate this weak demand as D in Figure 3A.7. As in our previous example, the supply of tickets is fixed by the size of the arena and is shown as vertical line S.

We represent the printed ticket price as P_1 in Figure 3A.7. In this case the printed price is much higher than the equilibrium price of P_2. At the printed ticket price, quantity supplied is Q_1 and quantity demanded is Q_2. So a surplus of tickets of ba $(= Q_1 - Q_2)$ occurs. No ticket scalping occurs and there are numerous empty seats. Only if the Olympic officials had priced the tickets at the lower price P_2 would the event have been a sellout. (Actually, the Olympic officials try to adjust to demand realities for curling contests by holding them in smaller arenas and by charging less for tickets. Nevertheless, the stands are rarely full for the preliminary contests, which compete against final events in other winter Olympic sports.)

APPENDIX SUMMARY

LO3.6 Illustrate how supply and demand analysis can provide insights on actual economic situations.

A decrease in the supply of a product increases its equilibrium price and reduces its equilibrium quantity. In contrast, an increase in the demand for a product boosts both its equilibrium price and its equilibrium quantity.

Simultaneous changes in supply and demand affect equilibrium price and quantity in various ways, depending on the relative magnitudes of the changes in supply and demand. Equal increases in supply and demand, for example, leave equilibrium price unchanged.

Sellers set prices of some items such as tickets in advance of the event. These items are sold in the primary market that involves the original seller and buyers. If preset prices turn out to be below the equilibrium prices, shortages occur and scalping in legal or illegal secondary markets arises. The prices in the secondary market then rise above the preset prices. In contrast, surpluses occur when the preset prices happen to exceed the equilibrium prices.

APPENDIX QUESTIONS

The following and additional problems can be found in ▣ **connect**

1. Why are shortages or surpluses more likely with preset prices, such as those on tickets, than flexible prices, such as those on gasoline? **LO3.6**

2. Most scalping laws make it illegal to sell—but not to buy—tickets at prices above those printed on the tickets. Assuming that is the case, use supply and demand analysis to explain why the equilibrium ticket price in an illegal secondary market tends to be higher than in a legal secondary market. **LO3.6**

3. Go to the website of the Energy Information Administration, www.eia.doe.gov, and follow the links to find the current retail price of gasoline. How does the current price of regular gasoline compare with the price a year ago? What must have happened to either supply, demand, or both to explain the observed price change? **LO3.6**

4. Suppose the supply of apples sharply increases because of perfect weather conditions throughout the growing season. Assuming no change in demand, explain the effect on the equilibrium price and quantity of apples. Explain why quantity demanded increases even though demand does not change. **LO3.6**

5. Assume the demand for lumber suddenly rises because of a rapid growth of demand for new housing. Assume no change in supply. Why does the equilibrium price of lumber rise? What would happen if the price did not rise under the demand and supply circumstances described? **LO3.6**

6. Suppose both the demand for olives and the supply of olives decline by equal amounts over some time period. Use graphical analysis to show the effect on equilibrium price and quantity. **LO3.6**

7. Assume that both the supply of bottled water and the demand for bottled water rise during the summer but that supply increases more rapidly than demand. What can you conclude about the directions of the impacts on equilibrium price and equilibrium quantity? **LO3.6**

APPENDIX PROBLEMS

1. Demand and supply often shift in the retail market for gasoline. Here are two demand curves and two supply curves for gallons of gasoline in the month of May in a small town in Maine. Some of the data are missing. **LO3.6**

Price	Quantities Demanded		Quantities Supplied	
	D_1	D_2	S_1	S_2
$4.00	5,000	7,500	9,000	9,500
____	6,000	8,000	8,000	9,000
2.00	____	8,500	____	8,500
____	____	9,000	5,000	____

a. Use the following facts to fill in the missing data in the table. If demand is D_1 and supply is S_1, the equilibrium quantity is 7,000 gallons per month. When demand is D_2 and supply is S_1, the equilibrium price is $3.00 per gallon. When demand is D_2 and supply is S_1, there is an excess demand of 4,000 gallons per month at a price of $1.00 per gallon. If demand is D_1 and supply is S_2, the equilibrium quantity is 8,000 gallons per month.

b. Compare two equilibriums. In the first, demand is D_1 and supply is S_1. In the second, demand is D_1 and supply is S_2. By how much does the equilibrium quantity change? By how much does the equilibrium price change?

c. If supply falls from S_2 to S_1 while demand declines from D_2 to D_1, does the equilibrium price rise, fall, or stay the same? What if only supply falls? What if only demand falls?

d. Suppose that supply is fixed at S_1 and that demand starts at D_1. By how many gallons per month would demand have to increase at each price level such that the equilibrium price per gallon would be $3.00? $4.00?

2. The table below shows two demand schedules for a given style of men's shoe—that is, how many pairs per month will be demanded at various prices at a men's clothing store in Seattle called Stromnord.

Price	D_1 Quantity Demanded	D_2 Quantity Demanded
$75	53	13
70	60	15
65	68	18
60	77	22
55	87	27

Suppose that Stromnord has exactly 65 pairs of this style of shoe in inventory at the start of the month of July and will not receive any more pairs of this style until at least August 1. LO3.6

a. If demand is D_1, what is the lowest price that Stromnord can charge so that it will not run out of this model of shoe in the month of July? What if demand is D_2?

b. If the price of shoes is set at $75 for both July and August and demand will be D_2 in July and D_1 in August, how many pairs of shoes should Stromnord order if it wants to end the month of August with exactly zero pairs of shoes in its inventory? What if the price is set at $55 for both months?

3. Use the table below to answer the questions that follow: LO3.6

a. If this table reflects the supply of and demand for tickets to a particular World Cup soccer game, what is the stadium capacity?

b. If the preset ticket price is $45, would we expect to see a secondary market for tickets? Would the price of a ticket in the secondary market be higher than, the same as, or lower than the price in the primary (original) market?

c. Suppose for some other World Cup game the quantity of tickets demanded is 20,000 lower at each ticket price than shown in the table. If the ticket price remains $45, would the event be a sellout?

Quantity Demanded, Thousands	Price	Quantity Supplied, Thousands
80	$25	60
75	35	60
70	45	60
65	55	60
60	65	60
55	75	60
50	85	60

Elasticity of Demand and Supply

Learning Objectives

LO4.1 Discuss price elasticity of demand and how it can be measured.

LO4.2 Explain how price elasticity of demand affects total revenue.

LO4.3 Describe price elasticity of supply and how it can be measured.

LO4.4 Apply price elasticity of demand and supply to real-world situations.

LO4.5 Explain income elasticity of demand and cross-elasticity of demand and how they can be applied.

Why do buyers of some products respond to price increases by substantially reducing their purchases while buyers of other products respond by only slightly cutting back their purchases? Why do price hikes for some goods cause producers to greatly increase their output while price hikes on other products barely cause any output increase? Why does the demand for some products rise a great deal when household incomes increase while the demand for other products rises just a little? How can we tell whether a given pair of goods are complements, substitutes, or unrelated to each other?

Elasticity extends our understanding of markets by letting us know the degree to which changes in prices and incomes affect supply and demand. Sometimes the responses are substantial, other times minimal or even nonexistent. But by knowing what to expect, businesses and the government can do a much better job in deciding what to produce, how much to charge, and, surprisingly, what items to tax.

Price Elasticity of Demand

The law of demand tells us that, other things equal, consumers will buy more of a product when its price declines and less of it when its price increases. But how much more or less will they buy? The amount varies from product to product and over different price ranges for the same product. And such variations matter. For example, a firm contemplating a price hike will want to know how consumers will respond. If they remain highly loyal and continue to buy, the firm's revenue will rise. But if consumers defect en masse to other sellers or other products, its revenue will tumble.

The responsiveness of the quantity of a product demanded by consumers when the product price changes is measured by a product's **price elasticity of demand.** For some products (for example, restaurant meals), consumers are highly responsive to price changes. Modest price changes cause very large changes in the quantity purchased. Economists say that the demand for such products is *relatively elastic* or simply *elastic.*

For other products (for example, medical care), consumers pay much less attention to price changes. Substantial price changes cause only small changes in the amount purchased. The demand for such products is *relatively inelastic* or simply *inelastic.*

> **price elasticity of demand** The ratio of the percentage change in quantity demanded of a product or resource to the percentage change in its price; a measure of the responsiveness of buyers to a change in the price of a product or resource.

The Price-Elasticity Coefficient and Formula

Economists measure the degree of price elasticity or inelasticity of demand with the coefficient E_d, defined as

$$E_d = \frac{\text{percentage change in quantity demanded of X}}{\text{percentage change in price of X}}$$

The percentage changes in the equation are calculated by dividing the *change* in quantity demanded by the original quantity demanded and by dividing the *change* in price by the original price. So we can restate the formula as

$$E_d = \frac{\text{change in quantity demanded of X}}{\text{original quantity demanded of X}} \div \frac{\text{change in price of X}}{\text{original price of X}}$$

Using Averages   Unfortunately, an annoying problem arises in computing the price-elasticity coefficient. A price change from, say, $4 to $5 along a demand curve is a 25 percent (= $1/$4) increase, but the opposite price change from $5 to $4 along the same curve is a 20 percent (= $1/$5) decrease. Which percentage change in price should we use in the denominator to compute the price-elasticity coefficient? And when quantity changes, for example, from 10 to 20, it is a 100 percent (= 10/10) increase. But when quantity falls from 20 to 10 along the identical demand curve, it is a 50 percent (= 10/20) decrease. Should we use 100 percent or 50 percent in the numerator of the elasticity formula? Elasticity should be the same whether price rises or falls!

The simplest solution to the problem is to use the averages of the two prices and the two quantities as the reference points for computing the percentages. That is

$$E_d = \frac{\text{change in quantity}}{\text{sum of quantities}/2} \div \frac{\text{change in price}}{\text{sum of prices}/2}$$

For the same $5–$4 price range, the price reference is $4.50 [= ($5 + $4)/2], and for the same 10–20 quantity range, the quantity reference is 15 units [= (10 + 20)/2]. The percentage change in price is now $1/$4.50, or about 22 percent, and the percentage change in quantity is 10/15, or about 67 percent. So E_d is about 3. This solution eliminates the "up versus down" problem. All the elasticity coefficients that follow are calculated using averages, also known as the *midpoints approach*.

Elimination of Minus Sign Because demand curves slope downward, the price-elasticity coefficient of demand E_d will always be a negative number. As an example, if price declines, quantity demanded will increase. This means that the numerator in our formula will be positive and the denominator negative, yielding a negative E_d. For an increase in price, the numerator will be negative but the denominator positive, again producing a negative E_d.

Economists usually ignore the minus sign and simply present the absolute value of the elasticity coefficient to avoid an ambiguity that might otherwise arise. It can be confusing to say that an E_d of −4 is greater than one of −2. This possible confusion is avoided when we say an E_d of 4 reveals greater elasticity than an E_d of 2. In what follows, we ignore the minus sign in the coefficient of price elasticity of demand and show only the absolute value.

Interpretations of E_d

We can interpret the coefficient of price elasticity of demand as follows.

Elastic Demand Demand is **elastic** if a specific percentage change in price results in a larger percentage change in quantity demanded. In such cases, E_d will be greater than 1. Example: Suppose that a 2 percent decline in the price of cut flowers results in a 4 percent increase in quantity demanded. Then demand for cut flowers is elastic and

$$E_d = \frac{.04}{.02} = 2$$

elastic demand Product or resource demand whose price elasticity is greater than 1. This means the resulting change in quantity demanded is greater than the percentage change in price.

Inelastic Demand If a specific percentage change in price produces a smaller percentage change in quantity demanded, demand is **inelastic.** In such cases, E_d will be less than 1. Example: Suppose that a 2 percent decline in the price of tea leads to only a 1 percent increase in quantity demanded. Then demand is inelastic and

$$E_d = \frac{.01}{.02} = .5$$

inelastic demand Product or resource demand for which the elasticity coefficient for price is less than 1. This means the resulting percentage change in quantity demanded is less than the percentage change in price.

Unit Elasticity The case separating elastic and inelastic demands occurs where a percentage change in price and the resulting percentage change in quantity demanded are the same. Example: Suppose that a 2 percent drop in the price of chocolate causes a 2 percent increase in quantity demanded. This special case is termed **unit elasticity** because E_d is exactly 1, or unity. In this example,

$$E_d = \frac{.02}{.02} = 1$$

unit elasticity Demand or supply for which the elasticity coefficient is equal to 1; means that the percentage change in the quantity demanded or supplied is equal to the percentage change in price.

Extreme Cases When we say demand is "inelastic," we do not mean that consumers are completely unresponsive to a price change. In that extreme situation, where a price change results in no change whatsoever in the quantity demanded, economists say that demand is **perfectly inelastic.** The price-elasticity coefficient is zero because there is no response to a change in price. Approximate examples include an acute diabetic's demand for insulin or an addict's demand for heroin. A line parallel to the vertical axis, such as D_1 in Figure 4.1a, shows perfectly inelastic demand graphically.

perfectly inelastic demand Product or resource demand in which price can be of any amount at a particular quantity of the product or resource demanded; quantity demanded does not respond to a change in price; graphs as a vertical demand curve.

FIGURE 4.1 Perfectly inelastic and elastic demands. Demand curve D_1 in (a) represents perfectly inelastic demand ($E_d = 0$). A price increase will result in no change in quantity demanded. Demand curve D_2 in (b) represents perfectly elastic demand. A price increase will cause quantity demanded to decline from an infinite amount to zero ($E_d = \infty$).

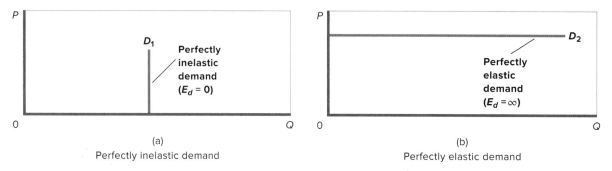

(a)
Perfectly inelastic demand

(b)
Perfectly elastic demand

perfectly elastic demand Product or resource demand in which quantity demanded can be of any amount at a particular product price; graphs as a horizontal demand curve.

total revenue The total number of dollars received by a firm (or firms) from the sale of a product; equal to the total expenditures for the product produced by the firm (or firms); equal to the quantity sold (demanded) multiplied by the price at which it is sold.

Conversely, when we say demand is "elastic," we do not mean that consumers are completely responsive to a price change. In that extreme situation, where a small price reduction causes buyers to increase their purchases from zero to all they can obtain, the elasticity coefficient is infinite (∞) and economists say demand is **perfectly elastic.** A line parallel to the horizontal axis, such as D_2 in Figure 4.1b, shows perfectly elastic demand. Such a demand curve, for example, faces wheat growers who can sell all or none of their wheat at the equilibrium market price.

The Total-Revenue Test

The importance of elasticity for firms relates to the effect of price changes on total revenue and thus on profits (total revenue minus total costs).

Total revenue (TR) is the total amount the seller receives from the sale of a product in a particular time period; it is calculated by multiplying the product price (P) by the quantity demanded and sold (Q). In equation form

$$TR = P \times Q$$

PHOTO OP Elastic versus Inelastic Demand

The demand for expensive leisure activities such as cruise vacations is elastic; the demand for surgery or other nonelective medical care is inelastic.

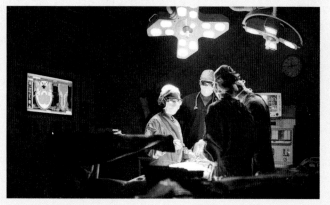

ILLUSTRATING THE IDEA

A Bit of a Stretch

The following analogy might help you remember the distinction between "elastic" and "inelastic." Imagine two objects: (1) an Ace elastic bandage used to wrap injured joints and (2) a relatively firm rubber tie-down used for securing items for transport. The Ace bandage stretches a great deal when pulled with a particular force; the rubber tie-down stretches some, but not a lot.

Similar differences occur for the quantity demanded of various products when their prices change. For some products, a price change causes a substantial "stretch" of quantity demanded. When this stretch in percentage terms exceeds the percentage change in price, demand is elastic. For other products, quantity demanded stretches very little in response to the price change. When this stretch in percentage terms is less than the percentage change in price, demand is inelastic.

In summary:

- Elastic demand displays considerable "quantity stretch" (as with the Ace bandage).
- Inelastic demand displays relatively little "quantity stretch" (as with the rubber tie-down).

And through extension:

- Perfectly elastic demand has infinite quantity stretch.
- Perfectly inelastic demand has zero quantity stretch.

QUESTION: Which do you think has the most quantity stretch, given an equal percentage increase in price—toothpaste or townhouses?

Graphically, total revenue is represented by the $P \times Q$ rectangle lying below a point on a demand curve. At point a in Figure 4.2a, for example, price is \$2 and quantity demanded is 10 units. So total revenue is \$20 (= \$2 × 10), shown by the rectangle composed of the yellow and green areas under the demand curve. We know from basic geometry that the area of a rectangle is found by multiplying one side by the other. Here, one side is "price" (\$2) and the other is "quantity demanded" (10 units).

Total revenue and the price elasticity of demand are related. In fact, the easiest way to infer whether demand is elastic or inelastic is to employ the **total-revenue test.**

Here is the test: Note what happens to total revenue when price changes. If total revenue changes in the opposite direction from price, demand is elastic. If total revenue changes in the same direction as price, demand is inelastic. If total revenue does not change when price changes, demand is unit-elastic.

Elastic Demand If demand is elastic, a decrease in price will increase total revenue. Even though a lesser price is received per unit, enough additional units are sold to more than make up for the lower price. For an example, look at demand curve D_1 in Figure 4.2a. We have already established that at point a, total revenue is \$20 (= \$2 × 10), shown as the yellow plus green area.

If the price declines from \$2 to \$1 (point b), the quantity demanded becomes 40 units and total revenue is \$40 (= \$1 × 40). As a result of the price decline, total revenue has

total-revenue test A test to determine elasticity of demand between any two prices: Demand is elastic if total revenue moves in the opposite direction from price; it is inelastic when it moves in the same direction as price; and it is of unitary elasticity when it does not change when price changes.

FIGURE 4.2 **The total-revenue test for price elasticity.** (a) Price declines from $2 to $1, and total revenue increases from $20 to $40. So demand is elastic. The gain in revenue (blue area) exceeds the loss of revenue (yellow area). (b) Price declines from $4 to $1, and total revenue falls from $40 to $20. So demand is inelastic. The gain in revenue (blue area) is less than the loss of revenue (yellow area). (c) Price declines from $3 to $1, and total revenue does not change. Demand is unit-elastic. The gain in revenue (blue area) equals the loss of revenue (yellow area).

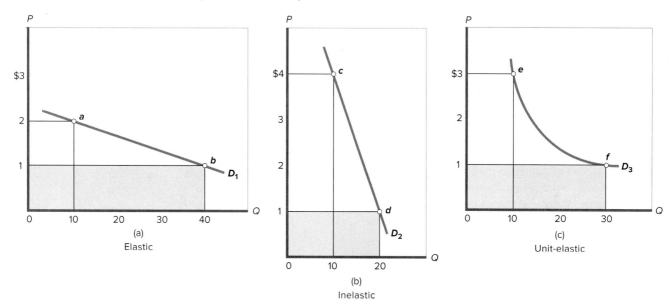

increased from $20 to $40. Total revenue has increased in this case because the $1 decline in price applies to 10 units, with a consequent revenue loss of $10 (the yellow area). But 30 more units are sold at $1 each, resulting in a revenue gain of $30 (the blue area). Visually, it is apparent that the gain of the blue area exceeds the loss of the yellow area. As indicated, the overall result is a net increase in total revenue of $20 (= $30 − $10).

The analysis is reversible: If demand is elastic, a price increase will reduce total revenue. The revenue gained on the higher-priced units will be more than offset by the revenue lost from the lower quantity sold. Bottom line: Other things equal, when price and total revenue move in opposite directions, demand is elastic. E_d is greater than 1, meaning the percentage change in quantity demanded is greater than the percentage change in price.

Inelastic Demand If demand is inelastic, a price decrease will reduce total revenue. The increase in sales will not fully offset the decline in revenue per unit, and total revenue will decline. To see this, look at demand curve D_2 in Figure 4.2b. At point c on the curve, price is $4 and quantity demanded is 10. So total revenue is $40, shown by the combined yellow and green rectangle. If the price drops to $1 (point d), total revenue declines to $20, which obviously is less than $40. Total revenue has declined because the loss of revenue (the yellow area) from the lower unit price is larger than the gain in revenue (the blue area) from the accompanying increase in sales. Price has fallen, and total revenue has also declined.

Our analysis is again reversible: If demand is inelastic, a price increase will increase total revenue. So, other things equal, when price and total revenue move in the same direction, demand is inelastic. E_d is less than 1, meaning the percentage change in quantity demanded is less than the percentage change in price.

Unit Elasticity In the special case of unit elasticity, an increase or a decrease in price leaves total revenue unchanged. The loss in revenue from a lower unit price is exactly offset by the gain in revenue from the accompanying increase in sales. Conversely, the gain in revenue from a higher unit price is exactly offset by the revenue loss associated with the accompanying decline in the amount demanded.

In Figure 4.2c (demand curve D_3), we find that at the $3 price, 10 units will be sold, yielding total revenue of $30. At the lower $1 price, a total of 30 units will be sold, again resulting in $30 of total revenue. The $2 price reduction causes the loss of revenue shown by the yellow area, but this is exactly offset by the revenue gain shown by the blue area. Total revenue does not change. In fact, that would be true for all price changes along this particular curve.

Other things equal, when price changes and total revenue remains constant, demand is unit-elastic (or unitary). E_d is 1, meaning the percentage change in quantity equals the percentage change in price.

Price Elasticity along a Linear Demand Curve

Now a major confession! Although the demand curves depicted in Figure 4.2 nicely illustrate the total-revenue test for elasticity, two of the graphs involve specific movements along linear (straight-line) demand curves. That presents no problem for explaining the total-revenue test. However, you need to know that elasticity typically varies over different price ranges of the same demand curve. (The exception is the curve in Figure 4.2c. Elasticity is 1 along the entire curve.)

Consider columns 1 and 2 of the table in Figure 4.3, which shows hypothetical data for movie tickets. We plot these data as demand curve D in the accompanying graph. The notation above the curve correctly suggests that demand is more price-elastic toward the upper left (here, the $5–$8 price range of D) than toward the lower right (here, the $4–$1 price range of D). This fact is confirmed by the elasticity coefficients in column (3) of the table: The coefficients decline as price falls. Also, note from column (4) that total revenue first rises as price falls and then eventually declines as price falls further. Column (5) employs the total-revenue test to show that elasticity declines as price falls along a linear demand curve.

The demand curve in Figure 4.3 illustrates that the slope of a demand curve (its flatness or steepness) is an unreliable basis for judging elasticity. The slope of the curve is computed from *absolute* changes in price and quantity, while elasticity involves *relative* or *percentage* changes in price and quantity. The demand curve in Figure 4.3 is linear, which

FIGURE 4.3 Price elasticity of demand along a linear demand curve as measured by the elasticity coefficient and the total-revenue test. Demand curve D is based on columns (1) and (2) of the table and is labeled to show that the hypothetical weekly demand for movie tickets is elastic at higher price ranges and inelastic at lower price ranges. That fact is confirmed by the elasticity coefficients (column 3) as well as the total-revenue test (columns 4 and 5) in the table.

(1) Total Quantity of Tickets Demanded per Week, Thousands	(2) Price per Ticket	(3) Elasticity Coefficient (E_d)	(4) Total Revenue, (1) × (2)	(5) Total-Revenue Test
1	$8		$ 8,000	
		5.00		Elastic
2	7		14,000	
		2.60		Elastic
3	6		18,000	
		1.57		Elastic
4	5		20,000	
		1.00		Unit elastic
5	4		20,000	
		0.64		Inelastic
6	3		18,000	
		0.38		Inelastic
7	2		14,000	
		0.20		Inelastic
8	1		8,000	

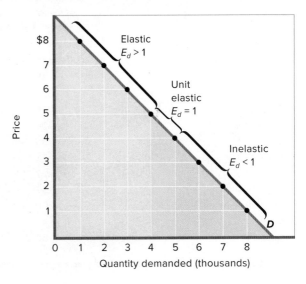

means its slope is constant throughout. But this linear curve is elastic in its high-price ($8–$5) range and inelastic in its low-price ($4–$1) range.

Determinants of Price Elasticity of Demand

We cannot say what will determine the price elasticity of demand in each individual situation, but the following generalizations are often helpful.

Substitutability Generally, the larger the number of substitute goods that are available, the greater is the price elasticity of demand. Mercedes, BMWs, and Lincolns are effective substitutes for Cadillacs, making the demand for Cadillacs elastic. At the other extreme, we saw earlier that the diabetic's demand for insulin is highly inelastic because there simply are no close substitutes.

The elasticity of demand for a product depends on how narrowly the product is defined. Demand for Reebok sneakers is more elastic than is the overall demand for shoes. Many other brands are readily substitutable for Reebok sneakers, but there are few, if any, good substitutes for shoes.

Proportion of Income Other things equal, the higher the price of a product relative to one's income, the greater the price elasticity of demand for it. A 10 percent increase in the price of low-priced pencils or chewing gum amounts to a very small portion of most people's incomes, and quantity demanded will probably decline only slightly. Thus, price elasticity for such low-priced items tends to be low. But a 10 percent increase in the price of relatively high-priced automobiles or houses means additional expenditures of perhaps $3,000 or $20,000. That price increase is a significant fraction of the incomes and budgets of most families, and the number of units demanded will likely diminish significantly. The price elasticities for such items tend to be high.

Luxuries versus Necessities In general, the more that a good is considered to be a "luxury" rather than a "necessity," the greater is the price elasticity of demand. Electricity is generally regarded as a necessity; it is difficult to get along without it. A price increase will not significantly reduce the amount of lighting and power used in a household. (Note the very low price-elasticity coefficient of these goods in Table 4.1.) An extreme

TABLE 4.1 Selected Price Elasticities of Demand

Product or Service	Coefficient of Price Elasticity of Demand (E_d)	Product or Service	Coefficient of Price Elasticity of Demand (E_d)
Newspapers	.10	Milk	.63
Electricity (household)	.13	Household appliances	.63
Bread	.15	Liquor	.70
Major League Baseball tickets	.23	Movies	.87
Cigarettes	.25	Beer	.90
Telephone service	.26	Shoes	.91
Sugar	.30	Motor vehicles	1.14
Medical care	.31	Beef	1.27
Eggs	.32	China, glassware, tableware	1.54
Legal services	.37	Residential land	1.60
Automobile repair	.40	Restaurant meals	2.27
Clothing	.49	Lamb and mutton	2.65
Gasoline	.60	Fresh peas	2.83

Source: Compiled from numerous studies and sources reporting price elasticity of demand.

case: A person does not decline emergency heart bypass surgery because the physician's fee has just gone up by 10 percent.

On the other hand, vacation travel and jewelry are luxuries that can easily be forgone. If the prices of vacation travel and jewelry rise, a consumer need not buy them and will suffer no great hardship without them.

What about the demand for a common product like salt? It is highly inelastic on three counts: There are few good substitutes available; salt is a negligible item in the family budget; and it is a "necessity" rather than a luxury.

Time   Generally, product demand is more elastic the longer the time period under consideration. Consumers often need time to adjust to changes in prices. For example, consumers may not immediately reduce their purchases very much when the price of beef rises by 10 percent, but in time they may shift to chicken, pork, or fish.

Another consideration is product durability. Studies show that "short-run" demand for gasoline is more inelastic ($E_d = .2$) than is "long-run" demand ($E_d = .7$). In the short run, people are "stuck" with their present cars and trucks, but with rising gasoline prices they eventually replace them with smaller, more fuel-efficient vehicles.

Table 4.1 shows estimated price-elasticity coefficients for a number of products. Each reflects some combination of the elasticity determinants just discussed.

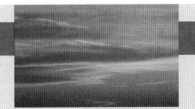

APPLYING THE ANALYSIS

Price Elasticity of Demand and College Tuition

For some goods and services, for-profit firms or not-for-profit institutions may find it advantageous to determine differences in price elasticity of demand for different groups of customers and then charge different prices to the different groups. Price increases for groups that have inelastic demand will increase total revenue, as will price decreases for groups that have elastic demand.

It is relatively easy to observe differences between group elasticities. Consider tuition pricing by colleges and universities. Prospective students from low-income families generally have more elastic demand for higher education than similar students from high-income families. This is true because tuition is a much larger proportion of household income for a low-income student or family than for his or her high-income counterpart. Desiring a diverse student body, colleges charge different *net* prices (= tuition *minus* financial aid) to the two groups on the basis of elasticity of demand. High-income students pay full tuition, unless they receive merit-based scholarships. Low-income students receive considerable financial aid in addition to merit-based scholarships and, in effect, pay a lower *net* price.

It is common for colleges to announce a large tuition increase and immediately cushion the news by emphasizing that they also are increasing financial aid. In effect, the college is increasing the tuition for students who have inelastic demand by the full amount and raising the *net* tuition of those with elastic demand by some lesser amount or not at all. Through this strategy, colleges boost revenue to cover rising costs while maintaining affordability for a wide range of students.

QUESTION: What are some other examples of charging different prices to different groups of customers on the basis of differences in elasticity of demand? (Hint: Think of price discounts based on age or time of purchase.)

Decriminalization of Illegal Drugs

In recent years proposals to legalize drugs have been widely debated, and recreational use of marijuana has been decriminalized in some states. Proponents contend that drugs should be treated like alcohol; they should be made legal for adults and regulated for purity and potency. The current war on drugs, it is argued, has been unsuccessful, and the associated costs—including enlarged police forces, the construction of more prisons, an overburdened court system, and untold human costs—have increased markedly. Legalization would allegedly reduce drug trafficking significantly by taking the profit out of it. Crack cocaine and heroin, for example, are cheap to produce and could be sold at low prices in legal markets. Because the demand of addicts is highly inelastic, the amounts consumed at the lower prices would increase only modestly. Addicts' total expenditures for cocaine and heroin would decline, and so would the street crime that finances those expenditures.

Opponents of legalization say that the overall demand for cocaine and heroin is far more elastic than proponents think. In addition to the inelastic demand of addicts, there is another market segment whose demand is relatively elastic. This segment consists of the occasional users or "dabblers," who use hard drugs when their prices are low but who abstain or substitute, say, alcohol when their prices are high. Thus, the lower prices associated with the legalization of hard drugs would increase consumption by dabblers. Also, removal of the legal prohibitions against using drugs might make drug use more socially acceptable, increasing the demand for cocaine and heroin.

Many economists predict that the legalization of cocaine and heroin would reduce street prices by up to 60 percent, depending on if and how much they were taxed. According to one study, price declines of that size would increase the number of occasional users of heroin by 54 percent and the number of occasional users of cocaine by 33 percent. The total quantity of heroin demanded would rise by an estimated 100 percent, and the quantity of cocaine demanded would rise by 50 percent.* Moreover, many existing and first-time dabblers might in time become addicts. The overall result, say the opponents of legalization, would be higher social costs, possibly including an increase in street crime.

QUESTION: In what ways do drug rehabilitation programs increase the elasticity of demand for illegal drugs?

*Henry Saffer and Frank Chaloupka, "The Demand for Illegal Drugs," *Economic Inquiry,* July 1999, pp. 401–411.

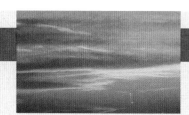

Excise Taxes and Tax Revenue

The government pays attention to elasticity of demand when it selects goods and services on which to levy *excise taxes* (taxes levied on the production of a product or on the quantity of the product purchased). If a $1 tax is levied on a product and 10,000 units are sold, tax revenue will be $10,000 (= $1 × 10,000 units sold). If the government raises the tax to $1.50, but the higher price that results reduces sales (quantity demanded) to 4,000 because demand is elastic, tax revenue will decline to $6,000 (= $1.50 × 4,000 units sold). So a higher tax on a product that has an elastic demand will bring in less tax revenue.

In contrast, if demand is inelastic, the tax increase from $1 to $1.50 will boost tax revenue. For example, if sales fall from 10,000 to 9,000, tax revenue will rise from $10,000 to $13,500 (= $1.50 × 9,000 units). Little wonder that legislatures tend to seek out products such as liquor, gasoline, cigarettes, and phone service when levying and raising taxes. Those taxes yield high tax revenues.

QUESTION: Under what circumstance might a reduction of an excise tax actually produce more tax revenue?

APPLYING THE ANALYSIS

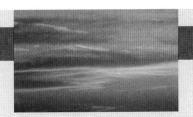

Fluctuating Farm Income

Inelastic demand for farm products and year-to-year changes in farm supply combine to produce highly volatile farm prices and incomes. Let's see why.

In industrially advanced economies, the price elasticity of demand for agricultural products is low. For farm products in the aggregate, the elasticity coefficient is between .20 and .25. These figures suggest that the prices of agricultural products would have to fall by 40 to 50 percent for consumers to increase their purchases by a mere 10 percent. Consumers apparently put a low value on additional farm output compared with the value they put on additional units of alternative goods.

Why is this so? Recall that a basic determinant of elasticity of demand is substitutability. When the price of one product falls, the consumer tends to substitute that product for other products whose prices have not fallen. But in relatively wealthy societies, this substitution is very modest for food. Although people may eat more, they do not switch from three meals a day to, say, five or six meals a day in response to a decline in the relative prices of farm products. Real biological factors constrain an individual's capacity to substitute food for other products.

Farm supply tends to fluctuate from year to year, mainly because farmers have limited control over their output. Floods, droughts, unexpected frost, insect damage, and similar disasters can mean poor crops, while an excellent growing season means bumper crops (extraordinarily large crops). Such natural phenomena are beyond the control of farmers, yet those phenomena exert an important influence on output.

In addition to natural phenomena, the highly competitive nature of agriculture makes it difficult for farmers to form huge combinations to control production. If the thousands of widely scattered and independent producers happened to plant an unusually large or an abnormally small portion of their land one year, an extra-large or a very small farm output would result even if the growing season were normal.

Combining inelastic demand with the instability of supply, we can see why farm prices and incomes are unstable. Even if the market demand for some crop such as barley remains fixed, its price inelasticity will magnify small changes in output into relatively large changes in farm prices and income. For example, suppose that a "normal" barley crop of 100 million bushels results in a "normal" price per bushel of $3 and a "normal" farm income of $300 million (= $3 × 100 million).

A bumper crop of barley will cause large deviations from these normal prices and incomes because of the inelasticity of demand. Suppose that a good growing season occurs and that the result is a large crop of 110 million bushels. As farmers watch their individual crops mature, little will they realize that their collectively large crop, when harvested, will drive the price per bushel down to, say, $2.50. Their revenue will fall from $300 million in the normal year to $275 million (= $2.50 × 110 million bushels) this year. When demand is inelastic, an increase in the quantity sold will be accompanied by a more-than-proportionate decline in price. The net result is that total revenue, that is, total farm income, will decline disproportionately.

Similarly, a small crop of 90 million bushels, perhaps caused by drought, might boost the price to $3.50. Total farm income will rise to $315 million (= $3.50 × 90 million bushels) from the normal level of $300 million. A decline in supply will cause a more-than-proportionate increase in price and in income when demand is inelastic. Ironically, for farmers as a group, a poor crop may be a blessing and a bumper crop a hardship.

QUESTION: How might government programs that pay farmers to take land out of production in order to achieve conservation goals (such as erosion control and wildlife protection) increase crop prices and farm income?

Price Elasticity of Supply

The concept of price elasticity also applies to supply. If the quantity supplied by producers is relatively responsive to price changes, supply is elastic. If it is relatively insensitive to price changes, supply is inelastic.

We measure the degree of price elasticity or inelasticity of supply with the coefficient E_s, defined almost like E_d except that we substitute "percentage change in quantity supplied" for "percentage change in quantity demanded":

$$E_s = \frac{\text{percentage change in quantity supplied of X}}{\text{percentage change in price of X}}$$

For reasons explained earlier, the averages, or midpoints, of the before and after quantities supplied and the before and after prices are used as reference points for the percentage changes. Suppose an increase in the price of a good from $4 to $6 increases the quantity supplied from 10 units to 14 units. The percentage change in price would be 2/5, or 40 percent, and the percentage change in quantity would be 4/12, or 33 percent:

$$E_s = \frac{.33}{.40} = .83$$

In this case, supply is inelastic because the price-elasticity coefficient is less than 1. If E_s is greater than 1, supply is elastic. If it is equal to 1, supply is unit-elastic. Also, E_s is never negative, since price and quantity supplied are directly related. Thus, there are no minus signs to drop, as was necessary with elasticity of demand.

price elasticity of supply The ratio of the percentage change in quantity supplied of a product or resource to the percentage change in its price; a measure of the responsiveness of producers to a change in the price of a product or resource.

The degree of **price elasticity of supply** depends mainly on how easily and quickly producers can shift resources between alternative uses to alter production of a good. The easier and more rapid the transfers of resources, the greater is the price elasticity of supply. Take the case of a producer of surfboards. The producer's response to an increase in the price of surfboards depends on its ability to shift resources from the production of other products such as wakeboards, skateboards, and snowboards (whose prices we assume

PHOTO OP Elastic versus Inelastic Supply

The supply of automobiles is elastic, whereas the supply of Monet paintings is inelastic.

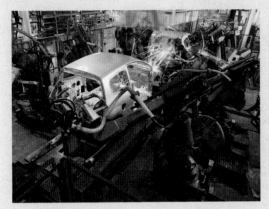

©Shutterstock/supergenijalac

Source: Courtesy National Gallery of Art, Washington

remain constant) to the production of surfboards. And shifting resources takes time: The longer the time, the greater the transferability of resources. So there will be a greater production response, and therefore greater elasticity of supply, the longer a firm has to adjust to a price change.

In analyzing the impact of time on elasticity, economists distinguish among the immediate market period, the short run, and the long run.

Price Elasticity of Supply: The Market Period

The **market period** is the period that occurs when the time immediately after a change in market price is too short for producers to respond with a change in the amount they supply. Suppose a farmer brings to market one truckload of tomatoes that is the entire season's output. The supply curve for the tomatoes is perfectly inelastic (vertical); the farmer will sell the truckload whether the price is high or low. Why? Because the farmer can offer only one truckload of tomatoes even if the price of tomatoes is much higher than anticipated. The farmer might like to offer more tomatoes, but tomatoes cannot be produced overnight. Another full growing season is needed to respond to a higher-than-expected price by producing more than one truckload. Similarly, because the product is perishable, the farmer cannot withhold it from the market. If the price is lower than anticipated, the farmer will still sell the entire truckload.

The farmer's costs of production, incidentally, will not enter into this decision to sell. Though the price of tomatoes may fall far short of production costs, the farmer will nevertheless sell everything brought to market to avoid a total loss through spoilage. In the market period, both the supply of tomatoes and the quantity of tomatoes supplied are fixed. The farmer offers only one truckload, no matter how high or low the price.

Figure 4.4a shows the farmer's vertical supply curve during the market period. Supply is perfectly inelastic because the farmer does not have time to respond to a change in demand, say, from D_1 to D_2. The resulting price increase from P_0 to P_m simply determines which buyers get the fixed quantity supplied; it elicits no increase in output.

market period A period in which producers of a product are unable to change the quantity produced in response to a change in its price and in which there is a perfectly inelastic supply.

FIGURE 4.4 Time and the elasticity of supply. The greater the amount of time producers have to adjust to a change in demand, here from D_1 to D_2, the greater will be their output response. In the immediate market period (a) there is insufficient time to change output, and so supply is perfectly inelastic. In the short run (b) plant capacity is fixed, but changing the intensity of its use can alter output; supply is therefore more elastic. In the long run (c) all desired adjustments, including changes in plant capacity, can be made, and supply becomes still more elastic.

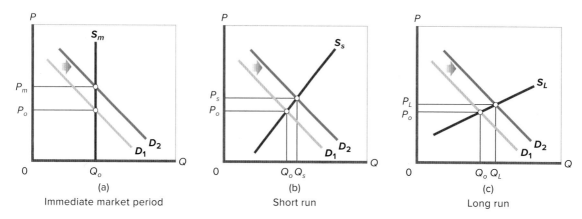

However, not all supply curves are perfectly inelastic immediately after a price change. If the product is not perishable and the price rises, producers may choose to increase quantity supplied by drawing down their inventories of unsold, stored goods. This will cause the market supply curve to attain some positive slope. For our tomato farmer, the market period may be a full growing season; for producers of goods that can be inexpensively stored, there may be no market period at all.

Price Elasticity of Supply: The Short Run

short run (1) In microeconomics, a period of time in which producers are able to change the quantities of some but not all of the resources they employ; a period in which some resources (usually plant) are fixed and some are variable. (2) In macroeconomics, a period in which nominal wages and other input prices do not change in response to a change in the price level.

The **short run** in microeconomics is a period of time too short to change plant capacity but long enough to use the fixed-size plant more or less intensively. In the short run, our farmer's plant (land and farm machinery) is fixed. But he does have time in the short run to cultivate tomatoes more intensively by applying more labor and more fertilizer and pesticides to the crop. The result is a somewhat greater output in response to a presumed increase in demand; this greater output is reflected in a more elastic supply of tomatoes, as shown by S_s in Figure 4.4b. Note now that the increase in demand from D_1 to D_2 is met by an increase in quantity (from Q_0 to Q_s), so there is a smaller price adjustment (from P_0 to P_s) than would be the case in the market period. The equilibrium price is therefore lower in the short run than in the market period.

Price Elasticity of Supply: The Long Run

long run (1) In microeconomics, a period of time long enough to enable producers of a product to change the quantities of all the resources they employ; period in which all resources and costs are variable and no resources or costs are fixed. (2) In macroeconomics, a period sufficiently long for nominal wages and other input prices to change in response to a change in the nation's price level.

The **long run** in microeconomics is a time period long enough for firms to adjust their plant sizes and for new firms to enter (or existing firms to leave) the industry. In the "tomato industry," for example, our farmer has time to acquire additional land and buy more machinery and equipment. Furthermore, other farmers may, over time, be attracted to tomato farming by the increased demand and higher price. Such adjustments create a larger supply response, as represented by the more elastic supply curve S_L in Figure 4.4c. The outcome is a smaller price rise (P_0 to P_L) and a larger output increase (Q_0 to Q_L) in response to the increase in demand from D_1 to D_2.

There is no total-revenue test for elasticity of supply. Supply shows a positive or direct relationship between price and amount supplied; the supply curve is upsloping. Regardless of the degree of elasticity or inelasticity, price and total revenue always move together.

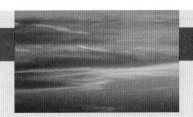

APPLYING THE ANALYSIS

Antiques and Reproductions

The *Antiques Roadshow* is a popular PBS television program in which people bring antiques to a central location for appraisal by experts. Some people are pleased to learn that their old piece of furniture or funky folk art is worth a large amount, say, $30,000 or more.

The high price of a particular antique is due to strong demand and limited, highly inelastic supply. Because a genuine antique can no longer be reproduced, its quantity supplied either does not rise or rises only slightly as its price goes up. The higher price might prompt the discovery of a few more of the remaining originals and thus add to the quantity available for sale, but this quantity response is usually quite small. So the supply of antiques and other collectibles tends to be inelastic. For one-of-a-kind antiques, the supply is perfectly inelastic.

Factors such as increased population, higher income, and greater enthusiasm for collecting antiques have increased the demand for antiques over time. Because the supply of antiques is limited and inelastic, those increases in demand have greatly boosted the prices of antiques.

Contrast the inelastic supply of original antiques with the elastic supply of modern "made-to-look-old" reproductions. Such faux antiques are quite popular and widely available at furniture stores and knickknack shops. When the demand for reproductions increases, the firms making them simply boost production. Because the supply of reproductions is highly elastic, increased demand raises their prices only slightly.

QUESTION: How does the reluctance to sell antiques add to their inelastic supply?

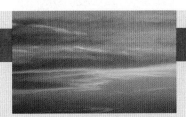

APPLYING THE ANALYSIS

Volatile Gold Prices

The price of gold is quite volatile, sometimes rocketing upward one period and plummeting downward the next. The main sources of these fluctuations are shifts in demand and highly inelastic supply. Gold production is a costly and time-consuming process of exploration, mining, and refining. Moreover, the physical availability of gold is highly limited. For both reasons, increases in gold prices do not elicit substantial increases in quantity supplied. Conversely, gold mining is costly to shut down, and existing gold bars are expensive to store. Price decreases therefore do not produce large drops in the quantity of gold supplied. In short, the supply of gold is inelastic.

The demand for gold is partly derived from the demand for its uses, such as for jewelry, dental fillings, and coins. But people also demand gold as a speculative financial investment. They increase their demand for gold when they fear general inflation or domestic or international turmoil that might undermine the value of currency and more traditional investments. They reduce their demand when events settle down. Because of the inelastic supply of gold, even relatively small changes in demand produce relatively large changes in price.

QUESTION: What is the current price of gold? (See www.goldprices.com.) What were the highest and the lowest prices over the last 12 months?

Income Elasticity of Demand

income elasticity of demand
The ratio of the percentage change in the quantity demanded of a good to a percentage change in consumer income; measures the responsiveness of consumer purchases to income changes.

Income elasticity of demand measures the degree to which the quantity of a product demanded responds, positively or negatively, to a change in consumers' incomes. The coefficient of income elasticity of demand E_i is determined with the formula

$$E_i = \frac{\text{percentage change in quantity demanded}}{\text{percentage change in income}}$$

Normal Goods

For most goods, the income elasticity coefficient E_i is positive, meaning that more of them are demanded as income rises. Such goods are called *normal* or *superior goods* (and were first described in Chapter 3). But the value of E_i varies greatly among normal goods. For example, income elasticity of demand for automobiles is about +3, while income elasticity for most farm products is only about +0.20.

Inferior Goods

A negative income elasticity coefficient designates an inferior good. Used mattresses, long-distance bus tickets, used clothing, and some frozen meals are likely candidates. Consumers decrease their purchases of inferior goods as their incomes rise.

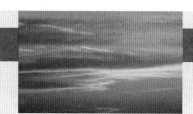

APPLYING THE ANALYSIS

Which Consumer Products Suffer the Greatest Demand Decreases during Recessions?

Coefficients of income elasticity of demand provide insights into how recessions impact the sales of different consumer products. A recession is defined as two or more consecutive quarters (six months) of falling real output and is typically characterized by rising unemployment rates, lower profits for business firms, falling consumer incomes, and weaker demand for products. In December 2007, the U.S. economy entered its tenth recession since 1950. Because of a worsening mortgage debt crisis, the recession continued through 2008 and into 2009. When recessions occur and incomes fall, coefficients of income elasticity of demand help predict which products will experience more rapid declines in demand than other products.

Products with relatively high income elasticity coefficients such as automobiles ($E_i = +3$), housing ($E_i = +1.5$), and restaurant meals ($E_i = +1.4$) are generally hit hardest by recessions. Those with low or negative income elasticity coefficients are much less affected. For example, food products ($E_i = +0.20$) respond relatively little to income fluctuations. When incomes drop, purchases of food (and toothpaste and toilet paper) drop little compared to purchases of movie tickets, luxury vacations, and wide-screen TVs. Products we view as essential tend to have lower income elasticity coefficients than products we view as luxuries. When our incomes fall, we cannot easily eliminate or postpone the purchase of essential products.

QUESTION: Why did discount clothing stores (such as Kohl's) suffer less than high-end clothing stores (such as Nordstrom) during the 2007–2009 U.S. recession?

Cross-Elasticity of Demand

Cross-elasticity of demand measures how the quantity of a product demanded (say, X) responds to a change in the price of some other product (say, Y). We calculate the coefficient of cross-elasticity of demand E_{xy} just as we do the coefficient of simple price elasticity, except that we relate the percentage change in the consumption of X to the percentage change in the price of Y:

$$E_{xy} = \frac{\text{percentage change in quantity demanded of product X}}{\text{percentage change in price of product Y}}$$

This cross-elasticity (or cross-price-elasticity) concept allows us to quantify and more fully understand substitute and complementary goods, introduced in Chapter 3.

> **cross-elasticity of demand** The ratio of the percentage change in *quantity demanded* of one good to the percentage change in the price of some other good. A positive coefficient indicates the two products are *substitute goods;* a negative coefficient indicates they are *complementary goods.*

Substitute Goods

If cross-elasticity of demand is positive, meaning that sales of X move in the same direction as a change in the price of Y, then X and Y are substitute goods. An example is Evian water (X) and Dasani water (Y). An increase in the price of Dasani causes consumers to buy more Evian, resulting in a positive cross-elasticity. The larger the positive cross-elasticity coefficient, the greater is the substitutability between the two products.

Complementary Goods

When cross-elasticity is negative, we know that X and Y "go together"; an increase in the price of one decreases the demand for the other. This indicates that the two are complementary goods. For example, a decrease in the price of digital cameras will increase the number of memory sticks purchased. The larger the negative cross-elasticity coefficient, the greater is the complementarity between the two goods.

Independent Goods

A zero or near-zero cross-elasticity suggests that the two products being considered are unrelated or independent goods. An example is textbooks and plums: We would not expect a change in the price of textbooks to have any effect on purchases of plums, and vice versa.

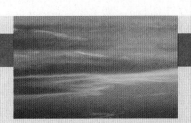

APPLYING THE ANALYSIS

Using Cross-Elasticity to Make Business and Regulatory Decisions

The degree of substitutability of products, measured by the cross-elasticity coefficient, is important to businesses and government. For example, suppose that Coca-Cola is considering whether or not to lower the price of its Sprite brand. Not only will it want to know something about the price elasticity of demand for Sprite (will the price cut increase or decrease total revenue?), but it also will be interested in knowing if the increased sales of Sprite will come at the expense of its Coke brand. How sensitive are the sales of one of its products (Coke) to a change in the price of another of its products (Sprite)? By how much will the increased sales of Sprite "cannibalize" the sales of Coke? A low cross-elasticity would indicate that Coke and Sprite are weak substitutes for each other and that a lower price for Sprite would have little effect on Coke sales.

Government also implicitly uses the idea of cross-elasticity of demand in assessing whether a proposed merger between two large firms will substantially reduce competition and therefore violate the antitrust laws. For example, the cross-elasticity between Coke and Pepsi is high, making them strong substitutes for each other. In addition, Coke and Pepsi together sell about 75 percent of all carbonated cola drinks consumed in the United States. Taken together, the high cross-elasticities and the large market shares suggest that the government would likely block a merger between Coke and Pepsi because the merger would substantially lessen competition. In contrast, the cross-elasticity between cola and gasoline is low or zero. A merger between Coke and Shell Oil Company would have a minimal effect on competition. So government would let that merger happen.

QUESTION: Prior to the 2007–2009 recession, why did sales of sport utility vehicles (SUVs) decline dramatically, while sales of hybrid vehicles rose significantly? Relate your answer to cross-elasticity of demand.

SUMMARY

LO4.1 Discuss price elasticity of demand and how it can be measured.

Price elasticity of demand measures the responsiveness of the quantity of a product demanded when the price changes. If consumers are relatively sensitive to price changes, demand is elastic. If they are relatively unresponsive to price changes, demand is inelastic.

The price-elasticity coefficient E_d measures the degree of elasticity or inelasticity of demand. The coefficient is found by the formula

$$E_d = \frac{\text{percentage change in quantity demanded of X}}{\text{percentage change in price of X}}$$

Economists use the averages of prices and quantities under consideration as reference points in determining percentage changes in price and quantity. If E_d is greater than 1, demand is elastic. If E_d is less than 1, demand is inelastic. Unit elasticity is the special case in which E_d equals 1.

Perfectly inelastic demand is graphed as a line parallel to the vertical axis; perfectly elastic demand is shown by a line above and parallel to the horizontal axis.

Elasticity varies at different price ranges on a demand curve, tending to be elastic in the upper-left segment and inelastic in the lower-right segment. Elasticity cannot be judged by the steepness or flatness of a demand curve.

The number of available substitutes, the size of an item's price relative to one's budget, whether the product is a luxury or a necessity, and the length of time to adjust are all determinants of elasticity of demand.

LO4.2 Explain how price elasticity of demand affects total revenue.

Total revenue (TR) is the total number of dollars received by a firm from the sale of a product in a particular period. It is found by multiplying price times quantity. Graphically, TR is shown as the $P \times Q$ rectangle under a point on a demand curve.

If total revenue changes in the opposite direction from prices, demand is elastic. If price and total revenue change in the same direction, demand is inelastic. Where demand is of unit elasticity, a change in price leaves total revenue unchanged.

LO4.3 Describe price elasticity of supply and how it can be measured.

The elasticity concept also applies to supply. The coefficient of price elasticity of supply is found by the formula

$$E_s = \frac{\text{percentage change in quantity supplied of X}}{\text{percentage change in price of X}}$$

The averages of the prices and quantities under consideration are used as reference points for computing percentage changes.

Elasticity of supply depends on the ease of shifting resources between alternative uses, which varies directly with the time producers have to adjust to a price change.

LO4.4 Apply price elasticity of demand and supply to real-world situations.

Price elasticity of demand and supply have numerous private and public sector applications. For example, they inform pricing and output decisions by firms, and government policies regarding the legalization and taxation of goods.

LO4.5 Explain income elasticity of demand and cross-elasticity of demand and how they can be applied.

Income elasticity of demand indicates the responsiveness of consumer purchases to a change in income. The coefficient of income elasticity of demand is found by the formula

$$E_i = \frac{\text{percentage change in quantity demanded}}{\text{percentage change in income}}$$

The coefficient is positive for normal goods and negative for inferior goods.

Cross-elasticity of demand indicates the responsiveness of consumer purchases of one product (X) to a change in the price of some other product (Y). The coefficient of cross-elasticity is found by the formula

$$E_{xy} = \frac{\text{percentage change in quantity demanded of product X}}{\text{percentage change in price of product Y}}$$

The coefficient is positive if X and Y are substitute goods and negative if X and Y are complements.

TERMS AND CONCEPTS

price elasticity of demand	perfectly elastic demand	short run
elastic demand	total revenue (TR)	long run
inelastic demand	total-revenue test	income elasticity of demand
unit elasticity	price elasticity of supply	cross-elasticity of demand
perfectly inelastic demand	market period	

QUESTIONS

The following and additional problems can be found in ▤ connect

1. What is the formula for measuring price elasticity of demand? What does it mean (in terms of relative price and quantity changes) if the price-elasticity coefficient is less than 1? Equal to 1? Greater than 1? **LO4.1**

2. Graph the accompanying demand data, and then use the price-elasticity formula (midpoints approach) for E_d to determine price elasticity of demand for each of the four possible $1 price changes. What can you conclude about the relationship between the slope of a curve and its elasticity? **LO4.1**

Product Price	Quantity Demanded
$5	1
4	2
3	3
2	4
1	5

3. What are the major determinants of price elasticity of demand? Use those determinants and your own reasoning in judging whether demand for each of the following products is probably elastic or inelastic: (a) bottled water; (b) toothpaste; (c) Crest toothpaste; (d) ketchup; (e) diamond bracelets; (f) Microsoft Windows operating system. **LO4.1**

4. What effect would a rule stating that university students must live in university dormitories have on the price elasticity of demand for dormitory space? What impact might this in turn have on room rates? **LO4.1**

5. Calculate total-revenue data from the demand schedule in question 2. Referring to changes in price and total revenue, describe the total-revenue test for elasticity. **LO4.2**

6. How would the following changes in price affect total revenue? That is, would total revenue increase, decrease, or remain unchanged? **LO4.2**
   a. Price falls and demand is inelastic.
   b. Price rises and demand is elastic.
   c. Price rises and supply is elastic.
   d. Price rises and supply is inelastic.
   e. Price rises and demand is inelastic.
   f. Price falls and demand is elastic.
   g. Price falls and demand is of unit elasticity.

7. You are chairperson of a state tax commission responsible for establishing a program to raise new revenue through excise taxes. Why would elasticity of demand be important to you in determining the products on which the taxes should be levied? **LO4.4**

8. In 2015, Paul Gauguin's painting *When Will You Marry* sold for $300 million. Portray this sale in a demand and supply diagram, and comment on the elasticity of supply. Comedian George Carlin once mused, "If a painting can be forged well enough to fool some experts, why is the original so valuable?" Provide an answer. **LO4.4**

9. Because of a legal settlement over state health care claims, in 1999 the U.S. tobacco companies had to raise the average price of a pack of cigarettes from $1.95 to $2.45. The decline in cigarette sales was estimated at 8 percent. What does this imply for the elasticity of demand for cigarettes? Explain. **LO4.4**

10. The income elasticities of demand for movies, dental services, and clothing have been estimated to be +3.4, +1, and +0.5, respectively. Interpret these coefficients. What does it mean if an income-elasticity coefficient is negative? **LO4.5**

11. Suppose the cross-elasticity of demand for products A and B is +3.6, and for products C and D is −5.4. What can you conclude about how products A and B are related? Products C and D? **LO4.5**

PROBLEMS

1. Look at the demand curve in Figure 4.2a. Use the midpoint formula and points *a* and *b* to calculate the elasticity of demand for that range of the demand curve. Do the same for the demand curves in Figures 4.2b and 4.2c using, respectively, points *c* and *d* for Figure 4.2b and points *e* and *f* for Figure 4.2c. **LO4.1**

2. Investigate how demand elastiticities are affected by increases in demand. Shift each of the demand curves in Figures 4.2a, 4.2b, and 4.2c to the right by 10 units. For example, point *a* in Figure 4.2a would shift rightward from location (10 units, $2) to (20 units, $2), while point *b* would shift rightward from location (40 units, $1) to (50 units, $1). After making these shifts, apply the midpoint formula to calculate the demand elasticities for the shifted points. Are they larger or smaller than the elasticities you calculated in problem 1 for the original points? In terms of the midpoint formula, what explains the change in elasticities? **LO4.1**

3. Suppose that the total revenue received by a company selling basketballs is $600 when the price is set at $30 per basketball and $600 when the price is set at $20 per basketball. Without using the midpoint formula, can you tell whether demand is elastic, inelastic, or unit-elastic over this price range? **LO4.2**

4. Danny "Dimes" Donahue is a neighborhood's 9-year-old entrepreneur. His most recent venture is selling homemade brownies that he bakes himself. At a price of $1.50 each, he sells 100. At a price of $1.00 each, he sells 300. Is demand elastic or inelastic over this price range? If demand had the same elasticity for a price decline from $1.00 to $0.50 as it does for the decline from $1.50 to $1.00, would cutting the price from $1.00 to $0.50 increase or decrease Danny's total revenue? **LO4.2**

5. What is the formula for measuring the price elasticity of supply? Suppose the price of apples goes up from $20 to $22 a box. In direct response, Goldsboro Farms supplies 1,200 boxes of apples instead of 1,000 boxes. Compute the coefficient of price elasticity (midpoints approach) for Goldsboro's supply. Is its supply elastic, or is it inelastic? **LO4.3**

6. **ADVANCED ANALYSIS** Currently, at a price of $1 each, 100 popsicles are sold per day in the perpetually hot town of Rostin. Consider the elasticity of supply. In the short run, a price increase from $1 to $2 is unit-elastic ($E_s = 1.0$). So how many popsicles will be sold each day in the short run if the price rises to $2 each? In the long run, a price increase from $1 to $2 has an elasticity of supply of 1.50. So how many popsicles will be sold per day in the long run if the price rises to $2 each? (Hint: Apply the midpoints approach to the elasticity of supply.) **LO4.3**

7. Lorena likes to play golf. The number of times per year that she plays depends on both the price of playing a round of golf as well as Lorena's income and the cost of other types of entertainment—in particular, how much it costs to go see a movie instead of playing golf. The three demand schedules in the table below show how many rounds of golf per year Lorena will demand at each price under three different scenarios. In scenario D_1, Lorena's income is $50,000 per year and movies cost $9 each. In scenario D_2, Lorena's income is also $50,000 per year, but the price of seeing a movie rises to $11. And in scenario D_3, Lorena's income goes up to $70,000 per year, while movies cost $11. **LO4.5**

	Quantity Demanded		
Price	D_1	D_2	D_3
$50	15	10	15
35	25	15	30
20	40	20	50

a. Using the data under D_1 and D_2, calculate the cross-elasticity of Lorena's demand for golf at all three prices. (To do this, apply the midpoints approach to the cross-elasticity of demand.) Is the cross-elasticity the same at all three prices? Are movies and golf substitute goods, complementary goods, or independent goods?

b. Using the data under D_2 and D_3, calculate the income elasticity of Lorena's demand for golf at all three prices. (To do this, apply the midpoints approach to the income elasticity of demand.) Is the income elasticity the same at all three prices? Is golf an inferior good?

Market Failures: Public Goods and Externalities

Learning Objectives

LO5.1 Differentiate between demand-side market failures and supply-side market failures.

LO5.2 Explain consumer surplus and producer surplus, and discuss how properly functioning markets maximize their sum while optimally allocating resources.

LO5.3 Identify how public goods are distinguished from private goods, and explain the method for determining the optimal quantity of a public good.

LO5.4 Explain how positive and negative externalities cause under- and overallocations of resources, and how they might be corrected.

LO5.5 Show why we normally won't want to pay what it would cost to eliminate every last bit of a negative externality.

Competitive markets usually do a remarkable job of allocating society's scarce resources to their highest-valued uses. But markets have certain limitations. In some circumstances, economically desirable goods are not produced at all. In other situations, they are either overproduced or underproduced. This chapter examines **market failure,** which occurs when the competitive market system (1) does not allocate any resources whatsoever to the production of certain goods or (2) either underallocates or overallocates resources to the production of certain goods.

market failure The inability of a market to bring about the allocation of resources that best satisfies the wants of society; in particular, the overallocation or underallocation of resources to the production of a particular good or service because of spillovers or informational problems or because markets do not provide desired public goods.

Where private markets fail, an economic role for government may arise. In this chapter, we will examine that role as it relates to public goods and so-called externalities—situations where market failures lead to suboptimal outcomes that the government may be able to improve upon by using its powers to tax, spend, and regulate. We conclude the chapter by noting potential government inefficiencies that can hinder government's economic efforts.

Market Failures in Competitive Markets[1]

Competitive markets usually produce an assignment of resources that is "right" from an economic perspective. Unfortunately, the presence of robust competition involving many buyers and many sellers may not be enough to guarantee that a market will allocate resources correctly. Market failures sometimes happen in competitive markets. The focus of this chapter is to explain how and why such market failures can arise, and how they might be corrected.

Fortunately, the broad picture is simple. Market failures in competitive markets fall into just two categories:

- **Demand-side market failures** happen when demand curves do not reflect consumers' full willingness to pay for a good or service.
- **Supply-side market failures** occur when supply curves do not reflect the full cost of producing a good or service.

Demand-Side Market Failures

demand-side market failures
Underallocations of resources that occur when private demand curves understate consumers' full willingness to pay for a good or service.

supply-side market failures
Overallocations of resources that occur when private supply curves understate the full cost of producing a good or service.

Demand-side market failures arise because it is impossible in certain cases to charge consumers what they are willing to pay for a product. Consider outdoor fireworks displays. People enjoy fireworks and would therefore be *willing* to pay to see a fireworks display if the only way to see it was to have to pay for the right to do so. But because such displays are outdoors and in public, people don't actually *have* to pay to see the display because there is no way to exclude those who haven't paid from also enjoying the show. Private firms will therefore be unwilling to produce outdoor fireworks displays, as it will be nearly impossible for them to raise enough revenue to cover production costs.

Supply-Side Market Failures

Supply-side market failures arise in situations in which a firm does not have to pay the full cost of producing its output. Consider a coal-burning power plant. The firm running the plant will have to pay for all of the land, labor, capital, and entrepreneurship that it uses to generate electricity by burning coal. But if the firm is not charged for the smoke that it releases into the atmosphere, it will fail to pay another set of costs—the costs that its pollution imposes on other people. These include future harm from global warming, toxins that affect wildlife, and possible damage to agricultural crops downwind.

A market failure arises because it is not possible for the market to correctly weigh costs and benefits in a situation in which some of the costs are completely unaccounted for. The coal-burning power plant produces more electricity and generates more pollution than it would if it had to pay for each ton of smoke that it released into the atmosphere. The extra units that are produced are units of output for which the costs are *greater than* the benefits. Obviously, these units should not be produced.

---

[1]Other market failures arise when there are not enough buyers or sellers to ensure competition. In those situations, the lack of competition allows either buyers or sellers to restrict purchases or sales below optimal levels for their own benefit. As an example, a monopoly—a firm that is the only producer in its industry—can restrict the amount of output that it supplies in order to drive up the market price and thereby increase its own profit.

Efficiently Functioning Markets

The best way to understand market failure is to first understand how properly functioning competitive markets achieve economic efficiency.

A competitive market not only makes private goods available to consumers but also allocates society's resources efficiently to the particular product. Competition among producers forces them to use the best technology and right mix of productive resources. Otherwise, lower-cost producers will drive them out of business. The result is **productive efficiency:** the production of any particular good in the least costly way. When society produces, say, bottled water at the lowest achievable per-unit cost, it is expending the smallest amount of resources to produce that product and therefore is making available the largest amount of resources to produce other desired goods. Suppose society has only $100 worth of resources available. If it can produce a bottle of water using only $1 of those resources, then it will have available $99 of resources to produce other goods. This is clearly better than producing the bottle of water for $5 and having only $95 of resources available for alternative uses.

Competitive markets also produce **allocative efficiency:** the *particular mix* of goods and services most highly valued by society (minimum-cost production assumed). For example, society wants high-quality mineral water to be used for bottled water, not for gigantic blocks of refrigeration ice. It wants devices and services for streaming music, not phonographs that play 45-rpm records. Moreover, society does not want to devote all its resources to bottled water and music streaming devices. It wants to assign some resources to automobiles and personal computers. Competitive markets make those proper assignments, as we will demonstrate.

Two conditions must hold if a competitive market is to produce efficient outcomes: The demand curve in the market must reflect consumers' full willingness to pay and the supply curve in the market must reflect all the costs of production. If these conditions hold, then the market will produce only units for which benefits are at least equal to costs. It also will maximize the amount of "benefit surpluses" that are shared between consumers and producers.

productive efficiency The production of a good in the least costly way; occurs when production takes place at the output at which average total cost is a minimum and marginal product per dollar's worth of input is the same for all inputs.

allocative efficiency The apportionment of resources among firms and industries to obtain the production of the products most wanted by society (consumers); the output of each product at which its marginal cost and price or marginal benefit are equal.

Consumer Surplus

The benefit surplus received by a consumer or consumers in a market is called **consumer surplus.** It is defined as the difference between the maximum price a consumer is (or consumers are) willing to pay for a product and the actual price that they do pay.

Suppose that the maximum Ted is willing to pay for an apple is $1.25. If Ted is charged any market price less than $1.25, he will receive a consumer surplus equal to the difference between the $1.25 maximum price that he would have been willing to pay and the lower market price. For instance, if the market price is $.50 per apple, Ted will receive a consumer surplus of $.75 per apple (= $1.25 − $.50). In nearly all markets, consumers individually and collectively gain greater total utility or satisfaction in dollar terms from their purchases than the amount of their expenditures (= product price × quantity). This utility surplus arises because each consumer who buys the product only has to pay the equilibrium price even though many of them would have been willing to pay more than the equilibrium price to obtain the product.

The concept of maximum willingness to pay also gives us another way to understand demand curves. Consider Table 5.1, where the first two columns show the maximum amounts that six consumers would each be willing to pay for a bag of oranges. Bob, for instance, would be willing to pay a maximum of $13 for a bag of oranges. Betty, by contrast, would only be willing to pay a maximum of $8 for a bag of oranges.

The maximum prices that these individuals are willing to pay represent points on a demand curve because the lower the market price, the more bags of oranges will be

consumer surplus The difference between the maximum price a consumer is (or consumers are) willing to pay for a product and the actual price paid.

TABLE 5.1 **Consumer Surplus**

(1) Person	(2) Maximum Price Willing to Pay	(3) Actual Price (Equilibrium Price)	(4) Consumer Surplus
Bob	$13	$8	$5 (= $13 − $8)
Barb	12	8	4 (= $12 − $8)
Bill	11	8	3 (= $11 − $8)
Bart	10	8	2 (= $10 − $8)
Brent	9	8	1 (= $ 9 − $8)
Betty	8	8	0 (= $ 8 − $8)

demanded. At a price of $12.50, for instance, Bob will be the only person listed in the table who will purchase a bag. But at a price of $11.50, both Bob and Barb will want to purchase a bag. The lower the price, the greater the total quantity demanded as the market price falls below the maximum prices of more and more consumers.

Lower prices also imply larger consumer surpluses. When the price is $12.50, Bob only gets $.50 in consumer surplus because his maximum willingness to pay of $13 is only $.50 higher than the market price of $12.50. But if the market price were to fall to $8, then his consumer surplus would be $5 (= $13 − $8). The third and fourth columns of Table 5.1 show how much consumer surplus each of our six consumers will receive if the market price of a bag of oranges is $8. Only Betty receives no consumer surplus because her maximum willingness to pay exactly matches the $8 equilibrium price.

It is easy to show on a graph the consumer surplus received by buyers in a market. Consider Figure 5.1, which shows the market equilibrium price P_1 = $8 as well as the downsloping demand curve D for bags of oranges. Demand curve D includes not only the six consumers named in Table 5.1 but also every other consumer of oranges in the market. The individual consumer surplus of each particular person who is willing to buy at the $8 market price is simply the vertical distance from the horizontal line that marks the $8 market price up to that particular buyer's maximum willingness to pay. The collective consumer surplus obtained by all of our named and unnamed buyers is found by adding together each of their individual consumer surpluses. To obtain the Q_1 bags of oranges represented, consumers collectively are willing to pay the total amount shown by the sum of the green triangle and yellow rectangle under the demand curve and to the left of Q_1. But consumers need pay only the amount represented by the yellow rectangle (= $P_1 \times Q_1$). So the green triangle is the consumer surplus in this market. It is the sum of the vertical distances between the demand curve and the $8 equilibrium price at each quantity up to Q_1.

FIGURE 5.1 Consumer surplus.
Consumer surplus—shown as the green triangle—is the difference between the maximum price consumers are willing to pay for a product and the lower equilibrium price, here assumed to be $8. For quantity Q_1, consumers are willing to pay the sum of the amounts represented by the green triangle and the yellow rectangle. Because they need to pay only the amount shown as the yellow rectangle, the green triangle shows consumer surplus.

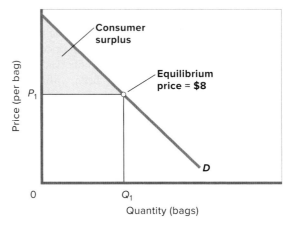

Thus, consumer surplus can also be defined as the area that lies below the demand curve and above the price line that extends horizontally from P_1.

Consumer surplus and price are inversely (negatively) related. Given the demand curve, higher prices reduce consumer surplus; lower prices increase it. When price goes up, the gap narrows between the maximum willingness to pay and the actual price; a price decline widens the gap.

Producer Surplus

Like consumers, producers also receive a benefit surplus in markets. This **producer surplus** is the difference between the actual price a producer receives (or producers receive) and the minimum acceptable price that a consumer would have to pay the producer to make a particular unit of output available.

A producer's minimum acceptable price for a particular unit will equal the producer's marginal cost of producing that particular unit. That marginal cost will be the sum of the rent, wages, interest, and profit that the producer will need to pay in order to obtain the land, labor, capital, and entrepreneurship required to produce that particular unit. In this section, we are assuming that the marginal cost of producing a unit will include *all* of the costs of production. Unlike the coal-burning power plant mentioned previously, the producer must pay for all of its costs, including the cost of pollution. In later sections, we will explore the market failures that arise in situations where firms do not have to pay all their costs.

The size of the producer surplus earned on any particular unit will be the difference between the market price that the producer actually receives and the producer's minimum acceptable price. Consider Table 5.2, which shows the minimum acceptable prices of six different orange growers. With a market price of $8, Carlos, for instance, has a producer surplus of $5, which is equal to the market price of $8 minus his minimum acceptable price of $3. Chad, by contrast, receives no producer surplus because his minimum acceptable price of $8 just equals the market equilibrium price of $8.

Carlos's minimum acceptable price is lower than Chad's minimum acceptable price because Carlos is a more efficient producer than Chad, by which we mean that Carlos produces oranges using a less-costly combination of resources than Chad uses. The differences in efficiency between Carlos and Chad are likely due to differences in the type and quality of resources available to them.

The minimum acceptable prices that producers are willing to accept form points on a supply curve because the higher the price, the more bags of oranges will be supplied. At a price of $3.50, for instance, only Carlos would be willing to supply a bag of oranges. But at a price of $5.50, Carlos, Courtney, and Chuck would all be willing to supply a bag of oranges. The higher the market price, the more oranges will be supplied, as the market price surpasses the marginal costs and minimum acceptable prices of more and more

producer surplus The difference between the actual price a producer receives (or producers receive) and the minimum acceptable price.

TABLE 5.2 Producer Surplus

(1) Person	(2) Maximum Acceptable Price	(3) Actual Price (Equilibrium Price)	(4) Producer Surplus
Carlos	$3	$8	$5 (= $8 − $3)
Courtney	4	8	4 (= $8 − $4)
Chuck	5	8	3 (= $8 − $5)
Cindy	6	8	2 (= $8 − $6)
Craig	7	8	1 (= $8 − $7)
Chad	8	8	0 (= $8 − $8)

FIGURE 5.2 Producer surplus.
Producer surplus—shown as the blue triangle—is the difference between the actual price producers receive for a product (here $8) and the lower minimum payment they are willing to accept. For quantity Q_1, producers receive the sum of the amounts represented by the blue triangle plus the yellow area. Because they need receive only the amount shown by the yellow area to produce Q_1, the blue triangle represents producer surplus.

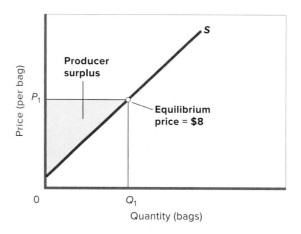

producers. Thus, supply curves shown in this competitive market are both marginal-cost curves and minimum-acceptable-price curves.

The supply curve in Figure 5.2 includes not only the six producers named in Table 5.2 but also every other producer of oranges in the market. At the market price of $8 per bag, Q_1 bags are produced because only those producers whose minimum acceptable prices are less than $8 per bag will choose to produce oranges with their resources. Those lower acceptable prices for each of the units up to Q_1 are shown by the portion of the supply curve lying to the left of and below the assumed $8 market price.

The individual producer surplus of each of these sellers is thus the vertical distance from each seller's respective minimum acceptable price on the supply curve up to the $8 market price. Their collective producer surplus is shown by the blue triangle in Figure 5.2. In that figure, producers collect revenues of $P_1 \times Q_1$, which is the sum of the blue triangle and the yellow area. As shown by the supply curve, however, revenues of only those illustrated by the yellow area would be required to entice producers to offer Q_1 bags of oranges for sale. The sellers therefore receive a producer surplus shown by the blue triangle. That surplus is the sum of the vertical distances between the supply curve and the $8 equilibrium price at each of the quantities to the left of Q_1.

There is a direct (positive) relationship between equilibrium price and the amount of producer surplus. Given the supply curve, lower prices reduce producer surplus; higher prices increase it. The gaps between minimum acceptable payments and actual prices widen when the price increases.

Efficiency Revisited

In Figure 5.3 we bring together the demand and supply curves of Figures 5.1 and 5.2 to show the equilibrium price and quantity and the previously described regions of consumer and producer surplus. All markets that have downsloping demand curves and upsloping supply curves yield consumer and producer surplus.

Because we are assuming in Figure 5.3 that the demand curve reflects buyers' full willingness to pay and the supply curve reflects all of the costs facing sellers, the equilibrium quantity in Figure 5.3 reflects both components of economic efficiency: productive efficiency and allocative efficiency.

- *Productive efficiency* is achieved because competition forces orange growers to use the best technologies and combinations of resources available. Doing so minimizes the per-unit cost of the output produced.
- *Allocative efficiency* is achieved because the correct quantity of oranges—Q_1—is produced relative to other goods and services.

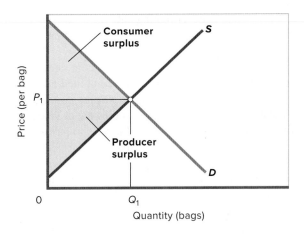

FIGURE 5.3 **Efficiency: maximum combined consumer and producer surplus.** At quantity Q_1 the combined amount of consumer surplus, shown as the green triangle, and producer surplus, shown as the blue triangle, is maximized. Efficiency occurs because, at Q_1, maximum willingness to pay, indicated by the points on the demand curve, equals minimum acceptable price, shown by the points on the supply curve.

There are two ways to understand why Q_1 is the correct quantity of oranges. Both involve realizing that any resources directed toward the production of oranges are resources that could have been used to produce other products. Thus, the only way to justify taking any amount of any resource (land, labor, capital, entrepreneurship) away from the production of other products is if it brings more utility or satisfaction when devoted to the production of oranges than it would if it were used to produce other products.

The first way to see why Q_1 is the allocatively efficient quantity of oranges is to note that demand and supply curves can be interpreted as measuring marginal benefit (MB) and marginal cost (MC). Recall from the discussion relating to Figure 1.3 that optimal allocation is achieved at the output level where MB = MC. We have already seen that supply curves are marginal cost curves. As it turns out, demand curves are marginal benefit curves. This is true because the maximum price that a consumer would be willing to pay for any particular unit is equal to the benefit that she would get if she were to consume that unit. Thus, each point on a demand curve represents both some consumer's maximum willingness to pay as well as the marginal benefit that he or she would get from consuming the particular unit in question.

Combining the fact that supply curves are MC curves with the fact that demand curves are MB curves, we see that points on the demand curve in Figure 5.3 measure the marginal benefit of oranges at each level of output, while points on the supply curve measure the marginal cost of oranges at each level of output. As a result, MB = MC where the demand and supply curves intersect—which means that the equilibrium quantity Q_1 must be allocatively efficient.

The second way to see why Q_1 is the correct quantity of oranges is based on our analysis of consumer and producer surplus and the fact that we can interpret demand and supply curves in terms of maximum willingness to pay and minimum acceptable price. In Figure 5.3, the maximum willingness to pay on the demand curve for each bag of oranges up to Q_1 exceeds the corresponding minimum acceptable price on the supply curve. Thus, each of these bags adds a positive amount (= maximum willingness to pay *minus* minimum acceptable price) to the *total* of consumer and producer surplus.

The fact that maximum willingness to pay exceeds minimum acceptable price for every unit up to Q_1 means that people gain more utility from producing and consuming those units than they would if they produced and consumed anything else that could be made with the resources that went into making those units. Only at the equilibrium quantity Q_1— where the maximum willingness to pay exactly equals the minimum acceptable price— does society exhaust all opportunities to produce units for which benefits exceed costs (including opportunity costs). Producing Q_1 units therefore achieves allocative efficiency because the market is producing and distributing only those units that make people happier with bags of oranges than they would be with anything else that could be produced with the same resources.

Geometrically, producing Q_1 units maximizes the combined area of consumer and producer surplus in Figure 5.3. In this context, the combined area is referred to as *total surplus*. Thus, when Q_1 units are produced, total surplus is equal to the large triangle formed by the green consumer surplus triangle and the blue producer surplus triangle.

When demand curves reflect buyers' full willingness to pay and when supply curves reflect all the costs facing sellers, competitive markets produce equilibrium quantities that maximize the sum of consumer and producer surplus. Allocative efficiency occurs at the market equilibrium quantity where three conditions exist simultaneously:

- MB = MC (Figure 1.3).
- Maximum willingness to pay = minimum acceptable price.
- Total surplus (= sum of consumer and producer surplus) is at a maximum.

Economists are enamored with markets because properly functioning markets automatically achieve allocative efficiency. Other methods of allocating resources—such as government central planning—do exist. But because other methods cannot do any better than properly functioning markets—and may in many cases do much worse—economists usually prefer that resources be allocated through markets whenever properly functioning markets are available.

Efficiency Losses (or Deadweight Losses)

efficiency (deadweight) loss A reduction in combined consumer and producer surplus caused by an underallocation or overallocation of resources to the production of a good or service.

Figures 5.4a and 5.4b demonstrate that **efficiency losses**—reductions of combined consumer and producer surplus—result from both underproduction and overproduction. First, consider Figure 5.4a, which analyzes the case of underproduction by considering what happens if output falls from the efficient level Q_1 to the smaller amount Q_2. When that happens, the sum of consumer and producer surplus, previously *abc*, falls to *adec*. So the combined consumer and producer surplus declines by the amount of the gray triangle to the left of Q_1. That triangle represents an efficiency loss to buyers and sellers. And because buyers and sellers are members of society, it represents an efficiency loss (or a so-called **deadweight loss**) to society.

FIGURE 5.4 Efficiency losses (deadweight losses). Quantity levels either less than or greater than the efficient quantity Q_1 create efficiency losses. In (a), triangle *dbe* shows the efficiency loss associated with underproduction at output Q_2. Triangle *bfg* in (b) illustrates the efficiency loss associated with overproduction at output level Q_3.

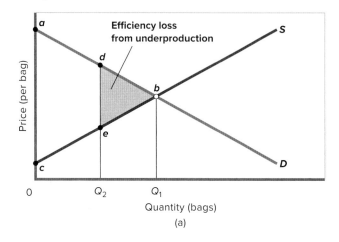

(a)

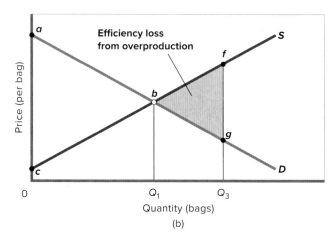

(b)

For output levels from Q_2 to Q_1, consumers' maximum willingness to pay (as reflected by points on the demand curve) exceeds producers' minimum acceptable price (as reflected by points on the supply curve). By failing to produce units of this product for which a consumer is willing to pay more than a producer is willing to accept, society suffers a loss of net benefits. As a concrete example, consider a particular unit for which a consumer is willing to pay $10 and a producer is willing to accept $6. The $4 difference between those values is a net benefit that will not be realized if this unit is not produced. In addition, the resources that should have gone to producing this unit will go instead to producing other products that will not generate as much utility as if those resources had been used here to produce this unit of this product. The triangle *dbe* in Figure 5.4a shows the total loss of net benefits that results from failing to produce the units from Q_2 to Q_1.

In contrast, consider the case of overproduction shown in Figure 5.4b, in which the number of oranges produced is Q_3 rather than the efficient level Q_1. In Figure 5.4b the combined consumer and producer surplus therefore declines by *bfg*—the gray triangle to the right of Q_1. This triangle subtracts from the total consumer and producer surplus of *abc* that would occur if the quantity had been Q_1. That is, for all units from 0 to Q_1, benefits exceed costs, so that those units generate the economic surplus shown by triangle *abc*. But the units from Q_1 to Q_3 are such that costs exceed benefits. Thus, they generate an economic loss shown by triangle *bfg*. The total economic surplus for all units from 0 to Q_3 is therefore the economic surplus given by *abc* for the units from 0 to Q_1 *minus* the economic loss given by *bfg* for the units from Q_1 to Q_3.

Producing any unit beyond Q_1 generates an economic loss because the willingness to pay for such units on the part of consumers is less than the minimum acceptable price to produce such units on the part of producers. As a concrete example, note that producing an item for which the maximum willingness to pay is, say, $7 and the minimum acceptable price is, say, $10 subtracts $3 from society's net benefits. Such production is uneconomical and creates an efficiency loss (or deadweight loss) for society. Because the net benefit of each bag of oranges from Q_1 to Q_3 is negative, we know that the benefits from these units are smaller than the opportunity costs of the other products that could have been produced with the resources that were used to produce these bags of oranges. The resources used to produce the bags from Q_1 to Q_3 could have generated net benefits instead of net losses if they had been directed toward producing other products. The gray triangle *bfg* to the right of Q_1 in Figure 5.4b shows the total efficiency loss from overproduction at Q_3.

The magic of markets is that when demand reflects consumers' full willingness to pay and when supply reflects all costs, the market equilibrium quantity will automatically equal the allocatively efficient output level. Under these conditions, the market equilibrium quantity will ensure that there are neither efficiency losses from underproduction nor efficiency losses from overproduction. As we are about to see, however, such losses do happen when either demand does not reflect consumers' full willingness to pay or supply does not reflect all costs.

Private and Public Goods

Demand-side market failures arise in competitive markets when demand curves fail to reflect consumers' full willingness to pay for a good or service. In such situations, markets fail to produce all of the units for which there are net benefits because demand curves underreport how much consumers are willing and able to pay. This underreporting problem reaches its most extreme form in the case of a public good: Markets may fail to produce *any* of the public good because its demand curve may reflect *none* of its consumers' willingness to pay.

To understand public goods, we first need to understand the characteristics that define private goods.

Private Goods Characteristics

private good A good or service that is individually consumed and that can be profitably provided by privately owned firms because they can exclude nonpayers from receiving the benefits.

Certain goods called **private goods** are produced through the market system. Private goods encompass the full range of goods offered for sale in stores and shops. Examples include automobiles, clothing, personal computers, household appliances, and sporting goods. Private goods have two characteristics: rivalry and excludability.

- *Rivalry* (in consumption) means that when one person buys and consumes a product, it is not available for another person to buy and consume. When Adams purchases and drinks a bottle of mineral water, it is not available for Benson to purchase and consume.
- *Excludability* means that sellers can keep people who do not pay for a product from obtaining its benefits. Only people who are willing and able to pay the market price for bottles of water can obtain these drinks and the benefits they confer.

Profitable Provision

Consumers fully express their personal demands for private goods in the market. If Adams likes bottled mineral water, that fact will be known by her desire to purchase the product. Other things equal, the higher the price of bottled water, the fewer bottles she will buy. So Adams' demand for bottled water will reflect an inverse relationship between the price of bottled water and the quantity of it demanded. This is simply *individual* demand, as described in Chapter 3.

The *market* demand for a private good is the horizontal summation of the individual demand schedules (review Figure 3.2). Suppose there are just two consumers in the market for bottled water and the price is $1 per bottle. If Adams will purchase 3 bottles and Benson will buy 2, the market demand will reflect that consumers demand 5 bottles at the $1 price. Similar summations of quantities demanded at other prices will generate the market demand schedule and curve.

Suppose the equilibrium price of bottled water is $1. Adams and Benson will buy a total of 5 bottles, and the sellers will obtain total revenue of $5 (= $1 × 5). If the sellers' cost per bottle is $.80, their total cost will be $4 (= $.80 × 5). So sellers charging $1 per bottle will obtain $5 of total revenue, incur $4 of total cost, and earn $1 of profits for the 5 bottles sold.

Because firms can profitably "tap market demand" for private goods, they will produce and offer them for sale. Consumers demand private goods, and profit-seeking suppliers produce goods that satisfy the demand. Consumers willing to pay the market price obtain the goods; nonpayers go without. A competitive market not only makes private goods available to consumers but also allocates society's resources efficiently to the particular product. There is neither underproduction nor overproduction of the product.

Public Goods Characteristics

public good A good or service that is characterized by nonrivalry and nonexcludability; a good or service with these characteristics provided by government.

Public goods have the opposite characteristics of private goods. Public goods are distinguished by nonrivalry and nonexcludability.

- *Nonrivalry* (in consumption) means that one person's consumption of a good does not preclude consumption of the good by others. Everyone can simultaneously obtain the benefit from a public good such as a global positioning system, national defense, street lighting, and environmental protection.
- *Nonexcludability* means there is no effective way of excluding individuals from the benefit of the good once it comes into existence.

free-rider problem The inability of potential providers of an economically desirable good or service to obtain payment from those who benefit because of nonexcludability.

These two characteristics create a **free-rider problem.** Once a producer has provided a public good, everyone including nonpayers can obtain the benefit. Because most people do

PHOTO OP Private versus Public Goods

Apples, distinguished by rivalry (in consumption) and excludability, are examples of private goods. In contrast, streetlights, distinguished by nonrivalry (in consumption) and nonexcludability, are examples of public goods.

©Marc Bruxelle/123RF

©Spaces Images/Blend Images

not voluntarily pay for something that they can obtain for free, most people become free riders. Free riders would be willing to pay for the public good if producers could somehow force them to pay—but nonexcludability means that there is no way for producers to withhold the good from the free riders without also denying it to the few who do pay. As a result, free riding means that the willingness to pay of the free riders is not expressed in the market. From the viewpoint of producers, free riding reduces demand. The more free riding, the less demand. And if all consumers free ride, demand will collapse all the way to zero.

The low or even zero demand caused by free riding makes it virtually impossible for private firms to profitably provide public goods. With little or no demand, firms cannot effectively "tap market demand" for revenues and profits. As a result, they will not produce public goods. Society will therefore suffer efficiency losses because goods for which marginal benefits exceed marginal costs are not produced. Thus, if society wants a public good to be produced, it will have to direct government to provide it. Because the public good will still feature nonexcludability, the government won't have any better luck preventing free riding or charging people for it. But because the government can finance the provision of the public good through the taxation of other things, the government does not have to worry about profitability. It can therefore provide the public good even when private firms can't.

A significant example of a public good is homeland defense. The vast majority of Americans think this public good is economically justified because they perceive the benefits as exceeding the costs. Once homeland defense efforts are undertaken, however, the benefits accrue to all Americans (nonrivalry). And there is no practical way to exclude any American from receiving those benefits (nonexcludability).

No private firm will undertake overall homeland defense because the free-rider problem means that benefits cannot be profitably sold. So here we have a service that yields substantial net benefits but to which the market system will not allocate sufficient resources. Like national defense in general, homeland defense is a public good. Society signals its desire for such goods by voting for particular political candidates who support their provision. Because of the free-rider problem, government provides these goods and finances them through compulsory charges in the form of taxes.

ILLUSTRATING THE IDEA

Art for Art's Sake

Suppose an enterprising sculptor creates a piece of art costing $600 and, with permission, places it in the town square. Also suppose that Jack gets $300 of enjoyment from the art and Diane gets $400. Sensing this enjoyment and hoping to make a profit, the sculptor approaches Jack for a donation equal to his satisfaction. Jack falsely says that, unfortunately, he does not particularly like the piece. The sculptor then tries Diane, hoping to get $400 or so. Same deal: Diane professes not to like the piece either. Jack and Diane have become free riders. Although feeling a bit guilty, both reason that it makes no sense to pay for something when anyone can receive the benefits without paying for them. The artist is a quick learner; he vows never to try anything like that again.

QUESTION: What is the rationale for government funding for art placed in town squares and other public spaces?

Optimal Quantity of a Public Good If consumers need not reveal their true demand for a public good in the marketplace, how can society determine the optimal amount of that good? The answer is that the government has to try to estimate the demand for a public good through surveys or public votes. It can then compare the marginal benefit of an added unit of the good against the government's marginal cost of providing it. Adhering to the MB = MC rule, it can provide the "right" amount of the public good.

Measuring Demand Suppose that Adams and Benson are the only two people in the society and that their willingness to pay for a public good, this time the war on terrorism, is as shown in columns 1 and 2 and columns 1 and 3 in Table 5.3. Economists might have discovered these schedules through a survey asking hypothetical questions about how much each citizen was willing to pay for various types and amounts of public goods rather than go without them.

   Notice that the schedules in the first four columns of Table 5.3 are price-quantity schedules, meaning they are demand schedules. Rather than depicting demand in the usual way—the quantity of a product someone is willing to buy at each possible price—these schedules show the price someone is willing to pay for the extra unit of each possible quantity. That is, Adams is willing to pay $4 for the first unit of the public good, $3 for the second, $2 for the third, and so on.

TABLE 5.3 **Optimal Quantity of a Public Good, Two Individuals**

(1) Quantity of Public Good	(2) Adams' Willingness to Pay (Price)		(3) Benson's Willingness to Pay (Price)		(4) Collective Willingness to Pay (Price)	(5) Marginal Cost
1	$4	+	$5	=	$9	$3
2	3	+	4	=	7	4
3	2	+	3	=	5	5
4	1	+	2	=	3	6
5	0	+	1	=	1	7

Suppose the government produces 1 unit of this public good. Because of nonrivalry, Adams' consumption of the good does not preclude Benson from also consuming it, and vice versa. So both people consume the good, and neither volunteers to pay for it. But from Table 5.3 we can find the amount these two people would be willing to pay, together, rather than do without this 1 unit of the good. Columns 1 and 2 show that Adams would be willing to pay $4 for the first unit of the public good, whereas columns 1 and 3 reveal that Benson would be willing to pay $5 for it. Adams and Benson therefore are jointly willing to pay $9 (= $4 + $5) for this first unit.

For the second unit of the public good, the collective price they are willing to pay is $7 (= $3 from Adams + $4 from Benson); for the third unit they will pay $5 (= $2 + $3); and so on. By finding the collective willingness to pay for each additional unit (column 4), we can construct a collective demand schedule (a willingness-to-pay schedule) for the public good. Here we are *not* adding the quantities demanded at each possible price, as with the market demand for a private good. Instead, we are adding the prices that people are willing to pay for the last unit of the public good at each possible quantity demanded.

What does it mean in columns 1 and 4 of Table 5.3 that, for example, Adams and Benson are collectively willing to pay $7 for the second unit of the public good? It means that they jointly expect to receive $7 of extra benefit or utility from that unit. Column 4, in effect, reveals the collective marginal benefit of each unit of the public good.

Comparing Marginal Benefit and Marginal Cost

Now let's suppose the marginal cost of providing the public good is as shown in column 5 of Table 5.3. As explained in Chapter 1, marginal cost tends to rise as more of a good is produced. In view of the marginal-cost data shown, how much of the good should government provide? The optimal amount occurs at the quantity where marginal benefit equals marginal cost. In Table 5.3 that quantity is 3 units, where the collective willingness to pay for the third unit—the $5 marginal benefit—just matches that unit's $5 marginal cost. As we saw in Chapter 1, equating marginal benefit and marginal cost efficiently allocates society's scarce resources.

APPLYING THE ANALYSIS

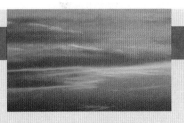

Cost-Benefit Analysis

The above example suggests a practical means, called **cost-benefit analysis,** for deciding whether to provide a particular public good and how much of it to provide. Like our example, cost-benefit analysis (or marginal-benefit–marginal-cost analysis) involves a comparison of marginal costs and marginal benefits.

Suppose the federal government is contemplating a highway construction plan. Because the economy's resources are limited, any decision to use more resources in the public sector will mean fewer resources for the private sector. There will be both a cost and a benefit. The cost is the loss of satisfaction resulting from the accompanying decline in the production of private goods; the benefit is the extra satisfaction resulting from the output of more public goods. Should the needed resources be shifted from the private to the public sector? The answer is yes if the benefit from the extra public goods exceeds the cost that results from having fewer private goods. The answer is no if the cost of the forgone private goods is greater than the benefit associated with the extra public goods.

Cost-benefit analysis, however, can indicate more than whether a public program is worth doing. It can also help the government decide on the extent to which a project should

cost-benefit analysis A comparison of the marginal costs of a government project or program with the marginal benefits to decide whether or not to employ resources in that project or program and to what extent.

TABLE 5.4 **Cost-Benefit Analysis for a National Highway Construction Project (in Billions)**

(1) Plan	(2) Total Cost of Project	(3) Marginal Cost	(4) Total Benefit	(5) Marginal Benefit	(6) Net Benefit (4) − (2)
No new construction	$ 0		$ 0		$ 0
		$ 4		$ 5	
A: Widen existing highways	4		5		1
		6		8	
B: New 2-lane highways	10		13		3
		8		10	
C: New 4-lane highways	18		23		5
		10		3	
D: New 6-lane highways	28		26		−2

be pursued. Real economic questions cannot usually be answered simply by "yes" or "no" but, rather, involve questions such as "how much" or "how little."

Roads and highways can be run privately, as excludability is possible with toll gates. However, the federal highway system is almost entirely nonexclusive because anyone with a car can get on and off most federal highways without restriction anytime they want. Federal highways therefore satisfy one characteristic of a public good: nonexcludability. The other characteristic, nonrivalry, is also satisfied by the the fact that unless a highway is already extremely crowded, one person's driving on the highway does not preclude another person's driving on the highway. Thus, the federal highway system is effectively a public good. This leads us to ask: Should the federal government expand the federal highway system? If so, what is the proper size or scope for the overall project?

Table 5.4 lists a series of increasingly ambitious and increasingly costly highway projects: widening existing two-lane highways; building new two-lane highways; building new four-lane highways; building new six-lane highways. The extent to which government should undertake highway construction depends on the costs and benefits. The costs are largely the costs of constructing and maintaining the highways; the benefits are improved flows of people and goods throughout the nation.

The table shows that total annual benefit (column 4) exceeds total annual cost (column 2) for plans A, B, and C, indicating that some highway construction is economically justifiable. We see this directly in column 6, where total costs (column 2) are subtracted from total annual benefits (column 4). Net benefits are positive for plans A, B, and C. Plan D is not economically justifiable because net benefits are negative.

But the question of optimal size or scope for this project remains. Comparing the marginal cost (the change in total cost) and the marginal benefit (the change in total benefit) relating to each plan determines the answer. The guideline is well known to you from previous discussions: Increase an activity, project, or output as long as the marginal benefit (column 5) exceeds the marginal cost (column 3). Stop the activity at, or as close as possible to, the point at which the marginal benefit equals the marginal cost. Do not undertake a project for which marginal cost exceeds marginal benefit.

In this case plan C (building new four-lane highways) is the best plan. Plans A and B are too modest; the marginal benefits exceed the marginal costs. Plan D's marginal cost ($10 billion) exceeds the marginal benefit ($3 billion) and therefore cannot be justified; it overallocates resources to the project. Plan C is closest to the theoretical optimum because its marginal benefit ($10 billion) still exceeds marginal cost ($8 billion) but approaches the MB = MC (or MC = MB) ideal.

This marginal-cost–marginal-benefit rule tells government which plan provides the maximum excess of total benefits over total costs or, in other words, the plan that provides society with the maximum net benefit. You can confirm directly in column 6 that the maximum net benefit ($5 billion) is associated with plan C.

QUESTION: Do you think it is generally easier to measure the costs of public goods or their benefits? Explain your reasoning.

Externalities

In addition to providing public goods, governments also can improve the allocation of resources in the economy by correcting for market failures caused by externalities. An *externality* occurs when some of the costs or the benefits of a good or service are passed onto or "spill over" to someone other than the immediate buyer or seller. Such spillovers are called externalities because they are benefits or costs that accrue to some third party that is external to the market transaction.

Negative Externalities

Production or consumption costs inflicted on a third party without compensation are called **negative externalities** or *spillover costs*. Environmental pollution is an example. When a chemical manufacturer or a meatpacking plant dumps its wastes into a lake or river, water users such as swimmers, fishers, and boaters suffer negative externalities. When a petroleum refinery pollutes the air with smoke or a paper mill creates obnoxious odors, the community experiences negative externalities for which it is not compensated.

Figure 5.5a illustrates how negative externalities affect the allocation of resources. When producers shift some of their costs onto the community as spillover costs, producers' marginal costs are lower than they would be if they had to pay for these costs. So their supply curves do not include or "capture" all the costs legitimately associated with the production of their goods. A supply curve such as S in Figure 5.5a therefore understates the total cost of production for a polluting firm. Its supply curve lies to the right of (or below) the full-cost supply curve S_t which would include the negative externality. Through polluting and thus transferring cost to society, the firm enjoys lower production costs and has the supply curve S.

The resource allocation outcome is shown in Figure 5.5a, where equilibrium output Q_e is larger than the optimal output Q_o. This is a market failure because resources are *overallocated* to the production of this commodity; too many units of it are produced. In fact, there is a net loss to society for every unit from Q_0 to Q_e because, for those units, the supply curve that accounts for all costs, S_t, lies above the demand curve. Therefore, MC exceeds MB for those units. The resources that went into producing those units should have been used elsewhere in the economy to produce other things.

In terms of our previous analysis, the negative externality results in an efficiency loss represented by triangle *abc*.

Positive Externalities

Sometimes spillovers appear as external benefits. The production or consumption of certain goods and services may confer spillover or external benefits on third parties or on the community at large without compensating payment. Immunization against measles and

negative externalities Spillover production or consumption costs imposed on third parties without compensation to them.

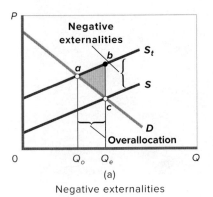

(a)
Negative externalities

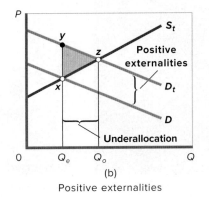

(b)
Positive externalities

FIGURE 5.5 Negative externalities and positive externalities. (a) With negative externalities borne by society, the producers' supply curve S is to the right of (below) the total-cost supply curve S_t. Consequently, the equilibrium output Q_e is greater than the optimal output Q_o, and the efficiency loss is *abc*. (b) When positive externalities accrue to society, the market demand curve D is to the left of (below) the total-benefit demand curve D_t. As a result, the equilibrium output Q_e is less than the optimal output Q_o, and the efficiency loss is *xyz*.

positive externalities Spillover production or consumption benefits conferred on third parties without compensation from them.

polio results in direct benefits to the immediate consumer of those vaccines. But it also results in widespread substantial positive externalities to the entire community.

Education is another example of **positive externalities.** Education benefits individual consumers: Better-educated people generally achieve higher incomes than less-well-educated people. But education also benefits society through a more versatile and more productive labor force, on the one hand, and smaller outlays for crime prevention, law enforcement, and welfare programs, on the other.

Figure 5.5b shows the impact of positive externalities on resource allocation. When positive externalities occur, the market demand curve D lies to the left of (or below) the full-benefits demand curve, D_t. That is, D does not include the positive externalities of the product, whereas D_t does. Consider inoculations against a communicable disease. When John gets vaccinated against a disease, this is a benefit not only to himself (because he can no longer contract the disease) but also to everyone else around him (because they know that in the future he will never be able to infect them). These other people would presumably be willing to pay some positive amount of money for the benefit they receive when John is vaccinated. But because there is no way to make them pay, the market demand curve reflects only the direct, private benefits to John. It does not reflect the positive externalities—the spillover benefits—to those around John, which are included in D_t.

The outcome, as shown in Figure 5.5b, is that the equilibrium output Q_e is less than the optimal output Q_o. The market fails to produce enough vaccinations, and resources are *underallocated* to this product. The underproduction implies that society is missing out on potential net benefits. For every unit from Q_e to Q_o, the demand curve that accounts for all benefits, D_t, lies above the supply curve that accounts for all costs—including the opportunity cost of producing other items with the resources that would be needed to produce these units. Therefore, MB exceeds MC for each of these units and society should redeploy some of its resources away from the production of other things in order to produce these units that generate net benefits.

In terms of our previous analysis, the positive externality results in an efficiency loss represented by triangle *xyz*.

Economists have explored several approaches to the problems of negative and positive externalities. Sometimes private parties work out their own solutions to externality problems; other times government intervention is warranted.

PHOTO OP   Positive and Negative Consumption Externalities

Homeowners create positive externalities when they put up nice holiday lighting displays. Not only does the homeowner benefit from consuming the sight, but so do people who pass by the house. In contrast, when people consume roads (drive) during rush hour, it creates a negative externality. This takes the form of traffic congestion, imposing time and fuel costs on other drivers.

©Design Pics/Corey Hochachka

©Shutterstock/XXLPhoto

ILLUSTRATING THE IDEA

Beekeepers and the Coase Theorem

Economist Ronald Coase received the Nobel Prize for his so-called **Coase theorem,** which pointed out that under the right conditions, private individuals could often negotiate their own mutually agreeable solutions to externality problems through *private bargaining* without the need for government interventions like pollution taxes.

This is a very important insight because it means that we shouldn't automatically call for government intervention every time we see a potential externality problem. Consider the positive externalities that bees provide by pollinating farmers' crops. Should we assume that beekeeping will be underprovided unless the government intervenes with, for instance, subsidies to encourage more hives and hence more pollination?

As it turns out, no. Research has shown that farmers and beekeepers long ago used private bargaining to develop customs and payment systems that avoid free riding by farmers and encourage beekeepers to keep the optimal number of hives. Free riding is avoided by the custom that all farmers in an area simultaneously hire beekeepers to provide bees to pollinate their crops. And farmers always pay the beekeepers for their pollination services because if they didn't, then no beekeeper would ever work with them in the future—a situation that would lead to massively reduced crop yields due to a lack of pollination.

The "Fable of the Bees" is a good reminder that it is a fallacy to assume that the government must always get involved to remedy externalities. In many cases, the private sector can solve both positive and negative externality problems on its own.

Coase theorem The idea, first stated by economist Ronald Coase, that externality problems may be resolved through private negotiations of the affected parties.

QUESTIONS: Suppose that in a town a large number of home gardeners need pollination services for their fruit and vegetable crops, but none can individually afford to pay a professional beekeeper. How might that affect the contracting of beekeepers? Would it suggest a possible role for government?

Government Intervention

Government intervention may be called upon to achieve economic efficiency when externalities affect large numbers of people or when community interests are at stake. Government can use direct controls and taxes to counter negative externalities (spillover costs); it may provide subsidies or public goods to deal with positive externalities (spillover benefits).

Direct Controls   The direct way to reduce negative externalities from a certain activity is to pass legislation limiting that activity. Such direct controls force the offending firms to incur the actual costs of the offending activity. To date, this approach has dominated public policy in the United States. Clean-air legislation has created uniform emission standards—limits on allowable pollution—and has forced factories and businesses to install "maximum achievable control technology" to reduce emissions of toxic chemicals. It has also mandated reductions in (1) tailpipe emissions from automobiles, (2) use of chlorofluorocarbons (CFCs) that deplete the ozone layer, and (3) emissions of sulfur dioxide by coal-burning utilities to prevent the acid-rain destruction of lakes and forests. Also, clean-water legislation has limited the amounts of heavy metals and detergents that firms can discharge into rivers and bays. Toxic-waste laws dictate special procedures and dump sites for disposing of contaminated soil and solvents. Violating these laws means fines and, in some cases, imprisonment.

FIGURE 5.6 **Correcting for negative externalities.** (a) Negative externalities (spillover costs) result in an overallocation of resources. (b) Government can correct this overallocation in two ways: (1) using direct controls, which would shift the supply curve from S to S_t and reduce output from Q_e to Q_o, or (2) imposing a specific tax T, which would also shift the supply curve from S to S_t, eliminating the overallocation of resources and thus the efficiency loss.

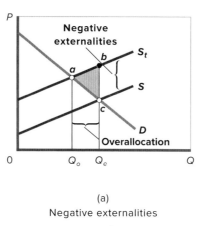

(a)
Negative externalities

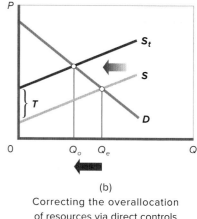

(b)
Correcting the overallocation
of resources via direct controls
or via a tax

Direct controls raise the marginal cost of production because the firms must operate and maintain pollution-control equipment. The supply curve S in Figure 5.6b, which does not reflect the negative externalities, shifts leftward (upward) to the full-cost supply curve, S_t. Product price increases, equilibrium output falls from Q_e to Q_o, and the initial overallocation of resources shown in Figure 5.6a is corrected. Observe that the efficiency loss shown by triangle abc in Figure 5.6a disappears after the overallocation is corrected in Figure 5.6b.

Pigovian Taxes

Pigovian taxes A tax or charge levied on the production of a product that generates negative externalities. If set correctly, the tax will precisely offset the overallocation (overproduction) generated by the negative externality.

A second policy approach to negative externalities is for government to levy taxes or charges specifically on the related good. These targeted tax assessments are often referred to as **Pigovian taxes,** in honor of A. C. Pigou, the first economist to study externalities. For example, the government has placed a manufacturing excise tax on CFCs, which deplete the stratospheric ozone layer protecting the earth from excessive solar ultraviolet radiation. Facing such an excise tax, manufacturers must decide whether to pay the tax or expend additional funds to purchase or develop substitute products. In either case, the tax raises the marginal cost of producing CFCs, shifting the private supply curve for this product leftward (or upward).

In Figure 5.6b, a tax equal to T per unit increases the firm's marginal cost, shifting the supply curve from S to S_t. The equilibrium price rises, and the equilibrium output declines from Q_e to the economically efficient level Q_o. The tax thus eliminates the initial overallocation of resources, and therefore the efficiency loss, associated with the negative externality.

Subsidies and Government Provision

What policies might be useful in dealing with *positive* externalities? Where positive externalities are large and diffuse, as in our earlier example of inoculations, government has three options for correcting the underallocation of resources:

- *Subsidies to buyers*   Figure 5.7a again shows the supply-demand situation for positive externalities. Government could correct the underallocation of resources, for example, to inoculations, by subsidizing consumers of the product. It could give each new mother in the United States a discount coupon to be used to obtain a series of inoculations for her child. The coupon would reduce the "price" to the mother by, say, 50 percent. As shown in Figure 5.7b, this program would shift the demand curve for inoculations from too low D to the appropriate D_t. The number of inoculations would rise from Q_e to the economically optimal Q_o, eliminating the underallocation of resources and efficiency loss shown in Figure 5.7a.

- *Subsidies to producers*   A subsidy to producers is a tax in reverse. Taxes impose an extra cost on producers, while subsidies reduce producers' costs. As shown in

FIGURE 5.7 **Correcting for positive externalities.** (a) Positive externalities (spillover benefits) result in an underallocation of resources. (b) Government can correct this underallocation through a subsidy to consumers, which shifts market demand from D to D_t and increases output from Q_e to Q_o. (c) Alternatively, government can eliminate the underallocation by giving producers a subsidy of U, which shifts their supply curve from S_t to S_t', increasing output from Q_e to Q_o.

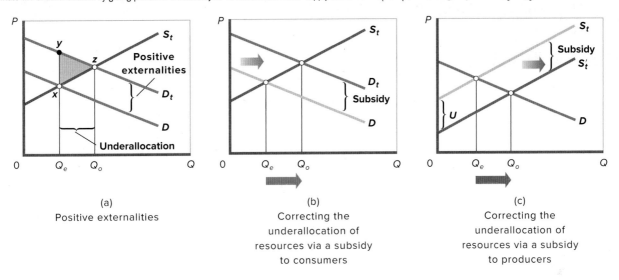

(a)
Positive externalities

(b)
Correcting the
underallocation of
resources via a subsidy
to consumers

(c)
Correcting the
underallocation of
resources via a subsidy
to producers

Figure 5.7c, a subsidy of U per inoculation to physicians and medical clinics would reduce their marginal costs and shift their supply curve rightward from S_t to S_t'. The output of inoculations would increase from Q_e to the optimal level Q_o, correcting the underallocation of resources and efficiency loss shown in Figure 5.7a.

- *Government provision* Finally, where positive externalities are extremely large, the government may decide to provide the product for free or for a minimal charge. Government provides many goods that could be produced and delivered in such a way that exclusion would be possible. Such goods, called **quasi-public goods,** include education, streets and highways, police and fire protection, libraries and museums, preventive medicine, and sewage disposal. They could all be priced and provided by private firms through the market system because the free-rider problem would be minimal. But because spillover benefits extend well beyond the individual buyer, the market system may underproduce them. Therefore, government often provides quasi-public goods.

Table 5.5 lists several methods for correcting externalities, including those we have discussed thus far.

quasi-public good A good or service to which excludability could apply but that has such a large spillover benefit that government sponsors its production to prevent an underallocation of resources.

TABLE 5.5 **Methods for Dealing with Externalities**

Problem	Resource Allocation Outcome	Ways to Correct
Negative externalities (spillover costs)	Overproduction of output and therefore overallocation of resources	1. Private bargaining 2. Liability rules and lawsuits 3. Tax on producers 4. Direct controls 5. Market for externality rights
Positive externalities (spillover benefits)	Underproduction of output and therefore underallocation of resources	1. Private bargaining 2. Subsidy to consumers 3. Subsidy to producers 4. Government provision

APPLYING THE ANALYSIS

Lojack: A Case of Positive Externalities

Economists Ayres and Levitt point out that some forms of private crime prevention simply redistribute crime rather than reduce it. For example, car alarm systems that have red blinking warning lights may simply divert professional auto thieves to vehicles that do not have such lights and alarms. The owner of a car with such an alarm system benefits through reduced likelihood of theft but imposes a cost on other car owners who do not have such alarms. Their cars are more likely to be targeted for theft by thieves because other cars have visible security systems.

In contrast, some private crime prevention measures actually reduce crime, rather than simply redistribute it. One such measure is installation of a Lojack (or some similar) car retrieval system. Lojack is a tiny radio transmitter that is hidden in one of many possible places within the car. When an owner reports a stolen car, the police can remotely activate the transmitter. Police then can determine the car's precise location and track its subsequent movements.

The owner of the car benefits because the 95 percent retrieval rate on cars with the Lojack system is higher than the 60 percent retrieval rate for cars without the system. But according to a study by Ayres and Levitt, the benefit to the car owner is only 10 percent of the total benefit. Ninety percent of the total benefit is external; it is a spillover benefit to other car owners in the community.

There are two sources of this positive externality. First, the presence of the Lojack device sometimes enables police to intercept the car while the thief is still driving it. For example, in California the arrest rate for cars with Lojack was three times greater than that for cars without it. The arrest puts the car thief out of commission for a time and thus reduces subsequent car thefts in the community. Second, and far more important, the device enables police to trace cars to "chop shops," where crooks disassemble cars for resale of the parts. When police raid the chop shop, they put the entire theft ring out of business. In Los Angeles alone, Lojack has eliminated 45 chop shops in just a few years. The purging of the chop shop and theft ring reduces auto theft in the community. So auto owners who do not have Lojack devices in their cars benefit from car owners who do. Ayres and Levitt estimate the *marginal social benefit* of Lojack—the marginal benefit to the Lojack car owner *plus* the spillover benefit to other car owners—is 15 times greater than the marginal cost of the device.

We saw in Figure 5.7a that the existence of positive externalities causes an insufficient quantity of a product and thus an underallocation of scarce resources to its production. The two general ways to correct the outcome are to subsidize the consumer, as shown in Figure 5.7b, or to subsidize the producer, as shown in Figure 5.7c. Currently, there is only one form of government intervention in place: state-mandated insurance discounts for people who install auto retrieval systems such as Lojack. In effect, those discounts on insurance premiums subsidize the consumer by lowering the "price" of the system to consumers. The lower price raises the number of systems installed. But on the basis of their research, Ayres and Levitt contend that the current levels of insurance discounts are far too small to correct the underallocation that results from the positive externalities created by Lojack.

QUESTION: Other than mandating lower insurance premiums for Lojack users, what might government do to increase the use of Lojack devices in automobiles?

Source: Based on Ian Ayres and Steven D. Levitt, "Measuring Positive Externalities from Unobservable Victim Precaution: An Empirical Analysis of Lojack," *Quarterly Journal of Economics*, February 1998, pp. 43–77. The authors point out that Lojack did not fund their work; nor do they have any financial stake in Lojack.

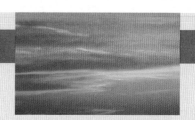

APPLYING THE ANALYSIS

Reducing Greenhouse Gases

Climate change, to the extent it is caused by human-generated greenhouse gases, is a negative externality problem. Suggested policies to reduce carbon emissions, a major greenhouse gas, include carbon taxes and a cap-and-trade program.

A tax imposed on each ton of carbon emitted would increase the marginal cost of production to all firms that release carbon into the air through their production processes. Because of the added marginal cost, the supply curves within affected markets would shift to the left (as illustrated by the move from S to S_t in Figure 5.5a). The reduced market supply would increase equilibrium price and reduce equilibrium quantity. With the lower output, carbon emissions in these industries would fall.

A carbon tax would require minimum government interference in the economy once the tax was in place. The federal government could direct the revenues from the tax to research on cleaner production technologies or simply use the new revenues to reduce other taxes. But there would be no free lunch here: According to a 2007 study, a proposed $15 tax per ton of carbon dioxide emitted would add an estimated 14 cents to a gallon of gasoline, 1.63 cents to a kilowatt hour of electricity, $28.50 to a ton of coal, and $6.48 to a barrel of crude oil.

An alternative approach is a cap-and-trade program, which creates a market for the right to discharge a particular pollutant into the air or water. These rights, allocated in the form of a fixed quantity of pollution permits, can be bought or sold in a permit market. Each permit specifies the amount of the pollutant that can be emitted. The decision to buy or sell permits depends on how costly it is for a company to reduce its pollution relative to the market price of the permits. Permit buyers, for example, are those whose costs to reduce emissions exceed the costs of the permits that allow them to pollute.

As it currently does with sulfur dioxide emissions, the federal government could place a cap or lid on total carbon emissions and then either hand out emission rights or auction them off. In ways previously discussed, the cap-and-trade program would reduce society's overall cost of lowering carbon emissions. In that regard, it would be more efficient than direct controls requiring each producer of greenhouse gas to reduce emissions by a fixed percentage amount. Existing cap-and-trade programs—including current European markets for carbon certificates—prove that this program can work. But such programs require considerable government oversight and enforcement of the rules.

QUESTION: Why would rising prices of emission rights increase the incentive for firms to use cleaner production methods?

Society's Optimal Amount of Externality Reduction

Negative externalities such as pollution reduce the utility of those affected. These spillovers are not economic goods but economic "bads." If something is bad, shouldn't society eliminate it? Why should society allow firms or municipalities to discharge *any* impure waste into public waterways or to emit *any* pollution into the air?

Economists answer these questions by pointing out that reducing pollution and negative externalities is not free. There are costs as well as benefits to reducing pollution. As a result, the correct question to ask when it comes to cleaning up negative externalities is not, "Do we pollute a lot or pollute zero?" That is an all-or-nothing question that ignores marginal costs and marginal benefits. Instead, the correct question is, "What is the optimal amount to clean up—the amount that equalizes the marginal cost of cleaning up with the marginal benefit of a cleaner environment?"

Reducing a negative externality has a "price." Society must decide how much of a reduction it wants to "buy." High costs may mean that totally eliminating pollution might not be desirable, even if it is technologically feasible. Because of the law of diminishing returns, cleaning up the second 10 percent of pollutants from an industrial smokestack normally is more costly than cleaning up the first 10 percent. Eliminating the third 10 percent is more costly than cleaning up the second 10 percent, and so on. Therefore, cleaning up the last 10 percent of pollutants is the most costly reduction of all.

The marginal cost (MC) to the firm and hence to society—the opportunity cost of the extra resources used—rises as pollution is reduced more and more. At some point MC may rise so high that it exceeds society's marginal benefit (MB) of further pollution abatement (reduction). Additional actions to reduce pollution will therefore lower society's well-being; total cost will rise more than total benefit.

MC, MB, and Equilibrium Quantity
Figure 5.8 shows both the rising marginal-cost curve, MC, for pollution reduction and the downsloping marginal-benefit curve, MB, for pollution reduction. MB slopes downward because of the law of diminishing marginal utility: The more pollution reduction society accomplishes, the lower the utility (and benefit) of the next unit of pollution reduction.

The **optimal reduction of an externality** occurs when society's marginal cost and marginal benefit of reducing that externality are equal (MC = MB). In Figure 5.8 this optimal amount of pollution abatement is Q_1 units. When MB exceeds MC, additional abatement moves society toward economic efficiency; the added benefit of cleaner air or water exceeds the benefit of any alternative use of the required resources. When MC exceeds MB, additional abatement reduces economic efficiency; there would be greater benefits from using resources in some other way than to further reduce pollution.

optimal reduction of an externality
The reduction of a negative externality such as pollution to a level at which the marginal benefit and marginal cost of reduction are equal.

FIGURE 5.8 Society's optimal amount of pollution abatement. The optimal amount of externality reduction—in this case, pollution abatement—occurs at Q_1, where society's marginal cost MC and marginal benefit MB of reducing the spillover are equal.

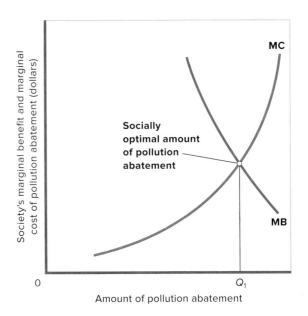

In reality, it is difficult to measure the marginal costs and benefits of pollution control. Figure 5.8 demonstrates that some pollution may be economically efficient. This is so not because pollution is desirable but because beyond some level of control, further abatement may reduce society's net well-being. As an example, it would cost the government billions of dollars to clean up every last piece of litter in America. Thus, it would be better to tolerate some trash blowing around if the money saved by picking up less trash would yield larger net benefits when spent on other things.

Shifts in Locations of the Curves   The locations of the marginal-cost and marginal-benefit curves in Figure 5.8 are not forever fixed. They can, and probably do, shift over time. For example, suppose that the technology of pollution-control equipment improved noticeably. We would expect the cost of pollution abatement to fall, society's MC curve to shift rightward, and the optimal level of abatement to rise. Or suppose that society were to decide that it wanted cleaner air and water because of new information about the adverse health effects of pollution. The MB curve in Figure 5.8 would shift rightward, and the optimal level of pollution control would increase beyond Q_1. Test your understanding of these statements by drawing the new MC and MB curves in Figure 5.8.

Government's Role in the Economy

Along with providing public goods and correcting externalities, government's economic role includes setting the rules and regulations for the economy, redistributing income when desirable, and taking macroeconomic actions to stabilize the economy.

Market failures can be used to justify government interventions in the economy. The inability of private-sector firms to break even when attempting to provide public goods and the over- and underproduction problems caused by positive and negative externalities mean that government can have an important role to play if society's resources are to be efficiently allocated to the goods and services that people most highly desire.

Correcting for market failures is not, however, an easy task. To begin with, government officials must correctly identify the existence and the cause of any given market failure. That by itself may be difficult, time-consuming, and costly. But even if a market failure is correctly identified and diagnosed, government may still fail to take appropriate corrective action due to the fact that government undertakes its economic role in the context of politics.

To serve the public, politicians need to get elected. To stay elected, officials (presidents, senators, representatives, mayors, council members, school board members) need to satisfy their particular constituencies. At best, the political realities complicate government's role in the economy; at worst, they produce undesirable economic outcomes.

In the political context, overregulation can occur in some cases; underregulation, in others. Some public goods and quasi-public goods can be produced not because their benefits exceed their costs but because their benefits accrue to firms located in states served by powerful elected officials. Inefficiency can easily creep into government activities because of the lack of a profit incentive to hold down costs. Policies to correct negative externalities can be politically blocked by the very parties that are producing the spillovers. In short, the economic role of government, although critical to a well-functioning economy, is not always perfectly carried out.

Economists use the term "government failure" to describe economically inefficient outcomes caused by shortcomings in the public sector.

SUMMARY

LO5.1 Differentiate between demand-side market failures and supply-side market failures.

A market failure happens in a particular market when the market produces an equilibrium level of output that either overallocates or underallocates resources to the product being traded in the market. In competitive markets that feature many buyers and many sellers, market failures can be divided into two types: Demand-side market failures occur when demand curves do not reflect consumers' full willingness to pay; supply-side market failures occur when supply curves do not reflect all production costs, including those that may be borne by third parties.

Properly functioning competitive markets ensure that private goods are (a) available, (b) produced in the least costly way, and (c) produced and sold in the "right" amounts.

LO5.2 Explain consumer surplus and producer surplus, and discuss how properly functioning markets maximize their sum while optimally allocating resources.

Consumer surplus is the difference between the maximum price that a consumer is willing to pay for a product and the lower price actually paid; producer surplus is the difference between the minimum price that a producer is willing to accept for a product and the higher price actually received. Collectively, consumer surplus is represented by the triangle under the demand curve and above the actual price, whereas producer surplus is shown by the triangle above the supply curve and below the actual price.

Graphically, the combined amount of producer and consumer surplus is represented by the triangle to the left of the intersection of the supply and demand curves that is below the demand curve and above the supply curve. At the equilibrium price and quantity in competitive markets, marginal benefit equals marginal cost, maximum willingness to pay equals minimum acceptable price, and the combined amount of consumer surplus and producer surplus is maximized.

Output levels that are either less than or greater than the equilibrium output create efficiency losses, also called deadweight losses. These losses are reductions in the combined amount of consumer surplus and producer surplus. Underproduction creates efficiency losses because output is not being produced for which maximum willingness to pay exceeds minimum acceptable price. Overproduction creates efficiency losses because output is being produced for which minimum acceptable price exceeds maximum willingness to pay.

LO5.3 Identify how public goods are distinguished from private goods, and explain the method for determining the optimal quantity of a public good.

Public goods are distinguished from private goods. Private goods are characterized by rivalry (in consumption) and excludability. One person's purchase and consumption of a private good precludes others from also buying and consuming it. Producers can exclude nonpayers (free riders) from receiving the benefits. In contrast, public goods are characterized by nonrivalry (in consumption) and nonexcludability. Public goods are not profitable to private firms because nonpayers (free riders) can obtain and consume those goods without paying. Government can, however, provide desirable public goods, financing them through taxation.

The collective demand schedule for a particular public good is found by summing the prices that each individual is willing to pay for an additional unit. The optimal quantity of a public good occurs where the society's willingness to pay for the last unit—the marginal benefit of the good—equals the marginal cost of the good.

LO5.4 Explain how positive and negative externalities cause under- and overallocations of resources, and how they might be corrected.

Externalities cause the output of certain goods to vary from society's optimal output. Negative externalities (spillover costs) result in an overallocation of resources to a particular product. Positive externalities (spillover benefits) are accompanied by an underallocation of resources to a particular product.

Direct controls and Pigovian taxes can improve resource allocation in situations where negative externalities affect many people and community resources. Both direct controls (for example, smokestack emission standards) and Pigovian taxes (for example, taxes on firms producing toxic chemicals) increase production costs and hence product price. As product price rises, the externality, overallocation of resources, and efficiency loss are reduced since less of the output is produced.

Government can correct the underallocation of resources and therefore the efficiency losses that result from positive externalities in a particular market either by subsidizing consumers (which increases market demand) or by subsidizing producers (which increases market supply). Such subsidies increase the equilibrium output, reducing or eliminating the positive externality and consequent underallocation of resources and efficiency loss.

The Coase theorem suggests that under the right circumstances private bargaining can solve externality problems. Thus, government intervention is not always needed to deal with externality problems.

LO5.5 Show why we normally won't want to pay what it would cost to eliminate every last bit of a negative externality.

The socially optimal amount of externality abatement occurs where society's marginal cost and marginal benefit of reducing the externality are equal. With pollution, for example, this optimal amount of pollution abatement is likely to be less than a 100 percent reduction. Changes in technology or changes in society's attitudes toward pollution can affect the optimal amount of pollution abatement.

Market failures present government with opportunities to improve the allocation of society's resources and thereby enhance society's total well-being. But even when government correctly identifies the existence and cause of a market failure, political pressures may make it difficult or impossible for government officials to implement a proper solution.

TERMS AND CONCEPTS

market failures	producer surplus	negative externality
demand-side market failures	efficiency (deadweight) loss	positive externality
supply-side market failures	private goods	Coase theorem
productive efficiency	public goods	Pigovian taxes
allocative efficiency	free-rider problem	quasi-public goods
consumer surplus	cost-benefit analysis	optimal reduction of an externality

QUESTIONS

The following and additional problems can be found in ■ **connect**

1. Explain the two causes of market failures. Given their definitions, could a market be affected by both types of market failures simultaneously? **LO5.1**

2. Draw a supply and demand graph and identify the areas of consumer surplus and producer surplus. Given the demand curve, what impact will an increase in supply have on the amount of consumer surplus shown in your diagram? Explain why. **LO5.2**

3. Use the ideas of consumer surplus and producer surplus to explain why economists say competitive markets are efficient. Why are below- or above-equilibrium levels of output inefficient, according to these two sets of ideas? **LO5.2**

4. Contrast the characteristics of public goods with those of private goods. Why won't private firms produce public goods? **LO5.3**

5. Draw a production possibilities curve with public goods on the vertical axis and private goods on the horizontal axis. Assuming the economy is initially operating on the curve, indicate how the production of public goods might be increased. How might the output of public goods be increased if the economy is initially operating at a point inside the curve? **LO5.3**

6. Use the distinction between the characteristics of private and public goods to determine whether the following should be produced through the market system or provided by government: (a) French fries, (b) airport screening, (c) court systems, (d) mail delivery, and (e) medical care. State why you answered as you did in each case. **LO5.3**

7. What divergences arise between equilibrium output and efficient output when (a) negative externalities and (b) positive externalities are present? How might government correct these divergences? Cite an example (other than the text examples) of an external cost and an external benefit. **LO5.4**

8. Why are spillover costs and spillover benefits also called negative and positive externalities? Show graphically how a tax can correct for a negative externality and how a subsidy to producers can correct for a positive externality. How does a subsidy to consumers differ from a subsidy to producers in correcting for a positive externality? **LO5.4**

9. An apple grower's orchard provides nectar to a neighbor's bees, while the beekeeper's bees help the apple grower by pollinating his apple blossoms. Use Figure 5.5b to explain why this situation of dual positive externalities might lead to an underallocation of resources to both apple growing and beekeeping. How might this underallocation get resolved via the means suggested by the Coase theorem? **LO5.4**

10. Explain the following statement, using the MB curve in Figure 5.8 to illustrate: "The optimal amount of pollution abatement for some substances, say, dirty water from storm drains, is very low; the optimal amount of abatement for other substances, say, cyanide poison, is close to 100 percent." **LO5.5**

11. Explain why zoning laws, which allow certain land uses only in specific locations, might be justified in dealing with a problem of negative externalities. Explain why in areas where buildings sit close together tax breaks to property owners for installing extra fire prevention equipment might be justified in view of positive externalities. Explain why excise taxes on beer might be justified in dealing with a problem of external costs. **LO5.5**

PROBLEMS

1. Refer to Table 5.1. If the six people listed in the table are the only consumers in the market and the equilibrium price is $11 (not the $8 shown), how much consumer surplus will the market generate? **LO5.2**

2. Refer to Table 5.2. If the six people listed in the table are the only producers in the market and the equilibrium price is $6 (not the $8 shown), how much producer surplus will the market generate? **LO5.2**

10,18,5

3. Look at Tables 5.1 and 5.2 together. What is the total surplus if Bob buys a unit from Carlos? If Barb buys a unit from Courtney? If Bob buys a unit from Chad? If you match up pairs of buyers and sellers so as to maximize the total surplus of all transactions, what is the largest total surplus that can be achieved? LO5.2

4. **ADVANCED ANALYSIS** Assume the following values for Figures 5.4a and 5.4b. $Q_1 = 20$ bags. $Q_2 = 15$ bags. $Q_3 = 27$ bags. The market equilibrium price is $45 per bag. The price at a is $85 per bag. The price at c is $5 per bag. The price at f is $59 per bag. The price at g is $31 per bag. Apply the formula for the area of a triangle (Area = ½ × Base × Height) to answer the following questions. LO5.2

   a. What is the dollar value of the total surplus (producer surplus plus consumer surplus) when the allocatively efficient output level is being produced? How large is the dollar value of the consumer surplus at that output level?

   b. What is the dollar value of the deadweight loss when output level Q_2 is being produced? What is the total surplus when output level Q_2 is being produced?

   c. What is the dollar value of the deadweight loss when output level Q_3 is produced? What is the dollar value of the total surplus when output level Q_3 is produced?

5. The accompanying table relating to a public good provides information on the prices Young and Zorn are willing to pay for various quantities of that public good. These two people are the only members of society. Determine the price that society is willing to pay for the public good at each quantity of output. If the government's marginal cost of providing this public good is constant at $7, how many units of the public good should government provide? LO5.3

Young		Zorn		Society	
P	Q_d	P	Q_d	P	Q_d
$8	0	$8	1	$ 13	1
7	0	7	2	11	2
6	0	6	3	9	3
5	1	5	4	7	4
4	2	4	5	5	5
3	3	3	6	3	6
2	4	2	7	2	7
1	5	1	8	1	8

6. The table below shows the total costs and total benefits in billions for four different antipollution programs of increasing scope. Use cost-benefit analysis to determine which program should be undertaken. LO5.3

Program	Total Cost	Total Benefit
A	$ 3	$ 7
B	7	12
C	12	16
D	18	19

7. On the basis of the three individual demand schedules in the following table, assuming these three people are the only ones in the society, determine (a) the market demand schedule on the assumption that the good is a private good and (b) the collective demand schedule on the assumption that the good is a public good. LO5.3

P	$Q_d(D_1)$	$Q_d(D_2)$	$Q_d(D_3)$
$8	0	1	0
7	0	2	0
6	0	3	1
5	1	4	2
4	2	5	3
3	3	6	4
2	4	7	5
1	5	8	6

8. Use your demand schedule for a public good, determined in problem 7, and the following supply schedule to ascertain the optimal quantity of this public good. LO5.3

P	Q_s
$19	10
16	8
13	6
10	4
7	2
4	1

9. Look at Tables 5.1 and 5.2, which show, respectively, the willingness to pay and willingness to accept of buyers and sellers of bags of oranges. For the following questions, assume that the equilibrium price and quantity will depend on the indicated changes in supply and demand. Assume that the only market participants are those listed by name in the two tables. LO5.4

   a. What are the equilibrium price and quantity for the data displayed in the two tables?

   b. What if, instead of bags of oranges, the data in the two tables dealt with a public good like fireworks displays? If all the buyers free ride, what will be the quantity supplied by private sellers?

   c. Assume that we are back to talking about bags of oranges (a private good), but that the government has decided that tossed orange peels impose a negative externality on the public that must be rectified by imposing a $2-per-bag tax on sellers. What are the new equilibrium price and quantity? If the new equilibrium quantity is the optimal quantity, by how many bags were oranges being overproduced before?

PART THREE

Product Markets

3

©Tatiana Belova/Shutterstock

6 Chapter

Businesses and Their Costs

Learning Objectives

LO6.1 Identify features of the corporate form of business organization that have made it so dominant.

LO6.2 Explain why economic costs include both explicit (revealed and expressed) costs and implicit (present but not obvious) costs.

LO6.3 Relate the law of diminishing returns to a firm's short-run production costs.

LO6.4 Describe the distinctions between fixed and variable costs and among total, average, and marginal costs.

LO6.5 Use economies of scale to link a firm's size and its average costs in the long run.

In market economies, a wide variety of businesses produce an even greater variety of goods and services. Each of those businesses needs economic resources in order to produce its product. In obtaining and using resources, a business makes monetary payments to resource owners (for example, workers) and incurs opportunity costs when using resources that it already owns (for example, entrepreneurial talent). Those payments and opportunity costs constitute the firm's *costs of production*.

This chapter describes the U.S. business population and identifies the costs faced by firms in producing products. Then, in the next several chapters, we bring demand, product price, and revenue into the analysis and explain how businesses compare revenues and costs to decide how much to produce. Our ultimate purpose is to show how those comparisons relate to profits, losses, and allocative efficiency.

The Business Population

Like households, businesses are a major element in the circular flow diagram that we discussed in Chapter 2. In discussing businesses, it will be useful to distinguish among a plant, a firm, and an industry:

- A *plant* is an establishment—a factory, farm, mine, store, website, or warehouse—that performs one or more functions in fabricating and distributing goods and services.
- A *firm* is an organization that employs resources to produce goods and services for profit and operates one or more plants.
- An *industry* is a group of firms that produce the same, or similar, products.

The organizational structures of firms are often complex and varied. *Multiplant firms* may be organized horizontally, with several plants performing much the same function. Examples are the multiple bottling plants of Coca-Cola and the many individual Walmart stores. Firms also may be *vertically integrated,* meaning they own plants that perform different functions in the various stages of the production process. For example, oil companies such as Shell own oil fields, refineries, and retail gasoline stations. Some firms are *conglomerates*, so named because they have plants that produce products in several separate industries. For example, Pfizer makes prescription medicines (Lipitor, Viagra) but also chewing gum (Trident, Dentyne), razors (Schick), cough drops (Halls), breath mints (Clorets, Certs), and antacids (Rolaids).

The business population ranges from giant corporations such as Walmart, Exxon, and IBM, with hundreds of thousands of employees and billions of dollars of annual sales, to neighborhood specialty shops with one or two employees and daily sales of only a few hundred dollars. As shown in Figure 2.3, only 18 percent of U.S. firms are corporations, yet they account for 82 percent of all sales (output).

Advantages of Corporations

Certain advantages of the corporate form of business enterprise have catapulted it into a dominant sales and profit position in the United States. The corporation is by far the most effective form of business organization for raising money to finance the expansion of its facilities and capabilities. The corporation employs unique methods of finance—the selling of stocks and bonds—that enable it to pool the financial resources of large numbers of people.

A common **stock** represents a share in the ownership of a corporation. The purchaser of a stock certificate has the right to vote for corporate officers and to share in dividends. If you buy 1,000 of the 100,000 shares issued by OutTell, Inc. (OT), then you own 1 percent of the company, are entitled to 1 percent of any dividends declared by the board of directors, and control 1 percent of the votes in the annual election of corporate officials.

stock (corporate) An ownership share in a corporation.

In contrast, a corporate **bond** does not bestow any corporate ownership on the purchaser. A bond purchaser is simply lending money to a corporation. A bond is an IOU, in acknowledgment of a loan, whereby the corporation promises to pay the holder a fixed amount set forth on the bond at some specified future date and other fixed amounts (interest payments) every year up to the bond's maturity date. For example, you might purchase a 10-year OutTell bond with a face value of $1,000 and a 5 percent rate of interest. This means that, in exchange for your $1,000, OT promises you a $50 interest payment for each of the next 10 years and then repays your $1,000 principal at the end of that period.

bond A financial device through which a borrower (a firm or government) is obligated to pay the principal and interest on a loan at a specific date in the future.

Financing through sales of stocks and bonds also provides other advantages to those who purchase these *corporate securities.* An individual investor can spread risks by buying the securities of several corporations. And it is usually easy for holders of corporate securities to sell their holdings. Organized stock exchanges and bond markets simplify the transfer of securities from sellers to buyers. This "ease of sale" increases the willingness of savers to make financial investments in corporate securities. Besides, corporations have easier access to bank credit than do other types of business organizations. Corporations are better risks and are more likely to become profitable clients of banks.

limited liability Restriction of the maximum loss to a predetermined amount for the owners (stockholders) of a corporation. The maximum loss is the amount they paid for their shares of stock.

Corporations provide **limited liability** to owners (stockholders), who risk only what they paid for their stock. Their personal assets are not at stake if the corporation defaults on its debts. Creditors can sue the corporation as a legal entity but cannot sue the owners of the corporation as individuals.

Because of their ability to attract financial capital, successful corporations can easily expand the scope of their operations and realize the benefits of expansion. For example, they can take advantage of mass-production technologies and division of labor. A corporation can hire specialists in production, accounting, and marketing functions and thus improve efficiency.

As a legal entity, the corporation has a life independent of its owners and its officers. Legally, at least, corporations are immortal. The transfer of corporate ownership through inheritance or the sale of stock does not disrupt the continuity of the corporation. Corporations have permanence that lends itself to long-range planning and growth.

The Principal-Agent Problem

Many of the world's corporations are extremely large. In 2017, 434 of the world's corporations had annual revenue of more than $25 billion, 181 firms had revenue exceeding $50 billion, and 53 firms had revenue greater than $100 billion. U.S.-based Walmart alone had revenue of over $485 billion in 2017.

principal-agent problem A conflict of interest that occurs when agents (workers or managers) pursue their own objectives to the detriment of the principals' (stockholders') goals.

But large size creates a potential problem. In sole proprietorships and partnerships, the owners of the real and financial assets of the firm enjoy direct control of those assets. But ownership of large corporations is spread over tens or hundreds of thousands of stockholders. The owners of a corporation usually do not manage it—they hire others to do so.

That practice can create a **principal-agent problem.** The *principals* are the stockholders who own the corporation and who hire executives as their *agents* to run the business on their behalf. But the interests of these managers (the agents) and the wishes of the owners (the principals) do not always coincide. The owners typically want maximum company profit and stock price. However, the agents may want the power, prestige, and pay that often accompany control over a large enterprise, independent of its profitability and stock price.

So a conflict of interest may develop. For example, executives may build expensive office buildings, enjoy excessive perks such as corporate jets, and pay too much to acquire other corporations. Consequently, the firm's costs will be excessive, and the firm will fail to maximize profits and stock prices for its owners.

Economic Costs

economic cost A payment that must be made to obtain and retain the services of a resource; the income a firm must provide to a resource supplier to attract the resource away from an alternative use; equal to the quantity of other products that cannot be produced when resources are instead used to make a particular product.

Firms face costs because the resources they need to produce their products are scarce and have alternative uses. Because of scarcity, firms wanting a particular resource have to bid it away from other firms. That process is costly for firms because it requires a payment to the resource owner. This reality causes economists to define **economic cost** as the payment that must be made to obtain and retain the services of a resource. It is the income the firm must provide to resource suppliers to attract resources away from alternative uses.

This section explains how firms incorporate opportunity costs to calculate economic costs. If you need a refresher on opportunity costs, a brief review of the section on opportunity costs in Chapter 1 might be useful before continuing on with the rest of this section.

APPLYING THE ANALYSIS

Unprincipled Agents

In the 1990s many corporations addressed the principal-agent problem by providing a substantial part of executive pay either as shares of the firm's stock or as stock options. *Stock options* are contracts that allow executives or other key employees to buy shares of their employers' stock at fixed, lower prices when the stock prices rise. The idea was to align the interest of the executives and other key employees more closely with those of the broader corporate owners. By pursuing high profits and share prices, the executives would enhance their own wealth as well as that of all the stockholders.

This "solution" to the principal-agent problem had an unexpected negative side effect. It prompted a few unscrupulous executives to inflate their firm's share prices by hiding costs, overstating revenues, engaging in deceptive transactions, and, in general, exaggerating profits. These executives then sold large quantities of their inflated stock, making quick personal fortunes. In some cases, "independent" outside auditing firms turned out to be "not so independent" because they held valuable consulting contracts with the firms being audited.

When the stock market bubble of the late 1990s burst, many instances of business manipulations and fraudulent accounting were exposed. Several executives of large U.S. firms were indicted, and a few large firms collapsed, among them Enron (energy trading), WorldCom (communications), and Arthur Andersen (accounting and consulting). General stockholders of those firms were left holding severely depressed or even worthless stock.

In 2002, Congress strengthened the laws and penalties against executive misconduct. Also, corporations have improved their accounting and auditing procedures. Despite these steps, corporate wrongdoing persists. In 2016, it was found that Wells Fargo (banking) employees had opened more than 2 million bank or credit card accounts using existing customer information, but without customers' knowledge or consent. In this case, the agents were the employees attempting to meet the sales goals of the executives. This example further illustrates that the principal-agent problem is not easy to solve.

QUESTION: Why are accurate accounting and independent auditing so crucial in reducing the principal-agent problem?

Explicit and Implicit Costs

To properly calculate a firm's economic costs, you must remember that *all* of the resources used by the firm have an opportunity cost. This is true both for the resources that a firm purchases from outsiders as well as for the resources that it already owns. As a result, *all* of the resources that a firm uses have economic costs. Economists refer to these two types of economic costs as *explicit costs* and *implicit costs:*

- A firm's **explicit costs** are the monetary payments it makes to those from whom it must purchase resources that it does not own. Because these costs involve an obvious cash transaction, they are referred to as explicit costs. Be sure to remember that explicit costs are opportunity costs because every monetary payment used to purchase outside resources necessarily involves forgoing the best alternatives that could have been purchased with the money.

> **explicit cost** The monetary payment a firm must make to an outsider to obtain a resource.

implicit cost The monetary income a firm sacrifices when it uses a resource it owns rather than supplying the resource in the market; equal to what the resource could have earned in the best-paying alternative employment; includes a normal profit.

- A firm's **implicit costs** are the opportunity costs of using the resources that it already owns to make the firm's own product rather than selling those resources to outsiders for cash. Because these costs are present but not obvious, they are referred to as implicit costs.

A firm's economic costs are the sum of its explicit costs and its implicit costs:

$$\frac{\text{Economic}}{\text{costs}} = \frac{\text{explicit}}{\text{costs}} + \frac{\text{implicit}}{\text{costs}}$$

The following example makes clear how both explicit costs and implicit costs affect firm profits and firm behavior.

Accounting Profit and Normal Profit

Suppose that after working as a sales representative for a large T-shirt manufacturer, you decide to open your own retail T-shirt shop. As we explain in Chapter 2, you will be providing two different economic resources to your new enterprise: labor and entrepreneurial ability. The part of your job that involves providing labor includes routine tasks that help run the business—things like answering customer e-mails, taking inventory, and sweeping the floor. The part of your job that involves providing entrepreneurial ability includes any nonroutine tasks involved with organizing the business and directing its strategy—things like deciding how to promote your business, what to include in your product mix, and how to decorate your store to maximize its appeal to potential customers.

You begin providing entrepreneurial ability to your new firm by making some initial organizational decisions. You decide to work full time at your new business, so you quit your old job that paid you $22,000 per year. You invest $20,000 of savings that has been earning $1,000 per year. You decide that your new firm will occupy a small retail space that you own and had been previously renting out for $5,000 per year. Finally, you decide to hire one clerk to help you in the store. She agrees to work for you for $18,000 per year.

After a year in business, you total up your accounts and find the following:

Total sales revenue		$120,000
Cost of T-shirts	$40,000	
Clerk's salary	18,000	
Utilities	5,000	
Total (explicit) costs		63,000
Accounting profit		$ 57,000

accounting profit The total revenue of a firm less its explicit costs.

These numbers look very good. In particular, you are happy with your $57,000 **accounting profit**, the profit number that accountants calculate by subtracting total explicit costs from total sales revenue. This is the profit (or net income) that would appear on your accounting statement and that you would report to the government for tax purposes.

But don't celebrate yet! Your $57,000 accounting profit overstates the economic success of your business because it ignores your implicit costs. The true measure of success is doing as well as you possibly can—that is, making more money in your new venture selling T-shirts than you could pursuing any other business venture.

To figure out whether you are achieving that goal, you must take into account *all* of your opportunity costs—both your implicit costs as well as your explicit costs. Doing so will indicate whether your new business venture is earning more money than what you could have earned in any other business venture.

To see how these calculations are made, let's continue with our example.

By providing your own financial capital, retail space, and labor, you incurred three different implicit costs during the year: $1,000 of forgone interest, $5,000 of forgone rent, and $22,000 of forgone wages. But don't forget that there is another implicit cost that you must also take account of—how much income you chose to forgo by applying your entrepreneurial abilities to your current retail T-shirt venture rather than applying them to other potential business ventures.

But what dollar value should we place on the size of the profits that you might have made if you had provided your entrepreneurial ability to one of those other ventures?

The answer is given by estimating a **normal profit,** the typical (or "normal") amount of accounting profit that you would most likely have earned in your next-best-alternative business venture. For the sake of argument, let us assume that with your particular set of skills and talents your entrepreneurial abilities would have on average yielded a normal profit of $5,000 in one of the other potential ventures. Knowing that value, we can take all of your implicit costs properly into account by subtracting them from your accounting profit:

> **normal profit** The payment made by a firm to obtain and retain entrepreneurial ability; the minimum income entrepreneurial ability must receive to induce it to perform entrepreneurial functions for a firm.

Accounting profit	$57,000
Forgone interest	$ 1,000
Forgone rent	5,000
Forgone wages	22,000
Forgone entrepreneurial income	5,000
Total implicit costs	33,000
Economic profit	$24,000

Economic Profit

After subtracting your $33,000 of implicit costs from your accounting profit of $57,000, we are left with an *economic profit* of $24,000.

Please distinguish clearly between accounting profit and economic profit. Accounting profit is the result of subtracting only explicit costs from revenue: *Accounting Profit = Revenue − Explicit Costs*. By contrast, **economic profit** is the result of subtracting all of your economic costs—both explicit costs and implicit costs—from revenue: *Economic Profit = Revenue − Explicit Costs − Implicit Costs*.

> **economic profit** The total revenue of a firm less its economic costs (which include both explicit costs and implicit costs); also called *pure profit* and *above-normal profit.*

By subtracting all of your economic costs from your revenue, you determine how your current business venture compares with your best alternative business venture. In our example, the fact that you are generating an economic profit of $24,000 means that you are making $24,000 more than you could expect to make in your best alternative business venture.

By contrast, suppose that you had instead done poorly in business, so that this year your firm generated an economic loss (a negative economic profit) of $8,000. This would mean that you were doing worse in your current venture than you could have done in your best alternative venture. You would, as a result, wish to switch to that alternative.

Generalizing this point, we see that there is an important behavioral threshold at $0 of economic profit. If a firm is breaking even (that is, earning exactly $0 of economic profit), then its entrepreneurs know that they are doing exactly as well as they could expect to do in their best alternative business venture. They are earning enough to cover all their explicit and implicit costs, including the normal profit that they could expect to earn in other business ventures. Thus, they have no incentive to change. By contrast, entrepreneurs running a positive economic profit know they are doing better than they could in alternative ventures and will want to continue doing what they are doing or maybe even expand their business. And entrepreneurs running an economic loss (a negative economic profit) know that they could do better by switching to something else.

FIGURE 6.1 Economic profit versus accounting profit. Economic profit is equal to total revenue less economic costs. Economic costs are the sum of explicit and implicit costs and include a normal profit to the entrepreneur. Accounting profit is equal to total revenue less accounting (explicit) costs.

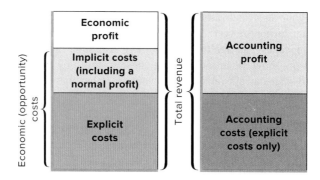

It is for this reason that economists focus on economic profits rather than accounting profits. Simply put, economic profits direct how resources are allocated in the economy. Entrepreneurs running economic losses close their current businesses, thereby freeing up the land, labor, capital, and entrepreneurial ability that they had been using. These resources are freed up to be used by firms that are generating positive economic profits or that are at least breaking even. Resources thus flow from producing goods and services with lower net benefits toward producing goods and services with higher net benefits. Allocative efficiency increases as firms are led by their profit signals to produce more of what consumers want the most.

Figure 6.1 shows the relationship among the various cost and profit concepts that we have just discussed. To test yourself, you might want to enter cost data from our example in the appropriate blocks.

Short Run and Long Run

When the demand for a firm's product changes, the firm's profitability may depend on how quickly it can adjust the amounts of the various resources it employs. It can easily and quickly adjust the quantities employed of many resources such as hourly labor, raw materials, fuel, and power. It needs much more time, however, to adjust its *plant capacity*—the size of the factory building, the amount of machinery and equipment, and other capital resources. In some heavy industries such as aircraft manufacturing, a firm may need several years to alter plant capacity. Because of these differences in adjustment time, economists find it useful to distinguish between two conceptual periods: the short run and the long run. We will discover that costs differ in these two time periods.

Short Run: Fixed Plant
In microeconomics, the **short run** is a period too brief for a firm to alter its plant capacity yet long enough to permit a change in the degree to which the fixed plant is used. The firm's plant capacity is fixed in the short run. However, the firm can vary its output by applying larger or smaller amounts of labor, materials, and other resources to that plant. It can use its existing plant capacity more or less intensively in the short run.

If Boeing hires 1,000 extra workers for one of its commercial airline plants or adds an entire shift of workers, we are speaking of the short run. Both are *short-run adjustments*.

Long Run: Variable Plant
From the viewpoint of an existing firm, the **long run** is a period long enough for it to adjust the quantities of all the resources that it employs, including plant capacity. From the industry's viewpoint, the long run also includes enough time for existing firms to dissolve and leave the industry or for new firms to be created and enter the industry. While the short run is a "fixed-plant" period, the long run is a "variable-plant" period. If Boeing adds a new production facility or merges with a supplier, we are referring to the long run. Both are *long-run adjustments*.

short run (1) In microeconomics, a period of time in which producers are able to change the quantities of some but not all of the resources they employ; a period in which some resources (usually plant) are fixed and some are variable. (2) In macroeconomics, a period in which nominal wages and other input prices do not change in response to a change in the price level.

long run (1) In microeconomics, a period of time long enough to enable producers of a product to change the quantities of all the resources they employ; period in which all resources and costs are variable and no resources or costs are fixed. (2) In macroeconomics, a period sufficiently long for nominal wages and other input prices to change in response to a change in the nation's price level.

PHOTO OP Long-Run Adjustments by Firms

An apparel manufacturer can make long-run adjustments to add production capacity in a matter of days by leasing another building and ordering and installing extra sewing machines. In contrast, an oil firm may need 2 to 3 years to construct a new refinery to increase its production capacity.

©Roberto Westbrook/Blend Images

©Steve Allen/Brand X Pictures

The short run and the long run are conceptual periods rather than calendar time periods. As indicated in the Photo Op, light-manufacturing industries can accomplish changes in plant capacity almost overnight. But for heavy industry the long run is a different matter. A firm may require several years to construct a new facility.

Short-Run Production Relationships

A firm's costs of producing a specific output depend on the prices of the needed resources and the quantities of those resources (inputs) needed to produce that output. Resource supply and demand determine resource prices. The technological aspects of production, specifically the relationships between inputs and output, determine the quantities of resources needed. Our focus will be on the *labor*-output relationship, given a fixed plant capacity. But before examining that relationship, we need to define three terms:

- **Total product (TP)** is the total quantity, or total output, of a particular good or service produced.
- **Marginal product (MP)** is the extra output or added product associated with adding a unit of a variable resource, in this case labor, to the production process. Thus,

$$\text{Marginal product} = \frac{\text{change in total product}}{\text{change in labor input}}$$

- **Average product (AP),** also called *labor productivity,* is output per unit of labor input:

$$\text{Average product} = \frac{\text{total product}}{\text{units of labor}}$$

In the short run, a firm for a time can increase its output by adding units of labor to its fixed plant. But by how much will output rise when it adds the labor? Why do we say "for a time"?

total product The total output of a particular good or service produced by a firm (or a group of firms or the entire economy).

marginal product The additional output produced when 1 additional unit of a resource is employed (the quantity of all other resources employed remaining constant); equal to the change in total product divided by the change in the quantity of a resource employed.

average product The total output produced per unit of a resource employed (total product divided by the quantity of that employed resource).

law of diminishing returns The principle that as successive increments of a variable resource are added to a fixed resource, the marginal product of the variable resource will eventually decrease.

Law of Diminishing Returns

The answers are provided in general terms by the **law of diminishing returns.** This law assumes that technology is fixed and thus the techniques of production do not change. It states that as successive units of a variable resource (say, labor) are added to a fixed resource (say, capital or land), beyond some point the extra, or marginal, product that can be attributed to each additional unit of the variable resource will decline. For example, if additional workers are hired to work with a constant amount of capital equipment, output will eventually rise by smaller and smaller amounts as more workers are hired. Diminishing returns will eventually occur.

Relevancy for Firms

The law of diminishing returns is highly relevant for production within firms. As producers add successive units of a variable input such as labor to a fixed input such as capital, the marginal product of labor eventually declines. Diminishing returns will occur sooner or later. Total product eventually will rise at a diminishing rate, then reach a maximum, and finally decline.

What is true for study time is true for producers. Suppose a farmer has a fixed resource—80 acres of land—planted in corn. If the farmer does not cultivate the cornfields (clear the weeds) at all, the yield will be 40 bushels per acre. If he cultivates the land once, output may rise to 50 bushels per acre. A second cultivation may increase output to 57

ILLUSTRATING THE IDEA

Diminishing Returns from Study

The following noneconomic example of a relationship between "inputs" and "output" may help you better understand the idea. Suppose for an individual that

> Total course learning = f(intelligence, quality of course materials, instructor effectiveness, class time, and study time)

where f means "function of" or "depends on." So this relationship supposes that total course learning depends on intelligence (however defined), the quality of course materials such as the textbook, the effectiveness of the instructor, the amount of class time, and the amount of personal study time outside the class.

For analytical purposes, let's assume that one's intelligence, the quality of course materials, the effectiveness of the instructor, and the amount of class time are *fixed*—meaning they do not change over the length of the course. Now let's add units of study time per day over the length of the course to "produce" greater course learning. The first hour of study time per day increases total course learning. Will the second hour enhance course learning by as much as the first? By how much will the third, fourth, fifth, . . . or fifteenth hour of study per day contribute to total course learning relative to the *immediately previous hour?*

We think you will agree that eventually diminishing returns to course learning will set in as successive hours of study are added each day. At some point the marginal product of an extra hour of study time will decline and, at some further point, become zero.

QUESTION: Given diminishing returns to study time, why devote any extra time to study?

bushels per acre, a third to 61, and a fourth to 63. Succeeding cultivations will add less and less to the land's yield. If this were not so, the world's needs for corn could be fulfilled by extremely intense cultivation of this single 80-acre plot of land. Indeed, if diminishing returns did not occur, the world could be fed out of a flowerpot. Why not? Just keep adding more seed, fertilizer, and harvesters!

The law of diminishing returns also holds true in nonagricultural industries. Assume a wood shop is manufacturing furniture frames. It has a specific amount of equipment such as lathes, planers, saws, and sanders. If this shop hired just one or two workers, total output and productivity (output per worker) would be very low. The workers would have to perform many different jobs, and the advantages of specialization would not be realized. Time would be lost in switching from one job to another, and machines would stand idle much of the time. In short, the plant would be understaffed, and production would be inefficient because there would be too much capital relative to the amount of labor.

The shop could eliminate those difficulties by hiring more workers. Then the equipment would be more fully used, and workers could specialize in doing a single job. Time would no longer be lost switching from job to job. As more workers were added, production would become more efficient and the marginal product of each succeeding worker would rise.

But the rise could not go on indefinitely. Beyond a certain point, adding more workers would cause overcrowding. Since workers would then have to wait in line to use the machinery, they would be underused. Total output would increase at a diminishing rate because, given the fixed size of the plant, each worker would have less capital equipment to work with as more and more labor was hired. The marginal product of additional workers would decline because there would be more labor in proportion to the fixed amount of capital. Eventually, adding still more workers would cause so much congestion that marginal product would become negative and total product would decline. At the extreme, the addition of more and more labor would exhaust all the standing room, and total product would fall to zero.

Note that the law of diminishing returns assumes that all units of labor are of equal quality. Each successive worker is presumed to have the same innate ability, motor coordination, education, training, and work experience. Less-skilled or less-energetic workers are not the cause of diminishing returns. Rather, marginal product ultimately diminishes because more workers are being used relative to the amount of plant and equipment available.

Tabular and Graphical Representations

The table at the top of Figure 6.2 is a numerical illustration of the law of diminishing returns. Column 2 shows the total product, or total output, resulting from combining each level of a variable input (labor) in column 1 with a fixed amount of capital, using the existing technology.

Column 3 shows the marginal product (MP), the change in total product associated with each additional unit of labor. Note that with no labor input, total product is zero; a plant with no workers will produce no output. The first 3 units of labor reflect increasing marginal returns, with marginal products of 10, 15, and 20 units, respectively. But beginning with the fourth unit of labor, marginal product diminishes continuously, becoming zero with the seventh unit of labor and negative with the eighth.

Average product, or output per labor unit, is shown in column 4. It is calculated by dividing total product (column 2) by the number of labor units needed to produce it (column 1). At 5 units of labor, for example, AP is 14 (=70/5).

Figure 6.2 also shows the diminishing-returns data graphically and further clarifies the relationships between total, marginal, and average products. (Marginal product in

FIGURE 6.2 The law of diminishing returns. (a) As a variable resource (labor) is added to fixed amounts of other resources (land or capital), the total product that results will eventually increase by diminishing amounts, reach a maximum, and then decline. (b) Marginal product is the change in total product associated with each new unit of labor. Average product is simply output per labor unit. Note that marginal product intersects average product at the maximum average product.

(1) Units of the Variable Resource (Labor)	(2) Total Product (TP)	(3) Marginal Product (MP), Change in (2)/ Change in (1)		(4) Average Product (AP), (2)/(1)
0	0			—
1	10	10	Increasing marginal returns	10.00
2	25	15		12.50
3	45	20		15.00
4	60	15	Diminishing marginal returns	15.00
5	70	10		14.00
6	75	5		12.50
7	75	0	Negative marginal returns	10.71
8	70	−5		8.75

(a)
Total product

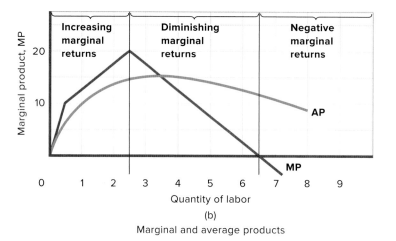

(b)
Marginal and average products

ILLUSTRATING THE IDEA

Exam Scores

The relationship between "marginal" and "average" shown in Figure 6.2b is a mathematical necessity. If you add to a total a number larger than the current average of that total, the average must rise. And if you add to a total a number smaller than the current average of that total, the average must fall. You raise your average examination grade only when your score on an additional (marginal) examination is greater than the average of all your past scores. You lower your average when your grade on an additional exam is below your current average. In our production example, when the amount an extra worker adds to total product exceeds the average product of all workers currently employed, average product will rise. Conversely, when the amount an extra worker adds to total product is less than the current average product, average product will decrease.

QUESTION: Suppose your average exam score for the first three exams is 80 and you receive a 92 on your fourth exam. What is your marginal score? What is your new average score? Why did your average go up?

Figure 6.2b is plotted halfway between the units of labor, since it applies to the addition of each labor unit.)

Note first in Figure 6.2a that total product, TP, goes through three phases: It rises initially at an increasing rate; then it increases, but at a diminishing rate; finally, after reaching a maximum, it declines.

Geometrically, marginal product—shown by the MP curve in Figure 6.2b—is the slope of the total-product curve. Marginal product measures the change in total product associated with each succeeding unit of labor. Thus, the three phases of total product are also reflected in marginal product. Where total product is increasing at an increasing rate, marginal product is rising. Here, extra units of labor are adding larger and larger amounts to total product. Similarly, where total product is increasing but at a decreasing rate, marginal product is positive but falling. Each additional unit of labor adds less to total product than did the previous unit. When total product is at a maximum, marginal product is zero. When total product declines, marginal product becomes negative.

Average product, AP (Figure 6.2b), displays the same tendencies as marginal product. It increases, reaches a maximum, and then decreases as more and more units of labor are added to the fixed plant. But note the relationship between marginal product and average product: Where marginal product exceeds average product, average product rises. And where marginal product is less than average product, average product declines. It follows that marginal product intersects average product where average product is at a maximum.

Short-Run Production Costs

Production information such as that in Figure 6.2 must be coupled with resource prices to determine the total and per-unit costs of producing various levels of output. We know that in the short run, resources associated with the firm's plant are fixed. Other resources, however, are variable in the short run. As a result, short-run costs can be either fixed or variable.

FIGURE 6.3 **A firm's cost curves.** AFC falls as a given amount of fixed costs is apportioned over a larger and larger output. AVC initially falls because of increasing marginal returns but then rises because of diminishing marginal returns. The marginal-cost (MC) curve eventually rises because of diminishing returns and cuts through the average-total-cost (ATC) curve and the average-variable-cost (AVC) curve at their minimum points.

Total-Cost Data				Average-Cost Data			Marginal Cost
(1)	(2)	(3)	(4)	(5)	(6)	(7)	(8)
Total Product (Q)	Total Fixed Cost (TFC)	Total Variable Cost (TVC)	Total Cost (TC) TC = TFC + TVC	Average Fixed Cost (AFC) AFC = $\dfrac{TFC}{Q}$	Average Variable Cost (AVC) AVC = $\dfrac{TVC}{Q}$	Average Total Cost (ATC) ATC = $\dfrac{TC}{Q}$	Marginal Cost (MC) MC = $\dfrac{change\ in\ TC}{change\ in\ Q}$
0	$100	$ 0	$ 100				
1	100	90	190	$100.00	$90.00	$190.00	$ 90
2	100	170	270	50.00	85.00	135.00	80
3	100	240	340	33.33	80.00	113.33	70
4	100	300	400	25.00	75.00	100.00	60
5	100	370	470	20.00	74.00	94.00	70
6	100	450	550	16.67	75.00	91.67	80
7	100	540	640	14.29	77.14	91.43	90
8	100	650	750	12.50	81.25	93.75	110
9	100	780	880	11.11	86.67	97.78	130
10	100	930	1030	10.00	93.00	103.00	150

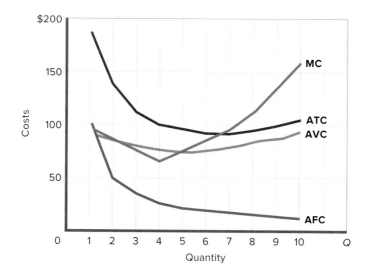

Fixed, Variable, and Total Costs

Let's see what distinguishes fixed costs, variable costs, and total costs from one another.

fixed cost Any cost that in total does not change when the firm changes its output; the cost of fixed resources.

Fixed Costs   **Fixed costs** are costs that do not vary with changes in output. Fixed costs are associated with the very existence of a firm's plant and therefore must be paid even if its output is zero. Such costs as rental payments, interest on a firm's debts, a portion of depreciation on equipment and buildings, and insurance premiums are generally fixed costs; they are fixed and do not change even if a firm produces more. In column 2 of Figure 6.3's table, we assume that the firm's total fixed cost is $100. By definition, this fixed cost is

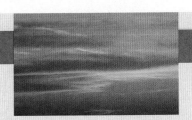

APPLYING THE ANALYSIS

Sunk Costs

Some of a firm's costs are not only *fixed* (recurring, but unrelated to the level of output) but *sunk* (unrecoverable). It is a deep-seated human tendency to drag these sunk costs into marginal-benefit, marginal-cost calculations. Doing so is known as the *sunk cost fallacy*.

Sunk costs are like sunken ships on the ocean floor: Once these costs are incurred, they cannot be recovered. For example, suppose a firm spends $1 million on R&D to bring out a new product, only to discover that the product sells very poorly. Should the firm continue to produce the product at a loss even when there is no realistic hope for future success? Obviously, it should not. In making this decision, the firm realizes that the amount it has spent in developing the product is irrelevant; it should stop production of the product and cut its losses. In fact, many firms have dropped products after spending millions of dollars on their development. For example, in 2007 Pfizer withdrew its novel insulin inhaler from the market because of poor sales and concerns about long-term side effects. The product had cost an estimated $2.8 billion to develop and market.

The emotional tendency that drives the sunk cost fallacy is the desire to "get one's money's worth" out of a past expenditure. But giving in to that emotion can lead to "throwing good money after bad." Both individuals and firms should ignore any cost that it cannot partly or fully recoup through a subsequent choice. Such costs are sunk costs. They are irrelevant in making future-oriented business decisions. Or, as the saying goes, don't cry over spilt milk.

QUESTION: Which is a sunk cost, rather than simply a recurring fixed cost: (1) a prior expenditure on a business computer that is now outdated or (2) a current monthly payment on an equipment lease that runs for 6 more months? Explain.

incurred at all levels of output, including zero. The firm cannot avoid paying fixed costs in the short run.

Variable Costs Unlike fixed costs, **variable costs** are costs that change with the level of output. They include payments for materials, fuel, power, transportation services, most labor, and similar variable resources. In column 3 of the table in Figure 6.3, we find that the total of variable costs changes directly with output.

> **variable cost** A cost that in total increases when the firm increases its output and decreases when the firm reduces its output.

Total Cost Total cost is the sum of fixed cost and variable cost at each level of output. It is shown in column 4 of the table in Figure 6.3. At zero units of output, total cost is equal to the firm's fixed cost. Then for each unit of the 10 units of production, total cost increases by the same amount as variable cost.

> **total cost** The sum of fixed cost and variable cost.

$$TC = TFC + TVC$$

The distinction between fixed and variable costs is significant to the business manager. Variable costs can be controlled or altered in the short run by changing production levels. Fixed costs are beyond the business manager's current control; they are incurred in the short run and must be paid regardless of output level.

Per-Unit, or Average, Costs

Producers are certainly interested in their total costs, but they are equally concerned with per-unit, or average, costs. In particular, average-cost data are more meaningful for making comparisons with product price, which is always stated on a per-unit basis. Average fixed cost, average variable cost, and average total cost are shown in columns 5 to 7 of the table in Figure 6.3.

average fixed cost A firm's total fixed cost divided by output (the quantity of product produced).

AFC   Average fixed cost (AFC) for any output level is found by dividing total fixed cost (TFC) by that output (Q). That is,

$$AFC = \frac{TFC}{Q}$$

Because the total fixed cost is, by definition, the same regardless of output, AFC must decline as output increases. As output rises, the total fixed cost is spread over a larger and larger output. When output is just 1 unit in Figure 6.3's table, TFC and AFC are the same at $100. But at 2 units of output, the total fixed cost of $100 becomes $50 of AFC or fixed cost per unit; then it becomes $33.33 per unit as $100 is spread over 3 units, and $25 per unit when spread over 4 units. This process is sometimes referred to as "spreading the overhead." Figure 6.3 shows that AFC graphs as a continuously declining curve as total output is increased.

average variable cost A firm's total variable cost divided by output (the quantity of product produced).

AVC   Average variable cost (AVC) for any output level is calculated by dividing total variable cost (TVC) by that output (Q):

$$AVC = \frac{TVC}{Q}$$

Due to increasing and then diminishing returns, AVC declines initially, reaches a minimum, and then increases again. A graph of AVC is a U-shaped or saucer-shaped curve, as shown in Figure 6.3.

Because total variable cost reflects the law of diminishing returns, so must AVC, which is derived from total variable cost. Because marginal returns increase initially, it takes fewer and fewer additional variable resources to produce each of the first 4 units of output. As a result, variable cost per unit declines. AVC hits a minimum with the fifth unit of output, and beyond that point AVC rises because diminishing returns require more and more variable resources to produce each additional unit of output.

You can verify the U or saucer shape of the AVC curve by returning to the production table in Figure 6.2. Assume the price of labor is $10 per unit. Labor cost per unit of output is then $10 (the price per unit of labor in this example) divided by average product (output per labor unit). Because we have assumed labor to be the only variable input, the labor cost per unit of output is the variable cost per unit of output, or AVC. When average product is initially low, AVC is high. As workers are added, average product rises and AVC falls. When average product is at its maximum, AVC is at its minimum. Then, as still more workers are added and average product declines, AVC rises. The "hump" of the average-product curve is reflected in the saucer or U shape of the AVC curve.

average total cost A firm's total cost divided by output (the quantity of product produced); equal to average fixed cost plus average variable cost.

ATC   Average total cost (ATC) for any output level is found by dividing total cost (TC) by that output (Q) or by adding AFC and AVC at that output:

$$ATC = \frac{TC}{Q} = \frac{TFC}{Q} + \frac{TVC}{Q} = AFC + AVC$$

Graphically, we can find ATC by adding vertically the AFC and AVC curves, as in Figure 6.3. Thus, the vertical distance between the ATC and AVC curves measures AFC at any level of output.

Marginal Cost

One final and very crucial cost concept remains: **Marginal cost (MC)** is *the extra, or additional, cost of producing 1 more unit of output.* MC can be determined for each added unit of output by noting the change in total cost which that unit's production entails:

$$MC = \frac{\text{change in TC}}{\text{change in } Q}$$

marginal cost The extra (additional) cost of producing 1 more unit of output; equal to the change in total cost divided by the change in output (and, in the short run, to the change in total variable cost divided by the change in output).

Calculations   In column 4 of Figure 6.3's table, production of the first unit of output increases total cost from $100 to $190. Therefore, the additional, or marginal, cost of that first unit is $90 (column 8). The marginal cost of the second unit is $80 (= $270 − $190); the MC of the third is $70 (= $340 − $270); and so forth. The MC for each of the 10 units of output is shown in column 8.

MC can also be calculated from the total-variable-cost column because the only difference between total cost and total variable cost is the constant amount of fixed costs ($100). Thus, the change in total cost and the change in total variable cost accompanying each additional unit of output are always the same.

Marginal Decisions   Marginal costs are costs the firm can control directly and immediately. Specifically, MC designates all the cost incurred in producing the last unit of output. Thus, it also designates the cost that can be "saved" by not producing that last unit. Average-cost figures do not provide this information. For example, suppose the firm is undecided whether to produce 3 or 4 units of output. At 4 units the table in Figure 6.3 indicates that ATC is $100. But the firm does not increase its total costs by $100 by producing the fourth unit, nor does it save $100 by not producing that unit. Rather, the change in costs involved here is only $60, as the MC column in the table reveals.

A firm's decisions as to what output level to produce are typically marginal decisions, that is, decisions to produce a few more or a few less units. Marginal cost is the change in costs when 1 more or 1 less unit of output is produced. When coupled with marginal revenue (which, as you will see in Chapter 7, indicates the change in revenue from 1 more or 1 less unit of output), marginal cost allows a firm to determine if it is profitable to expand or contract its production. The analysis in the next three chapters focuses on those marginal calculations.

Graphical Portrayal   Marginal cost is shown graphically in Figure 6.3. Marginal cost at first declines sharply, reaches a minimum, and then rises rather abruptly. This reflects the fact that variable costs, and therefore total cost, increase first by decreasing amounts and then by increasing amounts.

Relation of MC to AVC and ATC   Figure 6.3 shows that the marginal-cost curve MC intersects both the AVC and the ATC curves at their minimum points. As noted earlier, this marginal-average relationship is a mathematical necessity. When the amount (the marginal cost) added to total cost is less than the current average total cost, ATC will fall. Conversely, when the marginal cost exceeds ATC, ATC will rise. This means in Figure 6.3 that as long as MC lies below ATC, ATC will fall, and whenever MC lies above ATC, ATC will rise. Therefore, at the point of intersection where MC equals ATC, ATC has just ceased to fall but has not yet begun to rise. This, by definition, is the minimum point on the

Rising Gasoline Prices

Changes in supply and demand often lead to rapid increases in the price of gasoline. Because gasoline is used to power most motor vehicles, including those used by businesses, increases in the price of gasoline lead to increases in firms' short-run variable costs, marginal costs, and average total costs. In terms of our analysis, their AVC, MC, and ATC curves all shift upward when an increase in the price of gasoline increases their production costs.

The extent of these upward shifts depends upon the relative importance of gasoline as a variable input in the various firms' individual production processes. Package-delivery companies like FedEx that use a lot of gasoline-powered vehicles will see substantial upward shifts while software companies like Symantec (Norton) that mainly deliver their products through Internet downloads may see only small upward shifts.

QUESTION: If rising gasoline prices increase the cost for delivery to firms such as FedEx, how would that affect the cost curves for Internet retailers such as Amazon, that ship a lot of packages?

ATC curve. The marginal-cost curve intersects the average-total-cost curve at the ATC curve's minimum point.

Marginal cost can be defined as the addition either to total cost or to total variable cost resulting from 1 more unit of output; thus, this same rationale explains why the MC curve also crosses the AVC curve at the AVC curve's minimum point. No such relationship exists between the MC curve and the average-fixed-cost curve because the two are not related; marginal cost includes only those costs that change with output, and fixed costs by definition are those that are independent of output.

Long-Run Production Costs

In the long run, an industry and its individual firms can undertake all desired resource adjustments. That is, they can change the amount of all inputs used. The firm can alter its plant capacity; it can build a larger plant or revert to a smaller plant than that assumed in Figures 6.2 and 6.3. The industry also can change its overall capacity; the long run allows sufficient time for new firms to enter or for existing firms to leave an industry. We will discuss the impact of the entry and exit of firms to and from an industry in the next chapter; here we are concerned only with changes in plant capacity made by a single firm. Let's couch our analysis in terms of average total cost (ATC), making no distinction between fixed and variable costs because all resources, and therefore all costs, are variable in the long run.

Firm Size and Costs

Suppose a manufacturer with a single plant begins on a small scale and, as the result of successful operations, expands to successively larger plant sizes with larger output capacities. What happens to average total cost as this occurs? For a time, successively larger

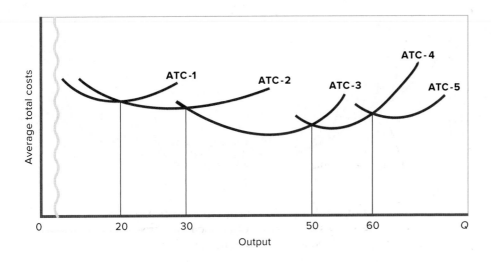

FIGURE 6.4 The long-run average-total-cost curve: five possible plant sizes. The long-run average-total-cost curve is made up of segments of the short-run cost curves (ATC-1, ATC-2, etc.) of the various-size plants from which the firm might choose. Each point on the bumpy planning curve shows the lowest unit cost attainable for any output when the firm has had time to make all desired changes in its plant size.

plants will reduce average total cost. However, eventually the building of a still larger plant may cause ATC to rise.

Figure 6.4 illustrates this situation for five possible plant sizes. ATC-1 is the short-run average-total-cost curve for the smallest of the five plants, and ATC-5, the curve for the largest. Constructing larger plants will lower the minimum average total costs through plant size 3. But then larger plants will mean higher minimum average total costs.

The Long-Run Cost Curve

The vertical lines perpendicular to the output axis in Figure 6.4 indicate the outputs at which the firm should change plant size to realize the lowest attainable average total costs of production. These are the outputs at which the per-unit costs for a larger plant drop below those for the current, smaller plant. For all outputs up to 20 units, the lowest average total costs are attainable with plant size 1. However, if the firm's volume of sales expands beyond 20 units but less than 30, it can achieve lower per-unit costs by constructing a larger plant, size 2. Although total cost will be higher at the expanded levels of production, the cost per unit of output will be less. For any output between 30 and 50 units, plant size 3 will yield the lowest average total costs. From 50 to 60 units of output, the firm must build the size-4 plant to achieve the lowest unit costs. Lowest average total costs for any output over 60 units require construction of the still larger plant, size 5.

Tracing these adjustments, we find that the long-run ATC curve for the enterprise is made up of segments of the short-run ATC curves for the various plant sizes that can be constructed. The long-run ATC curve shows the lowest average total cost at which *any output level* can be produced after the firm has had time to make all appropriate adjustments in its plant size. In Figure 6.4 the red, bumpy curve is the firm's long-run ATC curve or, as it is often called, the firm's *planning curve.*

In most lines of production, the choice of plant size is much wider than in our illustration. In many industries the number of possible plant sizes is virtually unlimited, and in time quite small changes in the volume of output will lead to changes in plant size. Graphically, this implies an unlimited number of short-run ATC curves, one for each output level, as suggested by Figure 6.5. Then, rather than being made up of segments of short-run ATC curves as in Figure 6.4, the long-run ATC curve is made up of all the points of tangency of the unlimited number of short-run ATC curves from which the long-run ATC curve is derived. Therefore, the planning curve is smooth rather than bumpy. Each point on it tells us the minimum ATC of producing the corresponding level of output.

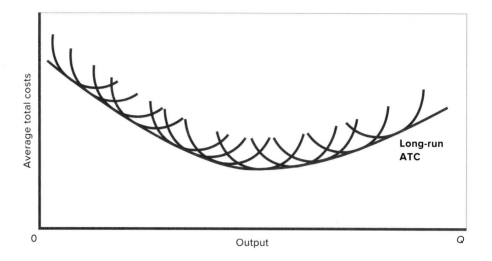

FIGURE 6.5 The long-run average-total-cost curve: unlimited number of plant sizes. If the number of possible plant sizes is very large, the long-run average-total-cost curve approximates a smooth curve. Economies of scale, followed by diseconomies of scale, cause the curve to be U-shaped.

Economies and Diseconomies of Scale

We have assumed that, for a time, larger and larger plant sizes will lead to lower unit costs but that, beyond some point, successively larger plants will mean higher average total costs. That is, we have assumed the long-run ATC curve is U-shaped. But why should this be? It turns out that the U shape is caused by economies and diseconomies of large-scale production, as we explain in a moment. But before we do, please understand that the U shape of the long-run average-total-cost curve *cannot* be the result of rising resource prices or the law of diminishing returns. First, our discussion assumes that resource prices are constant. Second, the law of diminishing returns does not apply to production in the long run. This is true because the law of diminishing returns only deals with situations in which a productive resource or input is held constant. Under our definition of "long run," all resources and inputs are variable.

economies of scale Reductions in the average total cost of producing a product as the firm expands the size of plant (its output) in the long run; the economies of mass production.

Economies of Scale
Economies of scale, or *economies of mass production,* explain the downsloping part of the long-run ATC curve, as indicated in Figure 6.6, graphs (a), (b), and (c). As plant size increases, a number of factors will, for a time, lead to lower average costs of production.

Labor Specialization
Increased specialization in the use of labor becomes more achievable as a plant increases in size. Hiring more workers means jobs can be divided and subdivided. Each worker may now have just one task to perform instead of five or six. Workers can work full time on the tasks for which they have special skills. By contrast, skilled machinists in a small plant may spend half their time performing unskilled tasks, leading to higher production costs.

Further, by working at fewer tasks, workers become even more proficient at those tasks. The jack-of-all-trades doing five or six jobs is not likely to be efficient in any of them. Concentrating on one task, the same worker may become highly efficient.

Finally, greater labor specialization eliminates the loss of time that occurs whenever a worker shifts from one task to another.

Managerial Specialization
Large-scale production also means better use of, and greater specialization in, management. A supervisor who can handle 20 workers is underused in a small plant that employs only 10 people. The production staff could be doubled with no increase in supervisory costs.

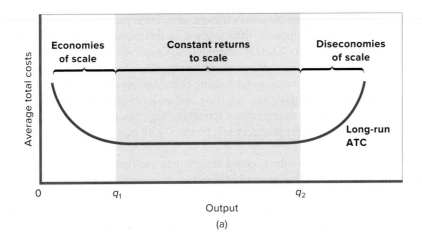

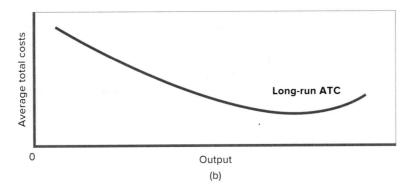

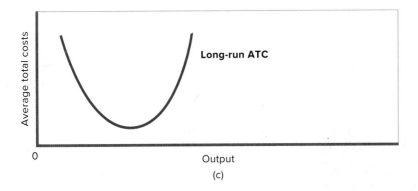

Small firms cannot use management specialists to the best advantage. For example, a sales specialist working in a small plant may have to spend some of her time on functions outside of her area of expertise—marketing, personnel, and finance. A larger scale of operations would allow her to supervise marketing full time, while different specialists perform other managerial functions. Greater efficiency and lower unit costs are the net result.

Efficient Capital   Small firms often cannot afford the most efficient equipment. In many lines of production, such machinery is available only in very large and extremely expensive units. Furthermore, effective use of the equipment demands a high volume of production, and that again requires large-scale producers.

In the automobile industry the most efficient fabrication method employs robotics and elaborate assembly-line equipment. Effective use of this equipment demands an annual output of perhaps 200,000 to 400,000 automobiles. Only very-large-scale producers can afford to purchase and use this equipment efficiently. The small-scale producer is faced with a dilemma. To fabricate automobiles using other equipment is inefficient and therefore more costly per unit. But so, too, is buying and underutilizing the equipment used by the large manufacturers. Because it cannot spread the high equipment cost over very many units of output, the small-scale producer will be stuck with high costs per unit of output.

Other Factors Many products entail design and development costs, as well as other "start-up" costs, which must be incurred irrespective of projected sales. These costs decline per unit as output is increased. Similarly, advertising costs decline per auto, per computer, per stereo system, and per box of detergent as more units are produced and sold. Also, the firm's production and marketing expertise usually rises as it produces and sells more output. This *learning by doing* is a further source of economies of scale.

All these factors contribute to lower average total costs for the firm that is able to expand its scale of operations. Where economies of scale are possible, an increase in all resources of, say, 10 percent will cause a more-than-proportionate increase in output of, say, 20 percent. The result will be a decline in ATC.

In many U.S. manufacturing industries, economies of scale have been of great significance. Firms that have expanded their scale of operations to obtain economies of mass production have survived and flourished. Those unable to expand have become relatively high-cost producers, doomed to a struggle to survive.

PHOTO OP   Economies of Scale

Economies of scale are extensive in the automobile industry, where the capital required is large and expensive and many workers are needed to perform the numerous, highly specialized tasks. Economies of scale in copying keys are exhausted at low levels of output; production usually occurs in small shops, the capital involved is relatively small and inexpensive, and a small number of workers (often only one) perform all of the labor and managerial functions of the business. There would be little, if any, cost advantage to establishing a key copying "factory" with hundreds of stations.

©RainerPlendl/Getty Images

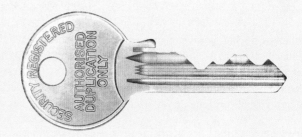

APPLYING THE ANALYSIS

The Verson Stamping Machine

In 1996 Verson (a U.S. firm located in Chicago) introduced a 49-foot-tall metal-stamping machine that is the size of a house and weighs as much as 12 locomotives. This $30 million machine, which cuts and sculpts raw sheets of steel into automobile hoods and fenders, enables automakers to make new parts in just 5 minutes compared with 8 hours for older stamping presses. A single machine is designed to make 5 million auto parts per year. So, to achieve the cost saving from the machine, an auto manufacturer must have sufficient auto production to use all these parts. By allowing the use of this cost-saving piece of equipment, large firm size achieves economies of scale.

QUESTION: Do you see any potential problems for a company that relies too heavily on just a few large machines for fabricating millions of its critical product parts?

Diseconomies of Scale
In time the expansion of a firm may lead to diseconomies and therefore higher average total costs.

The main factor causing **diseconomies of scale** is the difficulty of efficiently controlling and coordinating a firm's operations as it becomes a large-scale producer. In a small plant, a single key executive may make all the basic decisions for the plant's operation. Because of the firm's small size, the executive is close to the production line, understands the firm's operations, and can make efficient decisions because the small plant size requires only a relatively small amount of information to be examined and understood in optimizing production.

This neat picture changes as a firm grows. One person cannot assemble, digest, and understand all the information essential to decision making on a large scale. Authority must be delegated to many vice presidents, second vice presidents, and so forth. This expansion of the management hierarchy leads to problems of communication and cooperation, bureaucratic red tape, and the possibility that decisions will not be coordinated. At the same time, each new manager must be paid a salary. Thus, declining efficiency in making and executing decisions goes hand-in-hand with rising average total costs as bureaucracy expands beyond a certain point.

Also, in massive production facilities, workers may feel alienated from their employers and care little about working efficiently. Opportunities to shirk, by avoiding work in favor of on-the-job leisure, may be greater in large plants than in small ones. Countering worker alienation and shirking may require additional worker supervision, which increases costs.

Where diseconomies of scale are operative, an increase in all inputs of, say, 10 percent will cause a less-than-proportionate increase in output of, say, 5 percent. As a consequence, ATC will increase. The rising portion of the long-run cost curves in Figure 6.6 illustrates diseconomies of scale.

Constant Returns to Scale
In some industries there may exist a rather wide range of output between the output at which economies of scale end and the output at which diseconomies of scale begin. That is, there may be a range of **constant returns to scale** over which long-run average cost does not change. The q_1q_2 output range of Figure 6.6a is an

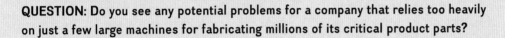

diseconomies of scale Increases in the average total cost of producing a product as the firm expands the size of its plant (its output) in the long run.

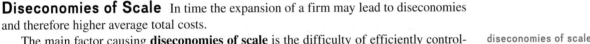

constant returns to scale No changes in the average total cost of producing a product as the firm expands the size of its operations (output) in the long run.

example. Here a given percentage increase in all inputs of, say, 10 percent will cause a proportionate 10 percent increase in output. Thus, in this range ATC is constant.

Minimum Efficient Scale and Industry Structure

minimum efficient scale (MES) The lowest level of output at which a firm can minimize long-run average total cost.

Economies and diseconomies of scale are an important determinant of an industry's structure. Here we introduce the concept of **minimum efficient scale (MES),** which is the lowest level of output at which a firm can minimize long-run average costs. In Figure 6.6a that level occurs at q_1 units of output. Because of the extended range of constant returns to scale, firms producing substantially greater outputs could also realize the minimum attainable long-run average costs. Specifically, firms within the q_1q_2 range would be equally efficient. So we would not be surprised to find an industry with such cost conditions to be populated by firms of quite different sizes. The apparel, banking, furniture, snowboard, wood products, food processing, and small-appliance industries are examples. With an extended range of constant returns to scale, relatively large and relatively small firms can coexist in an industry and be equally successful.

Compare this with Figure 6.6b, where economies of scale continue over a wide range of outputs and diseconomies of scale appear only at very high levels of output. This pattern of declining long-run average total cost occurs in the automobile, aluminum, steel, and other heavy industries. The same pattern holds in several of the new industries related to information technology, for example, computer microchips, operating system software, and Internet service provision. Given consumer demand, efficient production will be achieved with a few large-scale producers. Small firms cannot realize the minimum efficient scale and will not be able to compete.

Where economies of scale are few and diseconomies come into play quickly, the minimum efficient size occurs at a low level of output, as shown in Figure 6.6c. In such industries, a particular level of consumer demand will support a large number of relatively small producers. Many retail trades and some types of farming fall into this category. So do certain kinds of light manufacturing, such as the baking, clothing, and shoe industries. Fairly small firms are more efficient than larger-scale producers would be if they were present in such industries.

Our point here is that the shape of the long-run average-total-cost curve is determined by technology and the economies and diseconomies of scale that result. The shape of the long-run ATC curve, in turn, can be significant in determining whether an industry is populated by a relatively large number of small firms or is dominated by a few large producers, or lies somewhere in between.

But we must be cautious in our assessment because industry structure does not depend on cost conditions alone. Government policies, the geographic size of markets, managerial strategy and skill, and other factors must be considered in explaining the structure of a particular industry.

APPLYING THE ANALYSIS

Aircraft Assembly Plants versus Concrete Plants

Why are there only three plants in the United States (all operated by Boeing) that produce large commercial aircraft and thousands of plants (owned by hundreds of firms) that produce ready-mix concrete? The simple answer is that MES is radically different in the two industries. Why is that? First, while economies of scale are extensive in assembling large commercial aircraft, they are only very modest in mixing concrete. Manufacturing airplanes is a complex process that requires huge facilities, thousands of workers, and very expensive, specialized machinery. Economies of scale extend to huge plant sizes. But mixing Portland cement, sand, gravel, and water to produce concrete requires only a handful of workers and relatively inexpensive equipment. Economies of scale are exhausted at relatively small size.

The differing MES also derives from the vastly different sizes of the geographic markets. The market for commercial airplanes is global, and aircraft manufacturers can deliver new airplanes anywhere in the world by flying them there. In contrast, the geographic market for a concrete plant is roughly the 50-mile radius within which the concrete can be delivered before it "sets up." So in the ready-mix concrete industry, thousands of small concrete plants are positioned close to their customers in hundreds of small and large cities.

QUESTION: Speculate as to why the MES of firms in the Portland cement industry is considerably larger than the MES of single ready-mix concrete plants.

SUMMARY

LO6.1 Identify features of the corporate form of business organization that have made it so dominant.

Corporations—the dominant form of business organizations—are legal entities, distinct and separate from the individuals who own them. They often have thousands, or even millions, of stockholders who jointly own them. They finance their operations and purchases of new plant and equipment partly through the issuance of stocks and bonds. Stocks are ownership shares of a corporation, and bonds are promises to repay a loan, usually at a set rate of interest.

A principal-agent problem may occur in corporations when the agents (managers) hired to represent the interest of the principals (stockholders) pursue their own objectives to the detriment of the objectives of the principals.

LO6.2 Explain why economic costs include both explicit (revealed and expressed) costs and implicit (present but not obvious) costs.

The economic cost of using a resource to produce a good or service is the value or worth that the resource would have had in its best alternative use. Economic costs include explicit costs, which flow to resources owned and supplied by others, and implicit costs, which are payments for the use of self-owned and self-employed resources. One implicit cost is a normal profit to the entrepreneur. Economic profit occurs when total revenue exceeds total cost (= explicit costs + implicit costs, including a normal profit).

In the short run, a firm's plant capacity is fixed. The firm can use its plant more or less intensively by adding or subtracting units of variable resources, but it does not have sufficient time in the short run to alter plant size.

LO6.3 Relate the law of diminishing returns to a firm's short-run production costs.

The law of diminishing returns describes what happens to output as a fixed plant is used more intensively. As successive units of a variable resource, such as labor, are added to a fixed plant, beyond some point the marginal product associated with each additional unit of a resource declines.

LO6.4 Describe the distinctions between fixed and variable costs and among total, average, and marginal costs.

Because some resources are variable and others are fixed, costs can be classified as variable or fixed in the short run. Fixed costs are independent of the level of output; variable costs vary with output. The total cost of any output is the sum of fixed and variable costs at that output.

Average fixed, average variable, and average total costs are fixed, variable, and total costs per unit of output. Average fixed cost declines continuously as output increases because a fixed sum is being spread over a larger and larger number of units of production. A graph of average variable cost is U-shaped, reflecting the law of diminishing returns. Average total cost is the sum of average fixed and average variable costs; its graph is also U-shaped.

Marginal cost is the extra, or additional, cost of producing 1 more unit of output. It is the amount by which total cost and total variable cost change when 1 more or 1 less unit of output is produced. Graphically, the marginal-cost curve intersects the ATC and AVC curves at their minimum points.

LO6.5 Use economies of scale to link a firm's size and its average costs in the long run.

The long run is a period of time sufficiently long for a firm to vary the amounts of all resources used, including plant size. In the long run, all costs are variable. The long-run ATC, or planning, curve is composed of segments of the short-run ATC curves, and it represents the various plant sizes a firm can construct in the long run.

The long-run ATC curve is generally U-shaped. Economies of scale are first encountered as a small firm expands. Greater specialization in the use of labor and management, the ability to use the most efficient equipment, and the spreading of start-up costs among more units of output all contribute to economies of scale. As the firm continues to grow, it will encounter diseconomies of scale stemming from the managerial complexities that accompany large-scale production. The ranges of output over which economies and diseconomies of scale occur in an industry are often an important determinant of the structure of that industry.

A firm's minimum efficient scale (MES) is the lowest level of output at which it can minimize its long-run average cost. In some industries, MES occurs at such low levels of output that numerous firms can populate the industry. In other industries, MES occurs at such high output levels that only a few firms can exist in the long run.

TERMS AND CONCEPTS

stock	economic profit	total cost
bond	short run	average fixed cost (AFC)
limited liability	long run	average variable cost (AVC)
principal-agent problem	total product (TP)	average total cost (ATC)
economic cost	marginal product (MP)	marginal cost (MC)
explicit costs	average product (AP)	economies of scale
implicit costs	law of diminishing returns	diseconomies of scale
accounting profit	fixed costs	constant returns to scale
normal profit	variable costs	minimum efficient scale (MES)

QUESTIONS

The following and additional problems can be found in ▣ connect

1. Distinguish between a plant, a firm, and an industry. Contrast a vertically integrated firm, a horizontally integrated firm, and a conglomerate. Cite an example of a horizontally integrated firm from which you have recently made a purchase. LO6.1

2. What major advantages of corporations have given rise to their dominance as a form of business organization? LO6.1

3. What is the principal-agent problem as it relates to corporate managers and stockholders? How did firms try to solve this problem in the 1990s? In what way did the "solution" backfire on some firms? LO6.1

4. Distinguish between explicit and implicit costs, giving examples of each. What are some explicit and implicit costs of attending college? LO6.2

5. Distinguish between accounting profit, economic profit, and normal profit. Does accounting profit or economic profit determine how entrepreneurs allocate resources between different business ventures? Explain. LO6.2

6. Which of the following are short-run and which are long-run adjustments? LO6.3

   a. Wendy's builds a new restaurant.
   b. Harley-Davidson Corporation hires 200 more production workers.
   c. A farmer increases the amount of fertilizer used on his corn crop.
   d. An Alcoa aluminum plant adds a third shift of workers.

7. Complete the following table by calculating marginal product and average product from the data given: LO6.3

Inputs of Labor	Total Product	Marginal Product	Average Product
0	0		
1	15	_____	_____
2	34	_____	_____
3	51	_____	_____
4	65	_____	_____
5	74	_____	_____
6	80	_____	_____
7	83	_____	_____
8	82	_____	_____

Explain why marginal product eventually declines and ultimately becomes negative. What bearing does the law of diminishing returns have on marginal costs? Be specific.

8. Why can the distinction between fixed costs and variable costs be made in the short run? Classify the following as fixed or variable costs: advertising expenditures, fuel, interest on company-issued bonds, shipping charges, payments for raw materials, real estate taxes, executive salaries, insurance premiums, wage payments, sales taxes, and rental payments on leased office machinery. LO6.4

9. A firm has fixed costs of $60 and variable costs as indicated in the accompanying table. LO6.4

   Complete the table and check your calculations by referring to question 3 at the end of Chapter 7.

   a. Graph the AFC, ATC, and MC curves. Why does the AFC curve slope continuously downward? Why does the MC curve eventually slope upward? Why does the MC curve intersect the ATC curve at its minimum point?

   b. Explain how the location of each curve graphed in question 9a would be altered if (1) total fixed cost had been $100 rather than $60 and (2) total variable cost had been $10 less at each level of output.

10. Indicate how each of the following would shift the (1) marginal-cost curve, (2) average-variable-cost curve, (3) average-fixed-cost curve, and (4) average-total-cost curve of a manufacturing firm. In each case, specify the direction of the shift. LO6.4

    a. A reduction in business property taxes.

    b. An increase in the hourly wage rates of production workers.

c. A decrease in the price of electricity.

d. An increase in transportation costs.

11. Suppose a firm has only three possible plant-size options, represented by the ATC curves shown in the accompanying figure. What plant size will the firm choose in producing (a) 50, (b) 130, (c) 160, and (d) 250 units of output? Draw the firm's long-run average-cost curve on the diagram and describe this curve. LO6.5

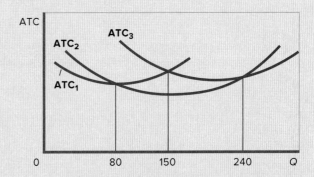

12. Use the concepts of economies and diseconomies of scale to explain the shape of a firm's long-run ATC curve. What is the concept of minimum efficient scale? What bearing can the shape of the long-run ATC curve have on the structure of an industry? LO6.5

Table for question 9:

Total Product	Total Fixed Cost	Total Variable Cost	Total Cost	Average Fixed Cost	Average Variable Cost	Average Total Cost	Marginal Cost
0	$_____	$ 0	$_____			$_____	$_____
1	_____	45	_____	$_____	$_____	_____	_____
2	_____	85	_____	_____	_____	_____	_____
3	_____	120	_____	_____	_____	_____	_____
4	_____	150	_____	_____	_____	_____	_____
5	_____	185	_____	_____	_____	_____	_____
6	_____	225	_____	_____	_____	_____	_____
7	_____	270	_____	_____	_____	_____	_____
8	_____	325	_____	_____	_____	_____	_____
9	_____	390	_____	_____	_____	_____	_____
10	_____	465	_____	_____	_____	_____	_____

PROBLEMS

1. Gomez runs a small pottery firm. He hires one helper at $12,000 per year, pays annual rent of $5,000 for his shop, and spends $20,000 per year on materials. He has $40,000 of his own funds invested in equipment (pottery wheels, kilns, and so forth) that could earn him $4,000 per year if alternatively invested. He has been offered $15,000 per year to work as a potter for a competitor. He estimates his entrepreneurial talents are worth $3,000 per year. Total annual revenue from pottery sales is $72,000. Calculate the accounting profit and the economic profit for Gomez's pottery firm. LO6.2

2. Imagine you have some workers and some handheld computers that you can use to take inventory at a warehouse. There are diminishing returns to taking inventory. If one worker uses one computer, he can inventory 100 items per hour. Two workers sharing a computer can together inventory 150 items per hour. Three workers sharing a computer can together inventory 160

items per hour. And four or more workers sharing a computer can together inventory fewer than 160 items per hour. Computers cost $100 each and you must pay each worker $25 per hour. If you assign one worker per computer, what is the cost of inventorying a single item? What if you assign two workers per computer? Three? How many workers per computer should you assign if you wish to minimize the cost of inventorying a single item? LO6.3

3. You are a newspaper publisher. You are in the middle of a one-year rental contract for your factory that requires you to pay $500,000 per month, and you have contractual labor obligations of $1 million per month that you can't get out of. You also have a marginal printing cost of $.25 per paper as well as a marginal delivery cost of $.10 per paper. If sales fall by 20 percent from 1 million papers per month to 800,000 papers per month, what happens to the AFC per paper, the MC per paper, and the minimum amount that you must charge to break even on these costs? LO6.4

4. There are economies of scale in ranching, especially with regard to fencing land. Suppose that barbed-wire fencing costs $10,000 per mile to set up. How much would it cost to fence a single property whose area is one square mile if that property also happens to be perfectly square, with sides that are each one mile long? How much would it cost to fence exactly four such properties, which together would contain four square miles of area? Now, consider how much it would cost to fence in four square miles of ranch land if, instead, it comes as a single large square that is two miles long on each side. Which is more costly—fencing in the four, one-square-mile properties or the single four-square-mile property? LO6.5

©Tatiana Belova/Shutterstock

Pure Competition

Learning Objectives

LO7.1 Give the names and summarize the main characteristics of the four basic market models.

LO7.2 List the conditions required for purely competitive markets.

LO7.3 Describe how purely competitive firms maximize profits or minimize losses.

LO7.4 Explain why the marginal-cost curve and supply curve of competitive firms are identical.

LO7.5 Describe how profits and losses drive the long-run adjustment process of pure competition.

LO7.6 Identify the differences between constant-cost, increasing-cost, and decreasing-cost industries.

LO7.7 Discuss how long-run equilibrium in pure competition produces economic efficiency.

In Chapter 4 we examined the relationship between product demand and total revenue, and in Chapter 6 we discussed businesses and their production costs. Now we want to connect revenues and costs to see how a business decides what price to charge and how much output to produce. But a firm's decisions concerning price and production depend greatly on the character of the industry in which it is operating. There is no "average" or "typical" industry. At one extreme is a single producer that dominates the market; at the other extreme are industries in which thousands of firms each produce a tiny fraction of market supply. Between these extremes are many other industries.

Since we cannot examine each industry individually, our approach will be to look at four basic *models* of market structure. Together, these models will help you understand how price, output, and profit are determined in the many product markets in the economy. They also will help you evaluate the efficiency or inefficiency of those markets. Finally, these four models will provide a crucial background for assessing public policies (such as antitrust policy) relating to certain firms and industries.

Four Market Models

Economists group industries into four distinct market structures: pure competition, pure monopoly, monopolistic competition, and oligopoly. These four market models differ in several respects: the number of firms in the industry, whether those firms produce a standardized product or try to distinguish their products from those of other firms, and how easy or how difficult it is for firms to enter the industry.

The four models are as follows, presented in order of degree of competition (most to least):

- *Pure competition* involves a very large number of firms producing a standardized product (that is, a product like cotton for which each producer's output is virtually identical to that of every other producer). New firms can enter or exit the industry very easily.

- *Monopolistic competition* is characterized by a relatively large number of sellers producing differentiated products (clothing, furniture, books). Present in this model is widespread *nonprice competition,* a selling strategy in which one firm tries to distinguish its product or service from all competing products on the basis of attributes such as design and workmanship (an approach called *product differentiation*). Either entry to or exit from monopolistically competitive industries is quite easy.

PHOTO OP   Standardized versus Differentiated Products

Wheat is an example of a standardized product, whereas Dove shampoo is an example of a differentiated product.

©Glow Images

©StockPhotosArt - Hygiene/Alamy

- *Oligopoly* involves only a few sellers of a standardized or differentiated product, so each firm is affected by the decisions of its rivals and must take those decisions into account in determining its own price and output.
- *Pure monopoly* is a market structure in which one firm is the sole seller of a product or service for which there is no good substitute (for example, a local electric utility or patented medical device). Since the entry of additional firms is blocked, one firm constitutes the entire industry. The pure monopolist produces a single unique product, so product differentiation is not an issue.

Pure Competition: Characteristics and Occurrence

Let's take a fuller look at **pure competition,** the focus of the remainder of this chapter:

- *Very large numbers* A basic feature of a purely competitive market is the presence of a large number of independently acting sellers, often offering their products in large national or international markets. Examples: markets for farm commodities, the stock market, and the foreign exchange market.
- *Standardized product* Purely competitive firms produce a standardized (identical or homogeneous) product. As long as the price is the same, consumers will be indifferent about which seller to buy the product from. Buyers view the products of firms B, C, D, and E as perfect substitutes for the product of firm A. Because purely competitive firms sell standardized products, they make no attempt to differentiate their products and do not engage in other forms of nonprice competition.
- *"Price takers"* In a purely competitive market, individual firms do not exert control over product price. Each firm produces such a small fraction of total output that increasing or decreasing its output will not perceptibly influence total supply or, therefore, product price. In short, the competitive firm is a **price taker:** It cannot change market price; it can only adjust to it. That means that the individual competitive producer is at the mercy of the market. Asking a price higher than the market price would be futile. Consumers will not buy from firm A at $2.05 when its 9,999 competitors are selling an identical product, and therefore a perfect substitute, at $2 per unit. Conversely, because firm A can sell as much as it chooses at $2 per unit, it has no reason to charge a lower price, say, $1.95. Doing that would shrink its profit.
- *Free entry and exit* New firms can freely enter and existing firms can freely leave purely competitive industries. No significant legal, technological, financial, or other obstacles prohibit new firms from selling their output in any competitive market.

Although pure competition is somewhat rare in the real world, this market model is highly relevant to several industries. In particular, we can learn much about markets for agricultural goods, fish products, foreign exchange, basic metals, and stock shares by studying the pure-competition model. Also, pure competition is a meaningful starting point for any discussion of how prices and output are determined. Moreover, the operation of a purely competitive economy provides a norm for evaluating the efficiency of the real-world economy.

Demand as Seen by a Purely Competitive Seller

To develop a model of pure competition, we first examine demand from a purely competitive seller's viewpoint and see how it affects revenue. This seller might be a wheat farmer, a strawberry grower, a sheep rancher, a foreign-currency broker, or some other pure

pure competition A market structure in which a very large number of firms sell a standardized product, into which entry is very easy, in which the individual seller has no control over the product price, and in which there is no nonprice competition; a market characterized by a very large number of buyers and sellers.

price taker A seller (or buyer) that is unable to affect the price at which a product or resource sells by changing the amount it sells (or buys).

FIGURE 7.1 A purely competitive firm's demand and revenue curves. The demand curve (*D*) of a purely competitive firm is a horizontal line (perfectly elastic) because the firm can sell as much output as it wants at the market price (here, $131). Because each additional unit sold increases total revenue by the amount of the price, the firm's total-revenue curve (TR) is a straight upward-sloping line and its marginal-revenue curve (MR) coincides with the firm's demand curve. The average-revenue curve (AR) also coincides with the demand curve.

Firm's Demand Schedule		Firm's Revenue Data	
(1) Product Price (*P*) (Average Revenue)	(2) Quantity Demanded (*Q*)	(3) Total Revenue (TR), (1) × (2)	(4) Marginal Revenue (MR)
$131	0	$ 0	
131	1	131	$131
131	2	262	131
131	3	393	131
131	4	524	131
131	5	655	131
131	6	786	131
131	7	917	131
131	8	1048	131
131	9	1179	131
131	10	1310	131

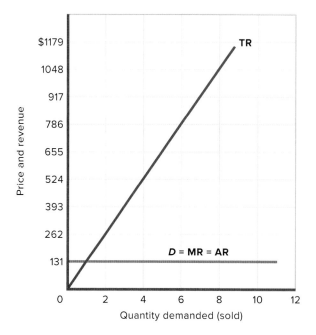

competitor. Because each purely competitive firm offers only a negligible fraction of total market supply, it must accept the price predetermined by the market. Pure competitors are price takers, not price makers.

Perfectly Elastic Demand

The demand schedule faced by the *individual firm* in a purely competitive industry is perfectly elastic at the market price, as demonstrated in Figure 7.1. As shown in column 1 of the table in Figure 7.1, the market price is $131. The firm represented cannot obtain a higher price by restricting its output, nor does it need to lower its price to increase its sales volume. Columns 1 and 2 show that the firm can produce and sell as many or as few units as it likes at the market price of $131.

We are *not* saying that *market* demand is perfectly elastic in a competitive market. Rather, market demand graphs as a downsloping curve. An entire industry (all firms producing a particular product) can affect price by changing industry output. For example, all firms, acting independently but simultaneously, can increase price by reducing output. But the individual competitive firm cannot do that because its output represents such a small fraction of its industry's total output. For the individual competitive firm, the market price is therefore a fixed value at which it can sell as many or as few units as it cares to. Graphically, this implies that the individual competitive firm's demand curve will plot as a straight, horizontal line such as *D* in Figure 7.1.

Average, Total, and Marginal Revenue

The firm's demand schedule is also its average-revenue schedule. Price per unit to the purchaser is also revenue per unit, or average revenue, to the seller. To say that all buyers must pay $131 per unit is to say that the revenue per unit, or **average revenue,** received by the seller is $131. Price and average revenue are the same thing.

The **total revenue** for each sales level is found by multiplying price by the corresponding quantity the firm can sell. (Column 1 multiplied by column 2 in the table in Figure 7.1 yields column 3.) In this case, total revenue increases by a constant amount, $131, for each additional unit of sales. Each unit sold adds exactly its constant price to total revenue.

When a firm is pondering a change in its output, it will consider how its total revenue will change as a result. **Marginal revenue** is the change in total revenue (or the extra revenue) that results from selling 1 more unit of output. In column 3 of the table in Figure 7.1, total revenue is zero when zero units are sold. The first unit of output sold increases total revenue from zero to $131, so marginal revenue for that unit is $131. The second unit sold increases total revenue from $131 to $262, and marginal revenue is again $131. Note in column 4 that marginal revenue is a constant $131, as is price. *In pure competition, marginal revenue and price are equal.*

Figure 7.1 shows the purely competitive firm's total-revenue, demand, marginal-revenue, and average-revenue curves. Total revenue (TR) is a straight line that slopes upward to the right. Its slope is constant because each extra unit of sales increases TR by $131. The demand curve (*D*) is horizontal, indicating perfect price elasticity. The marginal-revenue curve (MR) coincides with the demand curve because the product price (and hence MR) is constant. The average revenue equals price and therefore also coincides with the demand curve.

Profit Maximization in the Short Run

Because the purely competitive firm is a price taker, it cannot attempt to maximize its profit by raising or lowering the price it charges. With its price set by supply and demand in the overall market, the only variable that the firm can control is its output. As a result, the purely competitive firm attempts to maximize its economic profit (or minimize its economic loss) by adjusting its *output.* And in the short run, the firm has a fixed plant. Thus, it can adjust its output only through changes in the amount of variable resources (materials, labor) it uses. It adjusts its variable resources to achieve the output level that maximizes its profit.

More specifically, the firm compares the amounts that each *additional* unit of output would add to total revenue and to total cost. In other words, the firm compares the *marginal revenue* (MR) and the *marginal cost* (MC) of each successive unit of output. Assuming that producing is preferable to shutting down, the firm should produce any unit of output whose marginal revenue exceeds its marginal cost because the firm would gain more in revenue from selling that unit than it would add to its costs by producing it. Conversely, if the marginal cost of a unit of output exceeds its marginal revenue, the firm should not produce that unit. Producing it would add more to costs than to revenue, and profit would decline or loss would increase.

In the initial stages of production, where output is relatively low, marginal revenue will usually (but not always) exceed marginal cost. So it is profitable to produce through this

average revenue Total revenue from the sale of a product divided by the quantity of the product sold (demanded); equal to the price at which the product is sold when all units of the product are sold at the same price.

total revenue The total number of dollars received by a firm (or firms) from the sale of a product; equal to the total expenditures for the product produced by the firm (or firms); equal to the quantity sold (demanded) multiplied by the price at which it is sold.

marginal revenue The change in total revenue that results from the sale of 1 additional unit of a firm's product; equal to the change in total revenue divided by the change in the quantity of the product sold.

range of output. But at later stages of production, where output is relatively high, rising marginal costs will exceed marginal revenue. Obviously, a profit-maximizing firm will want to avoid output levels in that range. Separating these two production ranges is a unique point at which marginal revenue equals marginal cost. This point is the key to the output-determining rule: *In the short run, the firm will maximize profit or minimize loss by producing the output at which marginal revenue equals marginal cost (as long as producing is preferable to shutting down).* This profit-maximizing guide is known as the **MR = MC rule.** (For most sets of MR and MC data, MR and MC will be precisely equal at a fractional level of output. In such instances the firm should produce the last complete unit of output for which MR exceeds MC.)

> **MR = MC rule** The principle that a firm will maximize its profit (or minimize its losses) by producing the output at which marginal revenue and marginal cost are equal, provided product price is equal to or greater than average variable cost.

Keep in mind these three features of the MR = MC rule:

- As noted, the rule applies only if producing is preferable to shutting down. We will show shortly that if marginal revenue does not equal or exceed average variable cost, the firm will shut down rather than produce the amount of output at which MR = MC.
- The rule is an accurate guide to profit maximization for all firms whether they are purely competitive, monopolistic, monopolistically competitive, or oligopolistic.
- We can restate the rule as $P = MC$ when applied to a purely competitive firm. Because the demand schedule faced by a competitive seller is perfectly elastic at the going market price, product price and marginal revenue are equal. So under pure competition (and only under pure competition), we may substitute P for MR in the rule: *When producing is preferable to shutting down, the competitive firm that wants to maximize its profit or minimize its loss should produce at that point where price equals marginal cost ($P = MC$).*

Now let's apply the MR = MC rule or, because we are considering pure competition, the $P = MC$ rule.

Profit Maximization

The first five columns in the table in Figure 7.2 reproduce the AFC, AVC, ATC, and MC data derived for our product in Chapter 6. Here, we will compare the marginal-cost data of column 5 with price (equals marginal revenue) for each unit of output. Suppose first that the market price, and therefore marginal revenue, is $131, as shown in column 6.

What is the profit-maximizing output? Every unit of output up to and including the ninth unit represents greater marginal revenue than marginal cost of output. Each of the first 9 units therefore adds to the firm's profit and should be produced. The firm, however, should not produce the tenth unit. It would add more to cost ($150) than to revenue ($131).

We can calculate the economic profit realized by producing 9 units from the average-total-cost data. Price ($131) multiplied by output (9) yields total revenue of $1,179. Multiplying average total cost ($97.78) by output (9) gives us total cost of $880.[1] The difference of $299 (= $1,179 − $880) is the economic profit. Clearly, this firm will prefer to operate rather than shut down.

An alternative, and perhaps easier, way to calculate the economic profit is to determine the profit per unit by subtracting the average total cost ($97.78) from the product price ($131). Then multiply the difference (a per-unit profit of $33.22) by output (9). Take some time now to verify the numbers in column 7. You will find that any output other than that which adheres to the MR = MC rule will yield either profits below $299 or losses.

Figure 7.2 also shows price (= MR) and marginal cost graphically. Price equals marginal cost at the profit-maximizing output of 9 units. There the per-unit economic profit is

---

[1] Most of the unit-cost data are rounded figures from the total-cost figures presented in the previous chapter. Therefore, economic profits calculated from the unit-cost figures will typically vary by a few cents from the profits determined by subtracting actual total cost from total revenue. Here we simply ignore the few-cents differentials.

FIGURE 7.2 Short-run profit maximizing for a purely competitive firm. The MR = MC output enables the purely competitive firm to maximize profits or to minimize losses. In this case MR (= P in pure competition) and MC are equal at 9 units of output, Q. There P exceeds the average total cost A = \$97.78, so the firm realizes an economic profit of P − A per unit. The total economic profit is represented by the green rectangle and is 9 × (P − A).

(1) Total Product (Output)	(2) Average Fixed Cost (AFC)	(3) Average Variable Cost (AVC)	(4) Average Total Cost (ATC)	(5) Marginal Cost (MC)	(6) \$131 Price = Marginal Revenue (MR)	(7) Total Economic Profit (+) or Loss (−)
0						\$−100
				\$ 90	\$131	−59
1	\$100.00	\$90.00	\$190.00	80	131	
2	50.00	85.00	135.00			−8
				70	131	
3	33.33	80.00	113.33	60	131	+53
4	25.00	75.00	100.00			+124
				70	131	
5	20.00	74.00	94.00	80	131	+185
6	16.67	75.00	91.67			+236
				90	131	
7	14.29	77.14	91.43	110	131	+277
8	12.50	81.25	93.75			+298
				130	**131**	
9	**11.11**	**86.67**	**97.78**	150	131	**+299**
10	10.00	93.00	103.00			+280

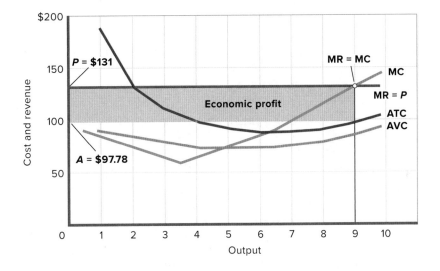

P − A, where P is the market price and A is the average total cost of 9 units of output. The total economic profit is 9 × (P − A), shown by the green rectangular area.

Loss Minimization and Shutdown

Now let's assume that the market price is \$81 rather than \$131. Should the firm still produce? If so, how much? And what will be the resulting profit or loss? The answers, respectively, are "Yes," "Six units," and "A loss of \$64."

The first five columns of the table in Figure 7.3 are the same as the first five columns of the table in Figure 7.2. But column 6 of the table in Figure 7.3 shows the new price (equal to MR) of \$81. Looking at columns 5 and 6, notice that the first unit of output adds \$90 to total cost but only \$81 to total revenue. One might conclude: "Don't produce—close down!" But that would be hasty. Remember that in the very early stages of production, marginal product is low, making marginal cost unusually high. The price–marginal cost relationship improves with increased production. For units 2 through 6, price exceeds marginal cost. Each of these 5 units adds more to revenue than to cost, and as shown in column 7, they decrease the total loss. Together they more than compensate for the "loss" taken on the first unit. Beyond 6

FIGURE 7.3 **Short-run loss minimization for a purely competitive firm.** If price P exceeds the minimum AVC (here, $74 at $Q = 5$) but is less than ATC, the MR = MC output (here, 6 units) will permit the firm to minimize its losses. In this instance the loss is $A - P$ per unit, where A is the average total cost at 6 units of output. The total loss is shown by the red area and is equal to $6 \times (A - P)$.

(1) Total Product (Output)	(2) Average Fixed Cost (AFC)	(3) Average Variable Cost (AVC)	(4) Average Total Cost (ATC)	(5) Marginal Cost (MC)	(6) $81 Price = Marginal Revenue (MR)	(7) Profit (+) or Loss (−), $81 Price
0						$-100
1	$100.00	$90.00	$190.00	$ 90	$81	−109
2	50.00	85.00	135.00	80	81	−108
3	33.33	80.00	113.33	70	81	−97
4	25.00	75.00	100.00	60	81	−76
5	20.00	74.00	94.00	70	81	−65
6	16.67	75.00	91.67	80	81	−64
7	14.29	77.14	91.43	90	81	−73
8	12.50	81.25	93.75	110	81	−102
9	11.11	86.67	97.78	130	81	−151
10	10.00	93.00	103.00	150	81	−220

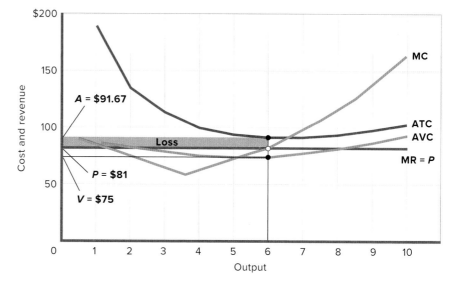

units, however, MC exceeds MR ($= P$). The firm should therefore produce 6 units. In general, the profit-seeking producer should always compare marginal revenue (or price under pure competition) with the rising portion of the marginal-cost schedule or curve.

Loss Minimization   Will production be profitable? No, because at 6 units of output the average total cost of $91.67 exceeds the price of $81 by $10.67 per unit. If we multiply that by the 6 units of output, we find the firm's total loss is $64. Alternatively, comparing the total revenue of $486 (= 6 × $81) with the total cost of $550 (= 6 × $91.67), we see again that the firm's loss is $64.

Then why produce? Because this loss is less than the firm's $100 of fixed costs, which is the $100 loss the firm would incur in the short run by closing down. The firm receives enough revenue per unit ($81) to cover its average variable costs of $75 and also provide $6 per unit, or a total of $36, to apply against fixed costs. Therefore, the firm's loss is only $64 (= $100 − $36), not $100.

This loss-minimizing case is illustrated in the graph in Figure 7.3. Wherever price P exceeds AVC but is less than ATC, the firm can pay part, but not all, of its fixed costs by producing. The firm minimizes its loss by producing the output at which MC = MR (here, 6 units). At that output, each unit contributes $P - V$ to covering fixed cost, where V is the AVC at 6 units of output. The per-unit loss is $A - P = \$10.67$, and the total loss is $6 \times (A - P)$, or \$64, as shown by the red area.

Shutdown   Suppose now that the market yields a price of only \$71. Should the firm produce? No, because at every output level the firm's average variable cost is greater than the price (compare columns 3 and 6 of the table in Figure 7.4). The smallest loss the firm can incur by producing is greater than the \$100 fixed cost it will lose by shutting down (as shown by column 7). The best action is to shut down.

You can see this shutdown situation in the graph in Figure 7.4, where the MR = P line lies below AVC at all points. The \$71 price comes closest to covering average

FIGURE 7.4   The short-run shutdown case for a purely competitive firm. If price P (here, \$71) falls below the minimum AVC (here, \$74 at $Q = 5$), the competitive firm will minimize its losses in the short run by shutting down. There is no level of output at which the firm can produce and realize a loss smaller than its total fixed cost.

(1) Total Product (Output)	(2) Average Fixed Cost (AFC)	(3) Average Variable Cost (AVC)	(4) Average Total Cost (ATC)	(5) Marginal Cost (MC)	(6) \$71 Price = Marginal Revenue (MR)	(7) Profit (+) or Loss (−), \$71 Price
0						\$−100
1	\$100.00	\$90.00	\$190.00	\$ 90	\$71	−119
2	50.00	85.00	135.00	80	71	−128
3	33.33	80.00	113.33	70	71	−127
4	25.00	75.00	100.00	60	71	−116
5	20.00	74.00	94.00	70	71	−115
6	16.67	75.00	91.67	80	71	−124
7	14.29	77.14	91.43	90	71	−143
8	12.50	81.25	93.75	110	71	−182
9	11.11	86.67	97.78	130	71	−241
10	10.00	93.00	103.00	150	71	−320

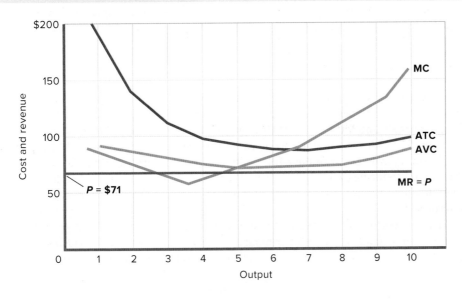

APPLYING THE ANALYSIS

The Still There Motel

Have you ever driven by a poorly maintained business facility and wondered why the owner does not either fix up the property or go out of business? The somewhat surprising reason is that it may be unprofitable to improve the facility yet profitable to continue for a time to operate the business as it deteriorates. Seeing why will aid your understanding of the "stay open or shut down" decision facing firms experiencing declining demand.

Consider the Still There Motel on Old Highway North, Anytown, USA. The owner built the motel on the basis of traffic patterns and competition existing several decades ago. But as interstate highways were built, the motel found itself located on a relatively untraveled stretch of road. Also, it faced severe competition from "chain" motels located much closer to the interstate highway.

As demand and revenue fell, Still There moved from profitability to loss ($P < $ ATC). But at first its room rates and annual revenue were sufficient to cover its total variable costs and contribute some to the payment of fixed costs such as insurance and property taxes ($P > $ AVC). By staying open, Still There lost less than it would have if it shut down. But since its total revenue did not cover its total costs (or $P < $ ATC), the owner realized that something must be done in the long run. The owner decided to lower average total costs by reducing annual maintenance. In effect, the owner opted to allow the motel to deteriorate as a way of regaining temporary profitability.

This renewed profitability of Still There cannot last because in time no further reduction in maintenance costs will be possible. The further deterioration of the motel structure will produce even lower room rates, and therefore even less total revenue. The owner of Still There knows that sooner or later total revenue will again fall below total cost (or P will again fall below ATC), even with an annual maintenance expense of zero. When that occurs, the owner will close down the business, tear down the structure, and sell the vacant property. But, in the meantime, the motel is still there—open, deteriorating, and profitable.

QUESTION: Why might even a well-maintained, profitable motel shut down in the long run if the land on which it is located becomes extremely valuable due to surrounding economic development?

variable costs at the MR ($= P$) $=$ MC output of 5 units. But even here, the table reveals that price or revenue per unit would fall short of average variable cost by $3 (= $74 − $71). By producing at the MR ($= P$) $=$ MC output, the firm would lose its $100 worth of fixed cost plus $15 (= $3 of variable cost on each of the 5 units), for a total loss of $115. This compares unfavorably with the $100 fixed-cost loss the firm would incur by shutting down and producing no output. So it will make sense for the firm to shut down rather than produce at a $71 price—or at any price less than the minimum average variable cost of $74.

The shutdown case reminds us of the qualifier to our MR ($= P$) $=$ MC rule. A competitive firm will maximize profit or minimize loss in the short run by producing that output at which MR ($= P$) $=$ MC, *provided that market price exceeds minimum average variable cost.*

Marginal Cost and Short-Run Supply

In the preceding section, we simply selected three different prices and asked what quantity the profit-seeking competitive firm, faced with certain costs, would choose to offer in the market at each price. This set of product prices and corresponding quantities supplied constitutes part of the supply schedule for the competitive firm.

Table 7.1 summarizes the supply schedule data for those three prices ($131, $81, and $71) and four others. This table confirms the direct relationship between product price and quantity supplied that we identified in Chapter 3. Note first that the firm will not produce at price $61 or $71 because both are less than the $74 minimum AVC. Then note that quantity supplied increases as price increases. Observe finally that economic profit is higher at higher prices.

Generalized Depiction

Figure 7.5 generalizes the MR = MC rule and the relationship between short-run production costs and the firm's supply behavior. The ATC, AVC, and MC curves are shown, along with several marginal-revenue lines drawn at possible market prices. Let's observe quantity supplied at each of these prices:

- Price P_1 is below the firm's minimum average variable cost, so at this price the firm won't operate at all. Quantity supplied will be zero, as it will be at all other prices below P_2.
- Price P_2 is just equal to the minimum average variable cost. The firm will supply Q_2 units of output (where $MR_2 = MC$) and just cover its total variable cost. Its loss will equal its total fixed cost. (Actually, the firm would be indifferent as to shutting down or supplying Q_2 units of output, but we assume it produces.)
- At price P_3 the firm will supply Q_3 units of output to minimize its short-run losses. At any other price between P_2 and P_4 the firm will minimize its losses by producing and supplying the MR = MC quantity.
- The firm will just break even at price P_4. There it will supply Q_4 units of output (where $MR_4 = MC$), earning a normal profit but not an economic profit. (Recall that a normal profit is a cost and included in the cost curves.) Total revenue will just cover total cost, including a normal profit, because the revenue per unit ($MR_4 = P_4$) and the total cost per unit (ATC) are the same.
- At price P_5 the firm will realize an economic profit by producing and supplying Q_5 units of output. In fact, at any price above P_4, the firm will obtain economic profit by producing to the point where MR (= P) = MC.

Note that each of the MR (= P) = MC intersection points labeled b, c, d, and e in Figure 7.5 indicates a possible product price (on the vertical axis) and the corresponding quantity that the firm would supply at that price (on the horizontal axis). Thus, points such

Price	Quantity Supplied	Maximum Profit (+) or Minimum Loss (−)
$151	10	$+480
131	9	+299
111	8	+138
91	7	−3
81	6	−64
71	0	−100
61	0	−100

TABLE 7.1 The Supply Schedule of a Competitive Firm Confronted with the Cost Data in the Table in Figure 7.2

FIGURE 7.5 The *P* = MC rule and the competitive firm's short-run supply curve. Application of the *P* = MC rule, as modified by the shutdown case, reveals that the (solid) segment of the firm's MC curve that lies above AVC is the firm's short-run supply curve.

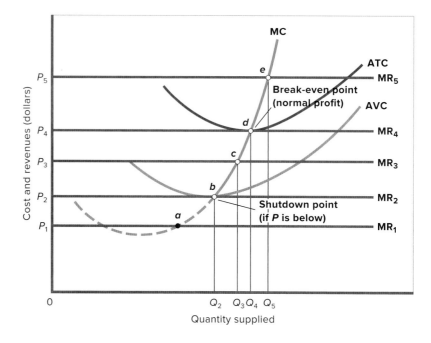

short-run supply curve A supply curve that shows the quantity of a product a firm in a purely competitive industry will offer to sell at various prices in the short run; the portion of the firm's short-run marginal cost curve that lies above its average-variable-cost curve.

as these are on the upsloping supply curve of the competitive firm. Note too that quantity supplied would be zero at any price below the minimum average variable cost (AVC). *We can conclude that the portion of the firm's marginal-cost curve lying above its average-variable-cost curve is its short-run supply curve.* In Figure 7.5, the solid segment of the marginal-cost curve MC *is* this firm's **short-run supply curve.** It tells us the amount of output the firm will supply at each price in a series of prices. It slopes upward because of the law of diminishing returns.

Table 7.2 summarizes the MR = MC approach to determining the competitive firm's profit-maximizing output level. It also shows the conditions under which a firm should decide to produce, and the circumstances that will generate economic profits.

Firm and Industry: Equilibrium Price

In the preceding section we established the competitive firm's short-run supply curve by applying the MR (= *P*) = MC rule. But which of the various possible prices will actually be the market equilibrium price?

From Chapter 3 we know that the market equilibrium price will be the price at which the total quantity supplied of the product equals the total quantity demanded. So to

TABLE 7.2 **Output Determination in Pure Competition in the Short Run**

Question	Answer
Should this firm produce?	Yes, if price is equal to, or greater than, minimum average variable cost. This means that the firm is profitable or that its losses are less than its fixed cost.
What quantity should this firm produce?	Produce where MR (= *P*) = MC; there, profit is maximized (TR exceeds TC by a maximum amount) or loss is minimized.
Will production result in economic profit?	Yes, if price exceeds average total cost (so that TR exceeds TC). No, if average total cost exceeds price (so that TC exceeds TR).

TABLE 7.3 **Firm and Market Supply and Market Demand**

(1) Quantity Supplied Single Firm	(2) Total Quantity Supplied, 1000 Firms	(3) Product Price	(4) Total Quantity Demanded
10	10,000	$151	4,000
9	9,000	131	6,000
8	**8,000**	**111**	**8,000**
7	7,000	91	9,000
6	6,000	81	11,000
0	0	71	13,000
0	0	61	16,000

determine the equilibrium price, we first need to obtain a total supply schedule and a total demand schedule. We find the total supply schedule by assuming a particular number of firms in the industry and supposing that each firm has the same individual supply schedule as the firm represented in Figure 7.5. Then we sum the quantities supplied at each price level to obtain the total (or market) supply schedule. Columns 1 and 3 in Table 7.3 repeat the supply schedule for the individual competitive firm, as derived in Table 7.1. Suppose 1,000 firms compete in this industry, all having the same total and unit costs as the single firm we discussed. This lets us calculate the market supply schedule (columns 2 and 3) by multiplying the quantity-supplied figures of the single firm (column 1) by 1,000.

Market Price and Profits To determine the equilibrium price and output, we must compare these total-supply data with total-demand data. Let's assume that total demand is as shown in columns 3 and 4 in Table 7.3. By comparing the total quantity supplied and the total quantity demanded at the seven possible prices, we determine that the equilibrium price is $111 and the equilibrium quantity is 8,000 units for the industry—8 units for each of the 1,000 identical firms.

Will these conditions of market supply and demand make this a profitable or unprofitable industry? Multiplying product price ($111) by output (8 units), we find that the total revenue of each firm is $888. The total cost is $750, found by looking at column 4 of the table in Figure 6.3. The $138 difference is the economic profit of each firm. For the industry, total economic profit is $138,000. This, then, is a profitable industry.

Another way of calculating economic profit is to determine per-unit profit by subtracting average total cost ($93.75) from product price ($111) and multiplying the difference (per-unit profit of $17.25) by the firm's equilibrium level of output (8). Again we obtain an economic profit of $138 per firm and $138,000 for the industry.

Figure 7.6 shows this analysis graphically. The individual supply curves of each of the 1,000 identical firms—one of which is shown as $s = MC$ in Figure 7.6a—are summed horizontally to get the total-supply curve $S = \Sigma MCs$ of Figure 7.6b. With total-demand curve D, it yields the equilibrium price $111 and equilibrium quantity (for the industry) 8,000 units. This equilibrium price is given and unalterable to the individual firm; that is, each firm's demand curve is perfectly elastic at the equilibrium price, as indicated by d in Figure 7.6a. Because the individual firm is a price taker, the marginal-revenue curve coincides with the firm's demand curve d. This $111 price exceeds the average total cost at the firm's equilibrium $MR = MC$ output of 8 units, so the firm earns an economic profit represented by the green area in Figure 7.6a.

Assuming no changes in costs or market demand, these diagrams reveal a genuine equilibrium in the short run. There are no shortages or surpluses in the market to cause price or total quantity to change. Nor can any firm in the industry increase its profit by

FIGURE 7.6 **Short-run competitive equilibrium for (a) a firm and (b) the industry.** The horizontal sum of the 1,000 firms' individual supply curves (s) determines the industry (market) supply curve (S). Given industry (market) demand (D), the short-run equilibrium price and output for the industry are $111 and 8,000 units. Taking the equilibrium price as given, the individual firm establishes its profit-maximizing output at 8 units and, in this case, realizes the economic profit represented by the green area.

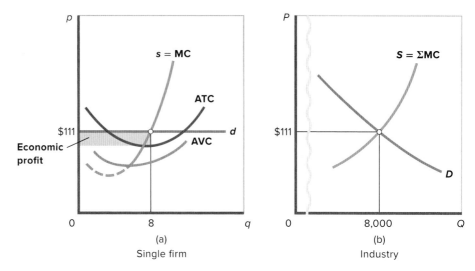

altering its output. Note, however, that weaker market demand or stronger market supply (and therefore lower prices) could shift the line *d* downward and change the situation to losses (P < ATC) or even to shutdown (P < AVC).

Firm versus Industry   Figure 7.6 underscores a point made earlier: Product price is a given fact to the individual competitive firm, but the supply plans of all competitive producers as a group are a basic determinant of product price. There is no inconsistency here. One firm, supplying a negligible fraction of total supply, cannot affect price. But the sum of the supply curves of all the firms in the industry constitutes the market supply curve, and that curve (along with demand) does have an important bearing on equilibrium price.

Profit Maximization in the Long Run

The entry and exit of firms in our market models can only take place in the long run. In the short run, the industry is composed of a specific number of firms, each with a plant size that is fixed and unalterable in the short run. Firms may shut down in the sense that they can produce zero units of output in the short run, but they do not have sufficient time to liquidate their assets and go out of business.

In the long run, by contrast, the firms already in an industry have sufficient time to either expand or contract their capacities. More important, the number of firms in the industry may either increase or decrease as new firms enter or existing firms leave.

The length of time constituting the long run varies substantially by industry, however, so that you should not fix in your mind any specific number of years, months, or days. Instead, focus your attention on the incentives provided by profits and losses for the entry and exit of firms into any purely competitive industry and, later in the chapter, on how those incentives lead to productive and allocative efficiency. The time horizons are far less important than how these long-run adjustments affect price, quantity, and profits, and the process by which profits and losses guide business managers toward the efficient use of society's resources.

Assumptions

We make three simplifying assumptions, none of which alters our conclusions:

- *Entry and exit only*   The only long-run adjustment in our graphical analysis is caused by the entry or exit of firms. Moreover, we ignore all short-run adjustments in order to concentrate on the effects of the long-run adjustments.

- *Identical costs* All firms in the industry have identical cost curves. This assumption lets us discuss an "average," or "representative," firm, knowing that all other firms in the industry are similarly affected by any long-run adjustments that occur.
- *Constant-cost industry* The industry is a constant-cost industry. This means that the entry and exit of firms does not affect resource prices or, consequently, the locations of the average-total-cost curves of individual firms.

Goal of Our Analysis

The basic conclusion we seek to explain is this: After all long-run adjustments are completed in a purely competitive industry, product price will be exactly equal to, and production will occur at, each firm's minimum average total cost.

This conclusion follows from two basic facts: (1) Firms seek profits and shun losses and (2) under pure competition, firms are free to enter and leave an industry. If market price initially exceeds minimum average total costs, the resulting economic profits will attract new firms to the industry. But this industry expansion will increase supply until price is brought back down to equality with minimum average total cost. Conversely, if price is initially less than minimum average total cost, resulting losses will cause firms to leave the industry. As they leave, total supply will decline, bringing the price back up to equality with minimum average total cost.

Long-Run Equilibrium

Consider the average firm in a purely competitive industry that is initially in long-run equilibrium. This firm is represented in Figure 7.7a, where MR = MC and price and minimum average total cost are equal at $50. Economic profit here is zero; the industry is in equilibrium or "at rest" because there is no tendency for firms to enter or to leave. The existing firms are just covering the explicit and implicit costs that are represented by their cost curves. Recall that the firm's cost curves include the normal profits that owners could expect to receive in their best alternative business ventures. The $50 market price is determined in Figure 7.7b by market or industry demand D_1 and supply S_1. (S_1 is a short-run supply curve; we will develop the long-run industry supply curve in our discussion.)

As shown on the quantity axes of the two graphs, equilibrium output in the industry is 100,000 while equilibrium output for the single firm is 100. If all firms in the industry are identical, there must be 1,000 firms (=100,000/100).

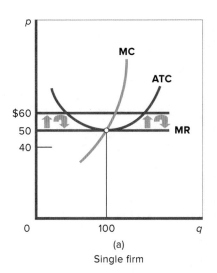

(a)
Single firm

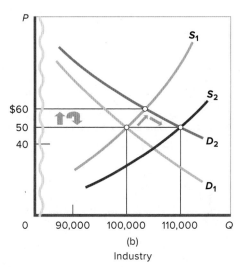

(b)
Industry

FIGURE 7.7 Temporary profits and the reestablishment of long-run equilibrium in (a) a representative firm and (b) the industry. A favorable shift in demand (D_1 to D_2) will upset the original industry equilibrium and produce economic profits. But those profits will entice new firms to enter the industry, increasing supply (S_1 to S_2) and lowering product price until economic profits are once again zero.

Entry Eliminates Economic Profits

Let's upset the long-run equilibrium in Figure 7.7 and see what happens. Suppose a change in consumer tastes increases product demand from D_1 to D_2. Price will rise to $60, as determined at the intersection of D_2 and S_1, and the firm's marginal-revenue curve will shift upward to $60. This $60 price exceeds the firm's average total cost of $50 at output 100, creating an economic profit of $10 per unit. This economic profit will lure new firms into the industry. Some entrants will be newly created firms; others will shift from less-prosperous industries.

As firms enter, the market supply of the product increases and the product price falls below $60. Economic profits persist, and entry continues until short-run supply increases to S_2. Market price falls to $50, as does marginal revenue for the firm. Price and minimum average total cost are again equal at $50. The economic profits caused by the boost in demand have been eliminated, and, as a result, the previous incentive for more firms to enter the industry has disappeared because the firms that remain are earning only a normal profit (zero economic profit). Entry ceases and a new long-run equilibrium is reached.

Observe in Figure 7.7a and 7.7b that total quantity supplied is now 110,000 units and each firm is producing 100 units. Now 1,100 firms rather than the original 1,000 populate the industry. Economic profits have attracted 100 more firms.

Exit Eliminates Losses

Now let's consider a shift in the opposite direction. We begin in Figure 7.8b with curves S_1 and D_1 setting the same initial long-run equilibrium situation as in our previous analysis, including the $50 price.

Suppose consumer demand declines from D_1 to D_3. This forces the market price and marginal revenue down to $40, making production unprofitable at the minimum ATC of $50. In time the resulting economic losses will induce firms to leave the industry. Their owners will seek a normal profit elsewhere rather than accept the below-normal profits (losses) now confronting them. As this exodus of firms proceeds, however, industry supply decreases, pushing the price up from $40 toward $50. Losses continue and more firms leave the industry until the supply curve shifts to S_3. Once this happens, price is again $50, just equal to the minimum average total cost. Losses have been eliminated so that the firms that remain are earning only a normal profit (zero economic profit). Since this is no better or worse than entrepreneurs could expect to earn in other business ventures, there is no longer any incentive to exit the industry. Long-run equilibrium is restored.

FIGURE 7.8 **Temporary losses and the reestablishment of long-run equilibrium in (a) a representative firm and (b) the industry.** An unfavorable shift in demand (D_1 to D_3) will upset the original industry equilibrium and produce losses. But those losses will cause firms to leave the industry, decreasing supply (S_1 to S_3) and increasing product price until all losses have disappeared.

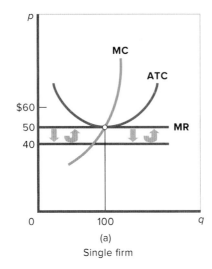

(a)
Single firm

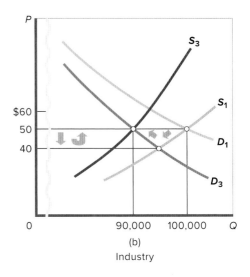

(b)
Industry

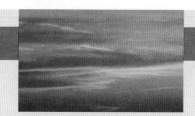

APPLYING THE ANALYSIS

The Exit of Farmers from U.S. Agriculture

The U.S. agricultural industry serves as a good example of how losses resulting from declining prices received by individual producers create an exit of producers from an industry.

A rapid rate of technological advance has significantly increased the *supply* of U.S. agricultural products over time. This technological progress has many roots: the mechanization of farms, improved techniques of land management, soil conservation, irrigation, development of hybrid crops, availability of improved fertilizers and insecticides, polymer-coated seeds, and improvements in the breeding and care of livestock. In 1950, each farmworker produced enough food and fiber to support about a dozen people. By 2011, that figure had increased to more than 100 people!

Increases in *demand* for agricultural products, however, have failed to keep pace with technologically created increases in the supply of the products. The demand for farm products in the United States is *income-inelastic*. Estimates indicate that a 10 percent increase in real per capita after-tax income produces about a 2 percent increase in consumption of farm products. Once consumers' stomachs are filled, they turn to the amenities of life that manufacturing and services, not agriculture, provide. So, as the incomes of Americans rise, the demand for farm products increases far less rapidly than the demand for products in general.

The consequences of the long-run supply and demand conditions just outlined have been those predicted by the long-run pure-competition model. Financial losses in agriculture have triggered a large decline in the number of farms and a massive exit of workers to other sectors of the economy. In 1950, there were about 5.4 million farms in the United States employing 9.3 million people. Today there are just over 2 million farms employing 1.8 million people. Since 1950, farm employment has declined from 15.8 percent of the U.S. workforce to just 1.2 percent. Moreover, the exodus of farmers would have been even larger in the absence of government subsidies that have enabled many farmers to remain in agriculture. Such subsidies were traditionally in the form of government price supports (price floors) but have more recently evolved to direct subsidy payments to farmers. Such payments have averaged more than $16 billion annually over the last decade.

QUESTION: Why is the exit of farmers from U.S. agriculture bad for the farmers who must leave but good for the farmers who remain?

In Figure 7.8a and 7.8b, total quantity supplied is now 90,000 units and each firm is producing 100 units. Only 900 firms, not the original 1,000, populate the industry. Losses have forced 100 firms out.

You may have noted that we have sidestepped the question of which firms will leave the industry when losses occur by assuming that all firms have identical cost curves. In the "real world," of course, managerial talents differ. Even if resource prices and technology are the same for all firms, less skillfully managed firms tend to incur higher costs and therefore are the first to leave an industry when demand declines. Similarly, firms with less-productive labor forces or higher transportation costs will be higher-cost producers and likely candidates to quit an industry when demand decreases.

Long-Run Supply for a Constant-Cost Industry

long-run supply curve A curve showing the prices at which a purely competitive industry will make various quantities of the product available in the long run.

We have established that changes in market supply through entry and exit create a long-run equilibrium in purely competitive markets. Although our analysis has dealt with the long run, we have noted that the market supply curves in Figures 7.7b and 7.8b are short-run curves. What then is the character of the **long-run supply curve** of a competitive industry? Our analysis points us toward an answer. The crucial factor here is the effect, if any, that changes in the number of firms in the industry will have on costs of the individual firms in the industry.

constant-cost industry An industry in which expansion by the entry of new firms has no effect on the prices firms in the industry must pay for resources and thus no effect on production costs.

In our discussion of long-run competitive equilibrium, we assumed that the industry under discussion was a **constant-cost industry.** This means that industry expansion or contraction will not affect resource prices and therefore production costs. Graphically, it means that the entry or exit of firms does not shift the long-run ATC curves of individual firms. This is the case when the industry's demand for resources is small in relation to the total demand for those resources. Then the industry can expand or contract without significantly affecting resource prices and costs.

What does the long-run supply curve of a constant-cost industry look like? The answer is contained in our previous analysis. There we saw that the entry and exit of firms changes industry output but always brings the product price back to its original level, where it is just equal to the constant minimum ATC. Specifically, we discovered that the industry would supply 90,000, 100,000, or 110,000 units of output, all at a price of $50 per unit. In other words, the long-run supply curve of a constant-cost industry is perfectly elastic.

Figure 7.9a demonstrates this graphically. Suppose industry demand is originally D_1, industry output is Q_1 (100,000 units), and product price is P_1 ($50). This situation, from Figure 7.7, is one of long-run equilibrium. We saw that when demand increases to D_2, upsetting this equilibrium, the resulting economic profits attract new firms. Because this is a constant-cost industry, entry continues and industry output expands until the price is driven back down to the level of the unchanged minimum ATC. This is at price P_2 ($50) and output Q_2 (110,000).

From Figure 7.8, we saw that a decline in market demand from D_1 to D_3 causes an exit of firms and ultimately restores equilibrium at price P_3 ($50) and output Q_3 (90,000 units).

FIGURE 7.9 Long-run supply: constant-cost industry versus increasing-cost industry. (a) In a constant-cost industry, the entry of firms does not affect resource prices or, therefore, unit costs. So an increase in demand (D_1 to D_2) or a decrease in demand (D_1 to D_3) causes a change in industry output (Q_1 to Q_2 or Q_1 to Q_3) but no alteration in price ($50). This means that the long-run industry supply curve (S) is horizontal through points Z_3, Z_1, and Z_2. (b) In an increasing-cost industry, the entry of new firms in response to an increase in demand (D_3 to D_1 to D_2) will bid up resource prices and thereby increase unit costs. As a result, an increased industry output (Q_3 to Q_1 to Q_2) will be forthcoming only at higher prices ($45 to $50 to $55). The long-run industry supply curve (S) therefore slopes upward through points Y_3, Y_1, and Y_2.

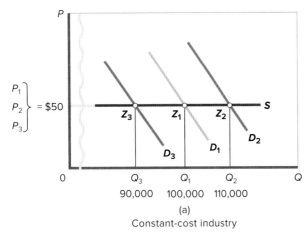

(a)
Constant-cost industry

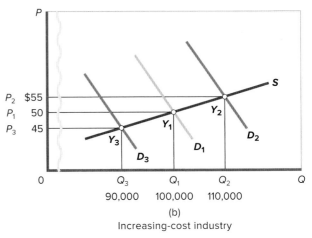

(b)
Increasing-cost industry

The points Z_1, Z_2, and Z_3 in Figure 7.9a represent these three price-quantity combinations. A line or curve connecting all such points shows the various price-quantity combinations that firms would produce if they had enough time to make all desired adjustments to changes in demand. This line or curve is the industry's long-run supply curve. In a constant-cost industry, this curve (straight line) is horizontal, as in Figure 7.9a, thus representing perfectly elastic supply.

Long-Run Supply for an Increasing-Cost Industry

Constant-cost industries are a special case. Most industries are **increasing-cost industries,** in which firms' ATC curves shift upward as the industry expands and downward as the industry contracts. The construction industry and medical care industries are examples.

Usually, the entry of new firms will increase resource prices, particularly in industries using specialized resources whose long-run supplies do not readily increase in response to increases in resource demand. Higher resource prices result in higher long-run average total costs for all firms in the industry. These higher costs cause upward shifts in each firm's long-run ATC curve.

Thus, when an increase in product demand results in economic profits and attracts new firms to an increasing-cost industry, a two-way squeeze works to eliminate those profits. As before, the entry of new firms increases market supply and lowers the market price. But now each firm's ATC curve also shifts upward. The overall result is a higher-than-original equilibrium price. The industry produces a larger output at a higher product price because the industry expansion has increased resource prices and the minimum average total cost.

Since greater output will be supplied at a higher price, the long-run industry supply curve is upsloping. Instead of supplying 90,000, 100,000, or 110,000 units at the same price of $50, an increasing-cost industry might supply 90,000 units at $45, 100,000 units at $50, and 110,000 units at $55. A higher price is required to induce more production because costs per unit of output increase as production increases.

Figure 7.9b nicely illustrates the situation. Original market demand is D_1 and industry price and output are P_1 ($50) and Q_1 (100,000 units), respectively, at equilibrium point Y_1. An increase in demand to D_2 upsets this equilibrium and leads to economic profits. New firms enter the industry, increasing both market supply and production costs of individual firms. A new price is established at point Y_2, where P_2 is $55 and Q_2 is 110,000 units.

Conversely, a decline in demand from D_1 to D_3 makes production unprofitable and causes firms to leave the industry. The resulting decline in resource prices reduces the minimum average total cost of production for firms that stay. A new equilibrium price is established at some level below the original price, say, at point Y_3, where P_3 is $45 and Q_3 is 90,000 units. Connecting these three equilibrium positions, we derive the upsloping long-run supply curve S in Figure 7.9b.

Long-Run Supply for a Decreasing-Cost Industry

In **decreasing-cost industries,** firms experience lower costs as their industry expands. The personal computer industry is an example. As demand for personal computers increased, new manufacturers of computers entered the industry and greatly increased the resource demand for the components used to build them (for example, memory chips, hard drives, monitors, and operating software). The expanded production of the components enabled the producers of those items to achieve substantial economies of scale. The decreased production costs of the components reduced their prices, which greatly lowered the computer manufacturers' average costs of production. The supply of personal computers increased by more than demand, and the price of personal computers declined. Although not shown in Figure 7.9, the long-run supply curve of a decreasing-cost industry is *downsloping*.

increasing-cost industry An industry in which expansion through the entry of new firms raises the prices firms in the industry must pay for resources and therefore increases their production costs.

decreasing-cost industry An industry in which expansion through the entry of firms lowers the prices that firms in the industry must pay for resources and therefore decreases their production costs.

PHOTO OP Increasing-Cost versus Decreasing-Cost Industries

Mining is an example of an increasing-cost industry, whereas electronics is an example of a decreasing-cost industry.

©rozpedowski/Getty Images

©Henrik Jonsson/Getty Images

Unfortunately, the industries that show decreasing costs also show increasing costs if output contracts. A decline in demand (say from foreign competition) makes production unprofitable and causes firms to leave the industry. Firms that remain face a greater minimum average total cost of production, implying a higher long-run equilibrium price in the market.

Pure Competition and Efficiency

Our final goal in this chapter is to examine the efficiency aspects of pure competition. Assuming a constant- or increasing-cost industry, the final long-run equilibrium positions of all firms have the same basic efficiency characteristics. As shown in Figure 7.10, price (and marginal revenue) will settle where it is equal to minimum average total cost: P (and MR) = minimum ATC. Moreover, since the marginal-cost curve intersects the average-total-cost curve at its minimum point, marginal cost and average total cost are equal: MC = minimum ATC. So in long-run equilibrium, a multiple equality occurs: P (and MR) = MC = minimum ATC. Thus, in long-run equilibrium, each firm produces at the output level that is associated with this triple equality.[2]

The triple equality tells us two very important things about long-run equilibrium. First, it tells us that although a competitive firm may realize economic profit or loss in the short run, it will earn only a normal profit by producing in accordance with the MR (= P) = MC rule in the long run. Second, the triple equality tells us that in long-run equilibrium, the profit-maximizing decision rule that leads each firm to produce the quantity at which P = MR also implies that each firm will produce at the output level that is associated with the minimum point on each identical firm's ATC curve.

This is very important because it suggests that pure competition leads to the most efficient possible use of society's resources. Indeed, subject only to Chapter 5's qualifications relating to public goods and externalities, an idealized purely competitive market economy composed of constant- or increasing-cost industries will generate both productive efficiency and allocative efficiency.

Productive efficiency requires that goods be produced in the least costly way. Allocative efficiency requires that resources be apportioned among firms and industries so as to

---

[2]This triple equality does not hold for decreasing-cost industries because MC always remains below ATC if average costs are decreasing. We will discuss this situation of "natural monopoly" in Chapter 8.

FIGURE 7.10 Long-run equilibrium: a competitive firm and market. (a) The equality of price (*P*), marginal cost (MC), and minimum average total cost (ATC) at output *Q_f* indicates that the firm is achieving productive efficiency and allocative efficiency. It is using the most efficient technology, charging the lowest price, and producing the greatest output consistent with its costs. It is receiving only a normal profit, which is incorporated into the ATC curve. The equality of price and marginal cost indicates that society allocated its scarce resources in accordance with consumer preferences. (b) In the purely competitive market, allocative efficiency occurs at the market equilibrium output *Q_e*. The sum of consumer surplus (green area) and producer surplus (blue area) is maximized.

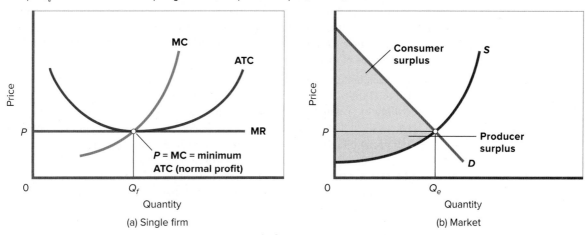

(a) Single firm   (b) Market

yield the mix of products and services that is most wanted by society (least-cost production assumed). Allocative efficiency has been realized when it is impossible to alter the combination of goods produced and achieve a net gain for society. Let's look at how productive and allocative efficiency would be achieved under purely competitive conditions.

Productive Efficiency: *P* = Minimum ATC

In the long run, pure competition forces firms to produce at the minimum average total cost of production and to charge a price that is just consistent with that cost. This is true because firms that do not use the best-available (least-cost) production methods and combinations of inputs will not survive.

To see why that is true, let's suppose that Figure 7.10 has to do with pure competition in the cucumber industry. In the final equilibrium position shown in Figure 7.10, suppose each firm in the cucumber industry is producing 100 units (say, pickup truckloads) of output by using $5,000 (equal to average total cost of $50 × 100 units) worth of resources. If any firm produced that same amount of output at any higher total cost, say $7,000, it would be wasting resources because all of the other firms in the industry are able to produce that same amount of output using only $5,000 worth of resources. Society would be faced with a net loss of $2,000 worth of alternative products. But this cannot happen in pure competition; this firm would incur a loss of $2,000, requiring it either to reduce its costs or go out of business.

Note, too, that consumers benefit from productive efficiency by paying the lowest product price possible under the prevailing technology and cost conditions. And the firm receives only a normal profit, which is part of its economic costs and thus incorporated in its ATC curve.

Allocative Efficiency: *P* = MC

Productive efficiency alone does not ensure the efficient allocation of resources. It does not guarantee that anyone will want to buy the items that are being produced in the least-cost manner. For all we know, consumers might prefer that the resources used to produce those items be redirected toward producing other products instead.

Fortunately, long-run equilibrium in pure competition also guarantees *allocative efficiency,* so we can be certain that society's scarce resources are directed toward producing the goods and services that people most want to consume. Stated formally, allocative efficiency occurs when it is impossible to produce any net gains for society by altering the combination of goods and services that are produced from society's limited supply of resources.

To understand how pure competition leads to allocative efficiency, recall the concept of opportunity cost while looking at Figure 7.10b, where Q_e total units are being produced in equilibrium by the firms in a purely competitive industry. For every unit up to Q_e, market demand curve D lies above market supply curve S. Recall from Chapter 5 what this means in terms of marginal benefits and marginal costs.

- For each unit of output on the horizontal axis, the point directly above it on demand curve D shows how many dollars' worth of other goods and services consumers are willing to give up to obtain that unit of output. Consequently, the demand curve shows the dollar value of the marginal benefit that consumers place on each unit.
- For each unit of output on the horizontal axis, the point directly above it on supply curve S shows how many dollars' worth of other products have to be sacrificed in order to direct the underlying resources toward producing each unit of this product. Consequently, the supply curve shows the dollar value of the marginal opportunity cost of each unit.

Keeping these definitions in mind, the fact that the demand curve lies above the supply curve for every unit up to Q_e means that marginal benefit exceeds marginal cost for every one of these units. It also implies that redirecting the necessary resources toward producing anything else would make people less happy.

The fact that pure competition yields allocative efficiency can also be understood by looking at the situation facing each individual firm in long-run equilibrium. To see this, take the market equilibrium price P that is determined in Figure 7.10b and see how it affects the behavior of the individual firm shown in Figure 7.10a. This profit-maximizing firm takes P as fixed and produces Q_f units, the output level at which $P = \text{MC}$.

By comparing the horizontal line at P with the upsloping MC curve, it is clear that for every unit up to Q_f, the price at which each unit can be sold exceeds the marginal cost of producing it. That is equivalent to saying that these units are worth more to consumers than they cost to make. Why? Because consumers are willing to forgo P dollars' worth of other goods and services when they pay P dollars for these units, but the firm uses less than P dollars' worth of resources to produce them. Thus, if these units are produced and consumed, there are net benefits and society comes out ahead. Allocative efficiency obtains because by spending their P dollars per unit on these units rather than anything else, consumers are indicating that they would rather have the necessary resources directed toward producing these units rather than anything else.

Maximum Consumer and Producer Surplus

We confirm the existence of allocative efficiency in Figure 7.10b, where we see that pure competition maximizes the sum of the "benefit surpluses" to consumers and producers. Recall from Chapter 5 that *consumer surplus* is the difference between the maximum prices that consumers are willing to pay for a product (as shown by the demand curve) and the market price of that product. In Figure 7.10b, consumer surplus is the green triangle, which is the sum of the vertical distances between the demand curve and equilibrium price. In contrast, *producer surplus* is the difference between the minimum prices that producers are willing to accept for a product (as shown by the supply curve) and the market price of the product. Producer surplus is the sum of the vertical distances between the equilibrium price and the supply curve. Here producer surplus is the blue area.

At the equilibrium quantity Q_e, the combined amount of consumer surplus and producer surplus is maximized. Allocative efficiency occurs because, at Q_e, marginal benefit, reflected by points on the demand curve, equals marginal cost, reflected by the points on the supply curve. At any output less than Q_e, the sum of consumer and producer surplus—the combined size of the green and blue area—would be less than that shown. At any output greater than Q_e, an efficiency loss (deadweight loss) would subtract from the combined consumer and producer surplus shown by the green and blue area.

After long-run adjustments, pure competition produces both productive and allocative efficiency. It yields a level of output at which $P =$ MC $=$ lowest ATC, marginal benefit $=$ marginal cost, maximum willingness to pay for the last unit $=$ minimum acceptable price for that unit, and combined consumer and producer surplus are maximized.

Dynamic Adjustments A further attribute of purely competitive markets is their ability to restore efficiency when disrupted by changes in the economy. A change in consumer tastes, resource supplies, or technology will automatically set in motion the appropriate realignments of resources. For example, suppose that cucumbers and pickles become dramatically more popular. First, the price of cucumbers will increase, and so, at current output, the price of cucumbers will exceed their marginal cost. At this point efficiency will be lost, but the higher price will create economic profits in the cucumber industry and stimulate its expansion. The profitability of cucumbers will permit the industry to bid resources away from now less-pressing uses, say, watermelons. Expansion of the industry will end only when the price of cucumbers and their marginal cost are equal—that is, when allocative efficiency has been restored.

Similarly, a change in the supply of a particular resource—for example, the field laborers who pick cucumbers—or in a production technique will upset an existing price–marginal-cost equality by either raising or lowering marginal cost. The resulting inequality will cause business managers, in either pursuing profit or avoiding loss, to reallocate resources until price once again equals marginal cost. In so doing, they will correct any inefficiency in the allocation of resources that the original change may have temporarily imposed on the economy.

"Invisible Hand" Revisited The highly efficient allocation of resources that a purely competitive economy promotes comes about because businesses and resource suppliers seek to further their self-interest. For private goods with no externalities (Chapter 5), the "invisible hand" (Chapter 2) is at work. The competitive system not only maximizes profits for individual producers but also, at the same time, creates a pattern of resource allocation that maximizes consumer satisfaction. The invisible hand thus organizes the private interests of producers in a way that is fully in sync with society's interest in using scarce resources efficiently. Striving for profit (and avoiding losses) produces highly desirable economic outcomes.

SUMMARY

LO7.1 Give the names and summarize the main characteristics of the four basic market models.

Economists group industries into four models based on their market structures: (a) pure competition, (b) monopolistic competition, (c) oligopoly, and (d) pure monopoly.

LO7.2 List the conditions required for purely competitive markets.

A purely competitive industry consists of a large number of independent firms producing a standardized product. Pure competition assumes that firms and resources are mobile among different industries.

LO7.3 Describe how purely competitive firms maximize profits or minimize losses.

In a competitive industry, no single firm can influence market price. This means that the firm's demand curve is perfectly elastic and price equals both marginal revenue and average revenue.

Provided price exceeds minimum average variable cost, a competitive firm maximizes profit or minimizes loss in the short run by producing the output at which price or marginal revenue equals marginal cost.

If price is less than minimum average variable cost, a competitive firm minimizes its loss by shutting down. If price is greater than average variable cost but is less than average total cost, a competitive firm minimizes its loss by producing the $P = MC$ amount of output. If price also exceeds average total cost, the firm maximizes its economic profit at the $P = MC$ amount of output.

LO7.4 Explain why the marginal-cost curve and supply curve of competitive firms are identical.

Applying the MR $(= P) = MC$ rule at various possible market prices leads to the conclusion that the segment of the firm's short-run marginal-cost curve that lies above the firm's average-variable-cost curve is its short-run supply curve.

LO7.5 Describe how profits and losses drive the long-run adjustment process of pure competition.

In the long run, the market price of a product will equal the minimum average total cost of production. At a higher price, economic profits would entice firms to enter the industry until those profits had been competed away. At a lower price, losses would force firms to exit the industry until the product price rose to equal average total cost.

LO7.6 Identify the differences between constant-cost, increasing-cost, and decreasing-cost industries.

The long-run supply curve is horizontal for a constant-cost industry, upsloping for an increasing-cost industry, and downsloping for a decreasing-cost industry.

LO7.7 Discuss how long-run equilibrium in pure competition produces economic efficiency.

The long-run equality of price and minimum average total cost means that competitive firms will use the most efficient known technology and charge the lowest price consistent with their production costs. That is, purely competitive firms will achieve productive efficiency.

The long-run equality of price and marginal cost implies that resources will be allocated in accordance with consumer tastes. Allocative efficiency will occur. In the market, the combined amount of consumer surplus and producer surplus will be at a maximum. The competitive price system will reallocate resources in response to a change in consumer tastes, in technology, or in resource supplies and will thereby maintain allocative efficiency over time.

TERMS AND CONCEPTS

pure competition

price taker

average revenue

total revenue

marginal revenue

MR = MC rule

short-run supply curve

long-run supply curve

constant-cost industry

increasing-cost industry

decreasing-cost industry

QUESTIONS

The following and additional problems can be found in ■ connect

1. Briefly state the basic characteristics of pure competition, pure monopoly, monopolistic competition, and oligopoly. Under which of these market classifications does each of the following most accurately fit? (a) a supermarket in your hometown; (b) the steel industry; (c) a Kansas wheat farm; (d) the commercial bank in which you or your family has an account; (e) the automobile industry. In each case, justify your classification. **LO7.1**

2. Use the demand schedule below to determine total revenue and marginal revenue for each possible level of sales: **LO7.2**
   a. What can you conclude about the structure of the industry in which this firm is operating? Explain.

Product Price	Quantity Demanded	Total Revenue	Marginal Revenue
$2	0	$____	
2	1	____	$____
2	2	____	____
2	3	____	____
2	4	____	____
2	5	____	____

   b. Graph the demand, total-revenue, and marginal-revenue curves for this firm.
   c. Why do the demand, marginal-revenue, and average-revenue curves coincide?
   d. "Marginal revenue is the change in total revenue associated with additional units of output." Explain verbally and graphically, using the data in the table.

3. "Even if a firm is losing money, it may be better to stay in business in the short run." Is this statement ever true? Under what condition(s)? **LO7.3**

4. Why is the equality of marginal revenue and marginal cost essential for profit maximization in all market structures? Explain why price can be substituted for marginal revenue in the MR = MC rule when an industry is purely competitive. **LO7.3**

5. "That segment of a competitive firm's marginal-cost curve that lies above its average-variable-cost curve constitutes the short-run supply curve for the firm." Explain using a graph and words. **LO7.4**

6. Explain: "The short-run rule for operating or shutting down is $P >$ AVC, operate; $P <$ AVC, shut down. The long-run rule for

continuing in business or exiting the industry is $P \geq$ ATC, continue; $P <$ ATC, exit." **LO7.5**

7. Using diagrams for both the industry and a representative firm, illustrate competitive long-run equilibrium. Assuming constant costs, employ these diagrams to show how (a) an increase and (b) a decrease in market demand will upset that long-run equilibrium. Trace graphically and describe verbally the adjustment processes by which long-run equilibrium is restored. Now rework your analysis for increasing- and decreasing-cost industries, and compare the three long-run supply curves. **LO7.6**

8. In long-run equilibrium, $P =$ minimum ATC $=$ MC. What is the significance of the equality of P and minimum ATC for society? The equality of P and MC? Distinguish between productive efficiency and allocative efficiency in your answer. **LO7.7**

9. Suppose that purely competitive firms producing cashews discover that P exceeds MC. Will their combined output of cashews be too little, too much, or just right to achieve allocative efficiency? In the long run, what will happen to the supply of cashews and the price of cashews? Use a supply-and-demand diagram to show how that response will change the combined amount of consumer surplus and producer surplus in the market for cashews. **LO7.7**

PROBLEMS

1. A purely competitive firm finds that the market price for its product is $20. It has a fixed cost of $100 and a variable cost of $10 per unit for the first 50 units and then $25 per unit for all successive units. Does price exceed average variable cost for the first 50 units? What about for the first 100 units? What is the marginal cost per unit for the first 50 units? What about for units 51 and higher? For each of the first 50 units, does MR exceed MC? What about for units 51 and higher? What output level will yield the largest possible profit for this purely competitive firm? **LO7.3**

2. A purely competitive wheat farmer can sell any wheat he grows for $10 per bushel. His five acres of land show diminishing returns because some are better suited for wheat production than others. The first acre can produce 1,000 bushels of wheat, the second acre 900, the third 800, and so on. Draw a table with multiple columns to help you answer the following questions. How many bushels will each of the farmer's five acres produce? How much revenue will each acre generate? What are the TR and MR for each acre? If the marginal cost of planting and harvesting an acre is $7,000 per acre for each of the five acres, how many acres should the farmer plant and harvest? **LO7.3**

3. Karen runs a print shop that makes posters for large companies. It is a very competitive business. The market price is currently $1 per poster. She has fixed costs of $250. Her variable costs are $1,000 for the first thousand posters, $800 for the second thousand, and then $750 for each additional thousand posters. What is her AFC per poster (not per thousand!) if she prints 1,000 posters? 2,000? 10,000? What is her ATC per poster if she prints 1,000? 2,000? 10,000? If the market price fell to 70 cents per poster, would there be *any* output level at which Karen would *not* shut down production immediately? **LO7.3**

4. Assume that the cost data in the table below are for a purely competitive producer: **LO7.3**

Total Product	Average Fixed Cost	Average Variable Cost	Average Total Cost	Marginal Cost
0				
				$45
1	$60.00	$45.00	$105.00	
				40
2	30.00	42.50	72.50	
				35
3	20.00	40.00	60.00	
				30
4	15.00	37.50	52.50	
				35
5	12.00	37.00	49.00	
				40
6	10.00	37.50	47.50	
				45
7	8.57	38.57	47.14	
				55
8	7.50	40.63	48.13	
				65
9	6.67	43.33	50.00	
				75
10	6.00	46.50	52.50	

a. At a product price of $56, will this firm produce in the short run? If it is preferable to produce, what will be the profit-maximizing or loss-minimizing output? What economic profit or loss will the firm realize per unit of output?

b. Answer the questions of 4a assuming product price is $41.

c. Answer the questions of 4a assuming product price is $32.

d. In the accompanying table, complete the short-run supply schedule for the firm (columns 1 and 2) and indicate the profit or loss incurred at each output (column 3).

(1) Price	(2) Quantity Supplied, Single Firm	(3) Profit (+) or Loss (−)	(4) Quantity Supplied 1,500 Firms
$26	_____	$_____	_____
32	_____	_____	_____
38	_____	_____	_____
41	_____	_____	_____
46	_____	_____	_____
56	_____	_____	_____
66	_____	_____	_____

e. Now assume that there are 1,500 identical firms in this competitive industry; that is, there are 1,500 firms, each of which has the cost data shown in the table. Complete the industry supply schedule (column 4).

f. Suppose the market demand data for the product are as follows:

Price	Total Quantity Demanded
$26	17,000
32	15,000
38	13,500
41	12,000
46	10,500
56	9,500
66	8,000

What will be the equilibrium price? What will be the equilibrium output for the industry? For each firm? What will profit or loss be per unit? Per firm? Will this industry expand or contract in the long run?

Pure Monopoly

Learning Objectives

LO8.1 List the characteristics of pure monopoly and discuss several barriers to entry that relate to monopoly.

LO8.2 Explain how a pure monopoly sets its profit-maximizing output and price.

LO8.3 Discuss the economic effects of monopoly.

LO8.4 Describe why a monopolist might prefer to charge different prices in different markets.

LO8.5 Identify the antitrust laws that are used to deal with monopoly.

We turn now from pure competition to pure monopoly (a single seller). You deal with monopolies—or near-monopolies—more often than you might think.

This happens when you see the Microsoft Windows logo after you turn on your computer and when you swallow a prescription drug that is under patent. Depending on where you live, you may be patronizing a local or regional monopoly when you make a local telephone call, turn on your lights, or subscribe to cable TV.

What precisely do we mean by "pure monopoly," and what conditions enable it to arise and survive? How does a pure monopolist determine what price to charge? Does a pure monopolist achieve the efficiency associated with pure competition? If not, what should the government try to do about it? A model of pure monopoly will help us answer these questions.

©Tatiana Belova/Shutterstock

An Introduction to Pure Monopoly

Pure monopoly exists when a single firm is the sole producer of a product for which there are no close substitutes. Here are the main characteristics of **pure monopoly:**

- *Single seller* A pure, or absolute, monopoly is an industry in which a single firm is the sole producer of a specific good or the sole supplier of a service; the firm and the industry are synonymous.
- *No close substitutes* A pure monopoly's product is unique in that there are no close substitutes. The consumer who chooses not to buy the monopolized product must do without it.
- *Price maker* The pure monopolist controls the total quantity supplied and thus has considerable control over price; it is a *price maker* (unlike a pure competitor, which has no such control and therefore is a *price taker*). The pure monopolist confronts the usual downward-sloping product demand curve. It can change its product price by changing the quantity of the product it produces. The monopolist will use this power whenever it is advantageous to do so.
- *Blocked entry* A pure monopolist faces no immediate competition because certain barriers keep potential competitors from entering the industry. Those barriers may be economic, technological, legal, or of some other type. But entry is totally blocked in pure monopoly.

Examples of *pure* monopoly are relatively rare, but there are excellent examples of less pure forms. In many cities, government-owned or government-regulated public utilities—natural gas and electric companies, the water company, the cable TV company, and the local telephone company—are all monopolies or virtually so.

There are also many "near-monopolies" in which a single firm has the bulk of sales in a specific market. Intel, for example, produces 80 percent of the central microprocessors used in personal computers. First Data Corporation, via its Western Union subsidiary, accounts for 80 percent of the market for money order transfers. Brannock Device Company has an 80 percent market share of the shoe-sizing devices found in shoe stores. Wham-O, through its Frisbee brand, sells 90 percent of plastic throwing disks. Google executes nearly 70 percent of all U.S. Internet searches and consequently controls nearly 75 percent of all the revenue generated by search ads in the United States.

Professional sports teams are, in a sense, monopolies because they are the sole suppliers of specific services in large geographic areas. With a few exceptions, a single major-league team in each sport serves each large American city. If you want to see a live major-league baseball game in St. Louis or Seattle, you must patronize the Cardinals or the Mariners, respectively. Other geographic monopolies exist. For example, a small town may be served by only one airline or railroad. In a small, extremely isolated community, the local barber shop, dry cleaner, or grocery store may approximate a monopoly.

Of course, there is almost always some competition. Satellite television is a substitute for cable, and amateur softball is a substitute for professional baseball. The Linux operating system can substitute for Windows, and so on. But such substitutes are typically in some way less appealing.

Barriers to Entry

The factors that prohibit firms from entering an industry are called **barriers to entry.** In pure monopoly, strong barriers to entry effectively block all potential competition. Somewhat weaker barriers may permit *oligopoly,* a market structure dominated by a few firms. Still weaker barriers may permit the entry of a fairly large number of competing firms, giving rise to *monopolistic competition.* And the absence of any effective entry barriers permits the entry of a very large number of firms, which provide the basis of pure competition. So barriers to entry are pertinent not only to the extreme case of pure monopoly but also to other market structures in which there are monopolylike characteristics or monopolylike behavior.

We will now discuss the four most prominent barriers to entry.

Economies of Scale

Modern technology in some industries is such that economies of scale—declining average total cost with added firm size—are extensive. In such cases, a firm's long-run average-cost schedule will decline over a wide range of output. Given market demand, only a few large firms or, in the extreme, only a single large firm can achieve low average total costs.

If a pure monopoly exists in such an industry, economies of scale will serve as an entry barrier and will protect the monopolist from competition. New firms that try to enter the industry as small-scale producers cannot realize the cost economies of the monopolist. They therefore will be undercut and forced out of business by the monopolist, which can sell at a much lower price and still make a profit because of its lower per-unit cost associated with its economies of scale. A new firm might try to start out big, that is, to enter the industry as a large-scale producer so as to achieve the necessary economies of scale. But the massive plant facilities required would necessitate huge amounts of financing, which a new and untried enterprise would find difficult to secure. In most cases, the financial obstacles and risks to "starting big" are prohibitive. This explains why efforts to enter such industries as automobiles, computer operating software, commercial aircraft, and basic steel are so rare.

In the extreme circumstance, in which the market demand curve cuts the long-run ATC curve where average total costs are still declining, the single firm is called a **natural monopoly.** It might seem that a natural monopolist's lower unit cost would enable it to charge a lower price than if the industry were more competitive. But that won't necessarily happen. As with any monopolist, a natural monopolist may, instead, set its price far above ATC and obtain substantial economic profit. In that event, the lowest-unit-cost advantage of a natural monopolist would accrue to the monopolist as profit and not as lower prices to consumers.

natural monopoly An industry in which economies of scale are so great that a single firm can produce the product at a lower average total cost than would be possible if more than one firm produced the product.

Legal Barriers to Entry: Patents and Licenses

Government also creates legal barriers to entry by awarding patents and licenses.

Patents A *patent* is the exclusive right of an inventor to use, or to allow another to use, her or his invention. Patents and patent laws aim to protect the inventor from rivals who would use the invention without having shared in the effort and expense of developing it. At the same time, patents provide the inventor with a monopoly position for the life of the patent. The world's nations have agreed on a uniform patent length of 20 years from the time of application. Patents have figured prominently in the growth of modern-day giants such as IBM, Pfizer, Kodak, Xerox, Intel, General Electric, and DuPont.

Research and development (R&D) is what leads to most patentable inventions and products. Firms that gain monopoly power through their own research or by purchasing the patents of others can use patents to strengthen their market position. The profit from one patent can finance the research required to develop new patentable products. In the pharmaceutical industry, patents on prescription drugs have produced large monopoly profits that have helped finance the discovery of new patentable medicines. So monopoly power achieved through patents may well be self-sustaining, even though patents eventually expire and generic drugs then compete with the original brand.

Licenses   Government may also limit entry into an industry or occupation through *licensing.* At the national level, the Federal Communications Commission licenses only so many radio and television stations in each geographic area. In many large cities, one of a limited number of municipal licenses is required to drive a taxicab. The consequent restriction of the supply of cabs creates economic profit for cab owners and drivers. New cabs cannot enter the industry to drive down prices and profits. In a few instances, the government might "license" itself to provide some product and thereby create a public monopoly. For example, in some states only state-owned retail outlets can sell liquor. Similarly, many states have "licensed" themselves to run lotteries.

Ownership or Control of Essential Resources

A monopolist can use private property as an obstacle to potential rivals. For example, a firm that owns or controls a resource essential to the production process can prohibit the entry of rival firms. At one time the International Nickel Company of Canada (now called Vale Canada Limited) controlled a large percentage of the world's known nickel reserves. A local firm may own all the nearby deposits of sand and gravel. And it is very difficult for new sports leagues to be created because existing professional sports leagues have contracts with the best players and have long-term leases on the major stadiums and arenas.

Pricing and Other Strategic Barriers to Entry

Even if a monopolist is not protected from entry by rivals by, say, extensive economies of scale or ownership of essential resources, entry may effectively be blocked by the way the monopolist responds to attempts by rivals to enter the industry. Confronted with a new entrant, the monopolist may "create an entry barrier" by slashing its price, stepping up its advertising, or taking other strategic actions to make it difficult for the entrant to succeed.

In 2005, for example, Dentsply, the dominant American maker of false teeth (70 percent market share), was found to have unlawfully precluded independent distributors of false teeth from carrying competing brands. The lack of access to the distributors deterred potential foreign competitors from entering the U.S. market. In another example of entry deterrence, in 2015, American Express was found guilty of an unlawful restraint of trade because it prohibited any merchant who had signed up to accept American Express credit cards from promoting rival credit cards, such as Visa and MasterCard, to their customers.

Monopoly Demand

Now that we have explained the sources of monopoly, we want to build a model of pure monopoly so that we can analyze its price and output decisions. Let's start by making three assumptions:

- Patents, economies of scale, or resource ownership secure our firm's monopoly.
- No unit of government regulates the firm.
- The firm is a single-price monopolist; it charges the same price for all units of output.

The crucial difference between a pure monopolist and a purely competitive seller lies on the demand side of the market. The purely competitive seller faces a perfectly elastic demand at the price determined by market supply and demand. It is a price taker that can sell as much or as little as it wants at the going market price. Each additional unit sold will add the amount of the constant product price to the firm's total revenue. That means that marginal revenue for the competitive seller is constant and equal to product price. (Review Figure 7.1 for price, marginal-revenue, and total-revenue relationships for the purely competitive firm.)

FIGURE 8.1 Demand, price, and marginal revenue in pure monopoly. (a) A pure monopolist (or any other imperfect competitor) must set a lower price in order to sell more output. Here, by charging $132 rather than $142, the monopolist sells an extra unit (the fourth unit) and gains $132 from that sale. But from this gain $30 is subtracted, which reflects the $10 less the monopolist received for each of the first 3 units. Thus, the marginal revenue of the fourth unit is $102 (= $132 − $30), considerably less than its $132 price. (b) Because a monopolist must lower the price on all units sold in order to increase its sales, its marginal-revenue curve (MR) lies below its downsloping demand curve (D).

Revenue Data			
(1) Quantity of Output	(2) Price (Average Revenue)	(3) Total Revenue, (1) × (2)	(4) Marginal Revenue
0	$172	$ 0	$162
1	162	162	142
2	152	304	122
3	142	426	102
4	132	528	82
5	122	610	62
6	112	672	42
7	102	714	22
8	92	736	2
9	82	738	−18
10	72	720	

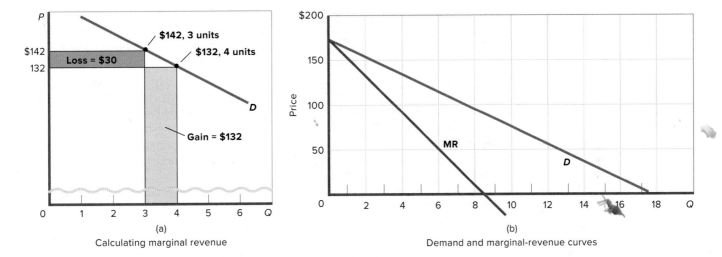

(a) Calculating marginal revenue

(b) Demand and marginal-revenue curves

The demand curve for the monopolist (or oligopolist or monopolistic competitor) is quite different from that of the pure competitor. Because the pure monopolist *is* the industry, its demand curve is *the market demand curve.* And because market demand is not perfectly elastic, the monopolist's demand curve is downsloping. Columns 1 and 2 in the table in Figure 8.1 illustrate this fact. Note that quantity demanded increases as price decreases.

In Chapter 7 we drew separate demand curves for the purely competitive industry and for a single firm in such an industry. But only a single demand curve is needed in pure monopoly because the firm and the industry are one and the same. We have graphed part of the demand data in the table in Figure 8.1 as demand curve *D* in Figure 8.1a. This is the monopolist's demand curve *and* the market demand curve. The downward-sloping demand curve has two implications that are essential to understanding the monopoly model.

Marginal Revenue Is Less Than Price

With a fixed downsloping demand curve, the pure monopolist can increase sales only by charging a lower price. Consequently, marginal revenue is less than price (average revenue) for every unit of output except the first. Why so? The reason is that the lower price of the extra unit of output also applies to all prior units of output. The monopolist could have sold these prior units at a higher price if it had not produced and sold the extra output. Each additional unit of output sold increases total revenue by an amount equal to its own price less the sum of the price cuts that apply to all prior units of output.

Figure 8.1a confirms this point. There, we have highlighted two price-quantity combinations from the monopolist's demand curve. The monopolist can sell 1 more unit at $132 than it can at $142 and that way obtain $132 of extra revenue (the blue area). But to sell that fourth unit for $132, the monopolist must also sell the first 3 units at $132 rather than $142. The $10 reduction in revenue on 3 units results in a $30 revenue loss (the red area). The net difference in total revenue from selling a fourth unit is $102: the $132 gain from the fourth unit minus the $30 forgone on the first 3 units. This net gain (marginal revenue) of $102 from the fourth unit is clearly less than the $132 price of the fourth unit.

Column 4 in the table shows that marginal revenue is always less than the corresponding product price in column 2, except for the first unit of output. We show the relationship between the monopolist's demand curve and marginal-revenue curve in Figure 8.1b. For this figure, we extended the demand and marginal-revenue data of columns 1, 2, and 4 in the table, assuming that successive $10 price cuts each elicit 1 additional unit of sales. That is, the monopolist can sell 11 units at $62, 12 units at $52, and so on. Note that the monopolist's MR curve lies below the demand curve, indicating that marginal revenue is less than price at every output quantity except the very first unit.

The Monopolist Is a Price Maker

All imperfect competitors, whether they are pure monopolists, oligopolists, or monopolistic competitors, face downsloping demand curves. As a result, any change in quantity produced causes a movement along their respective demand curves and a change in the price they can charge for their respective products. Economists summarize this fact by saying that firms with downsloping demand curves are *price makers*.

This is most evident in pure monopoly, where an industry consists of a single monopoly firm so that total industry output is exactly equal to whatever the single monopoly firm chooses to produce. As we just mentioned, the monopolist faces a downsloping demand curve in which each amount of output is associated with some unique price. Thus, in deciding on the quantity of output to produce, the monopolist is also indirectly determining the price it will charge. Through control of output, it can "make the price." From columns 1 and 2 in the table in Figure 8.1 we find that the monopolist can charge a price of $72 if it produces and offers for sale 10 units, a price of $82 if it produces and offers for sale 9 units, and so forth.

Output and Price Determination

At what specific price-quantity combination will a profit-maximizing monopolist choose to operate? To answer this question, we must add production costs to our analysis.

Cost Data

On the cost side, we will assume that although the firm is a monopolist in the product market, it hires resources competitively and employs the same technology and, therefore, has the same cost structure as the purely competitive firm that we studied in Chapter 7.

FIGURE 8.2 Profit maximization by a pure monopolist. The pure monopolist maximizes profit by producing the MR = MC output, here $Q_m = 5$ units. Then, as seen from the demand curve, it will charge price $P_m = \$122$. Average total cost is $A = \$94$, so per-unit profit is $P_m - A$ and total profit is $5 \times (P_m - A)$. Total economic profit is thus $140, as shown by the green rectangle.

	Revenue Data				Cost Data		
(1) Quantity of Output	**(2)** Price (Average Revenue)	**(3)** Total Revenue, (1) × (2)	**(4)** Marginal Revenue	**(5)** Average Total Cost	**(6)** Total Cost, (1) × (5)	**(7)** Marginal Cost	**(8)** Profit [+] or Loss [−]
0	$172	$ 0			$ 100		$−100
			$162	$190.00		$ 90	−28
1	162	162	142	135.00	190	80	+34
2	152	304	122	113.33	270	70	+86
3	142	426	102	100.00	340	60	+128
4	132	528	82	94.00	400	70	+140
5	**122**	**610**	62	**94.00**	**470**	**70**	**+140**
6	112	672	42	91.67	550	80	+122
7	102	714	22	91.43	640	90	+74
8	92	736	2	93.75	750	110	−14
9	82	738	−18	97.78	880	130	−142
10	72	720		103.00	1030	150	−310

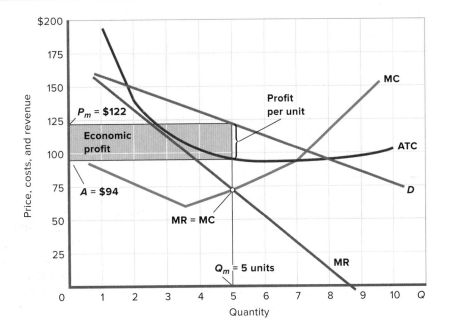

By using the same cost data that we developed in Chapter 6 and applied to the competitive firm in Chapter 7, we will be able to directly compare the price and output decisions of a pure monopoly with those of a pure competitor. Columns 5 through 7 in the table in Figure 8.2 restate the pertinent cost data from the table in Figure 7.2.

MR = MC Rule

A monopolist seeking to maximize total profit will employ the same rationale as a profit-seeking firm in a competitive industry. If producing is preferable to shutting down, it will produce up to the output at which marginal revenue equals marginal cost (MR = MC).

A comparison of columns 4 and 7 in the table in Figure 8.2 indicates that the profit-maximizing output is 5 units because the fifth unit is the last unit of output whose marginal revenue exceeds its marginal cost. What price will the monopolist charge? The demand schedule shown as columns 1 and 2 in the table indicates there is only one price at which 5 units can be sold: $122.

This analysis is shown in Figure 8.2, where we have graphed the demand, marginal-revenue, average-total-cost, and marginal-cost data from the table. The profit-maximizing output occurs at 5 units of output (Q_m), where the marginal-revenue (MR) and marginal-cost (MC) curves intersect. There, MR = MC.

To find the price the monopolist will charge, we extend a vertical line from Q_m up to the demand curve D. The unique price P_m at which Q_m units can be sold is $122. In this case, $122 is the profit-maximizing price. So the monopolist sets the quantity at Q_m to charge its profit-maximizing price of $122.

Columns 2 and 5 of the table show that at 5 units of output, the product price ($122) exceeds the average total cost ($94). The monopolist thus obtains an economic profit of $28 per unit, and the total economic profit is then $140 (= 5 units × $28). In the graph in Figure 8.2, per-unit profit is $P_m - A$, where A is the average total cost of producing Q_m units. Total economic profit of $140 (the green rectangle) is found by multiplying this per-unit profit by the profit-maximizing output Q_m.

Misconceptions Concerning Monopoly Pricing

Our analysis exposes three fallacies concerning monopoly behavior.

Not Highest Price   Because a monopolist can manipulate output and price, people often believe it "will charge the highest price possible." That is incorrect. There are many prices above P_m in Figure 8.2, but the monopolist shuns them because they yield a smaller-than-maximum total profit. The monopolist seeks maximum total profit, not maximum price. Some high prices that could be charged would reduce sales and total revenue too severely to offset any decrease in total cost.

Total, Not Unit, Profit   The monopolist seeks maximum *total* profit, not maximum *unit* profit. In Figure 8.2 a careful comparison of the vertical distance between average total cost and price at various possible outputs indicates that per-unit profit is greater at a point slightly to the left of the profit-maximizing output Q_m. This is seen in the table, where unit profit at 4 units of output is $32 (= $132 − $100) compared with $28 (= $122 − $94) at the profit-maximizing output of 5 units. Here the monopolist accepts a lower-than-maximum per-unit profit because additional sales more than compensate for the lower unit profit. A profit-seeking monopolist would rather sell 5 units at a profit of $28 per unit (for a total profit of $140) than 4 units at a profit of $32 per unit (for a total profit of only $128).

Possibility of Losses   The likelihood of economic profit is greater for a pure monopolist than for a pure competitor. In the long run, the pure competitor is destined to have only a normal profit, whereas barriers to entry mean that any economic profit realized by the monopolist can persist. In pure monopoly there are no new entrants to increase supply, drive down price, and eliminate economic profit.

But pure monopoly does not guarantee profit. Despite dominance in its market (as, say, a seller of home sewing machines), a monopoly enterprise can suffer a loss because of weak demand and relatively high costs. If the demand and cost situation faced by the monopolist is far less favorable than that in Figure 8.2, the monopolist can incur losses. Like the pure competitor, the monopolist will not persist in operating at a loss in the long run.

Faced with continuing losses, the firm's owners will move their resources to alternative industries that offer better profit opportunities. Like any firm, a monopolist must obtain a minimum of a normal profit in the long run or it will go out of business.

Economic Effects of Monopoly

Let's now evaluate pure monopoly from the standpoint of society as a whole. Our reference for this evaluation will be the outcome of long-run efficiency in a purely competitive market, identified by the triple equality $P = MC = $ minimum ATC.

Price, Output, and Efficiency

Figure 8.3 graphically contrasts the price, output, and efficiency outcomes of pure monopoly and a purely competitive *industry*. The $S = MC$ curve in Figure 8.3a reminds us that the market supply curve S for a purely competitive industry is the horizontal sum of the marginal-cost curves of all the firms in the industry. Suppose there are 1,000 such firms. Comparing their combined supply curve S with market demand D, we see that the purely competitive price and output are P_c and Q_c.

Recall that this price-output combination results in both productive efficiency and allocative efficiency. *Productive efficiency* is achieved because free entry and exit force firms to operate where their average total cost is at a minimum. The sum of the minimum-ATC outputs of the 1,000 pure competitors is the industry output, here, Q_c. Product price is at the lowest level consistent with minimum average total cost. The *allocative efficiency* of pure competition results because production occurs up to that output at which price (the measure of a product's value or marginal benefit to society) equals marginal cost (the worth of the alternative products forgone by society in producing any given commodity). In short: $P = MC = $ minimum ATC.

Now let's suppose that this industry becomes a pure monopoly (Figure 8.3b) as a result of one firm acquiring all its competitors. We also assume that no changes in costs

FIGURE 8.3 Inefficiency of pure monopoly relative to a purely competitive industry. (a) In a purely competitive industry, entry and exit of firms ensure that price (P_c) equals marginal cost (MC) and that the minimum average-total-cost output (Q_c) is produced. Both productive efficiency ($P = $ minimum ATC) and allocative efficiency ($P = $ MC) are obtained. (b) In pure monopoly, the MR curve lies below the demand curve. The monopolist maximizes profit at output Q_m, where MR = MC, and charges price P_m. Thus, output is lower (Q_m rather than Q_c) and price is higher (P_m rather than P_c) than they would be in a purely competitive industry. Monopoly is inefficient, since output is less than that required for achieving minimum ATC (here, at Q_c) and because the monopolist's price exceeds MC. Monopoly creates an efficiency loss (here, of triangle abc). There is also a transfer of income from consumers to the monopoly (here, of rectangle P_cP_mbd).

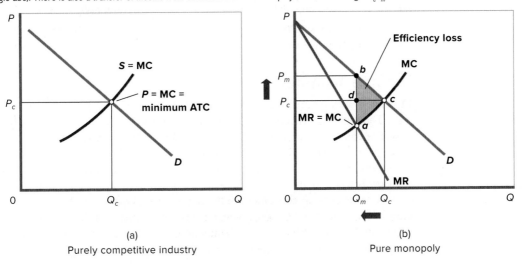

(a)
Purely competitive industry

(b)
Pure monopoly

or market demand result from this dramatic change in the industry structure. What formerly were 1,000 competing firms are now a single pure monopolist consisting of 1,000 noncompeting branches.

The competitive market supply curve S has become the marginal-cost curve (MC) of the monopolist, the summation of the individual marginal-cost curves of its many branch plants. The important change, however, is on the demand side. From the viewpoint of each of the 1,000 individual competitive firms, demand was perfectly elastic, and marginal revenue was therefore equal to the market equilibrium price P_c. So each firm equated its marginal revenue of P_c dollars per unit with its individual marginal-cost curve to maximize profits. But market demand and individual demand are the same to the pure monopolist. The firm *is* the industry, and thus the monopolist sees the downsloping demand curve D shown in Figure 8.3b.

This means that marginal revenue is less than price, that graphically the MR curve lies below demand curve D. In using the MR = MC rule, the monopolist selects output Q_m and price P_m. A comparison of both graphs in Figure 8.3 reveals that the monopolist finds it profitable to sell a smaller output at a higher price than do the competitive producers.

Monopoly yields neither productive nor allocative efficiency. The lack of productive efficiency can be understood most directly by noting that the monopolist's output Q_m is less than Q_c, the output at which average total cost is lowest. In addition, the monopoly price P_m is higher than the competitive price P_c that we know in long-run equilibrium in pure competition equals minimum average total cost. Thus, the monopoly price exceeds minimum average total cost, thereby demonstrating in another way that the monopoly will not be productively efficient.

The monopolist's underproduction also implies allocative inefficiency. One way to see this is to note that at the monopoly output level Q_m, the monopoly price P_m that consumers are willing to pay exceeds the marginal cost of production. This means that consumers value additional units of this product more highly than they do the alternative products that could be produced from the resources that would be necessary to make more units of the monopolist's product.

The monopolist's allocative inefficiency can also be understood by noting that for every unit between Q_m and Q_c, marginal benefit exceeds marginal cost because the demand curve lies above the supply curve. By choosing not to produce these units, the monopolist reduces allocative efficiency because the resources that should have been used to make these units will be redirected instead toward producing items that bring lower net benefits to society. The total dollar value of this efficiency loss (or *deadweight loss*) is equal to the area of the gray triangle labeled *abc* in Figure 8.3b. In monopoly, then

- *P* exceeds MC.
- *P* exceeds minimum ATC.

Income Transfer

In general, a monopoly transfers income from consumers to the owners of the monopoly. The income is received by the owners as revenue. Because a monopoly has market power, it can charge a higher price than would a purely competitive firm with the same costs. So the monopoly in effect levies a "private tax" on consumers. This private tax can often generate substantial economic profits that can persist because entry to the industry is blocked.

The transfer from consumers to the monopolist is evident in Figure 8.3b. For the Q_m units of output demanded, consumers pay price P_m rather than the price P_c that they would pay to a pure competitor. The total amount of income transferred from consumers to the monopolist is $P_m - P_c$ multiplied by the number of units sold, Q_m. So the total transfer is the dollar amount of rectangle P_cP_mbd. What the consumer loses, the monopolist gains. In contrast, the efficiency loss abc is a *deadweight* loss—society totally loses the net benefits of the Q_c minus Q_m units that are not produced.

Cost Complications

Our conclusion has been that, given identical costs, a purely monopolistic industry will charge a higher price, produce a smaller output, and allocate economic resources less efficiently than a purely competitive industry. These inferior results are rooted in the entry barriers present in monopoly.

Now we must recognize that costs may not be the same for purely competitive and monopolistic producers. The unit cost incurred by a monopolist may be either larger or smaller than that incurred by a purely competitive firm. There are four reasons why costs may differ: (1) economies of scale, (2) a factor called "X-inefficiency," (3) the need for monopoly-preserving expenditures, and (4) the "very long run" perspective, which allows for technological advance.

Economies of Scale Once Again
Where economies of scale are extensive, market demand may not be sufficient to support a large number of competing firms, each producing at minimum efficient scale (MES). In such cases, an industry of one or two firms would have a lower average total cost than would the same industry made up of numerous competitive firms. At the extreme, only a single firm—a natural monopoly—might be able to achieve the lowest long-run average total cost.

Some firms relating to new information technologies—for example, computer software, Internet service, and wireless communications—have displayed extensive economies of scale. As these firms have grown, their long-run average total costs have declined because of greater use of specialized inputs, the spreading of product development costs, and learning by doing. Also, *simultaneous consumption* and *network effects* have reduced costs.

A product's ability to satisfy a large number of consumers at the same time is called **simultaneous consumption.** Dell Inc. needs to produce a personal computer for each customer, but Microsoft needs to produce its Windows program only once. Then, at very low marginal cost, Microsoft delivers its program by disk or Internet to millions of consumers. Others able to deliver to additional consumers at low cost include Internet service providers, music producers, and wireless communication firms. Because marginal costs are so low, the average total cost of output typically declines as more customers are added.

Network effects are present if the value of a product to each user, including existing users, increases as the total number of users rises. Good examples are computer software, cell phones, and websites like Facebook where the content is provided by users. When other people have Internet service and devices to access it, a person can conveniently send e-mail messages to them. And when they have similar software, then documents, spreadsheets, and photos can be attached to the e-mail messages. The greater the number of persons connected to the system, the greater are the benefits of the product to each person.

Such network effects may drive a market toward monopoly because consumers tend to choose standard products that everyone else is using. The focused demand for these products permits their producers to grow rapidly and thus achieve economies of scale. Smaller firms, which have either higher-cost "right" products or "wrong" products, get acquired or go out of business.

Economists generally agree that some new information firms have not yet exhausted their economies of scale. But most economists question whether such firms are truly natural monopolies. Most firms eventually achieve their minimum efficient scale at less than the full size of the market. That means competition among firms is possible.

simultaneous consumption
A product's ability to satisfy a large number of consumers at the same time.

network effects Increases in the value of a product to each user, including existing users, as the total number of users rises.

But even if natural monopoly develops, it's unlikely that the monopolist will pass cost reductions along to consumers as price reductions. So, with perhaps a handful of exceptions, economies of scale do not change the general conclusion that monopoly industries are inefficient relative to competitive industries.

X-Inefficiency

In constructing all the average-total-cost curves used in this book, we have assumed that the firm uses the most efficient existing technology. This assumption is only natural because firms cannot maximize profits unless they are minimizing costs. **X-inefficiency** occurs when a firm produces output at a higher cost than is necessary to produce it. For example, in Figure 8.2 the ATC and MC curves might be located above those shown, indicating higher costs at each level of output.

X-inefficiency The production of output, whatever its level, at higher than the lowest average (and total) cost.

Why is X-inefficiency allowed to occur if it reduces profits? The answer harks back to our early discussion of the principal-agent problem. Managers may have goals, such as expanding power, having an easier work life, avoiding business risk, or giving jobs to incompetent relatives, that conflict with cost minimization. Or X-inefficiency may arise because a firm's workers are poorly motivated or ineffectively supervised. Or a firm may simply become lethargic and inert, relying on rules of thumb or intuition in decision making as opposed to relevant calculations of costs and revenues.

Presumably, monopolistic firms tend more toward X-inefficiency than competitive producers do. Firms in competitive industries are continually under pressure from rivals, forcing them to be internally efficient to survive. But monopolists are sheltered from such competitive forces by entry barriers, and that lack of pressure may lead to X-inefficiency.

Rent-Seeking Expenditures

Economists define **rent-seeking behavior** as any activity designed to transfer income or wealth to a particular firm or resource supplier at someone else's, or even society's, expense. We have seen that a monopolist can obtain an economic profit even in the long run. Therefore, it is no surprise that a firm may go to great expense to acquire or maintain a monopoly granted by government through legislation or an exclusive license. Such rent-seeking expenditures add nothing to the firm's output, but they clearly increase its costs. Taken alone, rent-seeking implies that monopoly involves higher costs and less efficiency than suggested in Figure 8.3b.

rent-seeking behavior The actions by persons, firms, or unions to gain special benefits from government at the taxpayers' or someone else's expense.

Technological Advance

In the very long run, firms can reduce their costs through the discovery and implementation of new technology. If monopolists are more likely than competitive producers to develop more efficient production techniques over time, then the inefficiency of monopoly might be overstated. The general view of economists is that a pure monopolist will not be technologically progressive. Although its economic profit provides ample means to finance research and development, it has little incentive to implement new techniques (or products). The absence of competitors means that there is no external pressure for technological advance in a monopolized market. Because of its sheltered market position, the pure monopolist can afford to be inefficient and lethargic; there is no major penalty for not being more efficient.

One caveat: Recall that entirely new products and new methods of production can suddenly supplant existing monopoly through the process of creative destruction (Chapter 2). Recognizing this threat, the monopolist may continue to engage in R&D and seek technological advance to avoid falling prey to future rivals. In this case technological advance is essential to the maintenance of monopoly. But forestalling creative destruction means that it is *potential* competition, not the monopoly market structure, that is driving the technological advance. By assumption, no such competition exists in the pure-monopoly model because entry is entirely blocked.

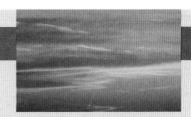

APPLYING THE ANALYSIS

Monopoly Power in the Internet Age

In the early 1990s, when the Internet was young, many analysts predicted that it would foster pure competition across a wide range of activities. Because the Internet allowed any user to publish text and images that could be read for free by any other user, they assumed that the Internet would create a level playing field for all types of media, communications, and commerce.

These predictions turned out to be wrong. One mistake was in not understanding that in a world awash in information, finding what you want becomes a huge problem. When the Internet started, there was no directory and there were no search engines. So it was nearly impossible to find what you were looking for.

Google solved that problem by creating the first effective search engine. Thanks to Google, people could easily locate what they were looking for. But this meant that anyone wishing to be found was now dependent on Google or some other search engine to be found.

If you were an advertiser, you would want to spend your money placing keyword ads on the most popular search engine so your ads would reach as many potential customers as possible. And if you were a customer who found ads helpful in finding what you were looking for, you would also want to utilize the most popular search engine so you could be exposed to the greatest number of helpful ads. Thus, Google quickly came to dominate search as the result of network effects.

Network effects created a barrier to entry that protects Google from competitors because both those searching for information and those wanting to provide it have an interest in sticking with whatever search engine has the most users. There are in fact many smaller search engines, but few want to use them because almost nobody else is using them. Consequently, Google controls about 70 percent of the U.S. search market and receives a majority of the revenue generated by search ads.

The network effects that help Google dominate search also drive the dominance of firms such as Facebook and Amazon. Facebook is a well-run website with lots of interesting things to do, but most people come back for the wall posts and other content generated by fellow users. If there were no fellow users, there would be little content and little reason to visit the site. That makes it hard for smaller social-networking sites to compete with Facebook. As a result, Facebook has come to dominate social media. With over a billion users, it enjoys the largest network effect and grows even bigger thanks to already being big.

The early predictions that the Internet would create a level playing field for all types of media, communications, and commerce have also been doomed by economies of scale. Consider Amazon. To the public, Amazon is the world's largest online retailer, with over $135 billion in annual sales. But behind the scenes, its success is driven by two activities that each enjoy massive economies of scale: data and logistics.

In terms of data, Amazon runs some of the world's largest server farms. These giant buildings are stacked top to bottom with tens of thousands of networked computers that store customer data, process payments, and keep track of inventory. The cost of building and running these server farms runs into the billions of dollars each year, including massive electricity bills. But because a larger server farm generates a lower cost per sale than a smaller server farm, Amazon enjoys economies of scale that allow it to undersell any rival operating on a smaller scale with smaller server farms.

The story with logistics is much the same. Amazon operates dozens of massive distribution warehouses that benefit from economies of scale because a warehouse that is twice as big costs less than twice as much to operate.

We should note, however, that Google, Facebook, and Amazon are not full-on monopolies, something we'll explore in Chapter 9. Each faces robust competition. While network effects and economies of scale benefit them greatly, those factors are not strong enough to guarantee them permanent dominance or even larger profits. In the fourth quarter of 2016, for example, Amazon's profit margin was only 1.71 percent.

QUESTION: Does simultaneous consumption also help explain the ability of Google and Facebook to achieve economies of scale? Explain. Use Figure 6.6 to demonstrate how economies of scale give Google, Facebook, and Amazon an advantage over smaller competitors.

Price Discrimination

We have thus far assumed that the monopolist charges a single price to all buyers. But under certain conditions the monopolist can increase its profit by charging different prices to different buyers. In so doing, the monopolist is engaging in **price discrimination,** the practice of selling a specific product at more than one price when the price differences are not justified by cost differences.

Price discrimination is a common business practice that rarely reduces competition and therefore is rarely challenged by government. The exception occurs when a firm engages in price discrimination as part of a strategy to block entry or drive out competitors.

price discrimination The selling of a product to different buyers at different prices when the price differences are not justified by differences in cost.

Conditions

The opportunity to engage in price discrimination is not readily available to all sellers. Price discrimination is possible when the following conditions are met:

- *Monopoly power* The seller must be a monopolist or, at least, must possess some degree of monopoly power, that is, some ability to control output and price.
- *Market segregation* At relatively low cost to itself, the seller must be able to segregate buyers into distinct classes, each of which has a different willingness or ability to pay for the product. This separation of buyers is usually based on different price elasticities of demand, as the examples below will make clear.
- *No resale* The original purchaser cannot resell the product or service. If buyers in the low-price segment of the market could easily resell in the high-price segment, the monopolist's price-discrimination strategy would create competition in the high-price segment. This competition would reduce the price in the high-price segment and undermine the monopolist's price-discrimination policy. This condition suggests that service industries such as the transportation industry or legal and medical services, where resale is impossible, are candidates for price discrimination.

Examples

Price discrimination is widely practiced in the U.S. economy. For example, airlines charge high fares to business travelers, whose demand for travel is inelastic, and offer lower highly restricted, nonrefundable fares to attract vacationers and others whose demands are more elastic.

Electric utilities frequently segment their markets by end uses, such as lighting and heating. The absence of reasonable lighting substitutes means that the demand for electricity for illumination is inelastic and that the price per kilowatt-hour for such use is high. But the availability of natural gas and petroleum for heating makes the demand for electricity for this purpose less inelastic and the price lower.

Movie theaters and golf courses vary their charges on the basis of time (for example, higher evening and weekend rates) and age (for example, lower rates for children, senior discounts). Railroads vary the rate charged per ton-mile of freight according to the market value of the product being shipped. The shipper of 10 tons of television sets or refrigerators is charged more than the shipper of 10 tons of gravel or coal.

The issuance of discount coupons, redeemable at purchase, is a form of price discrimination. It enables firms to give price discounts to their most price-sensitive customers who have elastic demand. Less price-sensitive consumers who have less elastic demand are not as likely to take the time to clip and redeem coupons. The firm thus makes a larger profit than if it had used a single-price, no-coupon strategy.

Finally, price discrimination often occurs in international trade. A Russian aluminum producer, for example, might sell aluminum for less in the United States than in Russia. In the United States, this seller faces an elastic demand because several substitute suppliers are available. But in Russia, where the manufacturer dominates the market and trade barriers impede imports, consumers have fewer choices and thus demand is less elastic.

Graphical Analysis

Figure 8.4 demonstrates price discrimination graphically. The two graphs are for a single pure monopolist selling its product, say, software, in two segregated parts of the market. For example, one segment might be small-business customers and the other students. Student versions of the software are identical to the versions sold to businesses but are available (1 per person) only to customers with a student ID. Presumably, students have lower ability to pay for the software and are charged a discounted price.

The demand curve D_b, in Figure 8.4a, represents the relatively inelastic demand for the product of business customers. The demand curve D_s, in Figure 8.4b, reflects the

FIGURE 8.4 Price discrimination to different groups of buyers. The price-discriminating monopolist represented here maximizes its total profit by dividing the market into two segments based on differences in elasticity of demand. It then produces and sells the MR = MC output in each market segment. (For visual clarity, average total cost (ATC) is assumed to be constant. Therefore, MC equals ATC at all output levels.) (a) The firm charges a higher price (here, P_b) to customers who have a less elastic demand curve and (b) a lower price (here, P_s) to customers with a more elastic demand. The price discriminator's total profit is larger than it would be with no discrimination and therefore a single price.

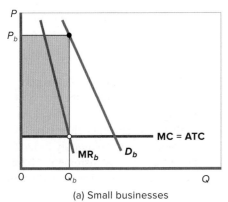

(a) Small businesses

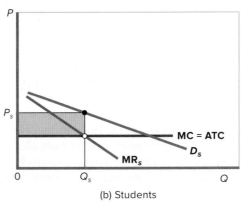

(b) Students

APPLYING THE ANALYSIS

Price Discrimination at the Ballpark

Professional baseball teams earn substantial revenues through ticket sales. To maximize profit, they offer significantly lower ticket prices for children (whose demand is elastic) than for adults (whose demand is inelastic). This discount may be as much as 50 percent.

If this type of price discrimination increases revenue and profit, why don't teams also price-discriminate at the concession stands? Why don't they offer half-price hot dogs, soft drinks, peanuts, and Cracker Jack to children? The answer involves the three requirements for successful price discrimination. All three requirements are met for game tickets: (1) The team has monopoly power; (2) it can segregate ticket buyers by age group, each group having a different elasticity of demand; and (3) children cannot resell their discounted tickets to adults.

It's a different situation at the concession stands. Specifically, the third condition is *not* met. If the team had dual prices, it could not prevent the exchange or "resale" of the concession goods from children to adults. Many adults would send children to buy food and soft drinks for them: "Here's some money, Billy. Go buy *10* hot dogs for all of us." In this case, price discrimination would reduce, not increase, team profit. Thus, children and adults are charged the same high prices at the concession stands.

QUESTION: Why are the prices for concessions at the games quite high compared to prices for the same or similar items at the local convenience store?

elastic demand of students. The marginal revenue curves (MR_b and MR_s) lie below their respective demand curves, reflecting the demand–marginal revenue relationship previously described.

For visual clarity, we have assumed that average total cost (ATC) is constant. Therefore, marginal cost (MC) equals average total cost (ATC) at all quantities of output. These costs are the same for both versions of the software and therefore appear as the single straight line labeled "MC = ATC."

What price will the pure monopolist charge to each set of customers? Using the MR = MC rule for profit maximization, the firm will offer Q_b units of the software for sale to small businesses. It can sell that profit-maximizing output by charging price P_b. Again using the MR = MC rule, the monopolist will offer Q_s units of software to students. To sell those Q_s units, the firm will charge students the lower price P_s.

Firms engage in price discrimination because it enhances their profit. The numbers (not shown) behind the curves in Figure 8.4 would reveal that the sum of the two profit rectangles shown in green exceeds the single profit rectangle the firm would obtain from a single monopoly price. How do consumers fare? In this case, students clearly benefit by paying a lower price than they would if the firm charged a single monopoly price; in contrast, the price discrimination results in a higher price for business customers. Therefore, compared to the single-price situation, students buy more of the software and small businesses buy less.

Monopoly and Antitrust Policy

Monopoly is a legitimate concern. Monopolists can charge higher-than-competitive prices that result in an underallocation of resources to the monopolized product. They can stifle innovation, engage in rent-seeking behavior, and foster X-inefficiency. Even when their costs are low because of economies of scale, there is no guarantee that the price they charge will reflect those low costs. The cost savings may simply accrue to the monopoly as greater economic profit.

Not Widespread

Fortunately, however, monopoly is not widespread in the United States. Barriers to entry are seldom completely successful. Although research and technological advances may strengthen the market position of a monopoly, technology may also undermine monopoly power. Over time, the creation of new technologies may work to destroy monopoly positions (creative destruction). For example, the development of courier delivery, fax machines, and e-mail has eroded the monopoly power of the U.S. Postal Service. Cable television monopolies are now challenged by satellite TV and by new technologies that permit the transmission of audio and visual signals over the Internet.

Similarly, patents eventually expire; and even before they do, the development of new and distinct substitutable products often circumvents existing patent advantages. New sources of monopolized resources sometimes are found, and competition from foreign firms may emerge. (See Global Snapshot 8.1.) Finally, if a monopoly is sufficiently fearful of future competition from new products, it may keep its prices relatively low so as to discourage rivals from developing such products. If so, consumers may pay nearly competitive prices even though competition is currently lacking.

GLOBAL SNAPSHOT 8.1

Competition from Foreign Multinational Corporations

Competition from foreign multinational corporations diminishes the market power of firms in the United States. Here are just a few of the hundreds of foreign multinational corporations that compete strongly with U.S. firms in certain American markets.

Company (Country)	Main Products
Bayer (Germany)	chemicals
Daimler (Germany)	automobiles
Michelin (France)	tires
Lenovo (China)	electronics
Nestlé (Switzerland)	food products
Nokia (Finland)	wireless phones
Panasonic (Japan)	electronics
Petrobras (Brazil)	gasoline
Royal Dutch Shell (Netherlands)	gasoline
Samsung (South Korea)	electronics
Toyota (Japan)	automobiles

Source: Compiled from the Fortune 500 listing of the world's largest firms, "FORTUNE Global 500," 2016, www.fortune.com.

Antitrust Policy

What should government do about monopoly when it arises and persists in the real world? Economists agree that government needs to look carefully at monopoly on a case-by-case basis. If the monopoly appears to be unsustainable over a long period of time, say, because of emerging new technology, society can simply choose to ignore it. In contrast, the government may want to file charges against a monopoly under the antitrust laws if the monopoly was achieved through anticompetitive actions, creates substantial economic inefficiency, and appears to be long-lasting. (Monopolies were once called "trusts.") The relevant antitrust law is the Sherman Act of 1890, which has two main provisions:

- *Section 1* "Every contract, combination in the form of a trust or otherwise, or conspiracy, in restraint of trade or commerce among the several States, or with foreign nations is declared to be illegal."
- *Section 2* "Every person who shall monopolize, or attempt to monopolize, or combine or conspire with any person or persons, to monopolize any part of the trade or commerce among the several States, or with foreign nations, shall be deemed guilty of a felony . . ." (as later amended from "misdemeanor").

In the 1911 Standard Oil case, the Supreme Court found Standard Oil guilty of monopolizing the petroleum industry through a series of abusive and anticompetitive actions. The Court's remedy was to divide Standard Oil into several competing firms. But the Standard Oil case left open an important question: Is every monopoly in violation of Section 2 of the Sherman Act or just those created or maintained by anticompetitive actions?

In the 1920 U.S. Steel case, the courts established a **rule of reason** interpretation of Section 2, saying that it is not illegal to be a monopoly. Only monopolies that "unreasonably" restrain trade violate Section 2 of the Sherman Act and are subject to antitrust action. Size alone was not an offense. Although U.S. Steel clearly possessed monopoly power, it was innocent of "monopolizing" because it had not resorted to illegal acts against competitors in obtaining that power nor had it unreasonably used its monopoly power. Unlike Standard Oil, which was a "bad trust," U.S. Steel was a "good trust" and therefore not in violation of the law. The rule of reason was attacked and once reversed by the courts, but today it is the accepted legal interpretation of the Sherman Act's monopoly provisions.

Today, the U.S. Department of Justice, the Federal Trade Commission, injured private parties, or state attorney generals can file antitrust suits against alleged violators of the Sherman Act. The courts can issue injunctions to prohibit anticompetitive practices (a behavioral remedy) or, if necessary, break up monopolists into competing firms (a structural remedy). Courts also can fine and imprison violators. Also, parties injured by monopolies can sue for *treble damages*—an award of three times the amount of the monetary injury done to them. In some cases, these damages have summed to millions or even billions of dollars.

The largest and most significant monopoly case of recent times is the Microsoft case, which is the subject of the application that follows.

rule of reason The rule stated and applied in the U.S. Steel case that only combinations and contracts unreasonably restraining trade are subject to actions under the antitrust laws and that size and possession of monopoly power are not illegal.

APPLYING THE ANALYSIS

United States v. Microsoft

In May 1998 the U.S. Justice Department, 19 individual states, and the District of Columbia (hereafter, "the government") filed antitrust charges against Microsoft under the Sherman Antitrust Act. The government charged that Microsoft had violated Section 2 of the act through a series of unlawful actions designed to maintain its "Windows" monopoly. It also charged that some of that conduct violated Section 1 of the Sherman Act, which prohibits actions that restrain trade or commerce.

Microsoft denied the charges, arguing it had achieved its success through product innovation and lawful business practices. Microsoft contended it should not be penalized for its superior foresight, business acumen, and technological prowess. It also insisted that its monopoly was highly transitory because of rapid technological advance.

In June 2000 the district court ruled that the relevant market was software used to operate Intel-compatible personal computers (PCs). Microsoft's 95 percent share of that market clearly gave it monopoly power. The court pointed out, however, that being a monopoly is not illegal. The violation of the Sherman Act occurred because Microsoft used anticompetitive means to maintain its monopoly power.

According to the court, Microsoft feared that the success of Netscape's Navigator, which allowed people to browse the Internet, might allow Netscape to expand its software to include a competitive PC operating system—software that would threaten the Windows monopoly. It also feared that Sun's Internet applications of its Java programming language might eventually threaten Microsoft's Windows monopoly.

To counter these and similar threats, Microsoft illegally signed contracts with PC makers that required them to feature its Internet Explorer on the PC desktop and penalized companies that promoted software products that competed with Microsoft products. Moreover, it gave friendly companies coding that linked Windows to software applications and withheld such coding from companies featuring Netscape. Finally, under license from Sun, Microsoft developed Windows-related Java software that made Sun's own software incompatible with Windows.

The district court ordered Microsoft to split into two competing companies, one initially selling the Windows operating system and the other initially selling Microsoft applications (such as Word, Hotmail, MSN, PowerPoint, and Internet Explorer). Both companies would be free to develop new products that compete with each other, and both could derive those products from the intellectual property embodied in the common products existing at the time of divestiture.

In late 2000 Microsoft appealed the district court decision to a U.S. court of appeals. In 2001 the higher court affirmed that Microsoft illegally maintained its monopoly, but tossed out the district court's decision to break up Microsoft. It agreed with Microsoft that the company was denied due process during the penalty phase of the trial and concluded that the district court judge had displayed an appearance of bias by holding extensive interviews with the press. The appeals court sent the remedial phase of the case to a new district court judge to determine appropriate remedies. The appeals court also raised issues relating to the wisdom of a structural remedy.

At the urging of the new district court judge, the federal government and Microsoft negotiated a proposed settlement. With minor modification, the settlement became the final court order in 2002. The breakup was rescinded and replaced with a behavioral remedy. It (1) prevents Microsoft from retaliating against any firm that is developing, selling, or using software that competes with Microsoft Windows or Internet Explorer or is shipping a personal computer that includes both Windows and a non-Microsoft operating system; (2) requires Microsoft to establish uniform royalty and licensing terms for computer manufacturers wanting to include Windows on their PCs; (3) requires that manufacturers be allowed to remove Microsoft icons and replace them with other icons on the Windows desktop; and (4) calls for Microsoft to provide technical information to other companies so those firms can develop programs that work as well with Windows as Microsoft's own products.

Microsoft's actions and conviction have indirectly resulted in billions of dollars of fines and payouts by Microsoft. Main examples: To AOL Time Warner (Netscape), $750 million; to the European Commission, $600 million in 2004 and $1.35 billion in 2008; to Sun Microsystems, $1.6 billion; to Novell, $536 million; to Brust.com, $60 million; to Gateway; $150 million; to interTrust, $440 million; to RealNetworks, $761 million; and to IBM, $850 million.

QUESTION: Why is the 2002 Microsoft settlement a behavioral remedy rather than a structural remedy?

Source: United States v. Microsoft (District Court Conclusions of Law), April 2000; *United States v. Microsoft* (court of appeals), June 2001; *United States v. Microsoft* (Final Judgment), November 2002; and Reuters and Associated Press news services.

SUMMARY

LO8.1 List the characteristics of pure monopoly and discuss several barriers to entry that relate to monopoly.

A pure monopolist is the sole producer of a good or service for which there are no close substitutes.

The existence of pure monopoly is explained by barriers to entry in the form of (a) economies of scale, (b) patent ownership and research, (c) ownership or control of essential resources, and (d) pricing and other strategic behavior.

LO8.2 Explain how a pure monopoly sets its profit-maximizing output and price.

The pure monopolist's market situation differs from that of a competitive firm in that the monopolist's demand curve is downsloping, causing the marginal-revenue curve to lie below the demand curve. Like the competitive seller, the pure monopolist will maximize profit by equating marginal revenue and marginal cost. Barriers to entry may permit a monopolist to acquire economic profit even in the long run. However, (a) the monopolist does not charge "the highest price possible"; (b) the price that yields maximum total profit to the monopolist rarely coincides with the price that yields maximum unit profit; and (c) high costs and a weak demand may prevent the monopolist from realizing any profit at all.

LO8.3 Discuss the economic effects of monopoly.

With the same costs, the pure monopolist will find it profitable to restrict output and charge a higher price than would sellers in a purely competitive industry. This restriction of output causes a misallocation of resources, as is evidenced by the fact that price exceeds marginal cost in monopolized markets.

Monopoly transfers income from consumers to monopolists because monopolists can charge a higher price than would a purely competitive firm with the same costs. So monopolists, in effect, levy a "private tax" on consumers and, if demand is strong enough, obtain substantial economic profits.

The costs monopolists and competitive producers face may not be the same. On the one hand, economies of scale may make lower unit costs available to monopolists but not to competitors. Also, pure monopoly may be more likely than pure competition to reduce costs via technological advance because of the monopolist's ability to realize economic profit, which can be used to finance research. On the other hand, X-inefficiency—the failure to produce with the least costly combination of inputs—is more common among monopolists than among competitive firms. Also, monopolists may make costly expenditures to maintain monopoly privileges that are conferred by government. Finally, the blocked entry of rival firms weakens the monopolist's incentive to be technologically progressive.

LO8.4 Describe why a monopolist might prefer to charge different prices in different markets.

A firm can increase its profit through price discrimination provided it (a) has monopoly pricing power, (b) can segregate buyers on the basis of elasticities of demand, and (c) can prevent its product or service from being readily transferred between the segregated markets.

LO8.5 Identify the antitrust laws that are used to deal with monopoly.

The cornerstone of antimonopoly law is the Sherman Act of 1890, particularly Section 2. According to the rule of reason, possession of monopoly power is not illegal. But monopoly that is unreasonably gained or unreasonably maintained is a violation of the law. If a company is found guilty of violating the Sherman Act, the government can either break up the monopoly into competing firms (a structural remedy) or prohibit it from engaging in specific anticompetitive business practices (a behavioral remedy).

TERMS AND CONCEPTS

pure monopoly	simultaneous consumption	rent-seeking behavior
barriers to entry	network effects	price discrimination
natural monopoly	X-inefficiency	rule of reason

QUESTIONS

The following and additional problems can be found in ▰ **connect**

1. "No firm is completely sheltered from rivals; all firms compete for consumer dollars. If that is so, then pure monopoly does not exist." Do you agree? Explain. LO8.1
2. Discuss the major barriers to entry into an industry. Explain how each barrier can foster either monopoly or oligopoly. Which barriers, if any, do you feel give rise to monopoly that is socially justifiable? LO8.1
3. How does the demand curve faced by a purely monopolistic seller differ from that confronting a purely competitive firm? Why does it differ? Of what significance is the difference? Why is the pure monopolist's demand curve typically not perfectly inelastic? LO8.2
4. Use the following demand schedule for a pure monopolist to calculate total revenue and marginal revenue at each quantity. Plot the monopolist's demand curve and marginal-revenue curve, and explain the relationships between them. Explain why the marginal revenue of the fourth unit of output is $3.50, even though its price is $5. What generalization can you make as to the relationship between the monopolist's demand and its marginal revenue? Suppose the marginal cost of successive units of output was zero. What output would the single-price monopolist produce, and what price would it charge? LO8.2

Price (P)	Quantity Demanded (Q)	Price (P)	Quantity Demanded (Q)
$7.00	0	$4.50	5
6.50	1	4.00	6
6.00	2	3.50	7
5.50	3	3.00	8
5.00	4	2.50	9

5. Assume a monopolistic publisher has agreed to pay an author 10 percent of the total revenue from the sales of a text. Will the author and the publisher want to charge the same price for the text? Explain. LO8.2
6. Assume that a pure monopolist and a purely competitive firm have the same unit costs. Contrast the two with respect to (a) price, (b) output, (c) profits, (d) allocation of resources, and (e) impact on the distribution of income. Since both monopolists and competitive firms follow the MR = MC rule in maximizing profits, how do you account for the different results? Why might the costs of a purely competitive firm and those of a monopolist be different? What are the implications of such a cost difference? LO8.3
7. Critically evaluate and explain each statement: LO8.3
   a. Because they can control product price, monopolists are always assured of profitable production by simply charging the highest price consumers will pay.
   b. The pure monopolist seeks the output that will yield the greatest per-unit profit.
   c. An excess of price over marginal cost is the market's way of signaling the need for more production of a good.
   d. The more profitable a firm, the greater its monopoly power.
   e. The monopolist has a pricing policy; the competitive producer does not.
   f. With respect to resource allocation, the interests of the seller and of society coincide in a purely competitive market but conflict in a monopolized market.
8. U.S. pharmaceutical companies charge different prices for prescription drugs to buyers in different nations, depending on elasticity of demand and government-imposed price ceilings. Explain why these companies, for profit reasons, oppose laws allowing reimportation of their drugs back into the United States. LO8.4
9. Why have firms such as Google, Facebook, and Amazon gained monopoly power in search, social media, and online retail, respectively, despite potential competitors having virtually unrestricted access to the Internet? What economic concepts explain their ability to monopolize these markets? LO8.1
10. Under what law and on what basis did the federal district court find Microsoft guilty of violating the Sherman Act? What was the initial district court's remedy? How did Microsoft fare with its appeal to the court of appeals? What was the final negotiated remedy? LO8.5

violated sect. 2 (Sherman Act

PROBLEMS

1. Assume that the most efficient production technology available for making vitamin pills has the cost structure given in the following table. Note that output is measured as the number of bottles of vitamins produced per day and that costs include a normal profit. **LO8.1**

Output	TC	MC
25,000	$100,000	$0.50
50,000	150,000	1.00
75,000	187,500	2.50
100,000	275,500	3.00

   a. What is ATC per unit for each level of output listed in the table?

   b. Is this a decreasing-cost industry? (Answer yes or no.)

   c. Suppose that the market price for a bottle of vitamins is $2.50 and that at that price the total market quantity demanded is 75,000,000 bottles. How many firms will there be in this industry?

   d. Suppose that, instead, the market quantity demanded at a price of $2.50 is only 75,000. How many firms do you expect there to be in this industry?

   e. Review your answers to parts b, c, and d. Does the level of demand determine this industry's market structure?

2. A new production technology for making vitamins is invented by a college professor who decides not to patent it. Thus, it is available for anybody to copy and put into use. The TC per bottle for production up to 100,000 bottles per day is given in the following table. **LO8.1**

Output	TC
25,000	$50,000
50,000	70,000
75,000	75,000
100,000	80,000

   a. What is ATC for each level of output listed in the table?

   b. Suppose that for each 25,000-bottle-per-day increase in production above 100,000 bottles per day, TC increases by $5,000 (so that, for instance, 125,000 bottles per day would generate total costs of $85,000 and 150,000 bottles per day would generate total costs of $90,000). Is this a decreasing-cost industry?

   c. Suppose that the price of a bottle of vitamins is $1.33 and that at that price the total quantity demanded by consumers is 75,000,000 bottles. How many firms will there be in this industry?

   d. Suppose that, instead, the market quantity demanded at a price of $1.33 is only 75,000. How many firms do you expect there to be in this industry?

   e. Review your answers to parts b, c, and d. Does the level of demand determine this industry's market structure?

   f. Compare your answer to part d of this problem with your answer to part d of problem 1. Do both production technologies show constant returns to scale?

3. Suppose a pure monopolist is faced with the demand schedule shown below and the same cost data as the competitive producer discussed in problem 4 at the end of Chapter 7. Calculate the missing total-revenue and marginal-revenue amounts, and determine the profit-maximizing price and profit-maximizing output for this monopolist. What is the monopolist's profit? Verify your answer graphically and by comparing total revenue and total cost. **LO8.2**

Price	Quantity Demanded	Total Revenue	Marginal Revenue
$115	0	$ _0_	$_120_
100	1	_100_	_100_
83	2	_166_	_47_
71	3	_213_	_39_
63	4	_252_	
55	5	_____	_____
48	6	_____	_____
42	7	_____	_____
37	8	_____	_____
33	9	_____	_____
29	10	_____	_____

4. Suppose that a price-discriminating monopolist has segregated its market into two groups of buyers. The first group is described by the demand and revenue data that you developed for problem 3. The demand and revenue data for the second group of buyers is shown in the table. Assume that MC is $13 in both markets and MC = ATC at all output levels. What price will the firm charge in each market? Based solely on these two prices, which market has the higher price elasticity of demand? What will be this monopolist's total economic profit? **LO8.4**

Price	Quantity Demanded	Total Revenue	Marginal Revenue
$71	0	$ 0	$63
63	1	63	47
55	2	110	34
48	3	144	24
42	4	168	17
37	5	185	13
33	6	198	5
29	7	203	

Monopolistic Competition and Oligopoly

Learning Objectives

LO9.1 List the characteristics of monopolistic competition.

LO9.2 Explain why monopolistic competitors earn only a normal profit in the long run.

LO9.3 Describe the characteristics of oligopoly.

LO9.4 Discuss how game theory relates to oligopoly.

LO9.5 Relate why the demand curve of an oligopolist may be kinked.

LO9.6 Compare the incentives and obstacles to collusion among oligopolists.

LO9.7 Contrast the positive and potential negative effects of advertising.

LO9.8 Discuss the efficiency of oligopoly and whether it is more or less efficient than monopoly.

In the United States, most industries have a market structure that falls somewhere between the two poles of pure competition (Chapter 7) and pure monopoly (Chapter 8). To begin with, most real-world industries usually have fewer than the large number of producers required for pure competition but more than the single producer that defines pure monopoly. In addition, most firms in most industries have both distinguishable rather than standardized products as well as some discretion over the prices they charge. As a result, competition often occurs on the basis of price, quality, location, service, and advertising. Finally, entry to most real-world industries ranges from easy to very difficult but is rarely completely blocked.

This chapter examines two models that more closely approximate these widespread industry structures. You will discover that *monopolistic competition* mixes a small amount of monopoly power with a large amount of competition. *Oligopoly,* in contrast, blends a large amount of monopoly power with both considerable rivalry among existing firms and the threat of increased future competition due to foreign firms and new technologies.

Monopolistic Competition

Let's begin by examining **monopolistic competition,** which is characterized by (1) a relatively large number of sellers, (2) differentiated products (often promoted by heavy advertising), and (3) easy entry into, and exit from, the industry. The first and third characteristics provide the "competitive" aspect of monopolistic competition; the second characteristic provides the "monopolistic" aspect. In general, however, monopolistically competitive industries are much more competitive than they are monopolistic.

Relatively Large Number of Sellers

Monopolistic competition is characterized by a fairly large number of firms, say, 25, 35, 60, or 70, not by the hundreds or thousands of firms in pure competition. Consequently, monopolistic competition involves:

- *Small market shares*   Each firm has a comparatively small percentage of the total market and consequently has limited control over market price.
- *No collusion*   The presence of a relatively large number of firms ensures that collusion by a group of firms to restrict output and set prices is unlikely.
- *Independent action*   With numerous firms in an industry, there is no feeling of interdependence among them; each firm can determine its own pricing policy without considering the possible reactions of rival firms. A single firm may realize a modest increase in sales by cutting its price, but the effect of that action on competitors' sales will be nearly imperceptible and will probably trigger no response.

Differentiated Products

In contrast to pure competition, in which there is a standardized product, monopolistic competition is distinguished by **product differentiation.** Monopolistically competitive firms turn out variations of a particular product. They produce products with slightly

monopolistic competition A market structure in which many firms sell a differentiated product, into which entry is relatively easy, in which the firm has some control over its product price, and in which there is considerable nonprice competition.

product differentiation A strategy in which one firm's product is distinguished from competing products by means of its design, related services, quality, location, or other attributes (except price).

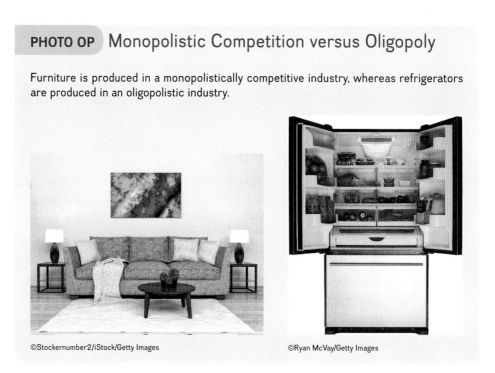

PHOTO OP   Monopolistic Competition versus Oligopoly

Furniture is produced in a monopolistically competitive industry, whereas refrigerators are produced in an oligopolistic industry.

©Stockernumber2/iStock/Getty Images   ©Ryan McVay/Getty Images

different physical characteristics, offer varying degrees of customer service, provide varying amounts of locational convenience, or proclaim special qualities, real or imagined, for their products.

These aspects of product differentiation require more attention.

Product Attributes Product differentiation may entail physical or qualitative differences in the products themselves. Real differences in functional features, materials, design, and workmanship are vital aspects of product differentiation. Personal computers, for example, differ in terms of storage capacity, speed, graphic displays, and included software. There are dozens of competing principles of economics textbooks that differ in content, organization, presentation and readability, pedagogical aids, and graphics and design. Most cities have a variety of retail stores selling men's and women's clothes that differ greatly in styling, materials, and quality of work. Similarly, one pizza place may feature its thin crust Neapolitan style pizza, while another may tout its thick-crust Chicago-style pizza.

Service Service and the conditions surrounding the sale of a product are forms of product differentiation too. One shoe store may stress the fashion knowledge and helpfulness of its clerks. A competitor may leave trying on shoes and carrying them to the register to its customers but feature lower prices. Customers may prefer 1-day over 3-day dry cleaning of equal quality. The prestige appeal of a store, the courteousness and helpfulness of clerks, the firm's reputation for servicing or exchanging its products, and the credit it makes available are all service aspects of product differentiation.

Location Products may also be differentiated through the location and accessibility of the stores that sell them. Small convenience stores manage to compete with large supermarkets, even though these minimarts have a more limited range of products and charge higher prices. They compete mainly on the basis of location—being close to customers and situated on busy streets. A motel's proximity to an interstate highway gives it a locational advantage that may enable it to charge a higher room rate than nearby motels in less convenient locations.

Brand Names and Packaging Product differentiation may also be created through the use of brand names and trademarks, packaging, and celebrity connections. Most aspirin tablets are very much alike, but many headache sufferers believe that one brand—for example, Bayer, Anacin, or Bufferin—is superior and worth a higher price than a generic substitute. A celebrity's name associated with watches, perfume, or athletic apparel may enhance the appeal of those products for some buyers. Many customers prefer one style of ballpoint pen to another. Packaging that touts "natural spring" bottled water may attract additional customers.

Some Control over Price Despite the relatively large number of firms, monopolistic competitors do have some control over their product prices because of product differentiation. If consumers prefer the products of specific sellers, then within limits they will pay more to satisfy their preferences. Sellers and buyers are not linked randomly, as in a purely competitive market. But the monopolistic competitor's control over price is quite limited since there are numerous potential substitutes for its product.

Easy Entry and Exit

Entry into monopolistically competitive industries is relatively easy compared to oligopoly or pure monopoly. Because monopolistic competitors are typically small firms, both absolutely and relatively, economies of scale are few and capital requirements are low. On the other hand, compared with pure competition, financial barriers may result from the need to develop and advertise a product that differs from rivals' products. Some firms may have trade secrets relating to their products or hold trademarks on their brand names, making it difficult and costly for other firms to imitate them.

Exit from monopolistically competitive industries is relatively easy. Nothing prevents an unprofitable monopolistic competitor from holding a going-out-of-business sale and shutting down.

Advertising

The expense and effort involved in product differentiation would be wasted if consumers were not made aware of product differences. Thus, monopolistic competitors advertise their products, often heavily. The goal of product differentiation and advertising—so-called **nonprice competition**—is to make price less of a factor in consumer purchases and make product differences a greater factor. If successful, the demand for the firm's product will increase. The firm's demand may also become less elastic because of the greater loyalty to the firm's product.

nonprice competition Competition based on distinguishing one's product by means of product differentiation and then advertising the distinguished product to consumers.

Monopolistically Competitive Industries

Several manufacturing industries approximate monopolistic competition. Examples of manufactured goods produced in monopolistically competitive industries are jewelry, asphalt, wood pallets, commercial signs, leather goods, plastic pipes, textile bags, and kitchen cabinets. In addition, many retail establishments in metropolitan areas are monopolistically competitive, including grocery stores, gasoline stations, hair salons, dry cleaners, clothing stores, and restaurants. Also, many providers of professional services such as medical care, legal assistance, real estate sales, and basic bookkeeping are monopolistic competitors.

Price and Output in Monopolistic Competition

How does a monopolistically competitive firm decide what quantity to produce and what price to charge? Initially, we assume that each firm in the industry is producing a specific differentiated product and engaging in a particular amount of advertising. Later we'll see how changes in the product and in the amount of advertising modify our conclusions.

The Firm's Demand Curve

Our explanation is based on Figure 9.1, which shows that the demand curve faced by a monopolistically competitive seller is highly, but not perfectly, elastic. It is precisely this feature that distinguishes monopolistic competition from both pure monopoly and pure competition. The monopolistic competitor's demand is more elastic than the demand faced by a pure monopolist because the monopolistically competitive seller has many competitors producing closely substitutable goods. The pure monopolist has no rivals at all. Yet, for two reasons, the monopolistic competitor's demand is not perfectly elastic like that of the pure competitor. First, the monopolistic competitor has fewer rivals; second, its products are differentiated, so they are not perfect substitutes.

The price elasticity of demand faced by the monopolistically competitive firm depends on the number of rivals and the degree of product differentiation. The larger the number of rivals and the weaker the product differentiation, the greater the price elasticity of each seller's demand, that is, the closer monopolistic competition will be to pure competition.

The Short Run: Profit or Loss

In the short run, monopolistically competitive firms maximize profit or minimize loss using exactly the same strategy as pure competitors and monopolists: They produce the level of output at which marginal revenue equals marginal cost (MR = MC). Thus, the

FIGURE 9.1 A monopolistically competitive firm: short run and long run. The monopolistic competitor maximizes profit or minimizes loss by producing the output at which MR = MC. The economic profit shown in (a) will induce new firms to enter, eventually eliminating economic profit. The loss shown in (b) will cause an exit of firms until normal profit is restored. After such entry and exit, the price will settle in (c) to where it just equals average total cost at the MR = MC output. At this price P_3 and output Q_3, the monopolistic competitor earns only a normal profit, and the industry is in long-run equilibrium.

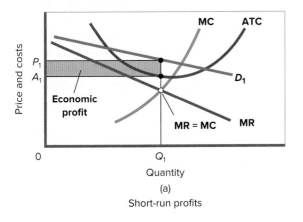

(a)
Short-run profits

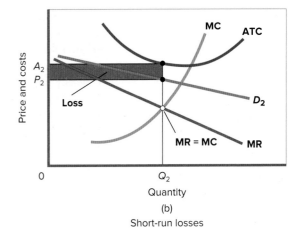

(b)
Short-run losses

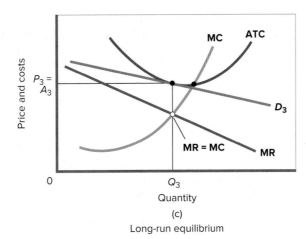

(c)
Long-run equilibrium

monopolistically competitive firm in Figure 9.1a produces output Q_1, where MR = MC. As shown by demand curve D_1, it then can charge price P_1. It realizes an economic profit, shown by the green area $[= (P_1 - A_1) \times Q_1]$.

But with less favorable demand or costs, the firm may incur a loss in the short run. We show this possibility in Figure 9.1b, where the firm's best strategy is to minimize its loss. It does so by producing output Q_2 (where MR = MC) and, as determined by demand curve D_2, by charging price P_2. Because price P_2 is less than average total cost A_2, the firm incurs a per-unit loss of $A_2 - P_2$ and a total loss represented as the red area $[= (A_2 - P_2) \times Q_2]$.

The Long Run: Only a Normal Profit

In the long run, firms will enter a profitable monopolistically competitive industry and leave an unprofitable one. So a monopolistic competitor will earn only a normal profit in the long run or, in other words, will only break even. (Remember that the cost curves include both explicit and implicit costs, including a normal profit.)

Profits: Firms Enter In the case of short-run profit (Figure 9.1a), economic profits attract new rivals because entry to the industry is relatively easy. As new firms enter, the demand curve faced by the typical firm shifts to the left (falls). Why? Because each firm has a smaller share of total demand and now faces a larger number of close-substitute products. This decline in the firm's demand reduces its economic profit. When entry of new firms has reduced demand to the extent that the demand curve is tangent to the average-total-cost curve at the profit-maximizing output, the firm is just making a normal profit. This situation is shown in Figure 9.1c, where demand is D_3 and the firm's long-run equilibrium output is Q_3. As Figure 9.1c indicates, any greater or lesser output will entail an average total cost that exceeds product price P_3, meaning a loss for the firm. At the tangency point between the demand curve and ATC, total revenue equals total costs. With the economic profit gone, there is no further incentive for additional firms to enter.

Losses: Firms Leave   When the industry suffers short-run losses, as in Figure 9.1b, some firms will exit in the long run. Faced with fewer substitute products and blessed with an expanded share of total demand, the surviving firms will see their demand curves shift to the right (rise), as to D_3. Their losses will disappear and give way to normal profits (Figure 9.1c). (For simplicity we have assumed a constant-cost industry; shifts in the cost curves as firms enter or leave would complicate our discussion slightly but would not alter our conclusions.)

Monopolistic Competition and Efficiency

We know from Chapter 7 that economic efficiency requires each firm to produce the amount of output at which $P = MC =$ minimum ATC. The equality of P and ATC yields *productive efficiency*. The good is being produced in the least costly way, and the price is just sufficient to cover average total cost, including a normal profit. The equality of P and MC yields *allocative efficiency*. The right amount of output is being produced, and thus the right amount of society's scarce resources is being devoted to this specific use.

How efficient is monopolistic competition, as measured against this triple equality? In particular, do monopolistically competitive firms produce the efficient output level associated with $P = MC =$ minimum ATC?

Neither Productive nor Allocative Efficiency

In monopolistic competition, neither productive nor allocative efficiency occurs in long-run equilibrium. Figure 9.2 enlarges part of Figure 9.1c and clearly shows this. First note that the profit-maximizing price P_3 slightly exceeds the lowest average total cost, A_4. In producing the profit-maximizing output Q_3, the firm's average total cost therefore is slightly higher than optimal from society's perspective—productive efficiency is not achieved. Also note that the profit-maximizing price P_3 exceeds marginal cost (here M_3), meaning that monopolistic competition causes an underallocation of resources. To measure the size of this inefficiency, note that the allocatively optimal amount of output is determined by point c, where demand curve D_3 intersects the MC curve. So for all units between Q_3 and the level of output associated with point c, marginal benefits exceed marginal costs. Consequently, by producing only Q_3 units, this monopolistic competitor creates an efficiency loss (deadweight loss) equal in size to area acd. The total efficiency loss for the industry as a whole will be the sum of the individual efficiency losses generated by each of the firms in the industry.

Excess Capacity

In monopolistic competition, the gap between the minimum-ATC output and the profit-maximizing output identifies **excess capacity:** plant and equipment that are underused

excess capacity Plant resources that are underused when imperfectly competitive firms produce less output than that associated with achieving minimum average total cost.

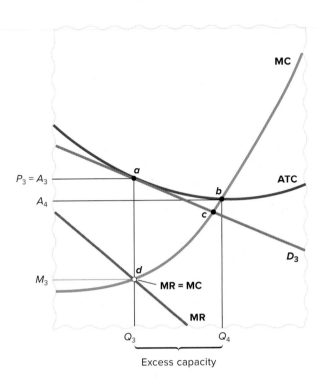

FIGURE 9.2 The inefficiency of monopolistic competition. In long-run equilibrium a monopolistic competitor achieves neither productive nor allocative efficiency. Productive efficiency is not realized because production occurs where the average total cost A_3 exceeds the minimum average total cost A_4. Allocative efficiency is not achieved because the product price P_3 exceeds the marginal cost M_3. The results are an underallocation of resources as well as an efficiency loss and excess production capacity at every firm in the industry. This firm's efficiency loss is area *acd* and its excess production capacity is $Q_4 - Q_3$.

because firms are producing less than the minimum-ATC output. This gap is shown as the distance between Q_4 and Q_3 in Figure 9.2. Note in the figure that the minimum ATC is at point *b*. If each monopolistic competitor could profitably produce at this point on its ATC curve, the lower average total cost would enable a lower price than P_3. More importantly, if each firm produced at *b* rather than at *a*, fewer firms would be needed to produce the industry output. But because monopolistically competitive firms produce at *a* in long-run equilibrium, monopolistically competitive industries are overpopulated with firms, each operating below its optimal capacity. This situation is typified by many kinds of retail establishments. For example, in most cities there is an abundance of small motels and restaurants that operate well below half capacity.

Product Variety and Improvement

But monopolistic competition also has two notable virtues. It promotes product variety and product improvement. A monopolistic competitor is rarely satisfied with the situation portrayed in Figure 9.1c because it means only a normal profit. Instead, it may try to regain its economic profit through further product differentiation and better advertising. By developing or improving its product, it may be able to re-create, at least for a while, the profit outcome of Figure 9.1a.

The product variety and product improvement that accompany the drive to regain economic profit in monopolistic competition are benefits for society—ones that may offset the cost of the inefficiency associated with monopolistic competition. Consumers have a wide diversity of tastes: Some people like Italian salad dressing, others prefer French dressing; some people like contemporary furniture, others prefer traditional furniture. If a product is differentiated, then at any time the consumer will be offered a wide range of types, styles, brands, and quality gradations of that product. Compared with pure competition, this provides an advantage to the consumer. The range of choice is widened, and producers more fully meet the wide variation in consumer tastes.

The product improvement promoted by monopolistic competition further differentiates products and expands choices. And a successful product improvement by one firm obligates rivals to imitate or improve on that firm's temporary market advantage or else lose business. So society benefits from new and improved products.

Oligopoly

In terms of competitiveness, the spectrum of market structures reaches from pure competition, to monopolistic competition, to oligopoly, to pure monopoly. We now direct our attention to **oligopoly,** a market dominated by a few large producers of a homogeneous or differentiated product. Because of their "fewness," oligopolists have considerable control over their prices, but each must consider the possible reaction of rivals to its own pricing, output, and advertising decisions.

A Few Large Producers

The phrase "a few large producers" is necessarily vague because the market model of oligopoly covers much ground, ranging between pure monopoly, on the one hand, and monopolistic competition, on the other. Oligopoly encompasses the U.S. aluminum industry, in which three huge firms dominate an entire national market, and the situation in which four or five much smaller auto-parts stores enjoy roughly equal shares of the market in a medium-size town. Generally, however, when you hear a term such as "Big Three," "Big Four," or "Big Six," you can be sure it refers to an oligopolistic industry. Examples of U.S. industries that are oligopolies are tires, beer, cigarettes, copper, greeting cards, lightbulbs, aircraft, motor vehicles, gypsum products, and breakfast cereals. There are numerous others.

Either Homogeneous or Differentiated Products

An oligopoly may be either a **homogeneous oligopoly** or a **differentiated oligopoly,** depending on whether the firms in the oligopoly produce standardized (homogeneous) or differentiated products. Many industrial products (steel, zinc, copper, aluminum, lead, cement, industrial alcohol) are virtually standardized products that are produced in oligopolies. Alternatively, many consumer goods industries (automobiles, tires, household appliances, electronic equipment, breakfast cereals, cigarettes, and many sporting goods) are differentiated oligopolies. These differentiated oligopolies typically engage in considerable nonprice competition supported by heavy advertising.

Control over Price, but Mutual Interdependence

Because firms are few in oligopolistic industries, each firm is a "price maker"; like the monopolist, it can set its price and output levels to maximize its profit. But unlike the monopolist, which has no rivals, the oligopolist must consider how its rivals will react to any change in its price, output, product characteristics, or advertising. Oligopoly is thus characterized by *strategic behavior* and *mutual interdependence*. By **strategic behavior,** we simply mean self-interested behavior that takes into account the reactions of others. Firms develop and implement price, quality, location, service, and advertising strategies to "grow their business" and expand their profits. But because rivals are few, there is **mutual interdependence:** a situation in which each firm's profit depends not just on its own price and sales strategies but also on those of the other firms in its highly concentrated industry. So oligopolistic firms base their decisions on how they think rivals will react. Example: In deciding whether to increase the price of its cosmetics, L'Oreal will try to predict the response of the other major producers, such as Clinique. Second example: In deciding on its advertising strategy, Burger King will take into consideration how McDonald's might react.

---

oligopoly A market structure in which a few firms sell either a standardized or a differentiated product, into which entry is difficult, in which the firm has limited control over product price because of mutual interdependence (except when there is collusion among firms), and in which there is typically nonprice competition.

homogeneous oligopoly An oligopoly in which the firms produce a standardized product.

differentiated oligopoly An oligopoly in which the firms produce a differentiated product.

strategic behavior Self-interested economic actions that take into account the expected reactions of others.

mutual interdependence A situation in which a change in price strategy (or in some other strategy) by one firm will affect the sales and profits of another firm (or other firms). Any firm that makes such a change can expect the other rivals to react to the change.

ILLUSTRATING THE IDEA

Creative Strategic Behavior

The following story, offered with tongue in cheek, illustrates a localized market that exhibits some characteristics of oligopoly, including strategic behavior.

Tracy Martinez's Native American Arts and Crafts store is located in the center of a small tourist town that borders on a national park. In its early days, Tracy had a minimonopoly. Business was brisk, and prices and profits were high.

To Tracy's annoyance, two "copycat" shops opened adjacent to her store, one on either side of her shop. Worse yet, the competitors named their shops to take advantage of Tracy's advertising. One was "Native Arts and Crafts"; the other, "Indian Arts and Crafts." These new sellers drew business away from Tracy's store, forcing her to lower her prices. The three side-by-side stores in the small, isolated town constituted a localized oligopoly for Native American arts and crafts.

Tracy began to think strategically about ways to boost profit. She decided to distinguish her shop from those on either side by offering a greater mix of high-quality, expensive products and a lesser mix of inexpensive souvenir items. The tactic worked for a while, but the other stores eventually imitated her product mix.

Then, one of the competitors next door escalated the rivalry by hanging up a large sign proclaiming "We Sell for Less!" Shortly thereafter, the other shop put up a large sign stating "We Won't Be Undersold!"

Not to be outdone, Tracy painted a colorful sign of her own and hung it above her door. It read "Main Entrance."

QUESTION: How do you think the two rivals will react to Tracy's strategy?

Entry Barriers

The same barriers to entry that create pure monopoly also contribute to the creation of oligopoly. Economies of scale are important entry barriers in a number of oligopolistic industries, such as the aircraft, rubber, and copper industries. In those industries, three or four firms might each have sufficient sales to achieve economies of scale, but new firms would have such a small market share that they could not do so. They would then be high-cost producers, and as such they could not survive. A closely related barrier is the large expenditure for capital—the cost of obtaining necessary plant and equipment—required for entering certain industries. The jet engine, automobile, commercial aircraft, and petroleum-refining industries, for example, are all characterized by very high capital requirements.

The ownership and control of raw materials help explain why oligopoly exists in many mining industries, including gold, silver, and copper. In the computer, chemicals, consumer electronics, and pharmaceutical industries, patents have served as entry barriers. Moreover, oligopolists can sometimes preclude the entry of new competitors through preemptive and retaliatory pricing and advertising strategies.

Mergers

Some oligopolies have emerged mainly through the growth of the dominant firms in a given industry (examples: breakfast cereals, chewing gum, candy bars). But for other industries the route to oligopoly has been through mergers (examples: steel, in its early history; and, more recently, airlines, banking, and entertainment). Section 7 of the Clayton Act (1914) outlaws mergers that *substantially* lessen competition. But the implied "rule of reason" leaves room for considerable interpretation. As a result, many mergers between firms in the same industry go unchallenged by government.

The combining of two or more firms in the same industry may significantly increase their market share, which may allow the new firm to achieve greater economies of scale. The merger also may increase the firm's monopoly power (pricing power) through greater control over market supply. Finally, because the new firm is a larger buyer of inputs, it may be able to obtain lower prices (costs) on its production inputs.

Oligopoly Behavior: A Game-Theory Overview

Oligopoly pricing behavior has the characteristics of certain games of strategy, such as poker, chess, and bridge. The best way to play such a game depends on the way one's opponent plays. Players (and oligopolists) must pattern their actions according to the actions and expected reactions of rivals. The study of how people or firms behave in strategic situations is called **game theory.**

game theory A means of analyzing the business behavior of oligopolists that uses the theory of strategy associated with games such as chess and bridge.

Now let's look at a more detailed prisoner's dilemma game, using the tools of game theory to analyze the pricing behavior of oligopolists. We assume that a duopoly, or two-firm oligopoly, is producing athletic shoes. Each of the two firms—for example, RareAir and Uptown—has a choice of two pricing strategies: price high or price low. The

ILLUSTRATING THE IDEA

The Prisoner's Dilemma

Games come in different forms, with many possible strategies and outcomes, and have numerous business, political, and personal applications. One frequently observed type of game is known as a *prisoner's dilemma game* because it is similar to a situation in which two people—let's call them Betty and Al—have committed a diamond heist and are being detained by the police as prime suspects. Unknown to the two, the evidence against them is weak so that the best hope that the police have for getting a conviction is if one or both of the thieves confess to the crime. The police place Betty and Al in separate holding cells and offer each the same deal: Confess to the crime and receive a lighter prison sentence.

Each detainee therefore faces a dilemma. If Betty remains silent and Al confesses, Betty will end up with a long prison sentence. If Betty confesses and Al says nothing, Al will receive a long prison sentence. What happens? Fearful that the other person will confess, both confess, even though they each would be better off saying nothing. In business, a form of the "confess–confess outcome" can occur when two oligopolists escalate their advertising budgets to high levels, even though both would earn higher profits at agreed-upon lower levels. In politics, it occurs when two candidates engage in negative advertising, despite claiming that, in principle, they are opposed to its use.

QUESTION: How might the prisoners' strategies or decisions be affected if the general prison population tends to punish those who are known to "rat out" (confess against) their partners?

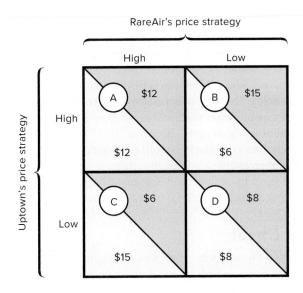

FIGURE 9.3 Profit payoff (in millions) for a two-firm oligopoly. Each firm has two possible pricing strategies. RareAir's strategies are shown in the top margin, and Uptown's in the left margin. Each lettered cell of this four-cell payoff matrix represents one combination of a RareAir strategy and an Uptown strategy and shows the profit that combination would earn for each firm. Assuming no collusion, the outcome of this game is cell D, with both parties using low-price strategies and earning $8 million of profits.

profit each firm earns will depend on the strategy it chooses *and* the strategy its rival chooses.

There are four possible combinations of strategies for the two firms, and a lettered cell in Figure 9.3 represents each combination. For example, cell C represents a low-price strategy for Uptown along with a high-price strategy for RareAir. Figure 9.3 is called a *payoff matrix* because each cell shows the payoff (profit) to each firm that would result from each combination of strategies. Cell C shows that if Uptown adopts a low-price strategy and RareAir a high-price strategy, then Uptown will earn $15 million (yellow portion) and RareAir will earn $6 million (blue portion).

Mutual Interdependence Revisited

The data in Figure 9.3 are hypothetical, but their relationships are typical of real situations. Recall that oligopolistic firms can increase their profits, and influence their rivals' profits, by changing their pricing strategies. Each firm's profit depends on its own pricing strategy and that of its rivals. This mutual interdependence of oligopolists is the most obvious point demonstrated by Figure 9.3. If Uptown adopts a high-price strategy, its profit will be $12 million provided that RareAir also employs a high-price strategy (cell A). But if RareAir uses a low-price strategy against Uptown's high-price strategy (cell B), RareAir will increase its market share and boost its profit from $12 million to $15 million. RareAir's higher profit will come at the expense of Uptown, whose profit will fall from $12 million to $6 million. Uptown's high-price strategy is a good strategy only if RareAir also employs a high-price strategy.

Collusion

Figure 9.3 also suggests that oligopolists often can benefit from **collusion**—that is, cooperation with rivals. Collusion occurs whenever firms in an industry reach an agreement to fix prices, divide up the market, or otherwise restrict competition among them. To see the benefits of collusion, first suppose that both firms in Figure 9.3 are acting independently and following high-price strategies. Each realizes a $12 million profit (cell A).

Note that either RareAir or Uptown could increase its profit by switching to a low-price strategy (cell B or C). The low-price firm would increase its profit to $15 million, and the

collusion A situation in which firms act together and in agreement (collude) to fix prices, divide a market, or otherwise restrict competition.

profit of the high-price firm would fall to $6 million. The high-price firm would be better off if it, too, adopted a low-price policy because its profit would rise from $6 million to $8 million (cell D). The effect of all this independent strategy shifting would be the reduction of both firms' profits from $12 million (cell A) to $8 million (cell D).

In real situations, too, independent action by oligopolists may lead to mutually "competitive" low-price strategies: Independent oligopolists compete with respect to price, and this leads to lower prices and lower profits. This outcome is clearly beneficial to consumers but not to the oligopolists, whose profits decrease.

How could oligopolists avoid the low-profit outcome of cell D? The answer is that they could collude, rather than establish prices competitively or independently. In our example, the two firms could agree to establish and maintain a high-price policy. So each firm will increase its profit from $8 million (cell D) to $12 million (cell A).

Incentive to Cheat

The payoff matrix also explains why an oligopolist might be strongly tempted to cheat on a collusive agreement. Suppose Uptown and RareAir agree to maintain high-price policies, with each earning $12 million in profit (cell A). Both are tempted to cheat on this collusive pricing agreement because either firm can increase its profit to $15 million by lowering its price. For instance, if Uptown secretly cheats and sells at the low price while RareAir keeps on charging the high price, the payoff would move from cell A to cell C so that Uptown's profit would rise to $15 million while RareAir's profit would fall to $6 million. On the other hand, if RareAir cheats and sets a low price while Uptown keeps the agreement and charges the high price, the payoff matrix would move from cell A to cell B so that RareAir would get $15 million while Uptown would get only $6 million. As you can see, cheating is both very lucrative to the cheater as well as very costly to the firm that gets cheated on. As a result, both firms will probably cheat so that the game will settle back to cell D, with each firm using its low-price strategy. This is another example of the prisoner's dilemma illustrated previously.

Kinked-Demand Model

Our game-theory discussion is helpful in understanding more traditional, graphical oligopoly models. We begin by examining a model in which rivals do not overtly collude to fix a common price. Such collusion is, in fact, illegal in the United States. Specifically, Section 1 of the Sherman Act of 1890 outlaws conspiracies to restrain trade. In antitrust law, these violations are known as **per se violations;** they are "in and of themselves" illegal, and therefore not subject to the rule of reason (Chapter 8). To gain a conviction, the government needs to show only that there was a conspiracy to fix prices, rig bids, or divide up markets, not that the conspiracy succeeded or caused serious damage to other parties.

per se violations Collusive actions, such as attempts to fix prices or divide markets, that are violations of the antitrust laws, even if the actions are unsuccessful.

Kinked-Demand Curve

Imagine an oligopolistic industry made up of three law-abiding firms (Arch, King, and Dave's), each having about one-third of the total market for a differentiated product. The question is, "What does each firm's demand curve look like?"

Let's focus on Arch, understanding that the analysis is applicable to each firm. Assume that the going price for the product is P_0 and Arch is currently selling output Q_0, as shown in Figure 9.4. Suppose Arch is considering a price increase. But if Arch raises its price above P_0 and its rivals ignore the price increase, Arch will lose sales significantly to its two rivals, who

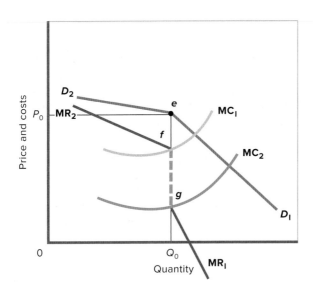

FIGURE 9.4 The kinked-demand curve. In all likelihood an oligopolist's rivals will ignore a price increase above the going price P_0 but follow a price cut below P_0. This causes the oligopolist's demand curve (D_2eD_1) to be kinked at e (price P_0) and the marginal-revenue curve to have a vertical break, or gap (fg). The firm will be highly reluctant to raise or lower its price. Moreover, any shift in marginal costs between MC_1 and MC_2 will cut the vertical (dashed) segment of the marginal-revenue curve and produce no change in price P_0 or output Q_0.

will be underpricing it. If that is the case, the demand and marginal-revenue curves faced by Arch will resemble the straight lines D_2 and MR_2 in Figure 9.4. Demand in this case is quite elastic: Arch's total revenue will fall. Because of product differentiation, however, Arch's sales and total revenue will not fall to zero when it raises its price; some of Arch's customers will pay the higher price because they have a strong preference for Arch's product.

And what about a price cut? It is reasonable to expect that King and Dave's will exactly match any price cut to prevent Arch from gaining an advantage over them. Arch's sales will increase only modestly. The small increase in sales that Arch (and its two rivals) will realize is at the expense of other industries; Arch will gain no sales from King and Dave's. So Arch's demand and marginal-revenue curves below price P_0 will look like the straight lines labeled D_1 and MR_1 in Figure 9.4.

Graphically, the D_2e "rivals ignore" segment of Arch's demand curve seems relevant for price increases, and the D_1e "rivals match" segment of demand seems relevant for price cuts. It is logical, then, or at least a reasonable assumption, that the noncollusive oligopolist faces the **kinked-demand curve** D_2eD_1, as shown in Figure 9.4. Demand is highly elastic above the going price P_0 but much less elastic or even inelastic below that price.

Note also that if rivals ignore a price increase but match a price decrease, the marginal-revenue curve of the oligopolist also will have an odd shape. It, too, will be made up of two segments: the left-hand marginal-revenue curve MR_2f in Figure 9.4 and the right-hand marginal-revenue curve MR_1g. Because of the sharp difference in elasticity of demand above and below the going price, there is a gap, or what we can simply treat as a vertical segment, in the marginal-revenue curve. This gap is the dashed segment fg in the combined marginal-revenue curve MR_2fgMR_1.

Price Inflexibility

This analysis helps explain why prices are generally stable in noncollusive oligopolistic industries. There are both demand and cost reasons.

On the demand side, the kinked-demand curve gives each oligopolist reason to believe that any change in price will be for the worse. If it raises its price, many of its customers will desert it. If it lowers its price, its sales will increase very modestly since rivals will match the lower price. Even if a price cut increases the oligopolist's total revenue somewhat, its costs may increase by a greater amount, depending on the price elasticity of demand. For instance, if its demand is inelastic to the right of Q_0, as it may well be, then

kinked-demand curve The demand curve for a noncollusive oligopolist, which is based on the assumption that rivals will match a price decrease and will ignore a price increase.

the firm's profit will surely fall. Its total revenue will decline at the same time that the production of a larger output increases its total cost.

On the cost side, the broken marginal-revenue curve suggests that even if an oligopolist's costs change substantially, the firm may have no reason to change its price. In particular, all positions of the marginal-cost curve between MC_1 and MC_2 in Figure 9.4 will result in the firm's deciding on exactly the same price and output. For all those positions, MR equals MC at output Q_0; at that output, it will charge price P_0.

Price Leadership

price leadership An informal method that firms in an oligopoly may employ to set the price of their product: One firm (the leader) is the first to announce a change in price, and the other firms (the followers) soon announce identical or similar changes.

The uncertainties of the reactions of rivals create a major problem for oligopolists. There are times when wages and other input prices rise beyond the marginal costs associated with MC_1 in Figure 9.4. If no oligopolist dare raise its price, profits for all rivals will be severely squeezed. In many industries, a pattern of price leadership has emerged to handle these situations. **Price leadership** involves an implicit understanding by which oligopolists can coordinate prices without engaging in outright collusion based on formal agreements and secret meetings. Rather, a practice evolves whereby the "dominant firm"—usually the largest or most efficient in the industry—initiates price changes and all other firms more or less automatically follow the leader. Many industries, including farm machinery, cement, copper, newsprint, glass containers, steel, beer, fertilizer, cigarettes, and tin, practice, or have in the recent past practiced, price leadership.

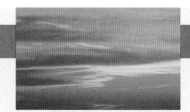

APPLYING THE ANALYSIS

Challenges to Price Leadership

Despite attempts to maintain orderly price leadership, price wars occasionally break out in oligopolistic industries. Sometimes price wars result from attempts to establish new price leaders; other times, they result from attempts to "steal" business from rivals.

Consider the breakfast cereal industry, in which Kellogg traditionally had been the price leader. General Mills countered Kellogg's leadership in 1995 by reducing the prices of its cereals by 11 percent. In 1996, another rival, Post, responded to General Mills' action with a 20 percent price cut. Kellogg then followed with a 20 percent cut of its own. Not to be outdone, Post reduced its prices by another 11 percent. In short, a full-scale price war broke out between General Mills, Post, and Kellogg.

As another example, in October 2009, with the Christmas shopping season just getting under way, Walmart cut its price on 10 highly anticipated new books to just $10 each. Within hours, Amazon.com matched the price cut. Walmart then retaliated by cutting its price for the books to just $9 each. Amazon.com matched that reduction—at which point Walmart went to $8.99! Then, out of nowhere, Target jumped in at $8.98, a price that Amazon.com and Walmart immediately matched. And that is where the price finally came to rest—at a level so low that each company was losing money on each book it sold.

Most price wars eventually run their course. After a period of low or negative profits, they again yield price leadership to one of the industry's dominant firms. That firm then begins to raise prices back to their previous levels, and the other firms willingly follow. Orderly pricing is then restored.

QUESTION: How might a low-cost price leader "enforce" its leadership through implied threats to rivals?

An examination of price leadership in a variety of industries suggests that the price leader is likely to observe the following tactics:

- ***Infrequent price changes***   Because price changes always carry the risk that rivals will not follow the lead, price adjustments are made only infrequently. The price leader does not respond to minuscule day-to-day changes in costs and demand. Price is changed only when cost and demand conditions have been altered significantly and on an industry basis as the result of, for example, industry wage increases, an increase in excise taxes, or an increase in the price of some basic input such as energy. In the automobile industry, price adjustments traditionally have been made when new models are introduced each fall.

- ***Communications***   The price leader often communicates impending price adjustments to the industry through speeches by major executives, trade publication interviews, or press releases. By publicizing "the need to raise prices," the price leader seeks agreement among its competitors regarding the actual increase.

- ***Avoidance of price wars***   Price leaders try to prevent price wars that can damage industry profits. Such wars can lead to successive rounds of price cuts as rivals attempt to maintain their market shares.

Collusion

The disadvantages and uncertainties of kinked-demand oligopolies and price leadership make collusion tempting. By controlling price through collusion, oligopolists may be able to reduce uncertainty, increase profits, and perhaps even prohibit the entry of new rivals. Collusion may assume a variety of forms. The most comprehensive form is the **cartel,** a group of producers that typically creates a formal written agreement specifying how much each member will produce and charge. The cartel members must control output—divide up the market—in order to maintain the agreed-upon price. The collusion is *overt,* or open to view, and typically involves a group of foreign nations or foreign producers. More common forms of collusion are *covert,* or hidden from view. They include conspiracies to fix prices, rig bids, and divide up markets. Such conspiracies sometimes occur even though they are illegal.

cartel A formal agreement among firms (or countries) in an industry to set the price of a product and establish the outputs of the individual firms (or countries) or to divide the market for the product geographically.

Joint-Profit Maximization

To see the benefits of a cartel or other form of collusion, assume there are three hypothetical oligopolistic firms (Gypsum, Sheetrock, and GSR) producing, in this instance, gypsum drywall panels for finishing interior walls. Suppose all three firms produce a homogeneous product and have identical cost, demand, and marginal-revenue curves. Figure 9.5 represents the position of each of our three oligopolistic firms.

What price and output combination should, say, Gypsum select? If Gypsum were a pure monopolist, the answer would be clear: Establish output at Q_0, where marginal revenue equals marginal cost; charge the corresponding price P_0; and enjoy the maximum profit attainable. However, Gypsum does have two rivals selling identical products, and if Gypsum's assumption that its rivals will match its price of P_0 proves to be incorrect, the consequences could be disastrous for Gypsum. Specifically, if Sheetrock and GSR actually charge prices below P_0, then Gypsum's demand curve D will shift sharply to the left as its potential customers turn to its rivals, which are now selling the same product at a lower price. Of course, Gypsum can retaliate by cutting its price too, but this will move all three firms down their demand curves, lowering their profits. It may even drive them to a point where average total cost exceeds price and losses are incurred.

So the question becomes, "Will Sheetrock and GSR want to charge a price below P_0?" Under our assumptions, and recognizing that Gypsum has little choice except to match any

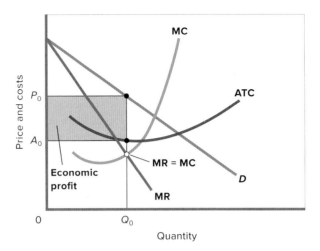

FIGURE 9.5 Collusion and the tendency toward joint-profit maximization. If oligopolistic firms face identical or highly similar demand and cost conditions, they may collude to limit their joint output and to set a single, common price. Thus, each firm acts as if it were a pure monopolist, setting output at Q_0 and charging price P_0. This price and output combination maximizes each firm's profit (green area) and thus the joint profits of all.

price they may set below P_0, the answer is no. Faced with the same demand and cost circumstances, Sheetrock and GSR will find it in their interest to produce Q_0 and charge P_0. This is a curious situation; each firm finds it most profitable to charge the same price, P_0, but only if its rivals actually do so! How can the three firms ensure the price P_0 and quantity Q_0 solution in which each is keenly interested? How can they avoid the less profitable outcomes associated with either higher or lower prices?

The answer is evident: They can collude. They can get together, talk it over, and agree to charge the same price, P_0. In addition to reducing the possibility of price wars, this will give each firm the maximum profit. For society, the result will be the same as would occur if the industry were a pure monopoly composed of three identical plants.

Obstacles to Collusion

Normally, cartels and similar collusive arrangements are difficult to establish and maintain. Below are several barriers to collusion beyond the antitrust laws.

Demand and Cost Differences
When oligopolists face different costs and demand curves, it is difficult for them to agree on a price. This is particularly the case in industries where products are differentiated and change frequently. Even with highly standardized products, firms usually have somewhat different market shares and operate with differing degrees of productive efficiency. Thus, it is unlikely that even homogeneous oligopolists would have the same demand and cost curves.

In either case, differences in costs and demand mean that the profit-maximizing price will differ among firms; no single price will be readily acceptable to all, as we assumed was true in Figure 9.5. So price collusion depends on compromises and concessions that are not always easy to obtain and hence act as an obstacle to collusion.

Number of Firms
Other things equal, the larger the number of firms, the more difficult it is to create a cartel or some other form of price collusion. Agreement on price by three or four producers that control an entire market may be relatively easy to accomplish. But such agreement is more difficult to achieve where there are, say, 10 firms, each with roughly 10 percent of the market, or where the Big Three have 70 percent of the market while a competitive fringe of 8 or 10 smaller firms battles for the remainder.

Cheating
As the game-theory model makes clear, there is a temptation for collusive oligopolists to engage in secret price cutting to increase sales and profit. The difficulty

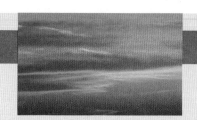

APPLYING THE ANALYSIS

Cartels and Collusion

Undoubtedly the most significant international cartel is the Organization of Petroleum Exporting Countries (OPEC), comprising 13 oil-producing nations (Saudi Arabia, Iran, Venezuela, UAE, Nigeria, Kuwait, Libya, Algeria, Angola, Ecuador, Qatar, Indonesia, and Iraq). OPEC produces about 34 percent of the world's oil and supplies about 34 percent of all oil traded internationally. OPEC has in some cases been able to drastically alter oil prices by increasing or decreasing supply. In the late 1990s, for instance, it caused oil prices to rise from $11 per barrel to $34 per barrel over a 15-month period.

That being said, most increases in the price of oil are not caused by OPEC. Between 2005 and 2008, for example, oil prices went from $40 per barrel to $140 per barrel due to rapidly rising demand from China and supply uncertainties related to armed conflict in the Middle East. But as the recession that began in December 2007 took hold, demand slumped and oil prices collapsed back down to about $40 per barrel. OPEC was largely a nonfactor in this rise and fall in the price of oil. But in those cases where OPEC can effectively enforce its production agreements, there is little doubt that it can hold the price of oil substantially above the marginal cost of production.

Because cartels among domestic firms are illegal in the United States, any collusion that exists is covert or secret. Yet there are numerous examples of collusion, as shown by evidence from antitrust (antimonopoly) cases. In 2011, U.S.-based Whirlpool, Japan-headquartered Panasonic, the Danish firm Danfoss, and the Italian company Appliance Components were fined over $200 million for attempting to run an international cartel that could rig the worldwide prices of refrigerator components. In 2012, several Japanese autoparts makers pleaded guilty to rigging the bids that they submitted to a major carmaker. The conspirators employed measures to keep their conduct secret, including using code names and instructing participants to destroy evidence of collusion.

There are many other relatively recent examples of price fixing: ConAgra and Hormel agreed to pay more than $21 million to settle their roles in a nationwide price-fixing case involving catfish. The U.S. Justice Department fined UCAR International $110 million for scheming with rivals to fix prices and divide the world market for graphite electrodes used in steel mills. The auction houses Sotheby's and Christy's were found guilty of conspiring over a 6-year period to set the same commission rates for sellers at auctions. Bayer AG pleaded guilty to, and was fined $66 million for, taking part in a conspiracy to divide up the market and set prices for chemicals used in rubber manufacturing.

QUESTION: In what way might mergers be an alternative to illegal collusion? In view of your answer, why is it important to enforce laws that outlaw mergers that substantially reduce competition?

with such cheating is that buyers who are paying a high price for a product may become aware of the lower-priced sales and demand similar treatment. Or buyers receiving a price concession from one producer may use the concession as a wedge to get even larger price concessions from a rival producer. Buyers' attempts to play producers against one another may precipitate price wars among the producers. Although secret price concessions are potentially profitable, they threaten collusive oligopolies over time. Collusion is more likely to succeed when cheating is easy to detect and punish. Then the conspirators are less likely to cheat on the price agreement.

Recession Long-lasting recession usually serves as an enemy of collusion because slumping markets increase average total cost. In technical terms, as the oligopolists' demand and marginal-revenue curves shift to the left in Figure 9.5 in response to a recession, each firm moves leftward and upward to a higher operating point on its average-total-cost curve. Firms find they have substantial excess production capacity, sales are down, unit costs are up, and profits are being squeezed. Under such conditions, businesses may feel they can avoid serious profit reductions (or even losses) by cutting price and thus gaining sales at the expense of rivals.

Potential Entry The greater prices and profits that result from collusion may attract new entrants, including foreign firms. Since that would increase market supply and reduce prices and profits, successful collusion requires that colluding oligopolists block the entry of new producers.

Oligopoly and Advertising

We have noted that oligopolists would rather not compete on the basis of price and may become involved in price collusion. Nonetheless, each firm's share of the total market is typically determined through product development and advertising, for two reasons:

- Product development and advertising campaigns are less easily duplicated than price cuts. Price cuts can be quickly and easily matched by a firm's rivals to cancel any potential gain in sales derived from that strategy. Product improvements and successful advertising, however, can produce more permanent gains in market share because they cannot be duplicated as quickly and completely as price reductions.
- Oligopolists have sufficient financial resources to engage in product development and advertising. For most oligopolists, the economic profits earned in the past can help finance current advertising and product development.

In 2016, U.S. firms spent an estimated $155 billion on advertising in the United States. *Advertising is prevalent in both monopolistic competition and oligopoly.* Table 9.1 lists the 10 leading U.S. advertisers in 2016.

TABLE 9.1 **The Largest U.S. Advertisers, 2016**

Company	Advertising Spending Millions of $
Comcast	$5,618
Procter & Gamble	4,312
General Motors	3,769
AT&T	3,601
Verizon	2,744
American Express	2,743
Amazon	2,637
Ford Motor	2,342
JP Morgan Chase	2,233
Walmart	2,175

Source: Advertising Age, www.adage.com. Copyright Global AdView Pulse lite, Copyright the Nielsen Company, 2016. Crain Communications.

Advertising may affect prices, competition, and efficiency either positively or negatively, depending on the circumstances. While our focus here is on advertising by oligopolists, the analysis is equally applicable to advertising by monopolistic competitors.

Positive Effects of Advertising

In order to make rational (efficient) decisions, consumers need information about product characteristics and prices. Media advertising may be a low-cost means for consumers to obtain that information. Suppose you are in the market for a high-quality camera and there is no advertising of such a product in newspapers or magazines. To make a rational choice, you may have to spend several days visiting stores to determine the availability, prices, and features of various brands. This search entails both direct costs (gasoline, parking fees) and indirect costs (the value of your time). By providing information about the available options, advertising reduces your search time and minimizes these direct and indirect costs.

By providing information about the various competing goods that are available, advertising diminishes monopoly power. In fact, advertising is frequently associated with the introduction of new products designed to compete with existing brands. Could Toyota and Honda have so strongly challenged U.S. auto producers without advertising? Could FedEx have sliced market share away from UPS and the U.S. Postal Service without advertising?

Viewed this way, advertising is an efficiency-enhancing activity. It is a relatively inexpensive means of providing useful information to consumers and thus lowering their search costs. By enhancing competition, advertising results in greater economic efficiency. By facilitating the introduction of new products, advertising speeds up technological progress. By increasing sales and output, advertising can reduce long-run average total cost by enabling firms to obtain economies of scale.

Potential Negative Effects of Advertising

Not all the effects of advertising are positive, of course. Much advertising is designed simply to manipulate or persuade consumers—that is, to alter their preferences in favor of the advertiser's product. A television commercial that indicates that a popular personality drinks a particular brand of soft drink—and therefore that you should too—conveys little or no information to consumers about price or quality. In addition, advertising is sometimes based on misleading and extravagant claims that confuse consumers rather than enlighten them. Indeed, in some cases advertising may well persuade consumers to pay high prices for much-acclaimed but inferior products, forgoing better but unadvertised products selling at lower prices. Example: *Consumer Reports* has found that heavily advertised premium motor oils and fancy additives provide no better engine performance and longevity than do cheaper brands.

Firms often establish substantial brand-name loyalty and thus achieve monopoly power via their advertising (see Global Snapshot 9.1). As a consequence, they are able to increase their sales, expand their market shares, and enjoy greater profits. Larger profits permit still more advertising and further enlargement of the firm's market share and profit. In time, consumers may lose the advantages of competitive markets and face the disadvantages of monopolized markets. Moreover, new entrants to the industry need to incur large advertising costs in order to establish their products in the marketplace; thus, advertising costs may be a barrier to entry.

Advertising can also be self-canceling. The advertising campaign of one fast-food hamburger chain may be offset by equally costly campaigns waged by rivals, so each firm's demand actually remains unchanged. Few, if any, extra burgers will be purchased, and all firms will experience higher costs, and either their profits will fall or, through successful price leadership, their product prices will rise.

GLOBAL SNAPSHOT 9.1

The World's Top 10 Brand Names

Here are the world's top 10 brands, based on four criteria: the brand's market share within its category, the brand's world appeal across age groups and nationalities, the loyalty of customers to the brand, and the ability of the brand to "stretch" to products beyond the original product.

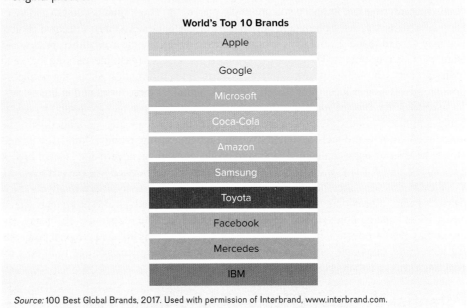

World's Top 10 Brands

- Apple
- Google
- Microsoft
- Coca-Cola
- Amazon
- Samsung
- Toyota
- Facebook
- Mercedes
- IBM

Source: 100 Best Global Brands, 2017. Used with permission of Interbrand, www.interbrand.com.

When advertising either leads to increased monopoly power or is self-canceling, economic inefficiency results.

Oligopoly and Efficiency

Is oligopoly, then, an efficient market structure from society's standpoint? How do the price and output decisions of the oligopolist measure up to the triple equality $P = \text{MC} = $ minimum ATC that occurs in pure competition?

Inefficiency

Many economists believe that the outcome of some oligopolistic markets is approximately as shown in Figure 9.5. This view is bolstered by evidence that many oligopolists sustain sizable economic profits year after year. In that case, the oligopolist's production occurs where price exceeds marginal cost and average total cost. Moreover, production is below the output at which average total cost is minimized. In this view, neither productive efficiency ($P = $ minimum ATC) nor allocative efficiency ($P = \text{MC}$) is likely to occur under oligopoly. A few observers assert that oligopoly is actually less desirable than pure monopoly because government usually regulates pure monopoly in the United States to guard against abuses of monopoly power. Informal collusion among oligopolists may yield price and output results similar to those under pure monopoly yet give the outward appearance of competition involving independent firms.

Qualifications

We should note, however, three qualifications to this view:

- *Increased foreign competition*   In recent decades foreign competition has increased rivalry in a number of oligopolistic industries—steel, automobiles, video games, electric shavers, outboard motors, and copy machines, for example. This has helped to break down such cozy arrangements as price leadership and to stimulate much more competitive pricing.

- *Limit pricing*   Recall that some oligopolists may purposely keep prices below the short-run profit-maximizing level in order to bolster entry barriers. In essence, consumers and society may get some of the benefits of competition—prices closer to marginal cost and minimum average total cost—even without the competition that free entry would provide.

- *Technological advance*   Over time, oligopolistic industries may foster more rapid product development and greater improvement of production techniques than would be possible if they were purely competitive. Oligopolists have large economic profits from which they can fund expensive research and development (R&D). Moreover, the existence of barriers to entry may give the oligopolist some assurance that it will reap the rewards of successful R&D. Oligopolists account for the bulk of the more than $400 billion that U.S. businesses spend on R&D each year. Thus, the short-run economic inefficiencies of oligopolists may be partly or wholly offset by the oligopolists' contributions to better products, lower prices, and lower costs over time.

APPLYING THE ANALYSIS

Internet Oligopolies

The Internet became accessible to the average person only in the mid-1990s. Over the past 20 years, it has evolved into a medium dominated by a few major firms. Chief among them are Google, Facebook, and Amazon. Other major players include Microsoft and Apple.

A key characteristic of each of these firms is that it holds a near-monopoly in a particular part of the tech business. Google dominates search. Facebook holds sway in social networking. Amazon rules the roost in online shopping. Microsoft holds a near monopoly on PC operating systems and business-productivity software. And Apple became the world's most valuable company in 2012 by way of being the planet's most profitable manufacturer of computers, mobile phones, and tablets—all of which run on Apple's own operating software.

But instead of just trying to maintain dominance in its own sector, each of these Internet titans has used the profits generated by its own near-monopoly to try to steal business from one or more of the other titans. The result has been intense oligopolistic competition between a few well-funded rivals.

Consider search. Google's 64 percent share of the search market creates massive amounts of advertising revenue for Google. In fact, Google's 2015 ad revenues of $16 billion exceeded the ad revenues received by all U.S. magazines and newspapers combined. So it may not be surprising that Microsoft created its Bing search engine to compete with Google. As of late 2015, Bing held 21 percent of the search market. Along with Yahoo, which held 13 percent, Bing maintains competitive pressure on Google, forcing ad rates lower.

Facebook is by far the largest social networking website, with more than 1 billion regular users. But in 2011, Google succeeded in creating a large enough social network to challenge

Facebook. Google did so by encouraging the users of its various free services—such as Gmail and YouTube—to join the Google+ social network. By late 2012, Google+ had 500 million total users and 235 million regular users—enough to compete credibly with Facebook.

Google+ was important for Google because Facebook had been encouraging advertisers to switch from using Google search ads to using Facebook banner ads that could be targeted at specific types of Facebook users (such as, "25–30-year-old males with pets living in Pittsburgh"). Google can now counter by offering its own social network on which advertisers can place those sorts of targeted ads.

Google has also challenged Apple by releasing its very popular Android operating system for mobile devices to compete with the iOS operating system that Apple uses on both its iPhone cell phones and its iPad tablet computers. By doing so, Google reduced the threat that Apple could at some point in the future substantially reduce Google's search revenues by directing searches done on Apple devices to a proprietary search engine of Apple's own design.

Apple's dominance in smartphones and tablets has also been challenged by some of the other Internet titans. In addition to licensing the Android operating system to any manufacturer who wants to use it on their own cell phones or tablets, Google launched its own line of Nexus mobile devices to compete with Apple's iPhone and iPad. Also seeking to challenge Apple in mobile devices, Microsoft updated its Windows operating system to handle phones and tablets, launched its Surface line of tablets to compete with the iPad, and attempted to compete with the iPhone by marketing its own Windows Phone, as well as by purchasing long-time cell-phone maker Nokia.

These are just a few examples of oligopoly competition resulting from Internet titans branching out of their own dominant sectors to compete with each other, and there's a simple reason for their aggressive competition. When a near-monopoly already dominates its own sector, its only chance for major profit growth is to invade a rival's sector.

QUESTION: Can you think of other industries where firms branch into new areas to offset dominance by potential competitors?

SUMMARY

LO9.1 List the characteristics of monopolistic competition.

The distinguishing features of monopolistic competition are (a) there are enough firms in the industry to ensure that each firm has only limited control over price, mutual interdependence is absent, and collusion is nearly impossible; (b) products are characterized by real or perceived differences so that economic rivalry entails both price and nonprice competition; and (c) entry to the industry is relatively easy. Many aspects of retailing, and some manufacturing industries in which economies of scale are few, approximate monopolistic competition.

LO9.2 Explain why monopolistic competitors earn only a normal profit in the long run.

Monopolistically competitive firms may earn economic profits or incur losses in the short run. The easy entry and exit of firms result in only normal profits in the long run.

The long-run equilibrium position of the monopolistically competitive producer is less efficient than that of the pure competitor. Under monopolistic competition, price exceeds marginal cost, suggesting an underallocation of resources to the product, and price exceeds minimum average total cost, indicating that consumers do not get the product at the lowest price that cost conditions might allow.

Nonprice competition provides a way that monopolistically competitive firms can offset the long-run tendency for economic profit to fall to zero. Through product differentiation, product development, and advertising, a firm may strive to increase the demand for its product more than enough to cover the added cost of such nonprice competition. Consumers benefit from the wide diversity of product choice that monopolistic competition provides.

In practice, the monopolistic competitor seeks the specific combination of price, product, and advertising that will maximize profit.

LO9.3 Describe the characteristics of oligopoly.

Oligopolistic industries are characterized by the presence of few firms, each having a significant fraction of the market. Firms thus situated engage in strategic behavior and are mutually interdependent: The behavior of any one firm directly affects, and is affected by, the actions of rivals. Products may be either virtually uniform or significantly differentiated. Various barriers to entry, including economies of scale, underlie and maintain oligopoly.

LO9.4 Discuss how game theory relates to oligopoly.

Game theory (a) shows the interdependence of oligopolists' pricing policies, (b) reveals the tendency of oligopolists to collude, and (c) explains the temptation of oligopolists to cheat on collusive arrangements.

LO9.5 Relate why the demand curve of an oligopolist may be kinked.

Noncollusive oligopolists may face a kinked-demand curve. This curve and the accompanying marginal-revenue curve help explain the price rigidity that often characterizes oligopolies; they do not, however, explain how the actual prices of products were first established.

LO9.6 Compare the incentives and obstacles to collusion among oligopolists.

Price leadership is an informal means of overcoming difficulties relating to kinked-demand curves whereby one firm, usually the largest or most efficient, initiates price changes and the other firms in the industry follow the leader.

Collusive oligopolists such as cartels maximize joint profits—that is, they behave like pure monopolists. Demand and cost differences, a "large" number of firms, cheating through secret price concessions, recessions, and the antitrust laws are all obstacles to collusive oligopoly.

Market shares in oligopolistic industries are usually determined on the basis of product development and advertising. Oligopolists emphasize nonprice competition because (a) advertising and product variations are less easy for rivals to match and (b) oligopolists frequently have ample resources to finance nonprice competition.

LO9.7 Contrast the positive and potential negative effects of advertising.

Advertising may affect prices, competition, and efficiency either positively or negatively. Positive: It can provide consumers with low-cost information about competing products, help introduce new competing products into concentrated industries, and generally reduce monopoly power and its attendant inefficiencies. Negative: It can promote monopoly power via persuasion and the creation of entry barriers. Moreover, it can be self-canceling when engaged in by rivals; then it boosts costs and creates inefficiency while accomplishing little else.

LO9.8 Discuss the efficiency of oligopoly and whether it is more or less efficient than monopoly.

Neither productive nor allocative efficiency is realized in oligopolistic markets, but oligopoly may be superior to pure competition in promoting research and development and technological progress.

TERMS AND CONCEPTS

monopolistic competition	homogeneous oligopoly	collusion
product differentiation	differentiated oligopoly	per se violation
nonprice competition	strategic behavior	kinked-demand curve
excess capacity	mutual interdependence	price leadership
oligopoly	game theory	cartel

QUESTIONS

The following and additional problems can be found in ≋ connect

1. How does monopolistic competition differ from pure competition in its basic characteristics? How does it differ from pure monopoly? Explain fully what product differentiation may involve. Explain how the entry of firms into its industry affects the demand curve facing a monopolistic competitor and how that, in turn, affects its economic profit. LO9.1
2. Compare the elasticity of the monopolistic competitor's demand with that of a pure competitor and a pure monopolist. Assuming identical long-run costs, compare graphically the prices and outputs that would result in the long run under pure competition and

under monopolistic competition. Contrast the two market structures in terms of productive and allocative efficiency. Explain: "Monopolistically competitive industries are characterized by too many firms, each of which produces too little." LO9.2
3. "Monopolistic competition is monopolistic up to the point at which consumers become willing to buy close-substitute products and competitive beyond that point." Explain. LO9.1, LO9.2
4. "Competition in quality and service may be just as effective as price competition in giving buyers more for their money." Do you

agree? Why? Explain why monopolistically competitive firms frequently prefer nonprice competition to price competition. LO9.2

5. Why do oligopolies exist? List five or six oligopolists whose products you own or regularly purchase. What distinguishes oligopoly from monopolistic competition? LO9.3

6. Explain the general meaning of the following profit payoff matrix for oligopolists X and Y. All profit figures are in thousands. LO9.4

X's possible prices

	$40	$35
Y's possible prices $40	$57 / $60	$59 / $55
$35	$50 / $69	$55 / $58

a. Use the payoff matrix to explain the mutual interdependence that characterizes oligopolistic industries.

b. Assuming no collusion between X and Y, what is the likely pricing outcome?

c. In view of your answer to part b, explain why price collusion is mutually profitable. Why might there be a temptation to cheat on the collusive agreement?

7. Construct a game-theory matrix to illustrate the text example of two firms and their decisions on high versus low advertising budgets and the effects of each on profits. Show a circumstance in which both firms select high advertising budgets even though both would be more profitable with low advertising budgets. Why won't they unilaterally cut their advertising budgets? Explain why this is an example of the prisoner's dilemma. LO9.4, LO9.7

8. What assumptions about a rival's response to price changes underlie the kinked-demand curve for oligopolists? Why is there a gap in the oligopolist's marginal-revenue curve? How does the kinked-demand curve explain price rigidity in oligopoly? LO9.5

9. Why might price collusion occur in oligopolistic industries? Assess the economic desirability of collusive pricing. What are the main obstacles to collusion? Speculate as to why price leadership is legal in the United States, whereas price fixing is not. LO9.6

10. Why is there so much advertising in monopolistic competition and oligopoly? How does such advertising help consumers and promote efficiency? Why might it be excessive at times? LO9.7, LO9.8

11. Why have tech firms with near monopolies in their own sectors sought to compete with tech firms that have extremely strong, near-monopoly positions in other sectors? LO9.4

PROBLEMS

1. Assume that in short-run equilibrium, a particular monopolistically competitive firm charges $12 for each unit of its output and sells 52 units of output per day. How much revenue will it take in each day? If its average total cost (ATC) for those 52 units is $10, will the firm (a) earn a short-run economic profit, (b) break even with only a normal profit, or (c) suffer an economic loss? If a profit or loss, what will be the amount? Next, suppose that entry or exit occurs in this monopolistically competitive industry and establishes a long-run equilibrium. If the firm's daily output remains at 52 units, what price will it be able to charge? What will be its economic profit? LO9.2

2. Suppose that a restaurant in an oligopolistic part of that industry is currently serving 230 meals per day (the output where MR = MC). At that output level, ATC per meal is $10 and consumers are willing to pay $12 per meal. What is the size of this firm's profit or loss? Will there be entry or exit? Will this restaurant's demand curve shift left or right? In long-run

equilibrium, suppose that this restaurant charges $11 per meal for 180 meals and that the marginal cost of the 180th meal is $8. What is the size of the firm's profit? Suppose that the allocatively efficient output level in long-run equilibrium is 200 meals. Is the deadweight loss for this firm greater than or less than $60? LO9.3

3. Suppose that an oligopolist is charging $21 per unit of output and selling 31 units each day. What is its daily total revenue? Also suppose that previously it had lowered its price from $21 to $19, rivals matched the price cut, and the firm's sales increased from 31 to 32 units. It also previously raised its price from $21 to $23, rivals ignored the price hike, and the firm's daily total revenue came in at $482. Which of the following is most logical to conclude? The firm's demand curve is (a) inelastic over the $21 to $23 price range, (b) elastic over the $19 to $21 price range, (c) a linear (straight) downsloping line, or (d) a curve with a kink in it? LO9.5

Resource Markets and Government

4

©Tatiana Belova/Shutterstock

Wage Determination

Learning Objectives

LO10.1 Explain why the firm's marginal revenue product curve is its labor demand curve.

LO10.2 List the factors that increase or decrease labor demand.

LO10.3 Discuss the determinants of elasticity of labor demand.

LO10.4 Demonstrate how wage rates are determined in competitive and monopsonistic labor markets.

LO10.5 Show how unions increase wage rates and how minimum wage laws affect labor markets.

LO10.6 Identify the major causes of wage differentials.

We now turn from the pricing and production of *goods and services* to the pricing and employment of *resources*. Although firms come in various sizes and operate under highly different market conditions, each has a demand for productive resources. They obtain those resources from households—the direct or indirect owners of land, labor, capital, and entre-preneurial resources. So, referring to the circular flow diagram (Figure 2.2), we shift our attention from the bottom loop (where businesses supply products that households demand) to the top loop (where businesses demand resources that households supply).

A Focus on Labor

The basic principles we develop in this chapter apply to land, labor, and capital resources, but we will emphasize the pricing and employment of labor. About 70 percent of all income in the United States flows to households in the form of wages and salaries. More than 146 million of us go to work each day in the United States. We have an amazing variety of jobs with thousands of different employers and receive large differences in pay. What determines our hourly wage or annual salary? Why is the salary of, say, a topflight major-league baseball player $15 million or more a year, whereas the pay for a first-rate schoolteacher is $50,000? Why are starting salaries for college graduates who major in engineering and accounting so much higher than those for graduates majoring in journalism and sociology?

Demand and supply analysis helps us answer these questions. We begin by examining labor demand and labor supply in a **purely competitive labor market.** In such a market,

- Numerous employers compete with one another in hiring a specific type of labor.
- Each of many workers with identical skills supplies that type of labor.
- Individual employers and individual workers are "wage takers" because neither can control the market wage rate.

purely competitive labor market A labor market in which a large number of similarly qualified workers independently offer their labor services to a large number of employers, none of whom can set the wage rate.

Labor Demand

Labor demand is the starting point for any discussion of wages and salaries. Labor demand is a schedule or a curve showing the amounts of labor that buyers are willing and able to purchase at various price levels (hourly wages) over some period of time. As with all resources, labor demand is a **derived demand,** meaning that the demand for labor is derived from the demand for the products that labor helps to produce. This is true because labor resources usually do not directly satisfy customer wants but do so indirectly through their use in producing goods and services. Almost nobody wants to directly consume the labor services of a software engineer, but millions of people do want to use the software that the engineer helps create.

derived demand The demand for a resource that depends on the demand for the products it helps to produce.

Marginal Revenue Product

Because resource demand is derived from product demand, the strength of the demand will depend on the productivity of the labor—its ability to produce goods and services—and the price of the good or service it helps produce. Other things equal, a resource that is highly productive in turning out a highly valued commodity will be in great demand. In contrast, a relatively unproductive resource that is capable of producing only a minimally valued commodity will be in little demand. And no demand whatsoever will exist for a resource that is phenomenally efficient in producing something that no one wants to buy.

Consider the table in Figure 10.1, which shows the roles of marginal productivity and product price in determining labor demand.

Productivity Columns 1 and 2 give the number of units of labor employed and the resulting total product (output). Column 3 provides the marginal product (MP), or additional output, resulting from using each additional unit of labor. Columns 1 through 3 remind us that the law of diminishing returns applies here, causing the marginal product of labor to fall beyond some point. For simplicity, we assume that these diminishing marginal returns—these declines in marginal product—begin with the second worker hired.

Product Price The derived demand for labor depends also on the market value (product price) of the good or service. Column 4 in the table in Figure 10.1 adds this price information to the mix. Because we are assuming a competitive product market, product price equals marginal revenue. The firm is a price taker and can sell units of output only at this market price. This price will also be the firm's marginal revenue. In this case, both price and marginal revenue are a constant $2.

Multiplying column 2 by column 4 provides the total-revenue data of column 5. These are the amounts of revenue the firm realizes from the various levels of employment. From these total-revenue data we can compute the **marginal revenue product (MRP)** of labor—the change in total revenue resulting from the use of each additional unit of labor. In equation form,

marginal revenue product (MRP) The change in a firm's total revenue when it employs 1 more unit of labor.

$$\text{Marginal revenue product} = \frac{\text{change in total revenue}}{\text{unit change in labor}}$$

The MRPs are listed in column 6 in the table.

FIGURE 10.1 The purely competitive seller's demand for labor. The MRP-of-labor curve is the labor demand curve; each of its points relates a particular wage rate (= MRP when profit is maximized) with a corresponding quantity of labor demanded. The downward slope of the D = MRP curve results from the law of diminishing marginal returns.

(1) Units of Labor	(2) Total Product (Output)	(3) Marginal Product (MP)	(4) Product Price	(5) Total Revenue, (2) × (4)	(6) Marginal Revenue Product (MRP)
0	0		$2	$ 0	
		7			$14
1	7		2	14	
		6			12
2	13		2	26	
		5			10
3	18		2	36	
		4			8
4	22		2	44	
		3			6
5	25		2	50	
		2			4
6	27		2	54	
		1			2
7	28		2	56	

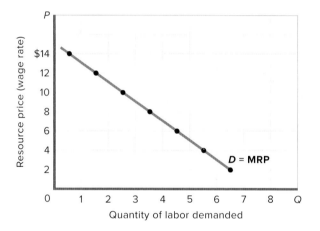

Rule for Employing Labor: MRP = MRC

The MRP schedule, shown as columns 1 and 6, is the firm's demand schedule for labor. To understand why, you must first know the rule that guides a profit-seeking firm in hiring any resource: To maximize profit, a firm should hire additional units of labor as long as each successive unit adds more to the firm's total revenue than to the firm's total cost.

Economists use special terms to designate what each additional unit of labor (or any other variable resource) adds to total revenue and what it adds to total cost. We have seen that MRP measures how much each successive unit of labor adds to total revenue. The **marginal resource cost (MRC)** The change in a firm's total cost when it employs 1 more unit of labor.

amount that each additional unit of labor adds to the firm's total cost is called its **marginal resource cost (MRC).** In equation form,

$$\begin{array}{c}\text{Marginal} \\ \text{resource} \\ \text{cost}\end{array} = \dfrac{\text{change in total (labor) cost}}{\text{unit change in labor}}$$

So we can restate our rule for hiring resources as follows: It will be profitable for a firm to hire additional units of labor up to the point at which labor's MRP is equal to its MRC. If the number of workers a firm is currently hiring is such that the MRP of the last worker exceeds his or her MRC, the firm can profit by hiring more workers. But if the number being hired is such that the MRC of the last worker exceeds his or her MRP, the firm is hiring workers who are not "paying their way" and it can increase its profit by discharging some workers. You may have recognized that this **MRP = MRC rule** is similar to the MR = MC profit-maximizing rule employed throughout our discussion of price and output determination. The rationale of the two rules is the same, but the point of reference is now *inputs* of a resource, not *outputs* of a product.

MRP = MRC rule The principle that to maximize profit a firm should expand employment until the marginal revenue product (MRP) of labor equals the marginal resource cost (MRC) of labor.

MRP as Labor Demand Schedule

In a competitive labor market, market supply and market demand establish the wage rate. Because each firm hires such a small fraction of the market supply of labor, an individual firm cannot influence the market wage rate; it is a wage taker, not a wage maker. This means that for each additional unit of labor hired, each firm's total labor cost increases by exactly the amount of the constant market wage rate. More specifically, the MRC of labor exactly equals the market wage rate. Thus, resource "price" (the market wage rate) and resource "cost" (marginal resource cost) are equal for a firm that hires labor in a competitive labor market. As a result, the MRP = MRC rule tells us that a competitive firm will hire units of labor up to the point at which the market *wage rate* (its MRC) is equal to its MRP.

In terms of the data in columns 1 and 6 of Figure 10.1's table, if the market wage rate is, say, $13.95, the firm will hire only one worker. This is the outcome because only the hiring of the first worker results in an increase in profits. To see this, note that for the first worker, MRP (= $14) exceeds MRC (= $13.95). Thus, hiring the first worker is profitable. For each successive worker, however, MRC (= $13.95) exceeds MRP (= $12 or less), indicating that it will not be profitable to hire any of those workers. If the wage rate is $11.95, by the same reasoning we discover that it will pay the firm to hire both the first and second workers. Similarly, if the wage rate is $9.95, three will be hired; if it is $7.95, four; if it is $5.95, five; and so forth. *The MRP schedule therefore constitutes the firm's demand for labor because each point on this schedule (or curve) indicates the quantity of labor units the firm would hire at each possible wage rate.* In the graph in Figure 10.1, we show the D = MRP curve based on the data in the table. The competitive firm's labor demand curve identifies an inverse relationship between the wage rate and the quantity of labor demanded, other things equal. The curve slopes downward because of diminishing marginal returns.[1]

Market Demand for Labor

We have now explained the individual firm's demand curve for labor. Recall that the total, or market, demand curve for a *product* is found by summing horizontally the demand curves of all individual buyers in the market. The market demand curve for a particular *resource* is derived in essentially the same way. Economists sum horizontally the individual labor demand curves of all firms hiring a particular kind of labor to obtain the market demand for that labor.

Changes in Labor Demand

What will alter the demand for labor (shift the labor demand curve)? The fact that labor demand is derived from *product demand* and depends on *resource productivity* suggests two "resource demand shifters." Also, our analysis of how changes in the prices of other products can shift a product's demand curve (Chapter 3) suggests another factor: changes in the *prices of other resources*.

---

[1]Note that we plot the points in Figure 10.1 halfway between succeeding numbers of labor units. For example, we plot the MRP of the second unit ($12) not at 1 or 2 but at 1½. This "smoothing" enables us to sketch a continuously downsloping curve rather than one that moves downward in discrete steps as each new unit of labor is hired.

Changes in Product Demand

Other things equal, an increase in the demand for a product will increase the demand for a resource used in its production, whereas a decrease in product demand will decrease the demand for that resource.

Let's see how this works. The first thing to recall is that a change in the demand for a product will normally change its price. In the table in Figure 10.1, let's assume that an increase in product demand boosts product price from $2 to $3. You should calculate the new labor demand schedule (columns 1 and 6) that would result, and plot it in the graph to verify that the new labor demand curve lies to the right of the old demand curve. Similarly, a decline in the product demand (and price) will shift the labor demand curve to the left. The fact that labor demand changes along with product demand demonstrates that labor demand is derived from product demand.

Example: With no offsetting change in supply, a decrease in the demand for new houses will drive down house prices. Those lower prices will decrease the MRP of construction workers, and therefore the demand for construction workers will fall. The labor demand curve will shift to the left.

Changes in Productivity

Other things equal, an increase in the productivity of a resource will increase the demand for the resource and a decrease in productivity will reduce the demand for the resource. If we doubled the MP data of column 3 in the table in Figure 10.1, the MRP data of column 6 also would double, indicating a rightward shift of the labor demand curve in the graph.

The productivity of any resource may be altered over the long run in several ways:

- *Quantities of other resources*   The marginal productivity of any resource will vary with the quantities of the other resources used with it. The greater the amount of capital and land resources used with labor, the greater will be labor's marginal productivity and, thus, labor demand.
- *Technological advance*   Technological improvements that increase the quality of other resources, such as capital, have the same effect. The better the *quality* of capital, the greater the productivity of labor used with it. Dockworkers employed with a specific amount of capital in the form of unloading cranes are more productive than dockworkers with the same amount of capital embodied in older conveyor-belt systems.
- *Quality of labor*   Improvements in the quality of labor will increase its marginal productivity and therefore its demand. In effect, there will be a new demand curve for a different, more skilled, kind of labor.

Changes in the Prices of Other Resources

Changes in the prices of other resources may change the demand for labor.

Substitute Resources   Suppose that labor and capital are substitutable in a certain production process. A firm can produce some specific amount of output using a relatively small amount of labor and a relatively large amount of capital, or vice versa. What happens if the price of machinery (capital) falls? The effect on the demand for labor will be the net result of two opposed effects: the substitution effect and the output effect.

- *Substitution effect*   The decline in the price of machinery prompts the firm to substitute machinery for labor. This allows the firm to produce its output at lower cost. So at the fixed wage rate, smaller quantities of labor are now employed. This **substitution effect** decreases the demand for labor. More generally, the substitution effect indicates that a firm will purchase more of an input whose relative price has declined and, conversely, use less of an input whose relative price has increased.

substitution effect The replacement of labor by capital when the price of capital falls.

- *Output effect*   Because the price of machinery has declined, the costs of producing various outputs also must decline. With lower costs, the firm can profitably produce and sell a greater output. The greater output increases the demand for all resources, including labor. So this **output effect** increases the demand for labor. More generally, the output effect means that the firm will purchase more of one particular input when the price of the other input falls and less of that particular input when the price of the other input rises.

- *Net effect*   The substitution and output effects are both present when the price of an input changes, but they work in opposite directions. For a decline in the price of capital, the substitution effect decreases the demand for labor and the output effect increases it. The net change in labor demand depends on the relative sizes of the two effects: If the substitution effect outweighs the output effect, a decrease in the price of capital decreases the demand for labor. If the output effect exceeds the substitution effect, a decrease in the price of capital increases the demand for labor.

> **output effect** An increase in the use of labor that occurs when a decline in the price of capital reduces a firm's production costs and therefore enables it to sell more output.

Complementary Resources   Resources may be complements rather than substitutes in the production process; an increase in the quantity of one of them also requires an increase in the amount of the other used, and vice versa. Suppose a small design firm does computer-assisted design (CAD) with relatively expensive personal computers as its basic piece of capital equipment. Each computer requires exactly one design engineer to operate it; the machine is not automated—it will not run itself—and a second engineer would have nothing to do.

Now assume that these computers substantially decline in price. There can be no substitution effect because labor and capital must be used in *fixed proportions:* one person for one machine. Capital cannot be substituted for labor. But there *is* an output effect. Other things equal, the reduction in the price of capital goods means lower production costs. It will therefore be profitable to produce a larger output. In doing so, the firm will use both more capital and more labor. When labor and capital are complementary, a decline in the price of capital increases the demand for labor through the output effect.

We have cast our analysis of substitute resources and complementary resources mainly in terms of a decline in the price of capital. Obviously, an *increase* in the price of capital causes the opposite effects on labor demand.

PHOTO OP   Substitute Resources versus Complementary Resources

Automatic teller machines (ATMs) and human tellers are substitute resources, whereas construction equipment and their operators are complementary resources.

©Onoky/SuperStock

©Steve Allen/Brand X Pictures

Occupational Employment Trends

Changes in labor demand are of considerable significance because they affect employment in specific occupations. Other things equal, increases in labor demand for certain occupational groups result in increases in their employment; decreases in labor demand result in decreases in their employment. For illustration, let's look at occupations that are growing and declining in demand.

Table 10.1 lists the 10 fastest-growing and 10 most rapidly declining U.S. occupations (in percentage terms) for 2016–2026, as projected by the Bureau of Labor Statistics. Notice that service occupations dominate the fastest-growing list. In general, the demand for service workers is rapidly outpacing the demand for manufacturing, construction, and mining workers in the United States.

Of the 10 fastest-growing occupations in percentage terms, five are related to health care. The rising demands for these types of labor are derived from the growing demand for

TABLE 10.1 The 10 Fastest-Growing and Most Rapidly Declining U.S. Occupations, in Percentage Terms, 2016–2026

Occupation	Employment, Thousands of Jobs		Percentage Change*
	2016	2026	
Fastest Growing			
Solar photovoltaic installers	11	23	105%
Wind turbine service technicians	6	11	96
Home health aides	912	1,343	47
Personal care aides	2,016	2,794	39
Physician assistants	106	146	37
Nurse practitioners	156	212	36
Statisticians	37	50	34
Physical therapist assistants	88	116	31
Software developer, applications	831	1,087	31
Mathematicians	3	4	30
Most Rapidly Declining			
Locomotive firers	1.2	0.3	−79
Respiratory therapy technicians	11	5	−56
Parking enforcement workers	9	6	−35
Word processors and typists	75	50	−33
Watch repairers	1.8	1.2	−30
Electronic equipment installers and repairers, motor vechicles	12.1	9	−26
Foundry mold and coremakers	12.5	9.5	−24
Pourers and casters, metal	8.4	6.5	−23
Computer operators	51	40	−23
Telephone operators	9	7	−23

*Percentages may not correspond with employment numbers due to rounding of the employment data and the percentages.
Source: Bureau of Labor Statistics, "Employment Projections," **www.bls.gov.**

health services, caused by several factors. The aging of the U.S. population has brought with it more medical problems, rising incomes have led to greater expenditures on health care, and the growing presence of private and public insurance has allowed people to buy more health care than most could afford individually.

Table 10.1 also lists the 10 U.S. occupations with the greatest projected job loss (in percentage terms) between 2016 and 2026. These occupations are more diverse than the fastest-growing occupations. Several of the occupations owe their declines mainly to "labor-saving" technological change. For example, automated or computerized equipment has greatly reduced the need for telephone operators and parking enforcement workers.

Two of the occupations in the declining-employment list are related to heavy manufacturing. The U.S. demand for these goods is increasingly being filled through imports. Those jobs are therefore rapidly disappearing in the United States.

QUESTION: Name an occupation (other than those listed) that you think will grow in demand over the next decade. Name an occupation that you think will decline in demand. In each case, explain your reasoning.

Elasticity of Labor Demand

The employment changes we have just discussed have resulted from shifts in the locations of labor demand curves. Such changes in demand must be distinguished from changes in the quantity of labor demanded caused by a change in the wage rate. Such a change is caused not by a shift of the demand curve but, rather, by a movement from one point to another on a fixed labor demand curve. Example: In Figure 10.1 we note that an increase in the wage rate from $5 to $7 will reduce the quantity of labor demanded from 5 units to 4 units. This is a change in the *quantity of labor demanded* as distinct from a *change in the demand for labor*.

The sensitivity of labor quantity to changes in wage rates along a fixed labor demand curve is measured by the **elasticity of labor demand** (or *wage elasticity of demand*). In coefficient form,

$$E_w = \frac{\text{percentage change in labor quantity demanded}}{\text{percentage change in wage rate}}$$

elasticity of labor demand A measure of the responsiveness of labor quantity to a change in the wage rate.

When E_w is greater than 1, labor demand is elastic; when E_w is less than 1, labor demand is inelastic; and when E_w equals 1, labor demand is unit-elastic. Several factors interact to determine the wage elasticity of demand.

Ease of Resource Substitutability

The greater the substitutability of other resources for labor, the more elastic is the demand for labor. As an example, the high degree to which computerized voice recognition systems are substitutable for human beings implies that the demand for human beings answering phone calls at call centers is quite elastic. In contrast, there are few good substitutes for physicians, so demand for them is less elastic or even inelastic.

Time can play a role in the input substitution process. For example, a firm's truck drivers may obtain a substantial wage increase with little or no immediate decline in employment. But over time, as the firm's trucks wear out and are replaced, that wage increase may motivate the company to purchase larger trucks and in that way deliver the same total output with fewer drivers.

Elasticity of Product Demand

The greater the elasticity of product demand, the greater is the elasticity of labor demand. The derived nature of resource demand leads us to expect this relationship. A small rise in the price of a product (caused by a wage increase) will sharply reduce output if product demand is elastic. So a relatively large decline in the amount of labor demanded will result. This means that the demand for labor is elastic.

Ratio of Labor Cost to Total Cost

The larger the proportion of total production costs accounted for by labor, the greater is the elasticity of demand for labor. In the extreme, if labor cost is the only production cost, then a 20 percent increase in wage rates will increase marginal cost and average total cost by 20 percent. If product demand is elastic, this substantial increase in costs will cause a relatively large decline in sales and a sharp decline in the amount of labor demanded. So labor demand is highly elastic. But if labor cost is only 50 percent of production cost, then a 20 percent increase in wage rates will increase costs by only 10 percent. With the same elasticity of product demand, this will cause a relatively small decline in sales and therefore in the amount of labor demanded. In this case the demand for labor is much less elastic.

Market Supply of Labor

Let's now turn to the supply side of a purely competitive labor market. The supply curve for each type of labor slopes upward, indicating that employers as a group must pay higher wage rates to obtain more workers. Employers must do this to bid workers away from other industries, occupations, and localities. Within limits, workers have alternative job opportunities. For example, they may work in other industries in the same locality, or they may work in their present occupations in different cities or states, or they may work in other occupations.

Firms that want to hire these workers must pay higher wage rates to attract them away from the alternative job opportunities available to them. They also must pay higher wages to induce people who are not currently in the labor force—who are perhaps doing household activities or enjoying leisure—to seek employment. In short, assuming that wages are constant in other labor markets, higher wages in a particular labor market entice more workers to offer their labor services in that market. This fact results in a direct relationship between the wage rate and the quantity of labor supplied, as represented by the upward-sloping market supply-of-labor curve S in Figure 10.2a.

FIGURE 10.2   A purely competitive labor market. In a purely competitive labor market (a), market labor supply S and market labor demand D determine the equilibrium wage rate W_c and the equilibrium number of workers Q_c. Each individual competitive firm (b) takes this competitive wage W_c as given. Thus, the individual firm's labor supply curve $s = $ MRC is perfectly elastic at the going wage W_c. Its labor demand curve, d, is its MRP curve (here labeled mrp). The firm maximizes its profit by hiring workers up to the point where MRP = MRC.

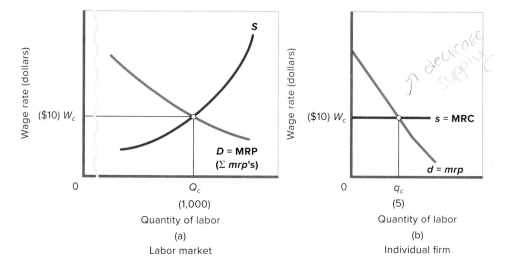

TABLE 10.2   **The Supply of Labor: Pure Competition in the Hire of Labor**

(1) Units of Labor	(2) Wage Rate	(3) Total Labor Cost (Wage Bill)	(4) Marginal Resource (Labor) Cost
0	$10	$ 0	
			$10
1	10	10	
			10
2	10	20	
			10
3	10	30	
			10
4	10	40	
			10
5	10	50	
			10
6	10	60	

Wage and Employment Determination

What determines the market wage rate and how do firms respond to it? Suppose 200 firms demand a particular type of labor, say, carpenters. These firms need not be in the same industry; industries are defined according to the products they produce and not the resources they employ. Thus, firms producing wood-framed furniture, wood windows and doors, houses and apartment buildings, and wood cabinets will demand carpenters. To find the total, or market, labor demand curve for a particular labor service, we sum horizontally the labor demand curves (the marginal revenue product curves) of the individual firms, as indicated in Figure 10.2. The horizontal summing of the 200 labor demand curves like d in Figure 10.2b yields the market labor demand curve D in Figure 10.2a.

The intersection of the market labor demand curve D and the market labor supply curve S in Figure 10.2a determines the equilibrium wage rate and the level of employment in this purely competitive labor market. Observe that the equilibrium wage rate is W_c ($10) and the number of workers hired is Q_c (1,000).

To the individual firm (Figure 10.2b) the market wage rate W_c is given at $10. Each of the many firms employs such a small fraction of the total available supply of this type of labor that no single firm can influence the wage rate. As shown by the horizontal line s in Figure 10.2b, the supply of labor faced by an individual firm is perfectly elastic. It can hire as many or as few workers as it wants to at the market wage rate. This fact is clarified in Table 10.2, where we see that the marginal cost of labor MRC is constant at $10 and is equal to the wage rate. Each additional unit of labor employed adds precisely its own wage rate (here, $10) to the firm's total resource cost.

Each individual firm will apply the MRP = MRC rule to determine its profit-maximizing level of employment. So the competitive firm maximizes its profit by hiring units of labor to the point at which its wage rate (= MRC) equals MRP. In Figure 10.2b the employer will hire q_c (5) units of labor, paying each worker the market wage rate W_c ($10). The other 199 firms (not shown) in this labor market will also each employ 5 workers and pay $10 per hour. The workers will receive pay based on their contribution to the firm's output and thus revenues.

Monopsony

In the purely competitive labor market, each firm can hire as little or as much labor as it needs at the market wage rate, as reflected in its horizontal labor supply curve. The

monopsony A market structure in which only a single buyer of a good, service, or resource is present.

situation is strikingly different when the labor market is a **monopsony,** a market structure in which there is only a single buyer. Labor market monopsony has the following characteristics:

- There is only a single buyer of a particular type of labor.
- The workers providing this type of labor have few employment options other than working for the monopsony either because they are geographically immobile or because finding alternative employment would mean having to acquire new skills.
- The firm is a "wage maker" because the wage rate it must pay varies directly with the number of workers it employs.

As is true of monopoly power, there are various degrees of monopsony power. In *pure* monopsony, such power is at its maximum because only a single employer hires labor in the labor market. The best real-world examples are probably the labor markets in towns that depend almost entirely on one major firm. For example, a silver-mining company may be almost the only source of employment in a remote Idaho town. A Wisconsin paper mill, a Colorado ski resort, or an Iowa food processor may provide most of the employment in its locale. In other cases, three or four firms may each hire a large portion of the supply of labor in a certain market and therefore have some monopsony power. Moreover, if they illegally act in concert in hiring labor, they greatly enhance their monopsony power.

Upward-Sloping Labor Supply to Firm

When a firm hires most of the available supply of a certain type of labor, its decision to employ more or fewer workers affects the wage rate it pays to those workers. Specifically, if a firm is large in relation to the size of the labor market, it will have to pay a higher wage rate to obtain more labor. Suppose that there is only one employer of a particular type of labor in a certain geographic area. In this pure monopsony situation, the labor supply curve for the *firm* and the total labor supply curve for the *labor market* are identical. The monopsonist's supply curve—represented by curve S in Figure 10.3—is upsloping because the firm must pay higher wage rates if it wants to attract and hire additional workers. This same curve is also the monopsonist's average-cost-of-labor curve. Each point on curve S indicates the wage rate (cost) per worker that must be paid to attract the corresponding number of workers.

FIGURE 10.3 Monopsony. In a monopsonistic labor market, the employer's marginal resource (labor) cost curve (MRC) lies above the labor supply curve S. Equating MRC with MRP at point b, the monopsonist hires Q_m workers (compared with Q_c under competition). As indicated by point c on S, it pays only wage rate W_m (compared with the competitive wage W_c).

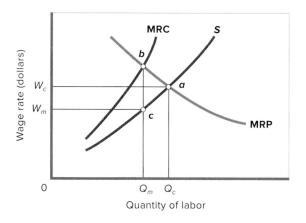

MRC Higher Than the Wage Rate

When a monopsonist pays a higher wage to attract an additional worker, it must pay that higher wage not only to the additional worker, but to all the workers it is currently employing at a lower wage. If not, labor morale will deteriorate, and the employer will be plagued with labor unrest because of wage-rate differences existing for the same job. Paying a uniform wage to all workers means that the cost of an extra worker—the marginal resource (labor) cost (MRC)—is the sum of that worker's wage rate and the amount necessary to bring the wage rate of all current workers up to the new wage level.

Table 10.3 illustrates this point. One worker can be hired at a wage rate of $6. But hiring a second worker forces the firm to pay a higher wage rate of $7. The marginal resource cost of the second worker is $8—the $7 paid to the second worker plus a $1 raise for the first worker. From another viewpoint, total labor cost is now $14 (= 2 × $7), up from $6 (= 1 × $6). So the MRC of the second worker is $8 (= $14 − $6), not just the $7 wage rate paid to that worker. Similarly, the marginal labor cost of the third worker is $10—the $8 that must be paid to attract this worker from alternative employment plus $1 raises, from $7 to $8, for the first two workers.

Here is the key point: Because the monopsonist is the only employer in the labor market, its marginal resource (labor) cost exceeds the wage rate. Graphically, the monopsonist's MRC curve lies above the average-cost-of-labor curve, or labor supply curve S, as is clearly shown in Figure 10.3.

Equilibrium Wage and Employment

How many units of labor will the monopsonist hire, and what wage rate will it pay? To maximize profit, the monopsonist will employ the quantity of labor Q_m in Figure 10.3 because at that quantity MRC and MRP are equal (point b). The monopsonist next determines how much it must pay to attract these Q_m workers. From the supply curve S, specifically point c, it sees that it must pay wage rate W_m. Clearly, it need not pay a wage equal to MRP; it can attract and hire exactly the number of workers it wants (Q_m) with wage rate W_m. And that is the wage that it will pay.

Contrast these results with those that would prevail in a competitive labor market. With competition in the hiring of labor, the level of employment would be greater (at Q_c) and the wage rate would be higher (at W_c). Other things equal, the monopsonist maximizes its profit by hiring a smaller number of workers and thereby paying a less-than-competitive wage rate. Society obtains a smaller output, and workers get a wage rate that is less by bc than their marginal revenue product.

TABLE 10.3 **The Supply of Labor: Monopsony in the Hiring of Labor**

(1) Units of Labor	(2) Wage Rate	(3) Total Labor Cost (Wage Bill)	(4) Marginal Resource (Labor) Cost
0	$ 5	$ 0	
			$ 6
1	6	6	
			8
2	7	14	
			10
3	8	24	
			12
4	9	36	
			14
5	10	50	
			16
6	11	66	

APPLYING THE ANALYSIS

Monopsony Power

Fortunately, monopsonistic labor markets are uncommon in the United States. In most labor markets, several potential employers compete for most workers, particularly for workers who are occupationally and geographically mobile. Also, where monopsony labor market outcomes might have otherwise occurred, unions have often sprung up to counter-act that power by forcing firms to negotiate wages. Nevertheless, economists have found some evidence of monopsony power in such diverse labor markets as the markets for nurses, professional athletes, public school teachers, newspaper employees, and some building-trade workers.

In the case of nurses, the major employers in most locales are a relatively small number of hospitals. Further, the highly specialized skills of nurses are not readily transferable to other occupations. It has been found, in accordance with the monopsony model, that, other things equal, the smaller the number of hospitals in a town or city (that is, the greater the degree of monopsony), the lower the beginning salaries of nurses.

Professional sports leagues also provide a good example of monopsony, particularly as it relates to the pay of first-year players. The National Football League, the National Basketball Association, and Major League Baseball assign first-year players to teams through "player drafts." That device prohibits other teams from competing for a player's services, at least for several years, until the player becomes a "free agent." In this way each league exercises monopsony power, which results in lower salaries than would occur under competitive conditions.

QUESTION: The salaries of star players often increase substantially when they become free agents. How does that fact relate to monopsony power?

Union Models

Our assumption thus far has been that workers compete with one another in selling their labor services. In some labor markets, however, workers unionize and sell their labor services collectively. In the United States, about 11 percent of wage and salary workers belong to unions. (As shown in Global Snapshot 10.1, this percentage is low relative to some other nations.)

Union efforts to raise wage rates are mainly concentrated on the supply side of the labor market.

Exclusive or Craft Union Model

Unions can boost wage rates by reducing the supply of labor, and over the years organized labor has favored policies to do just that. For example, labor unions have supported legislation that has (1) restricted permanent immigration, (2) reduced child labor, (3) encouraged compulsory retirement, and (4) enforced a shorter workweek.

Moreover, certain types of workers have adopted techniques designed to restrict the number of workers who can join their union. This is especially true of *craft unions,* whose members possess a particular skill, such as carpenters or brick masons or plumbers. Craft

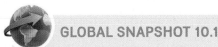

GLOBAL SNAPSHOT 10.1

Union Density, Selected Nations

The percentage of workers unionized varies considerably across countries, but sometimes this is due to differences in international practices, including some nations' legal restrictions preventing unionization in certain occupations. To adjust for these differences, alternative measures such as "union density," the rate of "actual" to "potential" membership, are used. Compared with most other industrialized nations, the percentage of potential wage and salary earners belonging to unions in the United States is small.

Trade Union Density, 2018

Sweden	
Denmark	
Norway	
Italy	
Ireland	
Canada	
Germany	
Japan	
Australia	
United States	
France	
Turkey	

0   10   20   30   40   50   60   70   80

Source: U.S. Bureau of Labor Statistics, *Union Membership Statistics in 24 Countries,* 2006, **www.bls.gov**

unions have frequently forced employers to agree to hire only union members, thereby gaining virtually complete control of the labor supply. Then, by following restrictive membership policies—for example, long apprenticeships, very high initiation fees, and limits on the number of new members admitted—they have artificially restricted labor supply. As indicated in Figure 10.4, such practices result in higher wage rates and constitute what is called **exclusive unionism.** By excluding workers from unions and therefore from the labor supply, craft unions succeed in elevating wage rates.

exclusive unionism The union practice of restricting the supply of skilled union labor to increase the wage rate received by union members.

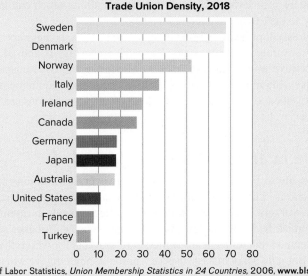

FIGURE 10.4 Exclusive or craft unionism. By reducing the supply of labor (say, from S_1 to S_2) through the use of restrictive membership policies, exclusive unions achieve higher wage rates (W_c to W_u). However, restriction of the labor supply also reduces the number of workers employed (Q_c to Q_u).

This craft union model is also applicable to many professional organizations, such as the American Medical Association, the National Education Association, the American Bar Association, and hundreds of others. Such groups seek to prohibit competition for their services from less-qualified labor suppliers. One way to accomplish that is through **occupational licensing.** Here, a group of workers in a given occupation pressure federal, state, or municipal government to pass a law that says that some occupational group (for example, barbers, physicians, lawyers, plumbers, cosmetologists, egg graders, pest controllers) can practice their trade only if they meet certain requirements. Those requirements might include level of education, amount of work experience, and the passing of an examination. Members of the licensed occupation typically dominate the licensing board that administers such laws. The result is self-regulation, which can lead to policies that restrict entry to the occupation and reduce labor supply.

occupational licensing Government laws that require a worker to satisfy certain specified requirements and obtain a license from a licensing board before engaging in a particular occupation.

The expressed purpose of licensing is to protect consumers from incompetent practitioners—surely a worthy goal. But such licensing, if abused, simply results in above-competitive wages and earnings for those in the licensed occupation (Figure 10.4). Moreover, licensing requirements often include a residency requirement, which inhibits the interstate movement of qualified workers. Some 1,100 occupations are now licensed in the United States.

Inclusive or Industrial Union Model

Instead of trying to limit their membership, however, most unions seek to organize all available workers. This is especially true of the *industrial unions,* such as those of the automobile workers and steelworkers. Such unions seek as members all available unskilled, semiskilled, and skilled workers in an industry. It makes sense for a union to be exclusive when its members are skilled craft workers for whom the employer has few substitutes. But it does not make sense for a union to be exclusive when trying to organize unskilled and semiskilled workers. To break a strike, employers could then easily substitute unskilled or semiskilled nonunion workers for the unskilled or semiskilled union workers.

By contrast, an industrial union that includes virtually all available workers in its membership can put firms under great pressure to agree to its wage demands. Because of its legal right to strike, such a union can threaten to deprive firms of their entire labor supply. And an actual strike can do just that. Further, with virtually all available workers in the union, it will be difficult in the short run for new nonunion firms to emerge and thereby undermine what the union is demanding from existing firms.

inclusive unionism The union practice of including as members all workers employed in an industry.

We illustrate such **inclusive unionism** in Figure 10.5. Initially, the competitive equilibrium wage rate is W_c and the level of employment is Q_c. Now suppose an industrial union is formed that demands a higher, above-equilibrium wage rate of, say, W_u. That wage rate W_u would create a perfectly elastic labor supply over the range ae in Figure 10.5. If firms wanted to hire any workers in this range, they would have to pay the union-imposed wage rate. If they decide against meeting this wage demand, the union will supply no labor at all, and the firms will be faced with a strike. If firms decide it is better to pay the higher wage rate than to suffer a strike, they will cut back on employment from Q_c to Q_u.

By agreeing to the union's W_u wage demand, individual employers become wage takers at the union wage rate W_u. Because labor supply is perfectly elastic over range ae, the marginal resource (labor) cost is equal to the union wage rate W_u over this range. The Q_u level of employment is the result of employers' equating this MRC (now equal to the union wage rate) with MRP, according to our profit-maximizing rule.

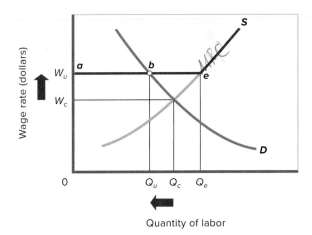

FIGURE 10.5 Inclusive or industrial unionism. By organizing virtually all available workers in order to control the supply of labor, inclusive industrial unions may impose a wage rate, such as W_u, that is above the competitive wage rate W_c. In effect, this changes the labor supply curve from S to aeS. At wage rate W_u, employers will cut employment from Q_c to Q_u.

Note from point e on labor supply curve S that Q_e workers desire employment at wage W_u. But as indicated by point b on labor demand curve D, only Q_u workers are employed. The result is a surplus of labor of $Q_e - Q_u$ (also shown by distance eb). In a purely competitive labor market without the union, the effect of a surplus of unemployed workers would be lower wages. Specifically, the wage rate would fall to the equilibrium level W_c where the quantity of labor supplied equals the quantity of labor demanded (each, Q_c). But this drop in wages does not happen because workers are acting collectively through their union. Individual workers cannot offer to work for less than W_u nor can employers pay less than that.

Wage Increases and Job Loss

Evidence suggests that union members on average achieve a 15-percent wage advantage over nonunion workers. But when unions are successful in raising wages, their efforts also have another major effect. As Figures 10.4 and 10.5 suggest, the wage-raising actions achieved by both exclusive and inclusive unionism reduce employment in unionized firms. Simply put, a union's success in achieving above-equilibrium wage rates thus tends to be accompanied by a decline in the number of workers employed. That result acts as a restraining influence on union wage demands. A union cannot expect to maintain solidarity within its ranks if it seeks a wage rate so high that 20–30 percent of its members lose their jobs.

Wage Differentials

Hourly wage rates and annual salaries differ greatly among occupations. In Table 10.4 we list average annual salaries for a number of occupations to illustrate such **wage differentials.** For example, observe that surgeons on average earn about nine times as much as retail salespersons. Not shown, there are also large wage differentials within some of the occupations listed. For example, some highly experienced surgeons earn several times as much income as surgeons just starting their careers. And, although average wages for retail salespersons are relatively low, some top salespersons selling on commission make several times the average wages listed for their occupation.

wage differential The differences between the wage received by one worker or group of workers and that received by another worker or group of workers.

TABLE 10.4 **Average Annual Wages in Selected Occupations, 2016**

Occupation	Average Annual Wages
Anesthesiologists	$269,600
Surgeons	252,900
Psychiatrists	200,220
Petroleum engineers	147,030
Law professors	134,530
Pharmacists	120,270
Dental hygienists	73,440
Registered nurses	72,180
Police officers	62,790
Electricians	59,840
Travel agents	39,900
Barbers	29,900
Retail salespersons	27,180
Bartenders	25,580
Child care workers	22,930
Fast-food cooks	20,570

Source: Bureau of Labor Statistics, **www.bls.gov**

What explains wage differentials such as these? Once again, the forces of demand and supply are highly revealing. As we demonstrate in Figure 10.6, wage differentials can arise on either the supply or the demand side of labor markets. Panels (a) and (b) in Figure 10.6 represent labor markets for two occupational groups that have identical *labor supply curves*. Labor market (a) has a relatively high equilibrium wage (W_a) because labor demand is very strong. In labor market (b) the equilibrium wage is relatively low (W_b) because labor demand is weak. Clearly, the wage differential between occupations (a) and (b) results solely from differences in the magnitude of labor demand.

Contrast that situation with panels (c) and (d) in Figure 10.6, where the *labor demand curves* are identical. In labor market (c) the equilibrium wage is relatively high (W_c) because labor supply is low. In labor market (d) labor supply is highly abundant, so the equilibrium wage (W_d) is relatively low. The wage differential between (c) and (d) results solely from the differences in the magnitude of labor supply.

Although Figure 10.6 provides a good starting point for understanding wage differentials, we need to know *why* demand and supply conditions differ in various labor markets. There are several reasons.

Marginal Revenue Productivity

The strength of labor demand—how far rightward the labor demand curve is located—differs greatly among occupations due to differences in how much various occupational groups contribute to the revenue of their respective employers. This revenue contribution, in turn, depends on the workers' productivity and the strength of the demand for the products they are helping to produce. Where labor is highly productive and product demand is strong, labor demand also is strong and, other things equal, pay is high. Top professional athletes, for example, are highly productive at producing sports entertainment, for which millions of people are willing to pay billions of dollars over the course of a season. Because the marginal revenue productivity of these players is so high, they are in very high demand by sports teams. This high demand leads to their extremely high salaries (as in

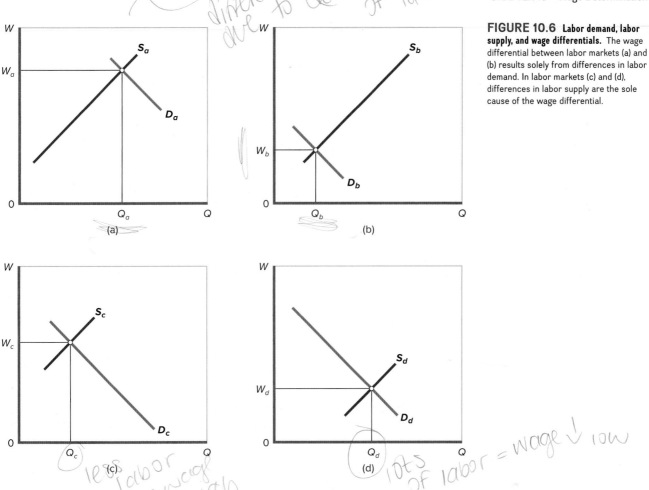

FIGURE 10.6 Labor demand, labor supply, and wage differentials. The wage differential between labor markets (a) and (b) results solely from differences in labor demand. In labor markets (c) and (d), differences in labor supply are the sole cause of the wage differential.

Figure 10.6a). In contrast, most workers generate much more modest revenue for their employers. This results in much lower demand for their labor and, consequently, much lower wages (as in Figure 10.6b).

Noncompeting Groups

On the supply side of the labor market, workers are not homogeneous; they differ in their mental and physical capacities and in their education and training. At any given time the labor force is made up of many noncompeting groups of workers, each representing several occupations for which the members of that particular group qualify. In some groups qualified workers are relatively few, whereas in others they are plentiful. Plus, workers in one group do not qualify for the occupations of other groups.

Ability Only a few workers have the ability or physical attributes to be brain surgeons, concert violinists, top fashion models, research chemists, or professional athletes. Because the supply of these particular types of labor is very small in relation to labor demand, their wages are high (as in Figure 10.6c). The members of these and similar groups do not compete with one another or with other skilled or semiskilled workers. The violinist does not compete with the surgeon, nor does the surgeon compete with the violinist or the fashion model.

FIGURE 10.7 Education levels and average annual income. Annual income by age is higher for workers with more education. Investment in education yields a return in the form of earnings differences enjoyed over one's work life. *Source:* U.S. Bureau of the Census, **www.census.gov.** Data are for both sexes in 2014.

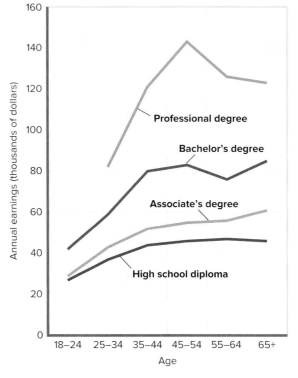

Education and Training   Another source of wage differentials is differing amounts of **human capital,** which is the personal stock of knowledge, know-how, and skills that enables a person to be productive and thus to earn income. Such stocks result from investments in human capital. Like expenditures on machinery and equipment, productivity-enhancing expenditures on education or training are investments. In both cases, people incur *present costs* with the intention that those expenditures will lead to a greater flow of *future earnings.*

human capital The accumulation of knowledge and skills that make a worker productive.

Figure 10.7 indicates that workers who have made greater investments in education achieve higher incomes during their careers. The reason is twofold: (1) There are fewer such workers, so their supply is limited relative to less-educated workers, and (2) more educated workers tend to be more productive and thus in greater demand. Figure 10.7 also indicates that the incomes of better-educated workers generally rise more rapidly than those of poorly educated workers. The primary reason is that employers provide more on-the-job training to the better-educated workers, boosting their marginal revenue productivity and therefore their earnings.

Although education yields higher incomes, it carries substantial costs. A college education involves not only direct costs (tuition, fees, books) but indirect or opportunity costs (forgone earnings) as well. Does the higher pay received by better-educated workers compensate for these costs? The answer is yes. Rates of return are estimated to be 10 to 13 percent for investments in secondary education and 8 to 12 percent for investments in college education. One generally accepted estimate is that each year of schooling raises a worker's wage by about 8 percent. Currently, college graduates on average earn about $1.70 for each $1 earned by high school graduates.

Compensating Differences

If the workers in a particular noncompeting group are equally capable of performing several different jobs, you might expect the wage rates to be identical for all these jobs. Not

ILLUSTRATING THE IDEA

My Entire Life

For some people, high earnings have little to do with actual hours of work and much to do with their tremendous skill, which reflects their accumulated stock of human capital. The point is demonstrated in the following story: It is said that a tourist once spotted the famous Spanish artist Pablo Picasso (1881–1973) in a Paris café. The tourist asked Picasso if he would do a sketch of his wife for pay. Picasso sketched the wife in a matter of minutes and said, "That will be 10,000 francs [roughly $2,000]." Hearing the high price, the tourist became irritated, saying, "But that took you only a few minutes."

"No," replied Picasso, "it took me my entire life!"

QUESTION: In general, how do the skill requirements of the highest-paying occupations in Table 10.4 compare with the skill requirements of the lowest-paying occupations?

so. A group of high school graduates may be equally capable of becoming salesclerks or general construction workers, but these jobs pay different wages. In virtually all locales, construction laborers receive much higher wages than salesclerks. These wage differentials are called **compensating differences** because they must be paid to compensate for non-monetary differences in various jobs.

The construction job involves dirty hands, a sore back, the hazard of accidents, and irregular employment, both seasonally and during recessions (the economywide economic slowdowns that periodically affect the economy). The retail sales job means clean clothing, pleasant air-conditioned surroundings, and little fear of injury or layoff. Other things equal, it is easy to see why workers would rather pick up a credit card than a shovel. So the amount of labor that is supplied to construction firms (as in Figure 10.6c) is smaller than that which is supplied to retail shops (as in Figure 10.6d). Construction firms must pay higher wages than retailers to compensate for the unattractive nonmonetary aspects of construction jobs.

Compensating differences play an important role in allocating society's scarce labor resources. If very few workers want to be garbage collectors, then society must pay high wages to garbage collectors to get the garbage collected. If many more people want to be salesclerks, then society need not pay them as much as it pays garbage collectors to get those services performed.

compensating differences Wage differentials received by workers to compensate them for nonmonetary disparities in their jobs.

APPLYING THE ANALYSIS

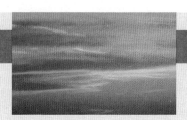

The Minimum Wage

Since the passage of the Fair Labor Standards Act in 1938, the United States has had a federal minimum wage. That wage has ranged between 35 and 50 percent of the average wage paid to manufacturing workers and was most recently raised to $7.25 in July 2009. Numerous states, however, have minimum wages considerably above the federal mandate.

For example, the 2018 minimum wage in the state of Washington was $11.50. The purpose of minimum wages is to provide a "wage floor" that will help less-skilled workers earn enough income to escape poverty.

Critics, reasoning in terms of Figure 10.5, contend that an above-equilibrium minimum wage (say, W_u) will simply cause employers to hire fewer workers. Downsloping labor demand curves are a reality. The higher labor costs may even force some firms out of business. In either case, some of the poor, low-wage workers whom the minimum wage was designed to help will find themselves out of work. Critics point out that a worker who is *unemployed* and desperate to find a job at a minimum wage of $7.25 per hour is clearly worse off than he or she would be if *employed* at a market wage rate of, say, $6.50 per hour.

A second criticism of the minimum wage is that it is "poorly targeted" to reduce household poverty. Critics point out that much of the benefit of the minimum wage accrues to workers, including many teenagers, who do not live in impoverished households.

Advocates of the minimum wage say that critics analyze its impact in an unrealistic context, specifically a competitive labor market (Figure 10.2). But in a less-competitive, low-pay labor market where employers possess some monopsony power (Figure 10.3), the minimum wage can increase wage rates without causing significant unemployment. Indeed, a higher minimum wage may even produce more jobs by eliminating the motive that monopsonistic firms have for restricting employment. For example, a minimum-wage floor of W_c in Figure 10.3 would change the firm's labor supply curve to $W_c aS$ and prompt the firm to increase its employment from Q_m workers to Q_c workers.

Moreover, even if the labor market is competitive, the higher wage rate might prompt firms to find more productive tasks for low-paid workers, thereby raising their productivity. Alternatively, the minimum wage may reduce *labor turnover* (the rate at which workers voluntarily quit). With fewer low-productive trainees, the *average* productivity of the firm's workers would rise. In either case, the alleged negative employment effects of the minimum wage might not occur.

Which view is correct? Unfortunately, there is no clear answer. All economists agree that firms will not hire workers who cost more per hour than the value of their hourly output. So there is some minimum wage so high that it would severely reduce employment. Consider $30 an hour, as an absurd example. Because the majority of U.S. workers earned roughly $22 per hour in 2017, a minimum wage that high would render the majority of workers unemployable because the minimum wage that they would have to be paid would far exceed their marginal revenue products.

It has to be remembered, though, that a minimum wage will only cause unemployment in labor markets where the minimum wage exceeds the equilibrium wage. Jobs in these labor markets are typically filled by unskilled or low-skilled workers. For members of such groups, recent research suggests that a 10 percent increase in the minimum wage will reduce employment of unskilled workers by about 1 to 3 percent. However, estimates of the employment effects of minimum wage laws vary from study to study, so significant controversy remains.

The overall effect of the minimum wage is thus uncertain. There seems to be a consensus emerging that, on the one hand, the employment and unemployment effects of the minimum wage are not as great as many critics fear. On the other hand, because a large part of its effect is dissipated on nonpoverty families, the minimum wage is not as strong an antipoverty tool as many supporters contend.

Voting patterns and surveys make it clear, however, that the minimum wage has strong political support. Perhaps this stems from two realities: (1) More workers are believed to be helped than hurt by the minimum wage and (2) the minimum wage gives society some assurance that employers are not "taking undue advantage" of vulnerable, low-skilled workers.

QUESTION: Have you ever worked for the minimum wage? If so, for how long? Would you favor increasing the minimum wage by $1? By $2? By $5? Explain your reasoning.

SUMMARY

LO10.1 Explain why the firm's marginal revenue product curve is its labor demand curve.

The demand for labor is derived from the product it helps produce. That means the demand for labor will depend on its productivity and on the market value (price) of the good it is producing.

Because the firm equates the wage rate and MRP in determining its profit-maximizing level of employment, the marginal revenue product curve is the firm's labor demand curve. Thus, each point on the MRP curve indicates how many labor units the firm will hire at a specific wage rate.

The competitive firm's labor demand curve slopes downward because of the law of diminishing returns. Summing horizontally the demand curves of all the firms hiring that resource produces the market demand curve for labor.

LO10.2 List the factors that increase or decrease labor demand.

The demand curve for labor will shift as the result of (a) a change in the demand for, and therefore the price of, the product the labor is producing; (b) changes in the productivity of labor; and (c) changes in the prices of substitutable and complementary resources.

LO10.3 Discuss the determinants of elasticity of labor demand.

The elasticity of demand for labor measures the responsiveness of labor quantity to a change in the wage rate. The coefficient of the elasticity of labor demand is

$$E_w = \frac{\text{percentage change in labor quantity demanded}}{\text{percentage change in wage rate}}$$

When E_w is greater than 1, labor demand is elastic; when E_w is less than 1, labor demand is inelastic; and when E_w equals 1, labor demand is unit-elastic.

The elasticity of labor demand will be greater (a) the greater the ease of substituting other resources for labor, (b) the greater the elasticity of demand for the product, and (c) the larger the proportion of total production costs attributable to labor.

LO10.4 Demonstrate how wage rates are determined in competitive and monopsonistic labor markets.

Specific wage rates depend on the structure of the particular labor market. In a competitive labor market, the equilibrium wage rate and level of employment are determined at the intersection of the labor supply curve and labor demand curve. For the individual firm, the market wage rate establishes a horizontal labor supply curve, meaning that the wage rate equals the firm's constant marginal resource cost. The firm hires workers to the point where its MRP equals its MRC.

Under monopsony, the marginal resource cost curve lies above the resource supply curve because the monopsonist must bid up the wage rate to hire extra workers and must pay that higher wage rate to all workers. The monopsonist hires fewer workers than are hired under competitive conditions, pays less-than-competitive wage rates (has lower labor costs), and thus obtains greater profit.

LO10.5 Show how unions increase wage rates and how minimum wage laws affect labor markets.

A union may raise competitive wage rates by (a) restricting the supply of labor through exclusive unionism or (b) directly enforcing an above-equilibrium wage rate through inclusive unionism. On average, unionized workers realize wage rates 15 percent higher than those of comparable nonunion workers.

Economists disagree about the desirability of the minimum wage. While it raises the income of some workers, it reduces the income of other workers whose skills are not sufficient to justify being paid the mandated wage.

LO10.6 Identify the major causes of wage differentials.

Wage differentials are largely explainable in terms of (a) marginal revenue productivity of various groups of workers; (b) noncompeting groups arising from differences in the capacities and education of different groups of workers; and (c) compensating wage differences, that is, wage differences that must be paid to offset nonmonetary differences in jobs.

TERMS AND CONCEPTS

purely competitive labor market	substitution effect	occupational licensing
derived demand	output effect	inclusive unionism
marginal revenue product (MRP)	elasticity of labor demand	wage differentials
marginal resource cost (MRC)	monopsony	human capital
MRP = MRC rule	exclusive unionism	compensating differences

QUESTIONS

The following and additional problems can be found in ▪connect

1. Explain the meaning and significance of the fact that the demand for labor is a derived demand. Why do labor demand curves slope downward? LO10.1

2. Complete the following table that shows the labor demand for a firm that is hiring labor competitively and selling its product in a purely competitive market. LO10.1

Units of Labor	Total Product	Marginal Product	Product Price	Total Revenue	Marginal Revenue Product
0	0		$2	$___	$___
1	17	17	2	34	34
2	31	14	2	62	28
3	43	12	2	86	24
4	53	10	2	106	20
5	60	7	2	120	14
6	65	5	2	130	10

a. How many workers will the firm hire if the market wage rate is $27.95? $19.95? Explain why the firm will not hire a larger or smaller number of units of labor at each of these wage rates.

b. Show in schedule form and graphically the labor demand curve of this firm.

3. In 2009 General Motors (GM) announced that it would reduce employment by 21,000 workers. What does this decision reveal about how GM viewed its marginal revenue product (MRP) and marginal resource cost (MRC)? Why didn't GM reduce employment by more than 21,000 workers? By less than 21,000 workers? LO10.2

4. How will each of the following affect the demand for resource A, which is being used to produce commodity Z? Where there is any uncertainty as to the outcome, specify the causes of that uncertainty. LO10.2

   a. An increase in the demand for product Z.
   b. An increase in the price of substitute resource B.
   c. A technological improvement in the capital equipment with which resource A is combined.
   d. A fall in the price of complementary resource C.
   e. A decline in the elasticity of demand for product Z due to a decline in the competitiveness of product market Z.

5. What effect would each of the following factors have on elasticity of demand for resource A, which is used to produce product Z? LO10.3

   a. There is an increase in the number of resources substitutable for A in producing Z.

   b. Due to technological change, much less of resource A is used relative to resources B and C in the production process.
   c. The elasticity of demand for product Z greatly increases.

6. Florida citrus growers say that the recent crackdown on illegal immigration is increasing the market wage rates necessary to get their oranges picked. Some are turning to $100,000 to $300,000 mechanical harvesting machines known as "trunk, shake, and catch" pickers, which vigorously shake oranges from the trees. If widely adopted, how will this substitution affect the demand for human orange pickers? What does that imply about the relative strengths of the substitution and output effects? LO10.2

7. Why is a firm in a purely competitive labor market a *wage taker*? What would happen if it decided to pay less than the going market wage rate? LO10.4

8. Contrast the methods used by inclusive unions and exclusive unions to raise union wage rates. LO10.5

9. What is meant by the terms "investment in human capital" and "compensating wage differences"? Use these concepts to explain wage differentials. LO10.6

10. Why might an increase in the minimum wage in the United States simply send some jobs abroad? Relate your answer to elasticity of labor demand. LO10.5

PROBLEMS

1. Suppose that marginal product tripled while product price fell by one-half in the table in Figure 10.1. What would be the new MRP values in the table for Figure 10.1? What would be the net impact on the location of the resource demand curve in Figure 10.1? LO10.2

2. Complete the following labor supply table for a firm hiring labor competitively: LO10.4

   a. Show graphically the labor supply and marginal resource (labor) cost curves for this firm. Are the curves the same or different? If they are different, which one is higher?

b. Plot the labor demand data of question 2 on the graph used in part *a* above. What are the equilibrium wage rate and level of employment?

Units of Labor	Wage Rate	Total Labor Cost	Marginal Resource (Labor) Cost
0	$14	$ ___	$ __14__
1	14	__14__	__14__
2	14	__28__	__14__
3	14	__42__	__14__
4	14	__56__	__14__
5	14	__70__	__14__
6	14	__84__	__14__

3. Assume a firm is a monopsonist that can hire its first worker for $6 but must increase the wage rate by $3 to attract each successive worker (so that the second worker must be paid $9, the third $12, and so on). LO10.4

   a. Draw the firm's labor supply and marginal resource cost curves. Are the curves the same or different? If they are different, which one is higher?

   b. On the same graph, plot the labor demand data of question 2. What are the equilibrium wage rate and level of employment?

c. Compare these answers with those you found in problem 2. By how much does the monoposonist reduce wages below the competitive wage? By how much does the monopsonist reduce employment below the competitive level?

4. Suppose that low-skilled workers employed in clearing woodland can each clear one acre per month if they are each equipped with a shovel, a machete, and a chainsaw. Clearing one acre brings in $1,000 in revenue. Each worker's equipment costs the worker's employer $150 per month to rent and each worker toils 40 hours per week for four weeks each month. LO10.5

   a. What is the marginal revenue product of hiring one low-skilled worker to clear woodland for one month?

   b. How much revenue per hour does each worker bring in?

   c. If the minimum wage were $6.20, would the revenue per hour in part *b* exceed the minimum wage? If so, by how much per hour?

   d. Now consider the employer's total costs. These include the equipment costs as well as a normal profit of $50 per acre. If the firm pays workers the minimum wage of $6.20 per hour, what will the firm's economic profit or loss be per acre?

   e. At what value would the minimum wage have to be set so that the firm would make zero economic profit from employing an additional low-skilled worker to clear woodland?

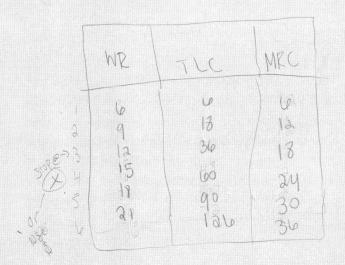

Income Inequality and Poverty

Learning Objectives

LO11.1 Explain how income inequality in the United States is measured and described.

LO11.2 Discuss the extent and sources of income inequality.

LO11.3 Demonstrate how income inequality has changed since 1975.

LO11.4 Debate the economic arguments for and against income inequality.

LO11.5 Describe how poverty is measured and its incidence by age, gender, ethnicity, and other characteristics.

LO11.6 Identify the major components of the income-maintenance program in the United States.

Evidence that suggests wide income disparity in the United States is easy to find. In 2017, musicians Diddy (Sean Combs) and Beyoncé earned $130 million and $105 million, respectively, while author J. K. Rowling earned $95 million, and television personality Sean Hannity earned $36 million. In contrast, the salary of the president of the United States is $400,000, and the typical schoolteacher earns around $57,500. A full-time minimum-wage worker at a fast-food restaurant makes about $20,000. Cash welfare payments to a mother with two children average $4,780.

At the end of 2016, about 40.6 million Americans—or 13 percent of the population—lived in poverty. An estimated 564,700 people were homeless in that year. The richest fifth of American households received about 51.5 percent of total income, while the poorest fifth received about 3.1 percent.

Facts about Income Inequality

Average household income in the United States is among the highest in the world; in 2016, it was $83,143 per household (one or more persons occupying a housing unit). But that average tells us nothing about income inequality. To learn about that, we must examine how income is distributed around the average.

Distribution by Income Category

One way to measure **income inequality** is to look at the percentages of households in a series of income categories. Table 11.1 shows that about 20.8 percent of all households had annual before-tax incomes of less than $25,000 in 2016, while another 27.7 percent had annual incomes of $100,000 or more. The data in the table suggest a wide dispersion of household income in the United States.

income inequality The unequal distribution of an economy's total income among households or families.

Distribution by Quintiles (Fifths)

A second way to measure income inequality is to divide the total number of individuals, households, or families (two or more persons related by birth, marriage, or adoption) into five numerically equal groups, or *quintiles,* and examine the percentage of total personal (before-tax) income received by each quintile. We do this for households in the table in Figure 11.1, where we also provide the upper income limit for each quintile. Any amount of income greater than that listed in each row of column 3 would place a household into the next-higher quintile.

The Lorenz Curve and Gini Ratio

We can display the quintile distribution of personal income through a **Lorenz curve.** In Figure 11.1, we plot the cumulative percentage of households on the horizontal axis and the cumulative percentage of income they obtain on the vertical axis. The diagonal line 0e

Lorenz curve A curve showing the distribution of income in an economy. The cumulated percentage of families (income receivers) is measured along the horizontal axis, and cumulated percentage of income is measured along the vertical axis.

TABLE 11.1 **The Distribution of U.S. Income by Households, 2016**

(1) Personal Income Category	(2) Percentage of All Households in This Category
Under $15,000	11.2
$15,000–$24,999	9.6
$25,000–$34,999	9.4
$35,000–$49,999	12.9
$50,000–$74,999	17.0
$75,000–$99,999	12.3
$100,000 and above	27.7
	100.0

Source: Bureau of the Census, **www.census.gov**

FIGURE 11.1   The Lorenz curve and Gini ratio. The Lorenz curve is a convenient way to show the degree of income inequality (here, household income by quintile in 2016). The area between the diagonal (the line of perfect equality) and the Lorenz curve represents the degree of inequality in the distribution of total income. This inequality is measured numerically by the Gini ratio—area *A* (shown in blue) divided by area *A* + *B* (the blue + green area). The Gini ratio for the distribution shown is 0.480.

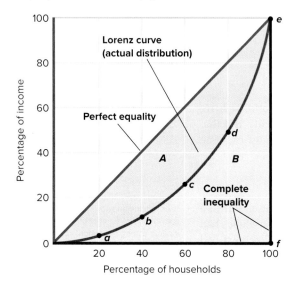

(1) Quintile	(2) Percentage of Total Income*	(3) Upper Income Limit
Lowest 20%	3.1	$ 24,002
Second 20%	8.2	45,600
Third 20%	14.3	74,869
Fourth 20%	23.2	121,018
Highest 20%	51.2	No limit
Total	100.0	

*Numbers do not add to 100 percent due to rounding.
Source: Bureau of the Census, **www.census.gov**

represents a *perfectly equal distribution of income* because each point along that line indicates that a particular percentage of households receive the same percentage of income. In other words, points representing 20 percent of all households receiving 20 percent of total income, 40 percent receiving 40 percent, 60 percent receiving 60 percent, and so on, all lie on the diagonal line.

By plotting the quintile data from the table in Figure 11.1, we obtain the Lorenz curve for 2016. Observe from point *a* that the bottom 20 percent of all households received 3.1 percent of the income; the bottom 40 percent received 11.3 percent (= 3.1 + 8.2), as shown by point *b*; and so forth. The blue area between the diagonal line and the Lorenz curve is determined by the extent that the Lorenz curve sags away from the diagonal and indicates the degree of income inequality. If the actual income distribution were perfectly equal, the Lorenz curve and the diagonal would coincide and the blue area would disappear.

At the opposite extreme is complete inequality, where all households but one have zero income. In that case, the Lorenz curve would coincide with the horizontal axis from 0 to point *f* (at 0 percent of income) and then would move immediately up from *f* to point *e* along the vertical axis (indicating that a single household has 100 percent of the total income). The entire area below the diagonal line (triangle 0*ef*) would indicate this extreme degree of inequality. So the farther the Lorenz curve sags away from the diagonal, the greater is the degree of income inequality.

We can easily transform the visual measurement of income inequality described by the Lorenz curve into the **Gini ratio**—a numerical measure of the overall dispersion of income:

Gini ratio A numerical measure of the overall dispersion of income among an economy's income receivers.

$$\text{Gini ratio} = \frac{\text{area between Lorenz curve and diagonal}}{\text{total area below the diagonal}}$$

$$= \frac{A \text{ (blue area)}}{A + B \text{ (blue + green area)}}$$

For the distribution of household income shown in Figure 11.1, the Gini ratio is 0.480. As the area between the Lorenz curve and the diagonal gets larger, the Gini ratio rises to reflect greater inequality. (Test your understanding of this idea by confirming that the Gini ratio for complete income equality is zero and for complete inequality is 1.)

Because Gini ratios are numerical, they are easier to use than Lorenz curves for comparing the income distributions of different ethnic groups and countries. For example, in 2014 the Gini ratio of U.S. household income for African Americans was 0.455; for Asians, 0.472; for whites, 0.463; and for Hispanics, 0.499.[1] Gini ratios for various nations range from 0.247 (Ukraine) to 0.608 (Haiti). Examples within this range include Denmark, 0.291; Italy, 0.352; Mexico, 0.481; and Honduras, 0.574.[2]

Income Mobility: The Time Dimension

The income data used so far have a major limitation: The income accounting period of one year is too short to be very meaningful. Because the Census Bureau data portray the distribution of income in only a single year, they may conceal a more equal distribution over a few years, a decade, or even a lifetime. If Brad earns $1,000 in year 1 and $100,000 in year 2, while Jenny earns $100,000 in year 1 and only $1,000 in year 2, do we have income inequality? The answer depends on the period of measurement. Annual data would reveal great income inequality, but there would be complete equality over the two-year period.

This point is important because evidence suggests considerable "churning around" in the distribution of income over time. Such movement of individuals or households from one income quintile to another over time is called **income mobility.** For most income receivers, income starts at a relatively low level during youth, reaches a peak during middle age, and then declines. It follows that if all people received exactly the same stream of income over their lifetimes, considerable income inequality would still exist in any specific year because of age differences. In any single year, the young and the old would receive low incomes while the middle-aged would receive high incomes.

income mobility The extent to which income receivers move from one part of the income distribution to another over some period of time.

If we change from a "snapshot" view of income distribution in a single year to a "time exposure" portraying incomes over much longer periods, we find considerable movement of income receivers among income classes. For instance, one study showed that between 1996 and 2005, half of the individuals in the lowest quintile of the U.S. income distribution in 1996 were in a higher income quintile in 2005. Almost 25 percent made it to the middle fifth and 5 percent achieved the top quintile. The income mobility moved in both directions. About 57 percent of the top 1 percent of income receivers in 1996 had dropped out of that category by 2005. Overall, income mobility between 1996 and 2005 was the same as it was the previous 10 years. All this correctly suggests that income is more equally distributed over a 5–, 10–, or 20–year period than in any single year.[3]

In short, there is significant individual and household income mobility over time; for many people, "low income" and "high income" are not permanent conditions.

Effect of Government Redistribution

The income data in the table in Figure 11.1 include wages, salaries, dividends, and interest. They also include all cash transfer payments such as Social Security,

---

[1]U.S. Census Bureau, *Historical Income Tables,* **www.census.gov.**

[2]*World Bank, 2013,* **www.worldbank.org.**

[3]U.S. Department of the *Treasury, Income Mobility in the U.S. from 1996–2005,* November 13, 2007, pp. 1–22.

FIGURE 11.2   The impact of taxes and transfers on U.S. income inequality. The distribution of income is significantly more equal after taxes and transfers are taken into account than before. Transfers account for most of the lessening of inequality and provide most of the income received by the lowest quintile of households.

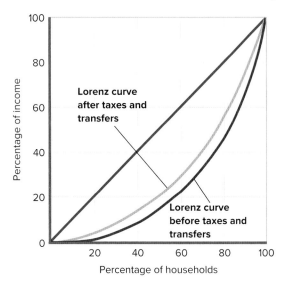

Quintile	Percentage of Total Income Received, 2011*	
	(1) Before Taxes and Transfers	(2) After Taxes and Transfers
Lowest 20 percent	5.3	6.3
Second 20 percent	9.6	10.9
Third 20 percent	14.1	15.2
Fourth 20 percent	20.4	21.0
Highest 20 percent	51.9	46.6

*The data include all money income from private sources, including realized capital gains and employer-provided health insurance. The "after taxes and transfers" data include the value of noncash transfers as well as cash transfers. Numbers may not add to 100 percent due to rounding.
Source: Congressional Budget Office, **www.cbo.gov**

noncash transfers Government transfer payments in the form of goods and services (or vouchers to obtain them) rather than money.

unemployment compensation benefits, and welfare assistance to needy households. The data are before-tax data and therefore do not take into account the effects of personal income and payroll (Social Security) taxes that are levied directly on income receivers. Nor do they include government-provided in-kind or **noncash transfers,** which make available specific goods or services rather than cash. Noncash transfers include such things as medical care, housing subsidies, subsidized school lunches, and food stamps. Such transfers are much like income because they enable recipients to "purchase" goods and services.

One economic function of government is to redistribute income, if society so desires. Figure 11.2 and its table reveal that government significantly redistributes income from higher- to lower-income households through taxes and transfers. Note that the U.S. distribution of household income before taxes and transfers are taken into account (dark red Lorenz curve) is substantially less equal than the distribution after taxes and transfers (light red Lorenz curve). Without government redistribution, the lowest 20 percent of households in 2011 would have received only 5.3 percent of total income. *With* redistribution, they received 6.3 percent, or 1.2 times as much.[4]

Which contributes more to redistribution, government taxes or government transfers? The answer is transfers. Because the U.S. tax system is only modestly progressive, nearly all of the reduction in income inequality is attributable to transfer payments. Together with job opportunities, transfer payments have been the most important means of alleviating poverty in the United States.

Causes of Income Inequality

There are several causes of income inequality in the United States. In general, the market system is permissive of a high degree of income inequality because it rewards individuals

---

[4]The data in this table are for 2011, whereas the data in Figure 11.1 are for 2016. Even if contemporaneous, the "before" data would differ from the data in Figure 11.1 because the latter include cash transfers. Also, the "after" data in Figure 11.2 are based on a broader concept of income than are the data in Figure 11.1.

on the basis of the contributions that they, or the resources that they own, make in producing society's output.

More specifically, the factors that contribute to income inequality are the following:

Ability

People have different mental, physical, and aesthetic talents. Some have inherited the exceptional mental qualities that are essential to such high-paying occupations as medicine, corporate finance, and law. Others are blessed with the physical capacity and coordination to become highly paid professional athletes. A few have the talent to become great artists or musicians or have the beauty to become top fashion models. Others have very weak mental endowments and may work in low-paying occupations or may be incapable of earning any income at all. The intelligence and skills of most people fall somewhere in between.

Education and Training

Native ability alone rarely produces high income; people must develop and refine their capabilities through education and training. Individuals differ significantly in the amount of education and training they obtain and thus in their capacity to earn income. Such differences may be a matter of choice: Chin enters the labor force after graduating from high school, while Rodriguez takes a job only after earning a college degree. Other differences may be involuntary: Chin and her parents may simply be unable to finance a college education.

People receive varying degrees of on-the-job training, which also contributes to income inequality. Some workers learn valuable new skills each year on the job and therefore experience significant income growth over time; others receive little or no on-the-job training and earn no more at age 50 than they did at age 30. Moreover, firms tend to select for advanced on-the-job training the workers who have the most formal education. That added training magnifies the education-based income differences between less-educated and better-educated individuals.

Discrimination

Discrimination in education, hiring, training, and promotion undoubtedly causes some income inequality. If discrimination confines certain racial, ethnic, or gender groups to lower-pay occupations, the supply of labor in those occupations will increase relative to demand and hourly wages and income in those lower-paying jobs will decline. Conversely, labor supply will be artificially reduced in the higher-pay occupations populated by "preferred" workers, raising their wage rates and income. In this way, discrimination can add to income inequality. In fact, economists cannot account for all racial, ethnic, and gender differences in work earnings on the basis of differences in years of education, quality of education, occupations, and annual hours of work. Many economists attribute the unexplained residual to discrimination.

Economists, however, do not see discrimination by race, gender, and ethnicity as a dominant factor explaining income inequality. The income distributions *within* racial or ethnic groups that historically have been targets of discrimination—for example, African Americans—are similar to the income distribution for whites. Other factors besides discrimination are obviously at work. Nevertheless, discrimination is an important concern since it harms individuals and reduces society's overall output and income.

Preferences and Risks

Incomes also differ because of differences in preferences for market work relative to leisure, market work relative to work in the household, and types of occupations. People who choose to stay home with children, work part-time, or retire early usually have less income than those who make the opposite choices. Those who are willing to take arduous, unpleasant jobs (for example, underground mining or heavy construction), to work long hours with great intensity, or to "moonlight" will tend to earn more.

Individuals also differ in their willingness to assume risk. We refer here not only to the race-car driver or the professional boxer but also to the entrepreneur. Although many entrepreneurs fail, many of those who develop successful new products or services realize very substantial incomes. That contributes to income inequality.

Unequal Distribution of Wealth

Income is a *flow;* it represents a stream of wage and salary earnings, along with rent, interest, and profits, as depicted in Chapter 2's circular flow diagram. In contrast, wealth is a *stock,* reflecting at a particular moment the financial and real assets an individual has accumulated over time. A retired person may have very little income and yet own a home, mutual fund shares, and a pension plan that add up to considerable wealth. A new college graduate may be earning a substantial income as an accountant, middle manager, or engineer but have yet to accumulate significant wealth.

The ownership of wealth in the United States is more unequal than the distribution of income. According to the most recent (2010) Federal Reserve wealth data, the wealthiest 10 percent of families owned 76.7 percent of the total wealth and the top 1 percent owned 35.4 percent. The bottom 90 percent held only 23.3 percent of the total wealth. This wealth inequality leads to inequality in rent, interest, and dividends, which in turn contributes to income inequality. Those who own more machinery, real estate, farmland, and stocks and bonds, and who have more money in savings accounts, obviously receive greater income from that ownership than people with less or no such wealth.

Market Power

The ability to "rig the market" on one's own behalf also contributes to income inequality. For example, in *resource* markets, certain unions and professional groups have adopted policies that limit the supply of their services, thereby boosting the incomes of those "on the inside." Also, legislation that requires occupational licensing for, say, doctors, dentists, and lawyers can bestow market power that favors the licensed groups. In *product* markets, "rigging the market" means gaining or enhancing monopoly power, which results in greater profit and thus greater income to the firms' owners.

Luck, Connections, and Misfortune

Other forces also play a role in producing income inequality. Luck and "being in the right place at the right time" have helped individuals stumble into fortunes. Discovering oil on a ranch, owning land along a major freeway interchange, and hiring the right press agent have accounted for some high incomes. Personal contacts and political connections are other potential routes to attaining high income.

In contrast, economic misfortunes such as prolonged illness, serious accident, the death of the family breadwinner, or unemployment may plunge a family into the low range of income. The burden of such misfortune is borne very unevenly by the population and thus contributes to income inequality.

Income inequality of the magnitude we have described is not exclusively an American phenomenon. Global Snapshot 11.1 compares income inequality in the United States (here by individuals, not by households) with that in several other nations. Income inequality tends to be greatest in South American nations, where land and capital resources are highly concentrated in the hands of very wealthy families.

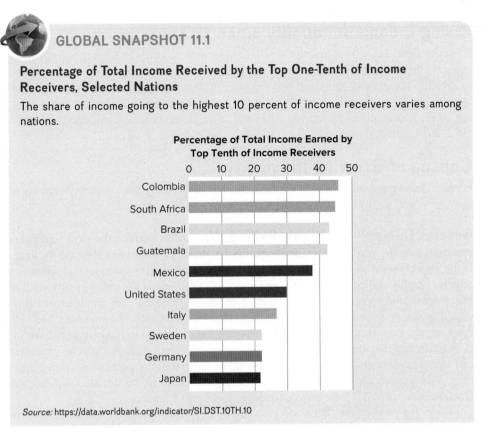

GLOBAL SNAPSHOT 11.1

Percentage of Total Income Received by the Top One-Tenth of Income Receivers, Selected Nations

The share of income going to the highest 10 percent of income receivers varies among nations.

Source: https://data.worldbank.org/indicator/SI.DST.10TH.10

Income Inequality over Time

Over a period of years, economic growth has raised incomes in the United States: In *absolute* dollar amounts, the entire distribution of income has been moving upward. But incomes may move up in *absolute* terms while leaving the *relative* distribution of income less equal, more equal, or unchanged. Table 11.2 shows how the distribution of household income has changed since 1975. This income is "before tax" and includes cash transfers but not noncash transfers.

TABLE 11.2 Percentage of Total Before-Tax Income Received by Each One-Fifth and by the Top 5 percent of Households, Selected Years*

Quintile	1975	1980	1985	1990	1995	2000	2005	2010	2016
Lowest 20%	4.3	4.2	3.9	3.8	3.7	3.6	3.4	3.3	3.1
Second 20%	10.4	10.2	9.8	9.6	9.1	8.9	8.6	8.5	8.3
Third 20%	17.0	16.8	16.2	15.9	15.2	14.8	14.6	14.6	14.2
Fourth 20%	24.7	24.7	24.4	24.0	23.3	23.0	23.0	23.4	22.9
Highest 20%	43.6	44.1	45.6	46.6	48.7	49.8	50.4	50.3	51.5
Total	100	100	100	100	100	100	100	100	100
Top 5%	16.5	16.5	17.6	18.5	21	22.1	22.2	21.3	22.6

*Numbers may not add to 100 percent due to rounding.
Source: Bureau of the Census, **www.census.gov**

Rising Income Inequality since 1975

It is clear from Table 11.2 that the distribution of income by quintiles has become more unequal since 1975. In 2016, the lowest 20 percent of households received 3.1 percent of total before-tax income, compared with 4.3 in 1975. Meanwhile, the income share received by the highest 20 percent rose from 43.2 in 1975 to 51.5 percent in 2016. Also, the percentage of income received by the top 5 percent of households rose significantly over the 1975–2016 period.

Causes of Growing Inequality

Economists suggest several major explanations for the growing U.S. income inequality of the past several decades.

Greater Demand for Highly Skilled Workers
Perhaps the most significant contributor to the growing income inequality has been an increasing demand by many firms for workers who are highly skilled and well educated. Moreover, several industries requiring highly skilled workers have either recently emerged or expanded greatly, such as the computer software, business consulting, biotechnology, health care, and Internet industries. Because highly skilled workers remain relatively scarce, their wages have been bid up. Consequently, the wage differences between them and less-skilled workers have increased. In fact, between 1980 and 2007, the wage difference between college graduates and high school graduates rose from 28 percent to 49 percent for women and from 22 percent to 44 percent for men. Despite some wage stagnation in the decade following the Great Recession, in 2017 the wage difference reached 49.5 percent.

The rising demand for skill also has shown up in rapidly rising pay for chief executive officers (CEOs), sizable increases in income from stock options, substantial increases in income for professional athletes and entertainers, and huge fortunes for successful entrepreneurs. This growth of "superstar" pay also has contributed to rising income inequality.

Demographic Changes
The entrance of large numbers of less-experienced and less-skilled "baby boomers" into the labor force during the 1970s and 1980s may have contributed to greater income inequality in those two decades. Because younger workers tend to earn less income than older workers, their growing numbers contributed to income inequality. There also has been a growing tendency for men and women with high earnings potential to marry each other, thus increasing family income among the highest income quintiles. Finally, the number of households headed by single or divorced women has increased greatly. That trend has increased income inequality because such households lack a second major wage earner and also because the poverty rate for female-headed households is very high.

International Trade, Immigration, and Decline in Unionism
Other factors are probably at work as well. Stronger international competition from imports has reduced the demand for and employment of less-skilled (but highly paid) workers in such industries as the automobile and steel industries. The decline in such jobs has reduced the average wage for less-skilled workers. It also has swelled the ranks of workers in already low-paying industries, placing further downward pressure on wages there.

Similarly, the transfer of jobs to lower-wage workers in developing countries has exerted downward wage pressure on less-skilled workers in the United States. Also, an upsurge in immigration of unskilled workers has increased the number of low-income households in the United States. Finally, the decline in unionism in the United States has undoubtedly contributed to wage inequality since unions tend to equalize pay within firms and industries.

Two cautions: First, when we note growing income inequality, we are not saying that the "rich are getting richer and the poor are getting poorer" in terms of absolute income. Both the rich and the poor are experiencing rises in real income. Rather, what has happened is that, while incomes have risen in all quintiles, income growth has been fastest in the top quintile. Second, increased income inequality is not solely a U.S. phenomenon. The recent rise of inequality also has occurred in several other industrially advanced nations.

The Lorenz curve can be used to contrast the distribution of income at different points in time. If we plotted Table 11.2's data as Lorenz curves, we would find that the curve shifted away from the diagonal between 1975 and 2016. The Gini ratio rose from 0.397 in 1975 to 0.446 in 2016.

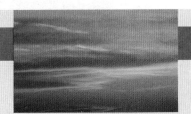

APPLYING THE ANALYSIS

Laughing at Shrek

Some economists say that the distribution of annual *consumption* is more meaningful for examining inequality of well-being than is the distribution of annual *income*. In a given year, people's consumption of goods and services may be above or below their income because they can save, draw down past savings, use credit cards, take out home mortgages, spend from inheritances, give money to charities, and so on. A recent study of the distribution of consumption finds that annual consumption inequality is less than income inequality. Moreover, consumption inequality has remained relatively constant over several decades, even though income inequality has increased.*

The Economist magazine extends the argument even further, pointing out that despite the recent increase in income inequality, the products consumed by the rich and the poor are far closer in functionality today than at any other time in history:

> More than 70 percent of Americans under the official poverty line own at least one car. And the distance between driving a used Hyundai Elantra and new Jaguar XJ is well nigh undetectable compared with the difference between motoring and hiking through the muck . . . A wide screen plasma television is lovely, but you do not need one to laugh at "Shrek". . .
>
> Those intrepid souls who make vast fortunes turning out ever higher-quality goods at ever lower prices widen the income gap while reducing the differences that really matter.†

Economists generally agree that products and experiences once reserved exclusively for the rich in the United States have, in fact, become more commonplace for nearly all income classes. But skeptics argue that *The Economist*'s argument is too simplistic. Even though both are water outings, there is a fundamental difference between yachting among the Greek isles on your private yacht and paddling on a local pond in your kayak.

QUESTION: How do the ideas of income inequality, consumption inequality, and wealth inequality differ?

*Dirk Krueger and Fabrizio Perri, "Does Income Inequality Lead to Consumption Inequality?" *Review of Economic Studies,* 2006, pp. 163–193.

†Source: *The Economist,* "Economic Focus: The New (Improved) Gilded Age," December 22, 2007, p. 122. © The Economist Newspaper Limited, London.

PHOTO OP The Rich and the Poor in America

Wide disparities of income and wealth exist in the United States.

©franckito/123RF

©DenisTangneyJr/Getty Images

Equality versus Efficiency

The main policy issue concerning income inequality is how much is necessary and justified. While there is no general agreement on the justifiable amount, we can gain insight by exploring the economic cases for and against greater equality.

The Case for Equality: Maximizing Total Utility

The basic economic argument for an equal distribution of income is that income equality maximizes the total consumer satisfaction (utility) from any particular level of output and income. The rationale for this argument is shown in Figure 11.3, in which we assume that the money incomes of two individuals, Anderson and Brooks, are subject to the **law of diminishing marginal utility.** In any time period, income receivers spend the first dollars received on the products they value most—products whose marginal utility (extra satisfaction) is high. As a consumer's most-pressing wants become satisfied, he or she then spends additional dollars of income on less-important, lower-marginal-utility goods. So marginal-utility-from-income curves slope downward, as in Figure 11.3. The identical diminishing curves (MU_A and MU_B) reflect the assumption that Anderson and Brooks have the same capacity to derive utility from income. Each point on one of the curves measures the marginal utility of the last dollar of a particular level of income.

Now suppose that there is $10,000 worth of income (output) to be distributed between Anderson and Brooks. According to proponents of income equality, the optimal distribution is an equal distribution, which causes the marginal utility of the last dollar spent to be the same for both persons. We can confirm this by demonstrating that if the income distribution is initially unequal, then distributing income more equally can increase the combined utility of the two individuals.

Suppose that the $10,000 of income initially is distributed such that Anderson gets $2,500 and Brooks $7,500. The marginal utility, *a,* from the last dollar received by Anderson is high and the marginal utility, *b,* from Brooks's last dollar of income is low. If a single dollar of income is shifted from Brooks to Anderson—that is, toward greater equality— then Anderson's utility increases by *a* and Brooks's utility decreases by *b*. The combined

law of diminishing marginal utility
The principle that the amount of extra satisfaction (marginal utility) from consuming a product declines as more of it is consumed.

FIGURE 11.3 **The utility-maximizing distribution of income.** With identical marginal-utility-of-income curves MU$_A$ and MU$_B$, Anderson and Brooks will maximize their combined utility when any amount of income (say, $10,000) is equally distributed. If income is unequally distributed (say, $2,500 to Anderson and $7,500 to Brooks), the marginal utility derived from the last dollar will be greater for Anderson than for Brooks, and a redistribution toward equality will result in a net increase in total utility. The utility gained by equalizing income at $5,000 each, shown by the blue area below curve MU$_A$ in panel (a), exceeds the utility lost, indicated by the red area below curve MU$_B$ in (b).

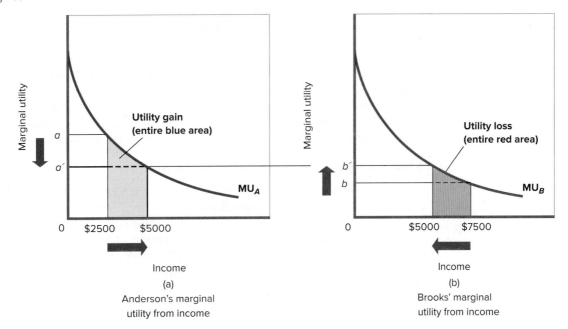

Anderson's marginal utility from income

(a)

Brooks' marginal utility from income

(b)

utility then increases by *a* minus *b* (Anderson's large gain minus Brooks's small loss). The transfer of another dollar from Brooks to Anderson again increases their combined utility, this time by a slightly smaller amount. Continued transfer of dollars from Brooks to Anderson increases their combined utility until the income is evenly distributed and both receive $5,000. At that time their marginal utilities from the last dollar of income are equal (at *a'* and *b'*), and any further income redistribution beyond the $2,500 already transferred would begin to create inequality and decrease their combined utility.

The area under the MU curve and to the left of the individual's particular level of income represents the total utility (the sum of the marginal utilities) of that income. Therefore, as a result of the transfer of the $2,500, Anderson has gained utility represented by the blue area below curve MU$_A$ and Brooks has lost utility represented by the red area below curve MU$_B$. The blue area exceeds the red area, so income equality yields greater combined total utility than does the initial income inequality.

The Case for Inequality: Incentives and Efficiency

Although the logic of the argument for equality is sound, critics attack its fundamental assumption that there is some fixed amount of output produced and therefore income to be distributed. Critics of income equality argue that the way in which income is distributed is an important determinant of the amount of output or income that is produced and is available for distribution.

Suppose once again in Figure 11.3 that Anderson earns $2,500 and Brooks earns $7,500. In moving toward equality, society (the government) must tax away some of Brooks's income and transfer it to Anderson. This tax and transfer process diminishes the income rewards of high-income Brooks and raises the income rewards of low-income Anderson; in so doing, it reduces the incentives of both to earn high incomes. Why should high-income

Brooks work hard, save and invest, or undertake entrepreneurial risks when the rewards from such activities will be reduced by taxation? And why should low-income Anderson be motivated to increase his income through market activities when the government stands ready to transfer income to him? Taxes are a reduction in the rewards from increased productive effort; redistribution through transfers is a reward for diminished effort.

In the extreme, imagine a situation in which the government levies a 100 percent tax on income and distributes the tax revenue equally to its citizenry. Why would anyone work hard? Why would anyone work at all? Why would anyone assume business risk? Or why would anyone save (forgo current consumption) in order to invest? The economic incentives to "get ahead" will have been removed, greatly reducing society's total production and income. That is, the way income is distributed affects the size of that income. The basic argument for income inequality is that inequality is an unavoidable consequence of maintaining the incentives needed to motivate people to produce output and income year after year.

The Equality–Efficiency Trade-off

equality–efficiency trade-off The decrease in economic efficiency that may accompany a decrease in income inequality; the presumption that some income inequality is required to achieve economic efficiency.

At the essence of the income equality-inequality debate is a fundamental trade-off between equality and efficiency. In this **equality–efficiency trade-off,** greater income equality (achieved through redistribution of income) comes at the opportunity cost of reduced production and income. And greater production and income (through reduced redistribution) come at the expense of less equality of income. The trade-off obligates society to choose how much redistribution it wants, in view of the costs. If society decides it wants to redistribute income, it needs to determine methods that minimize the adverse effects on economic efficiency.

ILLUSTRATING THE IDEA

Slicing the Pizza

The equality–efficiency trade-off might better be understood through an analogy. Assume that society's income is a huge pizza, baked year after year, *with the sizes of the pieces going to people on the basis of their contribution to making it.* Now suppose that, for fairness reasons, society decides some people are getting pieces that are too large and others are getting pieces too small. But when society redistributes the pizza to make the sizes more equal, they discover the result is a smaller pizza than before. Why participate in making the pizza if you get a decent-size piece without contributing?

The shrinkage of the pizza represents the efficiency loss—the loss of output and income—caused by the harmful effects of the redistribution on incentives to work, to save and invest, and to accept entrepreneurial risk. The shrinkage also reflects the resources that society must divert to the bureaucracies that administer the redistribution system.

How much pizza shrinkage will society accept while continuing to agree to the redistribution? If redistributing pizza to make it less unequal reduces the size of the pizza, what amount of pizza loss will society tolerate? Is a loss of 10 percent acceptable? 25 percent? 75 percent? This is the basic question in any debate over the ideal size of a nation's income redistribution program.

QUESTION: Why might "equality of opportunity" be a more realistic and efficient goal than an "equality of income" outcome?

The Economics of Poverty

We now turn from the broader issue of income distribution to the more specific issue of very low income, or "poverty." A society with a high degree of income inequality can have a high, moderate, or low amount of poverty. In fact, it could have no poverty at all. We therefore need a separate examination of poverty.

Definition of Poverty

Poverty is a condition in which a person or family does not have the means to satisfy basic needs for food, clothing, shelter, and transportation. The means include currently earned income, transfer payments, past savings, and property owned. The basic needs have many determinants, including family size and the health and age of its members.

The federal government has established minimum income thresholds below which a person or a family is "in poverty." In 2016 an unattached individual receiving less than $12,228 per year was said to be living in poverty. For a family of four, the poverty line was $24,563; for a family of six, it was $32,928. Based on these thresholds, in 2016 about 40.6 million Americans lived in poverty. In 2016, the **poverty rate**—the percentage of the population living in poverty—was 12.7 percent.

poverty rate The percentage of the population with incomes below the official poverty income levels that are established by the federal government.

Incidence of Poverty

The poor are heterogeneous: They can be found in all parts of the nation; they are whites and nonwhites, rural and urban, young and old. But as Figure 11.4 indicates, poverty is far from randomly distributed. For example, the poverty rate for African Americans is above the national average, as is the rate for Hispanics, while the rate for whites and Asians is below the average. In 2016 the poverty rates for African Americans and Hispanics were 22.0 and 19.4 percent, respectively; the rates for whites and Asians were 11.0 percent and 10.1 percent, respectively.

Figure 11.4 shows that female-headed households, foreign-born noncitizens, and children under 18 years of age have very high incidences of poverty. Marriage and full-time,

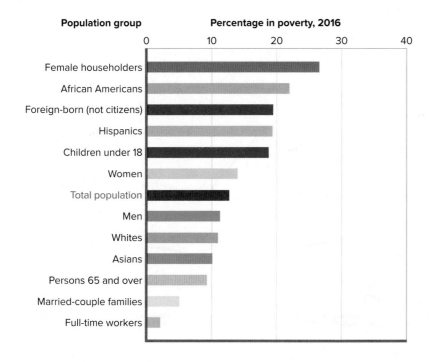

Population group   **Percentage in poverty, 2016**

FIGURE 11.4 Poverty rates among selected population groups, 2016. Poverty is disproportionately borne by African Americans, Hispanics, children, foreign-born residents who are not citizens, and families headed by women. People who are employed full-time or are married tend to have low poverty rates. *Source:* Bureau of the Census

year-round work are associated with low poverty rates, and because of the Social Security system, the incidence of poverty among the elderly is less than that for the population as a whole.

The high poverty rate for children is especially disturbing because poverty tends to breed poverty. Poor children are at greater risk for a range of long-term problems, including poor health and inadequate education, crime, drug use, and teenage pregnancy. Many of today's impoverished children will reach adulthood unhealthy and illiterate and unable to earn above-poverty incomes.

As many as half of people in poverty are poor for only 1 or 2 years before climbing out of poverty. But poverty is much more long-lasting among some groups than among others. In particular, African-American and Hispanic families, families headed by women, persons with little education and few labor market skills, and people who are dysfunctional because of drug use, alcoholism, or mental illness are more likely than others to remain in poverty. Also, long-lasting poverty is heavily present in depressed areas of cities, parts of the Deep South, and some Native American reservations.

Poverty Trends

As Figure 11.5 shows, the total poverty rate fell significantly between 1959 and 1969, stabilized at 11 to 13 percent over the next decade, and then rose in the early 1980s. In 1993, the rate was 15.1 percent, the highest since 1983. Between 1993 and 2000, the rate turned downward, falling to 11.3 percent in 2000. Because of recession and slow recovery, the rate rose to 11.7 percent in 2001, 12.1 percent in 2002, and 12.7 percent in 2004. During the second half of the 1990s, poverty rates plunged for African Americans, Hispanics, and Asians. Nevertheless, in 2016 African Americans and Hispanics still had poverty rates that were roughly double the rates for whites.

FIGURE 11.5 Poverty-rate trends, 1959–2016. Although the national poverty rate declined sharply between 1959 and 1969, it stabilized in the 1970s, only to increase significantly in the early 1980s. Between 1993 and 2000, it substantially declined, before rising slightly again in the immediate years following the 2001 recession. Although poverty rates for African Americans and Hispanics are much higher than the average, they significantly declined during the 1990s. Poverty rates rose in 2008 and 2009, in response to the recession that began in December 2007. By 2016, they had fallen to or below prerecession levels. *Source:* Bureau of the Census, **www.census.gov**

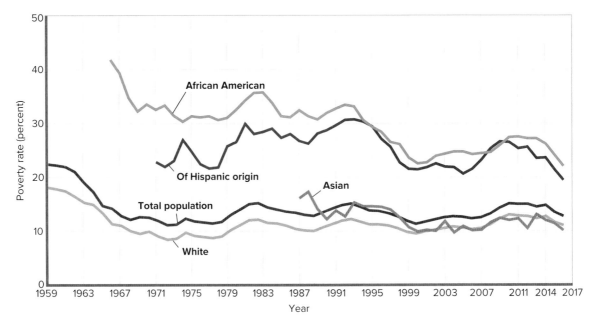

The recession that began in December 2007 increased poverty rates for all groups with, for instance, the Asian poverty rate rising from 10.2 percent in 2007 to 12.4 percent in 2009. As data become available for 2010 and 2011, many economists expect to see poverty rates rise further in response to the widespread and lingering unemployment caused by the so-called Great Recession. By 2016, poverty rates had fallen to or below prerecession levels.

Measurement Issues

The poverty rates and trends in Figures 11.4 and 11.5 need to be interpreted cautiously. The official income thresholds for defining poverty are necessarily arbitrary and therefore may inadequately measure the true extent of poverty in the United States.

Some observers say that the high cost of living in major metropolitan areas means that the official poverty thresholds exclude millions of families whose income is slightly above the poverty level but clearly inadequate to meet basic needs for food, housing, and medical care. These observers use city-by-city studies on "minimal income needs" to show there is much more poverty in the United States than is officially measured and reported.

In contrast, some economists point out that using income to measure poverty understates the standard of living of many of the people who are officially poor. When individual, household, or family *consumption* is considered rather than family *income,* some of the poverty in the United States disappears. Some low-income families maintain their consumption by drawing down past savings, borrowing against future income, or selling homes. Moreover, many poverty families receive substantial noncash benefits such as food stamps and rent subsidies that boost their living standards. Such "in-kind" benefits are not included in determining a family's official poverty status.

The U.S. Income-Maintenance System

Regardless of how poverty is measured, economists agree that considerable poverty exists in the United States. Helping those who have very low income is a widely accepted goal of public policy. A wide array of antipoverty programs, including education and training programs, subsidized employment, minimum-wage laws, and antidiscrimination policies, are designed to increase the earnings of the poor. In addition, there are a number of income-maintenance programs devised to reduce poverty, the most important of which are listed in Table 11.3. These programs involve large expenditures and numerous beneficiaries.

The U.S. income-maintenance system consists of two kinds of programs: (1) social insurance and (2) public assistance or "welfare." Both are known as **entitlement programs** because all eligible persons are legally entitled to receive the benefits set forth in the programs.

> **entitlement programs** Government programs such as social insurance, SNAP, Medicare, and Medicaid that guarantee particular levels of transfer payments or noncash benefits to all who fit the programs' criteria.

Social Insurance Programs

Social insurance programs partially replace earnings that have been lost due to retirement, disability, or temporary unemployment; they also provide health insurance for the elderly. The main social insurance programs are Social Security, unemployment compensation, and Medicare. Benefits are viewed as earned rights and do not carry the stigma of public charity. These programs are financed primarily out of federal payroll taxes. In these programs the entire population shares the risk of an individual's losing income because of retirement, unemployment, disability, or illness. Workers (and employers) pay a part of their wages to the government while they are working. The workers then receive benefits when they retire or face specified misfortunes.

TABLE 11.3 Characteristics of Major Income-Maintenance Programs

Program	Basis of Eligibility	Source of Funds	Form of Aid	Expenditures,* Billions	Beneficiaries, Millions
Social Insurance Programs					
Social Security	Age, disability, or death of parent or spouse; lifetime work earnings	Federal payroll tax on employers and employees	Cash	$911	61
Medicare	Age or disability	Federal payroll tax on employers and employees	Subsidized health insurance	$673	57
Unemployment compensation	Unemployment	State and federal payroll taxes on employers	Cash	$33	4.7
Public Assistance Programs					
Supplemental Security Income (SSI)	Age or disability; income	Federal revenues	Cash	$55	8.1
Temporary Assistance for Needy Families (TANF)	Certain families with children; income	Federal-state-local revenues	Cash and services	$13	2.8
Supplemental Nutrition Assistance Program (SNAP)	Income	Federal revenues	Cash via EBT cards	$67	44
Medicaid	Persons eligible for TANF or SSI and medically indigent	Federal-state-local revenues	Subsidized medical services	$566	74
Earned-income tax credit (EITC)	Low-wage working families	Federal revenues	Refundable tax credit, cash	$65	28

*Expenditures by federal, state, and local governments; excludes administrative expenses.
Source: Social Security Administration, Annual Statistical Supplement, 2017, **www.socialsecurity.gov**; U.S. Department of Agriculture, **www.fns.usda.gov**; Internal Revenue Service, **www.irs.gov/taxstats**; and other government sources. Latest data.

Social Security A federal pension program (financed by payroll taxes on employers and employees) that replaces part of the earnings lost when workers retire, become disabled, or die.

Medicare A federal program that helps finance the medical expenses of individuals covered by the Supplemental Security Income (SSI) and Temporary Assistance for Needy Families (TANF) programs.

Social Security and Medicare   The major social insurance program known as **Social Security** replaces earnings lost when workers retire, become disabled, or die. This gigantic program ($911 billion in 2016) is financed by compulsory payroll taxes levied on both employers and employees. Workers currently may retire at age 66 and receive full retirement benefits or retire early at age 62 with reduced benefits. When a worker dies, benefits accrue to his or her family survivors. Special provisions provide benefits for disabled workers.

Social Security covers over 90 percent of the workforce; some 59 million people receive Social Security benefits averaging about $1,230 per month. In 2016, those benefits were financed with a combined Social Security and Medicare payroll tax of 15.3 percent, with the worker and the employer each paying 7.65 percent on the worker's first $118,500 of earnings. The 7.65 percent taxes comprise 6.2 percent for Social Security and 1.45 percent for Medicare. Self-employed workers pay the full 15.3 percent.

Medicare provides hospital insurance for the elderly and disabled and is financed out of the payroll tax. This overall 2.9 percent tax is paid on all work income, not just on the first $118,500. Medicare also makes available a supplementary low-cost insurance program that helps pay doctor fees.

The number of retirees drawing Social Security and Medicare benefits is rapidly rising relative to the number of workers paying payroll taxes. As a result, Social Security and Medicare face serious long-term funding problems. These fiscal imbalances have spawned calls to reform the programs.

Unemployment Compensation All 50 states sponsor unemployment insurance programs called **unemployment compensation,** a federal-state program that makes income available to unemployed workers. This insurance is financed by a relatively small payroll tax, paid by employers, that varies by state and by the size of the firm's payroll. After a short waiting period, eligible wage and salary workers who become unemployed can receive benefit payments. The size of the payments varies from state to state. Generally, benefits approximate 33 percent of a worker's wages up to a certain maximum weekly payment, and last for a maximum of 26 weeks. In 2018, benefits averaged about $352 weekly. During recessions—when unemployment soars—Congress often provides supplemental funds to the states to extend the benefits for additional weeks.

> **unemployment compensation** A federal-state social insurance program (financed by payroll taxes on employers) that makes income available to workers who are unemployed.

Public Assistance Programs

Public assistance programs (welfare) provide benefits for those who are unable to earn income because of permanent disabilities or have no or very low income and also have dependent children. These programs are financed out of general tax revenues and are regarded as public charity. They include "means tests," which require that individuals and families demonstrate low incomes in order to qualify for aid. The federal government finances about two-thirds of the welfare program expenditures, and the rest is paid for by the states.

Many needy persons who do not qualify for social insurance programs are assisted through the federal government's **Supplemental Security Income (SSI)** program. The purpose of SSI is to establish a uniform, nationwide minimum income for the aged, blind, and disabled who are unable to work and who do not qualify for Social Security aid. Over half the states provide additional income supplements to the aged, blind, and disabled.

> **Supplemental Security Income (SSI)** A federally financed and administered program that provides a uniform nationwide minimum income for the aged, blind, and disabled who do not qualify for benefits under Social Security in the United States.

The **Temporary Assistance for Needy Families (TANF)** is the basic welfare program for low-income families in the United States. The program is financed through general federal tax revenues and consists of lump-sum payments of federal money to states to operate their own welfare and work programs. These lump-sum payments are called TANF funds, and in 2016 about 2.8 million people (including children) received TANF assistance. TANF expenditures in 2016 were about $13 billion.

> **Temporary Assistance for Needy Families (TANF)** The basic welfare program (financed through general tax revenues) for lowincome families in the United States.

In 1996, TANF replaced the six-decade-old Aid for Families with Dependent Children (AFDC) program. Unlike that welfare program, TANF established work requirements and placed limits on the length of time a family can receive welfare payments. Specifically, the TANF program

- Set a lifetime limit of 5 years on receiving TANF benefits and required able-bodied adults to work after receiving assistance for 2 years.
- Ended food-stamp eligibility for able-bodied persons age 18 to 50 (with no dependent children) who are not working or engaged in job-training programs.
- Tightened the definition of "disabled children" as it applies for eligibilty of low-income families for SSI assistance.
- Established a 5-year waiting period on public assistance for new legal immigrants who have not become citizens.

In 1996, about 12.6 million people were welfare recipients, including children, or 4.8 percent of the U.S. population. By the middle of 2007, those totals had declined to 4.5 million and 2 percent of the population. The recession that began in December 2007 pushed the number of welfare recipients up to about 4.4 million by December 2009. These recipients accounted for about 1.4 percent of the population in December 2009.

Supplemental Nutrition Assistance Program (SNAP) A government program that provides food money to low-income recipients by depositing electronic money onto special debit cards.

Medicare A federal program that is financed by payroll taxes and provides for (1) compulsory hospital insurance for senior citizens, (2) low-cost voluntary insurance to help older Americans pay physicians' fees, and (3) subsidized insurance to buy prescription drugs.

earned-income tax credit (EITC) A refundable federal tax credit provided to low-income wage earners to supplement their families' incomes and encourage work.

The welfare program has greatly increased the employment rate (= employment/population) for single mothers with children under age 6—a group particularly prone to welfare dependency. Today, that rate is about 13 percentage points higher than it was in 1996.

The **Supplemental Nutrition Assistance Program (SNAP)** was formerly known as the food-stamp program. SNAP is designed to provide all low-income Americans with a "nutritionally adequate diet." Under the program, eligible households receive monthly deposits of spendable electronic money on specialized debit cards known as Electronic Benefit Transfer (EBT) cards. The EBT cards are designed so that the deposits can only be spent on food. The amount deposited onto a family's EBT card varies inversely with the family's earned income.

Medicaid helps finance the medical expenses of individuals participating in the SSI and the TANF programs.

The **earned-income tax credit (EITC)** is a tax credit for low-income working families, with or without children. The credit reduces the federal income taxes that such families owe or provides them with cash payments if the credit exceeds their tax liabilities. The purpose of the credit is to offset Social Security taxes paid by low-wage earners and thus keep the federal government from "taxing families into poverty." In essence, EITC is a wage subsidy from the federal government that works out to be as much as $2 per hour for the lowest-paid workers with families. Under the program, many people owe no income tax and receive direct checks from the federal government once a year. According to the Internal Revenue Service, 28 million taxpayers received $65 billion in payments from the EITC in 2016.

Several other welfare programs are not listed in Table 11.3. Most provide help in the form of noncash transfers. Head Start provides education, nutrition, and social services to economically disadvantaged 3- and 4-year-olds. Housing assistance in the form of rent subsidies and funds for construction is available to low-income families. Pell grants provide assistance to college students from low-income families.

PHOTO OP Social Insurance versus Public Assistance Programs

Beneficiaries of social insurance programs such as Social Security have typically paid for at least a portion of that insurance through payroll taxes. Food stamps and other public assistance are funded from general tax revenue and are generally seen as public charity.

©kreinick/123RF

©Hero Images/Getty Images

SUMMARY

LO11.1 Explain how income inequality in the United States is measured and described.

The distribution of income in the United States reflects considerable inequality. The richest 20 percent of families receive 51.2 percent of total income, while the poorest 20 percent receive 3.1 percent.

The Lorenz curve shows the percentage of total income received by each percentage of households. The extent of the gap between the Lorenz curve and a line of total equality illustrates the degree of income inequality.

The Gini ratio measures the overall dispersion of the income distribution and is found by dividing the area between the diagonal and the Lorenz curve by the entire area below the diagonal. The Gini ratio ranges from zero to 1; higher ratios signify greater degrees of income inequality.

LO11.2 Discuss the extent and sources of income inequality.

Recognizing that the positions of individual families in the distribution of income change over time and incorporating the effects of noncash transfers and taxes would reveal less income inequality than do standard census data. Government transfers (cash and noncash) greatly lessen the degree of income inequality; taxes also reduce inequality, but not by nearly as much as transfers.

Causes of income inequality include differences in abilities, in education and training, and in job tastes, along with discrimination, inequality in the distribution of wealth, and an unequal distribution of market power.

LO11.3 Demonstrate how income inequality has changed since 1975.

Census data show that income inequality has increased significantly since 1975. The major cause of recent increases in income inequality is a rising demand for highly skilled workers, which has boosted their earnings significantly.

LO11.4 Debate the economic arguments for and against income inequality.

The basic argument for income equality is that it maximizes consumer satisfaction (total utility) from a particular level of total income. The main argument for income inequality is that it provides the incentives to work, invest, and assume risk and is necessary for the production of output, which, in turn, creates income that is then available for distribution.

LO11.5 Describe how poverty is measured and its incidence by age, gender, ethnicity, and other characteristics.

Recent statistics reveal that 12.7 percent of the U.S. population lived in poverty in 2016. Poverty rates are particularly high for female-headed families, young children, African Americans, and Hispanics.

LO11.6 Identify the major components of the income-maintenance program in the United States.

The present income-maintenance program in the United States consists of social insurance programs (Social Security, Medicare, and unemployment compensation) and public assistance programs (SSI, TANF, SNAP, Medicaid, and earned-income tax credit).

In 1996, Congress established the Temporary Assistance for Needy Families (TANF) program, which shifted responsibility for welfare from the federal government to the states. Among its provisions are work requirements for adults receiving welfare and a 5-year lifelong limit on welfare benefits. A generally strong economy and TANF have reduced the U.S. welfare rolls by more than one-half since 1996.

TERMS AND CONCEPTS

income inequality

Lorenz curve

Gini ratio

income mobility

noncash transfers

law of diminishing marginal utility

equality–efficiency trade-off

poverty rate

entitlement programs

Social Security

Medicare

unemployment compensation

Supplemental Security Income (SSI)

Temporary Assistance for Needy Families (TANF)

Supplemental Nutrition Assistance Program (SNAP)

Medicaid

earned-income tax credit (EITC)

QUESTIONS

The following and additional problems can be found in ▧**connect**

1. Use quintiles to briefly summarize the degree of income inequality in the United States. How and to what extent does government reduce income inequality? **LO11.1**

2. Assume that Al, Beth, Carol, David, and Ed receive incomes of $500, $250, $125, $75, and $50, respectively. Construct and interpret a Lorenz curve for this five-person economy. What percentages of total income are received by the richest quintile and by the poorest quintile? **LO11.1**

3. How does the Gini ratio relate to the Lorenz curve? Why can't the Gini ratio exceed 1? What is implied about the direction of income inequality if the Gini ratio declines from 0.42 to 0.35? How would one show that change of inequality in the Lorenz diagram? **LO11.1**

4. Why is the lifetime distribution of income more equal than the distribution in any specific year? **LO11.2**

5. Briefly discuss the major causes of income inequality. What factors have contributed to greater income inequality since 1975? **LO11.2, LO11.3**

6. Should a nation's income be distributed to its members according to their contributions to the production of that total income or according to the members' needs? Should society attempt to equalize income or economic opportunities? Are the issues of equity and equality in the distribution of income synonymous? To what degree, if any, is income inequality equitable? **LO11.4**

7. Comment on or explain: **LO11.4**
   a. Endowing everyone with equal income will make for very unequal enjoyment and satisfaction.
   b. Equality is a "superior good"; the richer we become, the more of it we can afford.
   c. The mob goes in search of bread, and the means it employs is generally to wreck the bakeries.
   d. Some freedoms may be more important in the long run than freedom from want on the part of every individual.
   e. Capitalism and democracy are really a most improbable mixture. Maybe that is why they need each other—to put some rationality into equality and some humanity into efficiency.
   f. The incentives created by the attempt to bring about a more equal distribution of income are in conflict with the incentives needed to generate increased income.

8. How do government statisticians determine the poverty rate? How could the poverty rate fall while the number of people in poverty rises? Which group in each of the following pairs has the higher poverty rate: (a) children or people age 65 or over? (b) African Americans or foreign-born noncitizens? (c) Asians or Hispanics? **LO11.5**

9. What are the essential differences between social insurance and public assistance programs? Why is Medicare a social insurance program whereas Medicaid is a public assistance program? Why is the earned-income tax credit considered to be a public assistance program? **LO11.6**

10. Prior to the implementation of welfare reforms through the Temporary Assistance for Needy Families (TANF) program, the old system (AFDC) was believed to be creating dependency, robbing individuals and family members of motivation and dignity. How did this reform (TANF) try to address those criticisms? Do you agree with the general thrust of the reform and with its emphasis on work requirements and time limits on welfare benefits? Has the reform reduced U.S. welfare rolls or increased them? **LO11.6**

PROBLEMS

1. In 2015 *Forbes* magazine listed Bill Gates, the founder of Microsoft, as the richest person in the United States. His personal wealth was estimated to be $76 billion. Given that there were about 322 million people living in the United States that year, how much could each person have received if Gates's wealth had been divided equally among the population of the United States? (Hint: A billion is a 1 followed by 9 zeros, while a million is a 1 followed by six zeros.) **LO11.1**

2. Imagine an economy with only two people. Larry earns $20,000 per year, while Roger earns $80,000 per year. As shown in the accompanying figure, the Lorenz curve for this two-person economy consists of two line segments. The first runs from the origin to point *a*, while the second runs from point *a* to point *b*. **LO11.1**

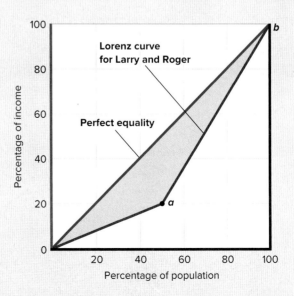

a. Calculate the Gini ratio for this two-person economy using the geometric formulas for the area of a triangle (= ½ × base × height) and the area of a rectangle (= base × height). (Hint: The area under the line segment from point *a* to point *b* can be thought of as the sum of the area of a particular triangle and the area of a particular rectangle.)

b. What would the Gini ratio be if the government taxed $20,000 away from Roger and gave it to Larry? (Hint: The figure will change.)

c. Start again with Larry earning $20,000 per year and Roger earning $80,000 per year. What would the Gini ratio be if both their incomes doubled? How much has the Gini ratio changed from before the doubling in incomes to after the doubling in incomes?

3. In 2015, many unskilled workers in the United States earned the federal minimum wage of $7.25 per hour. By contrast, average earnings in 2015 were about $23 per hour, and certain highly skilled professionals, such as doctors and lawyers, earned $100 or more per hour. LO11.6

a. If we assume that wage differences are caused solely by differences in productivity, how many times more productive was the average worker than a worker being paid the federal minimum wage? How many times more productive was a $100-per-hour lawyer compared to a worker earning minimum wage?

b. Assume that there are 20 minimum-wage workers in the economy for each $100-per-hour lawyer. Also assume that both lawyers and minimum-wage workers work the same number of hours per week. If everyone works 40 hours per week, how much does a $100-per-hour lawyer earn a week? How much does a minimum-wage worker earn a week?

c. Suppose that the government pairs each $100-per-hour lawyer with 20 nearby minimum-wage workers. If the government taxes 25 percent of each lawyer's income each week and distributes it equally among the 20 minimum-wage workers with whom each lawyer is paired, how much will each of those minimum-wage workers receive each week? If we divide by the number of hours worked each week, how much does each minimum-wage worker's weekly transfer amount to on an hourly basis?

d. What if instead the government taxed each lawyer 100 percent before dividing the money equally among the 20 minimum-wage workers with whom each lawyer is paired—how much per week will each minimum-wage worker receive? And how much is that on an hourly basis?

Public Finance: Expenditures and Taxes

Learning Objectives

LO12.1 Identify the main categories of government spending and the main sources of government revenue.

LO12.2 Summarize the different philosophies regarding the distribution of a nation's tax burden.

LO12.3 Explain the principles relating to tax shifting, tax incidence, and the efficiency losses caused by taxes.

LO12.4 Demonstrate how the distribution of income between rich and poor is affected by government taxes, transfers, and spending.

As discussed in Chapter 2, the U.S. economy relies heavily on the private sector (households and businesses) and the market system to decide what gets produced, how it gets produced, and who gets the

output. But the private sector is not the only entity in the decision process. The public sector (federal, state, and local government) also affects these economic decisions.

Government influences what gets produced and how it gets produced through laws that regulate the activities of private firms and also by directly producing certain goods and services, such as national defense and education. As discussed in Chapter 5, many of these government-produced goods and services are *public goods* that the private sector has trouble producing because of free-rider problems. Also, as seen in Chapter 11, government influences who receives society's output of goods and services through various taxes and through welfare and income-transfer payments that redistribute income from the rich to the poor.

Government-provided goods, services, and transfer payments are funded by taxes, borrowing, and *proprietary income*—the income that governments receive from running government-owned enterprises such as hospitals, utilities, toll roads, and lotteries.

Public finance is the subdiscipline of economics that studies the various ways in which governments raise and expend money. In this chapter we view the economy through the lens of public finance. Our main goal is to understand how taxes and income transfers not only pay for government-produced goods and services but also affect the distribution of income between rich and poor.

Government and the Circular Flow

In Figure 12.1 we integrate government into the circular flow model first shown in Figure 2.2. Here flows (1) through (4) are the same as the corresponding flows in that figure. Flows (1) and (2) show business expenditures for the resources provided by households. These expenditures are costs to businesses but represent wage, rent, interest, and profit income to households. Flows (3) and (4) show household expenditures for the goods and services produced by businesses.

Now consider what happens when we add government. Flows (5) through (8) illustrate that government makes purchases in both product and resource markets. Flows (5) and (6)

FIGURE 12.1 Government within the circular flow diagram. Government buys products from the product market and employs resources from the resource market to provide goods and services to households and businesses. Government finances its expenditures through the net taxes (taxes minus transfer payments) it receives from households and businesses.

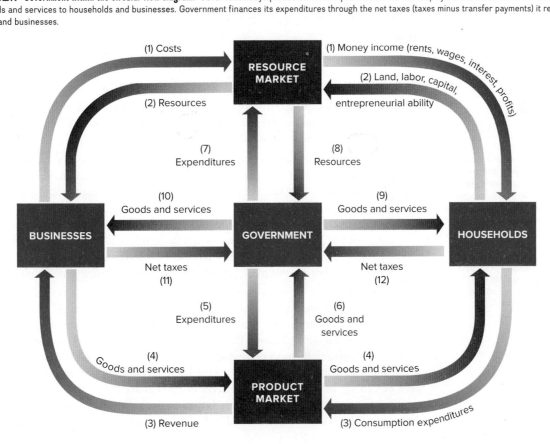

represent government purchases of such products as paper, computers, and military hardware from private businesses. Flows (7) and (8) represent government purchases of resources. The federal government employs and pays salaries to members of Congress, the armed forces, Justice Department lawyers, meat inspectors, and so on. State and local governments hire and pay teachers, bus drivers, police, and firefighters. The federal government might also lease or purchase land to expand a military base and a city might buy land on which to build a new elementary school.

Government then provides goods and services to both households and businesses, as shown by flows (9) and (10). Governments rely on three revenue sources to finance those goods and services: taxes, borrowing, and the proprietary income generated by government-run or government-sponsored businesses like public utilities and state lotteries. These revenues flowing from households and businesses to government are included in flows (11) and (12), which are labeled as "net taxes" for two reasons. First, the vast majority of the money raised by these three revenue sources comes from taxes; thus, it is sensible to have these labels refer to taxes. Second, the labels refer to *net taxes* to indicate that they also include "taxes in reverse" in the form of transfer payments to households and subsidies to businesses. Thus, flow (11) entails various subsidies to farmers, shipbuilders, and airlines as well as income, sales, and excise taxes paid by businesses to government. Most subsidies to business are "concealed" in the form of low-interest loans, loan guarantees, tax concessions, or public facilities provided at prices below their cost. Similarly, flow (12) includes not only taxes (personal income taxes, payroll taxes) collected by government from households but also transfer payments made by government to households. These include welfare payments and Social Security benefits.

Government Finance

How large is the U.S. public sector? What are the main expenditure categories of federal, state, and local governments? How are these expenditures financed?

Government Purchases and Transfers

We can get an idea of the size of government's economic role by examining government purchases of goods and services and government transfer payments. There is a significant difference between these two kinds of outlays:

government purchases Expenditures by government for goods and services that government consumes in providing public goods and for public capital that has a long lifetime; the expenditures of all governments in the economy for those final goods and services.

transfer payment A payment of money (or goods and services) by a government to a household or firm for which the payer receives no good or service directly in return.

- **Government purchases** are *exhaustive;* the products purchased directly absorb (require the use of) resources and are part of the domestic output. For example, the purchase of a missile absorbs the labor of physicists and engineers along with steel, explosives, and a host of other inputs.
- **Transfer payments** are *nonexhaustive;* they do not directly absorb resources or create output. Social Security benefits, welfare payments, veterans' benefits, and unemployment compensation are examples of transfer payments. Their key characteristic is that recipients make no current contribution to domestic output in return for them.

Federal, state, and local governments spent $7,169 billion (roughly $7.2 trillion) in 2017. Of that total, government purchases were $4,334 billion and government transfers were $2,835 billion. Figure 12.2 shows these amounts as percentages of U.S. domestic output for 2017 and compares them to percentages for 1960. Government purchases have declined from about 22 to 18 percent of output since 1960. But transfer payments have nearly tripled as a percentage of output—from 5 percent in 1960 to about 14 percent in 2017. Relative to U.S. output, total government spending is thus higher today than it was 55 years earlier. This means that the tax revenues required to finance government expenditures are also higher.

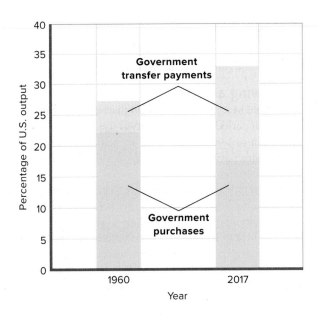

FIGURE 12.2 Government purchases, transfers, and total spending as percentages of U.S. output, 1960 and 2017. Government purchases have declined as a percentage of U.S. output since 1960. Transfer payments, however, have increased by more than this drop, raising total government spending (purchases plus transfers) from 27 percent of U.S. GDP in 1960 to about 33 percent today. *Source:* Compiled from Bureau of Economic Analysis data, **www.bea.gov**

Today, government spending and the tax revenues needed to finance it are about 33 percent of U.S. output. While it is not unusual to hear U.S. politicians and their constituents complain about high taxes, Global Snapshot 12.1 reveals that the tax burden in the United States is relatively low compared to many industrialized nations.

GLOBAL SNAPSHOT 12.1

Total Tax Revenue as a Percentage of Total Output, Selected Nations, 2016*

A nation's "tax burden" is its tax revenue from all levels of government as a percentage of its total output (GDP). Among the world's industrialized nations, the United States has a very moderate tax burden.

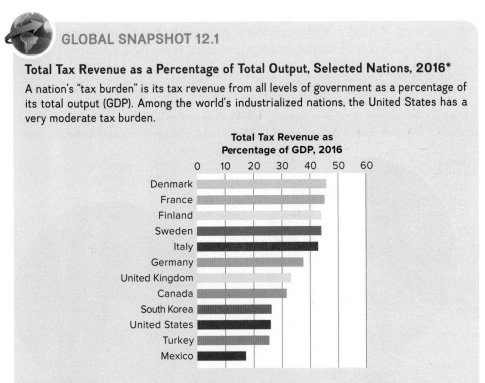

*Includes government nontax revenue from fees, charges, fines and sales of government property.

Source: OECD database, Tax Revenue Trends, 1965-2016, **www.oecdilibrary.org**, accessed April 10, 2018.

Government Revenues

The funds used to pay for government purchases and transfers come from three sources: taxes, proprietary income, and funds that are borrowed by selling bonds to the public.

Government Borrowing and Deficit Spending

The ability to borrow allows a government to spend more in a given time period than it collects in tax revenues and proprietary income during that period. This flexibility is useful during an economic downturn because a government can use borrowed funds to maintain high levels of spending on goods, services, and transfer payments even if tax revenues and proprietary income are falling due to the slowing economy.

Any money borrowed by a government, however, is money that cannot be put to other uses. During an economic downturn, this opportunity cost is likely to be small because any funds that the government does not borrow are likely to sit idle and unused by other parties due to the lack of economic activity during the downturn. But if the government borrows when the economy is doing well, many economists worry that the opportunity cost may be high. In particular, the government's borrowing may "crowd out" private-sector investment. As an example, a billion dollars borrowed and spent by the federal government on roads is a billion dollars that was not lent to private companies to fund the expansion of factories or the development of new technologies.

Government spending that is financed by borrowing is often referred to as *deficit spending* because a government's budget is said to be "in deficit" if the government's spending in a given time period exceeds the money that it collects from taxes and proprietary income during that period.

Federal Finance

Now let's look separately at each of the federal, state, and local units of government in the United States and compare their expenditures and taxes. Figure 12.3 tells the story for the federal government.

Federal Expenditures

Four areas of federal spending stand out: (1) pensions and income security, (2) national defense, (3) health, and (4) interest on the public debt. The *pensions and income security*

FIGURE 12.3 Federal expenditures and tax revenues, 2017. Federal expenditures are dominated by spending for pensions and income security, health, and national defense. A full 83 percent of federal tax revenue is derived from just two sources: the personal income tax and payroll taxes. The $666 billion difference between expenditures and revenues reflects a budget deficit. *Source:* U.S. Treasury, *Combined Statement of Receipts, Outlays, and Balances,* 2017, fms.treas.gov.

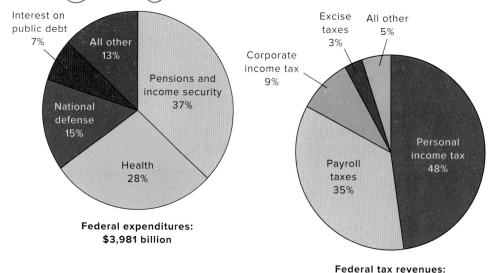

**Federal expenditures:
$3,981 billion**

**Federal tax revenues:
$3,315 billion**

category includes the many income-maintenance programs for the aged, persons with disabilities or handicaps, the unemployed, the retired, and families with no breadwinner. This category—dominated by the $911 billion pension portion of the Social Security program—accounts for 37 percent of total federal expenditures. *National defense* accounts for about 15 percent of the federal budget, underscoring the high cost of military preparedness. *Health* reflects the cost of government health programs for the retired (Medicare) and poor (Medicaid). *Interest on the public debt* accounts for 7 percent of federal spending.

Federal Tax Revenues

The revenue side of Figure 12.3 shows that the personal income tax, payroll taxes, and the corporate income tax are the largest revenue sources, accounting respectively for 48, 35, and 9 cents of each dollar collected.

Personal Income Tax   The **personal income tax** is the kingpin of the federal tax system and merits special comment. This tax is levied on *taxable income,* that is, on the incomes of households and unincorporated businesses after certain exemptions ($4,050 for each household member) and deductions (business expenses, charitable contributions, home mortgage interest payments, certain state and local taxes) are taken into account.

> **personal income tax** A tax levied on the taxable income of individuals, households, and unincorporated firms.

The federal personal income tax is a *progressive tax,* meaning that people with higher incomes pay a larger percentage of their incomes as taxes than do people with lower incomes. The progressivity is achieved by applying higher tax rates to successive layers or brackets of income.

Columns 1 and 2 in Table 12.1 show the mechanics of the income tax for a married couple filing a joint return in 2018. Note that a 10 percent tax rate applies to all taxable income up to $19,049 and a 12 percent rate applies to additional income up to $77,399. The rates on additional layers of income then go up to 22, 24, 32, 35, and 37 percent. These rates were established by the "Tax Cuts and Jobs Act" that was passed by congress in December 2017.

The tax rates shown in column 2 in Table 12.1 are marginal tax rates. A **marginal tax rate** is the rate at which the tax is paid on each *additional* unit of taxable income. Thus, if a couple's taxable income is $100,000, they will pay the marginal rate of 10 percent on each dollar from $1 to $19,049, 12 percent on each dollar from $19,050 to $77,399, and 22 percent on each dollar from $77,401 to $100,000. You should confirm that their total income tax is $13,879.

> **marginal tax rate** The tax rate paid on an additional dollar of income.

TABLE 12.1 Federal Personal Income Tax Rates, 2018*

(1) Total Taxable Income	(2) Marginal Tax Rate,%	(3) Total Tax on Highest Income in Bracket	(4) Average Tax Rate on Highest Income in Bracket,% (3) ÷ (1)
$1–$19,049	10	$ 1,905	10
$19,050–$77,399	12	8,907	11.5
$77,400–$164,999	22	28,179	17.1
$165,000–$314,999	24	67,179	20.4
$315,000–$399,999	32	94,379	23.6
$400,000–$599,999	35	164,379	27.3
Over $600,000	37		

*For a married couple filing a joint return.

average tax rate Total tax paid divided by total (taxable) income, as a percentage.

The marginal tax rates in column 2 overstate the personal income tax bite because the rising rates in that column apply only to the income within each successive tax bracket. To get a better idea of the tax burden, we must consider **average tax rates.** The average tax rate is the total tax paid divided by total taxable income. The couple in our previous example is in the 22 percent tax bracket because they pay a top marginal tax rate of 22 percent on the highest dollar of their income. But their *average tax rate* is 13.9 percent (= $13,879/$100,000).

As we will discuss in more detail shortly, a tax whose average rate rises as income increases is said to be a *progressive tax* because it claims both a progressively larger absolute amount of income as well as a progressively larger proportion of income as income rises. Thus we can say that the federal personal income tax is progressive.

payroll tax A tax levied on employers of labor equal to a percentage of all or part of the wages and salaries paid by them and on employees equal to a percentage of all or part of the wages and salaries received by them.

Payroll Taxes Social Security contributions are **payroll taxes**—taxes based on wages and salaries—used to finance two compulsory federal programs for retired workers: Social Security (an income-enhancement program) and Medicare (which pays for medical services). Employers and employees pay these taxes equally. In 2018, employees and employers each paid 7.65 percent on the first $128,400 of an employee's annual earnings and 1.45 percent each on all additional earnings. High income earners (over $250,000 for married couples filing jointly) paid an additional 0.9 percent in Medicare taxes.

corporate income tax A tax levied on the net income (accounting profit) of corporations.

Corporate Income Tax The federal government also taxes corporate income. The **corporate income tax** is levied on a corporation's profit—the difference between its total revenue and its total expenses. For almost all corporations, the tax rate is 21 percent, down from the 35 percent rate that existed prior to the passage of the "Tax Cuts and Jobs Act."

sales tax A tax levied on the cost (at retail) of a broad group of products.

excise tax A tax levied on the production of a specific product or on the quantity of the product purchased.

Excise Taxes Taxes on commodities or on purchases take the form of **sales** and **excise taxes.** The two differ primarily in terms of coverage. Sales taxes fall on a wide range of products, whereas excises are levied individually on a small, select list of commodities. An additional difference is that sales taxes are calculated as a percentage of the price paid for a product, whereas excise taxes are levied on a per-unit basis—for example, $2 per pack of cigarettes or $.50 per gallon of gasoline.

As Figure 12.3 suggests, the federal government collects excise taxes of various rates (on the sale of such commodities as alcoholic beverages, tobacco, and gasoline) but does not levy a general sales tax; sales taxes are, however, the primary revenue source of most state governments.

State and Local Finance

State and local governments have different mixes of revenues and expenditures than the federal government has.

State Finances

The primary sources of tax revenue for state governments are sales and excise taxes, which account for about 47 percent of all their tax revenue. State personal and corporate income taxes, which have much lower rates than the federal income tax, are the second most important source of state tax revenue. They bring in about 38 percent of total state tax revenue. License fees and other taxes account for most of the remainder of state tax revenue.

Education expenditures account for about 36 percent of all state spending. State expenditures on public welfare are next in relative weight, at about 31 percent of the total. States also spend heavily on health and hospitals (8 percent), highway maintenance and construction (7 percent), and public safety (4 percent). That leaves about 14 percent of all state spending for a variety of other purposes.

These tax and expenditure percentages combine data from all the states, so they reveal little about the finances of individual states. States vary significantly in the taxes levied.

APPLYING THE ANALYSIS

State Lotteries: A Good Bet?

State lotteries generated about $62.4 billion in revenue in 2013. Of that amount, $38.8 billion went to prizes and $3.2 billion went to administrative costs. That left $20.4 billion that could be spent by the states as they saw fit.

Though nowadays common, state lotteries are still controversial. Critics argue that (1) it is morally wrong for states to sponsor gambling; (2) lotteries generate compulsive gamblers who impoverish themselves and their families; (3) low-income families spend a larger portion of their incomes on lotteries than do high-income families; (4) as a cash business, lotteries attract criminals and other undesirables; and (5) lotteries send the message that luck and fate—rather than education, hard work, and saving—are the route to wealth.

Defenders contend that (1) lotteries are preferable to taxes because they are voluntary rather than compulsory; (2) they are a relatively painless way to finance government services such as education, medical care, and welfare; and (3) lotteries compete with illegal gambling and are thus socially beneficial in curtailing organized crime.

As a further point for debate, also note that state lotteries are monopolies, with states banning competing private lotteries. The resulting lack of competition allows many states to restrict prizes to only about half the money wagered. These payout rates are substantially lower than the 80–95 percent payout rates typically found in private betting operations such as casinos.

Thus, while lotteries are indeed voluntary, they are overpriced and underprovided relative to what would happen if there were a free market in lotteries. But, then again, a free market in lotteries would eliminate monopoly profits for state lotteries and possibly add government costs for regulation and oversight. Consequently, the alternative of allowing a free market in lottery tickets and then taxing the firms selling lottery tickets would probably net very little additional revenue to support state spending programs.

QUESTION: Lottery programs often warn potential participants that lottery games should only be played for entertainment and not as a form of financial investment. How do these warnings apply to the arguments both for and against lotteries?

Thus, although personal income taxes are a major source of revenue for all state governments combined, seven states do not levy a personal income tax. Also, there are great variations in the sizes of tax revenues and disbursements among the states, both in the aggregate and as percentages of personal income.

Forty-three states augment their tax revenues with state-run lotteries to help close the gap between their tax receipts and expenditures. Individual states also receive large intergovernmental grants from the federal government. In fact, about 25 percent of their total revenue is in that form. States also take in revenue from miscellaneous sources such as state-owned utilities and liquor stores.

Local Finances

The local levels of government include counties, municipalities, townships, and school districts as well as cities and towns. Local governments obtain about 73 percent of their tax revenue from **property taxes.** Sales and excise taxes contribute about 17 percent of all local government tax revenue.

property tax A tax on the value of property (capital, land, stocks and bonds, and other assets) owned by firms and households.

Federal versus State and Local Spending

Spending priorities vary across the different levels of government. The federal government spends a significant portion of its budget on national defense, and pensions and income security. State and local governments spend heavily on education and public welfare.

©Stocktrek Images/Getty Images   ©LWA/Dann Tardiff/Getty Images

About 46 percent of local government expenditures go to education. Welfare, health, and hospitals (13 percent); public safety (11 percent); housing, parks, and sewerage (9 percent); and streets and highways (6 percent) are also major spending categories.

The tax revenues of local government cover less than one-half of their expenditures. The bulk of the remaining revenue comes from intergovernmental grants from the federal and state governments. Also, local governments receive considerable amounts of proprietary income, for example, revenue from government-owned utilities providing water, electricity, natural gas, and transportation.

Local, State, and Federal Employment

In 2016, U.S. governments (local, state, and federal) employed about 22.2 million workers, or about 14 percent of the U.S. labor force. The types of jobs done by government workers depend on the level of government. Over half of state and local government employment is focused on education. The next largest sector is hospitals and health care, which accounts for about 12 percent of state and local government employment. Police and corrections make up another 11 percent. Smaller categories like highways, public welfare, and judicial together combine for less than 9 percent of state and local employment. The remaining employees work in areas such as parks and recreation, fire fighting, transit, and libraries.

Just over half of federal government jobs are in national defense or the postal service. A further 15 percent of government jobs are in hospitals or health care. Jobs in natural resources, police, and financial administration each account for between 4 and 7 percent of federal employment. The "other" category at the federal level is composed of workers in areas such as justice and law, corrections, air transportation, and social insurance administration.

Apportioning the Tax Burden

Taxes are the major source of funding for the goods and services provided by government and the wages and salaries paid to government workers. Without taxes, there would be no public schools, no national defense, no public highways, no courts, no police, and no other government-provided public and quasi-public goods. As stated by Supreme Court Justice Oliver Wendell Holmes, "Taxes are the price we pay for civilization."

Once government has decided on the total tax revenue it needs to finance its activities, including the provision of public and quasi-public goods, it must determine how to apportion the tax burden among the citizens. (By "tax burden" we mean the total cost of taxes imposed on society.) This apportionment question affects each of us. The overall level of taxes is important, but the average citizen is much more concerned with his or her share of taxes.

Benefits Received versus Ability to Pay

Two basic philosophies coexist on how the economy's tax burden should be apportioned.

Benefits-Received Principle

The **benefits-received principle** of taxation asserts that households should purchase the goods and services of government in the same way they buy other commodities. Those who benefit most from government-supplied goods or services should pay the taxes necessary to finance them. A few public goods are now financed on this basis. For example, money collected as gasoline taxes is typically used to finance highway construction and repairs. Thus people who benefit from good roads pay the cost of those roads. Difficulties immediately arise, however, when we consider widespread application of the benefits-received principle:

- How will the government determine the benefits that individual households and businesses receive from national defense, education, the court system, and police and fire protection? Recall from Chapter 5 that public goods are characterized by nonrivalry and nonexcludability. So benefits from public goods are especially widespread and diffuse. Even in the seemingly straightforward case of highway financing it is difficult to measure benefits. Good roads benefit owners of cars in different degrees. But others also benefit. For example, businesses benefit because good roads bring them workers and customers.

- The benefits-received principle cannot logically be applied to income redistribution programs. It would be absurd and self-defeating to ask poor families to pay the taxes needed to finance their welfare payments. It would also be self-defeating to tax only unemployed workers to finance the unemployment benefits they receive.

Ability-to-Pay Principle

The **ability-to-pay principle** of taxation asserts that the tax burden should be apportioned according to taxpayers' income and wealth. In practice, this means that individuals and businesses with larger incomes should pay more taxes in both absolute and relative terms than those with smaller incomes.

In justifying the ability-to-pay principle, proponents contend that each additional dollar of income received by a household yields a smaller amount of satisfaction or marginal utility when it is spent. Because consumers act rationally, the first dollars of income received in any time period will be spent on high-urgency goods that yield the greatest marginal utility. Successive dollars of income will go for less urgently needed goods and finally for trivial goods and services. This means that a dollar taken through taxes from a poor person who has few dollars represents a greater utility sacrifice than a dollar taken through taxes from a rich person who has many dollars. To balance the sacrifices that taxes impose on income receivers, taxes should be apportioned according to the amount of income a taxpayer receives.

This argument is appealing, but application problems arise here too. Although we might agree that the household earning $100,000 per year has a greater ability to pay taxes than a

benefits-received principle The idea that those who receive the benefits of goods and services provided by government should pay the taxes required to finance them.

ability-to-pay principle The idea that those who have greater income (or wealth) should pay a greater proportion of it as taxes than those who have less income (or wealth).

household receiving $10,000, we don't know exactly how much more ability to pay the first family has. Should the wealthier family pay the *same* percentage of its larger income, and hence a larger absolute amount, as taxes? Or should it be made to pay a *larger* percentage of its income as taxes? And how much larger should that percentage be? Who is to decide?

There is no scientific way of making utility comparisons among individuals and thus of measuring someone's relative ability to pay taxes. That is the main problem. In practice, the solution hinges on guesswork, the tax views of the political party in power, expediency, and how urgently the government needs revenue.

Progressive, Proportional, and Regressive Taxes

Any discussion of taxation leads ultimately to the question of tax rates. Taxes are classified as progressive, proportional, or regressive, depending on the relationship between average tax rates and taxpayer incomes. We focus on incomes because all taxes—whether on income, a product, a building, or a parcel of land—are ultimately paid out of someone's income.

progressive tax A tax whose average tax rate increases as the taxpayer's income increases and decreases as the taxpayer's income decreases.

regressive tax A tax whose average tax rate decreases as the taxpayer's income increases and increases as the taxpayer's income decreases.

proportional tax A tax whose average tax rate remains constant as the taxpayer's income increases or decreases.

- A tax is **progressive** if its average rate increases as income increases. Such a tax claims not only a larger absolute (dollar) amount but also a larger percentage of income as income increases.
- A tax is **regressive** if its average rate declines as income increases. Such a tax takes a smaller proportion of income as income increases. A regressive tax may or may not take a larger absolute amount of income as income increases. (You may want to derive an example to substantiate this fact.)
- A tax is **proportional** if its average rate *remains the same* regardless of the size of income. Proportional income taxes are often referred to as *flat taxes* or *flat-rate taxes* because their average rates do not vary with (are flat with respect to) income levels.

We can illustrate these ideas with the personal income tax. Suppose tax rates are such that a household pays 10 percent of its income in taxes regardless of the size of its income. This is a *proportional* income tax. Now suppose the rate structure is such that a household with an annual taxable income of less than $10,000 pays 5 percent in income taxes; a household with an income of $10,000 to $20,000 pays 10 percent; one with a $20,000 to $30,000 income pays 15 percent; and so forth. This is a *progressive* income tax. Finally, suppose the rate declines as taxable income rises: You pay 15 percent if you earn less than $10,000; 10 percent if you earn $10,000 to $20,000; 5 percent if you earn $20,000 to $30,000; and so forth. This is a *regressive* income tax.

In general, progressive taxes are those that fall relatively more heavily on people with high incomes; regressive taxes are those that fall relatively more heavily on the poor.

Applications   Let's examine the progressivity, or regressivity, of several taxes.

Personal Income Tax   As noted earlier, the federal personal income tax is progressive, with marginal tax rates (those assessed on additional income) ranging from 10 to 37 percent in 2018. Rules that allow individuals to deduct from income interest on home mortgages and property taxes and that exempt interest on state and local bonds from taxation tend to make the tax less progressive than these marginal rates suggest. Nevertheless, average tax rates rise with income.

Sales Taxes   At first thought, a general sales tax with, for example, a 5 percent rate would seem to be proportional. But in fact it is regressive with respect to income. A larger portion of a low-income person's income is exposed to the tax than is the case for a high-income person; the rich pay no tax on the part of income that is saved, whereas the poor are unable to save. Example: "Low-income" Smith has an income of $15,000 and spends it all. "High-income" Jones has an income of $300,000 but spends only $200,000 and saves the rest. Assuming a 5 percent sales tax applies to all expenditures of each individual, we find that Smith pays $750 (5 percent of $15,000) in sales taxes and Jones pays $10,000 (5 percent of $200,000). But Smith pays $750/$15,000, or 5 percent of income as sales taxes while Jones pays $10,000/$300,000, or 3.3 percent of income. The general sales tax therefore is regressive.

Corporate Income Tax   The federal corporate income tax is essentially a proportional tax with a flat 21 percent tax rate, as of 2018. In the short run, the corporate owners (shareholders) bear the tax through lower dividends and share values. In the long run, workers may bear some of the tax since it reduces the return on investment and therefore slows capital accumulation. It also causes corporations to relocate to other countries that have lower tax rates. With less capital per worker, U.S. labor productivity may decline and wages may fall. To the extent this happens, the corporate income tax may be somewhat regressive.

Payroll Taxes   Payroll taxes are taxes levied upon wages and salaries by certain states as well as by the federal government. The federal payroll tax is known as the FICA tax after the Federal Insurance Contributions Act, which mandated one payroll tax to fund the Social Security program and another to fund the Medicare program.

Both taxes are split between employer and employee. Thus, the 12.4 percent Social Security tax is split in half, with 6.2 percent paid by employees and an additional 6.2 percent paid by employers. In the same way, the 2.9 percent Medicare tax is split in half, with 1.45 percent paid by employees and 1.45 percent paid by employers.

Crucially, however, only the Medicare tax applies to all wage and salary income without limit. The Social Security tax, by contrast, is "capped," meaning that it applies only up to a certain limit, or cap. In 2018, the cap was $128,400.

The fact that the Social Security tax applies only on income below the cap implies that the FICA tax is regressive. To see this, consider a person with $128,400 in wage income. He would pay $9,822.60, or 7.65 percent (= 6.2 percent + 1.45 percent) of his wages in FICA taxes. By contrast, someone with twice that income, or $256,800, would pay $12,296.40 (= $9,822.60 on the first $128,400 + $2,473.80 on the second $128,400, of which $612 is from the 0.9 percent tax on earnings over $250,000 for married filing jointly), which is only 4.8 percent of his wage income. Thus, the average FICA tax falls as income rises, thereby confirming that the FICA tax is regressive.

But payroll taxes are even more regressive than suggested by this example because they only apply to wage and salary income. People earning high incomes tend to derive a higher percentage of their total incomes from nonwage sources like rents and dividends than do people who have incomes below the $128,400 cap on which Social Security taxes are paid. Thus, if our individual with the $256,800 of wage income also received $256,800 of nonwage income, his $12,296.40 of FICA tax would be only 2.4 percent of his total income of $513,600.

Property Taxes   Most economists conclude that property taxes on buildings are regressive for the same reasons as are sales taxes. First, property owners add the tax to the rents that tenants are charged. Second, property taxes, as a percentage of income, are higher for low-income families than for high-income families because the poor must spend a larger proportion of their incomes for housing.

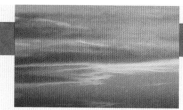

The VAT: A Very Alluring Tax?

A value-added tax (VAT) is like a retail sales tax except that it applies only to the *difference* between the value of a firm's sales and the value of its purchases from other firms. For instance, Intel would pay the VAT—say, 7 percent—only on the difference between the value of the microchips it sells and the value of the materials used to make them. Dell, Lenovo, and other firms that buy chips and other components to make computers would subtract the value of their materials from the value of their sales of personal computers. They would pay the 7 percent tax on that difference—on the value that *they* added.

Economists reason that because the VAT would apply to all firms, sellers could shift their VATs to buyers in the form of higher prices without having to worry that their higher prices might cause them to lose sales to competitors. Final consumers, who cannot shift the tax, would be the ones who ultimately end up paying the full VAT as 7 percent higher prices. So the VAT would amount to a national sales tax on consumer goods.

Most other nations besides the United States have a VAT in addition to other taxes. Why the attraction? Proponents argue that it encourages savings and investment because it penalizes consumption. Unlike income taxes and profits taxes, which reduce the returns to working and investing, the VAT only taxes consumption. Thus, people might be expected to save and invest more if the government switched from taxing income and profits to taxing consumption via a VAT.

Opponents counter, however, that the VAT discourages savings and investment just as much as do income and profit taxes because the whole point of working hard, saving, and investing is the ability to reward yourself in the future with increased consumption. By making consumption more expensive, the VAT reduces this future reward. Also, because VATs are regressive, opponents argue that VATs lead to higher and more progressive income taxes as governments try to use the progressivity of income taxes to counter the regressivity of the VAT. Finally, critics note that the VAT is deeply buried within product prices and therefore is a *hidden tax*. Such taxes are usually easier to increase than other taxes and therefore can result in excessively large government.

QUESTION: Would you rather pay an income tax or a value-added tax? Explain your reasoning.

Tax Incidence and Efficiency Loss

Determining whether a particular tax is progressive, proportional, or regressive is complicated because those on whom taxes are levied do not always pay the taxes. This is true because some or all of the value of the tax may be passed on to others. We therefore need an understanding of **tax incidence,** the degree to which a tax falls on a particular person or group. The tools of elasticity of supply and demand will help. Let's focus on a hypothetical excise tax levied on wine producers. Do the producers really pay this tax, or is some fraction of the tax shifted to wine consumers?

tax incidence The degree to which a tax falls on a particular person or group.

Elasticity and Tax Incidence

In Figure 12.4, S and D represent the pretax market for a certain domestic wine; the no-tax equilibrium price and quantity are $8 per bottle and 15 million bottles. Suppose that government levies an excise tax of $2 per bottle at the winery. Who will actually pay this tax?

Division of Burden Since the government imposes the tax on the sellers (suppliers), we can view the tax as an addition to the marginal cost of the product. Now sellers must get $2 more for each bottle to receive the same per-unit profit they were getting before the tax. While sellers are willing to offer, for example, 5 million bottles of untaxed wine at $4 per bottle, they must now receive $6 per bottle (= $4 + $2 tax) to offer the same 5 million bottles. The tax shifts the supply curve upward (leftward) as shown in Figure 12.4, where S_t is the "after-tax" supply curve.

The after-tax equilibrium price is $9 per bottle, whereas the before-tax equilibrium price was $8. So, in this case, consumers pay half the $2 tax as a higher price; producers pay the other half in the form of a lower after-tax per-unit revenue. That is, after remitting the $2 tax per unit to government, producers receive $7 per bottle, or $1 less than the $8 before-tax price. So, in this case, consumers and producers share the burden of the tax equally: Half of the $2 per-bottle tax is shifted to consumers in the form of a higher price and half is paid by producers.

Note also that the equilibrium quantity declines because of the tax levy and the higher price that it imposes on consumers. In Figure 12.4 that decline in quantity is from 15 million bottles to 12.5 million bottles per month.

Elasticities If the elasticities of demand and supply were different from those shown in Figure 12.4, the incidence of tax would also be different. Two generalizations are relevant.

With a specific supply, the more inelastic the demand for the product, the larger is the portion of the tax shifted to consumers. To verify this, sketch graphically the extreme cases

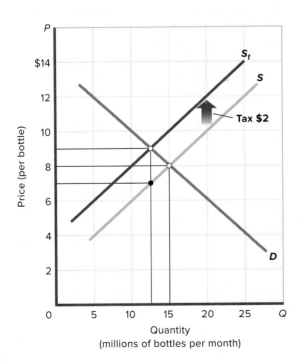

FIGURE 12.4 The incidence of an excise tax. An excise tax of a specified amount (here, $2 per unit) shifts the supply curve upward by the amount of the tax per unit: the vertical distance between S and S_t. This results in a higher price (here, $9) to consumers and a lower after-tax price (here, $7) to producers. Thus consumers and producers share the burden of the tax in some proportion (here, equally at $1 per unit).

FIGURE 12.5 **Demand elasticity and the incidence of an excise tax.** (a) If demand is elastic in the relevant price range, price rises modestly (P_1 to P_2) when an excise tax is levied. Hence, the producers bear most of the tax burden. (b) If demand is inelastic, the price increases substantially (P_4 to P_5) and most of the tax is borne by consumers.

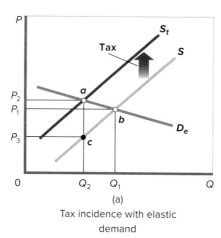

(a)

Tax incidence with elastic demand

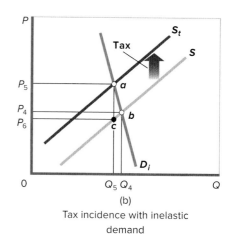

(b)

Tax incidence with inelastic demand

in which demand is perfectly elastic and perfectly inelastic. In the first case, the incidence of the tax is entirely on sellers; in the second, the tax is shifted entirely to consumers.

Figure 12.5 contrasts the more usual cases where demand is either relatively elastic or relatively inelastic in the relevant price range. With elastic demand (Figure 12.5a), a small portion of the tax ($P_2 - P_1$) is shifted to consumers and most of the tax ($P_1 - P_3$) is borne by the producers. With inelastic demand (Figure 12.5b), most of the tax ($P_5 - P_4$) is shifted to consumers and only a small amount ($P_4 - P_6$) is paid by producers. In both graphs the per-unit tax is represented by the vertical distance between S_t and S.

Note also that the decline in equilibrium quantity (from Q_1 to Q_2 in Figure 12.5a and from Q_4 to Q_5 in Figure 12.5b) is smaller when demand is more inelastic. This is the basis of our previous applications of the elasticity concept to taxation in earlier chapters: Revenue-seeking legislatures place heavy excise taxes on liquor, cigarettes, automobile tires, telephone service, and other products whose demand is thought to be inelastic. Since demand for these products is relatively inelastic, the tax does not reduce sales by much, so the tax revenue stays high.

The second generalization is that, with a specific demand, the more inelastic the supply, the larger is the portion of the tax borne by producers. When supply is elastic (Figure 12.6a), consumers bear most of the tax ($P_2 - P_1$) while producers bear only a small portion ($P_1 - P_3$) themselves. But where supply is inelastic (Figure 12.6b), the reverse is true: The

FIGURE 12.6 **Supply elasticity and the incidence of an excise tax.** (a) With elastic supply, an excise tax results in a large price increase (P_1 to P_2) and the tax is therefore paid mainly by consumers. (b) If supply is inelastic, the price rise is small (P_4 to P_5) and sellers bear most of the tax.

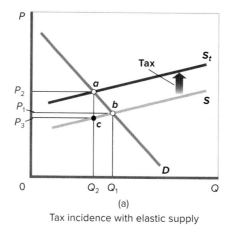

(a)

Tax incidence with elastic supply

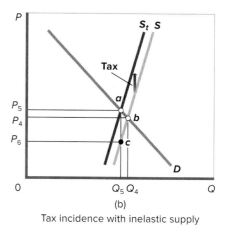

(b)

Tax incidence with inelastic supply

major portion of the tax $(P_4 - P_6)$ falls on sellers, and a relatively small amount $(P_5 - P_4)$ is shifted to buyers. The equilibrium quantity also declines less with an inelastic supply than it does with an elastic supply.

Gold is an example of a product with an inelastic supply and therefore one where the burden of an excise tax (such as an extraction tax) would mainly fall on producers. On the other hand, because the supply of baseballs is relatively elastic, producers would pass on to consumers much of an excise tax on baseballs.

Efficiency Loss of a Tax

We just observed that producers and consumers typically each bear part of an excise tax levied on producers. Let's now look more closely at the overall economic effect of the excise tax. Consider Figure 12.7, which is identical to Figure 12.4 but contains the additional detail we need for our discussion.

Tax Revenues In our example, a $2 excise tax on wine increases its market price from $8 to $9 per bottle and reduces the equilibrium quantity from 15 million bottles to 12.5 million. Government tax revenue is $25 million (= $2 × 12.5 million bottles), an amount shown as the rectangle *efac* in Figure 12.7. The elasticities of supply and demand in this case are such that consumers and producers each pay half this total amount, or $12.5 million apiece (= $1 × 12.5 million bottles). The government uses this $25 million of tax revenue to provide public goods and services. So this transfer of dollars from consumers and producers to government involves no loss of well-being to society.

Efficiency Loss The $2 tax on wine does more than require consumers and producers to pay $25 million of taxes; it also reduces the equilibrium amount of wine produced and consumed by 2.5 million bottles. The fact that consumers and producers demanded and supplied 2.5 million more bottles of wine before the tax means that those 2.5 million bottles provided benefits in excess of their production costs. This is clear from the following analysis.

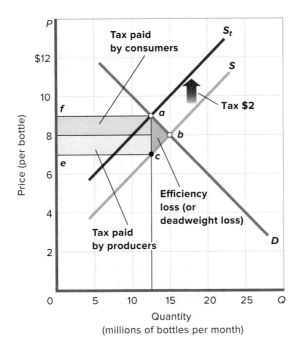

FIGURE 12.7 Efficiency loss (or deadweight loss) of a tax. The levy of a $2 tax per bottle of wine increases the price per bottle from $8 to $9 and reduces the equilibrium quantity from 15 million to 12.5 million. Tax revenue to the government is $25 million (area *efac*). The efficiency loss of the tax arises from the 2.5 million decline in output; the amount of that loss is shown as triangle *abc*.

efficiency (deadweight) loss of a tax The loss of net benefits to society because a tax reduces the production and consumption of a taxed good below the level of allocative efficiency.

Segment *ab* of demand curve *D* in Figure 12.7 indicates the willingness to pay—the marginal benefit—associated with each of the 2.5 million bottles consumed before (but not after) the tax. Segment *cb* of supply curve *S* reflects the marginal cost of each of the bottles of wine. For all but the very last one of these 2.5 million bottles, the marginal benefit (shown by a point on *ab*) exceeds the marginal cost (shown by a point on *cb*). Not producing these 2.5 million bottles of wine reduces well-being by an amount represented by the triangle *abc*. The area of this triangle identifies the **efficiency loss of the tax** (also called the *deadweight loss of the tax*). This loss is society's sacrifice of net benefit because the tax reduces production and consumption of the product below their levels of economic efficiency, where marginal benefit and marginal cost are equal.

Role of Elasticities

Most taxes create some degree of efficiency loss, but just how much depends on the supply and demand elasticities. Glancing back at Figure 12.5, we see that the efficiency loss area *abc* is greater in Figure 12.5a, where demand is relatively elastic, than in Figure 12.5b, where demand is relatively inelastic. Similarly, area *abc* is greater in Figure 12.6a than in Figure 12.6b, indicating a larger efficiency loss where supply is more elastic. Other things equal, the greater the elasticities of supply and demand, the greater the efficiency loss of a particular tax.

Two taxes yielding equal revenues do not necessarily impose equal costs on society. The government must keep this fact in mind in designing a tax system to finance beneficial public goods and services. In general, it should minimize the efficiency loss of the tax system in raising any specific dollar amount of tax revenue.

Qualifications

We must acknowledge, however, that other tax goals may be as important as, or even more important than, minimizing efficiency losses from taxes. Here are two examples:

- **Redistributive goals** Government may wish to impose progressive taxes as a way to redistribute income. The 10 percent excise tax the federal government placed on selected luxuries in 1990 was an example. Because the demand for luxuries is elastic, substantial efficiency losses from this tax were to be expected. However, Congress apparently concluded that the benefits from the redistribution effects of the tax would exceed the efficiency losses.

  Ironically, in 1993 Congress repealed the luxury taxes on personal airplanes and yachts, mainly because the taxes had reduced quantity demanded so much that widespread layoffs of workers were occurring in those industries. But the 10 percent tax on luxury automobiles remained in place until it expired in 2003.

- **Reducing negative externalities** Our analysis of the efficiency loss of a tax assumes no negative externalities arising from either the production or consumption of the product in question. Where such spillover costs occur, an excise tax on producers might actually improve allocative efficiency by reducing output and thus lessening the negative externality. For example, the $2 excise tax on wine in our example might be part of a broader set of excise taxes on alcoholic beverages. The government may have concluded that the consumption of these beverages produces certain negative externalities. Therefore, it might have purposely levied this $2 tax to shift the market supply curve in Figure 12.7 to increase the price of wine, decrease alcohol consumption, and reduce the amount of resources devoted to wine.

Excise taxes that are intended to reduce the production and consumption of products with negative externalities are sometimes referred to as *sin taxes*. This name captures the idea that governments are motivated to impose these taxes to discourage activities that are perceived to be harmful or sinful. Excise taxes on cigarettes and alcohol in particular are commonly referred to as sin taxes.

Probable Incidence of U.S. Taxes

Let's look now at the probable incidence of each of the major sources of tax revenue in the United States.

The incidence of the *personal income tax* generally is on the individual because there is little chance for shifting it. For every dollar paid to the tax, individuals have one less dollar in their pocketbooks. The same ordinarily holds true for inheritance taxes.

As discussed earlier, employees and employers in 2018 each paid 7.65 percent in *payroll taxes* on a worker's annual earnings up to the 2018 Social Security cap of $128,400 and then 1.45 percent on any additional earnings.

Workers bear the full burden of their share of the Social Security and Medicare payroll taxes. As is true for the income tax, they cannot shift the payroll taxes that they pay to anyone else.

But what about the portion of the FICA tax that is levied on employers? Who pays that? The consensus view is that part of the employers' share of the FICA tax gets shifted to workers in the form of lower before-tax wages. By making it more costly to hire workers, the payroll tax reduces the demand for labor relative to supply. That reduces the market wages that employers pay workers. In a sense, employers "collect" some of the payroll tax they owe from their workers.

In the short run, the incidence of the *corporate income tax* falls on the company's stockholders (owners), who bear the burden of the tax through lower dividends or smaller amounts of retained corporate earnings. A firm currently charging the profit-maximizing price and producing the profit-maximizing output will have no reason to change product price, output, or wages when a tax on corporate income (profit) is imposed. The price and output combination yielding the greatest profit before the tax will still yield the greatest profit after a fixed percentage of the firm's profit is removed by a corporate income tax. So, the company's stockholders will not be able to shift the tax to consumers or workers.

The situation may be different in the long run. Workers, in general, may bear a significant part of the corporate income tax in the form of lower wage growth. Because it reduces the return on investment, the corporate income tax may slow the accumulation of capital (plant and equipment). It also may prompt some U.S. firms to relocate abroad in countries that have lower corporate tax rates. In either case, the tax may slow the growth of U.S. labor productivity, which depends on American workers having access to more and better equipment. The growth of labor productivity is the main reason labor demand grows over time. If the corporate income tax reduces the growth of labor productivity, then labor demand and wages may rise less rapidly. In this indirect way—and over long periods of time—workers may bear part of the corporate income tax.

A *sales tax* is a general excise tax levied on a full range of consumer goods and services, whereas a *specific excise tax* is one levied only on a particular product. Sales taxes are usually transparent to the buyer, whereas excise taxes are often "hidden" in the price of the product. But whether they are hidden or clearly visible, both are often partly or largely shifted to consumers through higher equilibrium product prices (as in Figures 12.4, 12.5, and 12.6). Sales taxes and excise taxes may get shifted to different extents, however. Because a sales tax covers a much wider range of products than an excise tax, there is little chance for consumers to avoid the price boosts that sales taxes entail. They cannot reallocate their expenditures to untaxed, lower-priced products. Therefore, sales taxes tend to be shifted in their entirety from producers to consumers.

Excise taxes, however, fall on a select list of goods. Therefore, the possibility of consumers turning to substitute goods and services is greater. An excise tax on theater tickets that does not apply to other types of entertainment might be difficult to pass on to consumers via price increases. Why? The answer is provided in Figure 12.5a, where demand is

GLOBAL SNAPSHOT 12.2

Taxes on General Consumption as a Percentage of GDP, Selected Nations

A number of advanced industrial nations rely much more heavily on consumption taxes—sales taxes, specific excise taxes, and value-added taxes—than does the United States. A value-added tax, which the United States does not have, applies only to the difference between the value of a firm's sales and the value of its purchases from other firms. As a percentage of GDP, the highest tax rates on consumption are in countries that have value-added taxes.

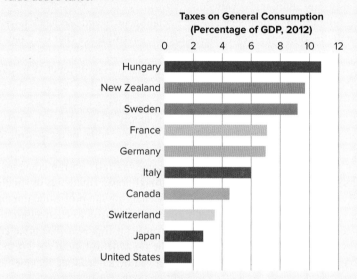

Source: Organization for Economic Cooperation and Development, *OECD Stat Extracts,* **stats.oecd.org.**

elastic. A price boost to cover the excise tax on theater tickets might cause consumers to substitute alternative types of entertainment. The higher price would reduce sales so much that a seller would be better off to bear all, or a large portion of, the excise tax.

With other products, modest price increases to cover taxes may have smaller effects on sales. The excise taxes on gasoline, cigarettes, and alcoholic beverages provide examples. Here consumers have few good substitute products to which they can turn as prices rise. For these goods, the seller is better able to shift nearly all the excise tax to consumers. Example: Prices of cigarettes have gone up nearly in lockstep with the recent, substantial increases in excise taxes on cigarettes.

As indicated in Global Snapshot 12.2, the United States depends less on sales and excise taxes for tax revenue than do several other nations.

Many *property taxes* are borne by the property owner because there is no other party to whom they can be shifted. This is typically true for taxes on land, personal property, and owner-occupied residences. Even when land is sold, the property tax is not likely to be shifted. The buyer will understand that future taxes will have to be paid on it, and this expected taxation would be reflected in the price the buyer is willing to offer for the land.

Taxes on rented and business property are a different story. Taxes on rented property can be, and usually are, shifted wholly or in part from the owner to the tenant by the process of boosting the rent. Business property taxes are treated as a business cost and are taken into account in establishing product price; hence such taxes are ordinarily shifted to the firm's customers.

Table 12.2 summarizes this discussion of the shifting and incidence of taxes.

TABLE 12.2 The Probable Incidence of Taxes

Type of Tax	Probable Incidence
Personal income tax	The household or individual on which it is levied.
Payroll taxes	Workers pay the full tax levied on their earnings and part of the tax levied on their employers.
Corporate income tax	In the short run, the full tax falls on owners of the businesses. In the long run, some of the tax may be borne by workers through lower wages.
Sales tax	Consumers who buy the taxed products.
Specific excise taxes	Consumers, producers, or both, depending on elasticities of demand and supply.
Property taxes	Owners in the case of land and owner-occupied residences; tenants in the case of rented property; consumers in the case of business property.

The U.S. Tax Structure

Is the overall U.S. tax structure—federal, state, and local taxes combined—progressive, proportional, or regressive? The question is difficult to answer. Estimates of the distribution of the total tax burden depend on the extent to which the various taxes are shifted to others, and who bears the burden is subject to dispute. But the majority view of economists who study taxes is as follows:

- ***The federal tax system is progressive.*** Overall, higher-income groups pay larger percentages of their income as federal taxes than do lower-income groups. Although federal payroll taxes and excise taxes are regressive, the federal income tax is sufficiently progressive to make the overall federal tax system progressive. About one-third of federal income tax filers owe no tax at all. In fact, because of fully refundable tax credits designed to reduce poverty and promote work, millions of households receive tax rebates even though their income tax bill is zero. Most of the federal income tax is paid by higher-income taxpayers. In 2015 (the latest year for which data have been compiled), the top 1 percent of income-tax filers paid 39 percent of the federal income tax; the top 5 percent paid 59.6 percent of the tax.

   The overall progressivity of the federal tax system is confirmed by comparing effective (average) tax rates, which are found by dividing the total of federal income, payroll, and excise taxes paid at various income levels by the total incomes earned by the people at those various income levels. In 2013, the 20 percent of the households with the lowest income paid an effective tax rate of 3.3 percent. The 20 percent of households with the highest income paid a 26.3 percent rate. The top 1 percent paid a 34.0 percent rate.[1]

   The "Tax Cuts and Jobs Act," passed in December 2017, reduced federal income tax rates for all but the lowest bracket, making the federal tax system less progressive.
- ***The state and local tax structures are largely regressive.*** As a percentage of income, property taxes and sales taxes fall as income rises. Also, state income taxes are generally less progressive than the federal income tax.
- ***The overall U.S. tax system is progressive.*** Higher-income people carry a substantially larger tax burden, as a percentage of their income, than do lower-income people.

   The income tax system cannot be relied upon by itself to substantially alter the distribution of income because the government might choose to spend the taxes collected from

[1]*The Distribution of Household Income and Federal Taxes, 2011,* Congressional Budget Office, November 2014.

the rich to pay for things that are used more by the rich than the poor. In actual fact, however, this does not happen in the United States because the government uses a large portion of the tax revenues collected from the rich to make income transfer payments to the poor and to pay for the provision of goods and services that are utilized more by the poor than the rich. The transfer payments by themselves are so large that they almost quadruple the incomes of the poorest fifth of U.S. households. Thus, the combined tax-transfer system levels the income distribution by much more than the tax system does on its own.

SUMMARY

LO12.1 Identify the main categories of government spending and the main sources of government revenue.

The funds used to pay for government purchases and transfers come from taxes, proprietary income, and borrowing. The ability to borrow allows governments to maintain high spending during economic downturns, but government borrowing when the economy is doing well may "crowd out" private-sector investment.

Government purchases exhaust (use up or absorb) resources; transfer payments do not. Government purchases have declined from about 22 percent of domestic output in 1960 to 18 percent today. Transfer payments, however, have grown rapidly. As a percentage of GDP, total government spending (purchases plus transfers) now stands at about 33 percent, up from 27 percent in 1960.

The main categories of federal spending are pensions and income security, national defense, health, and interest on the public debt; federal revenues come primarily from personal income taxes, payroll taxes, and corporate income taxes.

States derive their revenue primarily from sales and excise taxes and personal income taxes; major state expenditures go to education, public welfare, health and hospitals, and highways. Local communities derive most of their revenue from property taxes; education is their most important expenditure. State and local tax revenues are supplemented by sizable revenue grants from the federal government.

Slightly over half of state and local government employees work in education. Just over half of federal government employees work either for the postal service or in national defense.

LO12.2 Summarize the different philosophies regarding the distribution of a nation's tax burden.

The benefits-received principle of taxation states that those who receive the benefits of goods and services provided by government should pay the taxes required to finance them. The ability-to-pay principle states that those who have greater income should be taxed more, absolutely and relatively, than those who have less income.

The federal personal income tax is progressive. The corporate income tax is roughly proportional. General sales, excise, payroll, and property taxes are regressive.

LO12.3 Explain the principles relating to tax shifting, tax incidence, and the efficiency losses caused by taxes.

Excise taxes affect supply and therefore equilibrium price and quantity. The more inelastic the demand for a product, the greater is the portion of an excise tax that is borne by consumers. The greater the inelasticity of supply, the larger is the portion of the tax that is borne by the seller.

Taxation involves the loss of some output whose marginal benefit exceeds its marginal cost. The more elastic the supply and demand curves, the greater is the efficiency loss (or deadweight loss) resulting from a particular tax.

Some taxes are borne by those taxed; other taxes are shifted to someone else. The income tax, the payroll tax levied on workers, and the corporate income tax (in the short run) are borne by those taxed. In contrast, sales taxes are shifted to consumers, part of the payroll tax levied on employers is shifted to workers, and, in the long run, part of the corporate income tax is shifted to workers. Specific excise taxes may or may not be shifted to consumers, depending on the elasticities of demand and supply. Property taxes on owner-occupied property are borne by the owner; those on rental property are borne by tenants.

LO12.4 Demonstrate how the distribution of income between rich and poor is affected by government taxes, transfers, and spending.

The federal tax structure is progressive; the state and local tax structure is regressive; and the overall tax structure is progressive.

TERMS AND CONCEPTS

government purchases	marginal tax rate	corporate income tax
transfer payments	average tax rate	excise tax
personal income tax	payroll taxes	sales tax

property taxes

benefits-received principle

ability-to-pay principle

progressive tax

regressive tax

proportional tax

tax incidence

efficiency loss of a tax

QUESTIONS

The following and additional problems can be found in ⬛ connect

1. Use a circular flow diagram to show how the allocation of resources and the distribution of income are affected by each of the following government actions. LO12.1
   a. The construction of a new high school.
   b. A 2-percentage-point reduction of the corporate income tax.
   c. An expansion of preschool programs for disadvantaged children.
   d. The levying of an excise tax on polluters.
2. What do economists mean when they say government purchases are "exhaustive" expenditures whereas government transfer payments are "nonexhaustive" expenditures? Cite an example of a government purchase and a government transfer payment. LO12.1
3. What is the most important source of revenue and the major type of expenditure at the federal level? At the state level? At the local level? LO12.1
4. Distinguish between the benefits-received and the ability-to-pay principles of taxation. Which philosophy is more evident in our present tax structure? Justify your answer. To which principle of taxation do you subscribe? Why? LO12.2
5. What is meant by a progressive tax? A regressive tax? A proportional tax? Comment on the progressivity or regressivity of each of the following taxes, indicating in each case where you think the tax incidence lies: (a) the federal personal income tax, (b) a 4 percent state general sales tax, (c) a federal excise tax on automobile tires, (d) a municipal property tax on real estate, (e)

the federal corporate income tax, (f) the portion of the payroll tax levied on employers. LO12.3
6. What is the tax incidence of an excise tax when demand is highly inelastic? Highly elastic? What effect does the elasticity of supply have on the incidence of an excise tax? What is the efficiency loss of a tax, and how does it relate to elasticity of demand and supply? LO12.3
7. Given the inelasticity of cigarette demand, discuss an excise tax on cigarettes in terms of efficiency loss and tax incidence. LO12.3
8. **ADVANCED ANALYSIS** Suppose the equation for the demand curve for some product X is $P = 8 - .6Q$ and the supply curve is $P = 2 + .4Q$. What are the equilibrium price and quantity? Now suppose an excise tax is imposed on X such that the new supply equation is $P = 4 + .4Q$. How much tax revenue will this excise tax yield the government? Graph the curves, and label the area of the graph that represents the tax collection "TC" and the area that represents the efficiency loss of the tax "EL." Briefly explain why area EL is the efficiency loss of the tax but TC is not. LO12.3
9. Is it possible for a country with a regressive tax system to have a tax-spending system that transfers resources from the rich to the poor? LO12.4
10. Does a progressive tax system by itself guarantee that resources will be redistributed from the rich to the poor? Explain. Is the *tax* system in the United States progressive, regressive, or proportional? LO12.4

PROBLEMS

1. Suppose a tax is such that an individual with an income of $10,000 pays $2,000 of tax, a person with an income of $20,000 pays $3,000 of tax, a person with an income of $30,000 pays $4,000 of tax, and so forth. What is each person's average tax rate? Is this tax regressive, proportional, or progressive? LO12.3
2. Suppose in Fiscalville there is no tax on the first $10,000 of income, but a 20 percent tax on earnings between $10,000 and $20,000 and a 30 percent tax on income between $20,000 and $30,000. Any income above $30,000 is taxed at 40 percent. If your income is $50,000, how much will you pay in taxes? Determine your marginal and average tax rates. Is this a progressive tax? LO12.3
3. For tax purposes, "gross income" is all the money a person receives in a given year from any source. But income taxes are

levied on "taxable income" rather than gross income. The difference between the two is the result of many exemptions and deductions. To see how they work, suppose you made $50,000 last year in wages and $10,000 from investments, and were given $5,000 as a gift by your grandmother. Also assume that you are a single parent with one small child living with you. LO12.3
   a. What is your gross income?
   b. Gifts of up to $14,000 per year from any person are not counted as taxable income. Also, the "personal exemption" allows you to reduce your taxable income by $4,050 for each member of your household. Given these exemptions, what is your taxable income?
   c. Next, assume you paid $700 in interest on your student loans last year, put $2,000 into a health savings account

(HSA), and deposited $4,000 into an individual retirement account (IRA). These expenditures are all *tax exempt,* meaning that any money spent on them reduces taxable income dollar-for-dollar. Knowing that fact, what is now your taxable income?

d. Next, you can either take the so-called standard deduction or apply for itemized deductions (which involve a lot of tedious paperwork). You opt for the standard deduction that allows you as head of your household to exempt another $8,500 from your taxable income. Taking that into account, what is your taxable income?

e. Apply the tax rates shown in Table 12.1 to your taxable income. How much federal tax will you owe? What is the marginal tax rate that applies to your last dollar of taxable income?

f. As the parent of a dependent child, you qualify for the government's $1,000-per-child "tax credit." Like all tax credits, this $1,000 credit "pays" for $1,000 of whatever amount of tax you owe. Given this credit, how much money will you actually have to pay in taxes? Using that actual amount, what is your average tax rate relative to your taxable income? What about your average tax rate relative to your gross income?

International Trade and Exchange Rates

Learning Objectives

LO13.1 List and discuss several key facts about U.S. international trade.

LO13.2 Define comparative advantage and demonstrate how specialization and trade add to a nation's output.

LO13.3 Explain how exchange rates are determined in currency markets.

LO13.4 Analyze the validity of the most frequently presented arguments for protectionism.

LO13.5 Discuss the role played by free-trade zones and the World Trade Organization (WTO) in promoting international trade.

Backpackers in the wilderness like to think they are "leaving the world behind," but, like Atlas, they carry the world on their shoulders. Much of their equipment is imported—knives from Switzerland, rain gear from South Korea, cameras from Japan, aluminum pots from England, sleeping bags from China, and compasses from Finland. Moreover, they may have driven to the trailheads in Japanese-made Toyotas or German-made BMWs, sipping coffee from Brazil or snacking on bananas from Honduras.

International trade and the global economy affect all of us daily, whether we are hiking in the wilderness, driving our cars, listening to music, or working at our jobs. We cannot "leave the world behind." We are enmeshed in a global web of economic relationships—trading of goods and services, multinational corporations, cooperative ventures among the world's firms, and ties among the world's financial markets.

©Tatiana Belova/Shutterstock

Trade Facts

The following facts provide an "executive summary" of U.S. international trade:

- A *trade deficit* occurs when imports exceed exports. The United States has a trade deficit in goods. In 2017, U.S. imports of goods exceeded U.S. exports of goods by $835 billion.
- A *trade surplus* occurs when exports exceed imports. The United States has a trade surplus in services (such as air transportation services and financial services). In 2017, U.S. exports of services exceeded U.S. imports of services by $263 billion.
- Principal U.S. exports include chemicals, agricultural products, consumer durables, semiconductors, and aircraft; principal imports include petroleum, automobiles, metals, household appliances, and computers.
- Canada is the United States' most important trading partner quantitatively. In 2017, 15 percent of U.S. exported goods were sold to Canadians, who in turn provided 11 percent of the U.S. imports of goods.
- The United States has a sizable trade deficit with China. In 2017, U.S. imports of goods from China exceeded exports of goods to China by $375 billion.
- Starting in 2012, the shale oil boom in the Plains States greatly reduced U.S. dependence on foreign oil, as can be seen in the statistics that keep track of trade between the United States and the members of OPEC. In 2011, before the boom, the U.S. imported $191.5 billion of goods (mainly oil) from OPEC, while exporting $64.8 billion of goods to those countries. By 2015, U.S. imports had fallen to just $66.2 billion, while exports had risen to $72.8 billion. United States' oil usage had fallen so much that the United States ran its first-ever trade surplus with OPEC in 2015. It was not to last, however, as U.S. exports to OPEC fell and imports rose, so that in 2017 the United States had a trade deficit of $13 billion with OPEC.
- The United States leads the world in the combined volume of exports and imports, as measured in dollars. China, the United States, Germany, Japan, and the Netherlands were the top five exporters by dollar in 2016. The United States provides about 9.1 percent of the world's exports. (See Global Snapshot 13.1.)

 GLOBAL SNAPSHOT 13.1

Shares of World Exports, Selected Nations

China has the largest share of world exports, followed by the United States and Germany. The eight largest export nations account for about 48 percent of world exports.

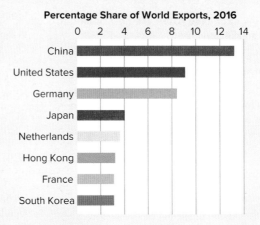

Source: World Trade Statistical Review 2017. WTO Publications.

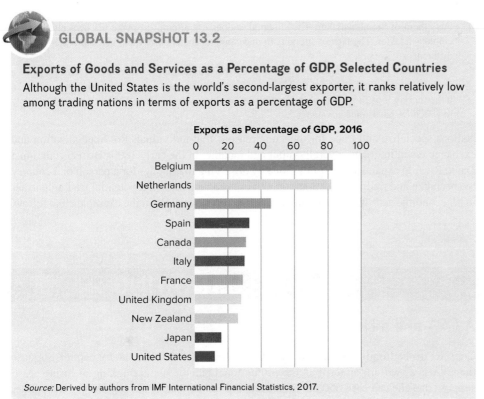

GLOBAL SNAPSHOT 13.2

Exports of Goods and Services as a Percentage of GDP, Selected Countries

Although the United States is the world's second-largest exporter, it ranks relatively low among trading nations in terms of exports as a percentage of GDP.

Exports as Percentage of GDP, 2016

Source: Derived by authors from IMF International Financial Statistics, 2017.

- Exports of goods and services make up about 12 percent of total U.S. output. That percentage is much lower than the percentage in many other nations, including Canada, Italy, France, and the United Kingdom (see Global Snapshot 13.2).
- China has become a major international trader, with an estimated $2.3 trillion of exports in 2017. Other Asian economies—including South Korea, Taiwan, and Singapore—are also active in international trade. Their combined exports exceed those of France, Britain, or Italy.
- International trade and finance are often at the center of economic policy.

With this information in mind, let's look more closely at the economics of international trade.

Comparative Advantage and Specialization

Given the presence of an *open economy*—one that includes the international sector—the United States produces more of certain goods (exports) and fewer of other goods (imports) than it would otherwise. Thus, U.S. labor and other resources are shifted toward export industries and away from import industries. For example, the United States uses more resources to make computers and to grow wheat and less to make sporting goods and clothing. So we ask: "Do shifts of resources like these make economic sense? Do they enhance U.S. total output and thus the U.S. standard of living?"

The answers are affirmative. Specialization and international trade increase the productivity of a nation's resources and allow for greater total output than would otherwise be possible. This idea is not new. Adam Smith had this to say in 1776:

> It is the maxim of every prudent master of a family, never to attempt to make at home what it will cost him more to make than to buy. The taylor does not attempt to make his own shoes, but

buys them of the shoemaker. The shoemaker does not attempt to make his own clothes, but employs a taylor. The farmer attempts to make neither the one nor the other, but employs those different artificers. . . .

What is prudence in the conduct of every private family, can scarce be folly in that of a great kingdom. If a foreign country can supply us with a commodity cheaper than we can make it, better buy it of them with some part of the produce of our own industry, employed in a way in which we have some advantage.[1]

Nations specialize and trade for the same reasons that individuals do: Specialization and exchange result in greater overall output and income. In the early 1800s British economist David Ricardo expanded on Smith's idea by observing that it pays for a person or a country to specialize and trade even if a nation is more productive than a potential trading partner in *all* economic activities. We demonstrate Ricardo's principle in the examples that follow.

ILLUSTRATING THE IDEA

A CPA and a House Painter

Consider the certified public accountant (CPA) who is also a skilled house painter. Suppose the CPA is a swifter painter than the professional painter she is thinking of hiring. Also suppose that she can earn $50 per hour as an accountant but would have to pay the painter $15 per hour. And say it would take the accountant 30 hours to paint her house but the painter would take 40 hours.

Should the CPA take time from her accounting to paint her own house, or should she hire the painter? The CPA's opportunity cost of painting her house is $1,500 (= 30 hours of sacrificed CPA time × $50 per CPA hour). The cost of hiring the painter is only $600 (= 40 hours of painting × $15 per hour of painting). Although the CPA is better at both accounting and painting, she will get her house painted at lower cost by specializing in accounting and using some of her earnings from accounting to hire a house painter.

Similarly, the house painter can reduce his cost of obtaining accounting services by specializing in painting and using some of his income to hire the CPA to prepare his income tax forms. Suppose it would take the painter 10 hours to prepare his tax return, while the CPA could handle the task in 2 hours. The house painter would sacrifice $150 of income (= 10 hours of painting time × $15 per hour) to do something he could hire the CPA to do for $100 (= 2 hours of CPA time × $50 per CPA hour). By specializing in painting and hiring the CPA to prepare his tax return, the painter lowers the cost of getting his tax return prepared.

We will see that what is true for our CPA and house painter is also true for nations. Specializing on the basis of comparative advantage enables nations to reduce the cost of obtaining the goods and services they desire.

QUESTION: How might the specialization described above change once the CPA retires? What generalization about the permanency of a particular pattern of specialization can you draw from your answer?

---

[1]Adam Smith, *The Wealth of Nations* (New York: Modern Library, 1937), p. 424. (Originally published in 1776.)

Comparative Advantage: Production Possibilities Analysis

Our simple example shows that the reason specialization is economically desirable is that it results in more efficient production. Now let's put specialization into the context of trading nations and use the familiar concept of the production possibilities table for our analysis.

Assumptions and Comparative Costs Suppose the production possibilities for one product in Mexico and for one product in the United States are as shown in Tables 13.1 and 13.2. Both tables reflect constant costs. Each country must give up a constant amount of one product to secure a certain increment of the other product. (This assumption simplifies our discussion without impairing the validity of our conclusions. Later we will allow for increasing costs.)

Also for simplicity, suppose that the labor forces in the United States and Mexico are of equal size. The data then tell us that the United States has an *absolute advantage* in producing both products. If the United States and Mexico use their entire (equal-size) labor forces to produce avocados, the United States can produce 90 tons compared with Mexico's 60 tons. Similarly, the United States can produce 30 tons of soybeans compared to Mexico's 15 tons. There are greater production possibilities in the United States, using the same number of workers as in Mexico. So labor productivity (output per worker) in the United States exceeds that in Mexico in producing both products.

Although the United States has an absolute advantage in producing both goods, gains from specialization and trade are possible. Specialization and trade are mutually beneficial or "profitable" to the two nations if the *comparative* costs of producing the two products within the two nations differ. What are the comparative costs of avocados and soybeans in Mexico? By comparing production alternatives A and B in Table 13.1, we see that Mexico must sacrifice 5 tons of soybeans ($= 15 - 10$) to produce 20 tons of avocados ($= 20 - 0$). Or, more simply, in Mexico it costs 1 ton of soybeans (S) to produce 4 tons of avocados (A); that is, $1S \equiv 4A$. (The "$\equiv$" sign simply means "equivalent to.") Because we assumed constant costs, this domestic opportunity cost will not change as Mexico expands the output of either product. This is evident from production possibilities B and C, where we see that 4 more tons of avocados ($= 24 - 20$) cost 1 unit of soybeans ($= 10 - 9$).

TABLE 13.1 **Mexico's Production Possibilities Table (in Tons)**

Product	Production Alternatives				
	A	B	C	D	E
Avocados	0	20	24	40	60
Soybeans	15	10	9	5	0

TABLE 13.2 **U.S. Production Possibilities Table (in Tons)**

Product	Production Alternatives				
	R	S	T	U	V
Avocados	0	30	33	60	90
Soybeans	30	20	19	10	0

Similarly, in Table 13.2, comparing U.S. production alternatives R and S reveals that in the United States it costs 10 tons of soybeans (= 30 − 20) to obtain 30 tons of avocados (= 30 − 0). That is, the domestic (internal) comparative-cost ratio for the two products in the United States is 1S ≡ 3A. Comparing production alternatives S and T reinforces this conclusion: an extra 3 tons of avocados (= 33 − 30) comes at the sacrifice of 1 ton of soybeans (= 20 − 19).

The comparative costs of the two products within the two nations are obviously different. Economists say that the United States has a **comparative advantage** over Mexico in soybeans. The United States must forgo only 3 tons of avocados to get 1 ton of soybeans, but Mexico must forgo 4 tons of avocados to get 1 ton of soybeans. In terms of opportunity costs, soybeans are relatively cheaper in the United States. *A nation has a comparative advantage in some product when it can produce that product at a lower opportunity cost than can a potential trading partner.* Mexico, in contrast, has a comparative advantage in avocados. While 1 ton of avocados costs $\frac{1}{3}$ ton of soybeans in the United States, it costs only $\frac{1}{4}$ ton of soybeans in Mexico. Comparatively speaking, avocados are cheaper in Mexico. We summarize the situation in Table 13.3. Be sure to give it a close look.

Because of these differences in comparative costs, Mexico should produce avocados and the United States should produce soybeans. If both nations specialize according to their comparative advantages, each can achieve a larger total output with the same total input of resources. Together they will be using their scarce resources more efficiently.

Terms of Trade The United States can shift production between soybeans and avocados at the rate of 1S for 3A. Thus, the United States would specialize in soybeans only if it could obtain *more than* 3 tons of avocados for 1 ton of soybeans by trading with Mexico. Similarly, Mexico can shift production at the rate of 4A for 1S. So it would be advantageous to Mexico to specialize in avocados if it could get 1 ton of soybeans for *less than* 4 tons of avocados.

Suppose that through negotiation the two nations agree on an exchange rate of 1 ton of soybeans for $3\frac{1}{2}$ tons of avocados. These **terms of trade** are mutually beneficial to both countries, since each can "do better" through such trade than through domestic production alone. The United States can get $3\frac{1}{2}$ tons of avocados by sending 1 ton of soybeans to Mexico, while it can get only 3 tons of avocados by shifting its own resources domestically from soybeans to avocados. Mexico can obtain 1 ton of soybeans at a lower cost of $3\frac{1}{2}$ tons of avocados through trade with the United States, compared to the cost of 4 tons if Mexico produced the 1 ton of soybeans itself.

comparative advantage A situation in which a person or country can produce a specific product at a lower opportunity cost than some other person or country; the basis for specialization and trade.

terms of trade The rate at which units of one product can be exchanged for units of another product; the price of a good or service; the amount of one good or service that must be given up to obtain 1-unit of another good or service.

TABLE 13.3 Comparative-Advantage Example: A Summary

Soybeans	Avocados
Mexico: Must give up 4 tons of avocados to get 1 ton of soybeans	**Mexico:** Must give up $\frac{1}{4}$ ton of soybeans to get 1 ton of avocados
United States: Must give up 3 tons of avocados to get 1 ton of soybeans	**United States:** Must give up $\frac{1}{3}$ ton of soybeans to get 1 ton of avocados
Comparative advantage: United States	**Comparative advantage:** Mexico

TABLE 13.4 Specialization According to Comparative Advantage and the Gains from Trade (in Tons)

Country	(1) Outputs before Specialization	(2) Outputs after Specialization	(3) Amounts Traded	(4) Outputs Available after Trade	(5) Gains from Specialization and Trade (4) − (1)
Mexico	24 avocados	60 avocados	−35 avocados	25 avocados	1 avocados
	9 soybeans	0 soybeans	+10 soybeans	10 soybeans	1 soybeans
United States	33 avocados	0 avocados	+35 avocados	35 avocados	2 avocados
	19 soybeans	30 soybeans	−10 soybeans	20 soybeans	1 soybeans

Gains from Specialization and Trade Let's pinpoint the gains in total output from specialization and trade. Suppose that, before specialization and trade, production alternative C in Table 13.1 and alternative T in Table 13.2 were the optimal product mixes for the two countries. That is, Mexico preferred 24 tons of avocados and 9 tons of soybeans (Table 13.1) and the United States preferred 33 tons of avocados and 19 tons of soybeans (Table 13.2) to all other available domestic alternatives. These outputs are shown in column 1 in Table 13.4.

Now assume that both nations specialize according to their comparative advantages, with Mexico producing 60 tons of avocados and no soybeans (alternative E) and the United States producing no avocados and 30 tons of soybeans (alternative R). These outputs are shown in column 2 in Table 13.4. Using our $1S \equiv 3\frac{1}{2}$ A terms of trade, assume that Mexico exchanges 35 tons of avocados for 10 tons of U.S. soybeans. Column 3 in Table 13.4 shows the quantities exchanged in this trade, with a minus sign indicating exports and a plus sign indicating imports. As shown in column 4, after the trade Mexico has 25 tons of avocados and 10 tons of soybeans, while the United States has 35 tons of avocados and 20 tons of soybeans. Compared with their optimal product mixes before specialization and trade (column 1), *both* nations now enjoy more avocados and more soybeans! Specifically, Mexico has gained 1 ton of avocados and 1 ton of soybeans. The United States has gained 2 tons of avocados and 1 ton of soybeans. These gains are shown in column 5.

Specialization based on comparative advantage improves global resource allocation. The same total inputs of world resources and technology result in a larger global output. If Mexico and the United States allocate all their resources to avocados and soybeans, respectively, the same total inputs of resources can produce more output between them, indicating that resources are being allocated more efficiently.

Through specialization and international trade a nation can overcome the production constraints imposed by its domestic production possibilities table and curve. Our discussion of Tables 13.1, 13.2, and 13.4 has shown just how this is done. The domestic production possibilities data (Tables 13.1 and 13.2) of the two countries have not changed, meaning that neither nation's production possibilities curve has shifted. But specialization and trade mean that citizens of both countries can enjoy increased consumption (column 5 of Table 13.4).

Trade with Increasing Costs

To explain the basic principles underlying international trade, we simplified our analysis in several ways. For example, we limited discussion to two products and two nations. But multiproduct and multinational analysis yields the same conclusions. We also assumed constant opportunity costs, which is a more substantive simplification. Let's consider the effect of allowing increasing opportunity costs to enter the picture.

As before, suppose that comparative advantage indicates that the United States should specialize in soybeans and Mexico in avocados. But now, as the United States begins to expand soybean production, its cost of soybeans will rise. It will eventually have to sacrifice more than 3 tons of avocados to get 1 additional ton of soybeans. Resources are no longer perfectly substitutable between alternative uses, as our constant-cost assumption implied. Resources less and less suitable to soybean production must be allocated to the U.S. soybean industry in expanding soybean output, and that means increasing costs—the sacrifice of larger and larger amounts of avocados for each additional ton of soybeans.

Similarly, Mexico will find that its cost of producing an additional ton of avocados will rise beyond 4 tons of soybeans as it produces more avocados. Resources transferred from soybean to avocado production will eventually be less suitable to avocado production.

At some point the differing domestic cost ratios that underlie comparative advantage will disappear, and further specialization will become uneconomical. And most importantly, this point of equal cost ratios may be reached while the United States is still producing some avocados along with its soybeans and Mexico is producing some soybeans along with its avocados. The primary effect of increasing opportunity costs is less-than-complete specialization. For this reason we often find domestically produced products competing directly against identical or similar imported products within a particular economy.

PHOTO OP   The Fruits of Free Trade*

Because of specialization and exchange, fruits and vegetables from all over the world appear in our grocery stores. For example, apples may be from New Zealand; bananas, from Ecuador; coconuts, from the Philippines; pineapples, from Costa Rica; avocados, from Mexico; plums, from Chile; and potatoes, from Peru.

©AGE Fotostock/Pixtal   ©Pixtal

*This example is from "The Fruits of Free Trade," 2002 Annual Report, by W. Michael Cox and Richard Alm, p. 3, Federal Reserve Bank of Dallas.

The Foreign Exchange Market

Buyers and sellers (whether individuals, firms, or nations) use money to buy products or to pay for the use of resources. Within the domestic economy, prices are stated in terms of the domestic currency and buyers use that currency to purchase domestic products. In Mexico, for example, buyers have pesos, and that is what sellers want.

International markets are different. Sellers set their prices in terms of their domestic currencies, but buyers often possess entirely different currencies. How many dollars does it take to buy a truckload of Mexican avocados selling for 3,000 pesos, a German automobile selling for 50,000 euros, or a Japanese motorcycle priced at 300,000 yen? Producers in Mexico, Germany, and Japan want payment in pesos, euros, and yen, respectively, so that they can pay their wages, rent, interest, dividends, and taxes.

A **foreign exchange market,** a market in which various national currencies are exchanged for one another, serves this need. The equilibrium prices in such currency markets are called **exchange rates.** An exchange rate is the rate at which the currency of one nation can be exchanged for the currency of another nation. (See Global Snapshot 13.3.)

The market price or exchange rate of a nation's currency is an unusual price; it links all domestic prices with all foreign prices. Exchange rates enable consumers in one country to translate prices of foreign goods into units of their own currency: They need only multiply the foreign product price by the exchange rate. If the U.S. dollar–yen exchange rate is $.01 (1 cent) per yen, a Sony television set priced at ¥20,000 will cost $200 (= 20,000 × $.01) in the United States. If the exchange rate rises to $.02 (2 cents) per yen, the television will cost $400 (= 20,000 × $.02) in the United States. Similarly, all other Japanese products would double in price to U.S. buyers in response to the altered exchange rate.

foreign exchange market A market in which the money (currency) of one nation can be used to purchase (can be exchanged for) the money of another nation.

exchange rate The rate of exchange of one nation's currency for another nation's currency.

GLOBAL SNAPSHOT 13.3

Exchange Rates: Foreign Currency per U.S. Dollar

The amount of foreign currency that a dollar will buy varies greatly from nation to nation and fluctuates in response to supply and demand changes in the foreign exchange market. The amounts shown here are for March 2018.

$1 Will Buy

64.8 Indian rupees
.72 British pounds
1.27 Canadian dollars
18.6 Mexican pesos
.94 Swiss francs
.81 European euros
108 Japanese yen
1,076 South Korean won
8.10 Swedish kronor
10 Venezuelan bolivares fuertes

Exchange Rates

Let's examine the rate, or price, at which U.S. dollars might be exchanged for British pounds. In Figure 13.1 we show the dollar price of 1 pound on the vertical axis and the quantity of pounds on the horizontal axis. The demand for pounds is D_1 and the supply of pounds is S_1 in this market for British pounds.

The *demand-for-pounds curve* is downward-sloping because all British goods and services will be cheaper to the United States if pounds become less expensive to the United States. That is, at lower dollar prices for pounds, the United States can obtain more pounds for each dollar and therefore buy more British goods and services per dollar. To buy those cheaper British goods, U.S. consumers will increase the quantity of pounds they demand.

The *supply-of-pounds curve* is upsloping because the British will purchase more U.S. goods when the dollar price of pounds rises (that is, as the pound price of dollars falls).

FIGURE 13.1 The market for foreign currency (pounds) The intersection of the demand-for-pounds curve D_1 and the supply-of-pounds curve S_1 determines the equilibrium dollar price of pounds, here, $2. That means that the exchange rate is $2 = £1. Not shown, an increase in demand for pounds or a decrease in the supply of pounds will increase the dollar price of pounds and thus cause the pound to appreciate. Also not shown, a decrease in demand for pounds or an increase in the supply of pounds will reduce the dollar price of pounds, meaning that the pound has depreciated.

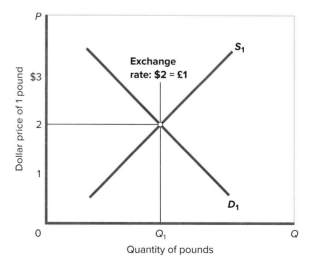

When the British buy more U.S. goods, they supply a greater quantity of pounds to the foreign exchange market. In other words, they must exchange pounds for dollars to purchase U.S. goods. So, when the dollar price of pounds rises, the quantity of pounds supplied goes up.

The intersection of the supply curve and the demand curve will determine the dollar price of pounds. In Figure 13.1, that price (exchange rate) is $2 for £1. At this exchange rate, the quantity of pounds supplied and demanded are equal; neither a shortage nor a surplus of pounds occurs.

Depreciation and Appreciation

An exchange rate determined by market forces can, and often does, change daily like stock and bond prices. These price changes result from changes in the supply of, or demand for, a particular currency. When the dollar price of pounds *rises,* for example, from $2 = £1 to $3 = £1, the dollar has *depreciated* relative to the pound (and the pound has appreciated relative to the dollar). A **depreciation** of a currency means that more units of it (dollars) are needed to buy a single unit of some other currency (a pound).

When the dollar price of pounds *falls,* for example, from $2 = £1 to $1 = £1, the dollar has *appreciated* relative to the pound. An **appreciation** of a currency means that it takes fewer units of it (dollars) to buy a single unit of some other currency (a pound). For example, the dollar price of pounds might decline from $2 to $1. Each British product becomes less expensive in terms of dollars, so people in the United States purchase more British goods. In general, U.S. imports from the United Kingdom rise. Meanwhile, because it takes more pounds to get a dollar, U.S. exports to the United Kingdom fall.

The central point is this: When the dollar depreciates (dollar price of foreign currencies rises), U.S. exports rise and U.S. imports fall; when the dollar appreciates (dollar price of foreign currencies falls), U.S. exports fall and U.S. imports rise.

In our U.S.-Britain illustrations, depreciation of the dollar means an appreciation of the pound, and vice versa. When the dollar price of a pound jumps from $2 = £1 to $3 = £1, the pound has appreciated relative to the dollar because it takes fewer pounds to buy $1. At $2 = £1, it took £1/2 to buy $1; at $3 = £1, it takes only £1/3 to buy $1. Conversely, when the dollar appreciates relative to the pound, the pound depreciates relative to the dollar. More pounds are needed to buy a U.S. dollar.

In general, the relevant terminology and relationships between the U.S. dollar and another currency are as follows:

- Dollar price of foreign currency increases ≡ dollar depreciates relative to the foreign currency ≡ foreign currency price of dollar decreases ≡ foreign currency appreciates relative to the dollar.
- Dollar price of foreign currency decreases ≡ dollar appreciates relative to the foreign currency ≡ foreign currency price of dollar increases ≡ foreign currency depreciates relative to the dollar.

Determinants of Exchange Rates

What factors would cause a nation's currency to appreciate or depreciate in the market for foreign exchange? Here are three generalizations (other things equal):

- If the demand for a nation's currency increases, that currency will appreciate; if the demand declines, that currency will depreciate.
- If the supply of a nation's currency increases, that currency will depreciate; if the supply decreases, that currency will appreciate.
- If a nation's currency appreciates, some foreign currency depreciates relative to it.

depreciation (of a currency) A decrease in the value of the dollar relative to another currency, so a dollar buys a smaller amount of the foreign currency and therefore of foreign goods.

appreciation (of a currency) An increase in the value of the dollar relative to the currency of another nation, so a dollar buys a larger amount of the foreign currency and thus of foreign goods.

With these generalizations in mind, let's examine the determinants of exchange rates—the factors that shift the demand or supply curve for a certain currency. As we do so, keep in mind that the other-things-equal assumption is always in force. Also note that we are discussing factors *that change the exchange rate,* not things that change *as a result of* a change in the exchange rate.

Tastes Any change in consumer tastes or preferences for the products of a foreign country may alter the demand for that nation's currency and change its exchange rate. If technological advances in U.S. MP3 players make them more attractive to British consumers and businesses, then the British will supply more pounds in the exchange market in order to purchase more U.S. MP3 players. The supply-of-pounds curve will shift to the right, causing the pound to depreciate and the dollar to appreciate.

In contrast, the U.S. demand-for-pounds curve will shift to the right if British woolen apparel becomes more fashionable in the United States. So the pound will appreciate and the dollar will depreciate.

Relative Income A nation's currency is likely to depreciate if its growth of national income is more rapid than that of other countries. Here's why: A country's imports vary directly with its income level. As total income rises in the United States, people there buy both more domestic goods and more foreign goods. If the U.S. economy is expanding rapidly and the British economy is stagnant, U.S. imports of British goods, and therefore U.S. demands for pounds, will increase. The dollar price of pounds will rise, so the dollar will depreciate.

Relative Inflation Rate Changes Other things equal, changes in the relative rates of inflation of two nations change their relative price levels and alter the exchange rate between their currencies. The currency of the nation with the higher inflation rate—the more rapidly rising price level—tends to depreciate. Suppose, for example, that inflation is zero percent in Great Britain and 5 percent in the United States so that prices, on average, are rising by 5 percent per year in the United States while, on average, remaining unchanged in Great Britain. U.S. consumers will seek out more of the now relatively lower-priced British goods, increasing the demand for pounds. British consumers will purchase less of the now relatively higher-priced U.S. goods, reducing the supply of pounds. This combination of increased demand for pounds and reduced supply of pounds will cause the pound to appreciate and the dollar to depreciate.

Relative Interest Rates Changes in relative interest rates between two countries may alter their exchange rate. Suppose that real interest rates rise in the United States but stay constant in Great Britain. British citizens will then find the United States a more attractive place in which to loan money directly or loan money indirectly by buying bonds. To make these loans, they will have to supply pounds in the foreign exchange market to obtain dollars. The increase in the supply of pounds results in depreciation of the pound and appreciation of the dollar.

Changes in Relative Expected Returns on Stocks, Real Estate, and Production Facilities
International investing extends beyond buying foreign bonds. It includes international investments in stocks and real estate as well as foreign purchases of factories and production facilities. Other things equal, the extent of this foreign investment depends on relative expected returns. To make the investments, investors in one country must sell their currencies to purchase the foreign currencies needed for the foreign investments.

For instance, suppose that investing in England suddenly becomes more popular due to a more positive outlook regarding expected returns on stocks, real estate, and production facilities there. U.S. investors therefore will sell U.S. assets to buy more assets in England. The U.S. assets will be sold for dollars, which will then be brought to the foreign exchange market and exchanged for pounds, which will in turn be used to purchase British assets. The increased demand for pounds in the foreign exchange market will cause the pound to appreciate and the dollar to depreciate.

Speculation Currency speculators are people who buy and sell currencies with an eye toward reselling or repurchasing them at a profit. Suppose that, as a group, speculators anticipate that the pound will appreciate and the dollar will depreciate. Speculators holding dollars will therefore try to convert them into pounds. This effort will increase the demand for pounds and cause the dollar price of pounds to rise (that is, cause the dollar to depreciate). A self-fulfilling prophecy occurs: The pound appreciates and the dollar depreciates because speculators act on the belief that these changes will in fact take place. In this way, speculation can cause changes in exchange rates.

Government and Trade

If people and nations benefit from specialization and international exchange, why do governments sometimes try to restrict the free flow of imports or encourage exports? What kinds of world trade barriers can governments erect, and why would they do so?

Trade Protections and Subsidies

Trade interventions by government take several forms. Excise taxes on imported goods are called **tariffs**. A *protective tariff* is implemented to shield domestic producers from foreign competition. These tariffs impede free trade by increasing the prices of imported goods and therefore shifting sales toward domestic producers. Although protective tariffs are usually not high enough to stop the importation of foreign goods, they put foreign producers at a competitive disadvantage. A tariff on imported shoes, for example, would make domestically produced shoes more attractive to consumers.

tariff A tax imposed by a nation on an imported good.

Import quotas are limits on the quantities or total value of specific items that may be imported in some period. Once a quota is "filled," further imports of that product are choked off. Import quotas are more effective than tariffs in impeding international trade. With a tariff, a product can go on being imported in large quantities; with an import quota, however, all imports are prohibited once the quota is filled.

import quota A limit imposed by a nation on the quantity (or total value) of a good that may be imported during some period of time.

Nontariff barriers (NTBs) include onerous licensing requirements, unreasonable standards pertaining to product quality, or excessive bureaucratic hurdles and delays in customs procedures. Some nations require that importers of foreign goods obtain licenses. By restricting the issuance of licenses, imports can be restricted. Although many nations carefully inspect imported agricultural products to prevent the introduction of potentially harmful insects, some countries use lengthy inspections to impede imports.

nontariff barriers All barriers other than protective tariffs that nations erect to impede international trade, including import quotas, licensing requirements, unreasonable product-quality standards, unnecessary bureaucratic detail in customs procedures, and so on.

A **voluntary export restriction (VER)** is a trade barrier by which foreign firms "voluntarily" limit the amount of their exports to a particular country. Exporters agree to a VER, which has the effect of an import quota, to avoid more stringent trade barriers. In the late 1990s, for example, Canadian producers of softwood lumber (fir, spruce, cedar, pine) agreed to a VER on exports to the United States under the threat of a permanently higher U.S. tariff.

voluntary export restrictions Voluntary limitations by countries or firms of their exports to a particular foreign nation to avoid enactment of formal trade barriers by that nation.

export subsidies Government payments to domestic producers to enable them to reduce the price of a good or service to foreign buyers.

Export subsidies consist of government payments to domestic producers of export goods. By reducing production costs, the subsidies enable producers to charge lower prices and thus to sell more exports in world markets. Example: The United States and other nations have subsidized domestic farmers to boost the domestic food supply. Such subsidies have lowered the market price of agricultural commodities and have artificially lowered their export prices.

Economic Impact of Tariffs

Tariffs, quotas, and other trade restrictions have a series of economic effects predicted by supply and demand analysis and observed in reality. These effects vary somewhat by type of trade protection. So to keep things simple, we will focus on the effects of tariffs.

Direct Effects
Because tariffs raise the price of goods imported to the United States, U.S. consumption of those goods declines. Higher prices reduce quantity demanded, as indicated by the law of demand. A tariff prompts consumers to buy fewer of the imported goods and reallocate a portion of their expenditures to less desired substitute products. U.S. consumers are clearly injured by the tariff.

U.S. producers—who are not subject to the tariff—receive the higher price (pretariff foreign price + tariff) on the imported product. Because this new price is higher than before, the domestic producers respond by producing more. Higher prices increase quantity supplied, as indicated by the law of supply. So domestic producers increase their output. They therefore enjoy both a higher price and expanded sales; this explains why domestic producers lobby for protective tariffs. But from a social point of view, the greater domestic production means the tariff allows domestic producers to bid resources away from other, more efficient, U.S. industries.

Foreign producers are hurt by tariffs. Although the sales price of the imported good is higher, that higher amount accrues to the U.S. government as tariff revenues, not to foreign producers. The after-tariff price, or the per-unit revenue to foreign producers, remains as before, but the volume of U.S. imports (foreign exports) falls.

Government gains revenue from tariffs. This revenue is a transfer of income from consumers to government and does not represent any net change in the nation's economic well-being. The result is that government gains a portion of what consumers lose by paying more for imported goods.

Indirect Effects
Tariffs have a subtle effect beyond those just mentioned. They also hurt domestic firms that use the protected goods as inputs in their production process. For example, a tariff on imported steel boosts the price of steel girders, thus hurting firms that build bridges and office towers. Also, tariffs reduce competition in the protected industries. With less competition from foreign producers, domestic firms may be slow to design and implement cost-saving production methods and introduce new products.

Because foreigners sell fewer imported goods in the United States, they earn fewer dollars and so must buy fewer U.S. exports. U.S. export industries must then cut production and release resources. These are highly efficient industries, as we know from their comparative advantage and their ability to sell goods in world markets.

Tariffs directly promote the expansion of inefficient industries that do not have a comparative advantage; they also indirectly cause the contraction of relatively efficient industries that do have a comparative advantage. Put bluntly, tariffs cause resources to be shifted in the wrong direction—and that is not surprising. We know that specialization and world trade lead to more efficient use of world resources and greater world output. But protective tariffs reduce world trade. Therefore, tariffs also reduce efficiency and the world's real output.

Net Costs of Tariffs

Tariffs impose costs on domestic consumers but provide gains to domestic producers and revenue to the federal government. The consumer costs of trade restrictions are calculated by determining the effect the restrictions have on consumer prices. Protection raises the price of a product in three ways: (1) The price of the imported product goes up; (2) the higher price of imports causes some consumers to shift their purchases to higher-priced domestically produced goods; and (3) the prices of domestically produced goods rise because import competition has declined.

Study after study finds that the costs to consumers substantially exceed the gains to producers and government. A sizable net cost or efficiency loss to society arises from trade protection. Furthermore, industries employ large amounts of economic resources to influence Congress to pass and retain protectionist laws. Because these efforts divert resources away from more socially desirable purposes, trade restrictions also impose that cost on society.

Conclusion: The gains that U.S. trade barriers produce for protected industries and their workers come at the expense of much greater losses for the entire economy. The result is economic inefficiency, reduced consumption, and lower standards of living.

So Why Government Trade Protections?

In view of the benefits of free trade, what accounts for the impulse to impede imports and boost exports through government policy? There are several reasons—some legitimate, most not.

Misunderstanding the Gains from Trade It is a commonly accepted myth that the greatest benefit to be derived from international trade is greater domestic sales and employment in the export sector. This suggests that exports are "good" because they increase domestic sales and employment, whereas imports are "bad" because they reduce domestic sales and deprive people of jobs at home. Actually, the true benefit created by international trade is the extra output obtained from abroad—the imports obtained for a lower opportunity cost than if they were produced at home.

One study suggests that the elimination of trade barriers since the Second World War has increased the income of the average U.S. household by at least $7,000 and perhaps by as much as $13,000. These income gains are recurring; they happen year after year.[2]

Political Considerations While a nation as a whole gains from trade, trade may harm particular domestic industries and particular groups of resource suppliers. In our earlier comparative-advantage example, specialization and trade adversely affected the U.S. avocado industry and the Mexican soybean industry. Understandably, those industries might seek to preserve their economic positions by persuading their respective governments to protect them from imports—perhaps through tariffs.

Those who directly benefit from import protection are relatively few in number but have much at stake. Thus, they have a strong incentive to pursue political activity to achieve their aims. Moreover, because the costs of import protection are buried in the price of goods and spread out over millions of citizens, the cost borne by each individual citizen is quite small. However, the full cost of tariffs and quotas typically greatly exceeds the benefits. It is not uncommon to find that it costs the public $250,000 or more a year to protect a domestic job that pays less than one-fourth that amount.

In the political arena, the voice of the relatively few producers and unions demanding *protectionism* is loud and constant, whereas the voice of those footing the bill is soft or

---

[2]Scott C. Bradford, Paul L.E. Grieco, and Gary C. Hufbauer, "The Payoff to America from Globalization," *The World Economy,* July 2006, pp. 893–916.

ILLUSTRATING THE IDEA

Buy American?

Will "buying American" make Americans better off? No, says Dallas Federal Reserve economist W. Michael Cox:

> A common myth is that it is better for Americans to spend their money at home than abroad. The best way to expose the fallacy of this argument is to take it to its logical extreme. If it is better for me to spend my money here than abroad, then it is even better yet to buy in Texas than in New York, better yet to buy in Dallas than in Houston . . . in my own neighborhood . . . within my own family . . . to consume only what I can produce. Alone and poor.*

*"The Fruits of Free Trade," 2002 Annual Report, by W. Michael Cox and Richard Alm, p. 16, Federal Reserve Bank of Dallas.

nonexistent. When political deal making is added in—"You back tariffs for the apparel industry in my state, and I'll back tariffs for the steel industry in your state"—the outcome can be a network of protective tariffs.

Three Arguments for Protection

Arguments for trade protection are many and diverse. Some—such as tariffs to protect "infant industries" or to create "military self-sufficiency"—have some legitimacy. But other arguments break down under close scrutiny. Three protectionist arguments, in particular, have persisted decade after decade in the United States.

Increased-Domestic-Employment Argument

Arguing for a tariff to "save U.S. jobs" becomes fashionable when the economy encounters a recession (such as the severe recession of 2007–2009 in the United States). In an economy that engages in international trade, exports involve spending on domestic output and imports reflect spending to obtain part of another nation's output. So, in this argument, reducing imports will divert spending on another nation's output to spending on domestic output. Thus domestic output and employment will rise. But this argument has several shortcomings.

While imports may eliminate some U.S. jobs, they create others. Imports may have eliminated the jobs of some U.S. steel and textile workers in recent years, but other workers have gained jobs unloading ships, flying imported aircraft, and selling imported electronic equipment. Import restrictions alter the composition of employment, but they may have little or no effect on the volume of employment.

The *fallacy of composition*—the false idea that what is true for the part is necessarily true for the whole—is also present in this rationale for tariffs. All nations cannot simultaneously succeed in restricting imports while maintaining their exports; what is true for one nation is not true for all nations. The exports of one nation must be the imports of another nation. To the extent that one country is able to expand its economy through an excess of exports over imports, the resulting excess of imports over exports worsens another economy's unemployment problem. It is no wonder that tariffs and import quotas meant to achieve domestic full employment are called "beggar my neighbor" policies: They achieve short-run domestic goals by making trading partners poorer.

Moreover, nations adversely affected by tariffs and quotas are likely to retaliate, causing a "trade-barrier war" that will choke off trade and make all nations worse off. The **Smoot-Hawley Tariff Act** of 1930 is a classic example. Although that act was meant to reduce imports and stimulate U.S. production, the high tariffs it authorized prompted adversely affected nations to retaliate with tariffs equally high. International trade fell, lowering the output and income of all nations. Economic historians generally agree that the Smoot-Hawley Tariff Act was a contributing cause of the Great Depression.

Finally, forcing an excess of exports over imports cannot succeed in raising domestic employment over the long run. It is through U.S. imports that foreign nations earn dollars for buying U.S. exports. In the long run a nation must import in order to export. The long-run impact of tariffs is not an increase in domestic employment but, at best, a reallocation of workers away from export industries and to protected domestic industries. This shift implies a less efficient allocation of resources.

> **Smoot-Hawley Tariff Act** Legislation passed in 1930 that established very high tariffs. Its objective was to reduce imports and stimulate the domestic economy, but it resulted only in retaliatory tariffs by other nations.

Cheap-Foreign-Labor Argument

The cheap-foreign-labor argument says that government must shield domestic firms and workers from the ruinous competition of countries where wages are low. If protection is not provided, cheap imports will flood U.S. markets and the prices of U.S. goods—along with the wages of U.S. workers—will be pulled down. That is, the domestic living standards in the United States will be reduced.

This argument can be rebutted at several levels. The logic of the argument suggests that it is not mutually beneficial for rich and poor persons to trade with one another. However, that is not the case. A relatively low-income mechanic may fix the Mercedes owned by a wealthy lawyer, and both may benefit from the transaction. And both U.S. consumers and Chinese workers gain when they "trade" a pair of athletic shoes priced at $30 as opposed to U.S. consumers being restricted to a similar shoe made in the United States for $60.

Also, recall that gains from trade are based on comparative advantage, not on absolute advantage. Again, think back to our U.S.-Mexico (soybean-avocado) example in which the United States had greater labor productivity than Mexico in producing both soybeans and avocados. Because of that greater productivity, wages and living standards will be higher for U.S. labor. Mexico's less productive labor will receive lower wages.

The cheap-foreign-labor argument suggests that, to maintain American living standards, the United States should not trade with low-wage Mexico. Suppose it forgoes trade with Mexico. Will wages and living standards rise in the United States as a result? Absolutely not! To obtain avocados, the United States will have to reallocate a portion of its labor from its relatively more-efficient soybean industry to its relatively less-efficient avocado industry. As a result, the average productivity of U.S. labor will fall, as will real wages and living standards for American workers. The labor forces of both countries will have diminished standards of living because without specialization and trade they will have less output available to them. Compare column 4 with column 1 in Table 13.4 to confirm this point.

Protection-against-Dumping Argument

The protection-against-dumping argument contends that tariffs are needed to protect domestic firms from "dumping" by foreign producers. **Dumping** is the sale of a product in a foreign country at prices either below cost or below the prices commonly charged at home.

Economists cite two plausible reasons for this behavior. First, with regard to below-cost dumping, firms in country A may dump goods at below cost into country B in an attempt

> **dumping** The sale of products in a foreign country at prices either below costs or below the prices charged at home.

to drive their competitors in country B out of business. If the firms in country A succeed in driving their competitors in country B out of business, they will enjoy monopoly power and monopoly prices and profits on the goods they subsequently sell in country B. Their hope is that the longer-term monopoly profits will more than offset the losses from below-cost sales that must take place while they are attempting to drive their competitors in country B out of business.

Second, dumping that involves selling abroad at a price that is below the price commonly charged in the home country (but which is still at or above production costs) may be a form of price discrimination, which is charging different prices to different customers. As an example, a foreign seller that has a monopoly in its home market may find that it can maximize its overall profit by charging a high price in its monopolized domestic market while charging a lower price in the United States, where it must compete with U.S. producers. Curiously, it may pursue this strategy even if it makes no profit at all from its sales in the United States, where it must charge the competitive price. So why bother selling in the United States? Because the increase in overall production that comes about by exporting to the United States may allow the firm to obtain the per unit cost savings often associated with large-scale production. These cost savings imply even higher profits in the monopolized domestic market.

Because dumping is an "unfair trade practice," most nations prohibit it. For example, where dumping is shown to injure U.S. firms, the federal government imposes tariffs called *antidumping duties* on the goods in question. But relatively few documented cases of dumping occur each year, and specific instances of unfair trade do not justify widespread, permanent tariffs. Moreover, antidumping duties can be abused. Often, what appears to be dumping is simply comparative advantage at work.

Trade Adjustment Assistance

A nation's comparative advantage in the production of a certain product is not forever fixed. As national economies evolve, the size and quality of their labor forces may change, the volume and composition of their capital stocks may shift, new technologies may develop, and even the quality of land and the quantity of natural resources may be altered. As these changes take place, the relative efficiency with which a nation can produce specific goods will also change. Also, new trade agreements can suddenly leave formerly protected industries highly vulnerable to major disruption or even collapse.

Shifts in patterns of comparative advantage and removal of trade protection can hurt specific groups of workers. For example, the erosion of the United States' once strong comparative advantage in steel has caused production plant shutdowns and layoffs in the U.S. steel industry. The textile and apparel industries in the United States face similar difficulties. Clearly, not everyone wins from free trade (or freer trade). Some workers lose.

Trade Adjustment Assistance Act
A U.S. law passed in 2002 that provides cash assistance, education and training benefits, health care subsidies, and wage subsidies (for persons age 50 or more) to workers displaced by imports or plant relocations abroad.

The **Trade Adjustment Assistance Act** of 2002 introduced some innovative policies to help those hurt by shifts in international trade patterns. The law provides cash assistance (beyond unemployment insurance) for up to 78 weeks for workers displaced by imports or plant relocations abroad. To obtain the assistance, workers must participate in job searches, training programs, or remedial education. There also are relocation allowances to help displaced workers move geographically to new jobs within the United States. Refundable tax credits for health insurance serve as payments to help workers maintain their insurance coverage during the retraining and job search period. Also, workers who are 50 years of age or older are eligible for "wage insurance," which replaces some of the difference in pay (if any) between their old and new jobs.

Many economists support trade adjustment assistance because it not only helps workers hurt by international trade but also helps create the political support necessary to reduce trade barriers and export subsidies.

But not all economists are keen on trade adjustment assistance. Loss of jobs from imports or plant relocations abroad is only a small fraction (about 4 percent in recent years) of total job loss in the economy each year. Many workers also lose their jobs because of changing patterns of demand, changing technology, bad management, and other dynamic aspects of a market economy. Some critics ask, "What makes losing one's job to international trade worthy of such special treatment, compared to losing one's job to, say, technological change or domestic competition?" There is no totally satisfying answer.

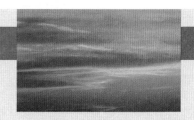

APPLYING THE ANALYSIS

Is Offshoring of Jobs Bad?

Not only are some U.S. jobs lost because of international trade, but some are lost because of globalization of resource markets. In recent years U.S. firms have found it increasingly profitable to outsource work abroad. Economists call this business activity **offshoring:** shifting work previously done by American workers to workers located in other nations. Offshoring is not a new practice but traditionally has involved components for U.S. manufacturing goods. For example, Boeing has long offshored the production of major airplane parts for its "American" aircraft.

Recent advances in computer and communications technology have enabled U.S. firms to offshore service jobs such as data entry, book composition, software coding, call-center operations, medical transcription, and claims processing to countries such as India. Where offshoring occurs, some of the value added in the production process occurs in foreign countries rather than the United States. So part of the income generated from the production of U.S. goods is paid to foreigners, not to American workers.

Offshoring is obviously costly to Americans who lose their jobs, but it is not generally bad for the economy. Offshoring simply reflects a growing international trade in services, or, more descriptively, "tasks." That trade has been made possible by recent trade agreements and new information and communication technologies. As with trade in goods, trade in services reflects comparative advantage and is beneficial to both trading parties. Moreover, the United States has a sizable trade surplus with other nations in services. The United States gains by specializing in high-valued services such as transportation services, accounting services, legal services, and advertising services, where it still has a comparative advantage. It then "trades" to obtain lower-valued services such as call-center and data entry work, for which comparative advantage has gone abroad.

Offshoring also increases the demand for complementary jobs in the United States. Jobs that are close substitutes for existing U.S. jobs are lost, but complementary jobs in the United States are expanded. For example, the lower price of offshore maintenance of aircraft and reservation centers reduces the price of airline tickets. That means more domestic and international flights by American carriers, which in turn means more jobs for U.S.-based pilots, flight attendants, baggage handlers, and check-in personnel. Moreover, offshoring encourages domestic investment and expansion of firms in the United States by reducing their costs and keeping them competitive worldwide. Some observers equate "offshoring jobs" to "importing competitiveness."

QUESTION: What has enabled white-collar labor services to become the world's newest export and import commodity even though such labor itself remains in place?

> **offshoring** The practice of shifting work previously done by American workers to workers located abroad.

Multilateral Trade Agreements and Free-Trade Zones

Being aware of the overall benefits of free trade, nations have worked to lower tariffs worldwide. Their pursuit of free trade has been aided by the growing power of free-trade interest groups: Exporters of goods and services, importers of foreign components used in "domestic" products, and domestic sellers of imported products all strongly support lower tariffs. And, in fact, tariffs have generally declined during the past half-century.

General Agreement on Tariffs and Trade

General Agreement on Tariffs and Trade (GATT) The international agreement reached in 1947 in which 23 nations agreed to give equal and nondiscriminatory treatment to one another, to reduce tariff rates by multinational negotiations, and to eliminate import quotas. It now includes most nations and has become the World Trade Organization.

Following the Second World War, the major nations of the world set upon a general course of liberalizing trade. In 1947 some 23 nations, including the United States, signed the **General Agreement on Tariffs and Trade (GATT).** GATT was based on the principles of equal, nondiscriminatory trade treatment for all member nations and the reduction of tariffs and quotas by multilateral negotiation. Basically, GATT provided a continuing forum for the negotiation of reduced trade barriers on a multilateral basis among nations.

Since 1947, member nations have completed eight "rounds" of GATT negotiations to reduce trade barriers. The *Uruguay Round* agreement of 1993 phased in trade liberalizations between 1995 and 2005.

World Trade Organization

World Trade Organization (WTO) An organization of 164 nations (as of 2017) that oversees the provisions of the current world trade agreement, resolves trade disputes stemming from it, and holds forums for further rounds of trade negotiations.

The Uruguay Round of 1993 established the **World Trade Organization (WTO)** as GATT's successor. In 2017, 164 nations belonged to the WTO, which oversees trade agreements and rules on disputes relating to them. It also provides forums for further rounds of trade negotiations. The ninth and latest round of negotiations—the **Doha Round**—was launched in Doha, Qatar, in late 2001. (The trade rounds occur over several years in several geographic venues but are named after the city or country of origination.) The negotiations are aimed at further reducing tariffs and quotas, as well as agricultural subsidies that distort trade.

Doha Round The latest, uncompleted (as of 2017) sequence of trade negotiations by members of the World Trade Organization; named after Doha, Qatar, where the set of negotiations began.

GATT and the WTO have been positive forces in the trend toward liberalized world trade. The trade rules agreed upon by the member nations provide a strong and necessary bulwark against the protectionism called for by the special-interest groups in the various nations. For that reason and because current WTO agreements lack strong labor standards and environmental protections, the WTO is controversial.

European Union

European Union (EU) An association of 28 European nations (as of 2017) that has eliminated tariffs and quotas among them, established common tariffs for imported goods from outside the member nations, eliminated barriers to the free movement of capital, and created other common economic policies.

Countries have also sought to reduce tariffs by creating regional *free-trade zones*—also called *trade blocs.* The most dramatic example is the **European Union (EU).** In 2007, the addition of Bulgaria and Romania, plus the 2013 addition of Croatia, expanded the EU to its present size of 28 nations, but the 2016 "Brexit" vote in the United Kingdom may soon reduce that number to 27.[3]

The EU has abolished tariffs and import quotas on nearly all products traded among the participating nations and established a common system of tariffs applicable to all goods received from nations outside the EU. It has also liberalized the movement of capital and labor within the EU and has created common policies in other economic

---

[3]The other 24 are France, Germany, Italy, Belgium, the Netherlands, Luxembourg, Denmark, Ireland, Greece, Spain, Portugal, Austria, Finland, Sweden, Poland, Hungary, Czech Republic, Slovakia, Lithuania, Latvia, Estonia, Slovenia, Malta, and Cyprus.

matters of joint concern, such as agriculture, transportation, and business practices. The EU is now a strong **trade bloc:** a group of countries having common identity, economic interests, and trade rules. Of the 28 EU countries, 19 used the **euro** as a common currency in 2017.

EU integration has achieved for Europe what the U.S. constitutional prohibition on tariffs by individual states has achieved for the United States: increased regional specialization, greater productivity, greater output, and faster economic growth. The free flow of goods and services has created large markets for EU industries. The resulting economies of large-scale production have enabled those industries to achieve much lower costs than they could have achieved in their small, single-nation markets.

North American Free Trade Agreement

In 1993, Canada, Mexico, and the United States formed a major trade bloc. The **North American Free Trade Agreement (NAFTA)** established a free-trade zone that has about the same combined output as the EU but encompasses a much larger geographic area. NAFTA has eliminated tariffs and other trade barriers between Canada, Mexico, and the United States for most goods and services.

Critics of NAFTA feared that it would cause a massive loss of U.S. jobs as firms moved to Mexico to take advantage of lower wages and weaker regulations on pollution and workplace safety. Also, there was concern that Japan and South Korea would build plants in Mexico and transport goods tariff-free to the United States, further hurting U.S. firms and workers.

In retrospect, critics were much too pessimistic. Since the passage of NAFTA in 1993, employment in the United States has increased by more than 25 million workers. Increased trade between Canada, Mexico, and the United States has enhanced the standard of living in all three countries.

Not all aspects of trade blocs are positive. By giving preferences to countries within their free-trade zones, trade blocs such as the EU and NAFTA tend to reduce their members' trade with non-bloc members. Thus, the world loses some of the benefits of a completely open global trading system. Eliminating that disadvantage has been one of the motivations for liberalizing global trade through the World Trade Organization. Its liberalizations apply equally to all 164 nations that belong to the WTO.

Recent U.S. Trade Deficits

As shown in Figure 13.2 the United States has experienced large and persistent trade deficits in recent years. These deficits rose rapidly between 2003 and 2006 before declining when consumers and businesses greatly curtailed their purchase of imports during the recession of 2007–2009. Even in 2009, however, the trade deficit on goods was still at $517 billion and the trade deficit on goods and services was $379 billion. As the economy began to recover, the trade deficit on goods rose to $738 billion in 2011, and the trade deficit on goods and services rose to $560 billion. Economists expect the trade deficits to continue to expand, absolutely and relatively, toward prerecession levels when the economic recovery strengthens and U.S. income and imports rise at a faster pace.

Causes of the Trade Deficits

The large U.S. trade deficits have several causes. First, the U.S. economy expanded more rapidly between 2001 and 2007 than the economies of several U.S. trading partners. The strong U.S. income growth that accompanied that economic growth enabled Americans to greatly increase their purchases of imported products. In contrast, Japan and some

trade bloc A group of nations that lower or abolish trade barriers among members. Examples include the European Union and the nations of the North American Free Trade Agreement.

euro The common currency unit used by 19 European nations as of 2017 (Austria, Belgium, Cyprus, Estonia, Finland, France, Germany, Greece, Ireland, Italy, Luxembourg, Malta, the Netherlands, Portugal, Slovakia, Slovenia, and Spain).

North American Free Trade Agreement (NAFTA) A 1993 agreement establishing, over a 15-year period, a free-trade zone composed of Canada, Mexico, and the United States.

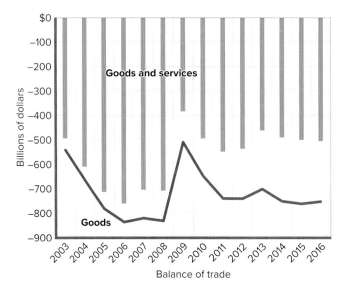

FIGURE 13.2 **U.S. trade deficits, 2003–2016.** The United States experienced large deficits in *goods* and in *goods and services* between 2003 and 2016. These deficits steadily increased until the recession of 2007–2009. Despite the decline, large trade deficits are expected to continue for many years to come. *Source:* Bureau of Economic Analysis, **www.bea.gov.**

European nations suffered recession or experienced relatively slow income growth over that same period. So consumers in those countries increased their purchases of U.S. exports much less rapidly than Americans increased their purchases of foreign imports.

Another factor explaining the large trade deficits is the enormous U.S. trade imbalance with China. In 2016, the United States imported $309 billion more of goods and services than it exported to China. Even in the recession year 2009, the trade deficit with China was $220 billion. The 2016 deficit with China was 65 percent larger than the combined deficits with Mexico ($63 billion), Germany ($67 billion), and Japan ($57 billion). The United States is China's largest export market, and although China has greatly increased its imports from the United States, its standard of living has not yet risen sufficiently for its households to afford large quantities of U.S. products. Adding to the problem, China's government has fixed the exchange rate of it currency, the yuan, to a basket of currencies that includes the U.S. dollar. Therefore, China's large trade surpluses with the United States have not caused the yuan to appreciate much against the U.S. dollar. Greater appreciation of the yuan would have made Chinese goods more expensive in the United States and reduced U.S. imports from China. In China a stronger yuan would have reduced the dollar price of U.S. goods and increased Chinese purchases of U.S. exports. That combination—reduced U.S. imports from China and increased U.S. exports to China—would have reduced the large U.S. trade imbalance.

Finally, a declining U.S. saving rate (= saving/total income) also contributed to the large U.S. trade deficits. Up until the recession of 2007–2009, the U.S. saving rate declined substantially, while its investment rate (= investment/total income) increased. The gap between U.S. investment and U.S. saving was filled by foreign purchases of U.S. real and financial assets. Because foreign savers were willing to finance a large part of U.S. investment, Americans were able to save less and consume more. Part of that added consumption spending was on imported goods. That is, the inflow of funds from abroad may be one cause of the trade deficits, not just a result of those deficits.

Implications of U.S. Trade Deficits

The prerecession U.S. trade deficits were the largest ever run by a major industrial nation. Whether the large trade deficits should be of significant concern to the United

States and the rest of the world is debatable. Most economists see both benefits and costs to trade deficits.

Increased Current Consumption At the time a trade deficit or a current account deficit is occurring, American consumers benefit. A trade deficit means that the United States is receiving more goods and services as imports from abroad than it is sending out as exports. Taken alone, a trade deficit allows the United States to consume outside its production possibilities curve. It augments the domestic standard of living. But here is a catch: The gain in present consumption may come at the expense of reduced future consumption.

Increased U.S. Indebtedness A trade deficit is considered "unfavorable" because it must be financed by borrowing from the rest of the world, selling off assets, or dipping into foreign currency reserves. Trade deficits are financed primarily by net inpayments of foreign currencies to the United States. When U.S. exports are insufficient to finance U.S. imports, the United States increases both its debt to people abroad and the value of foreign claims against assets in the United States. Financing of the U.S. trade deficit has resulted in a larger foreign accumulation of claims against U.S. financial and real assets than the U.S. claim against foreign assets. In 2015, foreigners owned about $7.4 trillion more of U.S. assets (corporations, land, stocks, bonds, loan notes) than U.S. citizens and institutions owned of foreign assets.

If the United States wants to regain ownership of these domestic assets, at some future time it will have to export more than it imports. At that time, domestic consumption will be lower because the United States will need to send more of its output abroad than it receives as imports. Therefore, the current consumption gains delivered by U.S. current account deficits may mean permanent debt, permanent foreign ownership, or large sacrifices of future consumption.

We say "may mean" above because the foreign lending to U.S. firms and foreign investment in the United States increase the stock of American capital. U.S. production capacity might increase more rapidly than otherwise because of a large inflow of funds to offset the trade deficits. We know that faster increases in production capacity and real GDP enhance the economy's ability to service foreign debt and buy back real capital, if that is desired.

Downward Pressure on the Dollar Finally, the large U.S. trade deficits place downward pressure on the exchange value of the U.S. dollar. The surge of imports requires the United States to supply dollars in the currency market in order to obtain the foreign currencies required for purchasing the imported goods. That flood of dollars into the currency market causes the dollar to depreciate relative to other currencies. Between 2002 and 2008, the dollar depreciated against most other currencies, including 43 percent against the European euro, 27 percent against the British pound, 37 percent against the Canadian dollar, 15 percent against the Chinese yuan, and 25 percent against the Japanese yen. In 2008, the U.S. dollar continued to depreciate against the Canadian dollar, the Chinese yuan, and the Japanese yen, but began appreciating relative to the euro and the pound. Some of this depreciation was fueled by the expansionary monetary policy (reduced real interest rates) undertaken by the Fed beginning in 2007 (discussed in Chapter 18). Subsequent appreciation of the U.S. dollar relative to most major currencies, including the Japanese yen, Canadian dollar, European euro and British pound, is largely attributed to continued economic weakness in those countries and their central banks pursuing monetary policy that was more expansionary than in the United States.

Economists feared that the decline in the dollar would contribute to inflation as imports became more expensive to Americans in dollar terms. Traditionally the Fed would need to react to that inflation with a tight monetary policy that raises real interest rates in the United States. However, because of the financial crisis and recession that began in 2007, the Fed chose to aggressively reduce interest rates, hoping to halt the downturn in the economy. In effect, it gambled that its actions would not ignite inflation because of the dampening effect of the severe economic recession on rising prices.

SUMMARY

LO13.1 List and discuss several key facts about U.S. international trade.

The United States leads the world in the volume of international trade, but trade is much larger as a percentage of GDP in many other nations.

LO13.2 Define comparative advantage and demonstrate how specialization and trade add to a nation's output.

Mutually advantageous specialization and trade are possible between any two nations if they have different domestic opportunity-cost ratios for any two products. By specializing on the basis of comparative advantage, nations can obtain larger real incomes with fixed amounts of resources. The terms of trade determine how this increase in world output is shared by the trading nations. Increasing costs lead to less-than-complete specialization for many tradable goods.

LO13.3 Explain how exchange rates are determined in currency markets.

The foreign exchange market establishes exchange rates between currencies. Each nation's purchases from abroad create a supply of its own currency and a demand for foreign currencies. The resulting supply-demand equilibrium sets the exchange rate that links the currencies of all nations. Depreciation of a nation's currency reduces its imports and increases its exports; appreciation increases its imports and reduces its exports.

Currencies will depreciate or appreciate as a result of changes in their supply or demand, which in turn depend on changes in tastes for foreign goods, relative changes in national incomes, relative changes in inflation rates, changes in interest rates, and the extent and direction of currency speculation.

LO13.4 Analyze the validity of the most frequently presented arguments for protectionism.

Trade barriers and subsidies take the form of protective tariffs, quotas, nontariff barriers, voluntary export restrictions, and export subsidies. Protective tariffs increase the prices and reduce the quantities demanded of the affected goods. Sales by foreign exporters diminish; domestic producers, however, gain higher prices and enlarged sales. Consumer losses from trade restrictions greatly exceed producer and government gains, creating an efficiency loss to society.

Three recurring arguments for free trade—increased domestic employment, cheap foreign labor, and protection against dumping—are either fallacies or overstatements that do not hold up under careful economic analysis.

Not everyone benefits from free (or freer) trade. The Trade Adjustment Assistance Act of 2002 provides cash assistance, education and training benefits, health care subsidies, and wage subsidies (for persons 50 years old or more) to workers who are displaced by imports or plant relocations abroad. But less than 4 percent of all job losses in the United States each year result from imports, plant relocations, or the offshoring of service jobs.

LO13.5 Discuss the role played by free-trade zones and the World Trade Organization (WTO) in promoting international trade.

In 1947 the General Agreement on Tariffs and Trade (GATT) was formed to encourage nondiscriminatory treatment for all member nations, to reduce tariffs, and to eliminate import quotas. The Uruguay Round of GATT negotiations (1993) reduced tariffs and quotas, liberalized trade in services, reduced agricultural subsidies, reduced pirating of intellectual property, and phased out quotas on textiles.

GATT's successor, the World Trade Organization (WTO), had 164 member nations in 2017. It implements WTO agreements, rules on trade disputes between members, and provides forums for continued discussions on trade liberalization. The latest round of trade negotiations—the Doha Development Agenda—began in late 2001 and as of 2017 was still in progress.

Free-trade zones (trade blocs) liberalize trade within regions but may at the same time impede trade with non-bloc members. Two examples of free-trade arrangements are the 28-member European Union (EU) and the North American Free Trade Agreement (NAFTA), comprising Canada, Mexico, and the United States. Nineteen of the EU nations (as of 2017) have abandoned their national currencies for a common currency called the euro.

U.S. trade deficits have produced current increases in the living standards of U.S. consumers. But the deficits have also increased U.S. debt to the rest of the world and increased foreign ownership of assets in the United States. This greater foreign investment in the United States, however, has undoubtedly increased U.S. production possibilities. The trade deficits also place extreme downward pressure on the international value of the U.S. dollar.

TERMS AND CONCEPTS

comparative advantage

terms of trade

foreign exchange market

exchange rates

depreciation

appreciation

tariffs

import quotas

nontariff barriers (NTBs)

voluntary export restriction (VER)

export subsidies

Smoot-Hawley Tariff Act

dumping

Trade Adjustment Assistance Act

offshoring

General Agreement on Tariffs and Trade (GATT)

World Trade Organization (WTO)

Doha Round

European Union (EU)

trade bloc

euro

North American Free Trade Agreement (NAFTA)

QUESTIONS

The following and additional problems can be found in ☰ **connect**

1. Quantitatively, how important is international trade to the United States relative to its importance to other nations? What country is the United States' most important trading partner, quantitatively? With what country does the United States have the largest current trade deficit? **LO13.1**

2. What effect do rising costs (rather than constant costs) have on the extent of specialization and trade? Explain. **LO13.2**

3. What is offshoring of white-collar service jobs, and how does it relate to international trade? Why has it recently increased? Why do you think more than half of all offshored jobs have gone to India? Give an example (other than that in the textbook) of how offshoring can eliminate some U.S. jobs while creating other U.S. jobs. **LO13.2**

4. Explain why the U.S. demand for Mexican pesos is downsloping and the supply of pesos to Americans is upsloping. Indicate whether each of the following would cause the Mexican peso to appreciate or depreciate: **LO13.3**
   a. The United States unilaterally reduces tariffs on Mexican products.
   b. Mexico encounters severe inflation.
   c. Deteriorating political relations reduce American tourism in Mexico.
   d. The U.S. economy moves into a severe recession.
   e. The United States engages in a high-interest-rate monetary policy.
   f. Mexican products become more fashionable to U.S. consumers.
   g. The Mexican government encourages U.S. firms to invest in Mexican oil fields.

5. Explain why you agree or disagree with the following statements: **LO13.3**
   a. A country that grows faster than its major trading partners can expect the international value of its currency to depreciate.
   b. A nation whose interest rate is rising more rapidly than interest rates in other nations can expect the international value of its currency to appreciate.
   c. A country's currency will appreciate if its inflation rate is less than that of the rest of the world.

6. If the European euro were to depreciate relative to the U.S. dollar in the foreign exchange market, would it be easier or harder for the French to sell their wine in the United States? Suppose you were planning a trip to Paris. How would depreciation of the euro change the dollar cost of your trip? **LO13.3**

7. What measures do governments take to promote exports and restrict imports? Who benefits and who loses from protectionist policies? What is the net outcome for society? **LO13.4**

8. Speculate as to why some U.S. firms strongly support trade liberalization while other U.S. firms favor protectionism. Speculate as to why some U.S. labor unions strongly support trade liberalization while other U.S. labor unions strongly oppose it. **LO13.4**

9. Explain: "Free-trade zones such as the EU and NAFTA lead a double life: They can promote free trade among members, but they pose serious trade obstacles for nonmembers." Do you think the net effects of trade blocs are good or bad for world trade? Why? How do the efforts of the WTO relate to these trade blocs? **LO13.5**

PROBLEMS

1. Assume that the comparative-cost ratios of two products—baby formula and tuna fish—are as follows in the nations of Canswicki and Tunata:

> Canswicki: 1 can baby formula ≡ 2 cans tuna fish
> Tunata: 1 can baby formula ≡ 4 cans tuna fish

In what product should each nation specialize? Which of the following terms of trade would be acceptable to both nations: (a) 1 can baby formula ≡ $2\frac{1}{2}$ cans tuna fish; (b) 1 can baby formula ≡ 1 can tuna fish; (c) 1 can baby formula ≡ 5 cans tuna fish? LO13.2

2. The accompanying hypothetical production possibilities tables are for New Zealand and Spain. Each country can produce apples and plums. Plot the production possibilities data for each of the two countries separately. Referring to your graphs, answer the following: LO13.2

New Zealand's Production Possibilities Table
(Millions of Bushels)

Product	A	B	C	D
	Production Alternatives			
Apples	0	20	40	60
Plums	15	10	5	0

Spain's Production Possibilities Table
(Millions of Bushels)

Product	R	S	T	U
	Production Alternatives			
Apples	0	20	40	60
Plums	60	40	20	0

a. What is each country's cost ratio of producing plums and apples?
b. Which nation should specialize in which product?
c. Show the trading possibilities lines for each nation if the actual terms of trade are 1 plum for 2 apples. (Plot these lines on your graph.)
d. Suppose the optimum product mixes before specialization and trade were alternative B in New Zealand and alternative S in Spain. What would be the gains from specialization and trade?

3. The following hypothetical production possibilities tables are for China and the United States. Assume that before specialization and trade the optimal product mix for China is alternative B and for the United States is alternative U. LO13.2

China Production Possibilities

Product	A	B	C	D	E	F
Apparel (in thousands)	30	24	18	12	6	0
Chemicals (in tons)	0	6	12	18	24	30

U.S. Production Possibilities

Product	R	S	T	U	V	W
Apparel (in thousands)	10	8	6	4	2	0
Chemicals (in tons)	0	4	8	12	16	20

a. Are comparative-cost conditions such that the two areas should specialize? If so, what product should each produce?
b. What is the total gain in apparel and chemical output that would result from such specialization?
c. What are the limits of the terms of trade? Suppose that the actual terms of trade are 1 unit of apparel for $1\frac{1}{2}$ units of chemicals and that 4 units of apparel are exchanged for 6 units of chemicals. What are the gains from specialization and trade for each nation?

4. Refer to the following table, in which Q_d is the quantity of yen demanded, P is the dollar price of yen, Q_s is the quantity of yen supplied in year 1, and Q_s' is the quantity of yen supplied in year 2. All quantities are in billions and the dollar-yen exchange rate is fully flexible. LO13.3

Q_d	P	Q_s	Q_s'
10	125	30	20
15	120	25	15
20	115	20	10
25	110	15	5

a. What is the equilibrium dollar price of yen in year 1?
b. What is the equilibrium dollar price of yen in year 2?
c. Did the yen appreciate or did it depreciate relative to the dollar between years 1 and 2?
d. Did the dollar appreciate or did it depreciate relative to the yen between years 1 and 2?
e. Which one of the following could have caused the change in relative values of the dollar and yen between years 1 and 2: (1) more rapid inflation in the United States than in Japan, (2) an increase in the real interest rate in the United States but not in Japan, or (3) faster income growth in the United States than in Japan.

5. Suppose that the current Canadian dollar (CAD) to U.S. dollar exchange rate is $.85 CAD = $1 US and that the U.S. dollar price of an Apple iPhone is $300. What is the Canadian dollar price of an iPhone? Next, suppose that the CAD to U.S. dollar exchange rate moves to $.96 CAD = $1 US. What is the new Canadian dollar price of an iPhone? Other things equal, would you expect Canada to import more or fewer iPhones at the new exchange rate? LO13.3

Behavioral Economics

Learning Objectives

LO14.1 Define behavioral economics and explain how it contrasts with neoclassical economics.

LO14.2 Discuss the evidence for the brain being modular, computationally restricted, reliant on heuristics, and prone to various forms of cognitive error.

LO14.3 Relate how prospect theory helps to explain many consumer behaviors, including framing effects, mental accounting, anchoring, loss aversion, and the endowment effect.

LO14.4 Describe how time inconsistency and myopia cause people to make suboptimal long-run decisions.

LO14.5 Define fairness and give examples of how it affects behavior in the economy and in the dictator and ultimatum games.

Scientific theories are judged by the accuracy of their predictions. As an example, nobody would take physics seriously if it weren't possible to use the equations taught in college physics classes to predict the best trajectory for putting a satellite into orbit or the best radio frequency to penetrate buildings and provide good indoor cellular service.

Conventional **neoclassical economics** makes many accurate predictions about human choice behavior, especially when it comes to financial incentives and how consumers and businesses respond to changing prices. On the other hand, a number of neoclassical predictions fail quite dramatically. These include predictions about how people deal with risk and uncertainty; choices that require willpower or commitment; and decisions that involve fairness, reciprocity, or trust.

neoclassical economics The dominant and conventional branch of economic theory that attempts to predict human behavior by building economic models based on simplifying assumptions about people's motives and capabilities. These include that people are fundamentally rational; motivated almost entirely by self-interest; good at math; and unaffected by heuristics, time inconsistency, and self-control problems.

Behavioral economics attempts to make better predictions about human choice behavior by combining insights from economics, psychology, and biology. This chapter introduces you to behavioral economics and the areas in which it has most dramatically increased our understanding of economic behavior. Among the highlights is prospect theory, which was such a large advance on our understanding of how people deal with risk and uncertainty that its inventor, Daniel Kahneman, received the Nobel Prize in economics.

Systematic Errors and the Origin of Behavioral Economics

behavioral economics The branch of economic theory that combines insights from economics, psychology, and biology to make more accurate predictions about human behavior than conventional neoclassical economics, which is hampered by its core assumptions that people are fundamentally rational and almost entirely self-interested. Behavioral economics can explain framing effects, anchoring, mental accounting, the endowment effect, status quo bias, time inconsistency, and loss aversion.

rational Behaviors and decisions that maximize a person's chances of achieving his or her goals.

systematic errors Suboptimal choices that (1) are not *rational* because they do not maximize a person's chances of achieving his or her goals and (2) occur routinely, repeatedly, and predictably.

We tend to think of ourselves as being very good at making decisions. While we may make a few mistakes here and there, we generally proceed through life with confidence, believing firmly that we will react sensibly and make good choices whenever decisions have to be made. In terms of economic terminology, we feel that our decisions are **rational,** meaning that they maximize our chances of achieving what we want.

Unfortunately, scientists have amassed overwhelming evidence to the contrary. People constantly make decision errors that reduce—rather than enhance—the likelihood of getting what they want. In addition, many errors are **systematic errors,** meaning that people tend to repeat them over and over, no matter how many times they encounter a similar situation.

Behavioral economics developed as a separate field of study because neoclassical economics could not explain why people make so many systematic errors. The underlying problem for neoclassical economics is that it assumes that people are fundamentally rational. Under that worldview, people might make some initial mistakes when encountering a new situation. But as they gain experience, they should learn and adapt to the situation. As a result, decision errors should be rare—and definitely not systematic or regularly repeated.

When evidence began to pile up in the late twentieth century that even highly experienced people made systematic errors, neoclassical economists assumed that people were just ignorant of what was in their best interests. They assumed that a little education would fix everything. But people often persisted in making the same error even after they were informed that they were behaving against their own interests.

As a result, several researchers realized that it would be necessary to drop the neoclassical assumption that people are fundamentally rational. With that assumption relaxed, economists could develop alternative theories that could make more accurate predictions about human behavior—including the tendency people have toward making systematic errors in certain situations. The result of those efforts is what we today refer to as behavioral economics. Its distinguishing feature is that it is based upon people's actual behavior—which is in many cases substantially irrational, prone to systematic errors, and difficult to modify.

Comparing Behavioral Economics with Neoclassical Economics

While rationality is the most fundamental point of disagreement between behavioral economics and neoclassical economics, it is not the only one. Behavioral economics also contends that neoclassical economics makes a number of highly unrealistic assumptions about human capabilities and motivations, including

- People have stable preferences that aren't affected by context.
- People are eager and accurate calculating machines.
- People are good planners who possess plenty of willpower.
- People are almost entirely selfish and self-interested.

Neoclassical economics made these "simplifying assumptions" for two main reasons. First, they render neoclassical models of human behavior both mathematically elegant and easy enough to solve. Second, they enable neoclassical models to generate very precise predictions about human behavior.

Unfortunately, precision is not the same thing as accuracy. As behavioral economist Richard Thaler has written, "Would you rather be elegant and precisely wrong—or messy and vaguely right?" Thaler received the Nobel Prize in Economics in 2017 for his contributions to behavioral economics.

Behavioral economists err on the side of being messy and vaguely right. As a result, behavioral economics replaces the simplifying assumptions made by neoclassical economics with much more realistic and complex models of human capabilities, motivations, and mental processes.

Table 14.1 summarizes how the two approaches differ in several areas.

Focusing on the Mental Processes behind Decisions Another major difference between behavioral economics and neoclassical economics is in the amount of weight and importance that they attach to predicting decisions on the one hand and in understanding the mental processes used to reach those decisions on the other. While neoclassical economics focuses almost entirely on predicting behavior, behavioral economics puts significant emphasis on the mental processes driving behavior.

Neoclassical economics focuses its attention on prediction because its assumption that people are rational allows it to fully separate what people do from how they do it. In particular, perfectly rational people will always choose the course of action that will maximize the likelihood of getting what they want. How they actually come to those optimal decisions might be interesting—but you don't need to know anything about that process to predict a perfectly rational person's behavior. He will simply end up doing whatever it is that will best advance his interests. Consequently, neoclassical economists have felt free to ignore the underlying mental processes by which people make decisions.

TABLE 14.1 **Major Differences between Behavioral Economics and Conventional Neoclassical Economics**

Topic	Neoclassical Economics	Behavioral Economics
Rationality	People are fundamentally rational and will adjust their choices and behaviors to best achieve their goals. Consequently, they will not make systematic errors.	People are irrational and make many errors that reduce their chances of achieving their goals. Some errors are regularly repeated systematic errors.
Stability of preferences	People's preferences are completely stable and unaffected by context.	People's preferences are unstable and often inconsistent because they depend on context (framing effects).
Capability for making mental calculations	People are eager and accurate calculators.	People are bad at math and avoid difficult computations if possible.
Ability to assess future options and possibilities	People are just as good at assessing future options as current options.	People place insufficient weight on future events and outcomes.
Strength of willpower	People have no trouble resisting temptation.	People lack sufficient willpower and often fall prey to temptation.
Degree of selfishness	People are almost entirely self-interested and self-centered.	People are often selfless and generous.
Fairness	People do not care about fairness and only treat others well if doing so will get them something they want.	Many people care deeply about fairness and will often give to others even when doing so will yield no personal benefits.

Behavioral economists disagree sharply with the neoclassical neglect of mental processes. To them, the fact that people are not perfectly rational implies two important reasons for understanding the underlying mental processes that determine decisions:

- It should allow us to make better predictions about behavior.
- It should provide guidance about how to get people to make better decisions.

Improving Outcomes by Improving Decision Making

Neoclassical economics and behavioral economics differ on how to improve human welfare. Neoclassical economics focuses its attention on providing people with more options. That's because a fully rational person can be trusted to select from any set of options the one that will make him best off. As a result, the only way to make him even happier would be to provide an additional option that is even better.

By contrast, the existence of irrationality leads behavioral economists to conclude that it may be possible to make people better off without providing additional options. In particular, improvements in utility and happiness may be possible simply by getting people to make better selections from the set of options that is already available to them.

This focus on improving outcomes by improving decisions is one of the distinguishing characteristics of behavioral economics. This chapter will review several instances where substantial benefits arise from helping people to make better choices from among the options that they already have.

Viewing Behavioral Economics and Neoclassical Economics as Complements

It would be hasty to view behavioral economics and neoclassical economics as fundamentally opposed or mutually exclusive. Instead, many economists prefer to think of them as complementary approaches that can be used in conjunction to help improve our understanding of human behavior.

As an example of their complementary nature, consider how using the two approaches in tandem can help us achieve a better understanding of how customers behave at a local supermarket.

Neoclassical Economics at the Supermarket The major neoclassical contribution to our understanding of the customers' shopping behavior can be summarized by the phrase "incentives matter." In particular, the customers will care a great deal about prices. When prices go up, they buy less. When prices go down, they buy more.

That insight goes a long way toward explaining how customers behave. But there are other shopping behaviors that neoclassical economics cannot explain with its emphasis on people reacting rationally to incentives and prices. In those cases, behavioral economics may be able to help us figure out what people are up to.

Behavioral Economics at the Supermarket A good example of a shopping behavior that neoclassical economics can't explain very well is that people tend to buy what they happen to see. This behavior is called *impulse buying* and it contradicts the neoclassical assumption that consumers carefully calculate marginal utilities and compare prices before making their purchases. On the other hand, it is a very common behavior that is regularly exploited by retailers.

For instance, nearly all supermarkets attempt to take advantage of impulse buying by placing staple products like milk and eggs against the back walls of their stores. Placing those products at the rear increases impulse buying by forcing customers to walk past hundreds of other items on the way to the milk and eggs. A few of those items will catch their eyes and thereby increase sales as customers end up purchasing products that they had no intention of buying when they first entered the store.

Marketers also know that impulse purchases are highest for items that are stacked on shelves at eye level. So, believe it or not, food manufacturers actively bid against each other and pay supermarkets for the privilege of having their brands stacked at eye level. In cereal aisles, the most expensive shelf space isn't at eye level for an adult, but a foot or two lower—at the eye level of a toddler sitting in a shopping cart or of a child walking with a parent. Because kids are even more prone to impulse buying than adults, cereal makers are more than happy to pay to have their products stacked at kid-friendly eye levels.

Complementary Explanations at the Supermarket   Behavioral economics explains impulse buying and other irrational behaviors as the result of a wide variety of underlying factors, including cognitive biases, heuristics, and ongoing battles between different areas of the brain.

You will learn about these underlying factors in the remainder of this chapter. But for now, take to heart the idea that we typically need both neoclassical *and* behavioral methods to figure out what people are doing. Some behaviors—including the fact that shoppers respond strongly to incentives and prices—can be explained very well by neoclassical models that assume people are perfectly rational. But other behaviors—including impulse buying—are very much inconsistent with rationality and are therefore better explained by using the methods of behavioral economics.

APPLYING THE ANALYSIS

Wanamaker's Lament

Source: Library of Congress, Prints & Photographs Division, Reproduction number LC-DIG-ggbain-04978 (digital file from original neg.)

Marketing experts try to increase sales or launch new products by applying what they think they know about consumer behavior. Many people find those efforts spooky and wonder if they are being constantly manipulated into purchasing products that they don't want. But how much do the marketing experts really know?

Judging by their success rate, not so much. Most advertising campaigns show little effect on sales. Eighty percent of newly launched consumer products fail within just three months. And the vast majority of Hollywood films end up as flops despite studios spending billions of dollars each year on market research and advertising.

The difficulties facing marketers were best described in the late nineteenth century by John Wanamaker, the marketing genius and department store entrepreneur who, among other things, invented the price tag and the money-back guarantee. He famously complained, "Half the money I spend on advertising is wasted—the trouble is, I don't know which half!"

A recent response to Wanamaker's lament has been to run lots of simple experiments to see if anything at all can increase sales. Amazon.com runs hundreds of experiments per month, systematically showing different groups of customers different versions of its website in order to see if any of those different versions can increase sales. Las Vegas casinos also run experiments, systematically varying the scents injected into their air-conditioning systems to see which ones cause the largest increases in gambling. Vanilla apparently works very well and some scents are said to increase revenues by up to 20 percent.

QUESTION: Consider some products or brands that you purchase regularly. Does the advertising for these products appeal to the rational side of the consumer or is it designed to prompt impulse buying?

Our Efficient, Error-Prone Brains

The human brain is one of the most complex objects in the known universe. One hundred billion neurons share 10,000 times as many connections. Working together, they allow you to observe your environment, think creatively, and interact with people and objects.

The brain, however, is rather error-prone. Its many weaknesses are most dramatically illustrated by visual illusions, such as the one shown in Figure 14.1. If you follow the instructions printed in that figure, you will quickly discover that your brain can't consistently tell what color an object is.

This inability to properly process visual information is especially informative about the brain's limitations because the brain devotes more neurons toward processing and interpreting visual information than it does anything else. So, if the brain makes errors with visual processing, we should expect to find errors in everything else it does, too.

Heuristics Are Energy Savers

The brain's information-processing limitations are the result of evolutionary pressures. In particular, it was normally very difficult for our ancestors to get enough food to eat. That matters because our brains are extremely energy intensive. In fact, while your brain accounts for just 5 percent of your body weight, it burns 20 percent of all the energy you consume each day. So back when our ancestors had to hunt and gather and scavenge to survive, getting enough energy was a constant challenge.

In response, the brain evolved many low-energy mental shortcuts, or **heuristics.** Because they are shortcuts, heuristics are not the most accurate mental-processing options. But in a world where calories were hard to come by, a low-energy "good enough" heuristic was superior to a "perfect but costly" alternative.

Your brain's susceptibility to the visual-processing failure demonstrated in Figure 14.1 is the result of your brain using a host of error-prone heuristics to process visual information. But think about what a good trade-off you are getting. In everyday life, the visual-processing failure demonstrated in Figure 14.1 hardly ever comes up. So, it would be a waste of resources to devote more brainpower to fixing the issue. Put in economic terms, there are diminishing returns to employing additional units of brainpower. Heuristics are used because the opportunity cost of perfection is too high.

Some Common Heuristics   The following examples will give you a sense of how the brain employs heuristics for nearly every type of action and decision we make.

Guesstimating Ranks with the Recognition Heuristic   Which German city has the larger population, Munich or Stuttgart?

heuristics The brain's low-energy mental shortcuts for making decisions. They are "fast and frugal" and work well in most situations but in other situations result in systematic errors.

FIGURE 14.1 A visual illusion. The human brain uses a large number of heuristics (shortcuts) to process both visual and other types of information. Many of them utilize context to interpret specific bits of information. When that context changes (as it does here when you put your finger horizontally across the middle of the image), so does the brain's heuristic-filtered interpretation.

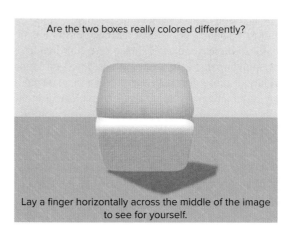

Are the two boxes really colored differently?

Lay a finger horizontally across the middle of the image to see for yourself.

Even people who know nothing about Germany tend to get the right answer to this question. They correctly guess "Munich" by employing the *recognition heuristic,* which says to assume that if one option is more easily recognized, it is probably more important or more highly ranked.

The recognition heuristic isn't foolproof, but it tends to work because relatively important people and places are much more likely to be mentioned in the media. Thus, whichever option is easier to recognize will probably be larger or more important.

Much of advertising is based on exploiting the recognition heuristic. Indeed, companies spend billions to ensure that consumers are familiar with their products because when it comes time to buy, consumers will be biased toward the products that seem the most familiar.

Interpreting Depth with the Shadow Heuristic The world is three-dimensional, but the light-sensing surfaces at the back of our eyes are two-dimensional. As a result, our brains are forced to use a cluster of heuristics to estimate depth when interpreting the two-dimensional images registered by our eyes.

Figure 14.2 shows how the *shadow heuristic* causes you to interpret shaded, two-dimensional circles as either humps or holes depending upon whether each circle is shaded on the top or on the bottom. Look at Figure 14.2 and count how many of the six shaded circles look like humps rather than holes. Now turn the picture upside down and count again. If your vision is typical, you will find that all the humps have become holes, and vice versa.

Here's what's happening. The shadow heuristic evolved back when sunlight was the only important source of light. As a result, it presumes that light always falls from above. Under that assumption, anything that sticks out from a surface will cast a shadow below it while anything indented will have a shadow on top due to the top of the recessed area casting a shadow on whatever lies below. Because your brain applies the shadow heuristic no matter what, you are tricked into believing that the shaded circles in Figure 14.2 are three-dimensional and either humps or holes depending upon whether they are shaded on the top or on the bottom.

Other common heuristics include the *gaze heuristic,* which allows a baseball player the judge the flight of a fly ball without complex calculations, and the *steering heuristic,* which kicks in automatically to help keep us upright when riding a bicycle. Whenever one forms an educated guess based on familiarity with past experiences, a form of heuristic is typically being used. We employ countless heuristics on a daily basis, often unaware of how they are guiding our decisions.

The Implications of Hardwired Heuristics
As you study the rest of the chapter, keep in mind that most heuristics appear to be hardwired into the brain, and, consequently, impossible to unlearn or avoid. That possibility has three important implications:

1. It may be very difficult for people to alter detrimental behaviors or routines even after you point out what they're doing wrong.

2. People may be easy prey for those who understand their hardwired tendencies.

3. If you want people to make a positive behavioral change, it might be helpful to see if you can put them in a situation where a heuristic will kick in and subconsciously lead them toward the desired outcome.

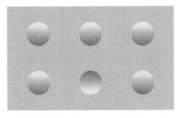

FIGURE 14.2 The shadow heuristic. The brain processes light with a heuristic that assumes that light always comes from above. Under that assumption, anything that sticks out will have a shadow on the bottom while anything that is recessed will have a shadow on top. As a result, your brain interprets five of the six shaded circles as humps that stick out while the bottom middle circle is interpreted as a recess. See what happens when you turn the picture upside down. Surprised?

Brain Modularity

The modern human brain is modular, so that specific areas deal with specific sensations, activities, and emotions—such as vision, breathing, and anger.

This modular structure is the result of millions of years of evolution, with the modern human brain evolving in stages from the much less complex brains of our hominid ancestors. The oldest parts of the brain are located in the back of the head, where the spine enters the skull. The newest parts are up front, near the forehead.

The older parts control subconscious activities like breathing and sweating as well as automatic emotional reactions such as fear and joy. The newer parts allow you to think creatively, imagine the future, and keep track of everyone in your social network. They are largely under conscious control.

System 1 and System 2 It is useful to think of the brain's decision-making systems as falling into two categories, which are informally referred to as System 1 and System 2. System 1 uses a lot of heuristics in the older parts of your brain to produce quick, unconscious reactions. If you ever get a "gut instinct," System 1 is responsible. By contrast, System 2 uses the newer parts of your brain to undertake slow, deliberate, and conscious calculations of costs and benefits. If you ever find yourself "thinking things over," you are using System 2.

Conflicts may sometimes arise between our unconscious System 1 intuitions and our conscious System 2 deliberations. For example, System 1 may urge you to eat an entire pile of cookies as fast as possible, while System 2 admonishes you to stick to your diet and have only one. That being said, a large body of evidence suggests that most decisions are probably either fully or mostly the result of System 1 intuitions and heuristics. That matters because those unconscious mental processes suffer from a variety of cognitive biases.

Cognitive Biases **Cognitive biases** are the misperceptions or misunderstandings that cause systematic errors.

There are a wide variety of cognitive biases, but they can be placed into two general categories. The first are mental-processing errors that result from faulty heuristics. As previously discussed, faulty heuristics are the result of evolution trading off accuracy for speed and efficiency.

The second category of cognitive biases consists of mental-processing errors that result from our brains not having any evolved capacities for dealing with modern problems and challenges, such as solving calculus problems or programming computers. Because our ancestors never encountered things like math, engineering, or statistics, our brains have a total absence of System 1 heuristics for dealing with those sorts of problems. In addition, our slower and more deliberative System 2 mental processes are also of only limited assistance because they were evolved to deal with other types of problems, such as keeping track of everyone in a social network or attempting to think through whether it would be better to go hunting in the morning or in the evening.

As a result, most people find recently developed mental challenges like math and physics to be very tiresome. In addition, cognitive biases often result because the System 2 processes that we are recruiting to solve modern problems were in fact designed for other purposes and don't work particularly well when directed at modern problems.

Psychologists have identified scores of cognitive biases. Here are a few that are relevant to economics and decision making.

Confirmation Bias The term *confirmation bias* refers to the human tendency to pay attention only to information that agrees with one's preconceptions. Information that contradicts those preconceptions is either ignored completely or rationalized away.

c. . biases Misperceptions or m   derstandings that cause systematic errors. Most result either (1) from heuristics that are prone to systematic errors or (2) because the brain is attempting to solve a type of problem (such as a calculus problem) for which it was not evolutionarily evolved and for which it has little innate capability.

Confirmation bias is problematic because it allows bad decisions to continue long after an impartial weighing of the evidence would have put a stop to them. When you see someone persisting with a failed policy or incorrect opinion despite overwhelming evidence that he or she should try something else, confirmation bias is probably at work.

Self-Serving Bias The term *self-serving bias* refers to people's tendency to attribute their successes to personal effort or personal character traits while at the same time attributing any failures to factors that were out of their control. While helping to preserve people's self-esteem, this bias makes it difficult for people to learn from their mistakes because they incorrectly assume that anything that went wrong was beyond their control.

Overconfidence Effect The *overconfidence effect* refers to people's tendency to be overly confident about how likely their judgments and opinions are to be correct. As an example, people who rated their answers to a particular quiz as being "99 percent likely to be right" were in fact wrong more than 40 percent of the time. Such overconfidence can lead to bad decisions because people will tend to take actions without pausing to verify if their initial hunches are actually true.

Hindsight Bias People engage in *hindsight bias* when they retroactively believe that they were able to predict past events. As an example, consider an election between candidates named Terence and Philip. Before the election happens, many people will predict that Terence will lose. But after Terence ends up winning, many of those same people will convince themselves that they "knew all along" that Terence was going to win. This faulty "I-knew-it-all-along" perspective causes people to massively overestimate their predictive abilities.

Availability Heuristic The *availability heuristic* causes people to base their estimates about the likelihood of an event not on objective facts but on whether or not similar events come to mind quickly and are readily available in their memories. Because vivid, emotionally charged images come to mind more easily, people tend to think that events like homicides, shark attacks, and lightning strikes are much more common than they actually are. At the same time, they underestimate the likelihood of unmemorable events.

As an example, you are five times more likely to die of stomach cancer than be murdered, but most people rate the likelihood of being murdered as much higher. They do this because they have many vivid memories of both real and fictional murders but almost no recollections whatsoever of anyone dying of stomach cancer.

The availability heuristic causes people to spend too much of their time and effort attempting to protect themselves against charismatic dangers of low actual probability while neglecting to protect themselves against dull threats of substantially higher probability.

Planning Fallacy The *planning fallacy* is the tendency people have to massively underestimate the time needed to complete a task. A good example is when last-minute test cramming gets really frantic. The student doing the cramming probably underestimated by many hours how much time he needed to prepare for the exam. The planning fallacy also helps to explain why construction projects, business initiatives, and government reform efforts all tend to come in substantially behind schedule.

Framing Effects **Framing effects** occur when a change in context (frame) causes people to react differently to a particular piece of information or to an otherwise identical situation.

Figure 14.3 gives an example of a framing effect. The middle symbol is identical in both rows, but it is interpreted differently depending upon whether it is surrounded by

framing effects In prospect theory, changes in people's decision making caused by new information that alters the context, or "frame of reference," that they use to judge whether options are viewed as gains or losses relative to the status quo.

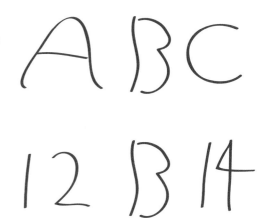

FIGURE 14.3 The letter illusion is the result of a framing effect. In each row, the middle symbol is the same. When that symbol is surrounded by the letters A and C in the top row, our brains tend to register the symbol as the letter B. But when it is surrounded by the numbers 12 and 14 in the bottom row, our brains tend to register it as the number 13. What our brain "sees" is largely a matter of context (frame).

letters or numbers. When surrounded by letters in the top row, the brain tends to interpret the symbol as the letter B. When surrounded by numbers in the bottom row, the brain tends to interpret the symbol as the number 13.

Changes in context can also cause extraordinary changes in behavior. Experiments have shown that ordinary people are twice as likely to litter, steal, or trespass if experimenters tag an area with graffiti and scatter lots of trash around. By changing the area's appearance from neat and orderly to rundown and chaotic, experimenters got ordinary people to subconsciously choose to engage in more crime.

Framing effects can also cause consumers to change their purchases. At the local supermarket, apples command a higher price if each one comes with a pretty sticker and meat sells faster if it is packaged in shiny plastic containers. At a high-end retailer, expensive packaging increases the perceived value of the shop's merchandise. So does having a nice physical space in which to shop. Thus, high-end retailers spend a lot on architecture and displays.

Prospect Theory

Neoclassical economics focuses much of its attention on consumer-choice situations in which people only have to deal with "goods" as opposed to "bads." When deciding on how to spend a budget, a consumer considers only items that would bring her positive marginal utility—that is, "good" things. She then uses marginal benefit–marginal cost analysis to select how much of each of those good things she should consume to get as much utility as possible from her limited budget.

Unfortunately, life often forces us to deal with bad things, too. Our houses may burn down. A potential investment may go bad. The money we lend out may not be repaid.

How people cope with negative possibilities is a central focus of behavioral economics. Many thousands of observations have been cataloged as to how people actually deal with the prospect of bad things as well as good things. Three very interesting facts summarize how people deal with goods and bads:

* People judge good things and bad things in relative terms, as gains and losses relative to their current situation, or **status quo.**
* People experience both diminishing marginal utility for gains (meaning that each successive unit of gain feels good, but not as good as the previous unit) as well as diminishing marginal disutility for losses (meaning that each successive unit of loss hurts, but less painfully than the previous unit).

status quo The existing state of affairs; in prospect theory, the current situation from which gains and losses are calculated.

- People experience **loss aversion,** meaning that for losses and gains near the status quo, losses are felt *much* more intensely than gains—in fact, about 2.5 times more intensely. Thus, for instance, the pain experienced by an investor who loses one dollar from his status quo level of wealth will be about 2.5 times more intense than the pleasure he would have felt if he had gained one dollar relative to his status quo level of wealth.

loss aversion In prospect theory, the property of most people's preferences that the pain generated by losses feels substantially more intense than the pleasure generated by gains.

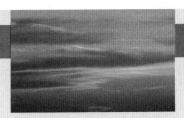

APPLYING THE ANALYSIS

©Kactus/Photographer's Choice/Getty Images

Rising Consumption and the Hedonic Treadmill

For many sensations, people's brains are wired to notice changes rather than states. For example, your brain can sense acceleration—your change in speed—but not speed itself. As a result, standing still feels the same as moving at a constant 50 miles per hour. And if you accelerate from one constant speed to another—say, from 50 miles per hour to 70 miles per hour—you will feel the acceleration only while it's happening. Once you settle down at the new higher speed, it will feel like you are standing still again.

Consumption appears to work in much the same way. If you are used to a given level of consumption—say, $50,000 per year—then you will get a lot of enjoyment for a while if your consumption accelerates to $100,000 per year. But, as time passes, you will get used to that higher level of consumption, so that $100,000 per year seems ordinary and doesn't bring you any more pleasure than $50,000 per year used to bring you when it was your status quo.

Economist Richard Easterlin coined the term *hedonic treadmill* (pleasure treadmill) to describe this phenomenon. Just as a person walking on a real treadmill gets nowhere, people trying to make themselves permanently happier by consuming more also get nowhere because they end up getting used to any higher level of consumption. Indeed, except for the extremely poor, people across the income spectrum report similar levels of happiness and satisfaction with their lives. This has led several economists, including Robert Frank, to argue that we should all stop trying to consume more because doing so doesn't make us any happier in the long run. What do you think? Should we all step off the hedonic treadmill?

QUESTION: Do you think the hedonic treadmill works in both directions? That is, will people suffering a loss of income return to their pre-loss level of happiness after they get used to a new, lower level of consumption?

prospect theory A behavioral economics theory of preferences having three main features: (1) people evaluate options on the basis of whether they generate gains or losses relative to the status quo; (2) gains are subject to diminishing marginal utility, while losses are subject to diminishing marginal disutility; and (3) people are prone to loss aversion.

These three facts about how people deal with goods and bads form the basis of **prospect theory,** which sheds important light on how consumers plan for and deal with life's ups and downs as well as why they often appear narrow-minded and fail to "see the big picture." To give you an idea of how powerful prospect theory is—and why its pioneer, Daniel Kahneman, was awarded the Nobel Prize in Economics—let's go through some examples of consumer behavior that would be hard to explain without the insights provided by prospect theory.

Losses and Shrinking Packages

Because people see the world in terms of gains and losses relative to the status quo situations that they are used to, businesses have to be very careful about increasing the prices they charge for their products. This is because once consumers become used to a given price, they will view any increase in the price as a loss relative to the status quo price they had been accustomed to.

The fact that consumers may view a price increase as a loss explains the otherwise curious fact that many food producers react to rising input costs by shrinking the sizes of their products. The company most famous for doing this is Hershey's chocolates. During its first decades of operation about 100 years ago, it would always charge exactly 5 cents for one of its Hershey's chocolate bars. But the size of the bars would increase or decrease depending on the cost of the company's inputs. When the cost of raw materials rose, the company would keep the price fixed at 5 cents but decrease the size of the bar. When the cost of raw materials fell, it would again keep the price fixed at 5 cents but increase the size of the bar.

This seems rather bizarre when you consider that consumers were not in any way *actually* being shielded from the changes in input prices. That is because what should rationally matter to consumers is the price per ounce that they are paying for Hershey's Bars. And that *does* go up and down when the price remains fixed but the size of the bars changes.

But people aren't being fully rational here. They mentally fixate on the product's price because that is the characteristic that they are used to focusing on when making their purchasing decisions. And because the 5-cent price had become the status quo that they were used to, Hershey's understood that any price increase would be mentally categorized as a loss. Thus, Hershey's wisely chose to keep the price of its product fixed at 5 cents even when input prices were rising.

Other companies employ the same strategy today. In the years following the 2007–2009 recession, the prices of many raw materials, including sugar, soybeans, and corn, rose substantially. Many major manufacturers reacted by reducing product sizes while keeping prices fixed. Häagen-Dazs reduced the size of its supermarket ice cream tubs from 16 to 14 ounces. Kraft reduced the number of slices of cheese in a package of Kraft Singles from 24 to 22 slices. A bottle of Tropicana orange juice shrank from 64 ounces (the traditional half-gallon size) to just 59 ounces. And Procter & Gamble reduced the size of Bounty paper towel rolls from 60 to 52 sheets.

Framing Effects and Advertising

Because people evaluate situations in terms of gains and losses, their decision making can be very sensitive to the mental frame that they use to evaluate whether a possible outcome should be viewed as a gain or a loss. Here are a couple of examples in which differences in the context or "frame" change the perception of whether a situation should be treated as a gain or loss. See how you react to them.

- Would you be happy with a salary of $100,000 per year? You might say yes. But what if your salary last year had been $140,000? Are you still going to say yes? Now that you know you are taking a $40,000 pay cut, does that $100,000 salary seem as good as it did before?

- Similarly, suppose you have a part-time job. One day, your boss Joe walks in and says that he is going to give you a 10 percent raise. Would that please you? Now, what if he also mentioned that *everyone else* at your firm would be getting a 15 percent raise. Are you still going to be just as pleased? Or does your raise now seem like a loss compared to what everyone else will be getting?

Prospect theory takes into account the fact that people's preferences can change drastically depending on whether contextual information causes them to define a situation as a gain or a loss. These framing effects are important to recognize because they can be manipulated by advertisers, lawyers, and politicians to try to alter people's decisions. For instance, would an advertising company be better off marketing a particular brand of hamburger as "20% fat" or as "80% lean"? Both phrases describe the same meat, but one frames the situation as a loss (20 percent fat) while the other frames it as a gain (80 percent lean).

And would you be more willing to take a particular medicine if you were told that 99.9 percent of the people who take it live or if you were told that 0.1 percent of the people who take it die? Continuing to live is a gain, whereas dying is clearly a loss. Which frame sounds better to you?

Framing effects have major consequences for consumer behavior because any frame that alters whether consumers consider a situation to be a gain or a loss *will* affect their consumption decisions!

Anchoring and Credit Card Bills

Before people can calculate their gains and losses, they must first define the status quo from which to measure those changes. But it turns out that irrelevant information can unconsciously influence people's feelings about the status quo. Here's a striking example. Find a group of people and ask each person to write down the last two digits of his or her Social Security number. Then ask each person to write down his or her best estimate of the value of some object that you display to them—say, a nice wireless keyboard. What you will find is that the people whose Social Security numbers end in higher numbers—say, 67 or 89— will give higher estimates for the value of the keyboard than people whose Social Security numbers end in smaller numbers like 18 or 37. The effect can be huge. Among students in one MBA class at MIT, those with Social Security numbers ending between 80 and 99 gave an average estimate of $56 for a wireless keyboard, while their classmates whose Social Security numbers ended between 00 and 20 gave an average estimate of just $16.

Psychologists and behavioral economists refer to this phenomenon as **anchoring** because people's estimates about the value of the keyboard are influenced, or "anchored," by the recently considered information about the last two digits of their Social Security numbers. Why irrelevant information can anchor subsequent valuations is not fully understood. But the anchoring effect is real and can lead people to unconsciously alter how they evaluate different options.

anchoring The tendency people have to unconsciously base, or "anchor," the valuation of an item they are currently thinking about on recently considered but logically irrelevant information.

Unfortunately, credit card companies have figured this out. They use anchoring to increase their profits by showing very small minimum-payment amounts on borrowers' monthly credit card statements. The companies could require larger minimum payments, but the minimum-payment numbers that they present are only typically about 2 percent of what a customer owes. Why such a small amount? Because it acts as an anchor that causes people to unconsciously make smaller payments each month. This can make a huge difference in how long it takes to pay off their bill and how much in total interest they will end up paying. For a customer who owes $1,000 on a credit card that charges the typical interest rate of 19 percent per year, it will take 22 years and $3,398.12 in total payments (including accumulated interest) to pay off the debt if he only makes 2 percent monthly payments. By showing such small minimum-payment amounts, credit card companies anchor many customers into the expensive habit of paying off their debts slowly rather than quickly.

Mental Accounting and Overpriced Warranties

mental accounting The tendency people have to create separate "mental boxes" (or "accounts") in which they deal with particular financial transactions in isolation rather than dealing with them as part of an overall decision-making process that would consider how to best allocate their limited budgets across all possible options by comparing marginal benefits and marginal costs (also called the *utility-maximizing rule*).

Neoclassical economics assumes that people compare marginal benefits and marginal costs across all of their potential consumption options simultaneously when trying to maximize the total utility attainable from their limited incomes. But as Richard Thaler famously noted, people sometimes look at consumption options in isolation, thereby irrationally failing to look at all their options simultaneously. Thaler coined the term **mental accounting** to describe this behavior because it was as if people arbitrarily put certain options into totally separate "mental accounts" that they dealt with without any thought to options outside of those accounts.

As an example of where this suboptimal tendency leads, consider the extended warranties offered by big electronic stores whenever customers purchase expensive products like plasma TVs. These warranties are very much overpriced given that the products they insure hardly ever break down. Personal financial experts universally tell people not to buy them. Yet many people do buy them because they engage in mental accounting.

They do this by mentally labeling their purchase of the TV as an isolated, individual transaction, sticking it into a separate mental account in their brain that might have a title like "Purchase of New TV." Viewing the purchase in isolation exaggerates the size of the potential loss that would come from a broken TV. Customers who view the transaction in isolation see the possibility of a $1,000 loss on their $1,000 purchase as a potential total loss—"Holy cow! I could lose $1,000 on a $1,000 TV!" By contrast, people who can see the big picture are able to compare the potential $1,000 loss with the much larger value of their entire future income stream. That allows them to realize that the potential loss is relatively minor—and thus not a good enough reason to purchase an expensive warranty.

The Endowment Effect and Market Transactions

endowment effect The tendency people have to place higher valuations on items they possess (are endowed with) than on identical items that they do not possess; perhaps caused by loss aversion.

Prospect theory also offers an explanation for the **endowment effect,** which is the tendency that people have to put a higher valuation on anything that they currently possess (are endowed with) than on identical items that they do not own but might purchase. For instance, if we show a person a new coffee mug and ask him what the maximum amount is that he would pay to buy it, he might say $10. But if we then give the mug to him so that he now owns it, and we then ask how much we would have to pay him to buy it back, he will very likely report a much higher value—say, $15.

The interesting thing is that he is not just bluffing or driving a hard bargain. Rather, the human brain appears wired to put a higher value on things we own than on things we don't. Economist John List has shown that this tendency can moderate if people are used to buying things for resale—that is, buying them with the intention of getting rid of them. But without such experience, the endowment effect can be quite strong. If it is, it can make market transactions between buyers and sellers harder because sellers will be demanding higher prices for the items they are selling ("Hey, *my* mug is worth $15 to me!") than the values put on those items by potential buyers ("Dude, *your* mug is only worth $10 to me").

Several researchers have suggested that loss aversion may be responsible for the endowment effect and the higher values demanded by sellers. They argue that once a person possesses something, the thought of parting with it seems like a potential loss. As a result, the person will demand a lot of money as compensation if he or she is asked to sell the item. On the other hand, potential purchasers do not feel any potential sense of loss, so they end up assigning lower values to the same items.

Status Quo Bias

Prospect theory also explains **status quo bias,** which is the tendency that people have to favor any option that is presented to them as being the default (status quo) option. As an example, consider Global Perspective 14.1. It shows, for a selection of European countries, the percentages of their respective populations that have indicated their willingness to participate in organ-donation programs.

As you can see, seven of the 11 countries have very high participation rates while the other four have low participation rates. You might suspect that cultural differences are at play, but that doesn't make sense when you note that countries like Germany and Austria that are culturally very similar still have massively different participation rates.

What is actually going on is a difference in the default option that people are presented with when they are asked whether they wish to participate. In the seven countries with high participation rates, the default option is participation, so that those who don't want to participate must explicitly check off a box indicating that they don't want to participate. By contrast, in the four countries with low participation rates, the default option is *not* participating, so that those wishing to participate must explicitly check off a box indicating that they want to participate.

status quo bias The tendency most people have when making choices to select any option that is presented as the default (status quo) option. Explainable by prospect theory and loss aversion.

GLOBAL PERSPECTIVE 14.1

Percent of Population Consenting to Be Organ Donors

People tend to stick with whatever option is presented as the default option. Thus, the seven countries with high percentages consenting to be organ donors have organ-donation programs in which the default option is participation. By contrast, the four countries with low percentages consenting to be organ donors have organ-donation programs where the default option is *not* participating.

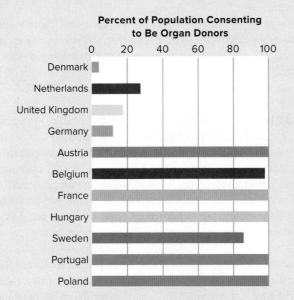

Source: Eric Johnson and Daniel Goldstein, "Defaults and Donation Decisions," *Transplantation* 78, no. 12, December 27, 2004.

What we see in all countries is that nearly everyone chooses to do nothing. They almost never check off the box that would indicate doing the opposite of the default option. Consequently, they end up agreeing to whatever the default option happens to be. Thus, the huge differences in participation rates among the 11 countries are driven almost entirely by what the default option happens to be.

Prospect theory explains this and other examples of status quo bias as a combination of the endowment effect and loss aversion. When people are put into a novel situation, they have no preexisting preferences for any of the options. As a result, the way the options are framed becomes very important because if any of them is presented as the default option, people will tend to treat it as an endowment that they wish to hold on to. At the same time, they will treat any other option as a prospect that could potentially cause a loss. Loss aversion then kicks in and causes most people to stick with the default option in order to avoid the possibility of incurring a loss. The result is a bias toward the status quo.

Status quo bias can be used to explain several consumer behaviors. Consider brand loyalty. If you have gotten used to eating Heinz ketchup, then status quo bias will make you reluctant to purchase any other brand of ketchup. Overcoming that feeling of potential loss is a difficult challenge for competing brands, as attested to by the fact that rivals seeking to challenge an established brand are often forced to resort to deep discounts or free samples to get consumers to even try their products.

Myopia and Time Inconsistency

Our ancient ancestors had little cause to spend much time worrying about anything that would happen in the distant future. Infectious diseases, predatory animals, and the constant threat of starvation made life extremely precarious. Consequently, they had to be almost entirely focused on the present moment and how to get through the next few weeks or the next few months.

Today, however, people living in industrialized countries only rarely die from infectious diseases, mostly see predatory animals in zoos, and are under no threat at all of starvation. Living past 80 is now routine and most of us will die of old age. As a result, long-run challenges like planning for retirement and saving for college are now common tasks that nearly everyone faces.

Unfortunately, our brains were designed for our ancestors' more immediate concerns. Thus, we often have difficulty with long-run planning and decisions that involve trade-offs between the present and the future. Two of the major stumbling blocks are myopia and time inconsistency.

Myopia

In biology, myopia, or nearsightedness, refers to a defect of the eye that makes distant objects appear fuzzy, out of focus, and hard to see. By analogy, economists use the word **myopia** to describe the fact that our brains have a hard time conceptualizing the future. Compared with the present, the future seems fuzzy, out of focus, and hard to see.

As an example, our brains are very good at weighing current benefits against current costs in order to make immediate decisions. But our brains almost seem "future blind" when it comes to conceptualizing either future costs or future benefits. As a result, we have difficulty evaluating possibilities that will occur more than a few weeks or months into the future.

The primary consequence of myopia is that when people are forced to choose between something that will generate benefits quickly and something that won't yield benefits for a long time, they will have a very strong tendency to favor the more immediate option. As an example, imagine that Terence has $1,000 that he can either spend on a vacation next month or save for his retirement in 30 years.

myopia Refers to the difficulty human beings have with conceptualizing the more distant future. Leads to decisions that overly favor present and near-term options at the expense of more distant future possibilities.

Myopia will cause him to have great difficulty imagining the additional spending power that he will be able to enjoy in 30 years if he saves the money. On the other hand, it is very easy for him to imagine all the fun he could have next month if he were to go on vacation. As a result, he will be strongly biased toward spending the money next month. With myopia obscuring the benefits of the long-term option, the short-term option will seem much more attractive.

Myopia also makes it hard to stick with a diet or follow an exercise plan. Compared with the immediate and clearly visible pleasures of eating doughnuts or hanging out, the future benefits from eating better or exercising consistently are just too hazy in most people's minds to be very attractive.

APPLYING THE ANALYSIS

©Shutterstock/Elena Elisseeva

A bright idea

In sunny areas, a solar panel can make up for the cost of its installation in just a few years by greatly reducing or even eliminating a household's electricity bill. After those years of payback are finished, there will be almost nothing but benefits because the solar panel will continue to provide free electricity at only modest maintenance costs. Consequently, nearly every household in sunny areas could rationally profit from installing solar panels.

Unfortunately, myopia discourages most people from wanting to reap the net benefits. Because people are myopic, they focus too strongly on the upfront costs of installing solar panels while at the same time discounting the long-run benefits from being able to generate their own electricity. The result is major inefficiency as most homeowners end up foregoing solar panels.

A company called Solar City has figured out a way to work with rather than against people's myopia. It does so by offering leasing and financing options that eliminate the need for consumers to pay for the upfront costs of installing a solar system. Instead, Solar City pays for the upfront costs and then makes its money by splitting the resulting savings on monthly electricity bills with consumers.

This arrangement actually benefits from myopia because consumers get to focus on instant savings rather than initial costs. The same strategy can also be used to promote other investments that would normally be discouraged by myopia, such as installing energy-efficient furnaces, air conditioners, and appliances.

QUESTION: Do college students suffer from myopia when assigned a term paper at the beginning of a semester? Explain. How could a professor structure the assignment to encourage students to work on the paper throughout the semester?

Time Inconsistency

time inconsistency The human tendency to systematically misjudge at the present time what will actually end up being desired at a future time.

Time inconsistency is the tendency to systematically misjudge at the present time what you will want to do at some future time. This misperception causes a disconnect between what you currently think you will want to do at some particular point in the future and what you actually end up wanting to do when that moment arrives. It is as though your present self does not understand what your future self will want.

Waking up early is a good example. At 8 p.m. on a Tuesday, you may really like the idea of waking up early the next morning so that you can exercise before starting the rest of your day. So you set your alarm 90 minutes earlier than you normally do. But when your alarm goes off the next morning at that earlier time, you loathe the concept, throw the alarm clock across the room, and go back to sleep. That switch in your preferences from the night before is the essence of time inconsistency. Your future self ends up disagreeing with your current self.

self-control problems Refers to the difficulty people have in sticking with earlier plans and avoiding suboptimal decisions when finally confronted with a particular decision-making situation. A manifestation of time inconsistency and potentially avoidable by using precommitments.

Self-Control Problems Time inconsistency is important because it is a major cause of **self-control problems.** To see why, imagine that before heading out to a restaurant with friends, you think that you will be happy sticking to your diet and only ordering a salad. After all, that particular restaurant has very tasty salads. But then, after you get there, you find the dessert menu overwhelmingly attractive and end up ordering two servings of cheesecake.

Because you were time inconsistent and didn't understand what your future self would want, you placed yourself into a situation in which it was very difficult for you to stick to your diet. If you had, instead, been able to correctly predict what your future self would want, you might have decided to stay home for the evening rather than putting yourself in temptation's way. Alternatively, you could have gone, but not before making your friends promise to prevent you from ordering dessert.

Time inconsistency also makes it hard for many workers to save money. Before their paychecks arrive, they mistakenly assume that their future selves will want to save money as much as their current selves do. But once the money becomes available, their future selves end up wanting to spend everything and save nothing.

precommittments Actions taken ahead of time that make it difficult for the future self to avoid doing what the present self desires. See *time inconsistency* and *self-control problems.*

Fighting Self-Control Problems with Precommitments The key to fighting time inconsistency and self-control problems is to have a good understanding of what your future self is likely to want. You can then make **precommitments** and take actions ahead of time to prevent your future self from doing much damage.

Hiding the Alarm Clock Consider again the problem of wanting to wake up 90 minutes early on Wednesday morning so that you can work out before starting the rest of your day. If you understand that your future self is not going to want to cooperate, you can take steps to prevent that future self from flaking out. Some people set multiple alarms. Others put their alarms on the other side of the room, underneath a pile of stuff that will have to be moved if the future self wants to turn the damned thing off. But the point is that each of these methods ensures that it will be nearly impossible for the future self to easily get back to sleep. They set things up so that the future self will be forced to do what the present self desires.

Automatic Payroll Deductions Precommitment strategies have also been used to help future selves save more. Consider automatic payroll deductions. If a worker named Blaire signs up for such a program, a fixed percentage will be automatically deducted from each of her paychecks and deposited directly into her retirement savings account. Because that money never gets to her checking account, there is no way for Blaire's future self to fall prey to temptation and spend it. As the old saying goes, "Out of sight, out of mind."

Salary Smoothing School teachers and college professors often have the choice of having their annual salaries paid out over 9 larger monthly installments (to match the length of the school year) or 12 smaller monthly installments (to match the length of the calendar year). If we observe which option they actually choose, we find that the vast majority opt to have their salaries spread out over 12 months rather than 9 months.

They do so because they fear self-control problems. In particular, they are afraid that if they opt to be paid over 9 months, they won't have the self-control to save enough money during the 9-month period when they will be getting paid to last them through the three months of summer vacation when they won't be getting paid. To avoid that situation, they opt to have their salaries spread out evenly over the entire calendar year. That precommitment ensures that their future selves are never given the chance to blow through all the money too quickly.

Early Withdrawal Penalties Sometimes, one cognitive bias can be used to offset another. Retirement accounts that have early-withdrawal penalties are a good example. They use loss aversion to offset time inconsistency and self-control problems.

In some cases, the penalties on these sorts of accounts are as high as 25 percent, meaning that if a saver wanted to withdraw $1,000 before reaching retirement, he would have to give up an additional $250 (= 25 percent of $1,000) as a penalty. While that amount is substantial in itself, loss aversion makes it even more painful to contemplate. As a result, most people can't bring themselves to make an early withdrawal.

Weight-Loss Competitions Loss aversion also drives the effectiveness of weight-loss competitions. For a person who has agreed to participate, the prospect of losing the competition can be a great motivator because loss aversion applies just as much to future selves as to present selves. Even after the future rolls around and the future self is in charge, the future self won't like the prospect of losing either. Thus, the present self can be confident that the future self will also be motivated to stick to the weight-loss goals that the present self wants to achieve.

APPLYING THE ANALYSIS

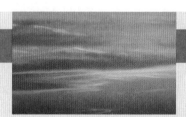

The Behavioral Insights Team

A Crack Team of Researchers Uses People's Behavioral Biases to "Nudge" Them Toward Making Better Decisions*

In 2010, the government of the United Kingdom established the Behavioral Insights Team. It was tasked with finding low-cost ways to gently nudge people toward making better choices for themselves and others.

A key feature of "nudges" is that they are subtle. This subtlety means that nudges can cause large changes in behavior without making people feel bullied or coerced—and also without imposing stringent new rules or having to offer people big monetary incentives or disincentives to get them to do something.

Consider tax collections. The Behavioral Insights Team (BIT) found that it could substantially increase the total amount of income tax collected each year in the United Kingdom by simply mailing letters to those who had not yet paid stating that most of their neighbors had already paid. That little bit of peer pressure was all it took to get many people to pay up. A similar experiment in Guatemala tripled tax collections.

*The term "nudge" was popularized by Richard Thaler and Cass Sunstein in their book *Nudge: Improving Decisions about Health, Wealth, and Happiness,* Yale University Press, 2008.

©rhouck13/iStock/Getty Images

Little personalized reminders are often all that is needed to make big changes in people's behavior. The BIT found that it could increase the attendance rates at adult literacy classes by over one-third just by sending students a text message each Sunday night that read, "I hope you had a good break, we look forward to seeing you next week. Remember to plan how you will get to your class."

The BIT uses randomized controlled trials to discover what works. Whenever it comes up with a potential nudge, it tests that potential nudge on a randomly selected group of people. At the same time, it also recruits a control (comparison) group who do not get the nudge. After waiting to see how both groups behave, the potential nudge is only deemed a success if the people receiving it make better choices than the people in the control group.

That was the case when it came to savings behavior in a poor rural area of the Philippines. The BIT worked with local researchers to see whether local people would save more at their local banks if they were offered a new type of "commitment" savings account. These commitment accounts restricted people from withdrawing money until they reached either a specific date or a specific savings target (that participants chose for themselves). By contrast, the people in the control group received ordinary savings accounts that had no such restrictions—meaning that people could withdraw money at any time they wanted and there were no savings targets.

The results of the experiment were startling. Over the course of one year, the people with ordinary accounts increased their stockpile of savings by only 12 percent. By contrast, the people randomized into having to use commitment accounts increased their savings by 82 percent—or nearly seven times more.

That large increase in savings is important because one of the surest ways out of poverty is for poorer people to pile up wealth that can be used for education, starting small businesses, and surviving periods of severe financial distress.

The introduction of commitment accounts made higher savings rates possible by providing locals with a simple way to overcome self-control problems. But please note that successful nudges can be viewed as a form of manipulation. That interpretation can be even more disturbing when you consider that the changes in behavior generated by successful nudges are most likely unconscious on the part of those being nudged. Keep this in mind as you consider for yourself whether it is morally or ethically acceptable to use nudges to guide people's behavior.

QUESTION: When dining out with friends, do the choices of others influence whether or not you have dessert? Would that constitute a nudge? What precommitment devices could you and your friends devise if you were trying to cut back on desserts?

Fairness and Self-Interest

Neoclassical models assume that people are purely self-interested. They do so because "pure self-interest" seems like a good basis for predicting many economic behaviors, especially those happening in market situations where people are dealing mostly with strangers and are, consequently, unlikely to be particularly sentimental or charity-minded.

Adam Smith, the founder of modern economics, put this line of thinking into words. The most-quoted passage from *The Wealth of Nations* reads,

> It is not from the benevolence of the butcher, the brewer, or the baker that we expect our dinner, but from their regard to their own interest. We address ourselves not to their humanity but to their self-love, and never talk to them of our own necessities but of *their* advantages.

Smith, however, did not believe that people are *exclusively* focused on self-love and their own interests. He believed that we are also strongly motivated by emotions such as charity, selflessness, and the desire to work for the common good. He expressed this view at length in his other influential book, *The Theory of Moral Sentiments*. The book's opening sentence reads:

> How selfish soever man may be supposed, there are evidently some principles in his nature which interest him in the fortune of others and render their happiness necessary to him though he derives nothing from it except the pleasure of seeing it.

What behavioral economists have discovered is that this human propensity to care about others extends into every type of economic behavior. While self-interest is always present, most people care deeply about others and how they are interacting with others. As a result, economic transactions are heavily influenced by moral and ethical factors.

Field Evidence for Fairness

Many real-world behaviors support the contention that economic transactions are heavily influenced by beliefs and values. This "field evidence" has helped behavioral economists identify the ethical and moral factors that appear to have the largest influence on economic behavior. Fairness is among the most important.

Fairness is a person's opinion as to whether a price, wage, or allocation is considered morally or ethically acceptable. Standards of fairness vary from person to person and economists generally take no stand on what people consider to be right or wrong. But fairness has been studied extensively because many everyday economic behaviors indicate that people care substantially about fairness and not just about maximizing what they can get for themselves.

Consider the following examples—none of which would be undertaken by a purely self-interested person.

- *Giving to Charity*   Each year, U.S. charities receive over $300 billion of cash donations and 8 billion hours of free labor. These donations of time and money are inconsistent with the idea that people are only interested in themselves. What is more, many of the cash donations are anonymous. That suggests that many donors have extremely pure motives and are not donating just to make themselves look good.
- *Obeying the Law*   In many countries, the large majority of citizens are law-abiding despite having many opportunities to break the law without getting caught. In the same way, the large majority of taxpayers complete their tax returns honestly despite having many opportunities to cut corners and hide income.
- *Fixing Prices*   During hurricanes and other natural disasters, shortages of crucial products such as gasoline and electric generators often develop. The shortages imply that retailers could raise prices, but they mostly keep prices fixed because they do not want to be thought of as taking advantage of the situation.

fairness A person's opinion as to whether a price, wage, or allocation is considered morally or ethically acceptable.

• **Purchasing "Fair-Trade" Products**   Many consumers are willing to pay premium prices to purchase products that have been certified by the Fair Trade organization as having been produced by companies that meet high standards with respect to workers' rights and environmental sustainability. These customers clearly care about more than just getting the lowest price.

Experimental Evidence for Fairness

Our understanding of fairness and how it affects economic transactions has been reinforced and refined in recent decades by examining experimental games that were specifically designed to test people's feelings about fairness.

The most important feature of these games is that they are played for real money. That matters because if people were only motivated by self-interest, you would expect everyone playing the games to utilize only those strategies that are most likely to maximize their own winnings.

As it turns out, however, only a few people behave that way. The majority actually play fairly and generously, often going out of their way to share with less-fortunate players even when they are under no compulsion to do so. That being said, their kindness only goes so far. If other players are acting selfishly, the average person will withhold cooperation and may even retaliate.

The Dictator Game   The strongest experimental evidence against the idea that people are only interested in what they can get for themselves comes from the **dictator game.**

dictator game A mutually anonymous behavioral economics game in which one person ("the dictator") unilaterally determines how to split an amount of money with the second player.

The Rules   In the game, two people interact anonymously. One of them is randomly designated as the "dictator." It is his job to split an amount of money that is put up for that purpose by the researcher running the game. A typical amount is $10.

The defining feature of the game is that the dictator can dictate whatever split he prefers. It could be to keep all the money for himself. It could be to give all the money to the other player. It could be to split it in any other possible way, such as $8.67 for himself and $1.33 for the other person.

Because the game is fully anonymous, the dictator doesn't have to worry about retaliation by the other person. He can get away with being as selfish as he wants.

How Players Behave   So what actually happens when people play the dictator game? After running the experiment many thousands of times in many different countries, experimenters have found that only one-third of dictators keep all of the money for themselves. The other two-thirds show substantial generosity, allocating an average of 42 percent of the money to the other player. In addition, 17 percent of all dictators split the money perfectly evenly and a little over 5 percent of all dictators give the other player everything.

Implications for Fairness   The way dictators behave suggests two important things about fairness.

First, the majority of people appear to be genuinely concerned about being fair to other people. They are willing to take less for themselves in order to ensure that the other player receives something, too. And they are willing to give substantially to the other player even though the game's guarantee of anonymity would allow them to take everything for themselves without fear of retaliation.

Second, generosity varies quite widely. Between the third of dictators who keep everything for themselves and the 5 percent who give everything to the other person lie the large majority who allocate some but not all of the money to the other person. Within that group, every possible split of the money can be found. As a result, behavioral economists believe that individuals vary widely in their beliefs about fairness. Some are incredibly selfish. Others are incredibly generous. And most of us lie somewhere in between.

To help get a better handle on how those widely divergent beliefs affect behavior in more realistic situations, economists designed a slightly more complex game.

The Ultimatum Game

Like the dictator game, the **ultimatum game** involves two players anonymously splitting an amount of money. But there is no longer a dictator who can arbitrarily decide how the money is split. Instead, both players need to agree on any proposed split if it is to take place.

That difference in the rules ensures that the ultimatum game mirrors the many real-world situations in which a project or proposal must obtain the consent and support of all parties if it is to be undertaken. As an example, consider a business transaction between a potential seller and a potential buyer. Even if there are substantial net benefits available to both parties, no transaction will take place unless the buyer and the seller can come to an agreement on the selling price.

The Rules As with the dictator game, the researcher puts up an amount of money to be split. This pot of money is similar in spirit to the net benefits that a buyer and a seller can split if they can agree on a price. It also represents the net benefits that will be forgone if the two parties cannot reach an agreement.

At the start of the experiment, one of the players is randomly assigned to be "the proposer" while the other player is randomly assigned to be "the responder." The game begins with the proposer proposing a split. As in the dictator game, the proposed split can range anywhere from suggesting that all the money go to the proposer to suggesting that all the money go to the responder.

The responder examines the proposed split and decides whether to accept it or reject it. If she accepts it, the split is made and both players are immediately paid their shares by the researcher. But if the responder rejects the proposed split, neither player gets anything. The game simply ends and both players go home without receiving any money at all—a situation similar to when a business negotiation fails and all the potential benefits are forgone.

How Players Behave When the ultimatum game is played, two behaviors stand out.

The more important is that the splits proposed by proposers in the ultimatum game are much more equal on average than the splits imposed by dictators in the dictator game. This is best seen by noting that whereas one-third of dictators keep all the money for themselves in the dictator game, almost no proposers suggest allocating all the money to themselves in the ultimatum game.

This extremely large difference in behavior arises because the people acting as proposers in the ultimatum game realize that suggesting a highly unequal split is almost certain to greatly offend a responder's sense of fairness and lead to a rejection. In addition, most proposers also seem to understand that even moderately unfair offers might also offend responders. As a result, the large majority of proposers suggest either perfectly equal splits or splits that are only slightly biased in the proposer's favor (such as 55 percent going to the proposer).

The second behavior that stands out is the decisiveness and emotional intensity with which responders reject offers that they consider unfair. Of particular interest is the fact that rejection decisions are not made in a cool and calculating fashion. Responders do *not* calmly weigh the costs and benefits of accepting an unfair offer. They actually become extremely angry and reject as a way of retaliating against the proposer. Their rejections are not just negative responses; they are acts of vengeance designed to hurt the proposer by denying him money.

The full extent to which unfair offers make responders angry can be gauged by looking at high-stakes versions of the ultimatum game in which proposers and responders attempt

ultimatum game A behavioral economics game in which a mutually anonymous pair of players interact to determine how an amount of money is to be split. The first player suggests a division. The second player either accepts that proposal (in which case the split is made accordingly) or rejects it (in which case neither player gets anything).

to split hundreds or even thousands of dollars. You might think that when such large amounts of money are on the line, responders would be willing to accept unfair splits. But what we actually see is responders continuing to reject splits that they consider to be unfair. Their preference for fair treatment is so strong that they will reject unfair offers even when doing so means giving up a *lot* of money.

Why the Threat of Rejection Increases Cooperation Some people won't offer anything to other people unless they are coerced into doing so. This is best understood by comparing the behavior of dictators in the dictator game with the behavior of proposers in the ultimatum game. In the dictator game, a full third of dictators award themselves all the money and leave nothing for the other player. In the ultimatum game, by contrast, nearly every proposer offers a substantial split to the responder.

That dramatic increase in generosity and fairness is, of course, related to the different rules used in the two games. When one person has total control over the split, selfish tendencies are given free reign. But when rejections become possible, the player in charge of proposing the split has to take the other player's feelings into account. That causes even selfish proposers to make generous offers because they quickly realize that the only way they can get any money for themselves is by making proposals that will not be rejected.

Implications for Market Efficiency The willingness of proposers to make more generous offers when faced with the threat of rejection can be thought of as the simplest expression of the invisible hand.

As we discussed in Chapter 2, the invisible hand is a metaphor that summarizes the tendency of the market system to align private interests with social interests and get people behaving in ways that benefit not only themselves but other people, too.

In the case of the ultimatum game, the threat of rejection helps to align private interests with social interests. It does so by motivating selfish people to make substantially more generous offers. The result is a higher level of cooperation and utility as offers get accepted and players split the money.

A similar process can be seen in the real world with respect to consumer sovereignty. As discussed in Chapter 2, consumer sovereignty is the right of consumers to spend their incomes on the goods and services that they are most willing and able to buy. Crucially, that right includes the ability to reject any product that does not meet the consumer's expectations.

That right of rejection leads to substantial social benefits because it motivates producers to work hard at producing products that will be acceptable to consumers. Over time, those efforts lead to increased allocative and productive efficiency as better products get produced at lower prices.

SUMMARY

LO14.1 Define behavioral economics and explain how it contrasts with neoclassical economics.

Neoclassical economics bases its predictions about human behavior on the assumption that people are fully rational decision makers who have no trouble making mental calculations and no problems dealing with temptation. While some of its predictions are accurate, many are not.

The key difficulty facing neoclassical economics is that people make systematic errors, meaning that they regularly and repeatedly engage in behaviors that reduce their likelihood of achieving what they want.

Behavioral economics attempts to explain systematic errors by combining insights from economics, psychology, and biology. Its goal is to make more accurate predictions about human choice behavior by taking into account the mental mistakes that lead to systematic errors.

LO14.2 Discuss the evidence for the brain being modular, computationally restricted, reliant on heuristics, and prone to various forms of cognitive error.

Our brains make systematic errors for two reasons. First, our brains were not prepared by evolution for dealing with many modern problems, especially those having to do with math, physics, and statistics. Second, our brains also make mistakes when dealing with long-standing challenges (like interpreting visual information) because caloric limitations forced our brains to adopt low-energy heuristics (shortcuts) for completing mental tasks.

Heuristics sacrifice accuracy for speed and low energy usage. In most cases, the lack of accuracy is not important because the errors that result are relatively minor. However, in some cases, those errors can generate cognitive biases that substantially impede rational decision making. Examples include confirmation bias, the overconfidence effect, the availability heuristic, and framing effects.

LO14.3 Relate how prospect theory helps to explain many consumer behaviors, including framing effects, mental accounting, anchoring, loss aversion, and the endowment effect.

Prospect theory is the behavioral economics theory that attempts to accurately describe how people deal with risk and uncertainty. Its key feature is that it models a person's preferences about uncertain outcomes as being based on whether those outcomes will cause gains or losses relative to the current status quo situation to which the person has become accustomed.

Prospect theory also accounts for loss aversion and the fact that most people perceive the pain of losing a given amount of money as being about 2.5 times more intense than the pleasure they would receive from an equal-sized gain.

LO14.4 Describe how time inconsistency and myopia cause people to make suboptimal long-run decisions.

Myopia refers to the difficulty that most people have in conceptualizing the future. It causes people to put insufficient weight on future outcomes when making decisions.

Time inconsistency refers to the difficulty that most people have in correctly predicting what their future selves will want. It causes self-control problems because people are not able to correctly anticipate the degree to which their future selves may fall prey to various sorts of temptation.

People sometimes utilize precommitments to help them overcome self-control problems. Precommitments are courses of action that would be very difficult for the future self to alter. They consequently force the future self to do what the present self desires.

LO14.5 Define fairness and give examples of how it affects behavior in the economy and in the dictator and ultimatum games.

Behavioral economists have found extensive evidence that people are *not* purely self-interested. Rather, they care substantially about fairness and are often willing to give up money and other possessions in order to benefit other people.

The field evidence for fairness includes donations to charity, law-abiding behavior, the reluctance of retailers to raise prices during natural disasters, and the willingness of many consumers to pay premium prices for Fair Trade products.

The dictator and ultimatum games provide experimental evidence on fairness by showing how pairs of people interact to split a pot of money that is provided by the researcher. In the dictator game, one person has total control over the split. In the ultimatum game, both players must agree to the split.

The dictator game shows that many people will share with others even when anonymity would allow them to be perfectly selfish and keep all the money for themselves. The ultimatum game shows that people put a very high value on being treated fairly. They would rather reject an unfair offer and get nothing than accept it and get something.

TERMS AND CONCEPTS

neoclassical economics	status quo	myopia
behavioral economics	loss aversion	time inconsistency
rational	prospect theory	self-control problems
systematic errors	anchoring	precommitments
heuristics	mental accounting	fairness
cognitive biases	endowment effect	dictator game
framing effects	status quo bias	ultimatum game

QUESTIONS

The following and additional problems can be found in ▪**connect**

1. Suppose that Joe enjoys and repeatedly does stupid things like getting heavily into debt and insulting police officers. Do these actions constitute systematic errors? If he gets what he wants each time, are his stupid actions even considered to be errors by economists? Explain. LO14.1

2. Which of the following are systematic errors? LO14.1
   a. A colorblind person who repeatedly runs red lights.
   b. An accountant whose occasional math errors are sometimes on the high side and sometimes on the low side.
   c. The tendency many people have to see faces in clouds.
   d. Miranda paying good money for a nice-looking apple that turns out to be rotten inside.
   e. Elvis always wanting to save more but then spending his whole paycheck, month after month.

3. Why do behavioral economists consider it helpful to base a theory of economic behavior on the actual mental processes that people use to make decisions? Why do neoclassical economists not care about whether a theory incorporates those actual mental processes? LO14.1

4. Identify each statement as being associated with neoclassical economics or behavioral economics. LO14.1
   a. People are eager and accurate calculators.
   b. People are often selfless and generous.
   c. People have no trouble resisting temptation.
   d. People place insufficient weight on future events and outcomes.
   e. People treat others well only if doing so will get them something they want.

5. Economist Gerd Gigerenzer characterizes heuristics as "fast and frugal" ways of reaching decisions. Are there any costs to heuristics being "fast and frugal"? Explain and give an example of how a fast and frugal method for doing something in everyday life comes at some costs in terms of other attributes forgone. LO14.2

6. "There's no such thing as bad publicity." Evaluate this statement in terms of the recognition heuristic. LO14.2

7. Label each of the following behaviors with the correct bias or heuristic. LO14.3
   a. Your uncle says that he knew all along that the stock market was going to crash in 2008.
   b. When Fred does well at work, he credits his intelligence. When anything goes wrong, he blames his secretary.
   c. Ellen thinks that being struck dead by lightning is much more likely than dying from an accidental fall at home.
   d. The sales of a TV that is priced at $999 rise after another very similar TV priced at $1,300 is placed next to it at the store.
   e. The sales of a brand of toothpaste rise after new TV commercials announce that the brand "is preferred by 4 out of 5 dentists."

8. For each of the following cognitive biases, come up with at least one example from your own life. LO14.2
   a. Confirmation bias.
   b. Self-serving bias.
   c. The overconfidence effect.
   d. Hindsight bias.
   e. The availability heuristic.
   f. The planning fallacy.
   g. Framing effects.

9. Suppose that Ike is loss averse. In the morning, Ike's stockbroker calls to tell him that he has gained $1,000 on his stock portfolio. In the evening, his accountant calls to tell him that he owes an extra $1,000 in taxes. At the end of the day, does Ike feel emotionally neutral since the dollar value of the gain in his stock portfolio exactly offsets the amount of extra taxes he has to pay? Explain. LO14.3

10. You just accepted a campus job helping to raise money for your school's athletic program. You are told to draft a fund-raising letter. The bottom of the letter asks recipients to write down a donation amount. If you want to raise as much money as possible, would it be better if the text of that section mentioned that your school is ranked third in the nation in sports or that you are better than 99 percent of other schools at sports? Explain. LO14.3

11. In the early 1990s, New Jersey and Pennsylvania both reformed their automobile insurance systems so that citizens could opt for either a less-expensive policy that did not allow people to sue if they got into accidents or a more-expensive policy that did allow people to sue if they got into accidents. In New Jersey, the default option was the less-expensive policy that did not allow suing. In Pennsylvania, the default option was the more-expensive policy that did allow suing. Given those options, which policy do you think most people in New Jersey ended up with? What about in Pennsylvania? Explain. LO14.3

12. Give an example from your own life of a situation where you or someone you know uses a precommitment to overcome a self-control problem. Describe why the precommitment is useful and what it compensates for. Avoid any precommitment that was mentioned in the book. LO14.4

13. Erik wants to save more, but whenever a paycheck arrives, he ends up spending everything. According to behavioral economists, which of the following strategies to help him overcome this tendency would be most effective? LO14.4
   a. Teach him about time inconsistency.
   b. Tell him that self-control problems are common.
   c. Have him engage in precommitments that will make it difficult for his future self to overspend.

14. What do you think of the ethics of using unconscious nudges to alter people's behavior? Before you answer, consider the

following argument made by economists Richard Thaler and Cass Sunstein, who favor the use of nudges. They argue that in most situations, we couldn't avoid nudging even if we wanted to because whatever policy we choose will contain some set of unconscious nudges and incentives that will influence people. Thus, they say, we might as well choose the wisest set of nudges. LO14.4

15. What does behavioral economics have to say about each of the following statements? LO14.5
    a. "Nobody is truly charitable—they just give money to show off."
    b. "America has a ruthless capitalist system. Considerations of fairness are totally ignored."
    c. "Selfish people always get ahead. It's like nobody even notices!"

16. Do people playing the dictator game show only self-interested behavior? How much divergence is there in the splits given by dictators to the other player? LO14.5

17. Evaluate the following statement. "We shouldn't generalize from what people do in the ultimatum game because $10 is a trivial amount of money. When larger amounts of money are on the line, people will act differently." LO14.5

18. Many proposers in the ultimatum game offer half to the responder with whom they are paired. This behavior could be motivated by (select as many as might apply): LO14.5
    a. Fear that an unequal split might be rejected by a fair-minded responder.
    b. A desire to induce the responder to reject the offer.
    c. A strong sense of fairness on the part of the proposers.
    d. Unrestrained greed on the part of the proposers.

PROBLEMS

1. One type of systematic error arises because people tend to think of benefits in percentage terms rather than in absolute dollar amounts. As an example, Samir is willing to drive 20 minutes out of his way to save $4 on a grocery item that costs $10 at a local market. But he is unwilling to drive 20 minutes out of his way to save $10 on a laptop that costs $400 at a local store. In percentage terms, how big is the savings on the grocery item? On the laptop? In absolute terms, how big is the savings on the grocery item? On the laptop? If Samir is willing to sacrifice 20 minutes of his time to save $4 in one case, shouldn't he also be willing to sacrifice 20 minutes of his time to save $10? LO14.2

2. Anne is a bargain-minded shopper. Normally, her favorite toothpaste costs the same at both of her local supermarkets, but the stores are having competing sales this week. At one store, there is a bonus offer: buy 2, get 1 free. At the other store, toothpaste is being sold at 40 percent off. Anne instantly opts for the first offer. Was that really the less-expensive choice? (Hint: Is "buy 2, get 1 free" the same as 50 percent off?) LO14.2

3. The coffee shop near the local college normally sells 10 ounces of roasted coffee beans for $10. But the shop sometimes puts the beans on sale. During some sales, it offers "33 percent more for free." Other weeks, it takes "33 percent off" the normal price. After reviewing the shop's sales data, the shop's manager finds that "33 percent more for free" sells a lot more coffee than "33 percent off." Are the store's customers making a systematic error? Which is actually the better deal? LO14.2

4. Angela owes $500 on a credit card and $2,000 on a student loan. The credit card has a 15 percent annual interest rate and the student loan has a 7 percent annual interest rate. Her sense of loss aversion makes her more anxious about the larger loan. As a result, she plans to pay it off first—despite the fact that professional financial advisors always tell people to pay off their highest-interest-rate loans first. Suppose Angela has only $500 at the present time to help pay down her loans and that this $500 will be the only money she will have for making debt payments for at least the next year. If she uses the $500 to pay off the credit card, how much interest will accrue on the other loan over the coming year? On the other hand, if she uses the $500 to pay off part of the student loan, how much in combined interest will she owe over the next year on the remaining balances on the two loans? By how many dollars will she be better off if she uses the $500 to completely pay off the credit card rather than partly paying down the student loan? (Hint: If you owe X dollars at an annual interest rate of Y percent, your annual interest payment will be $X \times Y$, where the interest rate Y is expressed as a decimal.) LO14.3

5. **ADVANCED ANALYSIS** In the algebraic version of prospect theory, the variable x represents gains and losses. A positive value for x is a gain, a negative value for x is a loss, and a zero value for x represents remaining at the status quo. The so-called value function, $v(x)$, has separate equations for translating gains and losses into, respectively, positive values (utility) and negative values (disutility). The gain or loss is typically measured in dollars while the resulting value (utility or disutility) is measured in utils. A typical person values gains ($x > 0$) using the function $v(x) = x^{0.88}$ and losses ($x < 0$) using the function $v(x) = -2.5*(-x)^{0.88}$. In addition, if she stays at the status quo ($x = 0$), then $v(x) = 0$. First use a scientific calculator (or a spreadsheet program) and the typical person's value functions for gains and

losses to fill out the missing spaces in the following table. Then answer the questions that follow. LO14.3

Gain or Loss	Total Value of Gain or Loss	Marginal Value of Gain or Loss
−3	−6.57	____
−2	____	−2.10
−1	−2.50	−2.50
0	0.00	____
1	____	1.00
2	1.84	____
3	____	0.79

a. What is the total value of gaining $1? Of gaining $2?

b. What is the marginal value of going from $0 to gaining $1? Of going from gaining $1 to gaining $2? Does the typical person experience diminishing marginal utility from gains?

c. What is the marginal value of going from $0 to losing $1? Of going from losing $1 to losing $2? Does the typical person experience diminishing marginal disutility from losses?

d. Suppose that a person simultaneously gains $1 from one source and loses $1 from another source. What is the person's total utility after summing the values from these two events? Can a *combination* of events that leaves a person with the same wealth as he started with be perceived negatively? Does this shed light on status quo bias?

e. Suppose that an investor has one investment that gains $2 while another investment simultaneously loses $1. What is the person's total utility after summing the values from these two events? Will an investor need to have gains that are bigger than her losses just to feel as good as she would if she did not invest at all and simply remained at the status quo?

6. Ted has always had difficulty saving money, so on June 1, Ted enrolls in a Christmas savings program at his local bank and deposits $750. That money is totally locked away until December 1 so that Ted can be certain that he will still have it once the holiday shopping season begins. Suppose that the annual rate of interest is 10 percent on ordinary savings accounts (that allow depositors to withdraw their money at any time). How much interest is Ted giving up by precommitting his money into the Christmas savings account for six months instead of depositing it into an ordinary savings account? (Hint: If you invest X dollars at an annual interest rate of Y percent, you will receive interest equal to $X \times Y$, where the interest rate Y is expressed as a decimal.) LO14.4

ability-to-pay principle   The idea that those who have greater income (or wealth) should pay a greater proportion of it as taxes than those who have less income (or wealth).

accounting profit   The total revenue of a firm less its explicit costs.

actual reserves   The funds that a bank has on deposit at the Federal Reserve Bank of its district (plus its vault cash).

aggregate   A collection of specific economic units treated as if they were one. For example, all prices of individual goods and services are combined into a price level, or all the units of output are aggregated into gross domestic product.

aggregate demand   A schedule or curve that shows the total quantity of goods and services demanded (purchased) at different price levels.

aggregate demand–aggregate supply model   The macroeconomic model that uses aggregate demand and aggregate supply to determine and explain the price level and the real domestic output.

aggregate supply   A schedule or curve showing the total quantity of goods and services supplied (produced) at different price levels.

aggregate supply shocks   Sudden, large changes in resource costs that shift an economy's aggregate supply curve.

allocative efficiency   The apportionment of resources among firms and industries to obtain the production of the products most wanted by society (consumers); the output of each product at which its marginal cost and price or marginal benefit are equal.

anchoring   The tendency people have to unconsciously base, or "anchor," the valuation of an item they are currently thinking about on recently considered but logically irrelevant information.

appreciation (of a currency)   An increase in the value of the dollar relative to the currency of another nation, so a dollar buys a larger amount of the foreign currency and thus of foreign goods.

asset demand   The amount of money people want to hold as a store of value; this amount varies inversely with the interest rate.

average fixed cost   A firm's total fixed cost divided by output (the quantity of product produced).

average product   The total output produced per unit of a resource employed (total product divided by the quantity of that employed resource).

average revenue   Total revenue from the sale of a product divided by the quantity of the product sold (demanded); equal to the price at which the product is sold when all units of the product are sold at the same price.

average tax rate   Total tax paid divided by total (taxable) income, as a percentage.

average total cost   A firm's total cost divided by output (the quantity of product produced); equal to average fixed cost plus average variable cost.

average variable cost   A firm's total variable cost divided by output (the quantity of product produced).

balance sheet   A statement of the assets, liabilities, and net worth of a firm or individual at some given time.

barrier to entry   Anything that artificially prevents the entry of firms into an industry.

barter   The exchange of one good or service for another good or service.

behavioral economics   The branch of economic theory that combines insights from economics, psychology, and biology to make more accurate predictions about human behavior than conventional neoclassical economics, which is hampered by its core assumptions that people are fundamentally rational and almost entirely self-interested. Behavioral economics can explain framing effects, anchoring, mental accounting, the endowment effect, status quo bias, time inconsistency, and loss aversion.

benefits-received principle   The idea that those who receive the benefits of goods and services provided by government should pay the taxes required to finance them.

Board of Governors   The seven-member group that supervises and controls the money and banking system of the United States; also called the *Board of Governors of the Federal Reserve System* and the *Federal Reserve Board.*

bond   A financial device through which a borrower (a firm or government) is obligated to pay the principal and interest on a loan at a specific date in the future.

budget deficit   The amount by which the expenditures of the federal government exceed its revenues in any year.

budget line   A line that shows the different combinations of two products a consumer can purchase with a specific money income, given the products' prices.

budget surplus   The amount by which the revenues of the federal government exceed its expenditures in any year.

built-in stabilizer   A mechanism that increases government's budget deficit (or reduces its surplus) during a recession and increases government's budget surplus (or reduces its deficit) during expansion without any action by policymakers. The tax system is one such mechanism.

business   A firm that purchases resources and provides goods and services to the economy.

business cycles   Recurring increases and decreases in the level of economic activity over periods of years; a cycle consists of peak, recession, trough, and expansion phases.

capital Human-made resources (buildings, machinery, and equipment) used to produce goods and services; goods that do not directly satisfy human wants; also called *capital goods* and *investment goods.*

capital goods Items that are used to produce other goods and therefore do not directly satisfy consumer wants.

cartel A formal agreement among firms (or countries) in an industry to set the price of a product and establish the outputs of the individual firms (or countries) or to divide the market for the product geographically.

change in demand A change in the quantity demanded of a good or service at every price; a shift of the demand curve to the left or right.

change in quantity demanded A movement from one point to another on a demand curve.

change in quantity supplied A movement from one point to another on a fixed supply curve.

change in supply A change in the quantity supplied of a good or service at every price; a shift of the supply curve to the left or right.

checkable deposit Any deposit in a commercial bank or thrift institution against which a check may be written.

circular flow diagram The flow of resources from households to firms and of products from firms to households. These flows are accompanied by reverse flows of money from firms to households and from households to firms.

Coase theorem The idea, first stated by economist Ronald Coase, that externality problems may be resolved through private negotiations of the affected parties.

cognitive biases Misperceptions or misunderstandings that cause systematic errors. Most result either (1) from heuristics that are prone to systematic errors or (2) because the brain is attempting to solve a type of problem (such as a calculus problem) for which it was not evolutionarily evolved and for which it has little innate capability.

collusion A situation in which firms act together and in agreement (collude) to fix prices, divide a market, or otherwise restrict competition.

command system A method of organizing an economy in which property resources are publicly owned and government uses central economic planning to direct and coordinate economic activities; command economy; communism.

commercial bank A firm that engages in the business of banking (accepts deposits, offers checking accounts, and makes loans).

comparative advantage A situation in which a person or country can produce a specific product at a lower opportunity cost than some other person or country; the basis for specialization and trade.

compensating differences Wage differentials received by workers to compensate them for nonmonetary disparities in their jobs.

competition The presence in a market of independent buyers and sellers competing with one another along with the freedom of buyers and sellers to enter and leave the market.

complementary goods Products and services that are used together. When the price of one falls, the demand for the other increases (and conversely).

constant opportunity cost An opportunity cost that remains the same for each additional unit as a consumer (or society) shifts purchases (production) from one product to another along a straight-line budget line (production possibilities curve).

constant returns to scale No changes in the average total cost of producing a product as the firm expands the size of its operations (output) in the long run.

constant-cost industry An industry in which expansion by the entry of new firms has no effect on the prices firms in the industry must pay for resources and thus no effect on production costs.

consumer goods Products and services that satisfy human wants directly.

Consumer Price Index (CPI) An index that measures the prices of a fixed "market basket" of some 300 goods and services bought by a "typical" consumer.

consumer sovereignty Determination by consumers of the types and quantities of goods and services that will be produced with the scarce resources of the economy; consumers' direction of production through their dollar votes.

consumer surplus The difference between the maximum price a consumer is (or consumers are) willing to pay for a product and the actual price paid.

contractionary fiscal policy A decrease in government purchases for goods and services, an increase in net taxes, or some combination of the two, for the purpose of decreasing aggregate demand and thus controlling inflation.

corporate income tax A tax levied on the net income (accounting profit) of corporations.

cost-benefit analysis A comparison of the marginal costs of a government project or program with the marginal benefits to decide whether or not to employ resources in that project or program and to what extent.

cost-push inflation Increases in the price level (inflation) resulting from an increase in resource costs (for example, raw-material prices) and hence in per-unit production costs; inflation caused by reductions in aggregate supply.

Council of Economic Advisers (CEA) A group of three persons that advises and assists the president of the United States on economic matters (including the preparation of the annual *Economic Report of the President*).

creative destruction The hypothesis that the creation of new products and production methods simultaneously destroys the market power of existing monopolies.

cross-elasticity of demand The ratio of the percentage change in *quantity demanded* of one good to the percentage change in the price of some other good. A positive coefficient indicates the two products are *substitute goods;* a negative coefficient indicates they are *complementary goods.*

crowding-out effect   A rise in interest rates and a resulting decrease in investment caused by the federal government's increased borrowing to finance budget deficits or debt.

cyclical asymmetry   The potential problem of monetary policy successfully controlling inflation during the expansionary phase of the business cycle but failing to expand spending and real GDP during the recessionary phase of the cycle.

cyclical deficit   A federal budget deficit that is caused by a recession and the consequent decline in tax revenues.

cyclical unemployment   A type of unemployment caused by insufficient total spending (or by insufficient aggregate demand).

cyclically adjusted budget   A measure of what the federal budget deficit or budget surplus would be with the existing tax and government spending programs if the economy had achieved full-employment GDP in the year.

decreasing-cost industry   An industry in which expansion through the entry of firms lowers the prices that firms in the industry must pay for resources and therefore decreases their production costs.

deflation   A decline in the economy's price level.

demand   A schedule showing the amounts of a good or service that buyers (or a buyer) wish to purchase at various prices during some time period.

demand curve   A curve illustrating demand.

demand shocks   Sudden, unexpected change in aggregate demand.

demand-pull inflation   Increases in the price level (inflation) resulting from an excess of demand over output at the existing price level, caused by an increase in aggregate demand.

demand-side market failures   Underallocations of resources that occur when private demand curves understate consumers' full willingness to pay for a good or service.

dependent variable   A variable that changes as a consequence of a change in some other (independent) variable; the "effect" or outcome.

depreciation (of a currency)   A decrease in the value of the dollar relative to another currency, so a dollar buys a smaller amount of the foreign currency and therefore of foreign goods.

derived demand   The demand for a resource that depends on the demand for the products it helps to produce.

determinants of aggregate demand   Factors such as consumption spending, investment, government spending, and net exports that, if they change, shift the aggregate demand curve.

determinants of aggregate supply   Factors such as input prices, productivity, and the legal-institutional environment that, if they change, shift the aggregate supply curve.

determinants of demand   Factors other than price that determine the quantities demanded of a good or service.

determinants of supply   Factors other than price that determine the quantities supplied of a good or service.

dictator game   A mutually anonymous behavioral economics game in which one person ("the dictator") unilaterally determines how to split an amount of money with the second player.

differentiated oligopoly   An oligopoly in which the firms produce a differentiated product.

direct relationship   The relationship between two variables that change in the same direction, for example, product price and quantity supplied.

discount rate   The interest rate that the Federal Reserve Banks charge on the loans they make to commercial banks and thrift institutions.

diseconomies of scale   Increases in the average total cost of producing a product as the firm expands the size of its plant (its output) in the long run.

disinflation   A reduction in the rate of inflation.

division of labor   The separation of the work required to produce a product into a number of different tasks that are performed by different workers; specialization of workers.

Doha Round   The latest, uncompleted (as of 2011) sequence of trade negotiations by members of the World Trade Organization; named after Doha, Qatar, where the set of negotiations began.

dollar votes   The "votes" that consumers and entrepreneurs cast for the production of consumer and capital goods, respectively, when they purchase those goods in product and resource markets.

dumping   The sale of products in a foreign country at prices either below costs or below the prices charged at home.

earned-income tax credit (EITC)   A refundable federal tax credit provided to low-income wage earners to supplement their families' incomes and encourage work.

easy money policy   Federal Reserve System actions to increase the money supply to lower interest rates and expand real GDP.

economic cost   A payment that must be made to obtain and retain the services of a resource; the income a firm must provide to a resource supplier to attract the resource away from an alternative use; equal to the quantity of other products that cannot be produced when resources are instead used to make a particular product.

economic growth   (1) An outward shift in the production possibilities curve that results from an increase in resource supplies or quality or an improvement in technology; (2) an increase of real output (gross domestic product) or real output per capita.

economic perspective   A viewpoint that envisions individuals and institutions making rational decisions by comparing the marginal benefits and marginal costs associated with their actions.

economic problem   The choices necessitated because society's economic wants for goods and services are unlimited but the resources available to satisfy these wants are limited (scarce).

economic profit   The total revenue of a firm less its economic costs (which include both explicit costs and implicit costs); also called *pure profit* and *above-normal profit*.

economic resources   The land, labor, capital, and entrepreneurial ability that are used in the production of goods and services; productive agents; factors of production.

economic system   A particular set of institutional arrangements and a coordinating mechanism for solving the economizing problem; a method of organizing an economy, of which the market system and the command system are the two general types.

economics   The study of how people, institutions, and society make economic choices under conditions of scarcity.

economies of scale   Reductions in the average total cost of producing a product as the firm expands the size of its plant (its output) in the long run; the economies of mass production.

efficiency (deadweight) loss   A reduction in combined consumer and producer surplus caused by an underallocation or overallocation of resources to the production of a good or service.

efficiency (deadweight) loss of a tax   The loss of net benefits to society because a tax reduces the production and consumption of a taxed good below the level of allocative efficiency.

elastic demand   Product or resource demand whose price elasticity is greater than 1. This means the resulting change in quantity demanded is greater than the percentage change in price.

elasticity of labor demand   A measure of the responsiveness of labor quantity to a change in the wage rate.

endowment effect   The tendency people have to place higher valuations on items they possess (are endowed with) than on identical items that they do not possess; perhaps caused by loss aversion.

entitlement programs   Government programs such as social insurance, SNAP, Medicare, and Medicaid that guarantee particular levels of transfer payments or noncash benefits to all who fit the programs' criteria.

entrepreneurial ability   The human resource that combines the other resources to produce a product, makes nonroutine decisions, innovates, and bears risks.

equality-efficiency trade-off   The decrease in economic efficiency that may accompany a decrease in income inequality; the presumption that some income inequality is required to achieve economic efficiency.

equilibrium price   The price in a competitive market at which the quantity demanded and the quantity supplied are equal, there is neither a shortage nor a surplus, and there is no tendency for price to rise or fall.

equilibrium price level   The price level at which the aggregate demand curve intersects the aggregate supply curve.

equilibrium quantity   (1) The quantity demanded and supplied at the equilibrium price in a competitive market; (2) the profit-maximizing output of a firm.

equilibrium real output   The gross domestic product at which the total quantity of final goods and services purchased (aggregate expenditures) is equal to the total quantity of final goods and services produced (the real domestic output); the real domestic output at which the aggregate demand curve intersects the aggregate supply curve.

euro   The common currency unit used by 19 European nations as of 2017 (Austria, Belgium, Cyprus, Estonia, Finland, France, Germany, Greece, Ireland, Italy, Luxembourg, Malta, the Netherlands, Portugal, Slovakia, Slovenia, and Spain).

European Union (EU)   An association of 28 European nations (as of 2017) that has eliminated tariffs and quotas among them, established common tariffs for imported goods from outside the member nations, eliminated barriers to the free movement of capital, and created other common economic policies.

excess capacity   Plant resources that are underused when imperfectly competitive firms produce less output than that associated with achieving minimum average total cost.

excess reserves   The amount by which a bank's or thrift's actual reserves exceed its required reserves; actual reserves minus required reserves.

exchange rate   The rate of exchange of one nation's currency for another nation's currency.

excise tax   A tax levied on the production of a specific product or on the quantity of the product purchased.

exclusive unionism   The union practice of restricting the supply of skilled union labor to increase the wage rate received by union members.

expansion   The phase of the business cycle in which output, income, and business activity rise.

expansionary fiscal policy   An increase in government purchases of goods and services, a decrease in net taxes, or some combination of the two, for the purpose of increasing aggregate demand and expanding real output.

explicit cost   The monetary payment a firm must make to an outsider to obtain a resource.

export subsidies   Government payments to domestic producers to enable them to reduce the price of a good or service to foreign buyers.

external public debt   Public debt owed to foreign citizens, firms, and institutions.

factors of production   Economic resources: land, capital, labor, and entrepreneurial ability.

fairness   A person's opinion as to whether a price, wage, or allocation is considered morally or ethically acceptable.

Federal funds rate   The interest rate banks and other depository institutions charge one another on overnight loans made out of their excess reserves.

Federal Open Market Committee (FOMC)   The 12-member group that determines the purchase and sale policies of the Federal Reserve Banks in the market for U.S. government securities.

Federal Reserve Banks The 12 banks chartered by the U.S. government to control the money supply and perform other functions. (Also known as *central bank, quasi-public bank, and bankers' bank.*)

Federal Reserve Note Paper money issued by the Federal Reserve Banks.

Federal Reserve System A central component of the U.S. banking system, consisting of the Board of Governors of the Federal Reserve and 12 regional Federal Reserve Banks.

final goods and services Goods and services that have been purchased for final use and not for resale or further processing or manufacturing.

financial services industry The broad category of firms that provide financial products and services to help households and businesses earn *interest,* receive *dividends,* obtain *capital gains,* insure against losses, and plan for retirement.

fiscal policy Changes in government spending and tax collections designed to achieve a full-employment and noninflationary domestic output; also called *discretionary fiscal policy.*

fixed cost Any cost that in total does not change when the firm changes its output; the cost of fixed resources.

foreign exchange market A market in which the money (currency) of one nation can be used to purchase (can be exchanged for) the money of another nation.

fractional reserve banking system A banking system in which banks and thrifts are required to hold less than 100 percent of their checkable deposit liabilities as cash reserves.

framing effects In prospect theory, changes in people's decision making caused by new information that alters the context, or "frame of reference," that they use to judge whether options are viewed as gains or losses relative to the status quo.

free-rider problem The inability of potential providers of an economically desirable good or service to obtain payment from those who benefit because of nonexcludability.

freedom of choice The freedom of owners of property resources to employ or dispose of them as they see fit, of workers to enter any line of work for which they are qualified, and of consumers to spend their incomes in a manner that they think is appropriate.

freedom of enterprise The freedom of firms to obtain economic resources, to use those resources to produce products of the firm's own choosing, and to sell their products in markets of their choice.

frictional unemployment A type of unemployment caused by workers voluntarily changing jobs and by temporary layoffs; unemployed workers between jobs.

game theory A means of analyzing the business behavior of oligopolists that uses the theory of strategy associated with games such as chess and bridge.

GDP gap Actual gross domestic product minus potential output; may be either a positive amount (a positive GDP gap) or a negative amount (a negative GDP gap).

General Agreement on Tariffs and Trade (GATT) The international agreement reached in 1947 in which 23 nations agreed to give equal and nondiscriminatory treatment to one another, to reduce tariff rates by multinational negotiations, and to eliminate import quotas. It now includes most nations and has become the World Trade Organization.

Gini ratio A numerical measure of the overall dispersion of income among an economy's income receivers.

government purchases Expenditures by government for goods and services that government consumes in providing public goods and for public capital that has a long lifetime; the expenditures of all governments in the economy for those final goods and services.

gross domestic product (GDP) The total market value of all final goods and services produced annually within the boundaries of the United States, whether by U.S.- or foreign-supplied resources.

gross private domestic investment Expenditures for newly produced capital goods (such as machinery, equipment, tools, and buildings) and for additions to inventories.

growth accounting The bookkeeping of the supply-side elements that contribute to changes in real GDP over some specific time period.

heuristics The brain's low-energy mental shortcuts for making decisions. They are "fast and frugal" and work well in most situations but in other situations result in systematic errors.

homogeneous oligopoly An oligopoly in which the firms produce a standardized product.

household An economic unit (of one or more persons) that provides the economy with resources and uses the income received to purchase goods and services that satisfy economic wants.

human capital The accumulation of knowledge and skills that make a worker productive.

immediate short-run aggregate supply curve An aggregate supply curve for which real output, but not the price level, changes when the aggregate demand curve shifts; a horizontal aggregate supply curve that implies an inflexible price level.

implicit cost The monetary income a firm sacrifices when it uses a resource it owns rather than supplying the resource in the market; equal to what the resource could have earned in the best-paying alternative employment; includes a normal profit.

import quota A limit imposed by a nation on the quantity (or total value) of a good that may be imported during some period of time.

inclusive unionism The union practice of including as members all workers employed in an industry.

income elasticity of demand The ratio of the percentage change in the quantity demanded of a good to a percentage change in consumer income; measures the responsiveness of consumer purchases to income changes.

income inequality The unequal distribution of an economy's total income among households or families.

income mobility The extent to which income receivers move from one part of the income distribution to another over some period of time.

increasing returns An increase in a firm's output by a larger percentage than the percentage increase in its inputs.

increasing-cost industry An industry in which expansion through the entry of new firms raises the prices firms in the industry must pay for resources and therefore increases their production costs.

independent variable The variable causing a change in some other (dependent) variable.

inelastic demand Product or resource demand for which the elasticity coefficient for price is less than 1. This means the resulting percentage change in quantity demanded is less than the percentage change in price.

inferior good A good or service whose consumption declines as income rises, prices held constant.

inflation A rise in the general level of prices in an economy.

inflexible prices Product prices that remain in place (at least for a while) even though supply or demand has changed; stuck prices or sticky prices.

information technology New and more efficient methods of delivering and receiving information through use of computers, fax machines, wireless phones, and the Internet.

infrastructure The capital goods usually provided by the public sector for the use of its citizens and firms (for example, highways, bridges, transit systems, wastewater treatment facilities, municipal water systems, and airports).

interest on excess reserves (IOER) Interest rate paid by the Federal Reserve on bank excess reserves.

intermediate goods Products that are purchased for resale or further processing or manufacturing.

inverse relationship The relationship between two variables that change in opposite directions, for example, product price and quantity demanded.

investment Spending for the production and accumulation of capital and additions to inventories.

investment demand curve A curve that shows the amounts of investment demanded by an economy at a series of real interest rates.

"invisible hand" The tendency of firms and resource suppliers that seek to further their own self-interests in competitive markets to also promote the interest of society.

kinked-demand curve The demand curve for a noncollusive oligopolist, which is based on the assumption that rivals will match a price decrease and will ignore a price increase.

labor People's physical and mental talents and efforts that are used to help produce goods and services.

labor force Persons 16 years of age and older who are not in institutions and who are employed or are unemployed and seeking work.

labor productivity Total output divided by the quantity of labor employed to produce it; the average product of labor or output per hour of work.

labor-force participation rate The percentage of the working-age population that is actually in the labor force.

Laffer Curve A curve relating government tax rates and tax revenues and on which a particular tax rate (between zero and 100 percent) maximizes tax revenues.

land Natural resources ("free gifts of nature") used to produce goods and services.

law of demand The principle that, other things equal, an increase in a product's price will reduce the quantity of it demanded, and conversely for a decrease in price.

law of diminishing marginal utility The principle that the amount of extra satisfaction (marginal utility) from consuming a product declines as more of it is consumed.

law of diminishing returns The principle that as successive increments of a variable resource are added to a fixed resource, the marginal product of the variable resource will eventually decrease.

law of increasing opportunity costs The principle that as the production of a good increases, the opportunity cost of producing an additional unit rises.

law of supply The principle that, other things equal, an increase in the price of a product will increase the quantity of it supplied, and conversely for a price decrease.

learning by doing Achieving greater productivity and lower average total cost through gains in knowledge and skill that accompany repetition of a task; a source of economies of scale.

legal tender A legal designation of a nation's official currency (bills and coins). Payment of debts must be accepted in this monetary unit, but creditors can specify the form of payment, for example, "cash only" or "check or credit card only."

limited liability Restriction of the maximum loss to a predetermined amount for the owners (stockholders) of a corporation. The maximum loss is the amount they paid for their shares of stock.

liquidity The ease with which an asset can be converted quickly into cash with little or no loss of purchasing power. Money is said to be perfectly liquid, whereas other assets have a lesser degree of liquidity.

liquidity trap A situation in a severe recession in which the Fed's injection of additional reserves into the banking system has little or no additional positive impact on lending, borrowing, investment, or aggregate demand.

long run (1) In microeconomics, a period of time long enough to enable producers of a product to change the quantities of all the resources they employ; period in which all resources and costs are variable and no resources or costs are fixed. (2) In macroeconomics, a period sufficiently long for nominal wages and other input prices to change in response to a change in the nation's price level.

long-run AD-AS model   A model in which the equilibrium price level and level of real GDP are determined by the intersection of the AD curve and the vertical long-run AS curve.

long-run aggregate supply curve   The aggregate supply curve associated with a time period in which input prices (especially nominal wages) are fully responsive to changes in the price level.

long-run supply curve   A curve showing the prices at which a purely competitive industry will make various quantities of the product available in the long run.

long-run vertical Phillips Curve   The Phillips Curve after all nominal wages have adjusted to changes in the rate of inflation; a line emanating straight upward at the economy's natural rate of unemployment.

Lorenz curve   A curve showing the distribution of income in an economy. The cumulated percentage of families (income receivers) is measured along the horizontal axis, and cumulated percentage of income is measured along the vertical axis.

loss aversion   In prospect theory, the property of most people's preferences that the pain generated by losses feels substantially more intense than the pleasure generated by gains.

M1   The most narrowly defined money supply, equal to currency in the hands of the public and the checkable deposits of commercial banks and thrift institutions.

M2   A more broadly defined money supply, equal to M1 plus noncheckable savings accounts (including money market deposit accounts), small-denominated time deposits (deposits of less than $100,000), and individual money market mutual fund balances.

macroeconomics   The part of economics concerned with the economy as a whole; with such major aggregates as the household, business, and government sectors; and with measures of the total economy.

marginal analysis   The comparison of marginal ("extra" or "additional") benefits and marginal costs, usually for decision making.

marginal cost   The extra (additional) cost of producing 1 more unit of output; equal to the change in total cost divided by the change in output (and, in the short run, to the change in total variable cost divided by the change in output).

marginal product   The additional output produced when 1 additional unit of a resource is employed (the quantity of all other resources employed remaining constant); equal to the change in total product divided by the change in the quantity of a resource employed.

marginal resource cost (MRC)   The change in a firm's total cost when it employs 1 more unit of labor.

marginal revenue   The change in total revenue that results from the sale of 1 additional unit of a firm's product; equal to the change in total revenue divided by the change in the quantity of the product sold.

marginal revenue product (MRP)   The change in a firm's total revenue when it employs 1 more unit of labor.

marginal tax rate   The tax rate paid on an additional dollar of income.

market   Any institution or mechanism that brings together buyers (demanders) and sellers (suppliers) of a particular good or service.

market failure   The inability of a market to bring about the allocation of resources that best satisfies the wants of society; in particular, the overallocation or underallocation of resources to the production of a particular good or service because of spillovers or informational problems or because markets do not provide desired public goods.

market period   A period in which producers of a product are unable to change the quantity produced in response to a change in its price and in which there is a perfectly inelastic supply.

market system   All the product and resource markets of a market economy and the relationships among them; a method that allows the prices determined in those markets to allocate the economy's scarce resources and to communicate and coordinate the decisions made by consumers, firms, and resource suppliers.

Medicaid   A federal program that helps finance the medical expenses of individuals covered by the Supplemental Security Income (SSI) and Temporary Assistance for Needy Families (TANF) programs.

Medicare   A federal program that is financed by payroll taxes and provides for (1) compulsory hospital insurance for senior citizens, (2) low-cost voluntary insurance to help older Americans pay physicians' fees, and (3) subsidized insurance to buy prescription drugs.

medium of exchange   Any item sellers generally accept and buyers generally use to pay for a good or service; money; a convenient means of exchanging goods and services without engaging in barter.

mental accounting   The tendency people have to create separate "mental boxes" (or "accounts") in which they deal with particular financial transactions in isolation rather than dealing with them as part of an overall decision-making process that would consider how to best allocate their limited budgets across all possible options by comparing marginal benefits and marginal costs (also called the *utility-maximizing rule*).

microeconomics   The part of economics concerned with such individual units as a household, a firm, or an industry and with individual markets, specific goods and services, and product and resource prices.

minimum efficient scale (MES)   The lowest level of output at which a firm can minimize long-run average total cost.

monetary multiplier   The multiple of its excess reserves by which the banking system can expand checkable deposits and thus the money supply by making new loans (or buying securities); equal to 1 divided by the reserve requirement.

monetary policy   A central bank's changing of the money supply to influence interest rates and assist the economy in achieving price stability, full employment, and economic growth.

money   Any item that is generally acceptable to sellers in exchange for goods and services.

money market The market in which the demand for and the supply of money determine the interest rate (or the level of interest rates) in the economy.

money market deposit account (MMDA) An interest-earning account (at a bank or thrift) consisting of short-term securities on which a limited number of checks may be written each year.

money market mutual funds (MMMFs) Interest-bearing accounts offered by investment companies, which pool depositors' funds for the purchase of short-term securities. Depositors may write checks in minimum amounts or more against their accounts.

monopolistic competition A market structure in which many firms sell a differentiated product, into which entry is relatively easy, in which the firm has some control over its product price, and in which there is considerable nonprice competition.

monopsony A market structure in which only a single buyer of a good, service, or resource is present.

moral hazard The possibility that individuals or institutions will change their behavior as the result of a contract or agreement.

mortgage-backed securities Bonds that represent claims to all or part of the monthly mortgage payments from the pools of mortgage loans made by lenders to borrowers to help them purchase residential property.

MR = MC rule The principle that a firm will maximize its profit (or minimize its losses) by producing the output at which marginal revenue and marginal cost are equal, provided product price is equal to or greater than average variable cost.

MRP = MRC rule The principle that to maximize profit a firm should expand employment until the marginal revenue product (MRP) of labor equals the marginal resource cost (MRC) of labor.

multiplier The ratio of a change in the equilibrium GDP to the change in *investment* or in any other component of *aggregate expenditures* or *aggregate demand;* the number by which a change in any such component must be multiplied to find the resulting change in the equilibrium GDP.

mutual interdependence A situation in which a change in price strategy (or in some other strategy) by one firm will affect the sales and profits of another firm (or other firms). Any firm that makes such a change can expect the other rivals to react to the change.

myopia Refers to the difficulty human beings have with conceptualizing the more distant future. Leads to decisions that overly favor present and near-term options at the expense of more distant future possibilities.

national income and product accounts (NIPA) The national accounts that measure overall production and income of the economy and other related aggregates for the nation as a whole.

natural monopoly An industry in which economies of scale are so great that a single firm can produce the product at a lower average total cost than would be possible if more than one firm produced the product.

near-money Financial assets, the most important of which are noncheckable savings accounts, time deposits, and U.S. short-term securities and savings bonds, which are not a medium of exchange but can be readily converted into money.

negative externalities Spillover production or consumption costs imposed on third parties without compensation to them.

neoclassical economics The dominant and conventional branch of economic theory that attempts to predict human behavior by building economic models based on simplifying assumptions about people's motives and capabilities. These include that people are fundamentally rational; motivated almost entirely by self-interest; good at math; and unaffected by heuristics, time inconsistency, and self-control problems.

net exports Exports minus imports.

network effects Increases in the value of a product to each user, including existing users, as the total number of users rises.

nominal GDP Gross domestic product measured in terms of the price level at the time of the measurement; GDP that is unadjusted for inflation.

nominal income The number of dollars received by an individual or group for supplying resources during some period of time; income that is not adjusted for inflation.

nominal interest rate The interest rate expressed in terms of annual amounts currently charged for interest and not adjusted for inflation.

noncash transfers Government transfer payments in the form of goods and services (or vouchers to obtain them) rather than money.

nonprice competition Competition based on distinguishing one's product by means of product differentiation and then advertising the distinguished product to consumers.

nontariff barriers All barriers other than protective tariffs that nations erect to impede international trade, including import quotas, licensing requirements, unreasonable product-quality standards, unnecessary bureaucratic detail in customs procedures, and so on.

normal good A good or service whose consumption increases when income increases and falls when income decreases, price remaining constant.

normal profit The payment made by a firm to obtain and retain entrepreneurial ability; the minimum income entrepreneurial ability must receive to induce it to perform entrepreneurial functions for a firm.

North American Free Trade Agreement (NAFTA) A 1993 agreement establishing, over a 15-year period, a free-trade zone composed of Canada, Mexico, and the United States.

occupational licensing Government laws that require a worker to satisfy certain specified requirements and obtain a license from a licensing board before engaging in a particular occupation.

offshoring The practice of shifting work previously done by American workers to workers located abroad.

offshoring The practice of shifting work previously done by American workers to workers located in other nations.

oligopoly A market structure in which a few firms sell either a standardized or a differentiated product, into which entry is difficult, in which the firm has limited control over product price because of mutual interdependence (except when there is collusion among firms), and in which there is typically nonprice competition.

open-market operations The buying and selling of U.S. government securities by the Federal Reserve Banks for purposes of carrying out monetary policy.

opportunity cost The value of the good, service, or time forgone to obtain something else.

optimal reduction of an externality The reduction of a negative externality such as pollution to a level at which the marginal benefit and marginal cost of reduction are equal.

other-things-equal assumption The assumption that factors other than those being considered are held constant; *ceteris paribus* assumption.

output effect An increase in the use of labor that occurs when a decline in the price of capital reduces a firm's production costs and therefore enables it to sell more output.

payroll tax A tax levied on employers of labor equal to a percentage of all or part of the wages and salaries paid by them and on employees equal to a percentage of all or part of the wages and salaries received by them.

per se violations Collusive actions, such as attempts to fix prices or divide markets, that are violations of the antitrust laws, even if the actions are unsuccessful.

perfectly elastic demand Product or resource demand in which quantity demanded can be of any amount at a particular product price; graphs as a horizontal demand curve.

perfectly inelastic demand Product or resource demand in which price can be of any amount at a particular quantity of the product or resource demanded; quantity demanded does not respond to a change in price; graphs as a vertical demand curve.

personal consumption expenditures The expenditures of households for durable and nondurable consumer goods and services.

personal income tax A tax levied on the taxable income of individuals, households, and unincorporated firms.

Phillips Curve A curve showing the relationship between the unemployment rate (on the horizontal axis) and the annual rate of increase in the price level (on the vertical axis).

Pigovian taxes A tax or charge levied on the production of a product that generates negative externalities. If set correctly, the tax will precisely offset the overallocation (overproduction) generated by the negative externality.

political business cycle The alleged tendency of presidential administrations and Congress to destabilize the economy by reducing taxes and increasing government expenditures before elections and to raise taxes and lower expenditures after elections.

positive externalities Spillover production or consumption benefits conferred on third parties without compensation from them.

potential output The real output (GDP) an economy can produce when it fully employs its available resources.

poverty rate The percentage of the population with incomes below the official poverty income levels that are established by the federal government.

precommittments Actions taken ahead of time that make it difficult for the future self to avoid doing what the present self desires. See *time inconsistency* and *self-control problems*.

price ceiling A legally established maximum price for a good or service.

price discrimination The selling of a product to different buyers at different prices when the price differences are not justified by differences in cost.

price elasticity of demand The ratio of the percentage change in quantity demanded of a product or resource to the percentage change in its price; a measure of the responsiveness of buyers to a change in the price of a product or resource.

price elasticity of supply The ratio of the percentage change in quantity supplied of a product or resource to the percentage change in its price; a measure of the responsiveness of producers to a change in the price of a product or resource.

price floor A legally determined price above the equilibrium price.

price leadership An informal method that firms in an oligopoly may employ to set the price of their product: One firm (the leader) is the first to announce a change in price, and the other firms (the followers) soon announce identical or similar changes.

price taker A seller (or buyer) that is unable to affect the price at which a product or resource sells by changing the amount it sells (or buys).

prime interest rate The benchmark interest rate that banks use as a reference point for a wide range of loans to businesses and individuals.

principal-agent problem A conflict of interest that occurs when agents (workers or managers) pursue their own objectives to the detriment of the principals' (stockholders') goals.

principles Statements about economic behavior that enable prediction of the probable effects of certain actions.

private good A good or service that is individually consumed and that can be profitably provided by privately owned firms because they can exclude nonpayers from receiving the benefits.

private property The right of private persons and firms to obtain, own, control, employ, dispose of, and bequeath land, capital, and other property.

producer surplus The difference between the actual price a producer receives (or producers receive) and the minimum acceptable price.

product differentiation A strategy in which one firm's product is distinguished from competing products by means of its design, related services, quality, location, or other attributes (except price).

product market A market in which products are sold by firms and bought by households.

production possibilities curve A curve showing the different combinations of two goods or services that can be produced in a full-employment, full-production economy where the available supplies of resources and technology are fixed.

productive efficiency The production of a good in the least costly way; occurs when production takes place at the output at which average total cost is a minimum and marginal product per dollar's worth of input is the same for all inputs.

productivity A measure of average output or real output per unit of input. For example, the productivity of labor is determined by dividing real output by hours of work.

progressive tax A tax whose average tax rate increases as the taxpayer's income increases and decreases as the taxpayer's income decreases.

property tax A tax on the value of property (capital, land, stocks and bonds, and other assets) owned by firms and households.

proportional tax A tax whose average tax rate remains constant as the taxpayer's income increases or decreases.

prospect theory A *behavioral economics* theory of preferences having three main features: (1) people evaluate options on the basis of whether they generate gains or losses relative to the *status quo;* (2) gains are subject to *diminishing marginal utility,* while losses are subject to diminishing marginal disutility; and (3) people are prone to *loss aversion.*

public debt The total amount owed by the federal government to the owners of government securities; equal to the sum of past government budget deficits less government budget surpluses.

public good A good or service that is characterized by nonrivalry and nonexcludability; a good or service with these characteristics provided by government.

public investments Government expenditures on public capital (such as roads, highways, bridges, mass-transit systems, and electric power facilities) and on human capital (such as education, training, and health).

pure competition A market structure in which a very large number of firms sell a standardized product, into which entry is very easy, in which the individual seller has no control over the product price, and in which there is no nonprice competition; a market characterized by a very large number of buyers and sellers.

pure monopoly A market structure in which one firm sells a unique product, into which entry is blocked, in which the single firm has considerable control over product price, and in which nonprice competition may or may not be found.

purely competitive labor market A labor market in which a large number of similarly qualified workers independently offer their labor services to a large number of employers, none of whom can set the wage rate.

quantitative easing (QE) An open-market operation in which bonds are purchased by a central bank in order to increase the quantity of excess reserves held by commercial banks and thereby (hopefully) stimulate the economy by increasing the amount of lending undertaken by commercial banks; undertaken when interest rates are near zero and, consequently, does not allow the central bank to further stimulate the economy with lower interest rates due to the zero lower bound problem.

quasi-public good A good or service to which excludability could apply but that has such a large spillover benefit that government sponsors its production to prevent an underallocation of resources.

rational Behaviors and decisions that maximize a person's chances of achieving his or her goals.

real GDP per capita Real output (GDP) divided by population.

real gross domestic product (GDP) Gross domestic product adjusted for inflation; gross domestic product in a year divided by the GDP price index for that year, the index expressed as a decimal.

real income The amount of goods and services that can be purchased with nominal income during some period of time; nominal income adjusted for inflation.

real interest rate The interest rate expressed in dollars of constant value (adjusted for inflation) and equal to the nominal interest rate less the expected rate of inflation.

recession A period of declining real GDP, accompanied by lower real income and higher unemployment.

regressive tax A tax whose average tax rate decreases as the taxpayer's income increases and increases as the taxpayer's income decreases.

rent-seeking behavior The actions by persons, firms, or unions to gain special benefits from government at the taxpayers' or someone else's expense.

repo A repurchase agreement (or "repo") is a short-term money loan made by a lender to a borrower that is collateralized with bonds pledged by the borrower. The name *repo* refers to how the lender would view the transaction. The same transaction when viewed from the perspective of the borrower would be called a *reverse repo.*

required reserves The funds that banks and thrifts must deposit with the Federal Reserve Bank (or hold as vault cash) to meet the legal reserve requirement; a fixed percentage of the bank's or thrift's checkable deposits.

reserve ratio The specified minimum percentage of its checkable deposits that a bank or thrift must keep on deposit at the Federal Reserve Bank in its district or hold as vault cash.

resource market A market in which households sell and firms buy resources or the services of resources.

reverse repo A reverse repurchase agreement (or "reverse repo") is a short-term money loan that the borrower obtains by pledging bonds as collateral. The name *reverse repo* refers to how the borrower would view the transaction. The same transaction when viewed by the lender would be called a *repo*.

rule of reason The rule stated and applied in the U.S. Steel case that only combinations and contracts unreasonably restraining trade are subject to actions under the antitrust laws and that size and possession of monopoly power are not illegal.

sales tax A tax levied on the cost (at retail) of a broad group of products.

savings account A deposit that is interest-bearing and that the depositor can normally withdraw at any time.

scientific method The procedure for the systematic pursuit of knowledge involving the observation of facts and the formulation and testing of hypotheses to obtain theories, principles, and laws.

securitization The process of aggregating many individual financial debts into a pool and then issuing new securities (financial instruments) backed by the pool. The holders of the new securities are entitled to receive debt payments made on the individual financial debts in the pool.

self-control problems Refers to the difficulty people have in sticking with earlier plans and avoiding suboptimal decisions when finally confronted with a particular decision-making situation. A manifestation of *time inconsistency* and potentially avoidable by using *precommitments*.

self-interest The most-advantageous outcome as viewed by each firm, property owner, worker, or consumer.

shocks Sudden, unexpected changes in demand (or aggregate demand) or supply (or aggregate supply).

short run (1) In microeconomics, a period of time in which producers are able to change the quantities of some but not all of the resources they employ; a period in which some resources (usually plant) are fixed and some are variable. (2) In macroeconomics, a period in which nominal wages and other input prices do not change in response to a change in the price level.

short-run aggregate supply curve An aggregate supply curve relevant to a time period in which input prices (particularly nominal wages) do not change in response to changes in the price level.

short-run supply curve A supply curve that shows the quantity of a product a firm in a purely competitive industry will offer to sell at various prices in the short run; the portion of the firm's short-run marginal cost curve that lies above its average-variable-cost curve.

shortage The amount by which the quantity demanded of a product exceeds the quantity supplied at a particular (below-equilibrium) price.

simultaneous consumption A product's ability to satisfy a large number of consumers at the same time.

slope of a straight line The ratio of the vertical change (the rise or fall) to the horizontal change (the run) between any two points on a line. The slope of an upward-sloping line is positive, reflecting a direct relationship between two variables; the slope of a downward-sloping line is negative, reflecting an inverse relationship between two variables.

Smoot-Hawley Tariff Act Legislation passed in 1930 that established very high tariffs. Its objective was to reduce imports and stimulate the domestic economy, but it resulted only in retaliatory tariffs by other nations.

Social Security A federal pension program (financed by payroll taxes on employers and employees) that replaces part of the earnings lost when workers retire, become disabled, or die.

Social Security trust fund A federal fund that saves excessive Social Security tax revenues received in one year to meet Social Security benefit obligations that exceed Social Security tax revenues in some subsequent year.

specialization The use of the resources of an individual, a firm, a region, or a nation to concentrate production on one or a small number of goods and services.

stagflation Inflation accompanied by stagnation in the rate of growth of output and an increase in unemployment in the economy; simultaneous increases in the inflation rate and the unemployment rate.

start-up firm A new firm focused on creating and introducing a particular new product or employing a specific new production or distribution method.

status quo The existing state of affairs; in prospect theory, the current situation from which gains and losses are calculated.

status quo bias The tendency most people have when making choices to select any option that is presented as the default (status quo) option. Explainable by prospect theory and loss aversion.

stock (corporate) An ownership share in a corporation.

store of value An asset set aside for future use; one of the three functions of money.

strategic behavior Self-interested economic actions that take into account the expected reactions of others.

structural unemployment Unemployment of workers whose skills are not demanded by employers, who lack sufficient skill to obtain employment, or who cannot easily move to locations where jobs are available.

subprime mortgage loans High-interest-rate loans to home buyers with above-average credit risk.

substitute goods Products or services that can be used in place of each other. When the price of one falls, the demand for the other product falls; conversely, when the price of one product rises, the demand for the other product rises.

substitution effect The replacement of labor by capital when the price of capital falls.

Supplemental Nutrition Assistance Program (SNAP) A government program that provides food money to low-income recipients by depositing electronic money onto special debit cards.

Supplemental Security Income (SSI) A federally financed and administered program that provides a uniform nationwide minimum income for the aged, blind, and disabled who do not qualify for benefits under Social Security in the United States.

supply A schedule showing the amounts of a good or service that sellers (or a seller) will offer at various prices during some period.

supply curve A curve illustrating supply.

supply shocks Sudden, unexpected changes in aggregate supply.

supply-side economics A view of macroeconomics that emphasizes the role of costs and aggregate supply in explaining inflation, unemployment, and economic growth.

supply-side market failures Overallocations of resources that occur when private supply curves understate the full cost of producing a good or service.

surplus The amount by which the quantity supplied of a product exceeds the quantity demanded at a specific (above-equilibrium) price.

systematic errors Suboptimal choices that (1) are not rational because they do not maximize a person's chances of achieving his or her goals and (2) occur routinely, repeatedly, and predictably.

tariff A tax imposed by a nation on an imported good.

tax incidence The degree to which a tax falls on a particular person or group.

Temporary Assistance for Needy Families (TANF) The basic welfare program (financed through general tax revenues) for lowin-come families in the United States.

terms of trade The rate at which units of one product can be exchanged for units of another product; the price of a good or service; the amount of one good or service that must be given up to obtain 1-unit of another good or service.

thrift institution A savings and loan association, mutual savings bank, or credit union.

tight money policy Federal Reserve System actions that contract, or restrict, the growth of the nation's money supply for the purpose of reducing or eliminating inflation.

time deposit An interest-earning deposit in a commercial bank or thrift institution that the depositor can withdraw without penalty after the end of a specified period.

time inconsistency The human tendency to systematically misjudge at the present time what will actually end up being desired at a future time.

token money Bills or coins for which the amount printed on the *currency* bears no relationship to the value of the paper or metal embodied within it; for currency still circulating, money for which the face value exceeds the commodity value.

total cost The sum of fixed cost and variable cost.

total demand for money The sum of the transactions demand for money and the asset demand for money.

total product The total output of a particular good or service produced by a firm (or a group of firms or the entire economy).

total revenue The total number of dollars received by a firm (or firms) from the sale of a product; equal to the total expenditures for the product produced by the firm (or firms); equal to the quantity sold (demanded) multiplied by the price at which it is sold.

total-revenue test A test to determine elasticity of demand between any two prices: Demand is elastic if total revenue moves in the opposite direction from price; it is inelastic when it moves in the same direction as price; and it is of unitary elasticity when it does not change when price changes.

Trade Adjustment Assistance Act A U.S. law passed in 2002 that provides cash assistance, education and training benefits, health care subsidies, and wage subsidies (for persons age 50 or more) to workers displaced by imports or plant relocations abroad.

trade bloc A group of nations that lower or abolish trade barriers among members. Examples include the European Union and the nations of the North American Free Trade Agreement.

transactions demand for money The amount of money people want to hold for use as a medium of exchange (to make payments); varies directly with nominal GDP.

transfer payment A payment of money (or goods and services) by a government to a household or firm for which the payer receives no good or service directly in return.

Troubled Asset Relief Program (TARP) A 2008 federal government program that authorized the U.S. Treasury to loan up to $700 billion to critical financial institutions and other U.S. firms that were in extreme financial trouble and therefore at high risk of failure.

U.S. securities Treasury bills, Treasury notes, Treasury bonds, and U.S. savings bonds issued by the federal government to finance expenditures that exceed tax revenues.

ultimatum game A behavioral economics game in which a mutually anonymous pair of players interact to determine how an amount of money is to be split. The first player suggests a division. The second player either accepts that proposal (in which case the split is made accordingly) or rejects it (in which case neither player gets anything).

unemployment compensation A federal-state social insurance program (financed by payroll taxes on employers) that makes income available to workers who are unemployed.

unemployment rate The percentage of the labor force unemployed at any time.

unit elasticity Demand or supply for which the elasticity coefficient is equal to 1; means that the percentage change in the quantity demanded or supplied is equal to the percentage change in price.

unit of account A standard unit in which prices can be stated and the value of goods and services can be compared; one of the three functions of money.

utility The want-satisfying power of a good or service; the satisfaction or pleasure a consumer obtains from the consumption of a good or service (or from the consumption of a collection of goods and services).

variable cost   A cost that in total increases when the firm increases its output and decreases when the firm reduces its output.

voluntary export restrictions   Voluntary limitations by countries or firms of their exports to a particular foreign nation to avoid enactment of formal trade barriers by that nation.

wage differential   The differences between the wage received by one worker or group of workers and that received by another worker or group of workers.

Wall Street Reform and Consumer Protection Act of 2010   A law that gave authority to the Federal Reserve to regulate all large-financial institutions, created an oversight council to look for growing risk to the financial system, established a process for the federal government to sell off the assets of large failing financial institutions, provided federal regulatory oversight of asset-backed securities, and created a financial consumer protection bureau within the Fed.

World Trade Organization (WTO)   An organization of 164 nations (as of 2017) that oversees the provisions of the current world trade agreement, resolves trade disputes stemming from it, and holds forums for further rounds of trade negotiations.

X-inefficiency   The production of output, whatever its level, at higher than the lowest average (and total) cost.

zero interest rate policy (ZIRP)   A monetary policy in which a central bank sets nominal interest rates at or near zero percent per year in order to stimulate the economy.

Note: Page numbers followed by n indicate notes.